Brothers in Arms

A Time of Terror, Part Three

By AJ Berry

Cover: Burning of The Valleys Re-enactment
at Fort Klock, September 2005

Previously published books by the author:

Foreword

The history of the people of the Mohawk Valley is intertwined with Native Americans and people from many countries. In this book, the story of the Native Americans, the French, the English, the Dutch, the Scots, the Irish are presented along with more pension applications from the Revolutionary War

Once more, the reader is cautioned to remember that the pension application transcription process is an uncertain one, due to the handwriting of that day, the age of the documents, non-standardized spelling and the memory of the service men. The men were in their seventies and eighties when they applied for a pension and often they were confused on the dates of events and officer's names. In addition, many could not read or write and had no way of keeping track of the dates when they served at various posts. Their memory of the superior officers is sometimes incorrect and so is the rank of a superior officer. In other words don't assume that your ancestor might have had a promotion, probably he did not.

The pension applications are on file mostly in the National Archives in Washington D.C., some at the House of Representatives and some in Albany, NY; and are the best source of original resource material available to the researcher. It is material that has never been assembled and published before. It is in this light that more of the applications for the men who served in this area are presented. Many thanks are due to James F. Morrison who generously shared his large supply of pension applications and answered my questions. One recent question he answered was in regards to substitutes. Who got the service credit, the substitute or the man he was substituting for? Jim answered: *"It would depend on what they agreed to. If a son went for his father it might be the father especially if the son was only 16. At other times the substitute would get the credit."*

At times the pension applications can ramble on and on, but then a gratifying surprise will appear. For instance, one soldier was sold in Canada to serve a family and he was forced to watch his father being flogged because his father tried to blow up an ammunition magazine. Sadly, his father died from the injuries he received during the flogging. Another man made application for pension on the basis of poverty under the 1818 Pension Law and was granted a pension. A neighbor informed the War Department that the soldier indeed served one year in the Continental service but then went to Canada and served five years there. While he was in the service of the British, he "painted" himself to look like an Indian and came back to wage war on his former neighbors. Because of the five years of service, he was granted bounty lands in Canada from England. Needless to say, his American pension ceased. John Ball tells a story about Colonel Willett and a detachment of 250 men that held off about 300 Tories, British, and Indians. Supposedly no one was scratched, even though they were fired upon. This is possible because the smooth bore muskets were not very accurate at a distance.

Notice the letters before the pension application numbers. "S" means a survivor is applying, "W" means a widow is applying, and "R" means the application was rejected.

A common fallacy is that the men believed firmly in what they were fighting for, but the truth of the matter is that some changed sides several times. When the war was going badly for the Americans, or rather when the farms and crops were burned, a soldier often lost his interest in fighting for the American side and he would desert. Desertion was a very common thing. When things were going well for the Americans, the men often came back to serve. It could be they simply wanted to be on the winning side and sometimes it was hard to discern which side that might be!

Some of the pension applications mention Debtor's Prison, something I was not familiar with. Apparently it is another subject that is not one people wish to remember. A small piece on the debtor's prison system is included in this book.

Book One in the Terror series is titled: <u>A Time of Terror, The Story of Colonel Jacob Klock's Regiment and The People They Protected, 1774-1783</u>, Book Two is titled: <u>So It Was Written, Part Two, A Time of Terror</u>, and Book Three: <u>Brothers In Arms, Part Three, A Time of Terror</u>.

The lists of the troop rosters were taken from <u>New York In The Revolution</u> by James A. Roberts, 1898. The book does not strictly follow alphabetical order and therefore the names are not strictly alphabetical in this book either. Charlotte County troops are not included in this book due to space limitations.

Because of the differences in printers between mine and Traffords, there is sometimes a difference in the pages and this will throw off the index slightly. Look a page ahead or beyond if necessary to find the name you seek.

Once again, thank you to my son Pieter Decker for his patient job of proof reading!

NOTE: Due to the limitation of only having 440 pages available with Create Space, the Index of Names, and some of the extra spacing has been eliminated. The individual pension applications were removed as well since they are available for a donation on line and are in the <u>Don't Shoot</u> pension books.   The fonts were also enlarged to make this book easier to read.   E-mail: berryenterprises@hotmail.com

Table of Contents

The Albany County Militia

The Continental Army

The Public Papers of George Clinton

The Loyalists

Appendix

The Local Scene

The Mohawk Valley has had a succession of people who have inhabited the lands of the Mohawk. The red man lived here followed by the French, Dutch, English and then the Palatines, Scots and Irish. Some of their stories are intertwined.

Algonquins and The Arrival of The French

The earliest record of the Mohawk Indians, whose aboriginal name, as given by the Jesuit priest, Jean Brebeuf, was Agnierrhonons, and it was shortened to Agniers, "the people of the flint," later called Mahaqua by the Algonquins, Maquas by the Dutch, and Mohawk by the English, is derived from Jacques Cartier's account of his voyage up the St. Lawrence to Hochelaga (Montreal) in 1535.

From their own oral traditions, the Mohawks were driven out of Canada by the Algonquins, probably during the latter part of the sixteenth century. Cartier described a large village that he visited in 1535 but by 1608, it was deserted and destroyed when Champlain visited this spot.

It is possible the Algonquins made their way directly to the Mohawk Valley, or the journey may have taken many years. The cautious Algonquins were small in numbers so they likely chose more secure secluded spots deep in the forest, four or five miles from the Mohawk River, to build their palisaded castles. Many of these palisaded sites have been located and studied.

One element of the life and survival of the Native Americans; is the constant watchfulness against enemies and the necessity of selecting a home, some in a very secluded spot which nature and their craftsmanship could make into a fortress. Ideally a spot of height was selected because defense was easier, arrows can be shot down a slop much farther than they can uphill.

One site is described by Max Reid in The Mohawk Valley, Its Legends and Its History. "The site of this ancient Indian fort is located on a high, broad point of land, between two ravines, which grow deeper as they approach the bed of the Cayudutta Creek, that flows by its western boundary. Both ravines run in a southerly direction and through the easterly ravine flows a small permanent stream. The approach to the high ground of the Indian village from the Cayudutta Creek seems to have been through the latter ravine, which becomes a narrow, slaty gorge as it approaches the flats of the Cayudutta Valley, and owing to the dense growth of small trees and underbrush the entrance is not easily seen from the creek below. The gorge itself is quite picturesque, and its present condition suggests a possible method of defence used by the Indians, large trees having been felled and thrown into the bed of the creek, forming a wall of rotten trunks so they presented an obstacle not easily overcome by the investigator. As you enter the gorge from below, you encounter a series of slaty ledges, over whose moss-covered surface the stream trickles slowly, making a series of slimy steps extending upward for twenty or thirty feet, or to the level of the higher ground of the forest. On the west side of the gorge these slaty steps have been worn smooth and rounded by countless footsteps, up to a point about ten feet from the entrance, where a trail is seen ascending the side of the hill to the plateau above. As the trail or path approaches the top, it is worn in some places from four to six inches deep along the edge of the hill, showing that the place had been occupied for a considerable space of time by a numerous population."

"The plateau itself extends north to a considerable distance and is well covered with trees of large size and the rotten trunks of many monarchs of the forest. The place suggests seclusion, and its stillness is almost oppressive. The only evidence of life observable was the scurry of a solitary partridge chick and the dismal croak of a pater familias crow, evidently solicitous for the safety of his little family in the top of one of the tall pines. Take it all in all, I would not recommend it as a very desirable place for a Sunday-school picnic. This spot has undoubtedly been visited by a *number of "diggers," as is seen by the upturned black earth, plentifully sprinkled with small fragments of fresh-water clam-shells and occasional bits of pottery."*

"It is evident that this spot was once an Indian fortification, as the line of the palisade is seen stretching across the plateau from ravine to ravine. Although I was unable to secure many relics of intrinsic value, my search was quite successful and resulted in unearthing a stone axe, a broken stone pestle, a few bone tools, and flint implements, together with forty fragments of as many decorated vessels of Indian pottery. One of the most interesting articles that have been unearthed is a brass or copper bead, about six inches long. This was found by Mr. A. G. Richmond a few years ago, and is valued from the fact that it enables archeologists to fix the probable date of the occupation of this secluded spot by the Indians. As this is the only article found there that would indicate that the occupants had ever come in contact with white men, it must have been occupied previous to 1609, and subsequent to the discovery of the river St. Lawrence, in 1535. Many archeologists are of the opinion that the Iroquois were the people whom Jacques Cartier met at Hochelaga, (Montreal) and Stadacone (Quebec) on the occasion of his ascent of the St. Lawrence in 1535, and they advance the theory that they were driven out of Canada between that time and 1609, when Champlain found a new people at Stadacone (Quebec) and Hochelaga (Montreal) entirely deserted."

Francis Parkman, in his <u>Pioneers of France in the New World</u>, Boston, Little & Brown 1885, the following in italics:

"When America was first made known to Europe, the part assumed by France on the borders of that new world was peculiar, and is little recognized. While the Spaniard roamed sea and land, burning for achievement, red-hot with bigotry and avarice, and while England, with soberer steps and a less dazzling result, followed in the path of discovery and gold hunting, it was from France that those barbarous shores first learned to serve the ends of peaceful commercial industry."

Another unidentified French writer, however, advances a more ambitious claim. *"In the year 1488, four years before the first voyage of Columbus, America, he maintains was found by a Frenchman. Cousin, a navigator of Dieppe, being at sea off the African coast, was forced westward; it is said, by winds and currents, to within sight of an unknown shore, where he presently described the mouth of a great river. On board his ship was one Pinzon, whose conduct became so mutinous that, on his return to Dieppe, he made complaint to the magistracy, who thereupon dismissed the offender from the maritime service of the town. Pinzon went to Spain, became known to Columbus, told him of his discovery, and joined him on his voyage in 1492."*

In the year 1535 Jacques Cartier, a Frenchman, sailed from the ancient town of St. Malo, France, and entered the bay of St. Lawrence, as Cartier named it, in August or September of the same year. Having with him the two Indian lads captured in his former visit to these shores, he found them of great assistance in communicating with the natives. They are supposed to have spoken the Mohawk dialect. It is said that the Indian name for the St. Lawrence River was Hochelaga, and that the present site of Quebec was called Stadacona, whose king's name was Donnacona. Cartier says that the country below Stadacona (Quebec) was called Saguenay, and that above, Hochelaga. At Stadacona, Cartier was told of a large Indian town, many days journey above, which was called Hochelaga, and had given the name to the river and country also. Passing up the river with a small galleon and two open boats and about fifty sailors, on the 2d of October, 1535, they reached the mysterious Hochelaga. Their landing was made just below the present quays of Montreal, and thronging the shores were a thousand or more Indians awaiting the strangers. The next morning they were conducted to the Indians' town, lying under the shadow of the mountain which Cartier named Mont Royal—Montreal; "hence the name of the busy city which now holds the site of the vanished Hochelaga. "

A later writer, Lescarbot, insists that the country on both sides of the St. Lawrence, from Hochelaga to its mouth, was called Canada. The derivation of the name Canada is undoubtedly Indian, and not Spanish, and it is a singular fact that in the vocabulary of the language of Hochelaga appended to the journal of Cartier's second voyage, Canada is set down as meaning town or village, and that it bears the same meaning in the Mohawk, and both languages are dialects of the Iroquois.

Quoting from Francis Parkman: *"That the Indians of Hochelaga belonged to the Huron-Iroquois family of tribes is evident from the affinities of their language and from the construction of their houses and defensive works. This was identical with the construction universal, or nearly so, among the Huron-Iroquois tribes." It is said that in 1860 a quantity of Indian remains were dug up at Montreal that evidently belonged to the Iroquois and not to the Algonquin type. There is said to be a tradition among the Agniers (Mohawks), one of the five nations of the Iroquois, that their ancestors were once settled at Quebec. A tradition recorded by Colden in his history of the Five Nations (Iroquois), that they were formerly settled near Montreal, is of interest. The tradition declares that they were driven thence by the Adirondacks, which was the distinctive name of the tribes of the Algonquins located in Canada."*

It is said that when Champlain, in 1603, passed up the St. Lawrence, sixty-eight years after Cartier's visit, *"Hochelaga and its savage population had vanished and in their place were a few wandering Algonquins of different tongues and lineage."*

Champlain, in 1609, met them again on the shores of Lake Champlain, called by the natives Iroquois Lake. Champlain's account of the meeting is interesting. Here are his own words about the meeting found in Francis Parkman's book, <u>Pioneers of France in the New World</u>:

"At nightfall we embarked in our canoes to continue our journey, and as we advanced very softly and noiselessly, we encountered a party of Iroquois, on the twenty-ninth of the month (July, 1609), about ten o'clock at night, at a point off a cape which juts into the lake on the west side. They and we began to shout, each seizing his arms. We withdrew towards the water and the Iroquois repaired on shore and arranged all their canoes, the one beside the other, and began to hew down trees with villainous axes, which they sometimes got in war, and others of stone, and fortified themselves securely."

"Our party, likewise, kept their canoes arranged, the one alongside the other, tied to poles so as not to run adrift, in order to fight all together, should need be. We were on the water about an arrow shot from their barricade."

"When they were armed and in order, they sent two canoes from the fleet, which consisted of twenty-four canoes and sixty savages, to know if their enemies wished to fight, who answered they desired nothing else; but that just then there was not much light, and that we must wait for day to distinguish each other, and they would give us battle at sunrise. This was agreed to by our party. Meanwhile the whole night was spent in dancing and singing, as well on one side as on the other, mingled with an infinitude of insults and other taunts such as the little courage they had; how powerless their resistance against our arms, and that when day would break they should experience this to their ruin. Ours, likewise, did not fail in repartee, telling them they should witness the effect of arms they had never seen before, and a multitude of speeches as is usual at a siege of a town. After the one and the other had sung, danced, and parliamented enough, day broke. My three companions and I were always concealed for fear the enemy should see us preparing our arms as best we could, being, however, separated, each in one of the canoes belonging to the savage Montagnaes."

"After being equipped with light armor, we took each an arquebus and went ashore. I saw the enemy leave their barricade; they were about 200 men, of strong and robust appearance, who were coming slowly towards us, with a gravity and assurance which greatly pleased me, led on by three chiefs. Ours were marching in similar order, and told us that those who bore three lofty plumes were the chiefs, and that there were but three, and they were to be recognized by those plumes, which were considerable larger than those of their companions, and that I must do all I could to kill them. I promised to do what I could, and that I was sorry they could not clearly understand me, so as to give them the order and plan of attacking their enemies, as we should undoubtedly defeat them all; but there was no help for that; that I was very glad to encourage them and to manifest to them my good will when we should be engaged."

"The moment we landed they began to run about two hundred paces toward their enemies, who stood firm, and had not yet perceived my companions, who went into the bush with some savages. Ours commenced calling me in a loud voice, and making way for me opened in two and placed me at their head marching, about twenty paces in advance, until I was within thirty paces of the enemy. The moment they saw me, they halted, gazing at me and I at them. When I saw them preparing to shoot at us, I raised my arquebus, and aiming directly at one of the three chiefs, two of them fell to the ground by this shot and one of their companions received a wound of which he died afterwards. I had put four balls in my arquebus. Ours on witnessing a shot so favorable for them, set up such tremendous shouts that thunder could not have been heard; and yet there was no lack of arrows on one side and the other."

"The Iroquois were greatly astonished seeing two men killed so instantaneously, notwithstanding they were provided with arrow proof armor, woven with cotton thread and wood; this frightened them very much. Whilst I was reloading, one of my companions in the bush fired a shot which so astonished them anew, seeing their chiefs slain, they lost courage, took to flight and abandoned the field and their fort, hiding themselves in the depths of the forest, whither pursuing them, I killed some others. Our savages also killed several of them and took ten or twelve prisoners. The rest carried off the wounded. Fifteen or sixteen of ours were wounded."

"After having gained the victory, they amused themselves plundering Indian corn and meal from the enemy; also their arms which they threw away in order to run better. And having feasted, danced and sung, we returned three hours afterward with the prisoners."

"The place where this battle was fought is in forty-three degrees, some minutes latitude, and I named it Lake Champlain."

Source Material:
<u>The Mohawk Valley Its Legends and its History</u>
by Max Reid
New York and London G. P. Putman's Sons
The Knickerbocker Press, 1901
<u>History of Montgomery and Fulton Counties, NY</u>
F. W. Beers & Co. 36 Vesey Street, 1878
<u>Pioneers of France in the New World,</u> by Francis Parkman, Boston, Little & Brown 1885

More French and then Dutch Arrive.
Then The English Arrive, Followed by More White People.

The French, from the day of their arrival in the St. Lawrence to the end of their power in America, were generally more successful in winning the confidence of the Indians with whom they came into immediate contact, than any other European people. Their traders traveled the forests and navigated the lakes and rivers, from the gulf of the St. Lawrence River to the delta of the Mississippi River. They had trading posts among them, adopted their habits, and intermarried with their women. Their missionaries went forth unarmed and alone, generally unharmed and gained the confidence of even the most savage Indians they encountered.

But there was one exception to this general success; the Iroquois. A long time after establishing trading posts in Canada, they finally succeeded in making contact with the Iroquois. This was probably due to a war the Iroquois Confederacy was involved in with the Hurons and Adirondacks.

The result of that alliance was a bitter hostility on the part of the Iroquois toward the French, which continued until after the conquest of New York when the Dutch in 1664 gave control of their colony to the English. During that long period even the fervent Jesuits failed to make a good impression upon them, especially upon the Mohawks at whose hands three Jesuits suffered terrible torture and martyrdom. More than once the Iroquois swept over the French settlements with the torch and tomahawk, leaving a path of blood almost to the gates of Quebec. But the French and then the Adirondacks successfully invaded the country of the Mohawks with a strong force in the spring of 1666. Peace came in the following year. This part will be followed in more depth in the following pages.

The first three English governors of the New York Colony, were Colonels Nicholls, Colonel Richard Lovelace, and Major Andross. The latter governor, Sir Edmund Andross, gave more attention to the Five Nations, but he did not understand the importance of their trade, or their friendship. Still the mortal hatred the Iroquois had for the French inclined them to the friendship of the English. But the Duke of York, because of his Catholic faith, shut his eyes to what the true policy of the English toward the Iroquois should have been, and envisioned handing the Confederates over to the Holy See as converts.

Efforts to mediate the peace between the Iroquois and the French in 1667, were followed by invitations from the English to the Jesuit missionaries to settle among the people of the Iroquois Confederation, along with efforts to persuade the Iroquois to receive the missionaries. The Mohawks were either too wise, or too bitter toward the French to listen. But not so with the other nations of the alliance; and the Oneidas, Onondagas, Cayugas and Senecas opened their arms to the strangers in holy garb, causing mischief in following years.

The peace of 1667 continued several years during which time both the English and French pursued a very profitable trade with the Indians.

The error made when the Jesuits were invited to come into the Iroquois Confederation was soon recognized by Colonel Dongan, the new governor who arrived in the colony as the successor of Major Andross in 1683. He was not at the head of the colony long before he recognized the mistakes of his predecessors in Indian relations. The Five Nations at that time had ten times more warriors than they did half a century afterward; and the governor saw their importance as a wall of separation between the English Colonies and the French. He also realized the importance of their trade, which the Jesuit priests were largely influential in directing to Canada.

Colonel Dongan lost no time in seeking to curtail the influence of the French, and to bring back the Iroquois to his own people. His instructions from home were to encourage the Jesuit missionaries. These directions he not only disregarded, but he ordered the missionaries away, and forbade the Five Nations to harbor them. It is true this order was never enforced to the letter. The priests, some of them at least, maintained a foothold at several points of the Confederacy. The attempts at conciliation adopted by Colonel Dongan made a strong and favorable impression upon the Indians.

Colonel Dongan was instrumental in organizing a convention of the Five Nations at Albany, in 1684, to meet Lord Howard of Effingham who was the Governor of Virginia. The difficulties with Virginia were resolved and a covenant made with Lord Howard for preventing further depredations. But what was of yet greater importance, Colonel Dongan succeeded in gaining the affections and trust of the Indians. They even asked that the coat of arms of the Duke of York might be put upon their castles. The governor thought convenient to think this was an act of at least partial submission to English authority, although it has been asserted that the Indians themselves looked upon the ducal insignia as a sort of charm to protect them against the French.

New York was at this time somewhat torn by the revolution which drove the Stuarts from the English throne, and ended the power of the Catholics in the colony. Because of this, the English could give the Indians no help in their invasion of Canada, otherwise that country would have been taken from the crown of France and this would have saved subsequent bloodshed in the future. During the civil feuds of the revolution, and those that followed, the Indian affairs of New York were neglected. Meantime, the New England colonies were becoming involved in a war with the Eastern Indians. A deputation was sent to invite the Five Nations to take up the hatchet and help with this cause; but the invitation was firmly declined.

The revolution which brought William and Mary upon the English throne was followed by war between England and France. This struggle between the two countries would be a factor in the future during our Revolutionary War when France came to assist us in the struggle. There is an old saying, "your newest best friend is your enemy's enemy".

The colonies were, of course, somewhat involved in the conflict even though the struggle was in Europe. Count Frontenac revived the policy of attempting to detach the Iroquois Confederates from the English interest. Through the efforts of a Jesuit residing among the Oneidas, all the Confederates but the Mohawks met the emissaries of the French in council at Onondaga. At the same time, to make a point with the Mohawks and to show the inability of the English to defend their own settlements against the arms of the French king, a secret expedition was set on foot against Schenectady. This resulted in a brutal massacre of the slumbering inhabitants on the night of February 8, 1690. More on this raid will be discussed later in this book.

But the Five Nations were not won to the interests of the French by the persuasive arguments of the French agents at Onondaga, or by the terrors of the scene at Schenectady. The Mohawks deeply sympathized with their suffering neighbors of Schenectady and attacked the invaders on their retreat north. Then they sent their war parties once more into Canada to attack the island of Montreal.

The Mohawk jealousies were far more easily awakened than eased; they became restless and unhappy. In spite of the alacrity with which the Mohawks had sought to avenge the murders of Schenectada in February 1690, the neglect they later experienced from the English caused them to turn against the English. The Mohawks went so far as to send an embassy of peace to Count Frontenac. Meantime, a council with the Four Nations of the Confederates was held, without the Mohawks and with good results. The plans of the Mohawks were frustrated and the covenant chain was renewed.

Colonel Henry Sloughter was commissioned to be the Governor of New York in January, 1689, but did not arrive until the nineteenth of March, 1691. The selection of Sloughter was not a good one. According to reports, he was utterly destitute of every qualification necessary for government and as a decent human being. He was licentious in his morals, avaricious for money and power, and crude in his behavior.

Jacob Leisler, who had administered the government after a fashion, since the departure of Dongan, was intoxicated with power, refused to surrender the government to Sloughter, and attempted to defend the fort in which he had taken refuge. He soon was forced to abandon the fort, and was arrested and with his son-in-law, Milburne, tried and executed for treason. Still, the conduct of Leisler during the revolution had been considered patriotic, and his sentence was considered very unjust and cruel. His enemies could not convince Sloughter to sign the warrant for his execution, so they got him intoxicated and in this condition he signed the death warrant. It was a murderous affair. Sloughter's administration was short and turbulent. He died July twenty-third, 1691.

The Canadian countryside was in a state of almost constant alarm by frequent incursions of war parties against the French settlements. Active hostilities were likewise pursued by the Confederates against the French traders and their posts on Lake Ontario. The celebrated Onondaga chief, Black-Kettle, was one of the bravest and most remarkable warriors and was the leader in that pursuit. He was captured and put to death by the most brutal torture.

Upon the death of Sloughter, Richard Ingoldsby, was made temporary president of the council. Colonel Benjamin Fletcher, arrived with a commission as governor in August, 1692. In the preceding month of June, Ingoldsby met with the Five Nations in council at Albany, during which occasion they declared their enmity to the French in the strongest possible terms. Their expressions of friendship for the English were also renewed. *"Brother Corlaer,"* said the sachem, *"we are all the subjects of one great king and queen; we have one head, one heart, one interest, and are all engaged in the same war."* They nevertheless condemned the English for their inactivity, telling them that *"the destruction of Canada would not make one summer's work, against their united strength, if ingeniously exerted."*

For help in conducting the Indian affairs of the colony, Colonel Fletcher took Major Peter Schuyler into his council and was guided by his opinions. No man understood those affairs better than Schuyler and his influence over the Indians was so great that whatever, Quider as they called Schuyler, recommended or disapproved had the force of a law. This power over them was supported by repeated acts of kindness and by his bravery and activity in the defense of his country. Through the influence of Quider, Colonel Fletcher was on good footing with the Indians, who conferred on him the name of *Cayenguinago*, or The Great Swift Arrow as a compliment for a rapid journey he made from New York to Schenectady on a sudden emergency.

Unable to make peace with the Five Nations, Count Frontenac decided to strike a blow on the Mohawks in their own country during in the month of February. For once the warriors were taken by surprise, two of their castles were entered and captured without much resistance because the warriors of both were absent at Schenectady. At the third or upper castle, the invaders met with a different reception. About forty warriors, were engaged in a war-dance, before departing for a war expedition. The warriors did not give up without a struggle and they killed about thirty of the attackers first.

The French took about 300 of the Mohawks prisoners in their invasion. The people of Schenectady were charged with bad conduct. They neither aided their neighbors nor told them of the coming danger, although they were informed of the fact. But Quider, the fast friend of the Indians, took the lead of the militia of Albany immediately after hearing of the invasion, and harassed the enemy sharply during their retreat. Except the unfortunate protection of a snowstorm, and the accidental resting of a cake of ice on the river which provided a bridge for their escape, the invaders would have been cut off.

The loss to the Mohawks by this incursion, added to dissatisfaction arising from the many unfulfilled promises made by the English discouraged the Indians so much that in the spring of 1693, the Oneidas sued the French for peace which was frustrated only by the promptness of Fletcher's movements. He presented a supply of presents to the Indians sent from England and this helped him to convene a council of the whole Iroquois Confederacy at Albany. With a liberal distribution of arms and ammunition, knives, hatchets, and clothing, they were pacified. To use their own figure of speech, made *"to roll and wallow in joy, by reason of the great favor the king and queen had done them."*

The tug of war for the control of the Indians was not over, but went on for many years with a lot of bloodshed. A Jesuit priest named Milet who lived among the Oneidas, succeeded in persuading all the nations except the Mohawks to open their ears to the propositions of certain representatives who were sent on the insidious errand to Onondaga. But the demands of the French, particularly for permission to rebuild the fort at Cadaraqui, were greater than the Indians were willing to concede and the war was renewed in 1694. Count de Frontenac sent an expedition of 300 men against the Five Nations in the region of the Niagara peninsula. The Five Nations also, renewed their incursions into Canada, and the fate of their brethren was avenged by a holocaust, in which ten of their Indian captives were burnt.

In the year 1696, the Count de Frontenac made another effort to subdue the Five Nations. An army consisting of two battalions of regular troops, four battalions of militia, together with the warriors of all the Indian tribes, assembled. The count ascended the St. Lawrence to Cadaraqui, and crossing to Oswego the troops fell upon the Onondagas unsuccessfully. The Indians had been told the French were bringing several small pieces of artillery against them. They had no defense against artillery, so they set fire to their towns and left with their women, children, and old men to live in the wilderness. All that remained to receive the invaders, was an old man whose head was white with the snows of a hundred winters. He refused to leave his lodge. The French were furious and took out their anger on the old man. He was put to death by torture, dying as bravely as he had lived. The death of the old sachem was the only death from the last campaign of the Count de Frontenac against the Iroquois. Not a single Onondaga captive was made, and the conquest was a field of smoldering ashes. A bitter victory indeed. Though the Onondagas were spared, 35 Oneidas were taken prisoners and carried into Canada. The Onondagas fell upon the rear of the army and cut off several bateaux. This was not all they did, the warriors of the Five Nations renewed their raids right up to the gates of Montreal, and by tomahawk and fire caused another famine in Canada.

The Peace of Ryswick in 1697, put an end to the killing. The Earl of Bellamont succeeded Colonel Fletcher in the government of New York and some problems arose between his lordship and the French Governor. In the following negotiations agreement was made for a mutual release of prisoners. In these negotiations the earl claimed the Iroquois as the subjects of the crown of Great Britain, a claim in which Count Frontenac was not in agreement.

Pending these diplomatic proceedings, the Count de Frontenac died.

Changes were under way in New York at the same time. Richard, Earl of Bellamont, was appointed Governor of New York, Massachusetts, and New Hampshire, in May of 1695, but he did not arrive in New York until May, 1698. He was appointed by King William with the command to stop piracy. New York was a ripe field for the pirates. The previous governor, Fletcher, and other officers in the colony had a good working agreement with the pirates, no doubt this was a paid arrangement. Kidd was given a ship by Bellamont, Robert Livingstone and several English noblemen to help counter the pirates. But instead of helping control the pirates, Kidd turned pirate himself with the shop he was given. Kidd was afterward arrested in Boston by the Earl of Bellamont, and sent home for trial.

In 1700 the French were far from giving up the idea of governing New York. To help this along, many Jesuit priests were working among the Indians to counter this movement, an act was passed by the provincial assembly for putting to death by hanging, every Popish priest coming voluntarily within the bounds of the colony.

In the spring of 1702, hostilities broke out between England, France, and Spain. Happily, the Five Nations had just previously concluded a treaty of neutrality with the Canadian French, and the murderous border raids from the Indians were not renewed.

But even threat of hanging was not enough to stop the Jesuits from making contact with the Five Nations of the Iroquois. In 1708, Lord Cornbury (Edward Hyde) who was then the head of the New York Colony, requested an appropriation to meet the Iroquois in council, and quiet them with presents. This timely measure was successful. In the next year, through Colonel Schuyler, (Quider) the Five Nations took part in Colonel Nicholson's expedition for the capture of Canada, at a vast cost to the colonies and to New York especially, the failure caused great embarrassment.

Colonel Schuyler was greatly beloved by the Five Nations. He excited the Iroquois at the prospect of the conquest of Canada, and in turn he bore much of the blame for the failure of Nicholson's expedition. Probably with the idea of diverting the attention of the Indians from their disappointment, he suggested a voyage to England to show the actual state of the country to England. His ideas were endorsed by the Colonial Assembly, and he took along five Iroquois Chiefs. The chiefs caused a big stir of excitement in England.

Schuyler returned with his chiefs in the autumn of the same year, 1710, his mission was successful. In turn, the chiefs were pleased with their voyage. The queen received them and treated them well. They had a chance to support the arguments of Quider for the speedy subduing of Canada, as the only permanent means of peace and security for the northern English colonies. The voyage accomplished something else, the chiefs came back with a good idea of how numerous the white men were on the other side of the ocean and they passed this piece of news on to their comrades.

Another expedition was tried in the next year, 1711, after making great preparations both by the parent government and the colonies. The French were equally active in preparing their measures of defense. The Iroquois were persuaded to take part in the expedition. The expedition resulted in another defeat, on the land and the sea. The Iroquois were discouraged, and once more they again began to "open their ears" to the French.

Brigadier-General Robert Hunter, was appointed next to the governor's position for New York. The peace of Utrecht was followed by several years of peace, the colonies were relieved of Indian hostilities. This was very helpful in the colony not to have to face the when, where, or how the enemy might strike. The people could concentrate on settling the land and raising their families and crops in this period of peace.

Meantime, the Iroquois Confederation, relieved of hostilities with the French directed their attention against their ancient enemies in the South, specifically to the Carolinas and to Georgia, where the Catawbas and the Cherokees lived. The most powerful nation in the midlands of Carolina were the Tuscaroras, their language bore a strong resemblance to that of the Five Nations. This resemblance caused the Iroquois to claim them as relatives; and with their consent, the Tuscaroras were transplanted north to the land of the Iroquois Confederacy thus becoming the Six Nations. It has been claimed that in 1708 the Tuscaroras had fifteen towns and had twelve hundred warriors. But the same sad event occurred with all the Indians and decimated their population, the white man's diseases; mostly the smallpox. The Native Americans never had these diseases to contend with and had no natural ability to counteract the disease. They died rapidly and in great numbers.

General Hunter continued at the head of the New York colonial administration until the summer of 1719, when he went back to England on leave of absence to look after his health and his private affairs.   He was in dire financial straits, the colonial government of New York refused to pay his salary and he was deeply in debt and unable to get any further loans. The person in charge after he left was the Hon. Peter Schuyler, as the oldest member of the council. He held a satisfactory treaty with the Six Nations at Albany but he was not successful in his efforts to persuade the Confederation to drive Joncaire, the French agent out of their country. This Jesuit emissary had long lived among the Senecas and had been adopted by the Indians. He was greatly beloved by the Onondagas but he was incessant in working for the French, helping the missionaries in their progress through the country, and contributing greatly in the withdrawal of the Indians from the English. Schuyler was aware of all this but he could not persuade them to discard Joncaire or at least to ignore his advice.

William Burnet became the next governor of the colony in the year 1720.   Immediately after the Peace of Utrecht, a brisk trade in goods for the Indian market was revived between Albany and Montreal. The Caughnawaga clan of the Mohawks residing near Montreal served as carriers. The chiefs of the Six Nations saw the danger from allowing that trade to pass around in that direction.   The Indians would of course be drawn exclusively to Montreal for their supplies, to be received immediately at the hands of the French, and they cautioned the English authorities against allowing this path of trade.

Mr. Hunter had indeed called the attention of the general assembly to the subject; but no action was taken until after Mr. Burnet had assumed firm control of the administration. The policy was at once to cut off trade with Montreal and bring the entire Indian trade within the limits and control of New York. An act was passed at his suggestion, subjecting the traders with Montreal to a forfeiture of their goods, and a penalty of one hundred pounds for each infraction of the law. It likewise entered into the policy of Mr. Burnet to win the confidence of the Caughnawagas, and reunite them with their kin in their native valley. But the ties by which the Catholic priests had bound the Caughnawagas to the interests of the French were too strong and the efforts of the governor were unsuccessful.

To develop Indian trade, not only with the Six Nations but to the remoter nations of the upper lakes, a trading post was established at Oswego in 1722. A trusted agent was also appointed to reside at the great council-fire of the Onondagas, the central nation of the Confederates. A congress of several of the colonies was held at Albany to meet the Six Nations, attended by Governor Alexander Spotswood, of Virginia, Sir William Keith, of Pennsylvania, and by Governor Burnet of New York. At this council the chiefs stipulated that in the future, during southern war expeditions they would not cross the Potomac and in their marches against their southern enemies their path would go westward of the great mountains (the Alleghany Mountains). Mr. Burnet again brightened the chain of friendship with them in the interests of the Colony of New York.

The benefits of Governor Burnet's policy were soon apparent. In the course of a single year more than forty young men plunged boldly into the Indian country as traders, acquired their languages and strengthened the friendship between the English and the more distant nations. Tribes of Indians previously unknown to the colonists, even from as far away as Michilimackinac visited Albany for purposes of traffic. Michilimackinac (Mich-ili-mac-i-naw) is located on the northern most lower peninsula of Michigan.

The establishment of an English post at Oswego made the French unhappy and they were determined to retake Niagara, rebuild the trading house, and repair their dilapidated fort. The consent of the Onondagas to do this work was obtained by the Baron de Longueil, who visited their country for that purpose, through the influence of Joncaire and his Jesuit associates. But the other members of the Confederacy, disapproved and declared the permission which was given to be void.

They dispatched messengers to Niagara to stop repairs. With an understanding of the importance of such an encroachment upon their territory, the Confederates met Governor Burnet in a council on the subject at Albany, in 1727.

"We come to you howling," said the chiefs; "and this is the reason why we howl, that the Governor of Canada encroaches on our land and builds thereon." Governor Burnet made a speech to them on this occasion, beautifully expressed in their own figurative language, which gave them great satisfaction.

The chiefs, declaring themselves unable to resist the invasion of the French, entreated the English for help and formally surrendered their country to the great king, "to be protected by him for their use," as heretofore stated.

Governor Burnet at that time was involved in political problems with an assembly that was too shortsighted to understand the importance of preserving the trust and friendship of the Indians for the colonial government. Burnet was allowed to do nothing more for the protection of the Indians than erect a small military defense at Oswego and to do this necessary work he had to use his own money. In the meantime the French completed their defense at Niagara without interference.

In the course 1727, Mr. Burnet, resigned from the government of New York, and accepted the governorship of Massachusetts and New Hampshire.

Montgomery succeeded him in New York, in 1728. He was a lazy man, without enough character to have opposition. He simply said what any person wanted to hear. The French who were enraged at the building of a fort at Oswego, were threatening the fort. The new governor met the Six Nations in council at Albany, to renew the covenant chain and to involve them in the defense of the fort. Large presents were distributed among them, and they declared their willingness to join the reinforcements detached from the independent companies for that service. Being told of the preparations, the French wisely gave up the idea of an invasion.

Much of the opposition to the administration of Governor Burnet had been from the residents of Albany who had been unable to do illicit trade in Indian goods with Montreal and also by the importers of those goods in New York City. Sustained by his council-board, and by Doctor Colden, Mr. Burnet had succeeded in putting Indian relations on a better footing or at he was able to limit the French ability to tamper with trade. But in December of the next year, all these advantages suddenly disappeared because of an act of the crown repealing the measures of Mr. Burnet which revived the Albany trade and reopened the door of intrigue between the French and the Six Nations. Montgomery was rapidly undoing all the good Burnet had done with resolving the French and Indian problems.

After the death of Colonel Montgomery, the duties of the colonial governor were taken over by Rip Van Dam, who was president of the council. His administration was noted for the infraction of the Treaty of Utrecht by the French, who invaded New York and built the fortress of St. Frederick at Crown Point. This gave them the command of Lake Champlain the highway between the English and French colonies.

The Commonwealth of Massachusetts was alarmed at this advance and called the attention of the authorities of New York to the problem, but the problem was treated with indifference. There was a regular military force in the colony strong enough to recover Crown Point at this time, but nothing was done.

During the stormy administration of Colonel Cosby, from 1732 to 1736, no attention seems to have been given to Indian affairs. The constant quarrels of this weak and avaricious man with the people and their representatives left him with no time to deal with the affairs of the colony.

The Six Nations once more resumed war against their enemies at the South. One of their expeditions against the Chickasaws was a disaster. They fell into an ambush and fought until all but two of a strong body of warriors was slain. Only one of those two returned to tell the tale. He headed off into the forest and supported himself by killing game along the way and succeeded in traveling the whole distance back to his own country without meeting a single human being. Another stronger expedition, was sent against the Catawbas and Cherokees. They met upon the banks of the Cumberland River, now in Kentucky, at a place called "the bloody lands." Seeing that their enemies were advancing to meet them, the Six Nations lured them into an ambush and a terrible two day battle followed in which the southern enemies were defeated with a loss of twelve hundred braves killed on the field.

After the death of Colonel Cosby, George Clarke, a member of the council became acting governor and afterward Lieutenant-Governor. He continued at the head of the colonial administration from the autumn of 1736 to 1743, a period of seven years. He was a man of strong common sense and of had a lot of tact. Because he had lived in the colony for many years and held several official positions, he was well acquainted with the state government and how to accomplish his agenda. His administration was popular and successful and his course was one of conciliation. In his first speech to the general assembly he referred to the unhappy divisions which had divided the colony, and he thought it was time to heal.

The English flour market was overstocked by large supplies furnished from other colonies and the attention of the assembly was directed to encouraging domestic manufacturing. To the Indian affairs of the colony, Mr. Clarke called special attention of the assembly. The military works of Fort Hunter were in a dilapidated condition. The necessary repairs were made on the fort and this gave protection to the settlements through the Mohawk Valley. Then the Lieutenant-Governor suggested the erection of a new fort at the carrying place between the Mohawk River and Wood Creek leading into Oneida Lake, and from there through the Oswego River into Lake Ontario. He suggested the transfer of the garrison from Fort Hunter to Oswego and recommended the repair of the blockhouse located at Oswego along with sending of smiths and other artificers into the Indian country, especially among the Senecas.

These recommendations were repeated in the executive speech to the assembly in the spring of 1737 and again to a new assembly which had been called in the summer of the same year. The Lieutenant-Governor further informed the new assembly that it had become necessary for him to meet the chiefs of the Six Nations in council at Albany as a result of certain negotiations pending between the Senecas and the French. The French were at the point of getting permission to erect a trading post at Tierondequot, which would enable them to intercept the fur-trade of the upper lakes on its way to Oswego.

To stop the movement of the French, and if possible to circumvent them by obtaining permission for the English to establish a trading-post at the same point, the meeting with the Confederate chiefs took place in Albany. The objectives of the interview were only partially successful. The Senecas agreed not to allow the French agent, John Coeur, to build at Tierondequot but neither would they permit the English to build there. Still they gladly entered into the proposition of the Lieutenant-Governor to send a gunsmith to reside among them. The smith could be used as an interpreter and with three other agents could assist in stopping the intrigues of the French. At the next session of the assembly, these measures were approved and provisions made for strengthening Oswego for the further encouragement of trade with the Indians.

The Lieutenant-Governor summoned a meeting of house and announced intelligence of a French scheme to establish themselves between the head or at the southern end of Lake

Champlain and the Hudson River. The governor asked to have a fort built there and to allow a colony of emigrants from Northern England to settle there to help with the defense of the northern frontier. The Lieutenant-Governor also announced in the same speech, that a delegation of the Senecas had left for Quebec to meet with M. Beauharnois, the governor of Canada. The delegation was to negotiate an agreement to allow the French to settle in the beautiful valley of the Tierondequot, a measure which "would put an end to the Oswego trade."

In conclusion the Lieutenant-Governor asked for an appropriation of money to enable him to frustrate the French plan. The assembly was suddenly dissolved a few days after the delivery of this speech so no steps were taken to either of its recommendations. They were once more proposed to the new assembly in spring of the next year, 1739.

The years 1738 and 1739, were marked by increasing political excitement, and division of those who sided with civil liberty on one side and those who recognized and wanted to protect the perogatives of the crown on the other. The administrations of the earlier English governors, Nicholls and Lovelace, were benevolent, and almost parental. The new governor, Edmond Andross, was a tyrant; and during his administration lines were formed much as they were in England over the questions of politics and religion. In England this brought the downfall of the Stuarts, and brought William and Mary to the English throne.

For nearly twenty years the colony was torn by personal, rather than political factions which had their origin in the controversy that accompanied the unhappy Leisler and his son-in-law Milborne. These factions died out over the years but other bigger issues appeared. The rights of the people, and the demands of the crown. Invariably the struggle centered on revenue, either in the levying or in its disposition, or both. Until the colony won its freedom, the struggle for revenue and its disbursement was almost perpetually before the people in one form or another. In some years, owing the obstinacy of the representatives of the crown on one side, and the inflexibility of the representatives of the people on the other, supplies were not granted at all.

In line with the monetary issues of the day, Mr. Clarke, was doomed to encounter the revenue problem. In a speech to the assembly in the autumn session of 1738, he complained that another year had passed without any provision being made for the support of his majesty's government in the province, the neglect having occurred by reason of "a practice not warranted by the usage any former general assemblies." He insisted upon the adoption of measures for the payment of salaries, for the payment of the public creditors for the general security of the public credit by the creation of a sinking fund for the redemption of the bills of the colony. The situation was not improved under the administration of Governor Andross.

The assembly was opposed. Instead of complying with the demands of Lieutenant-Governor Clarke and then the Governor Andross, the house resolved unanimously that they "would grant no supplies upon that principle; and in regard to a sinking fund for the redemption of the hills of credit afloat", and it further refused any other measure than a continuance of the existing excise. These resolutions gave offense to the representative of the crown and on the day following their adoption, the assembly was summoned to the fort and dissolved by a speech, declaring the said resolutions "to be such presumptuous, daring, and unprecedented steps that he could not look upon them but with astonishment, nor could he with honor suffer their authors to sit any longer."

The temper of the new assembly, summoned in the spring of the succeeding year, 1739, was no more in agreement with the desires of the Lieutenant-Governor than that of the previous assembly. The demand for a permanent supply bill was urged at several successive sessions, only to be met with refusals. This was followed by a long struggle between the official representative of the crown and the assembly. The lack of funding affected the defenses of the colony and every financial part of it.

Eventually supplies were granted, but only for the year and various appropriations were made for the defense of the colony. The Mohawks required that the dilapidated defense at Dyiondaroga (Fort Hunter) should be repaired or rebuilt and that a garrison should be stationed there. If this was not done there was a threat of the Mohawks leaving the country and moving to Canada. They were considered too important as a line of defense against the French to disregard their demand.

It is seldom that the wheels of revolution go backward, and the concession in which the general assembly allowed the funding for defense and supplies was claimed as the legal and known right of the crown and this appeased the popular party for a very short time. Nothing is more certain than the governed are never being satisfied with concessions and each successful demand only increases demand for more. Eventually the pendulum swings too far and then concessions have to be made to appease the other side.

The demand was made for the appropriations for a term of years. But the controversy was reopened in the spring of the following year, 1741, the Lieutenant-Governor delivered a speech listing the grievances of the crown because of the continued encroachments of the general assembly. The speech began by giving a review of the difficulties between the representatives of the crown and the assembly, in regard to the granting of supplies, and a lack of proper gratitude for the blessings which the colony enjoyed under the maternal care of the government. But it was not only in connection with the supplies that the assembly had invaded the rights of the crown. It was the undoubted prerogative of the crown to appoint the treasurer. The assembly had demanded the election of that officer. Not satisfied with that concession, they had claimed the right of choosing the auditor-general. Failing in that demand, they sought to accomplish their object by withholding the salary from that officer. They felt if they had to pay a public official, then they deserved the privilege of choosing said official. These inroads had been gradually increasing from year to year, until the concern was awakened in England "that the plantations are not without thoughts of throwing off their dependence on the crown." The assembly was urged to make sure the crown did not get the wrong impression "by giving to his majesty such revenue, and in such a manner, as will enable him to pay his own officers and servants". Of course the various assembly members denied they wished independence. But the assembly kept the financial purse firmly closed.

This clogged up the machinery of government. The independence principles were taking root in America and the seeds of the eventual rebellion were planted and slowly taking root and sprouting.

The Mohawks requested money for the rebuilding of their chapel but the assembly declined making the grant alleging that if the Christian converts in that nation were increasing, the funds required for a new chapel should be raised by private contributions and not by a government grant.

War had been declared by England against Spain and possibly a war was in the future with France. In anticipation of such an event, fortifications were required for the security of the harbor of New York and also for the strengthening of the defense of the frontiers, particularly Oswego. In the event of a war with France, the Lieutenant-Governor was concerned that this post would be taken and this would inflame the temper of the Six Nations. Appropriations were requested to enable the Lieutenant-Governor to appease a grand council of the Confederates at Albany. The Lieutenant-Governor's opening speech to the assembly of sachems and warriors was well received.

Clarke, first made an apology for not having met them earlier due to the spreading epidemic of smallpox in New York. He said he was concerned the infection might be spread among their people and he didn't want to bring the smallpox to them. He scolded them against the dangers arising from the trend of their young warriors to join the Indians who were supporting the interest of the French and in their hostile expeditions against the more distant tribes of their own kindred. The enticing of their young men in those expeditions, he argued, was a device of the French to divide and weaken them. "When united," said he, "you are like a strong rope, made of many strings and threads twisted together, but when separated, weak and easily broken. Thus they attempt to divide and weaken you, by leading your rash young men upon their distant wars. They hope to weaken you by degrees, to be able to conquer you. If they were lovers of liberty themselves, they ought not to try to enslave other nations."

The sachems were shrewd in their replies. In regard to Oswego, they wished "their brother Corlaer, would make powder and lead cheaper there, and pay the Indians better for helping to build their houses." Of the Tierondequot matter they replied: "You said that we had acted very wisely in not suffering the French to settle at Tierondequot, and that if they only had liberty to build a fishing hut there, they would soon build a fort. We perceive that both you and the French intend to settle that place, but we are fully resolved that neither you nor they shall do it. There is a jealousy between you and the Governor of Canada. If either should settle there it would breed mischief. Such near neighbors can never agree. "We think that the trading houses at Oswego and Niagara are near enough to each other." Touching the simile of the rope, they said it was their desire to make it strong by preserving friendship with as many nations as they could. "As our great father the great king has commanded us that we should be as one flesh and blood with the Indians to the southward and westward as far as the Mississippi, so we accept of them as brethren that we may be united as one heart and one flesh, according to the king's commandment. But we desire that some of the sachems of those southern Indians do come here, which will strengthen and confirm this treaty. We will give them two years time to come in, and in the meantime keep at home all our fighting men."

The council broke up amicably, and the Indians were well laden with presents when they returned to their homes, professing friendship which was to last so long as the Great Spirit should cause the grass to grow and the water to run. But however firm the grasp by which they purposed to hold on to their end of the covenant chain, their good resolutions were liable to be shaken by every trifling problem that awakened their unslumbering jealousy. Hoever in times of peril the steadfastness of the Indians; the Onondagas, Cayugas, and Senecas, was an object of big doubt inthe minds of the English. Still, the peace wrought by Mr. Clarke contributed largely to the peace with the Six Nations for the next two years, 1741 and 1742

A subject of local excitement during the year 1741 was the much discussed plan supposedly plotted by the Negroes toward the people New York City, to murder them and then and to ravage and burn the city.

The burning of the public buildings; the governor's residence, the secretary's office, the chapel and barracks in March, 1741 was first announced to the general assembly by the Lieutenant-Governor as the result of an accident. A plumber, who had been working on some repairs, left fire in a gutter between the house and chapel and it spread to other places. But several other fires occurred shortly afterward in different parts of the city, some of them under circumstances that could not be easily explained. This aroused suspicions that they were acts of incendiaries. Suspicion, to borrow the language of Shakespeare, "hath a ready tongue," and is "all stuck full of eyes which are easily put to sleep". Incidents and circumstances, ordinary and extraordinary, were seized upon and brought together by comparison, until it became obvious to all that there was actually a conspiracy with acts of arson to burn the entire city and murder the people. Nor was it long before the plot was fastened on the numerous Negro slaves. A Negro, with violent gesticulation had been heard to utter some terms of unintelligible jargon, in which the words "fire, fire, scorch, scorch," were heard or supposed to have been heard.

Terror is easy to spread. The terror of each man spread and became a source of terror to another. Universal panic spread and common sense was totally lost even among normally cautious and thoughtful people. A woman named Mary Burton confessed that she had heard Negroes talking privately about setting the town on fire. She at first only named Negroes; but afterward named several white persons among who were her landlord, his wife, another maidservant, and a Roman Catholic named Ury. Some other information was obtained from other informers, and numerous arrests were made and several strong apartments in the City Hall called "the jails," were crowded with prisoners, amounting to twenty-six whites and above one hundred and sixty slaves.

Numerous executions took place based on flimsy testimony; but jurors and magistrates were both panic-stricken and wild with the spreading terror. Among the condemned were landlord Hughson, his wife, the maidservant, and Ury Roman Catholic who was accused as a conspirator and for officiating as a priest by using an old law of the colony.

The whole summer was spent in the prosecutions, every new trial led to further accusations and spread the terror. A coincidence of slight circumstances was magnified by the general terror into stories of unbelievable proportions. Tales collected without doors, mingling with the proofs given at the bar and this poisoned the minds of the jurors. The terror of the day suffered no check until Mary, the chief informer, who was bewildered by frequent examinations and suggestions, began to name those who were above reproach. Then, as in the case of the Popish plot, and the prosecutions for witchcraft in Salem, the magistrates and jurors began to pause and think about their actions. This ended the terror for the people of New York City, but sadly many people had been sent to their final resting place by the wave which robbed people of their sanity.

Daniel Horsmanden the third Justice of the Supreme Court, published the history of this strange affair. Chief Justice De Lancey presided at least at some of the trials and he too, though he was an able and clear-minded man, was carried away by the perceived threats. Fear takes on a life of its own and takes over the minds of otherwise rational people and can cause a panic.

Here we will leave this part of the story and go on. There is just one little nagging detail to present in regards to the previous material. A bit troubling is the title Native American because it is not totally accurate since America had no native people. This is the title those people wish the world would use in referring to them, so it was done here.

So many pieces of stories from many countries contributed to the greater story of the settlement of New York. To summarize, there were a great many other peoples who settled New York and their stories were intertwined but for clarity sake, parts of the story were presented somewhat separate. The Native Americans, the English and the French history in New York has been presented. The eighteenth century Palatine movement was covered in the second book, So It Was Written, A Time of Terror, Part Two. There is no need to delve into the subject in this, the third book.

Now let's turn our attention to the story of the Dutch people in New York. We owe a great many of our freedoms and way of life to those sturdy settlers from long ago. I would highly recommend reading The Island at the Center of the World by Russell Shorto to gain a better understanding and respect for the early Dutch settlers.

The first settlers in the upper part of the Colony of New York were the Dutch who first settled at New Amsterdam (now the city of New York) and then established a trading post at Fort Orange, (now Albany).

Henry Hudson, working for the Dutch East India Company, explored the Hudson River in a ship called the *Half Moon* of 80 tons burthen, with a crew of 20 English and Dutch seamen. The purpose of his voyage was to find a northwest passage to the orient so ships leaving from a European port would not have to travel either around the tip of Africa as later explorations discovered, around the tip of South America. Finding a passage straight west from Europe to the Orient would make the Dutch East India Company very wealthy. Hudson's ship crossed the Atlantic and discovered the Hudson River in the autumn of 1609. From 1614 to 1664, a period of just fifty years, the Dutch held possession of the colony of New Netherland.

Captain Hudson went up the Hudson River above the present city of Hudson, and sent his mate with four hands in a small boat to survey the river further upstream. Probably the river was explored to the present site of Albany. As they traveled along the shores of the Hudson River, they saw many Indians by whom they were kindly treated. After passing through the Highlands, the captain sailed the stream the Five Nations called "Great River of the Mountains" or in their language, *Ca-ho-ha-ta-tea*. At first in colonial documents it was called the North River, to distinguish it from the Delaware, also discovered by Hudson and sometimes called the South River.

After the discovery by Captain Hudson, the Dutch immediately began to take advantage of their discovery. In 1610 at least one ship was sent by the East India Company for the very lucrative business of fur trading which was the principal commercial attraction to the new world. By 1624 a fort and trading post were built on the spot where Albany now stands and it was called Fort Orange. About the same time another fort and trading post was established on the southeast point of Manhattan Island called New Amsterdam. The whole colony received the name of New Netherland.

The position of Albany was first chosen by commercial people for a military post, convenient to trade with the Indians and about as far as a small ship could navigate up the river. Here a good ship channel was so close to the shore, it saved building docks. At Fort Orange they erected a stockade to guard against surprise attack by the Indians. The fort was later enlarged, better stockaded and the population slowly grew. By 1712 Albany contained nearly 4,000 inhabitants, a promising beginning for a city.

The first white woman in Albany was Catelyn Trico, who was a native of Paris. She said that in the year 1623, she came to this country in a ship called the *Unity*, the first ship sent by the West India Company. Upon arriving at New York two families and six men went to the Hartford River (the Connecticut); two families and eight men went to the Delaware River; eight men were left at New York to take possession of the entrance to the North River, and the rest of the passengers proceeded with the ship to Albany, then called Fort Orange. After arriving at Esopus (now called Kingston) which was the half way point to Albany, they lightened the ship by off loading onto some small boats which had been left the year before by Dutch traders. In this way the ship could proceed farther north on the river. She further stated that on arriving at Albany, there were eighteen families on board which settled themselves at that place and made a small fort. As soon as they made themselves huts of bark, the River Indians, those of the Five Nations, and some others came and made covenants with their commander, Jorise, bringing him presents of beaver and other peltry. Great numbers of Indians came to trade with them. (From Jeptha R. Simms, Frontiersman of New York, 1883.)

The settlement of several localities was referred to by Gov. Stuyvesant in his correspondence with Col. Nicholls when Nicholls demanded the surrender of New Netherland to the British Crown with four British men-of-war in the harbor of New Amsterdam. His letter was dated 2 September, 1664. He says the Dutch had enjoyed Fort Orange 48 or 50 years, Manhattan for 41 or 42 years, the South River settlement (the Delaware) for 40 years, and the Freshwater River (the Connecticut River) for about 36 years. This would make the beginning of these settlements arranged as follows Fort Orange, 1614; Manhattan, 1622; Delaware River, 1624; and Connecticut River, 1628.

<-Peter Stuyvesant's autograph.

Governor Stuyvesant was the last Dutch Governor of New Netherland, though the colony did not immediately settle down to English rule. For many years since ownership of the colony was switched back and forth between the Dutch and English. The little colony of New Netherland had no real defenses and when England surrounded the island and presented the articles of surrender, there was not much choice and no shots were fired. Then when the English were busy elsewhere, once more the Dutch resumed control.

Stuyvesant's administration began in 1648, and ended in 1664, when New Netherland became the English colony of New York. New Amsterdam also took the name New York, Richard Nicholls was the first English Governor of the colony. It was fortunate that the Dutch were the first settlers of the colony, because New Amsterdam became a city of refuge against the religious intolerance of the world and many of the freedoms we enjoy as a nation came from the Dutch Colony. The Dutch stamped their element of religious freedom on the colony which in time became part of the religious freedom guaranteed by our Constitution for the whole nation.

The administration of Governor Stuyvesant, was not generally noted for trouble with the natives. The relationship with the Indians is detailed in the book, <u>Documents Relative to the Colonial History of the State of New York</u>; Published 1855 procured in Holland, England, and France by John Romeyn Broadhead, Esq., Agent.

The book shows Stuyvesant's career at New Amsterdam was a thorny one.   In fact, his predecessors had their trials with neighboring white settlements and serious difficulties with the Indians surrounding them.   Not only was he constantly threatened with serious difficulty by the Indians in his immediate neighborhood; but he had a world of trouble with those around the pioneer settlement of Esopus, now Kingston. The safety of the pioneers received his personal attention in June 1658, when he found it necessary to enclose a village plot in palisades, and bring the adventurers from the boweries farms, to a residence within the palisades for their security. The enclosed town took on the name Wildwyck.

To look at the story of Stuyvesant's time in New Netherland, we can look at his writing Gov. Stuyvesant invariably called the natives "savages" which gives an idea about his low opinion of the red man.   Nearly all the serious difficulties between the Dutch and Indians started in a brandy bottle, (all liquor seems to have been called brandy at that period). So well known that liquor was the source of the problem. A city ordinance was eventually passed forbidding sale of brandy to the Indians. New Amsterdam tavern owner Sander Toursen and his wife violated this ordinance. They were arrested, banished from the country, and sent back to the fatherland. But there was a lot of money to be made from the Indians' great thirst for alcohol. Their inability to resist alcohol made it impossible to effectively stop the trade.

The Mohawks were generally friendly with the Dutch administration at Fort Orange or Beaverwyck, now Albany.   The earliest visit made by the Dutch into the Mohawk Valley is mentioned in a letter from Arent Van Corlaer, who was the director of the colony of Rensselaerwick to the Patroon in Holland in 1643. In the letter he says; *"I have been in the Maquaes (Mohawks) country last year with Labatie and Jacob Janson, of Amsterdam, where three Frenchmen are kept prisoners; among them a Jesuit, a very learned man, whom they treated very badly by cutting off his fingers and thumbs."* He spoke of visiting all their three castles, but named none of them or their location. VanCorlaer and his associates were welcomed by the natives, who went hunting and brought back some fine wild turkeys. Such game is mentioned as having been killed at Esopus. Van Corlaer offered a ransom of 600 florins for the three French captives. It was not taken but he extracted a promise that their lives would be spared.

On September 6, 1659 the Chiefs of the Mohawks at Fort Orange met the representatives of the government and renewed a treaty of friendship with the Dutch, bringing valuable presents of pelts and wampum. Sickness prevented Gov. Stuyvesant from being present at the conference, so he sent   representatives in his place.   He states that their first castle was Kaughnuwage, now Fonda. In the presence of the Chiefs, September 24, 1659, the conference was consummated with a gift of wampum, 75 lbs. of powder, 100 lbs. of lead, 15 axes and a quantity of knives. The Maquaes, which is what the Dutch called the Mohawks, had four towns or castles along the Mohawk River.

Spafford said regarding the settling of Schenectad in his <u>Gazetteer of New York</u>, in 1824, *"Some time previous to 1620, 15 or 20 persons, 12 of who came direct from Holland, and the rest from Albany, settled here in the fur trade."* He quoted no authority for what he said.   This statement, which was wide of the truth, has misled many early writers.   The volume of <u>Colonial Documents</u> mentioned previously, shows the place to have been settled after 1660, or more than 40 years later than the time given by Spafford.

In 1661, Arent Van Curler obtained permission from the Governor and Council for himself and others, to purchase from the natives the "Great Flat back of Fort Orange Inland" or the lands at and around Schenectada for their own occupancy. As soon as this became known at Beaverwyck (Albany) a protest went to the Governor stating that great damage might be done to that place if the settlers were allowed to trade with the Indians. The loss of profit and lessening of a portion of their fur trade was the real reason for the protest.

April 6, 1662 Van Curler wrote the Governor that he and his friends had secured the Indian title to the flats and he wanted the surveyor, Jacques Corteljou, sent up to survey and partition the lands.

A condition was set, at least twenty families must go upon the lands, while all trade was to be between the Albany residents and the Indians only. A few settlers had gone there, and on May 9, 1663, Surveyor Corteljou came up to partition the land only to be stopped by a protest from the Albany settlers, charging the settlers with having done some trading with the Indians.   This prompted the Governor to exact a written stipulation from those settlers that they were to have no dealings whatever with the natives.

Of course the Schenectada settlers were against signing this pledge and wanted the same privileges as other settlers in the colony.   A protest was signed by A. Van Corlaer, Philip Hendricksen, Sander Leendertsen Glen, Simon Volckertsen, Pieter Sogemaoklie, Tennis Cornelissen, William Teller, Gerret Bancker, Bastian De Winter who was authorized to sign the name of Cateleyn, the widow of Arent Andrissen, Pieter Jacobson Borsboom, Pieter Danielsen Van Olindee, Jan Barentsen Wemp and Jacques Cornelis.

Here are probably the names of the pioneer settlers of Schenectada, who had located there in the preceding two years. In September following, Jan B. Wemp and Martin Mauverensen contracted with Hendricksen to do general farm work at their bowery at "Schenechtede." The latter names were no doubt, those of two more permanent settlers and we may suppose that by this time the twenty families required as requisite for the settlement to have been made up. The master spirit of the place was Arent Van Corlaer.

In April, 1664, S. L. Glen, W. Teller and Harmen Tedder, on behalf of the settlement renewed the petition for a survey and Gov. Stuyvesant sent Sir Jacques Corteljou to survey and allot a share to each of those in the settlement. Schenectada became the westernmost town in the colony. The next September, the English captured New Netherland, but Albany prevented its becoming a place of trade.

As early as 1603, 200 ships were engaged in the New Foundland fishery, and employed at least 10,000 men. In the same year Samuel Champlain, sailed up the St. Lawrence, and in 1608 he planted a colony of his countrymen at Quebec. Other settlements soon began, and a lasting friendship established between the settlers and the Algonquin and other Canadian Indians along the St. Lawrence and its connecting chain of lakes.

The Dutch at New Netherland also formed friendly relations with the Indians in their vicinity, and mainly through the management at Fort Orange with the Mohawks and Senecas at first, and finally with the whole confederacy of the Five Nations and their allies, extending from central to western New York.

Schenectada was built on the site of a large castle once occupied by the Mohawks. The original Indian word signified, literally, *a great multitude collected together*.

The white man purchased ownership to the soil from the Indians, but the Indians still traveled their old hunting grounds in the forests surrounding their white neighbors. For a century the Indian settlements were mostly located in Western New York, and continued to be referred to as such until the close of the American Revolution. After losing the war, the red men were forced to leave their lands and retreat to Canada.

In 1690, Schenectada was the only white settlement west of Albany and was situated on the south bank of the Mohawk. By road it was nearly twenty miles from Albany to Schenectada. The place contained upwards of 80 well built and well furnished houses. Any one familiar with the present day cities of Albany and Schenectady will some of the early Dutch dwellings still standing.

The town in form, was an oblong shape and extended up and down the river. It had two entrance gates, one at each end of the enclosure. Its population was approximately 200.

The number of men sent to destroy this pioneer village of Schenectada in 1690 was about 200, 50 of whom were Indians and 150 were French. The Indians were mostly from the Caughnawaga tribe of the Mohawks who had become converts of the French Jesuits, and had settled near Montreal. The attackers started at mid winter, the troops having to carry upon their backs their own subsistence for the journey. They arrived at Schenectada the beginning of February on the 8th after a journey of 22 days. The last half of the journey was full of incredible suffering.

The destroyers arrived within a few miles of the doomed village. The French, who were suffering from cold and hunger, were thinking to surrender themselves prisoners of war; but the Indians learned that its inhabitants were not on guard. Security was so lax, the gates of the town were not even closed at night. A detachment went to the western gate, followed by the Indians under Agniez; while two junior officers led another party destined to enter at the eastern gate, but failing to find it they returned and joined their comrades at the western gate.

Entering the town unobserved, the troops were stationed at each dwelling. When the signal was given, the nighttime quiet was broken by one of the most frightful war whoops that ever greeted human ears, which was the signal for the terrible slaughter to begin. The greeting of the enemy awoke the little garrison at the fort, but the enemy forced their way in and either killed or captured its inmates. The fort was burned. Orders had been given to spare the minister, a Dutchman named Petrus Tasschemaker from whom the enemy hoped to obtain information, but in the confusion he was slain and burned in his house along with his papers. Some writers have stated that the place contained a church which was also burned.

At the end of two hours the destruction of the place was complete. The French account says only two houses were spared, but an account preserved in Albany, says the houses and barns were all burned except five or six, which were spared at the intercession of Capt. Alexander Glen, a brave man, who resided across the river. His wife had previously treated some French prisoners very humanely. Adam Vrooman, who was a courageous man, made a successful defense of his dwelling, seconded by the aid of a son who loaded guns for him; but his wife imprudently set a door ajar to let out the smoke of his firing. This gave an advantage to an Indian who shot through the door and killed her. A daughter fled early from the house with her infant child in her arms and was captured, the brains of the child dashed out.

The number murdered is 60; 11 Negro slaves, 7 soldiers of the garrison, 1 Mohawk Indian, and 1 French female prisoner. The captives made were 28, including 5 slaves, 3 soldiers, and an interpreter named Vielie. The little garrison, seems to have consisted of only ten men. Just how many escaped by flight to Albany is unknown; but several writers have stated that some 25 of them were more or less frost-bitten. In the confusion and darkness of the first attack, which was in the midst of a blinding snow-storm, it is possible that 40 or 50 escaped from the gate to Albany, scantily clothed. The snow on the ground was nearly knee deep and the fugitives suffered dreadfully.

The first bearer of Schenectada's doom to Albany was Simon Schemerhorn whose son Johannes perished in the attack. Schemerhorn arrived at five o'clock on Sunday morning on horseback. Several of the enemy fired upon him, but he escaped with a bullet through his thigh, which also wounded his horse. The news spread quickly through the town, it was believed the enemy would also visit the city and alarm guns were fired at the fort, one of which burst severely wounding a man named Sharpe. Messengers were sent to the towns along the Hudson for assistance but due to fear, a pursuit of the retreating enemy began three days after the attack, too late to catch them.

On Monday Capt. Bull, with a party of troops, was sent from Albany to bury the dead, protect the remaining citizens, and join in pursuit of the enemy. The French account says the lives of between 50 and 60 persons of Schenectada were spared, consisting of old men, women and children, who escaped the fury of the first attack.

After gaining possession of the town, the French officers took the precaution to destroy all the liquor they found, to prevent any of the troops from getting drunk. On their return march, among the plunder were 50 good horses, all but 16 being slaughtered for food before reaching Montreal. The French claimed, in this invasion, to have destroyed property at Schenectada valued at £400,000.

About 100 Mohawk Braves, with some 40 river Indians and about 50 white volunteers from Albany, pursued the enemy to Lake Champlain. The ice was solid and the enemy put their plunder on sleds, and with the stolen horses escaped. The pursuers gave chase and attacked their rear. A French account admitted a loss of 21 men during their trip back to Canada. Until the pursuers returned a report of their chase the Albany residents were so alarmed, that many of them were packing to move to New York City.

The names of the principal families which lost members at this time, were Wemp (now Wemple), Van Epps, Janse, Brat, Vielie, Teunise, Spoor, Vrooman, Meese, Marcellis, Gerritse de Goyer, Christoffelse, Aertse, Pieterse, Potman, Harmanse, Schaets, Schemerhorn, Teller, Groot, Vedder, Switts, Coon, Turmurent and Bouts.

The French through Jesuits with their settlement in Canada, introduced their own religious element, which in some instances enhanced the superstitious bent of the Indians.

The earliest Jesuit who made his way into the Mohawk valley was Isaac Jogues, who was born at Orleans, France, January 10th, 1607. In 1636, he was ordained a Priest and in the following July he arrived at Quebec. In August, 1662, he was captured on his way to the Huron Mission, by a party of Mohawks, and hurried to one of their castles, where he had to witness the terrible death of those captured with him.

After much suffering, he made his escape down the valley and reached Fort Orange, then occupied by the Dutch. The Mohawks pursued him and received a ransom for him and he was sent to New Amsterdam. (City of New York). Gov. Kieft supplied his needs and sent him to France. He was shipwrecked on the coast of England, and was destitute when he reached France. He was sent back by his superiors in France, to Canada, and was stationed at Montreal. On the conclusion of peace with the Mohawks, he was sent to their country as an ambassador.

May 16, 1646, he passed through Lakes Champlain and George and reached Fort Orange on June 4th and proceeded to the Mohawk's country. After a few days he returned to Three Rivers, where he arrived August 29. Again returning to the Mohawk Valley as a minister, he arrived at Gan-nu-wa-ge-Caughnawaga, October 17th, the place of his former captivity, and was again received unkindly. When he again left the Mohawks for Canada, he left a small box containing things of little value in a hut. When harvest time came it was found that a worm had destroyed much of the Indian's crop of corn. Superstition at once pointed attention the mysterious box of Father Jogues. The Indians were ready to sacrifice him to appease the evil spirits. On the evening of the day after his arrival he was struck on the head with a war club when he entered a lodge, then decapitated and his head was raised on a pole, ater which his body was thrown into the river. Thus perished the first Catholic missionary among the Mohawks.

The Mohawks sacrificed Father Jogues to their superstition, but at the end of a few decades, there were more converts in the Mohawk nation of the New York Confederacy than in any of the other nations. Many of the converts were persuaded to move to Canada so that at the end of a hundred years the converts had become quite a group near Montreal. Their settlement took the name of Caughnawaga, its people becoming known as the "praying Indians." It is difficult to determine whether or not this Canadian Jesuit religious element produced more good than evil among the Indians. It was often used as a cloak by the French to seduce the Indians who were friendly to the English colonies, to the interest of the French. They seemed to care more about the Indian fur-trade business and winning over the Indians from their English leanings than about saving their souls.

The colonies, from time to time, took stringent measures to counteract Jesuit influence. In 1647 the Legislature of Massachusetts passed an act against the Jesuits. In the year 1700 the Legislature of New York enacted a law to hang every Popish priest who should come voluntarily into the province. The same year the Legislature of Massachusetts passed an act against Jesuits and Popish priests, requiring them to leave the province by the 10th of September. The New York law was passed because a great number of French Jesuits were practicing their wiles on the Indians and inciting hostilities against the English Government.

The most serious disaster for the Mohawks was on the invasion of their country by the French and Canadian Indians. Gov. Frontenac dispatched from Montreal on January 15th, 1693, 625 men, consisting of 100 French soldiers, 200 Indians, and 325 active young Canadians, under the command of de Mantet, and 20 other French and Canadian officers. They were instructed to destroy the Mohawks, and commit as great ravages as possible around Fort Orange (Albany). The journey was made on snow-shoes by the men in front of the group with the army dragging their provisions after them on hand sleds over the frozen rivers and lakes. They entered the valley above Schenectada, but below all the Indian towns. On the first night of the invasion, John Baptist Van Eps, a young captive from the attack on Schenectada, a few years before, made his escape and brought the intelligence of the invasion to Schenectada and it was immediately sent on to Albany by an express rider. This brought a company of mounted troops to the assistance the next day.

The French on February 8, stormed the first Mohawk Castle, where there were only five men and some women and children, their other men were away and the five were all taken without opposition. The next fort was not far from the first, and it too was surprised without any opposition, both of them being small, and located next to the English, were not fortified. The war party arrived near the two Mohawk Villages, within fifteen leagues of Fort Orange, without being discovered. (A league is three miles.)

At night-fall, the Indians in company with some Frenchmen, went to enter two of the villages that were situated a short distance from the last castle they captured. On approaching them they heard the enemy singing so they waited until the Indians went to bed in order to surprise them while sleeping. The main body in the mean time advanced in two divisions, so as to be able to make a simultaneous attack on both villages. They were surrounded by strong palisades and closed with gates. Indians scaled the enclosure to open the gates. A crowd entered and became victors without resistance. The small village after having been burnt, was abandoned at daybreak, and the Indians and their families brought prisoners to the large village, where the commanders left a large force to guard them. Early the next morning, a party set off for the third village, seven or eight leagues distant, where they arrived in the evening and surprised it in the same manner they had the others. They set it on fire and brought the prisoners to the principal village.

By the French account we learn that the enemy only burned the small castle the first night, and the next evening they destroyed the Caughnawaga Castle; and on returning to Tienonderoga, where they had left their prisoners well guarded, they remained but one day. They not only feared to remain longer in an enemy's country, but softer weather warned them that their ice bridges over the rivers and lakes must be used soon if at all. After burning the principal village, with their prisoners and plunder they took the back track for Canada. We suppose this invasion to have been by the northern or Sacandaga route. On the first and second days, several hunters from the captured towns on learning that their wives and children were prisoners with the enemy, voluntarily became such and went with them to Canada.

On the third day an Iroquois scout overtook the enemy and had a parley with them, submitting certain peace propositions, and requesting them to halt and await the arrival of a pursuing party. The French looked upon this as a ruse, but their Indians prevailed on them to wait; in the meantime they threw up a breast work to protect them, and secure their prisoners. At this place Maj. Peter Schuyler, of Albany, with 250 whites and 290 Indians from the upper towns, arrived on the 17th; but fearing an ambuscade he approached the enemy by a circuitous route, and was saluted by three loud savage yells, which his Indians sent back with a will. There was little or no talk for peace, and Schuyler's men at once set about felling trees for a temporary defense. While busy with this task, the enemy made three attacks upon them, but each time they were repulsed with losses; neither party seeming anxious for a very general fight.

At this conjuncture Maj. Schuyler sent an express to Albany for more troops and provisions. The enemy moved forward on the 18th, a cold and stormy day, and a deserter arriving at the American camp said it would not be easy to follow them but the officers with 60 whites and a body of Mohawks pursued them until night with some success. They caught up with the enemy and when they came up to them, they released several prisoners to tell their pursuers that they would kill all their prisoners if compelled to abandon them. On the 19th the needed provisions and 80 men under Capt. Sims of the regular troops arrived at the American encampment, and the whole army moved forward. On the 20th, Major Schuyler was so straitened for food that he gave up the pursuit; and although meeting with some supplies and fresh troops he was afraid that the enemy would execute his threat and kill the prisoners as they threatened. The ice in the streams was becoming treacherous and all things considered, further pursuit was abandoned.

In the pursuit of the enemy, Schuyler lost four privates as many Indians, and two officers, and twelve Christians and Indians wounded. The whites were called Christians to distinguish them from Indians. The bodies of 20 dead were found by Schuyler's men, and so hungered were his Indian followers that they ate the bodies of the dead Frenchmen. Going among his Indian allies, Maj. Schuyler found them eating broth, which he was invited to share. He did so until he saw one of them ladle the broth from the kettle and a Frenchman's hand, was seen. This put an end to his desire to eat. Between 40 and 50 prisoners were rescued by the pursuers. The French admitted a loss in this expedition of 80 killed and 33 wounded. In their flight the enemy crossed a branch of the Hudson using a cake of ice, which had conveniently fastened itself from shore to shore

The enemy, on arriving at Lake Champlain left the lake shore to cross the country in the woods. Only about 50 of the prisoners were with the French at this time. They had stored food for later retrieval on way down for use on their return route. But the food had been spoiled by the rain, and the party nearly perished of hunger. They were out of food and were still fifty leagues from their nearest settlement. They were slowed down by having to carry their wounded. Never was there such distress in any army, which went four days without any food. Four Indians and a white man were sent forward for assistance and they reached Montreal in five days. One hundred and fifty men with provisions upon their backs, were hastened to the relief of the war party. One hundred and twenty were so overcome by fatigue and hunger, that they remained behind until they improved. Several died of hunger and many cast aside their arms and were almost unable to drag their heels after them. It is strange that they were not pursued in this weakened state.

In their great consternation at Albany, when the news of the invasion reached there, an express messenger was sent to New York to ask aid of Gov. Fletcher. By 8 A. M., the next day a regiment of volunteers were under arms and ready to march. When he asked who waswilling to go on this expedition, all threw up their hats in token of their readiness. The Hudson was open between New York and Albany, an event seldom seen so early in the season. The governor accompanied the troops, and preceded them to Schenectada, where the final preparation was made to give chase to the enemy, but by the time everything was in ready to move forward, they learned that Maj. Schuyler was on his return.

When the Mohawks came back from the pursuit of their enemies, Col. Fletcher made a speech to them and commiserated their misfortunes with promises of future assistance. The tardiness of the aid from Albany, when the enemy entered their valley displeased the Indians, who had so promptly rallied to revenge the burning of Schenectada. But the energetic and prompt action of the governor, did much to reconcile the Indians and in their answer to his speech, they called him *Cay-en-gui-ra-go*, signifying a great arrow on account of his alacrity in coming so far. But still, their chiefs told Col. Fletcher, that the French kept their Indian allies better armed than were the Mohawks, which accounted for the French having escaped in the late invasion.

In July, following this incursion of the French, Gov. Fletcher met the sachems of the five nations at Albany, and used a female interpreter. At this meeting, the best speaker of the Iroquois, *De-can-e-so-ra*, an Oneida, said: "We wish you gave less credit to rum-carriers than you do." This shows the contemptible character the Indian traders have among the Indians. They had from bitter experience learned to know that their troubles and quarrels not only came through the introduction of fire water among them, but that for a little of it they were literally robbed of their most valuable pelts. At a later period, through the administration of their affairs by Sir Wm Johnson, they made constant complaints and protests against the introduction of alcohol among them which they had discovered, demoralized them both physically and mentally, making them fit subjects for plunder and for all manner of immoral behavior and crime.

Near the beginning of the 1700s which was nearly an hundred years after a Dutch Indian trading post was established in Albany, the white settlers began mingling their homes among those of the red men along the water ways of Central New York and into the Mohawk Valley. The lands were more fertile, more plentiful, and the time was right for settlement. The Native American population was struggling with the white man's diseases and they were dying in great numbers. This ultimately helped defeat the red man.

The greatest average length of the Mohawk Valley settlements by 1740 or 1750 may have been 60 miles, and their greatest breadth 30 miles. While those of Schoharie Valley embracing Harpersfield extended some 40 miles in length by less than 20 in breadth. Many of the small settlements within those districts were miles and miles apart; well enough when only friends were abroad, but fearfully isolated and exposed to raids by the enemy.

All of these people and many more contributed to New York State. Truly it is the state that says:

Give me your tired, your poor, your huddled masses yearning to breathe free,
the wretched refuse of your teeming shore.
Send these, the homeless, tempest tossed to me.
I lift my lamp beside the golden door.

Inscription on the Statue of Liberty

Source Material:
The Life and Times of Sir William Johnson, Bart.,
by William L. Stone, Vol. I, Albany: J. Munsell, 78 State Street, 1865. CHAPTER I. 1534-1741.
The Frontiersmen of New York
by Jeptha R. Simms, Albany, NY 1883, Volume I, Page 13
Documents Relative to the Colonial History of the State of New York; procured in Holland, England and France
by John Romeyn Broadhead, Esq., Agent, Weed, Pasons and Company, Printers, 1855.
Fernow's, vol 12, New York Colonial History, 1877.
Frances D. Broderick's Papers, N.Y.S. Library-Manuscripts
A MILITARY JOURNAL During the American Revolutionary War, From 1775 to 1783. From the Original Manuscript by James Thacher, M. D., Boston, Published by Cottons & Barnard, 1827.
Smith's History of New York, vol II, pp. 70, 75
Bancroft's History of the United States, vol. III.

Wampum

Every now and then I hear someone say we cheated the Indians by buying land with beads. Well, yes and no. Those things were not called beads, but wampum.

When the white man first started settling the New World, an immediate problem arose. What to use for obtaining merchandise? The early colonists of course bartered things and in addition when they needed "money" various substitutes were used. Money was extremely rare and difficult to come by in the early colony. Any foreign coin would do and the thing the Indians used was wampum. They did not understand the white man's money and white man wanted to trade furs. The white man began making wampum which was what the Indians valued.

The role of wampum in conducting trade with the Indians is mentioned in a letter of August 11, 1628 by one of the earliest Dutch settlers, the Reverend Jonas Michaelius. Michaelius, having recently arrived in Manhattan and observed the Indians had products to sell, *but one who has no wares, such as knives, beads, and the like, or seewan [i.e. wampum], cannot come to any terms with them".*

In the winter of 1634 three West India Company employees were sent from Fort Orange to negotiate a price for furs with the Iroquois Indians, located west of the fort, in the Mohawk Valley. It seems some French traders from Lake Oneida had entered the area and were trying to gain control of the market. One of the three employees, a barber-surgeon named Harmen Meyndertsz van den Bogaert kept a journal of this adventure. On January 3, 1635 he was negotiating with the Iroquois, who offered to sell his company (the Dutch West India Company) all of their beaver pelts if they could agree to a price. Earlier, on December 30th, the Indians mentioned they had previously sold skins to French trappers. The Indians asked for four handfuls of wampum and four hand breaths of duffel cloth for each large beaver.

The importance of wampum to the Indian is best expressed in a letter from the Reverend Johannes Megapolensis, who was assigned to the fur trading center at Fort Orange, an outpost at present day Albany. On August 26, 1644, just over two years after Megapolensis had arrived at the fort, he wrote a short account of the Indians living in the region, the Mohawks. In this account he related the Indian attitude toward money as follows:

Their money consists of certain little bones, made of shells or cockles, which are found on the sea-beach; a hole is drilled through the middle of the little bones, and these they string upon thread, or they make of them belts as broad as a hand, or broader, and hang then on their necks, or around their bodies. They have also several holes in their ears, and there they likewise hang some. They value these little bones as highly as Christians do gold, silver and pearls; but they do not like our money, and esteem it no better than iron. I once showed one of their chiefs some money he asked how much it was worth among the Christians; and when I told him, he laughed exceedingly at us, saying we were fools to value a piece of iron so highly; and if he had such money, he would throw it into the river.

New Netherland Director General Peter Stuyvesant clearly expressed the importance of wampum to the directors of the West India Company in a letter he sent to them on April 21, 1660, where he stated: *wampum is the source and the mother of the beaver trade, and for goods only, without wampum, we cannot obtain beavers from the savages.*

Typically commodities were traded, such as cloth, metal utensils and liquor to the Indians for beaver pelts. Also, although there were regulations against it, guns and gunpowder were traded for pelts. When finalizing major agreements or large purchases the commodities would typically be given as gifts, then during the negotiations the Indians would be plied with liquor and a final agreement would specify an amount of wampum to be paid per pelt.

White man saw a profit in the making, he began producing "fake" wampum and flooded the market with it. Very soon, the substitute money, wampum, was abandoned. Whether the Indians received enough in Wampum to pay for Manhattan Island or not, well that is another story.

The Catholic Issue

In the name of their God, both Catholics and Protestants hastened to spread their version of the only truth as they saw it and convert the savages to their faith. The Protestants were very mindful of the terrible religious wars that had been waged over many long years in the old country and were determined not to be ruled by the Catholics and their ties to the Pope who was in that day, eager to make war in the name of God. Because of their old world experiences, the Protestants were very wary of the Catholics and suspected them of many devious deeds.

The religious climate in Europe was fractious and the people were forced to change their religious alliances along with their current ruler. It was not a matter of faith, but a matter of what they were told they had to believe. If they did not convert as they were told, they were persecuted for their ideology. Many were Lutherans, Calvinist, Zwingli and Reformed. All were fervently against what they considered the idolatrous bent of Roman Catholicism and endorsed the freedoms of the Protestant tenets.

America held great promise of religious freedom for Protestants. Queen Anne, the sponsor and benefactress of the Palatines was a fervent Protestant and at all costs was determined the Catholics were not to receive assistance from her. When it was discovered some Catholics had slipped through and gotten to America, they were shipped promptly back to The Netherlands.

Years later, Sir William Johnson shared this concern when he noticed the French Jesuits were invading further and further into the New York colony. He built the Anglican Mission church at Indian Castle at the Upper Castle to halt the march of Catholicism into the Mohawk Valley and the conversion of the Indians to that faith.

The war for the religious hearts of the people in America raged long and fierce for many years. From our point in time we simply do not understand such attitudes but this still is the case in many parts of the world. People are persecuted and hated for their religious affiliation.

The following is a list of the Catholic Palatines returned to The Netherlands. From:
Early Eighteenth Century Palatine Emigration
A British Government Redemptioner Project to Manufacture Naval Stores
by Walter Allen Knittle, Ph.D.
Published Philadelphia, 1937

Roman Catholic Palatines Returned to The Netherlands 1709 and 1711.

As mentioned previously, there was a deep suspicion harbored by the Protestants toward the Roman Catholics mostly because of the long religious wars in Europe. The Protestants did not want to live under the rule of the Roman See and were determined to keep Catholics out of the new world. Some lied about their religious persuasion to be allowed in America, but were sent back if they were determined to keep their Catholic beliefs.

The two lists presented were found in the Public Record Office, T 1/119, 136-153; T 1/132, 167-170. The first list is comprised of 2,257 Palatines sent back in 1709, the second includes those 618 returned early in 1711.

Because of the difference in the time of their sailing to The Netherlands, it has been considered desirable that the lists be given separately. Indeed, from the correspondence it appears that another list of about 900 Catholic Palatines should be found in the Treasury Papers in the Public Record Office. Such a list has not turned up and it may be that the 900 mentioned as sailing in 1710 were simply part of the 2,257 Palatines returned in 1709. The lists are not labeled carefully. As to their value generally, the disappointed Palatines may have found their own way eventually to the English colonies, particularly to Pennsylvania, as the large movement to that colony was to swell about 1717 and these people certainly had shown a desire to emigrate.

RETURNED to The Netherlands IN 1709

Abel, Michel, w. & 2 ch
Acht, Velden, w. & 2 ch

Anweyler, John, w. 2 ch
Anweyler, John, w. & 2 ch
Appel, John Jacob
Arnoldi, Philippus, w. & 1 ch
Arnolt, John, w. & 5 ch
Assenbreuer, Wolff
Bachteler, Michel, w. & 4 ch
Backer, Henry, w. & 8 ch
Bakkus, Ferdinand, w. & 1 ch
Balinger, Frantz, w. & 1 ch
Baseler, Frans, w. & 2 ch
Bauer, Andreas, w. & 6 ch
Baum, Feirig, w. & 4 ch
Baur, Peter, w. & 3 ch
Baur, Thomas, w. & 8 ch
Becker, Anthony, w.
Beckman, Michel, w, & 1 ch
Bekker, John, w.
Bekker, John w. & 1 ch
Bellesheim, Peter, w. & 1 ch.
Benedictus, Peter
Bergman, Nicolas, w. & 1 ch
Bernet, Matthias, w. & 2 ch
Berrier, John, w. & 2 ch
Bidsi, Adam, w. & 2 ch
Bidtiss, John Reidrich, w. & 1 ch
Biedliss, Henry, w. & 5 ch
Bietz, John's, widow and 3 ch
Bigerin, Elisabeth, & 1 ch
Bigerin, Magdalena, & 5 ch
Bilstein, Jacob, w & 4 ch
Binder, John, W & 3 ch
Birgh, Henry & 3 ch
Blaese, Christian, w. 1, Mary
Boepeleriter, Christian, w, & 3 ch
Borber, Philips
Bortholm, Matthias, w. & 2 ch
Braum, Ulrich, w. & 4 ch
Braune, Andries, w. & 2 ch
Brick, John, w. & 2 ch
Brieck, Matthias
Bruiner, John, w.
Brune, Philip, w. & 4 ch
Bucks, John Bernard, w. & 4 ch
Bug, Henry, w & 2 ch
Bug, John, w.
Bumri, Pancras, w & 3 ch
Bundersgell, John, w. & 4 ch
Calas, Lucas, w. & 3 ch
Catharina, Anna
Claes, Peter
Claes, Simon, w.
Claesen, John Dietrich, w, & 3 ch

Cobwasser, Anton, w, & 1 ch
Coenrad, Matthais
Collet, Michel, w. & 6 ch
Comas, Peter, W, & 4 ch
Conrads, Conrad, w. & 1 ch
Cosch, John Dam, W. & 4 ch
Crist, John, w. & 2 ch
Daniel, Anthony, w. & 5 ch
Dekker, John, w & 1 ch
Delman, John, w.
Diere, Hans Martin, w & 2 ch
Dietrich, Claes, W, & 7 ch
Dievedal, Hans Jurg
Diop, Abraham, w & 3 ch
Diwid, Frans, w.
Dohsban, Michael w. & 4 ch
Dol, John
Domas, Frans, w. & 1 ch
Domin, Anna & 3 ch
Eberhard, John w, & 4 ch
Edian, Bastian, w & 1 ch
Eeter, John, w & 4 ch
Ehrhard, Michel, w & 1 ch
Eiep, Conrad
Eigenman, John, w.
Einhorn, Caspar, w & 3 ch
Ellenbergerin, Eva
Engel, John Wm, w & 1 ch
Engle, Martin, W. & 2 ch
Engle, Peter, w & 2 ch
Engle, Robert, w & 4 ch
Eninghover, Philip, w
Erwein, John, w.
Eteler, Paulus, w & 3 ch
Euller, Jacob, w.
Eweling, John, w, & 3 ch
Eyg, Martin, w, & 4 ch
Eyler, Henry, w, & 2 ch
Feld, Hans Gerard, W & 6 ch
Fing, Adam, w & 1 ch
Fingin, Orsel, w & 1 ch
Finken, Elisabeth
Fischer, Gerhard, w & 3 ch
Fischer, Henry, w.
Fischer, John w, & 1 ch
Fischerin, Marg
Flohr, John w, & 4 ch
Flohr, Peter
Foog, Henry, w, & 1 ch
Forer, John, w & 2 ch
Franck, Michel
Friderick, Charles, w & 4 ch
Frisch, Nicolas, W, & 3 ch

Friss, John, w & 2 ch
Funck, Caspar, w & 1 ch
Gali, Andreas
Gali, Jacob
Gallobers, Gobeck, w, & 3 ch
Garino, Peter, w.
Gavas, Thomas, W. & 3 ch
Gevel, Anth., w. & 6 ch
Gevell, Henry, w, & 2 ch
Gerber, Jacob
Geres, John, w. & 2 ch
Gerhard, Hans Peter, w
Gieng, Elisabeth
Glasser, Bartholomeus, w & 2 ch
Graber, Peter, w.
Gress, Georg, w & 5 ch
Gress, Georg, Jun, w & 1 ch
Grosman, John, w & 3 ch
Gru, David, w
Gudt, John w & 2 ch
Guttien, Nicolas, w & 6 ch
Haen, Michael, w
Hag, Christian, w. & 3 ch
Hageboech, Dietrich, w. & 2 ch
Hain, Friedrich, w. & 2 ch
Hains, John Valentin, w & 2 ch
Hamer, John Wilhelm, w. & 4 ch
Han, Caspar, w. & 1 ch
Han, Matthias, w. & 2 ch
Hans, Michel
Hansen, Bernard, w. & 3 ch
Hansin, Anna Maria & 5 ch
Hansin, Eva
Hardman, John Conrad, w & 2 ch
Hardt, John
Hartman, Hans Jurg, w & 1 ch
Hartwig, Matth, w.
Hauff, Peter, w
Havig, Jost, w & 6 ch
Heber, Joseph
Heins, Nicolas, w. & 1 ch
Heiser, Jacob, w & 4 ch
Heiserin, Cristina
Hell, Balth, w & 5 ch
Helmschrodt, John, w
Hemerstorff, Haubert
Herbst, Hans Georg, w, & 3 ch
Herfener, John Steffen
Hergaet, Peter, w. & 1 ch
Herland, Conrad, w & 3 ch
Herman, Wikkert, w & 2 ch
Herr, John, w & 3 ch
Hersin, Margareta & 3 ch

Heyneman, John Henry, w & 2 ch
Hill, John, w. & 2 ch
Hoff, Peter, w & 5 ch
Hoffer, Christian
Hoffman, Jost, w & 2 ch
Hogenberger, John Nicolas, w & 4 ch
Holtzlender, Albertus, w & 5 ch
Heberin, Marg
Hulgas, Conrad, w & 4 ch
Jacks, Peter, w & 3 ch
Jagerin, Mary
Jener, Jorq, w. & 1 ch
Jkkert, Paltis, w & 2 ch
Jndepan, Stoffel, w & 1 ch
Jockim, John, w & 1 ch
Jong, John, w & 1 ch
Joon, Henry, w & 5 ch
Jorgo, Anthony, w & 5 ch
Joseph, Cornelis, w & 3 ch
Josten, Johannes, w, & 5 ch
Jrwitter, Francis, w & 2 ch
Justina, Margareta & 1 ch
Kaltdauer, Michel, w
Kaltdauer, Velten, w & 5 ch
Keers, Adam, w & 1 ch
Keiseler, Hans Jurg, w & 1 ch.
Keisser, Philippus, w & 1 ch
Kerger, John, w & 1 ch
Kern, Frederic, w & 1 ch
Kern, Michel, w & 2 ch
Kerpen, Nicolaes, w & 1 ch
Kert, Anthonius, w & 1 ch
Kesserling, Henry, w, & 1 ch
Keyer, John
Kien, Herman, w & 1 ch
Kien, John w, & 1 ch
Kies, John Jost, w & 3 ch
Kiffer, Philip, w & 7 ch
Kimmel, Hans Peter, w. & 5 ch
Klaes, William, w & 1 ch
Kle, Charles & 2 ch
Kleemans, Felte, w & 1 ch
Klees, John, w
Klein, Matth. W & 1 ch
Klein, William, w & 3 ch
Kleiss, Jorg, w
Klapper, Conrad, w & 3 ch
Kleyn, Michel, w & 5 ch
Klitter, Georg, w
Knauber, Paulus, w & 6 ch
Knedig, Jonas, w & 1 ch
Knees, Michael, w, & 3 ch
Knepel, Andreas, w & 3 ch

Knittelmeyer, Caspar
Kochin, Cath. & 3 ch
Kolb, Frans, w & 2 ch
Koll, Conrad
Koll, Peter
Kollet, Gerhard, w & 2 ch
Konig, Jacob, w & 8 ch
Kontenskein, Andreas, w & 3 ch
Koping, Cristoph
Korn, Michel, w & 8 ch
Kosserer, John, w & 4 ch
Kraft, Matthias, w & 3 ch
Krass, Philip, w & 4 ch
Krebs, Jost
Krehmer, Philip, w
Krielion, John, w & 1 ch
Kries, John, w & 5 ch
Krissilles, Dominick, w & 1 ch
Krissiles, Wm., w & 4 ch
Kristilles, Jurg, w
Kroebard, Matth. W, & 4 ch
Krumbs, Jacob, w & 1 ch
Kryss, Matth., w & 6 ch
Kryts, John, w & 2 ch
Kyrsteen, Martin
Kun, Mattheus, w & 1 ch
Kurtz, John, w & 2 ch.
Laan, Philip, w & 2 ch
Land, Anthon, w
Land, Philip, w
Lang, Christian, w, & 4 ch
Lang, Peter, w & 2 ch
Langin, Lea
Lans, Moritz, w & 4 ch
Laras, John, w & 6 ch
Lasara, Anna & her sister
Lassarig, John, w
Lauer, Hans Nicolas, w & 1 ch
Lauer, John, w & 3 ch
Lauer, John w, & 4 ch
Laurens, Michel, w & 4 ch
Lautwein, Henry, w & 4 ch
Leberd, Hans Jacob, w & 3 ch
Leborn, Matthias
Ledig, Hans Nickel, w & 1 ch
Leephaen, John & 1 ch
Leijdecker, Henry, w
Lenaker, Peter, w & 4 ch
Lens, Henry, w & 3 ch
Leonhard, Peter, w & 1 ch
Leonora, Barbara
Leora, Anna
Lerny, Matth., w. & 3 ch

Less, John Adam, w & 3 ch
Levin, Maria
Levin, Wm, w & 1 ch
Liber, John
Lindeboom, Peter, w & 1 ch
Linderin, Anna Maria
Littermeyer, Andreas, w & 3 ch
Loos, John, w & 2 ch
Loriss, Matthew, w & 3 ch
Loriss, Ulrich, w & 1 ch
Louka, Maria & 4 ch
Ludwig, Andreas
Ludwig, Anthony, w
Lut, Ulrich, w & 3 ch
Luts, John, w & 2 ch
Lutser, John, w & 2 ch
Lutz, John, w & 4 ch
Lux, Adam
Malena, Maria & 1 ch
Malleberger, Till, w
Mallefyn, John Peter, w & 1 ch
Mallerswed, Mastiaen
Mandernock, Wm
Marcks, Matth., w
Marg, Anna
Maria, a widow, 2 ch
Martin, Matth, w & 3 ch
Martin, Peter, w
Massia, Nicolas, w & 6 ch
Massin, Cath.
Matthew, Peter, w & 4 ch
Matthias, John, w & 3 ch
Matzer, Paulus, w
Maur, Hans, w & 5 ch
Maurer, John Jacob, w & 1 ch
Meenen, John
Meens, Anthony, w & 2 ch
Meerman, Jost, w
Megler, John Mattheus
Melchior, Frantz, w
Mellerd, John Nikel, w & 1 ch
Mengel, Hans Georg, w & 4 ch
Mets, Simon, w & 3 ch
Metshouer, John, w & 1 ch
Mey, Peter, w & 2 ch
Meyer, Hirg, w
Meyer, John Adam, w & 1 ch
Mayer, Paulus, w & 1 ch
Mieler, Caspar, w & 2 ch
Miller, Anna Marg
Miller, Peter, w & 2 ch
Min, John, w & 6 ch
Minek, Peter, w & 2 ch

Mini, Jor, w & 4 ch
Mitwig, Hermanus, w & 2 ch
Mondriaen, Salus, w & 3 ch
Moor, Gerhard, w & 4 ch
Morheister, Nicolas, w & 2 ch
Moriz, Dietrich, w & 3 ch
Mosi, Matthias, w & 5 ch
Mostert, Lambert, w & 3 ch
Mots, Frederick, w
Muller, Ehrhard, w & 1 ch
Muller, Hans Hurge, w
Muller, Henry, w & 4 ch
Muller, John, w & 1 ch
Muller, Kilian, w
Muller, Nicholaus, w & 4 ch
Muller, Philip, w & 3 ch
Mullerin, Barbara
Mullerin, Maria
Mullerin, Maria & 6 ch
Mulseberg, Dietrich, w & 6 ch
Musseler, Jacob, w & 1 ch
Negener, Michel, w & 1 ch
Neles, Michel, widow & 2 ch
Nelles, John Jacob, w & 3 ch
Nettel, Laurens Hagen
Neumenin, Maria
Neumeyer, Wentz, w & 2 ch
Neuss, Andreas
Nicola, Peter, w & 3 ch
Nilgen, Maria
Noll, Herbert
Notterman, John, w & 4 ch
Null, Herbert
Obel, John w & 1 ch
Obernheimer, Henry, w & 1 ch
Oberreidter, Hans Georg, w & 3 ch
Oberscheiner, Peter, w & 2 ch
Obert, Martin w & 1 ch
Oostwaltin, Otelia, & 1 ch
Opperdubble, John Jacob, w & 2 ch
Ortering, Nicolas, w & 4 ch
Otsbergerin, Anna Cath.
Otsenberger, John, w & 1 ch
Otterman, John w, & 4 ch
Palser, Jacob, w & 3 ch
Paner, Jacob w & 1 ch
Paulus, Michel
Paulusin, Agnes & 2 ch
Peer, Frederic, w
Peltemer, John, w & 2 ch
Pens, Jacob, w & 2 ch
Perkin, Elisabeth
Petri, Adam, w

Petri, Andreas, w & 3 ch
Petruzin, Remetius, w
Petter, Jacob, w
Pieck, Conrad
Pinheimer, Bartholome, w & 3 ch
Pleij, John, w & 3 ch
Pletseler, Georg, w & 2 ch
Plinling, Cristian, w & 4 ch
Poeck, Joseph
Polser, Henry, w & 2 ch
Pon, Hans William, w
Pons, Nicolas, w & 3 ch
Pooser, Nicolaes, w & 3 ch
Portman, Jost, w & 1 ch
Poself, John
Poster, Arend, w
Pouer, Matthew, w & 2 ch
Pras, Andreas, w & 2 ch
Preiss, John
Premer, Jacob w, & 4 ch
Pretser, Ulrich, w & 3 ch
Prietzgis, Friederic, w & 1 ch
Pritz, John w & 3 ch
Prol, Jost, w
Pross, Hans Peter, w & 3 ch
Pull, Nicolas
Quint, Anthony, w & 1 ch
Rauch, Matthias, & 4 ch
Rauch, Matthias, & 4 ch
Reggert, John Henry
Rehrer, Hans Jacob, w & 1 ch
Reicherd, Dietrich
Reidinger, Adam, w
Reinhart, Caspar, w & 1 ch
Reise, John Henry, w & 4 ch
Reinsenberg, Lorens, w
Reiter, Matth., w & 1 ch
Remer, John, w & 2 ch
Rick, Jacob, w & 2 ch
Riel, Jacob, w & 5 ch
Ries, Matthew
Riessen, Anna Catharina & 1 ch
Ring, Anthony, w & 1 ch
Ringer, Jacob, w & 1 ch
Ritterstein, Georg, w & 3 ch
Ritz, John
Ritz, Jorg, w
Ritzkorn, Hans Michel & 1 ch
Robbenicker, Nicolaes, w
Rodenfluger, John, w & 1 ch
Rose, Laurentz, w & 2 ch
Rosmarien, Catharina
Rosskops, Martin, w & 3 ch

Roth, Jacob, w & 2 ch
Rupen, Arnold
Rupix, Matth.
Ryes, Hans Georg, w & 2 ch.
Sachs, Bastian, w & ch
Sarton, Henry, w & 3 ch
Schadt, John Peter, w & 5 ch
Schaff, Bartholomeus, w & 1 ch
Schaffern, Marg & 3 ch
Schamerin, Catharina & 4 ch
Scharning, Andreas, w & 2 ch
Scheefer, Gerhard, w & 2 ch
Scheeser, Philip, w & 1 ch
Scheffer, John, w & 4 ch
Scheffer, Laurens
Scheffer, Reinhard, w & 2 ch
Scheffer, Servas, w & 1 ch
Scheffle, Henry, w & 1 ch
Scherner, Michael, w & 5 ch
Scheul, Flg, w & 2 ch
Schiffer, Nicholaus, w
Schilder, John, w
Schinkel, Hans Jacob, w & 3 ch
Schleyer, John, w & 1 ch
Schlitz, Martinitz, w & 1 ch
Schmidt, Hans Michel, w
Schmidt, Matthias, w
Schmidt, Nicolas, w & 4 ch
Schmidt, Peter
Schneider, Arnold, w & 2 ch
Schneider, Casper, w & 5 ch
Schneider, Hans Michel, w & 2 ch
Schneider, John, w & 2 ch
Schneider, Nicolas, w & 3 ch
Schneider, Peter, w & 2 ch
Schneider, Philip, w & 3 ch
Schnider, Philip, w & 4 ch
Schnell, Mattheus
Schofferin, Catharina
Scholt, John, w & 1 ch
Scholter, Tebalt, w & 4 ch
Schonberger, Bartholomeus, w & 1 ch
Schorin, Anna Cristina
Schreiner, John Martin
Schryver, Jacob, w & 6 ch
Schuch, Nicolas, w & 7 ch
Schuler, Matthais, w & 4 ch
Schuler, Peter, w & 5 ch
Seiger, John, w
Serbing, John, w & 1 ch
Sernart, John, Jr., w
Seyberger, w & 4 ch
Sider, John, w & 1 ch

Sieffer, Bastian, w
Sirin, Jurg Peter, w & 1 ch
Siss, Peter, w & 6 ch
Sissig, Herman, w & 3 ch
Sivin, John, w & 1 ch
Sleiss, Matth. W & 7 th
Slick, Martin, w
Smit, Hans Peter, w & 2 ch
Smit, Jaspar & 8 ch
Smit, John, w & 1 ch
Smit, Michel, w & 1 ch
Smit, Nicolas, w & 3 ch
Smith, Nicolas, w & 1 ch
Smonck, Joseph, w
Soeck, Peter, w & 2 ch
Soller, Dominicus, w & 6 ch
Sommer, Jacob w & 1 ch
Sondag, Francis, w & 2 ch
Sorg, Matthias, w & 3 ch
Spadt, Ludwig
Specht, John, w 2 ch
Speiss, Ferdinandus, w & 1 ch
Spierck, Martin, w & 6 ch
Spinler, Caspar, w & 4 ch
Spoor, Matth. W & 1 ch
Stahl, Didtrich, w & 1 ch
Stahl, Hans Georg, w & 3 ch
Stahl, Martin, w & 3 ch
Steenhouer, Christian, w & 4 ch
Steffing, Catharina
Stein, Hans Michel, w & 3 ch
Ster, Cristian, w & 1 ch
Steyn, John, w
Steyner, Michel, w
Stick, Herman, w & 2 ch
Sticker, Michel, [sic]
Stress, Michel
Stucker, John, [sic]
Sturtue, Caspar
Stutz, John, w & 4 ch
Swaebs, Philip
Swertel, Conrad, w & 4 ch
Syman, Simon, w & 4 ch
Taelem, Lambert, w & 1 ch
Taes, John, w & 3 ch
Tamper, Henry, w & 3 ch
Taub, Michel, w & 1 ch
Teiss, Thomas, W & 1 ch
Thibelhoffen, Jorg, w & 3 ch
Thilschneider, John, w & 2 ch
Thinkel, Andreas, w & 2 ch
Thomas, Johannes, w & 5 ch
Thomas, John

Thomas, Matth.
Thomas, Matth.
Thomasin, Barbara, & 2 ch
Tielman's widow & 3 ch (no other name)
Tielsbergen, Georg, w & 1 ch
Ties, Hand Peter
Tirstin (sic), w & 4 ch
Tirt, Hans Adam, w & 2 ch
Tragseil, Jacob, w & 5 ch
Trap, Laurens, w & 4 ch
Treeser, John, w & 2 ch
Tres, John, w
Trip, Matth., w
Tusch, John, w & 4 ch
Uder, Michel, w & 5 ch
Vagner, Nicolas, w & 1 ch
Valadin, John, w & 4 ch
Veigert, John Valentin
Veilandt, Peter, w & 1 ch
Viber, John Matth.
Visering, Anna Marie
Vogelsberger, Peter, w
Vogt, Daniel, w & 2 ch
Volck, John, w & 1 ch
Voltraut, John Matthias, w & 5 ch
von Bergen, Hans Peter, w & 1 ch
Voos, Serves, w & 5 ch
Vorbeck, Hane Georg, w & 2 ch
Vot, Hans Peter, w & 2 ch
Vuchs, Arnold, w & 3 ch
Wagener, Cath.
Wagener, Felte, w & 3 ch
Wagener, John, w & 1 ch
Wagener, John Eberhard, w & 2 ch
Wagener, Nicolas, w & 4 ch
Wald, Caspar Rickte, w & 2 ch
Waller, John, w
Walter, Adam w & 3 ch
Walter, Matth., w & 4 ch
Wanemacher, Henry, w & 1 ch
Warner, Andreas, w & 2 ch
Weber, Auinstin, w
Weber, Dietrich, w & 2 ch
Weber, Jacob, w & 3 ch
Weber, Matth., w
Weber, Michel, w & 2 ch
Weber, Philip
Weillmacher, Matthias, w & 3 ch
Weinberg, Conrad, w
Weisgerber, John, w & 2 ch
Wels, Jacob
Wenmer, John, w
Widi, Bernard, w & 4 ch

Widschlagem, Magdalena
Wikketey, Philip, w
Wilbert, Hans Martin, w & 4 ch
Wilhelmi, John, w & 3 ch
Will, John
Willer, Philips, w & 3 ch
Wimer, Simon
Wind, Peter, w & 3 ch
Wintenseimer, Christoph, w & 5 ch
Winter, Thomas, W & 3 ch
Wintzenehimer, Peter
Witer, Martin, w & 4 ch
Witner, Michel, w & 3 ch
Wolff, Caspar
Wolff, Henry, w
Wolff, Jorg, w & 4 ch
Wolffle, Peter, w
Wolschlager, Michel
Wyckel, Felte, w & 5 ch
Ysel, Anthony, w & 1 ch
Zirvas, Peter, w & 6 ch.

RETURNED to The Netherlands IN 1711.
ADDITIONAL PERSONS ARE SIGNIFIED BY PR. OR PRS.
Albrecht, Jacob
Altvader, Faltin, & 2 prs.
Alwinger, Hans Wilhelm
Apple, Christian & 5 prs.
Ascher, Jacob & 4 prs.
Baeker, Andreas, & 3 prs.
Bahr, Andreas & 1 pr.
Bath, George & 1 pr.
Bauman, Joost & 2 prs
Bauwer, Christiaen & 2 prs.
Becker, Frederick & 2 prs.
Bher, Peter & 1 pr.
Beihard, Eliz.
Bihm, Martin & 1 pr.
Braun, Dewald & 2 prs.
Brener, George & 1 pr.
Casner, Andreas & 5 prs.
Casnerin, Mar. Eliz, widow
Cleman, Bestian & 4 prs.
Cleman, Peter & 1 pr.
Cramer, Ludwick & 2 prs.
Craemer, Pieter
Creitzin, Eliz, wid. & 4 prs.
Dauhn, George & 2 prs.
Dhiel, Christiaan & 1 pr.
Diehl, Herman & 3 prs.
Dohrbach, Johan Jost
Donnerel, Jacob & 1 pr.

Eberech, Johannes, & 3 prs.

Eberhartin, Fronick, & 3 prs.

Ecker, Jacob & 2 prs.

Elberger, Hans George & 2 prs.

Emmel, Anthony & 4 prs.

Faller, Johannes & 5 prs.

Farey, Henrich & 4 prs.

Fatheyer, George & 4 prs.

Fatheyer, Martzele & 1 pr.

Feyersteen, Leonard, & 5 prs.

Fucs, Andreas & 4 prs.

Fuhrman, Mathias & 1 pr.

Frebes, Joh. Nicolaes & 7 prs.

Gerbie, Michael & 2 prs.

Gess, Godfried & 3 prs.

Getell, John. Peter & 1 pr.

Geyer, David, & 4 prs.

Gross, Frederick & 2 prs.

Gruberin, Marg.

Hahn, Mathias, & 1 pr.

Harnisch. Johannes & 2 prs.

Hatt, Conrad & 2 prs.

Hawel, Andreas, & 2 prs.

Hecht, Caspar & 7 prs.

Heck, Conrad & 3 prs.

Heck, Henrich & 3 prs.

Hein, Daniels

Herbert, Jacob & 3 prs.

Herman, Bastian & 1 pr.

Hern, Hans Henrich & 4 prs.

Hertzheimer, Henrik Thiel & 1 pr.

Hes, Jeremias & 3 prs.

Heym, Paul & 2 prs.

Heymaker, Johan Jacob & 1 pr.

Hillard, Marg.

Hiram, Christina & 1 pr.

Jacob, Christian & 3 prs.

Jacobs, Barth, & 2 prs.

Jager, Balthazer & 2 prs.

Jost, Christopher & 2 prs.

Kehl, Adam & 1 pr.

Kehl, Peter & 3 prs.

Khyn, Hendrick & 3 prs

Kiefer, Daniel & 2 prs

Klogner, Adam & 5 prs.

Klop, Nicolaes & 5 prs.

Klotter, Johan & 1 pr.

Koller, Jacob & 7 prs.

Kornman, Peter & 2 prs.

Kuts, George & 3 prs

Kyhn, Peter & 2 prs.

Kytter, Diedrick & 5 prs.

Labegeyer, Godfried & 1 pr.

Lang, Johannes & 5 prs.

Leiterman, Christopher & 1 pr.

Lingelbach, Barbara, widow & 3 prs.

Loch, Henrich & 4 prs.

Messer, Sylvester & 4 prs.

Meyer, Henrich & 3 prs.

Meyer, Leonard & 2 prs.

Mick, Johannes & 2 prs.

Mickel, Caspas & 4 prs.

Miller, Jacob & 2 prs.

Mittenbauer, Jacob & 3 prs.

Muller, Peter & 7 prs.

Muller, Valentin & 1 pr.

Musher, Jacob & 1 pr.

Netzel, Rudolph & 3 prs.

Neyman, Ludwick, & 3 prs.

Nonius, Johan Peter & 2 prs.

Ohness, Henrich & 2 prs.

duPre, Johan & 2 prs.

Reisser, Michael & 2 prs.

Retizner, Johannes & 1 pr.

Reuter, Wilhelm & 2 prs

Rinck, Melchior, & 4 prs

Ritte, Nicolaes

Roerbach, Christian & 2 prs.

Rohn, Johan & 7 prs.

Roop, Johannis & 1 pr.

Ropth, Johannes & 3 prs.

Roth, Johannes Jost & 3 prs.

Rottelin, Maria, widow & 6 prs.

Schaffer, Adam & 3 prs.

Schaffer, Conrad

Schelberger, Conrad & 2 prs.

Schenk, Nicholaes, & 1 pr.

Schenkin, Anna Maria & 1 pr.

Schick, Mathys & 2 prs.

Schickendanee, Christopher & 3 prs.

Schildebuck, Martin & 1 pr.

Schildt, Henrich, & 2 prs.

Schuck, Nicolaes & 5 prs.

Seydelmeyer, Mich. & 1 pr.

Shaffer, Johan & 2 prs.

Shaffer, Nicolaes & 4 prs.

Shaller, Jacob & 1 pr.

Sharr, Daniel & 2 prs.

Shober, Christiaen, & 3 prs.

Sieb, Michael & 2 prs.

Simon, Zacharias & 4 prs.

Sinkhaen, Conrad & 2 prs.

Sletzer, Jeremias & 5 prs.

Slingoff, Johannes & 4 prs.

Slisser, Andreas & 3 prs.

Smith, Caspar & 3 prs.

Smitzer, Martin & 2 prs.
Sneider, Peter & 2 prs.
Spengler, Frans & 1 pr.
Spengler, Fredr. & 4 prs.
Steyer, George & 4 prs.
Swartz, Christiaen, & 1 pr.
Swartz, Johannes & 3 prs.
Theyse, Peter & 2 prs.
Thiel, George & 4 prs.
Thiel, Johannes & 2 prs.
Tickert, Andires & 3 prs.
Umbach, Johan George & 3 prs.
Unverricht, Jacob & 5 prs.
Van der Myl, Philip & 8 prs.
Voight, Abraham & 5 prs.
Wabbel, Jacob & 5 prs.
Walter, Philip & 2 prs.

Waltman, Leonard & 3 prs.
Weber, Casper
Weber, Henrich & 5 prs.
Weisman, Henrick & 4 prs.
Weisner, Elisabeth, widow & 2 prs.
Weissin, Elisabeth & 1 pr.
Weyler, Andris & 4 prs.
Wickel, Jonas & 1 pr.
Windt, Henrich & 5 prs.
Wipff, Jacob & 1 pr.
Zents, Mathias & 1 pr.
Zieger, George & 3 prs.
Ziegler, Nicolaes & 4 prs.
Zinck, Rudolph & 4 prs.
Zittel, Jacob & 3 prs.
Zwartz, Jacob & 7 prs

The Melting Pot

America has always been known as the melting pot, a haven where people from many countries could settle and prosper. The Mohawk Valley also was such a place, the first people to come to the valley after the Native Americans were the Dutch and then the French followed by the Palatines. Here is information on still another group of people who came to live here in middle New York, the people from Scotland. They too, were fleeing terrible conditions in their homeland.

Scotland had a system called the Clan System. It owes its origin to the Celtic tribal tradition, and remains at its strongest north of the `Highland Line' where Gaelic was the primary language.

The introduction of the Norman Feudal System from the south altered the relationship between the clan chiefs and the king, in that lands which had previously been held by the clans were now deemed to belong to the monarch to be granted as he willed. The internal organization of the clans was little changed, and the chief, who succeeded according to the law of tanistry, dispensed justice in peacetime and led his clan in war. Each clan consisted of 'native men', related by blood, and `broken men' individuals or groups from other clans, who sought and obtained protection of the clan.

The Normans, who came north from England, adopted many of these customs; the great Sinclair clan in Caithness, for example, owes its size to the number of retainers who took to themselves the chief's name. The custom of fosterage, the mutual exchange of children (often including the chief's children) between families, did much to bind the clan together. The Gaelic proverb "Kindred to forty degrees, fosterage to a hundred", describes a feeling of clan loyalty and egalitarianism, which today stretches from Scotland to every country in the world.

Following are some of the clan names you might recognize (this is by no means all the names). Some of the names can also be from those of Irish descent:

Agnew, Armstrong, Baird, Barclay, Bisset, Boyd, Boyle, Bruce, Buchanan, Burnett, Cameron, Campbell, Carmichael, Carnegie, Cathcart, Chattan, Crawford, Crichton, Cummings, Cunningham, Davidson, Douglas, Drummond, Duncan, Dundas, Eliott, Farquharson, Ferguson, Fletcher, Forbes, Fraser, Gordon, Graham, Grant, Gunn, Guthrie, Haig, Hamilton, Hannay, Hay, Henderson, Home Hume, Irvine, Johnston, Keith, Kennedy, Kerr, Leslie, Lindsay, Livingstone,

Lockhard, (You can drop the "Mac" off these names and you will recognize them) MacAlister, MacAndrew (Anderson), MacArthur, MacAulay, MacDonald, MacDougall, MacDowall, MacDuff, MacDwen, MacFarlane, MacGregor, MacIntyre, MacKenzie, MacKintosh, MacLachlan, MacLean, MacLennan(Logan), MacLeod, MacMillan, MacNab, MacNaughton, MacNeil, MacNicol (Nicholson) MacPherson, MacQueen, MacSwan, MacRae, Maitland, Malcolm, Matheson, Maxwell, Menzies, Moffat, Montgomery, Morrison, Munor, Murray, Ramsey, Robertson, Rose, Ross, Scott, Shaw, Sinclair, Stewart, Stirling, Sutherland, Wallace.

The relationship between England and Scotland is still to this day an uneasy one. The Scots still fester and fret about being bound to England and now are trying to at least become self governing by being able to control their own Parliament.

In the past, England tried repeatedly to impose the Anglicans' form of worship and church government on the Scottish Kirk or church. The Scots took up arms against Charles I and when civil war broke out in England, they aided the Puritans against the king. After Oliver Cromwell executed Charles I without consulting the Scots, however, the Scots welcomed Charles's son as Charles II. Cromwell then marched into Scotland and imposed his rule. When Charles II was restored to the throne, persecution of Presbyterians continued.

Finally, after James II had been driven from the throne, Presbyterianism was firmly established as Scotland's national church. The Highlanders long remained loyal to the exiled Stuarts. In 1715 they attempted to restore the house of Stuart to the throne. James Stuart, known as the Old Pretender, was proclaimed James III. In 1745 they supported his son, Charles Edward, known as the Young Pretender and Bonnie Prince Charlie. The Young Pretender's quest for the throne ended in 1746 at the battle of Culloden when the Highland forces were defeated by the English and a great many of the men were simply slaughtered. The clan system of government was finished for good. The people were starving and life was very hard for the Scots during this period of time. America was a place of refuge and along with so many others seeking the means to survive, they made the difficult ocean voyage to America. Sir William Johnson and his son, Sir John Johnson, used a group of Scots who settled in the Johnstown area as their loyal guard. Sir William's and Sir John's idea of using the old feudal system was one the Scottish people understood and were comfortable using in this strange new land. The Clan chieftain ruled them and made decisions about who was the enemy and when they would fight them and they were very loyal to their new chief as they were to their old one across the sea.

If you would like to read an historically correct fiction, make sure to read Diana Gabaldon's Outlander series. The background information about Scotland and the clans is correct and it follows the story of a family to America before the Revolutionary War. The American part of the story is as correct as the Scottish part of the series; Governor Tryon appears as the Governor of North Carolina and as the Governor of New York.

The Scots In America

The author of the following mentioned book calls the people from Scotland, Scotch, which is the name of a whisky. I made the mistake of calling a Scottish man a Scotch at one time and was corrected, rightly so. The name is corrected where it appears in the article, but I can't change the title of the book.

The following history on the Scots is from:

Hanna, Charles A.
<u>The Scotch-Irish or the Scot in North Britain, North Ireland and North America</u>
Vol. 2. New York, NY, Putnam, 1902. (New York, privately printed, 1899.)

The extent to which the Presbyterian settlements of Scottish people had become spread over the American colonies down to the year 1760 may be inferred from the fact that there were 105 ministers on the roll of the Synod of New York and Philadelphia, which met in that year. It is stated by Dr. Alfred Nevin that there were at that time 200 Presbyterian congregations in the country. This estimate is below the actual number. 300 would be nearer right. There were more than 60 congregations in New Jersey; from 80 to 100 in Pennsylvania and Delaware; upwards of 40 in New England; about forty in Maryland and Virginia; more than 20 in New York; from 15 to 20 in North Carolina; and about 20 in South Carolina.

In the following list, the names of the ministers on the roll of the Synod in 1760 are given, with the names of the congregations under their care, and the probable date of organization of each congregation. From this data, we can determine approximately the time and the size of the settlement of many of these communities.

In this light the following list of churches is presented and you can see where the Scottish people settled.

Presbytery of New York.

Timothy Allen, Ashford, Mass.
Enos Ayres, Blooming Grove, Orange County, NY
David Bostwick, New York City (1707)
John Brainerd, Newark, N. J.
Abner Brush; Alexander Cumming, New York (1707) or Boston (1727)
John Darby, Jonathan Elmer, New Providence, NJ
Chauncey Graham, Rumbout (before 1748) and Poughkeepsie, N. Y.
Jacob Green, South Hanover (Madison), N. J. (1747)
Simon Horton, Newtown, L. I.
Timothy Johnes, Morristown, N. J. (1733)

Abraham Kettletas, Elizabethtown, N. J. (1667)
Hugh Knox, Saba Island, West Indies
Silas Leonard, Goshen, N. Y. (1720)
John Maltby, Bermuda Island
John Moffatt, Wallkill, Orange couny, N. Y. (1729)
John Piersen , Mendham (1735-38), NJ
Aaron Richards, Rahway, N. J. (1741)
Azel Roe, licensure reported 1760
Caleb Smith, Orange, N. J.
John Smith, Rye and White Plains, N. Y.
Nathaniel Whitaker, Chelsea, Conn.
Benjamin Woodruff

Vacancies in the NY Presbytery: Florida (1750); Pittsburgh (174?); Union (1743); Cherry Valley (1744); Albany (1760); Middlefield (1755); Cambridge (1761); Salem (1761-64).

Presbytery of Suffolk, Long Island.

Eliphalet Ball, Bedford, Westchester County, N. Y.
Moses Baldwin; James Brown, Bridgehampton, L. I.
Samuel Buel , East Hampton, L. I.
Thomas Lewis, Hopewell (1709)
and Maidenhead, N. J. (1709)
Ebenezer Prime, Huntington, L. I.
Abner Reeve, Moriches and Ketchabonock, L. I.
Samuel Sackett, Hanover and Crompond, N. Y.
Benjamin Talmage, Brookhaven, L. I.; Sylvanus White , Southampton, L. I.

Presbytery of New York

David Austin, ordained, 1788
Ebenezer Bradford, licensure reported, 1775

Mathias Burnet, licensure reported, 1774
John Burton (received from Scotland), 1785

Jedediah Chapman (received), 1766
Oliver Deeming, ordination reported, 1771
Thaddeus Dodd, ordination reported, 1778
Peter Fish, licensure reported, 1781
Lemuel Fordham, licensure reported, 1781
James Glassbrook (from England), 1786
Joseph Grover (from New England), 1774
Thomas Jackson (from Scotland), 1767
John Joline, ordination reported, 1781
Andrew King, first enrolled, 1778
Amzi Lewis (from New England), 1770
John Lindley, licensure reported, 1786

Samuel McCorkle, licensure reported, 1774
John McDonald (from Scotland), 1785
Alexander Miller, licensure reported, 1768
Jonathan Murdock, ordination reported, 1771
John Murray (from Ireland), 1764
Joseph Periam, licensure reported, 1774
Peter Stryker, ordained, 1788
James Thompson (from Scotland), 1786
James Tuttle, licensure received, 1767
James Wilson (from Scotland), 1785
James Wilson, 2d (licentiate from Scotland), 1786
John Young, first enrolled, 1788.

Presbytery of Suffolk, Long Island

Joseph Avery, licensure reported, 1771
Nehemiah Barker, first enrolled, 1764
John Blydenburgh, licensure reported, 1772
Wait Cornwall, ordination reported, 1788
John Davenport, ordination reported, 1775
Benjamin Goldsmith, licensure reported, 1763
Joshua Hart, ordination reported, 1772
Asa Hillyer, licensure reported, 1788
Samson Occam (an Indian), first enrolled, 1764
Thomas Payne (received), 1764

Elam Potter, ordination reported, 1767
Ezra Reeves, first enrolled 1761
David Rose, ordination reported, 1766
Thomas Russell, ordination reported, 1788
Noah Wetmore, first enrolled, 1788
Joshua Williams, ordination reported, 1786
Nathan Woodhull, ordination reported, 1786
William Woodhull, licensure reported, 1768
Aaron Woolworth (received from New England), 1788.

The General Assembly of the Presbyterian Church in the United States met at Philadelphia on the third Thursday of May 1789, succeeding the Synod of New York and Philadelphia, which had been divided the year before into the four Synods of New York and New Jersey, Philadelphia, Virginia, and the Carolinas. In the volume containing the published records of the General Assembly from 1789 to 1820, you will find the year to year reports of the various Presbyteries in the Assembly, showing the different congregations and ministers in each Presbytery. The reports show nearly all of the American Presbyterian congregations which were in existence at the close of the eighteenth century.

The Associate Presbytery of New York, which was organized in New York City, May 20, 1776, included in its territory not only the State of New York, but New England.

On October 31st, same year, upon the union of the Associate and Reformed Churches of America, this Presbytery became a part of the Synod of the Associate Reformed Presbyterian Church.

On June 2, 1786, the name of the Presbytery was changed from New York to Londonderry. In 1788 it was called the Associate Reformed Presbytery of New England.

In 1793, the Associate Reformed Presbytery of New England united with the Presbytery of Londonderry.

The Reformed Presbyterian Church in America was first organized into congregations by the Rev. John Cuthbertson, who came from Ulster in 1751, and labored as a missionary through the frontier settlements of Pennsylvania and New York for nearly forty years.

The Scottish in North Britain, North Ireland, and North America

In New York City, the Scottish and Scot-Irish emigrants began to settle before the year 1700. Francis Makemie preached to the Presbyterians in January, 1707, for which service he was arrested and imprisoned. The Presbyterian Congregation in New York was not formally organized until 1717. A number of Scot-Irish emigrants settled in the vicinity of Goshen, Orange County, New York, before 1720, and in that year their church at Goshen was organized. During the decade from 1720 to 1730 some forty families from Northern Ireland settled along the Wallkill River in what are now Orange and Ulster counties. At Bethlehem, in Orange County, and at Wallkill, in Ulster, these people organized two churches about 1729, and in September of that year applied to the Philadelphia Synod for ministers to preach to them. These settlers were joined in 1731 by a second colony from Northern Ireland, with which came Charles Clinton and his sister, Christiana Clinton Beatty, the former the father and grandfather of two Revolutionary generals and two governors of New York; the latter the mother of two noted Presbyterian divines, both named for her brother, Charles Clinton.

The dividing line between the French and English possessions in America was left in dispute by the Peace of Utrecht, and in 1731 the French governor of Canada made a movement to secure a large part of the disputed territory for France by building a fortress at Crown Point. Great alarm was felt along the northern frontier of New York; it was realized that in case of war much greater access would be given for the murderous expeditions of the French and Indians than ever before. The obvious counter movement would have been for New York to build a fort at Ticonderoga, but the Governor and the Assembly were in constant conflict with each other, and nothing was done. Even Fort Anne was left in ruins, and no defenses were erected at the head of Lake Champlain or Lake George. Fort Saratoga, however, was still kept up, though not in a proper manner. The only move towards counteracting the French advance was an attempt made to settle the territory above the Saratoga patent with a colony of fearless Scots. In 1735 a proclamation was issued by the governor inviting "loyal Protestant Highlanders" to settle the lands between the Hudson and the northern lakes, the men of the tartan and claymore being considered the best defenders that the province could have.

In 1737, Captain Lauchlin Campbell, of Islay, a Highland soldier of distinguished courage, came to America in response to this proclamation, and went over the Territory of Washington County to see if a colony could be located there. He was satisfied with the locality, and according to his statement, which was in all probability true, Lieutenant-Governor Clarke (acting governor at that time) promised him a grant of thirty thousand acres for the use of a colony, free of all expenses except surveying fees and quit rent.

Campbell returned to Scotland, sold his property there, and raised a company of four hundred and twenty-three adults, to come to America. In 1738 the first group of Scots crossed the Atlantic in anticipation of receiving the land grant. On his arrival, the governor insisted on his full fees and a share in the land. This Campbell refused to give to the governor, the fees he was perhaps unable to give. Governor Clarke pretended to be very anxious to aid the emigrants, and recommended the Legislature to grant them assistance. But the Legislature was, as usual, at war with the governor and refused to vote money to the emigrants, which they suspected with good reason, the latter would be required to pay to the colonial officials for fees. The members of the colony were obliged to separate to earn their living. Once again the New York Colonial government was given a chance to confound the plans for settlement of a good, honest and hard working group of people, and once more it did so.

A full account of this enterprise was set forth by a son of Lauchlin Campbell in a "Memorial" to the Lords of Trade, printed in the <u>Documentary and Colonial History of New York</u>, vol. Vii., p. 630, from which the following is included:

To the Right Honorable Lord Commissioners of Trade, etc., memorial of Lieut. Donald Campbell of the Province of New York Plantation, humbly showeth:

That in the year 1734, Colonel Cosby being then governor of the province of New York, by and with the advice and assent of his Council published a printed advertisement for encouraging the resort of Protestants from Europe to settle upon the northern frontier of the said province (in the route from Fort Edward to Crown Point) promising to each family two hundred acres of unimproved land out of one hundred thousand acres purchased from the Indians, without any fee or expenses whatsoever, except a very moderate charge for surveying, and liable only to the King's quit rent of one shilling and nine pence farthing per hundred acres, which settlement would at that time have been of the outmost utility to the province, and these proposals were looked upon as so advantageous that they could not fail of having a proper effect.

That these proposals, in 1737, falling into the hands of Captain Lauchlin Campbell, of the Island of Islay, he the same year went over to North America, and passing through the province of Pennsylvania, where he rejected many considerable offers that were made to him, he proceeded to New York, Cosby was deceased, George Clarke, Esq., then governor, assured him no part of the lands were as yet granted; importuned him and two or three persons that went over with him to go up and visit the lands, which they did, and were very kindly received and greatly caressed by the Indians.

On his return to New York he received the most solemn promises that he should have a thousand acres of land for every family that he brought over, and that each family should have, according to their number, from five hundred to one hundred and fifty acres, but declined making any grant till the families arrived, because, according to the constitution of that government, the names of the settlers were to be inserted in that grant. Captain Campbell accordingly returned to Islay, and brought from thence, at a very large expense, his own family and thirty other families, making in all one hundred and fifty-three souls.

Campbell went again to visit the lands, received all possible respect and kindness from the government, who proposed an old fort, Anne, to be repaired, to cover the new settlers from the French Indians. At the same time, the people of New York proposed to maintain the people already brought till Captain Campbell could return and bring more, alleging that it would be for the interest of the infant colony to settle upon the lands in a large body; that, covered by the fort, and assisted by the [friendly] Indians, they might be less liable to the incursions of enemies;

That to keep up the spirit of the undertaking, Governor Clarke, by a writing bearing date the 4th day of December, 1738 , declared his having promised Captain Campbell 30,000 acres of land at Wood Creek, free of charges, except the expenses of surveying and the King's quit rent, in consideration of his having already brought over thirty families, who, according to their respective numbers in each family, were to have from 150 to 500 acres. Encouraged by this declaration, he departed in the same month for Islay, and in August, 1740, brought over 40 families more; and under the faith of the same promises made a third voyage, from which he returned in November, 1740, bringing with him 13 families, the whole making 83 families, composed of 423 persons, all sincere and loyal Protestants, and very capable of forming a respectable frontier for the security of the province;

But after all these perilous and expensive voyages, and though there wanted but 17 families to complete the number for which he had undertaken, he found no longer the same countenance or protection, but on the contrary it was insinuated to him that he could have no land either for himself or the people but upon conditions in direct violation of the faith of government, and detrimental to those who upon his assurances had accompanied him into America [i. e., that he should bribe the officials for their assistance in securing legislative approval of the grant]. The people also were reduced to demand separate grants for themselves, which upon large promises some of them did, yet more of them never had so much as a foot of land, and many listed themselves to join the expedition to Cuba.

That Captain Campbell, having disposed of his whole fortune in the Island of Islay, expended the far greatest part of it from confidence in these fallacious promises, found himself at length constrained to employ the little he had left in the purchase of a small farm, 70 miles north of New York, for the subsistence of himself and his family, consisting of three sons and three daughters. He went over again into Scotland in 1745, and having the command of a company of Argyleshire men, served with reputation under his Royal Highness, the Duke, against the rebels. He went back to America in 1747, and not long after died of a broken heart.

In January, 1763, Donald, George, and James Campbell, sons of Lauchlin Campbell, presented a petition asking for a grant of a 100,000 acres between Batten Kill and Wood Creek. It is difficult to account for the seeming exorbitance of this request, as under the terms of his contract with Governor Clarke, Lauchlin Campbell would have been entitled to only 83,000 acres. It has been suggested that the Campbells intended, or claimed that they intended, to provide for the descendants of the colonists who had expected to settle under their father's direction. A more probable explanation, in view of what had happened before, would be, that it was designed to use a portion of the grant as a bribe to secure the passage of the act.

The petition was rejected on the ground that the orders of the English government positively forbade the granting of over a thousand acres to any one person. Nevertheless, it was felt that Captain Campbell had been very badly treated, and there was a disposition on the part of the colonial authorities to give some relief to his children. Accordingly, in the autumn of that year, a grant of ten thousand acres in the present township of Argyle, Washington County, was made to the three brothers before named, their three sisters, and four other persons, three of whom were also named Campbell.

On the 2d of March, 1764, Alexander McNaughton and 106 others of the original Campbell immigrants and their descendants petitioned for one thousand acres to be granted to each of them "to be laid out in a single tract between the head of South Bay and Kingsbury, and reaching east towards New Hampshire and westward to the mountains in Warren county." The committee of the Council to whom this petition was referred reported May 21, 1764, recommending that 47,700 acres should be granted to them, between the tract already granted to Schuyler and others Fort Edward, and the tract proposed to be granted to Turner and other Salem). The grant was made out in conformity with the recommendation of the Council, and specifies the amount of land that each individual of the petitioners was to receive, two hundred acres being the least and six hundred acres the most that any individual obtained. It also appoints five men as trustees, to divide and distribute the lands as directed. By the same instrument, the tract was incorporated as a township, to be named Argyle, and to have a supervisor, treasurer, collector, two assessors, two overseers of highways, two overseers of the poor, and six constables, to be elected annually by the inhabitants on the first day of May.

This grant included a large portion of what is now the northern half of the township of Greenwich, and a portion of the township of Fort Edward.

The townships in which these Scottish Highlanders settled were directly west of what is now Salem township, Washington county. Settlements were made in the latter township early in the year 1762, by James Turner, Alexander Conkey, Pelbam, in Massachusetts, to which reference has already been made. Salem Township consists largely of the tract of 25,000 acres, granted August 7, 1764, to James Turner and others. One-half of the land covered by the patent, however, in accordance with a not uncommon custom of the time, became the property of Oliver De Lancey and Peter Du Bois, two government officials, whose services presumably aided in securing the grant. De Lancey and Du Bois sold their share of the land in 1765 to the Rev. Thomas Clark and his Scots-Irish congregation, who had emigrated the year before from Ballybay, County Monaghan, Ireland.

Mr. Clark, a native of Scotland, was a follower of Ebenezer Erskine, and in 1748 had been called as their minister by a portion of Mr. Jackson's congregation in Ireland, which had seceded from the main body. At Ballybay he is said to have labored with great success, but amid many trials and persecutions. He refused to take an oath by "kissing the book," believing it to be unscriptural; and although he entered the army while a student, and fought against the Pretender, yet he would not take the Oath of Abjuration, because it recognized the King as the head of the Church.

Taking advantage of these things, some of his enemies had him arrested by the civil authorities in 1754, and he was imprisoned in the jail at Monaghan. From his place of confinement he preached every Sabbath to as many of his people as could convene. When the day of his trial came, it appeared that he had been imprisoned on a fraudulent charge, and he was released. In 1763 Mr. Clark received invitations to visit two settlements in America, one in Rhode Island and the other near Albany. Wearied with his contendings he regarded these calls favorably, and his Presbytery gave him leave of absence for one year. But when he came to sail from Newry on the 16th of May, 1764, it was found that the greater part of his congregation, some 300 persons, were ready to sail with him. They all embarked together, and after arriving in New York settled temporarily at Stillwater. Thence a portion of his parishioners removed to Abbeville district, South Carolina, but a majority of them settled with Mr. Clark at Salem. His pastoral relationship had never been disturbed; his church had simply been transplanted; and he continued at Salem as the pastor of the eight ruling elders and 150 communicants and their children, who had come with him from Ballybay. He resigned his ministry at Salem in 1782, and three years later removed to Abbeville district, where he was installed as minister of Cedar Spring and Long Cane congregations, dying there in 1792.

From 1764 to 1774 the township of Hebron, lying north of Salem in Washington county, was largely granted in patents of 2,000 acres each, issued to commissioned officers, and in lots of 200 acres each to non-commissioned officers, and lots of 50 acres each to privates who had served in the French and Indian War. These grants were made mostly to the officers and men of the 77th Regiment, Montgomery's Highlanders in America and for seven years they took part in the capture of Fort Duquesne and the reduction of Ticonderoga. Their term of service having expired, they were discharged in New York City. They took up the lands in Washington County, owing to a proclamation made by the King in October, 1763, offering land in America, without fees, to all officers and soldiers who had served on that continent, and who desired to establish their homes there.

The principal part of Cambridge Township, in the southern part of Washington County, was granted to Isaac Sawyer and others in 1761. To induce settlements on this land, the patentees gave 100 acres to each of the first 30 families who should become actual settlers. The names of these first settlers are nearly all Scot, and they probably came from the Scot-Irish settlements of

Coleraine and Pelham in Massachusetts and from Connecticut, as well as from the North of Ireland and Scotland direct. Many of the latter were Covenanters, and these were visited in 1764 by Rev. John Cuthbertson, the noted missionary, who spent forty years (1751-1790) between the scattered congregations of the Reformed Presbyterian Church, from Pennsylvania to New Hampshire. From a manuscript copy of Cuthbertson's diary, it appears that he visited Orange County, New York, in 1759, where he spent the month of September in missionary labor along the Wallkill. Returning in 1764, he continued his journey to Albany, and in August arrived at Cambridge. He made a second visit in 1766, and another in October, 1769, at which time he ordained two ruling elders. The Rev. Thomas Clark, of Salem, also visited and preached to the settlers at Cambridge, and in April, 1769, also ordained a number of elders at that place.

Besides the Scottish outpost planted near the head of Lake Champlain by Lieutenant-Governor Clarke, he also granted, in 1738, a tract of 8,000 acres in Otsego County, on what was then the western frontier of the province, covering the present township of Cherry Valley. This grant was made for the same reasons which had induced the authorities to promise the grant to Lauchlin Campbell, namely, the desire to obtain a population on the frontier which would protect the province from the incursions of the Indians and the encroachments of the French. The patent was issued to John Lindesay and three associates. Mr. Lindesay was a Scottish gentleman, of some fortune and distinction. He purchased the interest of his associates, and by his influence induced a settlement on the lands of several families, comprising about 30 persons, originally from Scotland and Ulster.

A few years afterwards small settlements were made at other points in the vicinity, along the valley of the Susquehanna River. Middlefield was settled by the Scots-Irish in 1755. These settlements increased very slowly in consequence of the fear of Indian hostilities. By 1765 there were about 40 families located at Cherry Valley, and ten years later the number of families was nearly 60. Mr. Lindesay began his settlement about 1740.

While in New York City, preparing for the removal of his family, he formed a friendship with the Rev. Samuel Dunlop, a young Presbyterian minister of Ulster birth, and persuaded him to join in the colonization of the land. Mr. Dunlop accordingly visited Londonderry, New Hampshire, and induced a number of his friends there to accompany him to the settlement. When about 1743, he established a classical school at his dwelling, the first school of the kind west of the Hudson. Cherry Valley was still a frontier settlement at the commencement of the Revolution. On October 11, 1778, it was attacked by the Tories and Indians, under the lead of Walter Butler and Joseph Brant. Thirty-two of the inhabitants, mostly women and children, were massacred in cold blood, and sixteen Continental officers and soldiers were killed. The remainder of the inhabitants were carried off as prisoners, and all the buildings in the settlement burned. For seven years the site remained waste, and it was not until 1784-85 that the survivors and friends of the victims began to return and rebuild.

Glen Township, Montgomery County, New York, was settled in 1740 by sixteen families from Ireland. These afterwards removed, from fear of the Indians.

Monroe Township, Orange County, was settled by a number of Scots-Irish families who came in 1742. Much of Orange County was first occupied by emigrants of Scottish descent from the North of Ireland, who began to make settlements along the Wallkill River as early as 1729 .

Harpersfield Township, Delaware County, was settled by emigrants from Scotland or Ulster in 1771. Kortright Township, in the same county, was also settled by Scottish emigrants before 1785, and Bovina Township by settlers from Scotland and Connecticut some ten years later.

Ballston Township, in Saratoga County, was settled in 1770 by a Presbyterian minister, Rev. Eliphalet Bal, and several members of his congregation, who removed from Bedford, New

York. Soon after their arrival a large number of Presbyterian emigrants came in from Scotland, Ireland, New Jersey, and New England, many of whom a few years later took an active part in the Battle of Saratoga. Stillwater Township, in the same county, was settled by Scottish and New England emigrants, many from the vicinity of Litchfield, Conn., in 1763 Broadalbin Township, in Fulton County, was settled by James McIntyre and other emigrants from Scotland, soon after the close of the Revolution.

New Scotland Township, Albany County, was settled by emigrants from Scotland who began to locate there before 1786.

Albany itself received a substantial emigration from Scotland and the North of Ireland before 1760. In that year, a Presbyterian Church was organized there, composed chiefly of members of Scottish descent.

Sir William Johnson, who had taken a prominent part in the defence of New York against the French at Crown Point and Lake George in 1755, received from the Crown a grant 100,000 acres of land north of the Mohawk River, in the vicinity of Johnstown, Tryon (now Fulton) County.

In order to secure tenants for this land, he appointed agents to visit the Scottish Highlands, where he obtained as many colonists as he desired, all of whom were of the Roman Catholic faith. They embarked for America during the month of August, 1773. The Gentleman's Magazine for September 30, 1773, in speaking of these emigrants, states: "Three gentlemen of the name of MacDonnell, with their families, and four hundred Highlanders from the counties [districts] of Glengarry, Glenmorison, Urquhart, and Strathglass, lately embarked for America, having obtained a grant of land in Albany." The three gentlemen here referred to were the MacDonnells of Aberchalder, Leek, and Collachie; there was also a fourth MacDonnell, of Scots. They had fought for the Pretender in 1745, and in order to mend their shattered fortunes were willing to remove to America. These men made their homes in what was then Tryon county, about thirty miles from Albany, where now stands the town of Gloversville. Tracts varying from one to five hundred acres were granted to certain families, all subjected to the lord of the manor as under the feudal system. Here the Highlanders settled, and they soon became deeply attached to the interests of Sir William Johnson and his family. On the death of the former in 1774, they transferred their allegiance to his son, Sir John Johnson; and on the breaking out of the Revolutionary War, followed their master into the British army. The majority of them served in the first and second battalions of the King's Royal Regiment of New York.

Not being permitted to remain in the United States after the Revolutionary War, the Scottish retainers of Sir John Johnson were granted lands in Canada by the British government. The officers and men of the first battalion settled in a body at Glengarry, Ontario, occupying the first five townships west of the boundary line of Quebec province, being the present townships of Lancaster, Charlottenburgh, Cornwall, Osnabruck, and Williamsburgh. Those of the second battalion removed farther west to the Bay of Quinte, settling in the counties of Lennox and Prince Edward. They were joined in the month of September, 1786, by five hundred of their kinsfolk from Knoydart who had sailed with the Rev. Alexander MacDonnell from Greenock, in the ship *MacDonald*.

In the first half of the seventeenth century Sir William Alexander, a favorite of James I, tried to found a New Scotland in America. The only existing memorial of that attempt is the name Nova Scotia, and the titles of a number of Scottish noblemen, whose ancestors of that period were created by James barons of Nova Scotia. A more successful attempt was made after the forced evacuation of the French from that province in 1755. About the year 1760, a party of Scots-Irishmen, many of them from Londonderry, New Hampshire, started a permanent settlement at

Truro, in Colchester County. Other Scot-Irish settlers followed, their descendants becoming numerous, and populating several neighboring towns.

Colonel Alexander McNutt, an agent of the British government, arrived in Halifax October 9, 1761, with more than 300 settlers from the North of Ireland. In the following spring, some of these moved to Londonderry, while many settled at Onslow and Truro.

The Hector was the first emigrant ship from Scotland to come to Nova Scotia. It arrived in the harbor of Pictou, September 15, 1773, bringing about 200 emigrants from Rossshire. The pioneers who came in that vessel formed the beginning of a stream of emigrants from Scotland, which flowed over the county of Pictou, the eastern portions of Nova Scotia, Cape Breton, Prince Edward Island, portions of New Brunswick, and some of the upper provinces. Simcoe County, Ontario, is almost entirely settled by men and women of Ulster or Scots descent. The County of Restigouche in Nova Scotia, is almost wholly Scottish, and the names of its townships—Glenelg, Glenlivet, Dunlee, and Campbelltown, show conclusively the very districts in Scotland from which its early settlers came. "The town and whole district of Pictou," says MacGregor, in his work on British America, "are decidedly Scots. In the streets, within the houses, in the shops, on board the vessels, and along the roads, we hear little but Gaelic and broad Scots."

The places in the maritime provinces of Canada where the Gaelic language prevails or is still largely spoken are the counties of Pictou and Antigonish; Earltown, the county of Colchester; a part of the county of Guysborough; the island of Cape Breton; Prince Edward Island; and some settlements along the Bay of Chaleur, in New Brunswick. In Glengarry County, Ontario, Gaelic still continues to be the language of the people, and it is there spoken as purely as it is in Dingwall or Lewis. According to a census taken in 1852 there were in Glengarry County 3228 McDonalds, 551 McMillans, 41 McDougalls, 40 McRaes, 473 McLeods, 415 Grants, 399 Camerons, 312 McLennans, 304 Campbells, 133 Chisholms, 50 Cattenachs, 262 McIntoshes, 176 Frasers, 114 McGregors, and representatives of nearly every other name peculiar to the Highlands of Scotland. A story told in Canada is to the effect that a Yankee who visited Ontario for the first time, concluded that he really was in Scotland, for the queen's representative was a Scot; the prime minister was a Scot; the members of the cabinet he met were Scots; he heard the Gaelic spoken in all the government offices; saw that all the large stores were owned by "Macs"; and that a large number of the towns he passed on the railway bore Scots names.

In 1772, John MacDonald of Glenaladale, with 200 persecuted Catholic Highlanders immigrated to Prince Edward Island, where he had purchased a tract of 40,000 acres on the north coast, at the head of Tracadie Bay, almost due north of Charlottetown. There, in 1776, he organized a company from his followers and Prince Edward Island in 1774, by Wellwood Waugh, of Lockerbie, Dumfriesshire. Their first crops were ruined by a visitation of locusts, and they removed to Pictou. After 1783, there were considerable additions to this colony, the largest number coming from the 82d, or Hamilton Regiment, which had been on duty under General McLean, at Halifax and in the United States. This regiment, which was composed almost entirely of Scots, was disbanded at Halifax, and had a large tract of land set apart for it in Pictou, known as the "82d Grant."

Concerning the Scots in the Northwest Territory, Dr. Peter Ross, in his book on Scotland and the Scots, quotes from Mr. David Scott as follows:

After the English Government found it necessary for the Hanoverian succession to disarm the Highlanders, and break up, so far as they could, the ancient loyalty of the clans to their chieftains, and the ancient protection which the chief, as in honor bound, extended to every member of his clan, a large number of Scottish gentlemen turned their attention toward Canada, as a country which offered many inducements in the way not only of exciting adventure but also of prosperous commerce. These emigrants of noble descent did not settle as cultivators of the soil, but banded together and formed themselves into a trading concern, which grew, in the course of years, into a vast partnership known as the "Northwest Company." Over the interior of the Canadas the merchants spread a great network of stations, each of them presided over by a clerk, who (if he behaved well) rose in the course of time to a junior partnership. The principal trade was in furs, and in order to obtain the furs it was necessary to barter with the Indians. So it came to pass that these pioneers of Canadian commerce bought from the old country cheap articles in the form of clothing, knives, muskets, and other commodities suitable for exchange with the Indians, and sent back valuable furs, which found their way to every available market in Europe . . . . . Once a year the whole company of shareholders met to transact business, and then the scene was like a gathering of the clans in the forests of the far West. The names of the old chieftains were those familiar among them—Cameron and Chisholm and Mackenzie –the free and rough hospitality was the same. . . . To this very day, though the reign of the first Northwest Company of Canada is long over, you may find relics of these old Celtic families among the citizens of Montreal and Toronto . . . . Instead of the grandness of the Northwest Company, places further north in Canada had been taken possession by a humbler class of countrymen, who were content to till the ground they owned for a livelihood. Whole villages of the Far West are Celtic in origin, and we may hear the Gaelic tongue almost as readily among the Canadian pines as in the glens of Inverness-shire or among the boatmen of Green Islay itself.

While the settlements of the Scot-Irish in New England, Virginia, and the Carolinas were numerous, and represented a population of many thousand families, the great majority of the Ulster emigrants to America first landed on the Delaware shore. Most of the passenger ships sailing from Ireland during the eighteenth century were bound for ports in the Quaker colony. Pennsylvania thus became the center of the Presbyterian settlements in the New World, and from that province, after 1735, a continuous stream of emigration flowed to the South and West.

The emigrants to Pennsylvania usually landed at one of the three ports, Lewes, Newcastle (both in Delaware, which was part of Pennsylvania), or Philadelphia. Presbyterian congregations were gathered in all of these towns before 1698. During the first decade of the eighteenth century the Scot-Irish made settlements along White Clay, Red Clay, and Brandywine Creeks in Newcastle County, Delaware, and at the head of Elk Creek on both sides of the Pennsylvania-Maryland boundary, at its intersection with the Delaware line. John McKnitt Alexander, who took a prominent part in the Mecklenburg (North Carolina) Convention of 1775, was descended from one of the four families of that name who had settled at New Munster on the east side of Elk creek, in Cecil county, Maryland, "some years before 1715 "—possibly as early as 1683, in which year the tract had been surveyed for Edwin O'Dwire, and "15 other Irishmen."

Witchcraft or Superstition

Witchcraft is one tradition which has generally fallen by the wayside so to speak. Or has it? Have you noticed some hex signs on the outside of a house, or indoors? Have you ever seen a Pennsylvania Dutch Quilt with all the good luck signs including one for fertility?

Perhaps now we put some of the good advice under folklore, but in the past it was attributed to witches, some evil and some good. A lot of old wisdom came from a witch. In the past, the good blessings were of course dealt by the heavens above, the bad events, well they perhaps came from a witch. This is another taboo subject among the folk who live in the valley now, but this again is part of the history of this special place.

The Palatines were very superstitious people and there is still evidence of the dark worries they had when they lived here almost 300 years ago. When a home is torn down, it will reveal secrets of the people who inhabited the house. Things were put in the walls of the home, things to keep the evil spirits away. Every person in the family put something in the wall, often it was a shoe, just one. If a person was very poor, perhaps a bottle of urine might be used and sealed in the wall. Anything personal from each person in the household was stored to ward off the evil eye.

This is a caution for those who have older homes, watch for the shoes. All across New England and New York shoes have been found in the walls. Why would shoes be deliberately built into a home or public building? Some have speculated that the tradition stems from the prehistoric custom of killing a person and placing the body in the foundation to insure that the building holds together. Could it be that later the shoes were used as a substitute for a human sacrifice? Shoes may have been chosen, because over time they take on and keep the shape of the wearer's foot. Shoes were hidden near openings in the home such as doors, windows, chimneys; these are the perceived weak places in the building that were thus protected from evil by the shoe owner's spirit.

About half the shoes in the wall are children's shoes. Women's shoes are more common than men's. Shoes are almost invariably well worn, perhaps because the donor didn't want to waste an expensive new shoe on the project, or perhaps because a well-worn shoe is more likely to retain the shape of the wearer's foot and hence his spirit. Though shoes are the common denominator, more than two hundred different personal possessions—coins, spoons, pots, goblets, food, knives, toys, gloves, pipes, even chicken and cat bones—have been found hidden with them and registered in the "shoes in the wall" research. Just type "shoes in the wall" in your web browser and you will find groups dedicated to researching this phenomenon.

I spent some time talking with men who tear down old homes and asked them if they ever found shoes in the walls. Several got a funny look on their face and said they thought they were just old shoes and bottles left there, garbage in other words. They didn't realize what they were looking at and that they had been left there deliberately. They said the shoes were worn, were women's and children's shoes, just one shoe and there were bottles with them but they were empty. The shoes are found near an opening to the house, a ledge in the chimney or near an outside door entrance.

Considering how widespread and long lasting this folk belief has been, it is curious that nowhere was it described in writing until references began to appear in mid-twentieth century archaeology literature in scholarly journals. Some speculate the tradition of hiding shoes was a male superstition, kept secret almost out of fear that telling about it would reduce its effectiveness. Others feel contemporary writers did not describe it since superstition ran counter to prevailing religious beliefs and the Puritans punishment of witchcraft and magic was well-known.

When removing walls especially around windows and doors, under roof rafters and behind old chimneys, homeowners should be aware of the possibility of turning up concealed shoes. While most are found in eighteenth and nineteenth century homes, a find hidden as late as 1935 has been reported. If shoes are found, they should be left exactly as they were discovered and photographed.

A local man, David Collins, deals with recycling parts of old historic homes and he was the one who pointed out the phenomenon of the shoes. Of course he would be aware of this because of his work with old homes. He showed me an article from the United Kingdom regarding the shoes. According to the article, over 1200 examples have been recorded, with the earliest reference to the use of shoes comes the 14th century. One of England's unofficial saints, John

Schorn from Buckinghamshire who was the rector of North Marston 1290-1314, is reputed to have cast the devil into a boot. The oldest concealed shoes date to about this time.

Witchcraft is the heritage of all humanity. Since barbarian days, fear of the supernatural has been instilled into the souls of men. So it was in the isolated hills of the Mohawk Valley. Immigrants from Europe brought with them centuries of their own folklore, superstitions, ghost stories, and books of witchcraft. These tales were all handed down within families and communities, and very often, changed to suit the area. A hundred years ago storytellers flourished among the Schoharie hill people and, as late as 1920, witchcraft was still a thing to be reckoned with in the isolated hill hamlets.

First, there are two varieties of witches: some who did only evil; and the others who had healing powers, were said to have second sight, and told fortunes – always happy ones of course.

Here are the folklore stories about the evil witches:

Among them was Granny Garlock whose favorite trick was bewitching milk churnings so the butter wouldn't come. There was Witch Lehman who had more butter to sell than her poor old scrub cows could possibly be responsible for; there was the Witch Philter, whose penetrating glance caused children to turn black and blue. Another was the witch-granny who could rise out of her old wrinkled skin when her soul was off witching. A rival witch doctor cured her of that trick by filling her skin with salt; the treatment was so powerful that the poor old girl died the next morning.

Evil witches made people do strange things; one bewitched a young woman into running around on all fours for a whole week and when the spell was finally broken, she didn't remember a thing. Today that would be called hypnotism. Another young girl walked up the panes of a tall, old fashioned window clear to the top. When she came down, she stuck needles through the window lights.

These witches of long ago cast their evil spells over animals. Cows wouldn't let down their milk, and calves cavorted as if inhabited by the devil, while nice old white horses sometimes sat back on their haunches and positively refused to work. One farmer went to the barn one morning and found his mare up in the hay mow, which could be reached only by a rickety ladder.

Witches sometimes climbed inside the bodies of animals. Great Grandpa Clapper proved this without a doubt, when his big black horse balked one day while doing the spring plowing. Grandpa was so furious that he whipped out his knife and slashed a chunk from the horse's right ear. The next day old Clapper happened to see the witch-woman and there was a chunk out of *her* right ear. What greater proof do we need than that?

Unlike European witches, the local variety didn't ride broomsticks; instead they stole horses or yearling calves, which they mounted then muttered these simple magic words: "Over thick and over thin; and away we go." The story goes that the animals were always brought back absolutely exhausted, and with a disease called "witches' stirrup", for which there was no cure. In the local area, the Town of Palatine had a witch trial, the records of the trial are in the Department of History and Archives in Fonda, NY. (See the Appendix, p. 471, for the transcript of the local witch trial.)

Back in those days one had to know how to protect one's self from witchcraft. A witch recommended that you just place a twig of ash or witch-hazel over the door; a broomstick laid across the threshold also kept the witches out of a home. Witches had no power over the first child born into a family, according to legend.

The good witches had many sterling qualities, and were very desirable in a community. They could divine water with a forked witch-hazel stick. The practice is still prevalent, I was shocked when a local church hired a water witch to find water before a well was drilled

The good witches could give the farmer helpful hints, for example:

When plum trees are in bloom, sew garden seeds.
When beech leaves are as big as mice's ears, it's time to plant corn.
Cucumbers will grow when you can sleep without quilts.
Never give a knife to a friend, it will cut your friendship.
If you have a wart, steal a dishcloth and bury it in your yard.

The good witches also told people to wear a red woolen string tied around the neck to prevent or stop nosebleeds. They maintained that a raw potato in the pocket would prevent rheumatism, and if you carried hen's teeth in your pocket, you would never have a toothache. There are many old wives tales giving advice about daily living, we call the advice old wives tales.
Source Material: http://j.w.d.home.comcast.net/whs/index.htm
http://threerivershms.com

Debtor's Prison

It was a bit of a surprise to discover New York had Debtor's Prison and that some of the men who served in the Revolutionary War had been in such a prison. There is very little written about it, much like some other distasteful subjects and it is hard to get information about the circumstances.

In the eighteenth century debt and the inability to pay was considered a moral issue, a sin. The rapid expansion of the country forced a different view on indebtedness and forced change. Probably credit has always been available for purchases, and it was certainly no exception during the period about the time of the war. Cash was a very scarce commodity, and there were many types of currency used. Foreign, state, and local banks all produced their own.

But just suppose you were in urgent need of something, but you were strapped for money, so you purchased it on credit. After all, when the crops came in, you could pay it back easily but what happened if the crops failed for lack of water? Some time later, your creditor wanted the money that you promised to pay and you simply didn't have the money.

Your creditor could proceed against you in a couple of different ways, but either way, assuming you still didn't have the money, you went to jail. And there you rotted, unless you had the means to buy your way out, in which case you wouldn't be there in the first place. In a notorious perversion of logic, a debtor, like any prisoner, was expected to feed and clothe himself while incarcerated. Conditions in Debtor's Prison were far worse than those in a regular prison. The state fed and clothed felons and criminals but not debtors. The enterprising debtor often would commit a greater crime to force transfer to the regular prison and therefore be fed and clothed. A pauper's grave, the so-called potter's field, was the lot for the debtor who died in prison. It could have been worse: under ancient Roman law, creditors were entitled to chunks of your actual body and there was no penalty for hacking off a disproportionate slice. Hence the expression, extract a pound of flesh! How things have changed in the world!

What changed this callous system? Not sentiment, but hard economic facts. For one thing, it was an ineffective arrangement. The creditor derived satisfaction from watching his debtor fade away in prison, but that didn't satisfy the debt. For another thing, the colonies suffered a chronic people shortage. They needed laborers and militiamen. Society couldn't afford to lose the prisoner's labor, or his ability to shoulder a musket and defend against Indian attacks. Nor could society afford to support the innocent wife and children "perishing with hunger & cold".

The system began to be modified in various ways. For some categories of debtors, single men who owed little, some colonies substituted indentured service for imprisonment. Another modification, applicable to petty debts, provided a release from prison and immunity from re-arrest if he swore he was impoverished, probably a more effective deterrent centuries ago when there was true shame associated with being a deadbeat. A third modification put clothing, furniture, eating utensils, and tools beyond the reach of attachment by the creditor.

None of this was of any help to the larger defaulters, the businessmen, and it was for their benefit (economic necessity, again) that colonial bankruptcy laws began to evolve. Interestingly, the colonies preferred voluntary proceedings, giving the right of action to the insolvent, in contrast to English bankruptcy practice, which sided with the creditor. Development of bankruptcy relief was by no means smooth because, many stern and rockbound colonists took a moral stance against it. Complicating matters was the requirement that until the Revolution, a debtor relief law and any colonial legislation had to be approved by the Crown, in this case the Board of Trade.

Congress repealed the bankruptcy act in 1803 before its scheduled expiration. The government worried about insufficient creditor control of the bankruptcy cases and that the creditors would not be able to be compensated for their losses. Regional reforms were made with different solutions, but the old Debtor's Prison was abolished.

Source Material:
http://www.beardbooks.com/debtors_and_creditors_in_america.html
http://www.jesbeard.com/w2.htm
http://www.eh.net/bookreviews/library/0740.shtml
http://www.mens-network.org/debt.html

Map of the Central Mohawk Valley
by John C. Devendorf (used with permission)

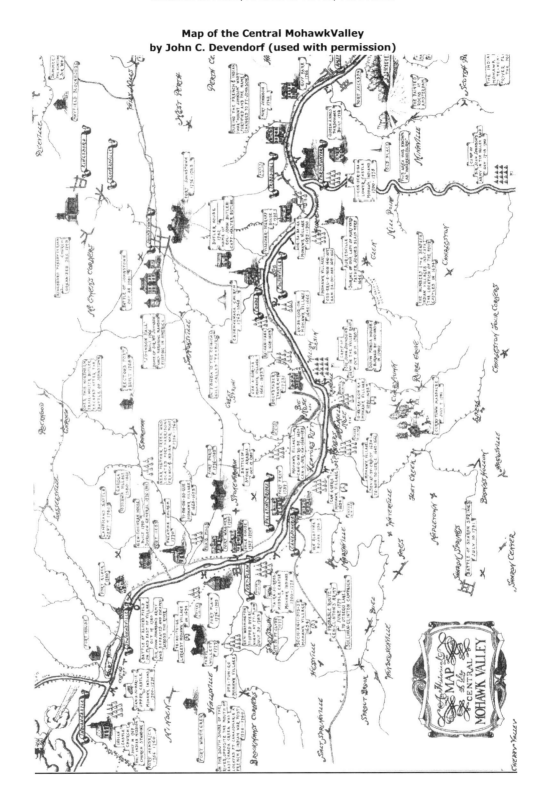

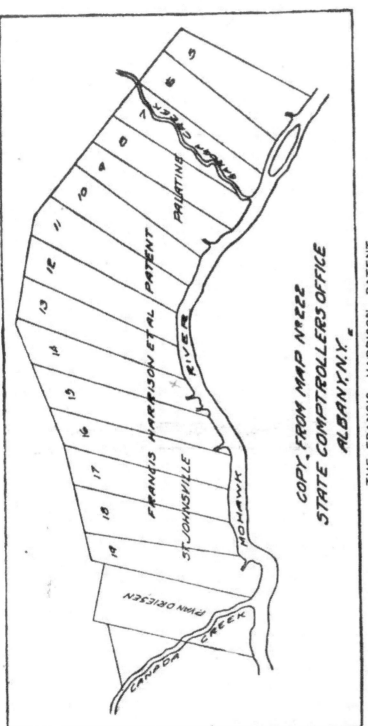

COPY. FROM MAP N°222
STATE COMPTROLLERS OFFICE
ALBANY, N.Y.

THE FRANCIS HARRISON PATENT

Purchased from the Mohawk Indians in 1722 for 700 Beaver skins, by Harrison and others "in the name and behoof of our sovereign lord, George III, by the Grace of God, of Great Britain, France and Ireland, King, defender of the faith, etc." and sold by the crown to the original patent holders. The patent embraced the land north of the Mohawk from below the Palatine line on the east to Canada Creek on the west. The lot holders given are as they stood after the revolutionary war. The tract to the west was a patent of 7423 acres granted in the year 1766 to John Van Driessen, the grandson of Dominie Petrius Honorias Van Driessen. The site of the first church edifice of the organization was upon the Petrius Van Driessen patent.

The Lot Owners

5. P. Warenmoth and Waggoner
6. P. Waggner
7. Ph. Fox and Geo. Fox
8. L. Helmer and H. W. Nellis
9. Hess and Bellinger

10. Phi. Nellis and Jo Hess
11. John Klock
12. Christr. Nellis
13. George G. Klock and Jacob Klock
14. Timmerman and Veeling
15. Timmerman and Veeling

16. J. G. Klock
17. Adam Woolraat and Geo. Klock
18. Timmerman and Veeling
19. Elisebeth Johnson
20. Pet. Vandriessen Patent

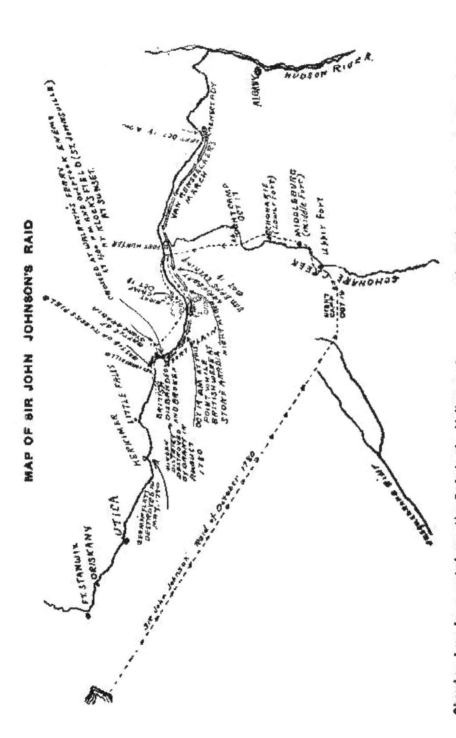

Showing how he swept down the Schoharie Valley and swung up the Mohawk leaving death and destruction in his wake. At St. Johnsville his force was shattered. Dotted line shows course taken by enemy. Parallel lines show march of General Van Rensselaer in pursuit.

S. A. Patent
Oct 1723
Sir Wm Johnston's Patent
1st Division
2nd
3rd
YEAR
1723 Green 51 Lotts of 50 A each
1733 BLUE 98 " 100 A Each
1753 Yellow 29
LOTT A - 100 ACRES
Town of Ephratah
Town of Johnstown
William Foos (Fox) 19
Adam Empie 18
John Lawyer 17
Sufferenus Deychert 16
Jacob Schnell 21
Johannes Schnell 25
Warner Deychert 24
William Coppernell 26
William Von Schelyune 23
Martin Seybert 27
John Lawyer 22
Garth Schaeffer 6
Christian Garlock
John Jost Schnell 5
Hendrick Frey 9
Theobold Garlock 11
Johan Gramps 13
William Nellis 14
Ephrata
Garoga Creek
Approx N
Alexander
Copied from
All lines are Approximate

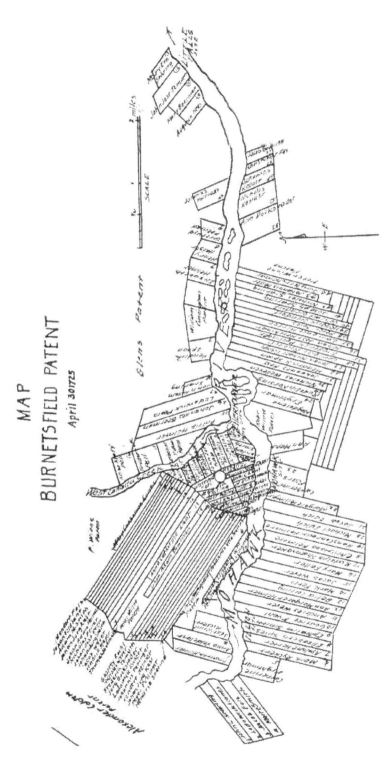

The original purchase from the Indians was for "24 English miles along the river and as far back on each side as they wished but the colonial Governor allowed each patentee only 100 acres. This was given in 30 acres, 30 acres as the town site and 70 acres wood lot. The names are as copied. Purchase was dated July 9, 1722. Petition for patent Jan. 17, 1723. Thirty or more families from Schoharie settled on the land in 1723 and were given land certificates. The patent was issued April 30, 1725. The petitioners were John Jost Petrie and Conrad Rickert in behalf of themselves and other patentees. There were 46 lots of 100 acres each side of the river. Some split as noted. The village of Herkimer now occupies part of the above patent. Copied for the Enterprise and News, by Boyd Ehle. C. E.

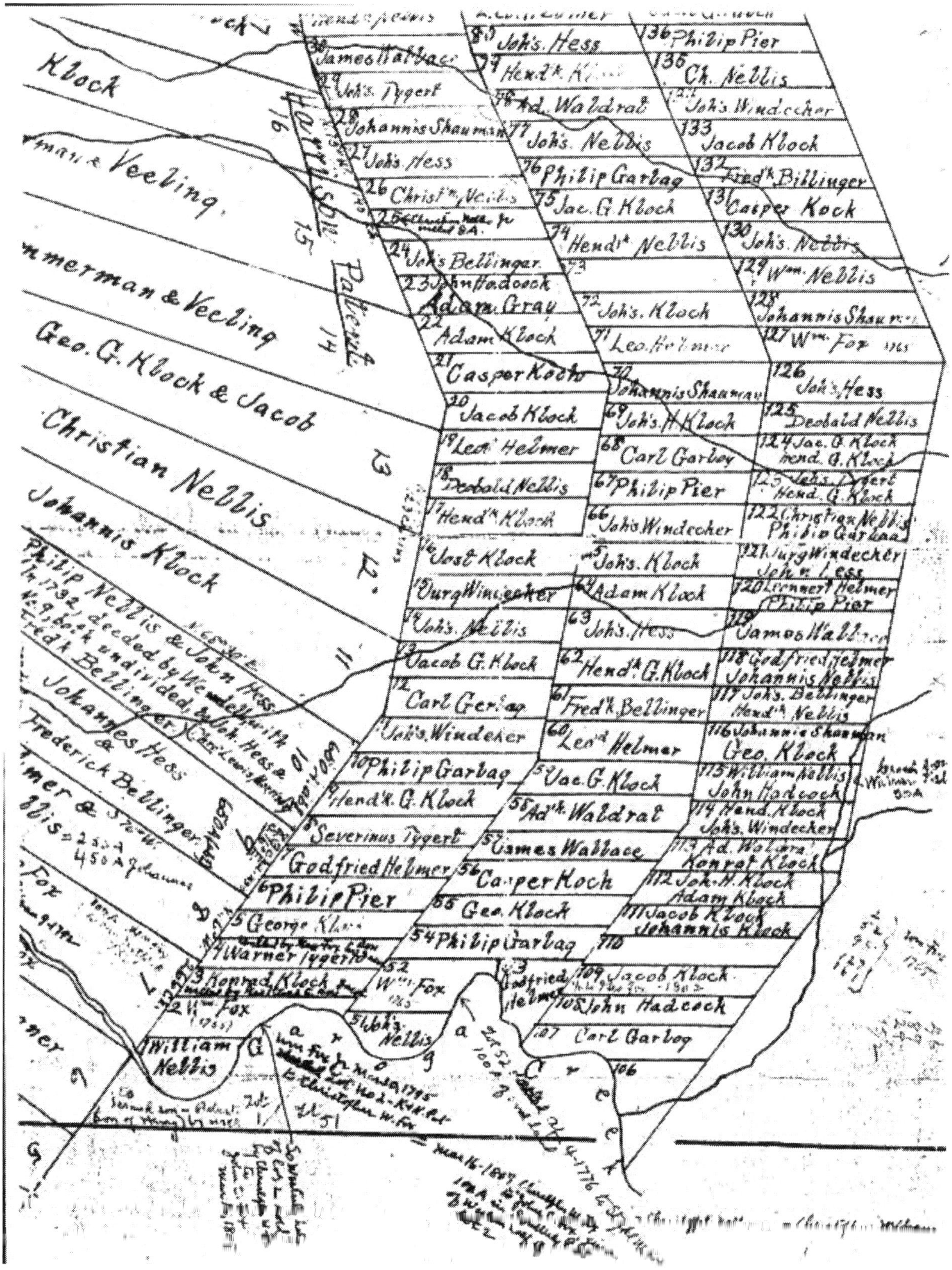
Klock
Veeling
mmerman & Veeling
Geo. G. Klock & Jacob
Christian Nellis
Johannis Klock
Philip Nellis & John Hess
Johannes Hess
Frederick Bellinger
Harrison Patent
16
15
14
11
30 James Wallace
29 Joh's. Tygert
28 Johannis Shaumin
27 Joh's. Hess
26 Christ'n Nellis
24 Joh's Bellingar.
23 John Hadcock
Adam Gray
22 Adam Klock
21 Casper Koch
20 Jacob Klock
19 Leo'. Helmer
18 Deobald Nellis
17 Hend'k Klock
16 Jost Klock
15 Jurg Windecker
14 Joh's. Nellis
13 Jacob G. Klock
12 Carl Gerbag
11 Joh's. Windeker
10 Philip Garbag
9 Hend'k. G. Klock
8 Severinus Tygert
7 Godfried Helmer
6 Philip Pier
5 George Klock
4 Warner Tygert
3 Konrad Klock
2 W'm. Fox
William Nellis
80 Joh's. Hess
79 Hend'k. Klock
78 Ad. Waldrat
77 Joh's. Nellis
76 Philip Garbag
75 Jac. G. Klock
74 Hend'k Nellis
73
72 Joh's. Klock
71 Leo. Helmer
70 Johannis Shaumin
69 Joh's. H. Klock
68 Carl Garbag
67 Philip Pier
66 Joh's Windecker
65 Joh's. Klock
64 Adam Klock
63 Joh's. Hess
62 Hend'k. G. Klock
61 Fred'k. Bellinger
60 Len'd. Helmer
59 Jac. G. Klock
58 Ad'k. Waldrat
57 James Wallace
56 Casper Koch
55 Geo. Klock
54 Philip Garbag
53 Godfried Helmer
52 W'm. Fox
51 Joh's. Nellis
136 Philip Pier
135 Ch. Nellis
134 Joh's Windecker
133 Jacob Klock
132 Fred'k. Billinger
131 Casper Kock
130 Joh's. Nellis
129 W'm. Nellis
128 Johannis Shaumin
127 W'm. Fox
126 Joh's. Hess
125 Deobald Nellis
124 Jac. G. Klock
Hend. G. Klock
123 Joh's. Tygert
Hend. G. Klock
122 Christian Nellis
Philip Garbag
121 Jurg Windecker
John'n Hess
120 Lennert Helmer
Philip Pier
119 James Wallace
118 Godfried Helmer
Johannis Nellis
117 Joh's. Bellinger
Hend'k. Nellis
116 Johannis Shauman
Geo. Klock
115 William Nellis
John Hadcock
114 Hend. Klock
Joh's. Windecker
113 Ad. Waldrat
Konrat Klock
112 Joh. H. Klock
Adam Klock
111 Jacob Klock
Johannis Klock
110
109 Jacob Klock
108 John Hadcock
107 Carl Garbag
106

KLOCK & NELLIS PATENT.
Montgomery Co. N.Y.
Granted, Dec. 21,
1754.

Lots 100 A. each.
Scale on this
tracing is
60 chains in an inch

Klock & Nellis Patent map with numbered lots including:

164 War. Tygert
Carl Garlag
163 Joh's Klock
Fred. Bellinger
162 Leon't. Helmer
Sever's Tygert
161 W'm Fox
Casper Koch
160 James Wallace
159 Hen. G. Klock
158 Leo. Helmer
157 Warner Tygert
156 Severinus Tygert
155 George Klock
154 Godfried Helmer
153 Konrad Klock
152 Joh's. Klock
151 Hend. Nellis
150 Joh's Bellinger
149 Leo. Helmer Jr.
148 Joh's. H. Klock
147 Adolph Walldron
146 Carl Garlag
145 Adam Klock
144 Jury Windecker
143 Hend. Klock
142 Johannis Dygert
141 Jost Klock
140
139 Philip Garlag
138 John Hadcock

Philip Pier
Christn Nellis
104
103 Jurg Windecker
102 Casper Koch
101 Godfried Helmer
100 Deobold Nellis
99 Jacob Klock
98 Wm. Fox
97 Joh's Windecker
96 Fred'k Bellinger
95 John Hadcock Wm Brass
94 Konrat Klock
93 James Wallace
92 Sever's Tygert
91 Christ'n Nellis
90 Joh's Bellinger
89 Wm. Nellis
88 Geo. Klock
87 Warner Dygert
86 Jurg Windecker
85 Jost Klock
84 Joh's Tygert
83 Hend. G. Klock

105
50
49 Joh's H Klock
48
47 Konrat Klock
46 Wm. Nellis
45 Joh's Bellinger
44 Deob'd. Hess
43 Sever's Tygert
42 Hend'k. Klock
41 Joh's Tygert
40 Johannis Shauman
39 Hend. Nellis
38 Warner Tygert
37 Leo. Helmer
36 Lev'd. Helmer
35 Fred'k. Bellinger
34 Hend'k Klock
33 Joh's Klock
32

North Creek

Teady Magin's Patent.
(His Lots were 11 chains & 26 ch.
& contained 626 acres, The
smaller lots contained 366.)

Van Driesen
(Patent 1731)

Bel't Johnson

Kremb's Kill

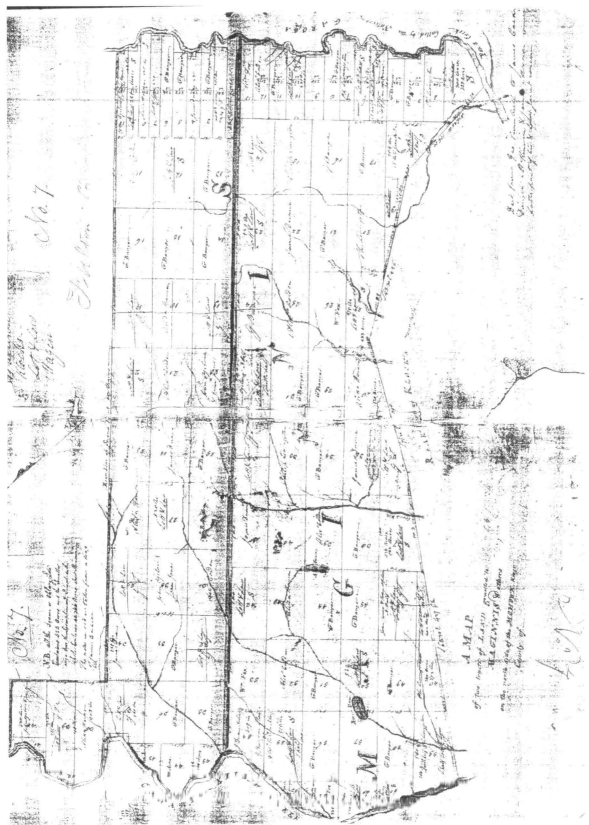

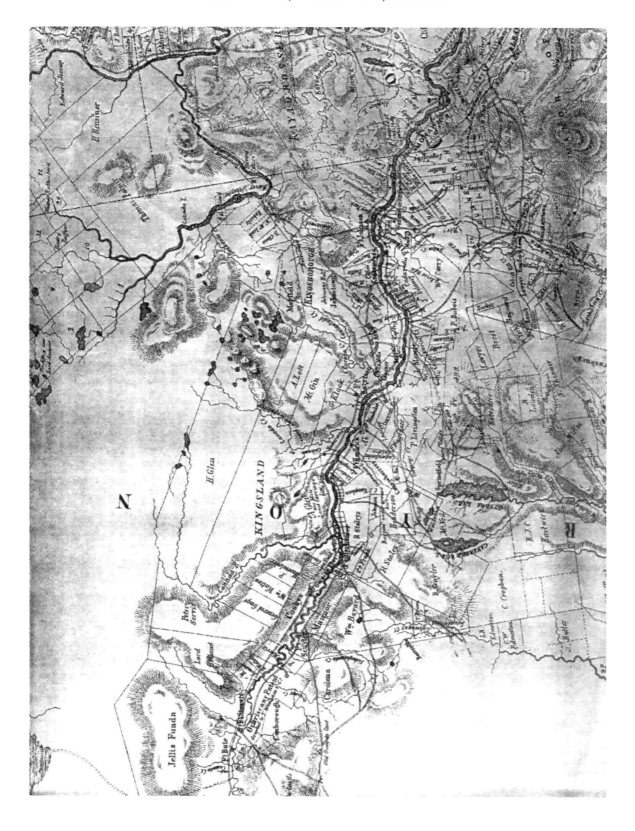

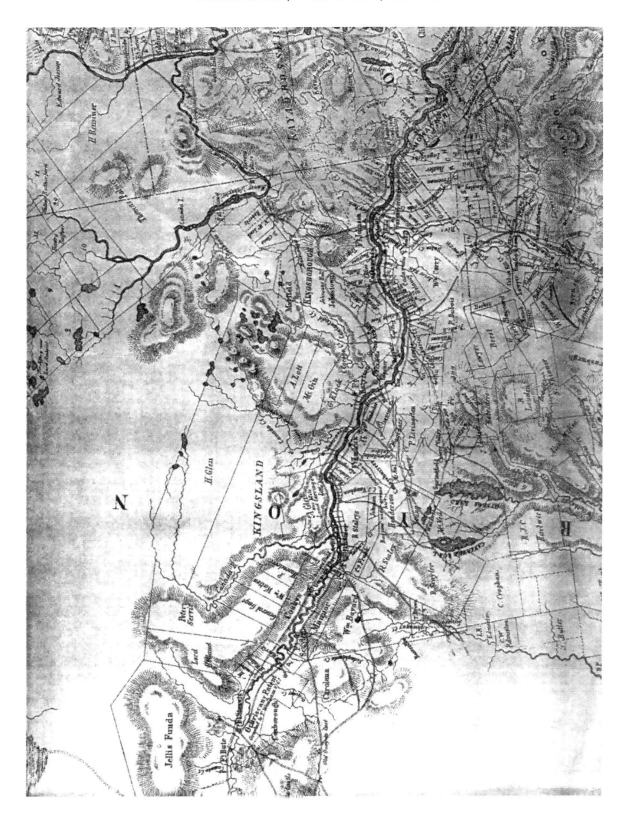

THE SNELL-TIMMERMAN PATENT, 1755

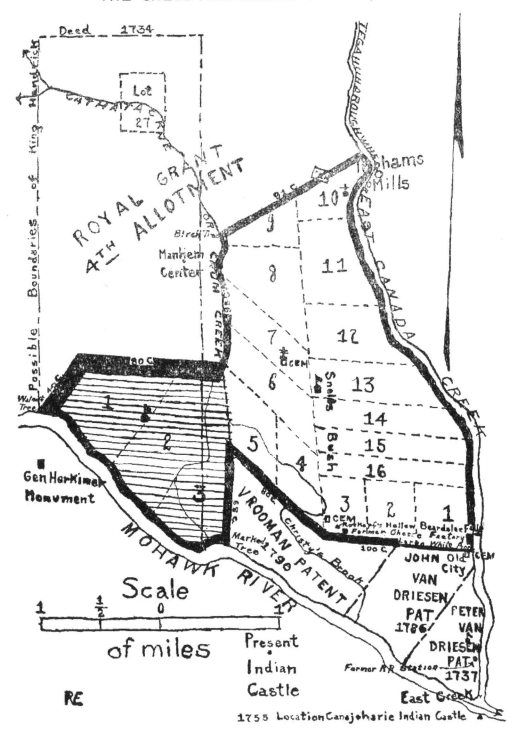

MAP OF THE SNELL-TIMMERMAN PATENT

(By Ralph Ehle, Ph D.)

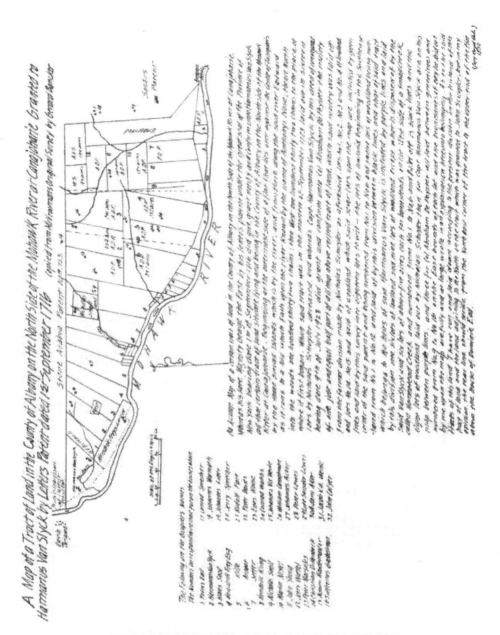

THE HARMANUS VAN SLYKE PATENT

Map of a tract of land on the north side of the Mohawk at Canajóharie, granted to Harmanus Van Slyke by letters patent, dated 1st September, 1716, from map now in possession of Boyd Ehle. Printed here for the first time.

S.

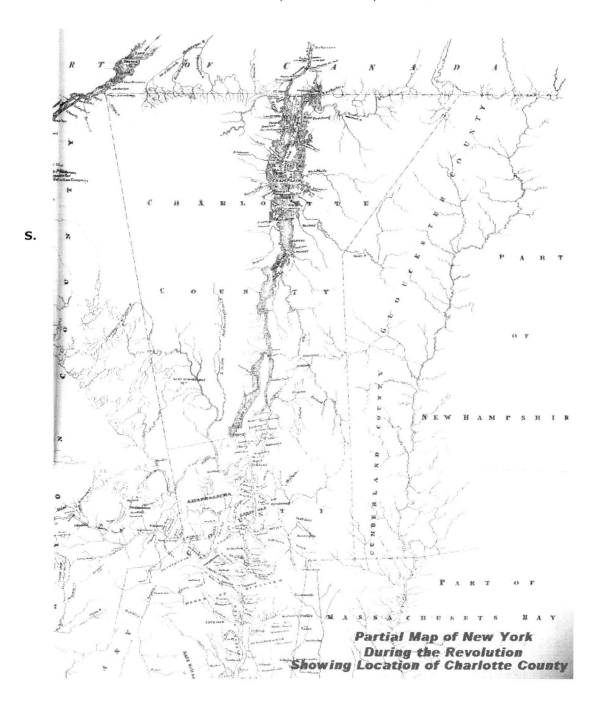

Partial Map of New York During the Revolution Showing Location of Charlotte County

Military Services

CLASSIFICATION AND PAY OF THE MILITARY FORCES.

The military forces of the Colony and State during the Revolutionary struggle were divided into three classes.

The Line; which regiments were in the United States service under General Washington. There were also regiments of artillery and an organization of "Green Mountain Boys " in the Line.

The Levies; which were drafts from the different militia regiments, and direct from the people as well, and which could be called upon to serve outside the tate during their entire term.

The Militia; which (then, as now), could only be called out of the state for three months at a time. Of the Line, 9 organizations are traced by these records; of Levies, 7 organizations; of militia, 68 organizations; in all 84 organizations.

Records are found of four privateers in the service and pay of the state-the schooner "General Putnam," the sloop "Montgomery," the sloop "Schuyler," and the frigate "Congress." These armed vessels took many prizes, and records are found of the division of the spoils.

Associated Exempts were a unique class and wire authorized by an act of April 3, 1778. They comprised: "All persons under the age of sixty who have held civil or military commissions and are not or shall not be reappointed to their respective proper ranks of office, and all persons between the ages of fifty and sixty." They could only be called out "in time of invasion or incursion of the enemy."

The militia regiments were designated, first by the colonels' names and next by their counties, as "Fisher's Regiment, of Tryon County." Instances crop up, here and there, in which a number was given to a regiment; as, for instance, "The Sixth Albany County," but it is a moot question if such was the general practice. Be that as it may, the name of the colonel is found to be quite sufficient for full identification.

The militia was called out when wanted; kept as long as wanted, and the soldiers then sent to their homes. Sometimes a regiment or a part of a regiment would be called out half a dozen times in the course of a year, and for half a dozen days at a time, and again it might not be needed in the entire year. Officers and men seem to have served in different organizations almost indiscriminately. At one call, they were in one regiment or company, and at another call, in another regiment or company. It is, therefore, very difficult to keep track of them on the different pay-rolls or "pay-books," as they were sometimes called. Nepotism, or family influence, was most marked, and some regiments contained as many as five and seven officers of the same family. (See Colonel Brinkerhoff's regiment, and the Millers', in Colonel Thomas' regiment.)

Counties were divided into districts, and the colonel of the regiment in each district was given almost unlimited jurisdiction in military matters. He was required to see that every male between the ages of sixteen and fifty was enrolled. Later, the age limit was extended to sixty. If an able-bodied man, he must serve when "warned" under penalty of fine and imprisonment; but if incapacitated, he must contribute toward furnishing and equipping another man - any person furnishing a substitute being exempt for the time that substitute served. Quakers, Moravians and United Brethren were enrolled, but exempted from service upon payment of money, which varied in amount as the war progressed until, in 1780, they were obliged to pay -£160 per year. One miller to each grist mill, three powder makers to each powder mill, five men to each furnace, three journeymen in each printing office, and one ferryman to each public ferry, were also exempt. Each soldier must present himself armed, and with a blanket, a powder-horn and a flint, and sometimes even a tomahawk was required. All officers in the cities of New York, Albany and Schenectady were ordered to wear their swords during divine service under a penalty of twenty shillings.

Rum, sugar and tea were regular rations, and the amount was gauged by the rank. A major-general was deemed to require, and was allowed each month, four gallons of rum, six pounds of sugar, and half a pound of tea. A brigadier-general, three gallons of rum, four pounds of sugar, and six ounces of tea. A colonel, a lieutenant-colonel, and a major, two and one-half gallons of rum, and the same amount of sugar and tea. A chaplain, ditto as to sugar and tea, but only two gallons of rum. The scale was continued until a noncommissioned officer and a private received one pound of sugar, two ounces of tea, and one pound of tobacco, but no rum. A colonel's pay was $75 per month, or one York £ per day; a lieutenant-colonel's pay was $60 per month; a major's pay was $50 per month, a captain's pay was $40 per month; an adjutant's pay was $40 per month; a lieutenant's pay was $26 per month; an ensign's pay was $20 per month; a sergeant's pay was $8 per month; a corporal's pay was $7 per month; a private's pay was $6 per month.

Nor was this, by any means, always in money. It was sometimes in state notes and sometimes in authority to "impress" articles or animals under supervision of some designated officer, who should give a receipt, in the name of the state, to the impressee. As late as 1784, the large majority of the soldiers were still unpaid for their services in 1776-1782. On April 27 of 1874, the legislature passed "An act for the settlement of the pay of the Levies and militia for their services in the late war." This statute provided that abstracts and pay-rolls of the different regiments and separate commands should be certified by the state auditor; he deducting for advances made to officers or privates by "impressing" or otherwise, and an allowance be made for the depreciation of the pay of such as had been in captivity, for the time they were in captivity. Upon receipt of these accounts from the auditor, the treasurer of the state was required to issue to persons, to whom pay should appear to be due, or to their legal representatives, certificates of indebtedness bearing five percent interest, and such certificates should be receivable for purchases of forfeited estates, or in payment for waste or "unappropriated lands," taxes, etc. Officers could not "throw up or quit" their commissions until they had served fifteen years.

All slaves killed in the service were to be paid for. In time of invasion, any slave, not in the military service, found one mile from his master's abode, without a certificate from his master showing his business, might be "shot or otherwise destroyed without fear of censure, impeachment or prosecution for the same." In 1781, it was provided that any slave who should enlist and serve "for three years, or until discharged," should be declared a freeman of the state.

LEAD

Lead was the most difficult of the warlike stores to secure. (See " Public Papers of George Clinton", Vol. II, pp. 489 and 498). As it was impossible to import lead, the troops from this state resorted to pewter dishes as material for their bullets. At Fort Montgomery, even the weights on fishing-nets were used for this purpose. Small quantities of lead were brought from Connecticut. Finally, early in 1776, a happy thought came over the Provincial Congress. Here is the story, as told by Peter T. Curtenius, in making up his accounts against the United States:-

The reason that their is no account of Purchaces Produced by P. T. C. is because by a Resolve of the Provincial Congress the Window Leads were taken out of the Windows of the Inhabitants in the City of New York & deliv'd to P T Curtenius then Commissary of the Provincial Congress amounting to Something above l00 Tons wt for which the Citizens were paid for by the Treasurer of the State after the War was over at 9d pr Ib this is the reason why It does not appear in P T C acct of Purchases-the 4 Ton 7.1 -was sent by P T C to Brig' Genl Geo Clintons Encampment at Westchester the 12 Ton was Sent up to Orange County as a place of Safety & afterwards was delivd to J Rudduch who was a Contin Officer & the remainder Say 6324 was Sent up to Albany & delivd to Phil Vanrenselaer who was a Millitary Store Keeper for the United States.

This is the form of Certificate that was given by Daniel Dunscomb:-

1776 State of New York to Paulus Banta Dr.
July. For 124 lb. Window Lead taken from my House by Order of Convention for
public use as pr Danl. Dunscomb's Certificate at 9d pr W..............£4.13.-

New York 7th Decem' 1784 I have examin'd the above account and allow to be due thereon the
Sum of Four Pounds thirteen shillings Currency which please pay Mr. Nicholas Bogart on his
producing Mr. Banta's Receipt on the Back of this Accot.
Gerard Bancker Esqr. Treasurer. Peter T. Curtenius State Audr.
[Indorsed, as follows]
Rece'd New York 7th Decent. 1784 from Gerard Bancker Treasurer of the State the Sum
of Four Pounds thirteen shillings in full of the within Account.
£4..I3.. 0 Paulus Banta.

New York the 7th Decem'. 174
I Certify that there was taken out of the house of Paulus Banta in Dey Street One hundred &
twenty four pounds of window leads tor Public service by order of Convention.
Peter T. Curtenius Esq'. Auditor. Daniel Dunscomb.

A deposition of Edward Blagge, made on Feb. 14, 1785, states "that sometime in the Month of July
in the year of 1776, a Number of Men came to the house of Capt George Codwise and took from
the Windows of the Dwelling House of the said George Codwise a Number of Leaden sash weights
& put them in a Cart with a Number of Others, & when this deponent ask'd what Authority they had
for so doing he was answer'd 'twas by Public Authority ".

The following is the only claim that appears from any locality outside the City of New
York:-

State of New York to Frederick Roorbach ...... Dr
For 91 1/4 lb Lead Weights delivered for public use as pr Certificate from Robert
Boyd, junr Chairman of Ulster County Committee a 9d pr Ib.................... £.3. 8. 3

I hereby certify that Mr Frederick Roorbach delivered to me as Chairman of the Committee for the
County of Ulster Ninety one pounds and a Quarter of lead, and that the same was made into
Bullets and used by the militia of the County aforesaid when going to Forts Montgomery and
Clinton in the Month of July 1776-
New York 30th December 1784. Robt. Boyd Junr.

[The account was allowed by the Auditor-General on Jan. 10, 1785; and paid the same date.]

Previous to the removal of the Window Leads belonging to the private citizens of New York, Samuel
Prince and two assistants, on June 5, 1776, took the Leads from the City Hall and the Exchange;
and, on July 12, 36 bars of Lead, weighing 1069 pounds, were taken from Jacobus Depeyster, John

Davis. July 17, 1776 charged the Committee of Poughkeepsie 9d per pound for 41 pounds of Lead. Daniel Dunscomb was paid by a law passed May 12, 1784.

Window Leads Were Taken From The Homes of These Citizens:

Abrams Andrew
Abrams Anthony
Ackly Anthony
Algier (Mrs.)
Alner John
Alsop John
Alstyne Elizabeth
Anderson Elbert
Anthony Nicholas
Anthony Nicholas N.
Aspinwall John
Bache Theophylaet
Bail Cornelia (Mrs.)
Bancker Adrian
Bancker Evert
Bancker John Banta Paulus
Barclay Andrew
Barclay Henry, Rev.
Barnes Mary
Barnes Phebe
Barrea Francis
Barrow Thomas
Bassett (Mrs.)
Bassett Francis
Bauman Sebastian, Maj.
Bayard Samuel
Beekman (Mrs.)
Beekman Abraham
Beekman Gerard G., Jr.
Beekman Gerard William
Beekman Henry
Beekman James
Beekman John
Beekman Samuel
Beekman Theo's
Beekman Wm. & Family
Bend Grove
Bender Matthew
Benson Benjamin
Benson Robert
Blake Jonathan
Blau Cornelia (Mrs.)
Bockee Abraham
Bogart Henry C.
Bogart Nicholas, Capt,
Bogert Cornelius

Bogert Elizabeth (Mrs.)
Bogert Jacobus
Bogert John
Bogert Nicholas
Bogert Peter
Bonta Jacob
Bouvelot James
Bowne Samuel
Brasher Abraham
Brasier Meads
Breested Andrew
Brevoort Elias
Brevoort Henry
Brewerton George
Brewerton Jacob
Brinckerhoff Abraham
Broome Samuel
Brower Abraham
Brower Jeremiah
Brower John
Brower Peter
Brown John
Brown Mary (Mrs.)
Brown Thomas
Brown John William
Buller Jane
Burke (Mrs.)
Burling Lancaster
Burras Lawrence
Butler William
Byvanck Evert
Byvanck John
Callow Stephen
Car Anthony
Carmer Henry
Carpenter Elizabeth
Carroll James
Cheesman Thomas
Clark John
Clarke James, Dr.
Clarke Thomas, Capt. Clarkson
David
Clopper Peter
Cockeroft William
Cockle Hannah (Mrs.)
Codwise George, Capt.
Cooley Francis

Cornelison Michael
Couwenhoven Nicholas
Covenhoven Edward
Crolius John
Crommelin Robert
Crooke Annahe (Mrs.)
Crooke Elizabeth (Mrs.)
Crosfield Stephen
Cruger Henry
Cruger John
Curtenius Peter T.
Dale Robert, Capt.
Davis Benjamin
Deall Samuel
Deane William
De Lancey John
De Lancey John Peter
De Lancey Peter
Delaplaine William
Denning William
De Peyster Cornelia (Mrs.)
De Peyster Nicholas
De Peyster William
Des Brosses Elias
Des Brosses James
Dickson David, Capt.
Dobson Thomas
Dodge Amos
Dodge Samuel
Drake Jasper
Duane (Mrs.)
Dudley John
Duncan George
Dunscomb Daniel
Dunscomb Edward
Dunscomb John
Dunscomb Samuel
Duryee Abraham
Duryee John
Dutch Church Convention
Duyckinck Gerardus
Eagles William
Ebbetts Daniel
Elliott John
Ellison Thomas
Elsworth Johannes (Mrs.)
Elsworth Theophilus

Elsworth William, sr.
Elsworth William, jr.
Fangere Lewis, Dr.
Farman Samuel
Farmer Maria
Fell John
Filkin Francis
Finch Alexander
Fine Frederick
Foght John M.
Forbes Gilbert
Forbes Joseph
Fox Mary (Mrs.)
Franklin James
Franklin John
Franklin Samuel
Franklin Walter
Fraunces Samuel
Gaine Hugh
Gautier Andrew
Girnng George
Gilbert John
Gilbert William
Goelet Peter
Gomez Moses
Graham Ennis
Gregg David
Griffith Robert
Griffiths John, Capt.
Grigg Henry
Griswold Joseph
Groesbeck Elizabeth (Mrs.)
Hallett James
Hallett Joseph
Halstead Phebe
Ham Coenrad W.
Hammond Elizabeth (Mrs.)
Hardenbrook Abel
Hardenbrook Theophilus
Hardenbrook William
Haring Elbert
Harris Richard
Harrison George
Harsin Garrit
Hayes (Mrs.)
Haynes Joseph
Henderson Thomas
Henshaw Daniel, Capt.
Heyer William, Col.
Hicks Whitehead
Hildreth Benjamin
Hitchcock Daniel
Hodgeson John

Holland Henry
Hopkins George
Hopper Matthew
Hopper Rynear
Housman Aurt
Howard Sheffield
Hoyer Peter
Hughes, Mary Walton
(Mrs.)
Hunt Davis
Hunt Jane
Hyer Walter
Jandine Charles
Jarvis James
Jauncey James, jr.
Jauncey John
Jauncey Mary (Mrs.)
Jay Frederick
Johnson Jane (Mrs.)
Johnson John, Capt.
Johnson Samuel
Johnson Simeon
Jones Humphrey
Jones Margaret (Mrs.)
Kelly William
Kemmeny Engelbart, Dr.
Kendall Mary (Mrs.)
Kennedy Archibald
Ketellas Abraham, Rev.
Ketellas Peter, jr.
Kibbel Stephen
Kiersted Rulef, Dr.
King Linus
Kip Abraham
Kip Henry
Kip Jane (Widow)
Kip Leonard
Kippin William
Kissick Philip
Knack Reinier
Kortright Lawrence
Laight Edward
Lasher John
Latham Daniel
Latham John
Latham Joseph
Lawrence Augustin
Lawrence Caleb
Lawrence Catharine (Mrs.)
Lawrence John
Lawrence Thomas
Leake Ann (Mrs.)
Leake John

Leary John, sr.
Leaycraft Viner
Lee John
Lefferts Jacobus
Lester Joseph
Lispenard Leonard
Livingston Elizabeth (Mrs)
Livingston John
Livingston Philip
Livingston Robert
Livingston Robert G.
Long John
Lott Abraham
Lott Abraham P.
Louden Samuel
Lowey Michael
Ludlow Cary
Ludlow Gabriel
Ludlow William
Lupton William
Lyng John Burt
Lynson Catharine (Mrs.)
McAdam William
McAlpin Robert
McCready James
McEvers Charles
McEvers James
McKenny John
McKinly William
Mallet Jonathan
Marsalis Peter
Marschalk Francis
Marston Nathaniel
Marston Thomas
Martin John
Masterton David
Matthewman Catharine
Maxwell William
Mead Isaac
Mercier William
Mesier Abraham
Mesier Peter
Milliner William
Misnard Daniel
Moncrieff Thomas
Montanye (Mrs.)
Montanye John
Montanye Joseph
Moore Benjamin, sr.
Moore John
Moore Lambert
Moore Michael
Moore Thomas William

Moore William
Morton John
Murray Robert
Myer John R.
Myers Myer
Neilson William
Nicoll Charles
Nicoll Edward
Oakes Thomas
Ogsbury Alexander
Oothout John
Oudenaarde Henry
Panton Francis
Parceles Abraham
Payne Ann (Mrs.)
Pearsall Thomas
Pearse William
Pell Samuel
Pettit Thomas
Phillips Charles
Phoenix Daniel
Pinto Rachel
Play Hannah (Mrs.)
Prince Samuel
Provoost David
Provoost Eve (Mrs.)
Provoost Peter
Puffendorf (Mrs.)
Quackenbos Walter
Quackenbush Johannes
Quackenbush Nicholas
Quick Abraham
Quick Jacobus
Quill Thomas, Capt.
Ramsay John
Randall Thomas
Rapalje Garret
Rapalje Rem
Ray John
Ray Robert
Reade John
Reed James
Remney William
Remsen (Mrs.)
Remsen George
Remsen Henry
Remsen Jacob
Richards Paul
Richards Stephen
Riker Andrew
Riker Henry
Riker John
Rivington James

Robert Christopher
Robertson Alexander
Roome Jacob
Roome Luke
Roorbach Frederick
Roorbach John
Roosevelt Isaac
Roosevelt Jacobus
Roosevelt Nicholas
Rutgers Elizabeth (Mrs.)
Rutgers Henry
Rutherford Walter, Maj.
Sackett Samuel
Sands Comfort
Sarly Jacob
Schermerhorn John, Capt.
Schuyler Elizabeth (Mrs.)
Schuyler John
Schuyler Samuel
Seaman Edmond
Sears Isaac
Sebring Bannat
Sebring Cornelius
Shand Mary
Sharp Richard
Shoals John, Capt.
Sickels Robert
Sickels Zachariah
Silvester Francis
Simson Solomon
Smith Abraham
Smith Ann (Mrs.)
Smith Barnardus
Smith Christopher
Smith John
Smith Thomas
Smith William
Smith William Peartree
Spraggs Samuel
Stagg John
Stanton George
Steele Stephen
Stephany John
Sebastian
Stevens John
Stewart Alexander
Steymets Benjamin
Steymets Christopher
Stiles Daniel
Stout Benjamin
Stoutenbergh Tobias
Stoutenburgh Isaac
Stoutenburgh Peter

Sweedland Christopher
Talman William
Taylor John
Ten Eyck Abraham
Ten Eyck Anthony
Ten Eyck Daniel
Ten Eyck Mary (Mrs,)
Teppet Stephen
Tetard John Peter
Thurman John, sr.
Thurman John, Jr.
Tiebout Teunis
Tillou Peter
Todd Sarah (Mrs.)
Tolmie Norman
Totten Joseph
Towt Robert
Troup John I.
Troup Robert, Capt.
Tucker Thomas
Turk Aha's
Turner John
Ustick Henry
Ustick William
Van Alstyne Abraham
Van Alstyne John
Van Alstyne Roome
Van Antwerp Jacobus
Van Buren Beekman. Dr.
Van Cortlandt Augustus
Van Cortlandt John
Van Cortlandt William
Van derbilt John
Van derspeigle John
Van der Voort Peter
Van der Water William
Van Dolsem John
Van Drill William
Van Dum Catarine
Van Dum Sarah
Van Dursen Peter
Van Dyck Abraham
Van Dyck Jacobus
Van Gelder Abraham
Van Gelder Colin
Van Home Augustus
Van Home David
Van Home Samuel
Van Keuren Margaret
(Mrs.)
Van Renst Catharine
(Mrs.)
Van Solingen Godardus

Van Varck Effie
Van Varck James
Van Varick Guilliam
Van Vleeck Henry
Ven Vleeck John
Van Vorhis Jacob
Van Wagenen Huybert
Van Wagenen Jacob
VanWyck Theodoras
Van Zandt Jacobus
Van Zandt Peter
Varick Guilliam
Varick John
Verplanck (Mrs.)
Verplanck Samuel
Vredenburgh John
Vredenburgh Matthias

Vredenburgh William
Waddle (Mrs.)
Waldron Kilah (Mrs.)
Waldron Richard
Waldron Sarah (Mrs.)
Walker John
Walton Cornelia
Walton Jacob
Walton William
Wardell Thomas
Watar Agnes
Watson Jacob
Watts John, jr.
Weeks Peezard
Wells James
Wendover Hercules
Wendover Thomas

Wessels Francis
Wetherhead Rachel (Mrs.)
Wetzell John
Whiteman Henry
Wickham William
Williams Erasmus
Williams William
Witter Thomas
Wolfe David
Wood John
Woodward John
Wright John G., Dr.
Yates Richard
Zuricker John

July, 1776, the Provincial Congress, or Convention, voted £40 to Nathaniel Sackett for transporting Lead in Dutchess County; £50 to Henry Wisner, jr., for transporting Lead to the Counties of Orange and Ulster; and £70 to Messrs. Marsh, Stevens and Sessions for transporting Lead to the Counties of Cumberland and Gloucester.

The 100 tons of Lead secured from the windows in New York City proved invaluable. The fate of the American cause might have been much more doubtful, had it not been (or this supply. From July to December, 1776, about 20 tons of this lead had been delivered to the Army. In July and August, a large part of it was shipped to Col. Levi Pawling, in Gen. James Cnnton's Encampment; to Nathaniel Sackett and Jonathan Platt, in Dutchess County; and to Henry Wisner, in Ulster and Orange Counties-£ 20. 0. 6 having been paid to the latter, Oct. 23, by the Treasurer of the Provincial Congress. The Committee of Ulster County, Oct. 25, paid 4/6 to Johannes Hardenbergh tor freight on Lead; and, also, the same amount to William Elsworth for freight paid for Lead Carried to Kingston from N. Y. of which the lower end of the County had none. Some of the last named Lead was afterward carted from Kingston to Newburgh.

1776 State of New York to Henry Bogart Dr.

Novr 10 To Cartage for Sash Leads from Hobuck & Newark .... £t3- 4.
To Cartage down to the Ferry..10.
To casting 15 ct Lead into Musket Ball @ 8/--..6.

1784 To 15 Boxes for the Ball - 2/-. 1.10
July 10 To my Wages going to Hackensack to dig up the Bullets & carting them
to the Landing 4 days @ l0/-...2.
To 9 New Boxes the old ones being rotten ....18.
To freight paid to the Boatman from Hackinsack including cartage to
the Barracks...£ 12.
14. I4.

This bill was audited and paid May 15, 1786. The State, May 29, 1777, paid a bill of the Committee of Newburgh Precinct, dated July 4, 1776, for 186 3/4 pounds of Lead, at 8d., delivered to Col Hasbrouck's Regiment at Fort Montgomery.

Muskets

Muskets were among the Military Stores that at first were furnished by Peter T. Curtenius, the Commissary of the Provincial Congress. Later they were collected by John Henry, the State Clothier, and forwarded to Col. John Lasher, Commissary, who thereafter had full charge of them

The Muskets were taken from Tories and Disaffected Persons; and, also, from the "Well-Affected " who could not use them.

The following comments of Mr. Curtenius, Commissary, show the way in which Muskets were taken and distributed:-

The Muskets of the Corporation [New York City] were taken out of the Armoury by a Number of Citizens under the Command of Capt Sears (shortly after the News arrived of the Lexington Battle) and carried into Capt Vandykes Fire Ally after which a Committee was appointed to deliver them into the hands of such Citizens as were well-affected to the freedom of America. In the month of June or July following the Provincial Congress passed a Resolve to Raise 4 Redgiments of Contini Troops and the troops being in want of Muskets the P. Congress published a Resolve that all Citizens possessed of Corporation muskets should deliver them to the proper officer at the Barracks which was done & Colol McDougalls Regimt had 434 of them & the remainder went up to New Windsor for Colol Clintons Redgiment as appears by Wm Tapps affidavit The Corporation applied last Winter to the Legislature of our State for payment In consequence of which the Legislature passed a Law to pay for them provided the United States should pass the amot of them to the Credit of the State of New York.

At about the same date, 500 other Muskets were taken out of New York, by the committee of the City and County, and sent to Gen. Schuyler, at the North. In the Campaign of 1775, 16 Guns were bought for the Continental Troops, and delivered to Capt. Henry B. Livingston. The price, for each, ranged from £1. to £7. On Sept. 14, 1776 Capt. Livingston loaned 69 "Fire-Locks" to the State of Connecticut. In May, of that year, and again in October, many Guns were taken from the inhabitants, by the Committee of Suffolk County, and delivered to Col. Livingston. (See " Suffolk County Committee "). On Dec. 9, 1776, 73 Muskets, many Bayonets and some Powder were brought from the Eastern end of Long Island, by Col Livingston, and delivered to Capt. Nathaniel Platt. Nearly all of the Muskets from Long Island belonged to the Refugees from that Island. (See the Refugees from Long Island to Connecticut, in "Provincial Congresses ").

A number of interesting events, relative to Small Arms, took place in 1776:-Jan 12, Cornelius Atherton made two written contracts, with bonds of £700 each, for the furnishing of, £700 worth of Muskets, with Bayonets, for which he was to be allowed £3.14. each; Feb. 2, the Committee of Safety ordered the payment of £700 to Jecamiah Allen for Muskets; Mar. 10, and July 6, the Committee on Conspiracies took many Arms from the Tories and Disaffected in New York City; in April, Capt. Thaddeus Noble made a contract for 30 Muskets, at $8 each; June 4, Lieut. Joseph Youngs charged £3.11.6 for 11 days' expenses in collecting 106 Arms from the Tories in Westchester County; in the same month, the brigantine " Grant" brought 263 Guns from Marseilles to the West Indies; July 19, William Duer authorized Peter T. Curtenius to buy 600 or 700 French Muskets, at $11 each; July 9, the Dutchess County Committee paid l0/ - for the " carriage of 14 Guns to Col. Humphrey ", and l2/ - for " Fetching 20 Guns from John Carpenter to Waters, the Gunsmith " ; Aug. 3, the same Committee paid Waters £14. 15. 11 for repairing Guns; Richard Ten Eyck was paid 6/- per day for directing the repair of Small Arms; David Howell sent in a bill of £48. 1.2 for repairing Arms, which the Auditor-General described as " moderately charged

", but Howell was not paid till June 4, 1792. The Auditor-General made this statement, relative to another claim:-" Danl Delavan's Claim 1140 for payment of Arms. By his own acct of the matter they were deposited in the Contin'l Store at Kings Ferry, therefore the U. S. must pay him ".

In 1776 and 1777, the Committee of Rumbout Precinct, in Dutchess County, delivered 431 Guns to the State. The Guns were afterward delivered to Colonels Harper, Willett, Van Cortlandt, and others. In March, 1777, these items were paid:-Jacob Hunt, £6.l0.0 for conveying Arms to Peekskill, Samuel Niely, £ 1.4.0, for repairing Arms; Robert Merrit, £1.7.0, for making Arm-Chests; William Jeffery, 16, for repairing Arms. William Ellsworth had a charge for cleaning 101 Muskets. The Provincial Congress, June 9, 1777, offered a Bounty of £20 for every 100 Muskets delivered to the County Committees.

Reed of Brig'r Genl James Clinton Fifty One Guns & barrels. Forty two Gun Ramrods & Ten Gun Stocks, without barrels, which was hid by Peter Cortenis at Hackinsack to prevent their falling into the Enemies hands - and taken up by Capt Daniel Tier, agreeable to Genl Clinton's Orders &c pr me John Varick Ramapough Clove, 6 July 1777 Expenses paid Daniel Tier A. Qr. Mr. G. for the hire of Waggon, Men's Expences &c in bringing up the within mentioned Guns &c £3.12.0. I certify that I employed Danl Tier to fetch the Guns. P. T. Curtenius Late Commiss'y to purchase Armes & Cloathing

1777 State of New York to Dan' Tier................Dr.

July 6 To Expences by me for the hire of Waggon & Men's Expences & bringing up 51 Gun barrels & 52 Ramrods from Hackinsack, where they were buried up to Mr. Sloots in the Clove, as pr Rect of John Varick who reed them from Gen. Clinton............................. £3. 12. 0

Danl Tier, being duly sworn, deposeth & saith that the above account is just & True & that he has received no compensation from the State of New York or the United States.

Sworn before me this 11th   Daniel Tier
Day of Febry 1786.
Bn Blagge, Alderman

Source Material for previous articles:

New York In The Revolution as Colony and State
by James A. Roberts, Comptroller
Second Edition 1898

The Militia Bill
The Militia Bill Adopted by The Prvincial Congress August 22d, 1775.

In Provincial Congress New York, Aug. 22d, 1775.

Whereas the well ordering and regulating the militia of this Colony is become an object of the greatest importance to the preservation of the lives and Liberties of its Inhabitants.

And Whereas, The Continental Congress held at Philadelphia on the 10th day of May last taking into consideration the necessity of such a regulation have recommended the same to the Inhabitants of the associated Colonies and Whereas this Congress on the ninth day of this instant August by several resolutions recommended to their constituents the expediency of forming themselves into Companies and chusing their Officers in the manner following vizt.

Resolved, that every County, City, Manor, Town, Precinct and District within this Colony, (where the same is not already done) be divided into districts or beats by their respective Committees in such manner, that out of each may be formed a military Company, ordinarily to consist of about eighty-three able bodied and effective men, Officers included, between 16 or 60 years of age. (The Battalion commanded by Col. Lasher, the Companies of artillery, Light horse and Hussars in the City and County of New York and the Troops of Horse, Companies of Grenadiers and associated Companies already formed within this Colony excepted.

Resolved secondly, That in each Company so to be formed there be chosen (in the manner hereinafter mentioned) one Captain, two Lieutenants, one Ensign, four Sergeants, four Corporals, one Clerk, one Drummer and one Fifer.

Resolved thirdly, That two Committeemen at the least attend in each district or beat on a day to be appointed for the purpose of chusing the above mentioned Officers, who shall be persons within such district or beat, who have signed the General Association recommended by this Congress.

That such choice or Election be made in the manner following, vizt—

After the Company is drawn up the Committee men, who preside at the Election, may repair to a station at some convenient distance from the Company,--then let the men pass in a single file between them, each man giving the name of the person he chooses to fill the office in question, the majority of such votes to determine the Election. But in case the votes shall be so divided, that no one has the majority, then the presiding Committeemen are to acquaint the Company therewith and call them to a new Election—the same to be repeated, till such majority be obtained or the Company agree upon some other mode of choosing the Officers. The names of the Captains, Lieutenants and Ensigns so chosen to be returned with all convenient speed to this or some future Provincial Congress of this Colony or during their recess to the Committee of Safety, to be commissioned by them.

Resolved fourthly, That whenever a vacancy shell happen in any Company by the promotion, death or resignation of an Officer, such vacancy to be filled up in the before mentioned manner.

Resolved fifthly, That those Companies in the above excepted Battalion, commanded by Col. Lasher, which are now under the direction of Field Officers shall for the future be commanded by Captains, who are to be chosen in the manner aforesaid.

Resolved sixthly, That for the purpose of completely carrying into execution the recommendation of the Continental Congress; after the whole militia is formed as above every fourth man of each Company be selected for Minute Men, or such persons, as are willing to enter into this necessary service. That the Officers of the militia make with all convenient speed a return of the names of those persons to the Committee of their respective Counties, who shall thereupon arrange those men into Companies their choice of their Officers in the manner above mentioned, provided that where whole Companies offer their services a Minute Men, they shall be commanded by the Officers already chosen and the remaining number of Minute Men shall be completed out of the other Companies as above.

Resolved seventhly, That the several Committees do return to the Secretary of the Provincial Congress of this Colony the names of such persons, as do refuse to conform to the above resolves.

1st. That the several Companies so formed be joined unto Regiments, each Regiment to consist of not less than five or more than ten Companies, (the Battalion commanded by Col. Lasher excepted.)

2d. That a Major General be appointed and commissioned by this Congress to command the militia of the Colony New York.

3d. That one Colonel, one Lieutenant Colonel, and two Majors, an Adjutant & Quarter Master be commissioned by this Congress for each Regiment.

4th. That the militia of this Colony be formed into Brigades in the following manner, to wit: The mlitia of the City and County of New York and Counties of Kings and Richmond. *One Brigade.*
The militia of the City and County of Albany and the County of Tryon. *One other Brigade.*
The militia of the Counties of Dutchess and Westchester. *One other Brigade.*
The militia of the Counties of Ulster and Orange. *One other Brigade.*
The militia of the Counties of Charlotte, Cumberland and Gloucester. *One other Brigade.*

5th. That a Brigadier General with a Major of Brigade be commissioned to the command of each Brigade.

6th. That every man between the ages of 16 and 50 do with all convenient speed furnish himself with a good Musket or firelock & Bayonet Sword or Tomahawk, a Steel Ramrod, Worm, Priming Wire and Brush fitted thereto, a Cartouch Box to contain 23 rounds of cartridges, 12 flints and a knapsack agreeable to the directions of the Continental Congress under forfeiture of five shillings for the want of a musket or firelock and of one shilling for the want of a bayonet, sword or tomahawk, cartridge box, cartridge or bullet, the whole to be judged by the Captain or next commanding officers.
     That every man shall at his place of abode be also provided with one pound of powder and three pounds of bullets of proper size to his musket or firelock.

7th. That each Company (not Minute Men) do meet the first Monday in every month and spend at least four hours in each of the said days to perfect themselves in military discipline. Provided, that if the commissioned Officers of any Company shall judge it inexpedient to meet on that day, they have power to put off the meeting to some other day, notifying the Company thereof.

8th. That the Colonels and commanding Officers of each Regiment do assemble and exercise their respective Regiments at least two days in every year at some convenient place to be fixed Upon by the Field Officers.

9th. That the several Companies of Horse already formed or to be formed in this Colony shall be under the direction of the Colonel of the Regiment, where their respective Captains do reside and be considered a part of such Regiment,--that the Officers and Privates shall assemble as often, as by these regulations it is required of the Companies of Foot (not Minute Men) and be subject to the same penalties and forfeitures for non-attendance,-- That every man belonging to the Horse shall, with all convenient speed, provide himself with a good serviceable horse, not less than 14 hands high, with a good saddle, bridle, hostlers, housings, breast plate and crupper, a case of pistols, a sword or hanger, one pound of gunpowder and 3 lbs. Of sizeable bullets, a pair of boots with suitable spurs and a carabine, well fixed with a good belt, swivel & buckle under the penalty of 10s for the want of a sizeable horse & 5 s. for the want of each or either of the articles of the Trooper's furniture. And also that every trooper be provided at their respective places of abode with 1 lb. of powder and 3 lbs. of bullets.

10th. That in case any persons shall refuse or neglect to serve as Sergeant, Corporal or Drummer in any Company being thereto requested by the Captain or commanding Officer or shall refuse or neglect to warn the men to appear under arms, when required by the Captain or commanding Officer, shall for every such neglect forfeit the sum of 40 shill.

11th. That all Officers commissioned by this Congress Do subscribe the following declaration:

We, the subscribers, the Officers of the _____ Battalion or Regiment in the County of _____ and the Colony of New York do hereby promise and engage under all the ties of religion, honour and regard to our country, that we will respectively duly observe and carry into execution to the utmost of our power, all and every the orders, rules and recommendations made or to be made by the Continental Congress and the Congress or Convention of this Colony. That we'll also give the Continental Congress and the Congress or Convention of this Colony. That we'll also give in our respective ranks due obedience to the regulations by them established for the forming of the militia of this Colony, as also due obedience to such Officers, who either by rank or superiority are placed above us in such order, as is directed by the said Continental or Provincial Congress.

12th. That the following penalties be inflicted on those, who do not attend and obey orders on the days appointed for exercise, not having a reasonable excuse to be allowed of by the Officer commanding, to wit: a Colonel 5 pounds, a Lieutenant Colonel 4 pounds, a Major 3 pounds, Captains, Lieutenants and Adjutants 30 s. each, Ensigns and Quartermaster 20s. each, Sergeants, Corporals, Drummers, Fifers and Privates 10s. each for the first default and double for the second. And in case any person make default three times successively or refuse to enlist and do duty, such person shall be advertised and held up as an enemy to his country. All fines under the degree of a Captain to be levied on the goods and chattels of the offender by warrant from the Captain directed to a Sergeant of the Company and those of a Captain and all Field Officers under the degree of a Colonel to be levied on the goods and chattels of the offender by a warrant from the Colonel of the Regiment directed to the Adjutant, and those of a Colonel by a warrant from a Brigadier General directed to the Major of the Brigade, and for want of the goods and chattels to take the body of the offender and him keep in safe custody, until such fine together with the charges be paid. The monies arising by the fines in any Company be applied by the Captain, (after paying for the Drum and Fife for the Company) towards purchasing Arms, Ammunition and Accoutrements for such persons in such Company, as are unable to furnish themselves. The monies arising by the fines of the Field Officers (after paying for a set of colours for each Battalion) be equally divided between the several Companies for the above mentioned use.

13th. That the members of his Majesty's Council, Justices of the Supreme Court, of the Vice Admiralty Court, of the Mayors Courts and Inferior Courts of Common Pleas, his majesty's Attorney General, Secretary of the Province or his Deputy, Clerks of the Courts, Collector,

Comptroller, Naval Officer and Searcher and Surveyor of his Majesty's Customs, Ministers of the Gospel, Physicians and Surgeons, Members of the Continental Congress and of the Provincial Congress and the several Committees, while immediately engaged in the public service, Sheriffs, Gaolers, Ferrymen, one Miller to each mill, and the people, Called Quakers, be excused from military duty, except in cases of invasion and in case of an invasion in any part of this Colony, the Physicians and Surgeons there or such of them as shall be directed by the Officers commanding the militia (that shall march to oppose the Enemy) shall attend with proper medicines, instruments and other necessaries to take care of the sick and wounded.

14th That the commissioned Officers of each Company of Minute Men form their Companies into four subdivisions in such manner, as they shall think most convenient for their frequent meetings. The subdivisions under their respective Officers to meet once in every week and to employ half a day or at least four hours each time in perfecting themselves in military discipline, the whole Companies to meet once every fortnight, to spend the same time for the same purpose. That the several Companies of Minute Men be formed into Regiments, to consist of about seven Companies each. That there be commissioned by the Congress to each Regiment, one Colonel, one Lieutenant Colonel, two Majors, and Adjutant and Quarter Master.

15th. That those Regiments be formed into Brigades, each Brigade to consist of about ____ Regiments. That there be commissioned by this Congress to each Brigade one Brigadier General and a Major of Brigade.

16th. That the whole body of Minute Men shall be under the direction of the Major General appointed by this Congress, while within the Colony, unless a Continental Officers of superior or equal rank be present.

17th. That the Minute Men, when called out in defence of their country shall be subject to the Articles of War established by the Continental Congress and be entitled to the same allowance as to pay and provisions with the continental forces. To be under the direction of the Commander in Chief of those Forces.

18th. That they be subject to the like penalties and forfeitures for not attending on the days appointed for exercise as above mentioned. The said fines to be levied and applied as above directed.

19th. That in case of any alarm, invasion or insurrection every sabaltern and soldier is immediately to repair properly armed and accoutred to his colours or Parade, (which Parade shall be understood to be the habitation of his Captain unless otherwise ordered) and the Captain or commanding Officer nearest to the place, where such invasion or insurrection shall be, shall immediately march his Company to oppose the enemy, at the same time send off an express to the commanding Officer of the Regiment or Brigade, to which he belongs, who is to march with the whole or part of the militia under his command, as he shall judge necessary, and use all possible diligence to prevent the Enemy from landing or penetrating into any part of the country and to quell every insurrection. That every non-commissioned Officer and Private, who shall neglect or refuse to perform his duty in this case, shall be subject to such pains, penalties and forfeitures, as shall be adjudged by a general Court Martial.

20th. That at least twice in every year the Captains or in their absence the next commanding Officer of every company of militia, as well as of the Minute Men as others, shall deliver to the Colonel of the Regiment a true and compleat Roll containing the names of all the men belonging to his Company, under the penalty of two pounds to be recovered and applied, as hereinbefore directed And the Colonels of the Regiments shall within one month after the receipt of every such roll deliver or send a copy of every such roll to the Brigadier General of the Brigade, to which he belongs, who is directed to send the same or a copy to the Major General of the Colony.

21st. That in case of an alarm or an invasion the Officer commanding in each district shall leave a proper detachment of his Company, to guard against the insurrection of slaves, or if judged more expedient and safe, may take the slaves or part of them with him and employ them in carrying baggage, dragging cannon or the like.

22nd. That all persons, as well Minute Men as others, able to bear arms, who shall leave or attempt to leave a place actually invaded without leave of the Officer commanding such place or who shall refuse to obey order in time of actual invasion or insurrection shall be liable to such punishment, as shall be inflicted by a Court Martial.

23rd. That in case it shall be judged necessary at any time and place by this Congress, by the Committee of Safety or by the several Committees of the respective Counties or districts, that a military watch be established, All persons able to bear arms, where such watch is judged to be necessary, shall upon due warning be obliged to serve on such watch under the penalty of the 12s. for every neglect, A commissioned Officer in turn to mount said guard in person under the penalty of 40s.

24th. That every Centinel, who shall leave his post, be found asleep, when he is posted, shall be liable to such punishment, as shall be inflicted by a Court Martial.

25th. That when the militia, as well Minute Men as others, in case of Invasion or Insurrection shall be called out on actual service, They shall be subject to the same Rules and Orders, as directed and ordered by the Continental Congress of the associated Colonies held at Philadelphia on the 10th day of May last for better government of the Continental Troops.

A letter from Capt. John Lamb, dated this day, soliciting this Congress to ascertain the pay of the Artillery Company under his command was read and filed.

Agreed and Ordered, That the Artillery Company raised in the Colony as part of the Continental Army and enlised under Capt. John Lamb shall have such pay, as the Continental Congress shall agree to and order, and that in the meantime Capt. Lamb's Company shall have the like pay, as the Rhode Island Company of Artillery are allowed,* until the Continental Congress shall have fixed and ascertained the pay of Capt. Lamb's Company. And ordered that Capt. John Lamb and his Company be considered as an additional Company to, and a part of Colo. McDougall's Regiment and subject to his commands.

*Capt. Lamb, in the letter mentioned, refers to the pay of the R. I. Company and points out as a mistake in that arrangement, that the pay of a 2d. Lieutenant and Lieut. Fireworker is not equal to the pay of Lieutenants of Foot Companies, also that a Bombardier receives more, than a Sergeant.

Note: There were subsequent revisions and additions to the able, but will not be included in this book except for a few interesting additions:

Page 105.   That the distinction between Minute Men and common militia which seems to be a consequence of the aforesaid Resolve of the Continental Congress be henceforth abolished, that thereby the militia of the Colony may be again reduced to one Common mass.   That all the commission for Minute Officers be forthwith recalled and that every private be placed under his proper militia Officer, leaving each Regiment of be Officered according to the Mode prescribed, that is to say, those under the degree of Field Officers by Election of the privates and those above that Degree by the appointment of the provincial Congress.

Source Material:
New York State Archives
New York In The Revolution
Prepared under direction of the Board of Regents
By Berthold Fernow.
Weed, Parsons and Company, Printers
Volume I, 1887

The following lists of regiments were taken from:
New York In The Revolution as Colony and State
by James A. Roberts, Comptroller
Compiled by Frederic G. Mather
Second Edition 1898

The Levies--(Willett's)

[Captain, Major, Lieutenant-Colonel, Colonel and Acting Brigadier General Marinus Willett was a gallant officer. He held many commands and his promotions were rapid. In 1775-6 he was a Captain in Colonel Alexander McDougal's Regiment, 1st N. Y. Line. On April 27, 1776, the Provincial Congress recommended him to the Continental Congress for Major of the same Regiment. In November of the same year he was recommended for Lieutenant- Colonel of the 3d Line, and in July, 1780, he was made Lieutenant-Colonel Commandant of the 5th Regiment of the Line. In 1781, as Lieutenant-Colonel, he commanded a Regiment of Levies, and in 1782 was made full Colonel of still another Regiment of Levies, After the death of General Nicholas Herkimer, Colonel Willett commanded the Tryon Co. Militia as Acting Brigadier General, and in the battles of Johnstown and Caughnawaga defeated the enemy most signally.]

COLONEL MARINUS WILLETT
LIEUT. COL. JOHN McKINSTRY
MAJOR ANDREW FINK, JR.
(MAJOR OF BRIGADE)

MAJOR LYMAN HITCHCOCK
(MUSTER MASTER)
MAJOR JOSIAH THROOP
MAJOR ELIAS VAN BUNSCHOTEN
ADJUTANT JELLES A. FONDA
ADJUTANT PLINY MOORE
QUARTER MASTER JOHN FONDEY
QUARTER MASTER MATTHEW TROTTER
QUARTER MASTER JACOB WINNEY
PAY MASTER ABRAHAM TEN EYCK
SURGEON CALVIN DELANO
SURGEON WILLIAM PETRY
SURGEON'S MATE GEORGE FAUGH
SURGEON'S MATE MOSES WILLARD
CHAPLAIN JOHN DANIEL GROS

CAPT. JAMES CANNON
" PHILIPP CONINE, JR.
" EDWARD CONNOR
" BENJAMIN DUBOIS
" HOLTHAM DUNHAM
" PETER ELSWORTH
" PETER B. FEARCE
" ABRAHAM FONDA
" FRANCIS
" ABNER FRENCH
" SILAS GRAY
" LAWRENCE GROS
" AARON HALE
" JOSEPH HARKISON
" NATHANIEL HENRY
" ABRAHAM LIVINGSTON
" ELIHU MARSHALL
" SIMEON NEWELL
" JOHN PERCY
" GERRIT PUTNAM
" JOSIAH SKINNER
" THOMAS SKINNER

CAPT. PETER B. TEARCE
" JOSEPH VAN INGEN
" PETER VAN RENSSELAER
" ANTHONY WELP
" ABRAHAM WESTFALL
" STEPHEN WHITE
" JOB WRIGHT
" GUY YOUNG
LIEUT. WILLIAM BLOODGOOD
" JACOB BOKEE
" GIDEON COWLES
" BENANIWELL DEUEL
" DUTTON
" EPHRAIM EATON
" NATHANIEL FORD
" BARTEL HENDRICKS
" JONATHAN HILTON
" JACOB HOCHSTRASSER, JK.
" CHRISTOPHER HUTTON
" TIMOTHY HUTTON
" PETER LOOP, JR.
" JOHN LOW

LIEUT. WILLIAM MOORE
" GERRIT NUKERK
" GEORGE PASSAGE
" VICTOR PUTNAM
" JOSIAH RICHARDSON
" ISAAC SALKILL
" JACOB SAMMONS
" JOHN CONRAD SHAFER
" JOHN SHAW
" JOHN SPENCER
" ABRAHAM TEN EYCK
" JOHN THORNTON
" WILLIAM VAN ARNUM
" PETER VAN BERGEN
" ISAAC VAN VALKENBURGH
" SIMON J. VROOMAN
" RICHARD RANDOLPH WILLSON
" WILLIAM WILLSON
" SOLOMON WOODWORTH

Additional Names on State Treasurer's Pay Books
Capt. Joel Gillett, Lieut. Storm A. Becerk, Lieut. Richard Bingham, Lieut Duncan Campbell, Lieut. John Frimper,
Lieut. Jesse Hubbell, Lieut. John Hudson, Lieut. Witter Johnson, Lieut. Oliver Newell, Lieut. Christian Peak,
Lieut. John Watson.

ENLISTED MEN

Adams Elijah	Allen Justus	Ammerman Derick
Adamy Peter	Allen William	Andrews Ichabod
Adkins William	Aller Jacob	Anthony George
Agers Henry Julius	Allison Samuel	Arewax Jacob A.
Albert White	Alter Jacob	Armstrong John
Allen Henry	Amberman Derick	Arnold Abram

Arnold David
Atwell Paul
Avery Abel
Babcock Benjamin
Backer Philip
Bagley David
Bailey David
Bailey Timothy
Baker Albert
Baker Albert, Jr.
Baker Andrew
Baker Barrant
Baker David
Baker Samuel
Baker William
Baldwin Alexander
Baldwin Hezekiah
Balse Andreas
Bamm Friterick
Banks David
Banter Hellebrant
Bareup Andrew
Barker Philip
Barnar Simon
Barnhard Harmanus
Barnum Israel
Barritt Bartholomew
Barritt Jonathan
Barrs John
Barstow Job
Bartholomew Dualt
Basly Andreas
Battle Joseph
Bauck William
Baxter Anson
Bearwonn Jonn
Beaty Samuel
Becker Barnett
Becker John D.
Beebe Peter
Beecraft Thomas
Be Gordis Nening
Bendick Frances
Benedict Uriah
Benjamin Breach
Benjamin Brush
Benjamin Ebenezer
Bennet Owen
Bennet Simon
Bernhet Herman
Berry David
Bersey Winning
Bertholemay Theobalt

Bervert John
Bester Joab
Betty Samuel
Beyer Fratz
Bidwell Daniel
Bishop John
Blacius Lawrence
Blacus Lawrence
Blaus Lawrence
Blesucs Lawrence
Bloemendale Jacob
Bloomingdall Jacob
Bogardus Hendrick
Bogardus Nanning
Bomehover George
Bonesteel Henry
Bonny John
Booke William, Jr.
Booldman John, Jr.
Boom Frederick
Borks Christian
Borst Christian
Borst Johanis
Boston Negro
Bottles Joseph
Bouchall Hopper
Boughhall Hooper
Boyer John, Jr,
Braat Shirmin
Bradt Storme
Brakemen Jacob
Braner Reuben
Brant Edward
Brantner Anthony
Bratt Storm
Breem John
Breemer Lodewick
Brewer John
Brewer William
Broomhower George
Brown Dorcs
Brown Edward
Brown John
Brown Ned
Brown Perias
Brown Tunis (colored)
Brown William
Buckley Andrew
Buell Jonathan
Bullick Charles
Bullock Charles
Bulman John
Bulson Henry

Buly Benjamin
Bunshead Frederick
Bunstead Frederick
Burck John
Burdick Gideon
Burk Aronor
Burk, George
Burk Henry
Burnk George
Burt Henry
Bush John
Bust John
Buysbow Andrew
Byer Francis
Byker Henry
Cabeneer John
Cady David
Caine John
Calver David
Cambell John
Camble John
Campbell John
Campbell Thomas
Cannan James
Carpenter Benjamin
Carpenter Warren
Carr John
Carr William
Carsin William
Carter John
Carts John
Casler Henry
Casler John
Casler Nicholas
Casseler Thomas
Casselman John
Casselman Peter
Casslar John
Cassler Adorn
Cassler Thomas
Cassoner William
Castleman Bartholomew
Caton Thomas
Caveneer John
Chapman Amos
Chapman Ezekiel
Chapman Herman
Chapman Noah
Child Solomon
Chiles Solomon
Christman Nicholas
Church Medad
Cianar William

Clapsadle William
Clark Waters
Clark William
Clause George
Claver Nicholas
Claves Nicholas
Cleightman Frederick
Cline Hennery
Clinton John
Clough George
Clowy George
Clute Garret
Clute Garret D.
Clyne Henry
Cole John
Cole Peter
Cole Simon Peter
Cole William
Coleve Oliver
Coll John
Colver David
Colver Josiah
Combs Barnard
Combs Barnet
Commins Philip
Cone Ichabod
Cone Jacobud
Conklen Isick
Conklin Ephraim
Conly Jacob
Cook Joseph
Cooly James
Cornmings Thomas
Cost Martin
Cotton Nathaniel
Covell David
Cowls Oliver
Crandel Martinus
Crandle William
Cranker John
Crannel Martin
Crawford Joseph
Crippen Ichabod
Crisman Nicholas
Crofford Joseph
Crooks John
Crossard John
Crosset John
Crowley William
Crukes John
Culp John
Culver Joshua
Cummins Jehu Obediah

Cunnel William
Cuphin Egbert
Curbey John
Curtis Allantis
Curtis Asahel
Curtis Jotham
Curtis Thomas
Dack Henry
Dale William
Dallaway John
Danels Thomas
Dannals Jacob
Dark John
Darro George, Jr.
Darrow Ammirus
Darrow Daniel
Darrow George
Darrow Jedidiah
Daudge Daniel
Davis Amos
Davis John
Day Aaron
Day Lewis
De Bevoise Charles
Debocker John
Deck Henry
Decker Jacob
Dedrick Frederick
Dedrick Thode
Degolan James
Degolin Joseph
De Groot Henry
Dekyn Leonar
Delamater Henry
Delamatter Benjamin
De Line Ryer
Delond David
Delong David
Delong Joseph
Demair John
Deniston William
Deuce Henery
Deven Henry
Devereux Theodorus
Devew Henry
Devine John
Devoe Henry
Dibble Hezekiah
Dick Henry
Dickerson James
Dickeson Gideon
Dickson James
Dickson Richard

Dilliwere John
Dimesa Gerret
Dingman Samuel
Dixon Gideon
Dodge Daniel
Dole William
Donnel John
Doty Isaac
Douglass Jonathan
Downen Cornelius
Downing Cornelius
Dox Peter
Doxley Klark
Driselmon Christian
Dubois Charles
Ducker Jacobus
Dunham John
Dusler Marcus
Eagars Julies
Eaker Nicoless
Earcher Edward
Earnest Jacob
Eatick George
Eaton Eleazer
Eaton James
Ecker Nicholas
Edick Conrat
Edwards Abel
Edwards Samuel
Ellis John
Ellison David
Elsworth John
Engles James
Engrum Humphrey
Esselstyn Jacob
Eveson John
Evins Andrew
Evins Samuel
Faling Lips
Faling Philip
Farguson James
Farris Aron
Felbush Jesse
Ferguson Caleb
Ferguson Hezekiah
Ferris Aaron
Filmore Richard
Fine Reuben
Flanburgh Antony
Flander Henry
Flander Jacob
Flansburgh Matthew
Flemeing Asa

Flicker John	Groesbeck Jacob	Hawley Zadok
Flipsen Hermennes	Groot Abraham	Haws John
Flounsburgh Anthony	Groot Andrew	Heath James
Folts Conrad	Grot Andrus	Heath Josiah
Fonda John	Guile Daniel	Hebzenger Michael
Fonk William	Guiles Henry	Hebzinger John
Foot John	Gurshie Edward	Heecock Guiles
Foot Simeon	Hackney George	Heermance John
Forgason James	Hagedorn Adam	Hendericks Peter
Forstor Watson	Hagedorn Bartholomew	Hendricks Peter
Fort John	Hagedorn John	Herkimer George
Foster John	Hager Henry	Hermans John
Fowler Mayers	Hager Joseph	Herrick Daniel
Fowler Morris	Haker Jesse	Herrington Isaac
Fox Benjamin	Hakes Jesse	Herrington William
Fox Peter	Hall Benjamin	Hervey Phillips
Fradenburg Abraham	Hall Isaac	Hess John
Fraer Peter	Hall William	Hewins Joseph
Frailenbury Abr'm	Hallenbeack Henry, Jr.	Heysser John
Frank Andrew	Hallenbeck Garret	Hgaboom James
Fratinbury Abraham	Hallenbeck Isaac	Hichcox Giles
Freeman Jonas	Hambleton William	Hicks Joseph
French Anesel	Hamilton William	Hids Daniel
Frisbee John	Hammen John C.	Higgins Enoch
Fry George	Hanby John	Hill Reuben
Fryer Peter	Handley John	Hill Samuel
Fuller Daniel	Hankey John J.	Hills Asa
Fuller Isaac	Hannes Jacob	Hillsinger John
Fuller Josiah	Hannis James	Hillsinger Michael
Fuller Varsel	Harkeman George	Himlin Adorn
Fulmer Christopher	Harman John Christopher	Hines Daniel
Fulmore Christian	Harms Jacob	Hines George
Funk William	Harrington Isaac	Histead Thaddeus
Ganse Benjamin	Harrington William	Hitchcock Zenos
Garret James	Harrison Peter	Hobbs Samuel
Garvey Thomas	Harson, Haramnius	Hodgson George
Gause Benjamin	Harson Harman	Hogoboom Jacob
Gibson John	Harson Peter	Hogoboom James
Gile Hennery	Harver Christian	Holdridge Amasa
Gipson John	Hary Phillip	Holdridge Amesiah
Goes Mathies	Hass John	Holdsberger Adam
Goose Mathisi	Hatch James	Holly Zadock
Goose Nicholas	Hatch Matthew	Holmes Rozel
Gott Story	Haugedom John	Holms Jedediah
Graft Philip	Haugedorn Samuel	Holms Roswell
Granger John	Haulenbeke Garrit	Holnbake Isack
Graves Mark	Haus Hendrick	Hoisted Ezekiel
Green Ebenezer	Hausman John	Hoos Nicholas
Greggs Evert	Haven Christian	Hopkins Thomas
Grime Henderick	Havens Benjamin	Hople George
Grime Henry	Havens Darius	Hopper John
Grippen Egbert	Havens Thomas	Horton William
Groat Abraham	Hawley James	Hough Zephaniah

House George
House Henry
Houseman John
How David
How Jesse
How Samuel
Howard Enos
Howard Jesse
Howber Felix
Howes Samuel
Howley James
Hubbard Samuel
Hubbart John
Hubberd John
Hubble Ithamer
Hudson Edward
Hudson William
Hugshan Nathan
Hull Isaac
Hunter James
Hunter John
Huntly Solomon
Husted Thaddeus
Hutchson William
Hyser John
Indian Anthony
Indian Nicholas
Ingels James
Ingham Humphrey
Ingram Humpry
Ittig Goerg
Jackson Ebenezer
Jackson Joseph
Jainkens Anthony
Jakeway Asael
Jenkins Anthony
Jerome Jason
Jerroms Jansen
Johnson Benjamin
Johnson Derick
Johnson John
Johnson Philip
Johnson Samuel
Johnston Benjamin
Johnston John
Johnston Philip
Jones Harmanus
Jones Richard
Jones William
Jonk Jacob
Kanedy Henry
Kasler John
Kasselman Johannis

Kellogg Eliphalet
Kelly Henry
Kelse John
Kelts George
Kenny Amous
Kesler John
Kessler Adam
Ketchum Benjamin
Ketchum Joel
Ketchum Nathaniel
Kill Christopher
King Leonard
King Thomas
Kinney Amos
Kipple George
Kitman Edward
Kittle Adam
Kittle Jocham
Kitts George
Klukman Frederick
Knapp Henry
Knapp William
Knox Frederick
Knox Joseph
Kolb John
Koll John
Lain Alexander
Lake William
Lally John
Lambert Peter
Lamon George
Lancaster Samuel
Lance John
Lane Alexander
Lansing John
Lansingh Evert
Lard William
Larraway Jacob
Laughaday John
Laughre John
Laveway Jacob
Lawrence Peter
Leifheat John
Lent Henry
Leonard Elijah
Lewes Ebuniser
Lewis Ebenezer
Libble Thomas
Lighthart Barnabas
Lint Henry
Livingston Richard
Loman George
Lonas John

Lonis John
Lord John
Lord Joseph
Lord Timothy
Lovejoy Daniel
Lovel John
Low John
Lummis Ezekiel
Lusk Jacob
Lusk Michael
Lusk William
Lyfhidt John
Lyons Nathaniel
Mabb John
McAntier Thomas
McChesney Samuel
McCollister Archable
McCoy John
McDaniel Henry
McDole George
McDowel George
McGee George
McGee William
McGill John
McGurfy Edward
McGurfy Robert
McGurshie Robert
McKeen Samuel
McKnot Jimmie
McMaster Robert
McMichel Ebenezer
McMickle Ebenezer
McNut James
McVane Daniel
McVey Daniel
McWiams John
McWilliams John
Makefee William
Malat Richard
Maloon John
Marshel Simeon
Martin Amasa
Mason John
Matherwson Warren
Matteson Warren
Mattice George
Mayer Lewis
Meer John
Meinger Timthy
Miler Peter
Miles William
Miller Andrew
Miller Eleazer

Miller George	Orendorf Daniel	Raspel Frederick
Miller James	Orsher Onies	Rattenam George
Miller Peter	Overbagh John, Jr.	Rattle Joseph
Miller William	Overpagh John	Ray William
Mob John	Pace Henry	Ray Zacherius
Mobs Peirs	Paddock John	Ray Zacheus
Moles Peeres	Paine John	Read John
Molloy Thomas	Palmer Amoziah	Reais Daniel
Monger Timothy	Parker Elisha	Redwood Prince
Montgomerie John	Parker Robert	Reman John
Montgomery John	Parker Ruben	Remaw John
Moon Jacob	Patrick James	Rexford Ensign
Moor Peres	Patrick Matthew	Rexford Joseph
Moor Peter	Paulay Benjamin	Rexford Joseph, Jr.
Moore Jacob	Payer John	Richards John
More Thomas	Payne John	Richardson George
Morris Nicholas	Peak Chris	Richardson Isaac
Morrison Nicholas	Pease Abner	Richarson James
Morroy James	Pease Asa	Richarson William
Mors Joshua	Peek Christopher	Richmond Benjamin
Moshier Thomas	Peelor Jacob	Richmond Silas
Moss Josiah	Permer Jacob	Richmond Silvester
Mower George	Perry David	Richtmeyer Johannes
Mower Peter	Peter Godlip	Ricker Hendrick
Moyer David	Peters Simeon	Rightmier John
Mudge Ebenezer	Peters Simon	Rightmire Henry
Mulley Thomas	Peterson John	Rihes Henry, Jr.
Murray Alexander	Pettit John	Rinehart William
Murry James	Peulay Benjamin	Ripley, Asa
Myer Lodewick	Phelps Amous	Ripley Piram
Myers Frederick	Philips Abner	Ritchanson James
Myers John	Philips Amos	Robb George
Nagar Joseph	Philips Isaac	Robbens James
Name Abraham	Philips Jacob	Robberds John
Nathan Rece	Philips Philip	Robbins Charles
Nestel Richard	Plum John	Roberson Charles
Nestle George	Powers Charles	Roberts John
Newell Chancey	Price George	Robertson Jeremiah
Newell Seth	Prime John	Robertson William
Newkirk Thomas	Primer Ludwig	Robins Jube
Newton Benjamin	Prince Negro (colored)	Robinson Hector
Nicholls Silas	Pudney Thorn	Robinson Jeremiah
Nickals John	Purchase Taberd	Rockefeller William
Nier Casper	Putnam David	Rogers George
Noor Peres	Puxley Crark	Rogers Jacob
Norton William	Quimbey Stephen	Roop John
Oakley Jonathan	Quin William	Roop Peter
O'Briant Cornelius	Quinby Stephen	Rosa Stonne
Olman Frederick	Radley Jacob	Rose Jacob
Omens Daniel	Randal Nathaniel	Rosed Storm
Orchard Thomas	Randell Benjamin	Rottinower George
Orcher Edward	Randle Matthew	Rowlee Jabish
Ore Jacob	Randle Matthias	Rowley Aron

Rowley Aaron, Jr.
Rowley Samuel
Rowley Samuel Ham
Rowley Seth
Rude Eli
Ruff Jonathan
Rumney John
Rumney John G.
Russel James
Russell Benjamin
Russman Conradt
Ryan Duncan
Ryker Henry
Rynhard William
Salbury Joseph
Salspury Gideon
Saltmarsh William
Saltmask William
Sanders John
Sanders Wat
Sanders Wat, Jr.
Saunders John
Savage Joel
Sayer Lambert
Scarbory William
Schall George
Schall John
Schank William
Scheneman Hendrick
Scheneman Henry
Schermehorn John
Scheyler John
Schmit Anton
Schmit Hendrick
Schoolcraft Peter
Schoolcraft Fitter
Schulgraft John
Schultze William
Schutt William
Schutt William, Jr.
Schuyler David
Schuyler David, Jr.
Schuyler Dirck
Schuyler John
Schuyler John Jost
Scott Cornelias
Scott Henry
Scribner Thaddeus
Scribner Thomas
Seeber John
Seeber John W.
Semister John
Senn Aaron

Shafer
Shafer John Conrad
Shall Hendrick
Shall Henry
Shattuck Thomas
Shaver John
Shaw
Shaw Comfort
Shaw Ebenezer
Shaw Jacob
Shaw William
Sheffield Nathan
Shepard James
Sherman Jenkins
Shifflebean Jacob
Shiltenberger Casparus
Shiltenburger Casper
Shoefelt Christopher
Sholl John
Shoolcraft John
Shoot William, Jr.
Show Jacob
Shults Henry
Shults William
Shute William
Shuts Abraham
Simonds Joshua
Simonds Joshua, Jr.
Simons John
Simson Joseph
Sits George
Skiltenberger Casparos
Skinner Jonathan
Skinner Micah
Skinner Michael
Sibury Joseph
Smith Adam
Smith Anthony
Smith Ezekiel
Smith Henry
Smith James
Smith John
Smith John Connat
Smith Joseph
Smith Nicholas
Smith Philip
Smith Thomas
Smith William
Smor Josams
Sole William
Sparbeck Conradt
Spaulding Nehemiah
Speed Henry

Spencer Truman
Spickerman Philip
Spike Daniel
Spoon John
Sprague Alexander
Stalker John
Stephen John
Stephens Daniel
Stephens Isaac
Stephens John
Stevens Isaac
Steward John
Steward Robert
Stewart James
Stewart John
Stolker John
Stoner Nicholas
Stopplebeen Jacob
Storm, David
Stormes David
Strobeck Adam
Strong John
Stuart John
Suits George
Suits Peter
Suits Henry
Suts Peter P.
Swayer Lammert
Taber William
Tacker John
Talman Thomas
Tanall Nicholas
Tancill Danyel
Tanner Jacob
Tansel Daniel
Tarbox Job
Tarbush Isaac
Tartle Joseph
Tawner Jacob
Taylor Ebenezer
Taylor Friend
Taylor Jasper
Taylor Johannis
Taylor Joseph
Taylor Samuel
Taylor Thomas
Teal John
Ten Eyck Barrent
Teneyck Gurney
Ter Bosh Isaac
Thomas Beriah
Thomas Buriel
Thompson Jack

Titus Philip
Tollman Thomas
Tortle Joseph
Townsen James
Trewax Abraham
Trewax Jacob
Trewax Jacob A.
Trim Walter
Tripp Charles
Tripp Job
Trisselman Christian
Troll John
Truax John
Trumble Judah
Tryon William
Tubbs Cyrus
Turner Lemuel
Tusler Marks
Tussler John
Tymoson Garret
Ullendorf Daniel
Ulroan Frederick
Utley Jarmiah
Valentine James
Valentine Stephen
Van Alstyne Cornelius
Van Alstyne John
Van Aps Samuel
Van Arnem William
Van Atter James
Van Camp Moses
Van Deboe Jacob
Vandebol Jacob
Van Deburgh Daniel
Van Der Car Richard
Van Der Hiden Gershom
Van Derhider David
Van Derhider Gershom
Van Der Wark John
Van Der Werken Henry
Vandeuse Aaron
Vandeuse William
Van Dusen Aaron
Van Dyck David
Van Dyck Jacob
Van Ess John
Van Hoosen Rynier
Van Ieven Thomas
Van Loon Albertus
Van Loon Benjamin
Vannetta Jacobus
Van Nist Janeson
Van Nist Jeranmus

Van Nist John
Van Schaack Nicholes
Van Sicker Rynier
Van Sikle David
Van Slycke George
Van Sycklar David
Van Valkenberg Jacob
Van Valkenburgh George
Van Valkenburgh Har-
manus
Van Valkenburgh Henry
Van Valkenburgh Joachim,
Sr.
Van Valkenburgh Joachim
Van Valkenburgh Leanor
Van Valker George
Van Vurman Cornelius
Van Worman Cornelius
Van Wormer Matthew
Van Yevern Thomas
Vedder Peter
Verty Thomas
Vestry Thomas
Vols Conrad
Von Herrman Johns Christian
Von Schleik Gorg
Vroman Adam
Vroman Peter
Wagenner Michael
Wagoner George
Wagonnit Hermanis
Waid James
Wallebure John
Walradt Adolphus
Walter George
Warren Nathaniel
Wart John
Wasson James
Wasson John
Waterman Elisha
Waterman Samuel
Watkins Edmund
Watson Jepson
Watson William
Watson Zephthah
Wauson John
Weat Nathaniel
Weaver David
Webster Peletiah
Weed William
Weever David
Welch Rozzel
Welch Thomas

Wells Abraham
Wells Philip
Welsh Thomas
Wemp Aron
Wemple Aron
Wentworth James
Wentworth Shuble
Werts John
Wheeler Abraham
Wheeler John
Wheever Nicholas
Whing Benjamin
Whing Daniel
White James
White John
White Nathaniel
White Perregreen
White Stephen
White Stephen, Jr.
White William
Whitehead Thomas
Whilbers John
Whitman Benjamin
Whitmore Christopher
Wilcocks Nathan
Wilcox Jeremiah
Wilcox Nathan
Wilcox Nathaniel
Wilcox Salvenus
Wiles John
Willer Amos
Williams Elias
Williams John
Williams William
Willson James
Willson Jesse
Willson John
Wilson Israel
Wiltsey John
Winne Johannis
Winney John
Winter John
Winters John
Winterscale Barnaby
Wintworth James
Witmer Christopher
Wolf Samuel
Wolsh Rosel
Wood Barnabas
Wood James
Wood Robert
Wood Samuel
Wood Thomas

Wood William	Woss Jacob	Young John
Woodard Ephraim	Wright David	Young Peter
Woodbeck Samuel	Wright Jacob	Young Peter, Jr.
Woolcott Joseph	Wyat Nathaniel	Young William
Woolsey Nathan	Yager Hendrick	Yucker John
Worden Ahithophel	Yatt James	Yuger Johannes
Wormwood John	Yett James	Yunger Henrick
Woss Gerrit	Young Henry	

The Levies--(Dubois')

COLONEL LEWIS DUBOIS
LIEUTENANT COLONEL BRINTON PAINE
MAJOR JAMES M. HUGHES
ADJUTANT HUGH McCONNELL
QUARTER MASTER JOHN BRADNER
PAY MASTER DANIEL GANG
SURGEON HENRY BUCK
SURGEON'S MATE SAMUEL ALLEN

Capt. JOSHUA BARNUM	Capt. THOMAS LEE	LIEUT. JOHN COPPERNOLL
" JOHN BRADBICK	" JOHN MCBRIDE	" ADAM HELMER
" JOHN BURNETT	" THOMAS MCKINSTRY	" JAMES OAKLEY
" COLBE CHAMBEBLAIN	" MCQUOW	" JACOB PECK
" MARK DE MONT	" JOHN ROLB	" JAMES PECK
" HENRY DODGE	" BENJAMIN STEVENSON	" JOHN BANDERBURGH
" BENJAMIN DUBOIS	LIEUT. JAMES BETTS	" SIMON J. BROOMAN
" JOHN M. FOGHT	" JACOB BOCKER	" WILLIAM WALLACE
" DANIEL GAMO	" JAMES BUTTERFIELD	

Additional names on State Treasurer's Pay Books
Lieut. Edmund Duvall, Lieut. Henry Vanderburgh

ENLISTED MEN

Adam Peter	Beckwith David	Brown Hezekiah
Adams Peter	Bellinger Adam P.	Brown Jonathan
Adriance Theodonis	Benjamin Cyrus	Brown Noah, Jr.
Adsit Benjamin	Benjamin Jonathan	Brown Samuel
Akins Stephen	Bennet Jeremiah	Buchiet John
Allen Reuben	Bishop John	Bump Sathuel
Allen Samuel	Biskney Francis	Burch Hezekiah
Allison Isaac	Bissell John	Burch Isiah
Armstrong George	Blaesdell Levi	Burch Jesse
Arnot Cornelius	Bloomerone Abraham	Burling Benjamin
Bader Francis	Bocrum William	Burlington Joel
Bailey Daniel	Bogardus Lewis	Burton Gilbert
Bairmore Michael	Bogart Gilbert	Campbell Robertson
Baker William	Bouman Abraham	Campbell William
Barch Rudolf	Bradner John	Canfield James
Barr John	Brooks George	Careley John
Beater Jacob	Brooks William	Carman John

Carney Barnabas
Carter Jabez
Carvender Joseph
Cashin William
Chase Benjamin
Church Jonathan
Churchill James
Clapsadle William
Clark William
Claver Nehemiah
Cleland William
Cline Jacob
Cole John
Concklin Samuel
Connell Benjamin
Cook Solomon
Cosier Joseph
Cowley Jonathan
Crook Coonrod
Crosby Reuben
Crover George
Culver Daniel
Cummins Jacob
Cummins John
Curtis James
Cutler Nathaniel
Cyeserton Manassa
Dalery Jeremiah
Darley Robert
Darling Benjamin
Davis Benjamin
Davison Alverson
Dealeway Jeremiah
Decker Jacob
Demoutt John
Dermott James
Dewel Benjamin
Dewel Emanuel
Dewit William
Drake Joshua
Dunbar William
Durgen Pattrick
Dymoot Dalrick
Edee Joshuh
Edesell Joseph
Engle George
Engle William
English Robert
Etch Jacob
Evans Amos
Evans William
Faden John
Felling Philip

Ferguson William
Fetterly John
Forbus Henry
Fowler Daniel
Fox George
Franck Henrich
Freeman Elijah
Fuller Daniel
Fullmore Christopher
Gale John
Galsschus Claus
Garlinghouse John
Garrit Benjamin
Ginson Richard
Graham George
Grant Peter
Green Caleb
Green Isaac
Griffin John
Hall Robert
Hamilton James
Hammill Nathaniel
Handley Mathew
Hans James
Hanson Arthur
Harris Joshua
Harrits Jonathan
Hart James
Hartman Adam
Hatch Joseph
Hatch Oliver
Hawk Frederick
Head Briton
Heberd Prime
Helmer Adam
Hess George
Hester Lawrence
Hewitt Joseph
Hewitt Samuel
Higney Joseph
Hill Nathaniel
Hills John
Hinckley Elkanah
Hock Rudolph
Hoff John
Holdren Daniel
Holenbeck Jacob
Holmes Daniel
Hoover Isaac
Horton William
Hothalin James
How John
Howard William

Howell Josiah
Hubberd Reuben
Hunter James
Irwin Robert
Jewit Alpheus
Johnson John
Johnson Samuel
Johnston William
Jones Richard Jost
Lake John
Lamphier John
Lane William
Lansing Everent W.
Lappius Daniel
Laughlin James
Letts David
Lewis John
Lowery John
Lua William
Lutts Coonrod
McClockin Joseph
McColley Hugh
McConnil Hugh
McCowan Duncan
McEwen Duncan
McGown Robert
McMaster James
McRoy Epraim
McWhorter Thomas
McWhorton James
Martin Archibald
Martin Thomas
Massy Andrew
Mead Israel
Mercy Andrew
Miles Benjamin
Millage Thomas
Millet Felix
Milligan Robert
Mills John
Miluan Robert
Moores Thomas
Morehouse Reuben
Morehouse Thomas
Morris John
Morse Josiah
Mosher Abner
Motts Joseph
Myer Lewis
Myer Peter
Myers Abraham
Myers John
Myers Lodewick

Nostrandt George
Oakman Presoine
Omsted Gideon
Oosterhoudt Gysbrt
Overbagh Jeremiah
Owen Solomon
Owens Isaac
Panter Jacob
Parmerton Abijah
Parshal James
Pease Asa
Pelhamn Eli
Pelham Elisha
Pellenger Adam
Perry David
Phillips Samuel
Pipar Elder
Prat William
Price Timothy
Purdy Josiah
Ralphin George
Randle Matthias
Rankins, James, Jr.
Relyea John
Reynolds Shubal
Reynolds Stephen
Richard Edward
Richardson William
Rickman Abraham
Robertson Nathaniel
Robins Elijah
Rock William
Roes John
Rogers Moses
Rood Ezra
Rosa Adert
Ross William
Russel Rowlins
Salisbury Lawrence
Salkill Isaac
Scheit Peter
Schonover Benjamin
Schonover James
Scott James
Scribner Aaron

Scribner Jonathan
Scribner Zadock
Seabury Cornelius
Sears Selah
Seeley John
Seloover Isaac
Sessee Abraham
Shail Peter
Shaw Ezra
Silsby David
Simon John
Simpson Fetter
Sits John
Slight Henry
Smith James
Smith John
Smith Joseph
Smith Ludlow
Smith Richard
Smith Thomas
Smith William
Snyder Cornelius
Soper Timothy
Spicer Jeremiah
Spragge Benjamin
Sprague Gideon
Stagg John
Stark Henry
Starks John
Stighter Adam
Stone Daniel
Stunter Ebenezer
Sufelt Christopher
Sutherland William
Targasor Benjamin
Taylor Jeremiah
Taylor Stephen
Taylor William
Tees John
Terry Usbany
Terwillegar Tunis
Terwilliger Abraham, Jr.
Thomas Richard
Thompson William
Thorington Thomas

Thorn Jacob
Tilwillegar James
Tingue John
Tippet Thomas
Titus Phillip
Totten Daniel
Twaghinans John
Van Aulstine Derrick
Vandebogart John
Vanderworker Hermanus
Van De Water Adolph
Van Etten Jacobus
Van Every Jacob
Vansize Hanyost
Vickery Ichabod
Von Netten James
Walbort Tobias
Walker John
Walsz Jacob
Walsz Kunrad
Weaver George
Webster Oliver
Wells David
Wells Gershom
Whaley Timothy
Wheeler Ira
White Nicholas
Wilkinson David
Willcox David
Williams Pompy
Wills Jesse
Winegar Samuel
Wood Job
Wood Solomon
Wood Timothy
Woolgert Joseph
Woolsee Sammon
Wright Edmund
Yongs Alexander
York Aaron
Young Henry
Young Richard
Young Zacharias

THE LEVIES (Harper's)
Colonel John Harper

QUARTER MASTER BARENT ROSEBOOM
QUARTER MASTER BARENT TEN EYCK
PAY MASTER ISAAC PARIS
SURGEON WILLIAM PETRIE

MAJOR JOHN CHIPMAN
MAJOR JAMES M. HUGHES
ADJUTANT JOHN BATEMAN
CAPT. LOTHROP ALLEN

" ISAAC BOGERT
" JOSHUA DRAKE
" JOSEPH HARRISON
" JONATHAN LAWRENCE, JR.
" GERRITT PUTNAM
" WALTER VROOMAN
LIEUT. ALBERTUS BECKER
LIEUT. THOMAS BRADSHAW
" EZRA BUELL
" JOHN DUNHAM
" CORNELIUS ECKERSON
" JOSEPH HARPER

" RICHARD LAWRENCE
" GEORGE PASSAGE
" OTHNIEL PHILIPS
LIEUT. MATTHEW POTAN
" VICTOR PUTNAM
" SETH SHERWOOD
" PETER B. TEN BROECK
" PETER VAN BERGEN
" SOLOMON WOODWORTH
" JAMES YULE
" JAMES YUYLE

ENSIGN THOMAS BOYCE
ADDITIONAL NAME ON STATE TREASURER'S PAY BOOKS

Acker George	Bollman John	Carter John
Ackerman John	Bollon Alexander	Carter William
Ackervon George	Bolton Alexander	Carty Solomon
Alien Henry	Bolton John	Ceaton Isaac
Allis John	Bolton Samuel	Chapman Edward
Allison Samuel	Boolman John	Chapman Samuel
Ambler Nathaniel	Bosliver Paul	Chatfield Cornelius
Ansom James	Boste Henry Julius	Christman John
Archey Annanis	Bowdish John	Clark John
Arsha Annanias	Bowen Timothy	Clark Samuel
Atwood Jonathan	Brandow Abraham	Clemments Philip
Aylworth Isaac	Brannon Abraham	Cleveland Samuel
Babark John	Branon Abraham	Cole John
Babcock John	Brockway Gideon	Coleman Andrew
Babcock Nehemiah	Brower Eldrick	Collins James
Babick Nighimie	Buckley Andrew	Collins William
Ballard Benoni	Burchard Nathaniel	Coltman William
Banker James	Burcher Nathaniel	Colver Joseph
Barnes Samuel	Burgess Stephen	Conklin John
Barns Nathaniel	Burhans Therck	Conklin Joseph
Barred Peter	Burley Elijah	Connore James
Barrington Lewis	Bursey Elijah	Cooper Elijah
Barry William	Burst Jacob	Cooper Henry
Bartlett Joseph	Burst Jacob I.	Cooper John
Baum Frederick	Bush Henry	Coplant Samuel Sun
Bell Matthew	Bush John	Coplin Samuel
Bellinger Christian	Bushanie Carrick	Cornelius John
Benedick Ellas	Bussey Elijah	Cost Martin
Benidick Oliver	Buzzle Jonathan	Crim Henry
Bernom Levi	Caine Thomas	Crisman John
Berry William	Camp Asa	Cross Daniel
Bertley Joseph	Campbell John	Cross John
Bicker Henry	Care Teunis	Cross Ruben
Billings Incrose	Carker Jacob	Culley Matthew
Biilins Ineris	Carpenter Thomas	Cummings Josiah
Blamely William	Carpner Thomas	Cuper Henry
Bogardus James	Carson William	Curtis Solomon

Darling John	Garmen James	Hyer Peter
Darrow Jedidiah	Gault Story	Hyser John
Davy Adam	Gautt John	Ikler Johannis
Day Aaron	Germaine James	Isden John
Day Jonathan	Ghospead Joseph	Jackson Lyman
Day Lewis	Gleson Joel	Johnson Benjamin
Debie Adam	Goart John	Jones Isaac
De Graff Jesse	Golding Benjamin	Keeler Isiah
De Groff Jesse	Goff Oliver	Kelley Elenezar
De Harsh Philip	Gooff Joseph	Kelly Henry
De Lavign Francis	Graham John	Ketchum Joel
De Long John	Gray James	Kidder Stephen
Demott John	Green Ebenezer	Killsey Ebenezer
De Narsh Philip	Griffen James	Kiner William
Densil Daniel	Griffis James	King Ruben
Deveraux Joseph	Hackman Thomas	Kisner William
Dickson Robert	Hadley Isaac	Kittle Adam
Dixon Robert	Hagedorn Samuel	Klein William
Dodge Andrew	Hammond Paul	Knap James
Dratt John	Hanrillor Silas	Knapp Silas
Dunbar Robert	Harper Archibald	Kronkheit John
Dunham Charles	Harrington John	Ladine John
Dunham John	Harris David	Ladoo John
Dunn Phineas	Harris Thomas	Larraby Elias
Dunnim Charles	Harrow Robert	Lattimore Francis
Dunnivan Daniel	Hatch William	Lewis James
Dutcher Henry	Haugudom Samuel	Leahy William
Dygart Severinus	Hawkins Stephen	Leak William
Dygerd Safrenes	Heath Simeon	Leeson Joel
Eastwood John	Helmes John	Lefoy Abraham
Ecker George	Hennion John	Lehigh William
Eckler Leonard	Henry Hugh	Lent Herculas
Edwards William	Herring Robert	Lepper Frederick
Eightler John	Hewitt James	Lemer Philip
Ekleman Jacob	Highly Seth	Lettimore Daniel
Ellis John	Hill Amos	Levine Francis
Ellison David	Hilssinger John	Loff David
Elson David	Hoard David	Long William
Elsworth Isaac	Hogeboom Peter	Lovejoy Andrew
Embler Nathaniel	Holiday Henry	Loyd William
Farnham Asa	Holmes John	Luner Philip
Felter Peter	Horsford Samuel	Lusk Jacob
Fetter Peter	House Cornelius	Lusk Michael
Fidler Godfrey	House Jesse	Lusk William
Fiedler Gottfried	House Peter	Lyon Nathaniel
Flamsted William	Houser Henry	McCauley Charles
Flansburgh William	Howel Jesse	McCaulley Robert
Fleming Asa	Hoyer Peter	McClallen James
Folmer Christian	Hubbard William	McColm John
Frank Henry	Hubble Ethamour	McMannis William
Frase Isaac	Humphris John	McNitt John
Fuller Daniel	Hunt David	Magee John
Gardinier Tunis	Hursie Thomas	Man James

Marks Jesse
Martin Robert
Mearanas Thomas
Menn James
Mervin Malkica
Middle Christian
Midler Christopher
Miller Jacobus
Miller James
Miller Zadoc
Mitchel Robert
Modian James
Monrose Jesse
Moon Matthew
Moran William
Moss Simon
Moss Timon
Murphy Timothy
Murray Nicholas
Murray Peter
Murray William
Myall Joseph
Myers David
Nestell George
Newcomb James
Newkerk John
Newkirk Jacob
Niles Nathan
Norton William
Nottingham Lewis
Oarchard Thomas
Omsted Aron
Orchard Edward
Order Peter V.
Ostrander Adam
Owens Elisha
Parker Robert
Patchin Samuel
Pease Abner
Perry David
Peters Simon
Peterson Peter
Phanton James
Phelps Ebenezer
Philips Ebenezer
Philips Jacobus
Philipse James
Phillips Isaac
Piearce John
Pitcher Godlip
Pool William
Porch Andrew
Post Cornelius

Potter Roland
Power Moses
Preston William
Price William
Prusnar Christian
Putnam David
Quant Frederick
Randell Joseph
Read Alphias
Reghmyre Johams
Renex Andrew
Resacker John P.
Rice David
Rickert Jacob
Riley John
Riley Philip
Roberts Ezekiel
Roberts John
Robinson Jesse
Rockwelt Simeon
Rockwell Symon
Romer James
Rose James
Rosliver Paul
Rowley Seth
Russell James
Sackett Benjamin
Sackett John
Sanlam Moses
Schoolcraft Johannis
Scot Benjamin
Scott Thomas
Scranton Merchan
Scribner John
Scutt Solomon, Jr.
Secaur Jonas
Seger Evart
Servis John
Shall John
Sharp Andrew
Sharp Peter
Shaver Adam
Shaw Henry
Shaw Jacob
Shay Malcom
Shepherd James
Sherror James
Sherwood James
Shutts Abraham
Simons James
Slils Amasa
Smith Garret
Smith John

Smith Joseph
Smith Nicholas
Smith Polly Carp
Soultis Jacob
Speed George
Sprague Alexander
Stalker William
Stark Nathan
Starkweather Roger
Starring George
Start Nathan
Start William
Steel Thomas
Stenbergh Peter
Stils Amasa
Storm Thomas
Strong Robert
Stuart Oliver
Suard Jedediah
Sueldes Jacob
Sweet James
Swett James
Tancill Daniel
Tanner Benjamin
Taylor Jasper
Tenner Gedion
Thomas Jacob
Thomas Peter
Thorn Zadok
Tice John
Trinker Guliup
Trull John
Truwax Isaac
Tuffs Zachariah
Valentine Alexander
Valentine Peter
Valkenburgh Joghem
Van Benthuysen Mark
Van Camp Moses
Vandanburgh Daniel
Van der Bogart Johannis
Van Dusen Aron
Van Dyck Cornelius
Van Dyck Peter
Van Horn John
Van Houten John
Van Ieveren Garret
Van Sickler Reynear
Van Sickles Reynear
Van Wagoner Andrew
Van Yeveren Garret
Van Zickler Bynier
Veader Peter

Virgen Abijah
Virgil Abijah
Vosburgh Peter
Ward Zadok
Warden Barnerd
Weed Phineas
Weed William
Wells Jamess
Wertham Warren
Wheeler John
Wholebur John

Willeber John
Williams Gilbert
Williamson John
Willis William
Willman John
Willson Silas
Wilmer John
Wilsiey James
Wilson William
Wincel John
Winchal Penctial

Winne Kelian
Winshell John
Witbeck Samuel
Woodworth Reuben
Wright Robert
Yat James
Yeat James
Young Jeremiah
Young John
Zitser George

THE LEVIES Wessenfel's

COLONEL FREDERICK WEISSENFELS
MAJOR THOMAS DE WITT
MAJOR SAMUEL LOGAN
ADJUTANT PETER WELSH
QUARTER MASTER EDWARD CONNER
QUARTER MASTER EBENEZER MOTT
"QUARTER MASTER PETER WELSH
PAY MASTER JOHN VAN DOZER
PAY MASTER ANDREW WHITE
SURGEON HENRY BUCK
SURGEON PETER VAN DER LYN
SURGEON'S MATE JOHN YOUNG
CAPT. PRENTICE BOWEN
″ HENRY BREWSTER, JR.
″ HENRY DODGE
″ HENRY GOODWIN
″ JOHN HORNBECK
″ THOMAS HUNT
″ GILBERT J. LIVINGSTON
″ HENRY PAWLING
″ DANIEL SHEPHARD
CAPT. ANDREW THOMPSON
″ ABRAHAM WESTFALL

" ANDREW WHITE
LIEUT. PETER BUNSCHOTEN
" CORNELIUS DU BOYS
" JOHN ELLSWORTH
" FINCH GILDERSLEEVE
" JONATHAN T. JANSEN
" JAMES JOHNSON
" McARTHUR
LIEUT. JAMES MYER
" WILLIAM NOTTINGHAM
" JOHN OSTRANDER
" ALDERT ROOSA
" CHARLES STUART, JR.
" AZARIAH TUTHILL
" THEODORUS VAN WYCK
" JONAH WEEKS
" SAMUEL YOUNGS

ADDITIONAL NAMES ON STATE TREASURER'S PAY BOOKS
LIEUT. JOHN BARR, LIEUT. GEORGE HARSON, LIEUT. GEORGE P. WEISSENFELS, LIEUT. JOHN FINCH, LIEUT. JOHN PUNDERSON

ENLISTED MEN

Ackerman Casparaus
Ackerman James
Adames Deliverance
Addams Major
Adsit Martin
Ager James

Aherd Jacob
Akard Jacob
Albeen Nathan
Aldridge Benjamin
Alexander Rufus
Aller John
Ambler Enos

Ambler Nathan
Anderson John
Annet Henry
Anson John
Armstrong John
Austin Lockwood
Avery Nehemiah

Babcock Amos
Babcock Elisha
Babcock John
Backer John
Bailey John
Bailey Samuel
Baker Jessy
Baker John
Baker Richard
Baker William
Balard Caleb
Baldwin Aaron
Baly Richart
Bardge Jonathan
Barlow Joseph
Barnes Gilliam
Barnes John
Barnet Nathaniel
Barns Glean
Barr Daniel
Barret John
Bartlet Haines
Bartlet Jacob
Bartley Jacob
Bassett Cesar
Bates Justus
Beard John
Bebrown Deliverance
Becker John
Beekman Benjamin
Belknap Thomas
Benedict Azariah
Benedict Thomas
Benedik Tom
Benjamin Cyrus
Bennet John
Berber Alisha
Berber Joseph
Beringer Jacob
Bernard Simon
Berringhas David
Berry Samuel
Besemer Michael
Bevier Andries
Bevier David
Bevier David, Jr.
Birch Josiah
" Black Walter " (colored)
Blanchard Justus
Blawvelt Cornelius
Bogardus Jacobus
Boice Hendrick
Bonker Solomon

Bowen Isaac
Bowen Prentice
Bowington John
Boyd Nathaniel
Boyles Walter
Brannon Reuben
" Brave Boy " (colored)
Brennen Michael
Bresin John
Brewster Jesse
Brinck John
Broadhead Henry
Brooks George
Broun Elijah
Brower Aaron
Brower Cornelius
Brower George
Brower Henry
Brower Jeremiah
Brower William
Brown Deliverance
Brown Elisha
Brown Halsey
Brown James
Brown James H.
Brown Reuben
Brown Samuel
Brundage Sollimon
Brush David
Brush Isaiah
Buckhout James
Buckingham William
Burges John
Burgess James
Burhans Jacob
Burr Daniel
Butts William
Byington David
Byington John
Calkins Ely
Camber John
Camble Archibald
Camble James
Cameron David
Campbell Archibald
Campbell John
Canfield Ebenezer
Cannon Amot
Carehart Jacob
Carhaday Nicholas
Carmer Samuel
Camel Henry
Currier Andrew

Carpenter Barnard
Catterling Nathaniel
Cee Moses
Cepinosa Anthony
Chanders Isaac
Chard Hugh
Chrispell Abraham
Claerwater John
Clark Benjamin
Clark John
Close Henry
Close Peter
Cochran Samuel
Cohoon Heman
Cole Cornelius
Cole Reuben
Colegrove Francis
Collins John
Colwell Arthur
Conare William
Conckling John
Conklin Jacob
Conkling Abraham
Connolly John
Constable Gerret
Conway Michael
Cook Darius
Cook David
Cook Henry
Cook Job
Cook Nathan
Coon Peter
Cooper Gerrit
Coovert John
Cornelison Michael
Coulter John
Covert James
Cowings Isaac
Coxwell Francis
Crans Christopher
Crawford James
Creed Aston
Crissy William
Cropsy Henry
Crosby Ebenezer
Crosby Richard
Cross William
Cry John
Cummins Daniel
Cunningham Benjamin
Cuper Henry
Currie Elijah
Curtis Ezra

David John
Davis Nathan
Davis Samuel
Davis William
Dea Cass Thomas
Dealy Samuel
Dean Ebenezer
Dean James
Dean Reuben
Decker Cornelius
Deforege Reuben
DeGrove William
Degrushie Elias
Delaney Dennis
Delano Thomas
Delavan Daniel
De Lavigne Francis
Demick Samuel
Deo Hugh
Derbishire Daniel
Derbishire James
Derbyshire David
Derly Philip
Devie Isaac
Devoo Anthony
De Witt Jacob
De Witt John L.
De Witt Peter, Jr.
De Witt William
Dimmuck Samuel
Dobbins Hugh
Dodge Daniel
Dolittle Hopkins
Dolleway Andrew
Donnovan Daniel
Doty Elias
Douglass James
Downy John
Doxy Stephen
Draper John
Drew Oliver
Du Bois Cornelius
Dubois John
Dubois Martin
Dubois Matthew
Duley Philip
Dumond Cornelius
Dunlap Thomas
Durling Benjamin
Dusenbury William
Dutcher Abraham
Dutcher David
Dutcher Henry

Dyer James
Eager James
Edwards John
Eigener Jacobus
Elliot Christopher
Elliott Thomas
Ellis Christopher
Ellison Jeremiah
Elmendorph Petrus
Elsworth John
English George
Ennest William
Ennis Peter
Ferdon Samuel
Ferguson Enos
Ferguson Jeremiah
Ferris Benjamin
Ferrison Silvenus
Finch Elnathan
Finch Philip
Fontaman Frederick
Forgerson Gilbert
Forsbag John
Fowler George
Fowler Nehemiah
Fox Martin
France Adam
Franklin Nathaniel
Fuller Joseph
Furman Samuel
Gardenir George
Gardinier James
Garison Jacob
Garrison Abraham
Garrison John
Garrison Joseph
Garrison Peter
Garvey Francis
Gay John
Geason Matthew
German James
Gerrison Jacob
Gifford John
Gildersleeve Joseph
Gilford Benjamin
Gillespey James
Glasby David
Graham Jacobus
Graham James
Graham John
Gray Jonathan
Green Isaac
Green Jehial

Green John
Green Joseph
Green Peter
Green Samuel
Griffin John
Grimes Shepherd
Gue Joseph
Gunsalon Samuel
Hadley Isaac
Hagaman Nicholas
Hager William
Haight Joseph
Hait Minnah
Hall Benjamin
Hall Boston
Hall Robert
Halleet William
Hallet Jeffery
Halley Robin
Haimer James
Hammel Nathaniel
Hanfield David
Hanna James D.
Hanmore David
Hansen William
Hardenbergh Cornelius
Hardifant Zur
Harington Alexander
Harris Squire
Harris Thomas
Hatch Solomon
Hay Nathaniel
Heevens Justice
Hennicum Elisha
Herdenbergh Lewis
Hergoman Nicholas
Herrick Elijah
Herrick Jonathan
Hicks John
Hillman Nicholas
Hines James
Hitt Dennis
Hodge Israel
Hoghtaling William
Holly William
Holmes Anthony
Holmes James
Holt William
Holtslandery Adam
Homan John
Homan Joshua
Homes Nathaniel
Hood John

Horton Thomas	Lane Jeremiah	McNamee William
Hosier Thomas	Lane Joshua	McSweeney Daniel
Hoskier Lawrence	Lane Samuel	Mahoney James
House Seth	Lane William	Maines Charles
Howe Timothy	Lassing George	Mapes Henry
Hoyt Elijah	Lattimore Roger	Mapes Henry, Jr.
Hubbard Prince	Laurence Alexander	Marks George
Hubbil Richard	Lawrence Samuel	Marrigut Jacob
Hubbill Gershom	Lawson Lawrence	Marshall Henry
Hughan John	Lawyer Adam	Martin Thomas
Hunt Aaron	Lee Jonathan	Mashanan James
Hunt Thomas	Legg Samuel	Masstin Thomas
Hunter Ebenezer	Lenared Robert	Matthews Peter
Huskins Asel	Lent Jacob	Mead Marshel
Hutchins Jacob	Le Roy Henry	Meed Lewis
Hyme Cornelius	Letts David	Middagh Daniel
Ingerson John	Lewes Galop	Midgley Joseph
Ingraham Justus	Linsey States	Miller Alexander
Irwin James	Liskum Samuel	Miller George
Ives Grigery	Lifts John	Miller Peter
Jackson James	Lloyd Elisha	Miller Samuel
Jameson Thomas	Lockwood Benjamin	Miller William
Jane John	Lockwood Job	Milligan Robert
Jansen Thomas	Lockwood John	Mingas David
Jansen Thomas, Jr.	Lockwood Moses	Minthorn Nathaniel
Jarvis Francis	Loden Pettit	Mires William
Jecocks Gershom	Loder Pettit	Monall James
Jenkins Ezekiel	Lossing Matthew	Montanye Peter
Jennings Stephen	Low John	Mooney Abraham
Jersey Richard	Lucas Jonathan Budd	Moor Martin
Johnson Josiah	Lucas William	Moore Martin
Johnson Richard	Lucky Robert	Moore Thomas
Johnson Thomas	Luddington William	Moore William
Jones Isaac	Lukky Jeffy	Mopps Frederick
Jonson Daniel	Lyke Hendrick	Morgan David
June Abraham	Lyons Michael	Morgan Seth
June John	McCann Cornelius	Morris Elijah
Jursey Richard	McCay John	Morris William
Keator Gideon	McClarning John	Morse Rufus
Keeler John	McClintock John	Mosher Cornelius
Kelly Dinnis	McCluer William	Moss Charlie
Kelly Isaac	McCormick James	Murdough Lackey
Kelly Sylvanut	McCoy Daniel	Murphy Thomas
Kelsey John	McCraney William	Mutz Johannes
Keslor Peter	McDaniel Daniel	Myer David
Kip Igness	McDonald James	Myer Henry
Kitcher John	McDugle Alexander	Myer William
Knap Joseph	McEuen Cornelius	Myers David
Knapp Shadrick	McHurter James	Nap Joseph
Koch John Henry	McKee Thomas	Neirn James
Lake Joshua	McKenzie Alexander	Nelson Absalom
Lamphier John	McLaning John	Nelson James
Lane Daniel	McMunn William	Nelson John

Newkirk Isaac
Newman William
Niemeyer John Henry
Noble Lyman
Nol Christian
Northrup Eli
O'Bradley Daniel
Odell Jonathan
Odie Richard
O'Ferrol Michael
Ogden Joseph
O'Kie Martin
Olcutt Isaac
Oosterhoudt Hendricus
Oosterhoudt Tounis
Oostorhout Aldert
Osterhout Jonathan
Otterman James
Outerman James
Owen John D.
Owens Amasa
Owens Thaddeus
Paddock Daniel
Paddock Peter
Palmer Henry
Palmer Solomon
Parigo Uzal
Parish Cyprian
Parish Ephraim
Parve Jonathan
Patterson James
Pawn Chance
Pearce Jonathan
Pembrook William
Penny John
Perry John
Perry Samuel
Phillips Isaac
Phillips James
Pine Timothy
Plough Henry, Jr.
Plugh Hendrick
Plumley Jonathan
Polden William
Pond Chance
Pool William
Post Martin, Jr.
Pots Martin, Jr.
Prince Richard
Prose Abraham
Ransom James
Ranson Barezillia
Reeve Daniel

Rennals John
Renshout John
Reynolds Stephen
Rice Isaac
Rice John
Richard Nathaniel
Richards Ezra
Richmond John
Riddle John
Rile James
Rinders James
Rinders John
Roach William
Robb Aaron
Robbins Lewis
Roberson Lewes
Roberts James
Roberts John
Robin (negro)
Robinson Ebenezer
Robinson Lewis
Robison James
Rock William
Rockwell Enos
Roff Christopher
Rogers Joseph
Rogers William
Romer Aaron
Rosa Abraham
Rosa Dirck
Rowley Subil
Rumsey Jonas
Rundle Elnathan
Runo Simon
Sampson George
Schoonmaker Hezekiah
Schoonmaker Isaac
Schoonmaker Peter
Schut Christian
Scofield Henry
Scott Archibald
Shadler John
Shaw Joshua
Shearer Robert
Sheldon William
Shepherd Benjamin
Sherwood Moses
Shippard Jonathan
Shoecraft John
Shoefelt John
Shoffer John
Shuts Frederick
Sidney James

Sidway James
Sillick James
Simmons John
Skeldin William
Slauson John
Slawson Samuel
Sleight Abraham
Sleight John
Slouter William
Slover Isaac
Sluyter Cornelius
Sluyter Daniel
Smith Alpheus
Smith Doctor
Smith Isaac
Smith James
Smith John
Smith Lemuel
Smith Peter
Smith Thomas
Smith Thomas, Jr.
Smith William
Smith Zacharias
Smyth Thomas
Snedeker James
Sneyder John
Snider John
Snoden Francis
Sooloy Coonradt
Southard Henry
Southerland Gurline
Spaningbergh Jacob
Sparks George
Sparks Robert
Spicer Jeremiah
Spragge Benjamin
Spraig John
Squier Ichabod
Stafford Richard
Starr Aaron
Stars Moses
Steenbergh Abraham
Steenrod Solomon
Stenebrander David
Stephens Justice
Stinard Drake
Stinard Oglisbery D.
Stirdavan Isaack
Stone Henry
Stonebrander David
Strong Joel
Strong Joseph
Sturges Abraham

Sullivan Michael
Suthard Henry
Sutharland Gurline
Sutherland Israel
Swartwout Jack (colored)
Swartwout Samuel
Swezey Joseph
Tailor Jeremiah
Tankus Isaac
Tappen Matthew
Taylor Ebenezer
Teater John
Ter Bush William
Terilleger William
Terry Benjamin
Terwilleger Cornelius
Terwilliger John
Terwilliger Josiah
Terwilliger Tunes
Thompson Jack (colored)
Tobius John
Trealiger Martin
Trim Ezra
Truesdell Jesse, Jr.
Trumbull James
Trusdell Thomas
Turner Jacob
Tuthill Azariah
Tuttel John
Tuttle Daniel
Vael Joseph
Vail John
Valantine Peter
Van Amber Joseph
Van Ass Solomon
Van Cleef Isaac
Van Cleift Gerritt
Van Cleift Joseph
Van De Bogart James
Vandenbogard Mindard
Vandervort John
Van De Waters Adolph
Van De Waters Harmanus
Van De Werken Martin
Van Fleet Joshauay

Van Kleeck Michael
Van Kleek George
Van Kleek James
Vannaker Nathaniel
Van Narden Hendrick
Van Nostrandt John
Van Scoy Jonething
Van Scoy Samuel
Van Steenbergh Benjamin
Van Steenburgh Peter
Van Stervelt John
Van Stienbergh John
Vantasel Isaac
Van Waggoner Garret
Van Zile Abraham
Veal John
Vernooy Abraham
Vinegar Samuel
Vines Jeremiah
Vredenburgh Thomas
Waddle Robert
Wade Joseph
Waldron Joseph
Waldron William
Wallace John
Ward Jesiass
Ward Joshua
Ward Josiah
Wardell Eliakim
Warner Thomas
Warren Mordica
Waterbury James
Way John
Webb Joseph
Webb William
Weed Charles
Weed John
Weeks James
Weelar John
Weissmiler Jeremiah
Wells Joseph
Wells Samuel
Westervelt John
Westfalls Levi
Whigham Robert

Whitaker Edward
White John
White Solomon (colored)
Whitlock Thaddcus
Whitney David
Whitney Silas
Wickson David
Wiggins William
Wilde Thomas
Wilkelow Jacob
Wilkison Thomas
Willbur Gideon
William Elias
Williams Abraham
Williams Daniel
Williams Uriah
Willson Andrew
Willson William
Wilson John
Winans John
Winfield Abram
Winfield Jacob
Winfield Simon
Wird John
Wixson John
Woldorf Henry
Wolf Simon
Wollf John
Wood Alexander
Wood Allickzander
Wood Vincent
Wordern George
Wrick James
Wyatt Joseph
Wynkoop Cornelius
Yeomans Nathan
Young John
Yuall John
Yune Abraham

The Levies--(Malcom)

Colonel William Malcom
Adjutant Isaac Requa
Major Elias Van Benschoten
Quaarter Master Alexander Stewart
Adjutant Joseph Hasbrouck, Jr.
Surgeon's Mate Peter Osborn

CAPT. JAMES BLAKSLEE
" ELIJAH BOSTWICK
" JOHN BURNET
" MOSES CANTINE
" DANIEL DELAVAN
" JOSHUA DRAKE
" JACOB LANSING
" JONATHAN LAWRENCE, JR.
" GILBERT J. LIVINGSTON
" THOMAS McKINSTRY
" MAGEE
" MILLER
" CHRISTOPHER MULLER
CAPT. ISAAC REQUA
" ADIEL SHERWOOD
" DANIEL WOOD
LIEUT. CORNELIUS ACKERSON
" CORNELIUS ADRIANCE
" CORNELIUS BALDWIN

" JOHN BOLTON
" ELIAS DELONG
" JOSHUA DRAKE
" ZACHARIAH GIBSON
" JOSIAH HALLETT
" JOSEPH JOY
" RICHARD LAWRENCE
LIEUT. JOHN I. LOW
" JEREMIAH MULLER
" WILLIAM NOTTINGHAM
" JOHN OSTRANDER
" HUGH PEACOCK
" JOSEPH REQUA
" JONAS RICE
" EZEKIEL ROBERTS
" DANIEL SACKETT
" PETER B. TEN BROECK.
" SAMUEL UTLEY
ENSIGN PATRICK CRONIM

Additional Name On State Treasurer's Pay Books

Lieut. Jacob Vermilla

Enlisted Men

Abrams John
Acker Francis
Ackerman John
Adair William
Adams Gilbert
Allen David
Allen James
Allen Samuel
Amberman Aurt
Andersen John
Andrews John
Andries Jacob
Anson James
Anthony Richard
Antis William
Archer James

Arnol William
Ausgood Nathaniel
Ayres Phelix
Ayres Thomas
Babcock Benjamin
Bacon James
Badcock David
Bailey Moses
Bailey Timothy
Baily Richard
Baker Bartholomew
Baker Conrad
Baker John
Baker Judah
Baker Thomas
Ball John

Barber William
Barkman John
Barnes Jacob
Barnet Alexander
Barret William
Bartley Abraham
Beatly Abram
Beckes Elijah
Beebe Constant
Beekman Henry
Beekman John
Bell John
Bell Robert
Bell William
Benjamin Daniel
Bennet Benjamin

Bennett William	Carner Andries	Crist Daniel
Benson John	Carningham John	Christ Matthew
Bently Joseph	Carr James	Crou Peter
Berger Jacob	Case William	Cry John
Berges Wilhelmea	Case Zenes	Cudberth Benjamin
Biles George	Cass William	Cumston David
Black Henry	Casswell David	Cunningham John
Black Jack	Cawline Joseph	Curington Enough
Black Robert	Chamberlain Gordon	Curniston David
Blackman Joel	Chase Robert	Curtus Naniad
Blakesley James	Chism Peter	Dains Abraham
Blakslee Nathaniel	Chithster Nathan	Daley Samuel
Blawvelt Cornelius	Christ Abraham	Darling Samuel
Blawvelt Isaac	Church James	Darrow Amarias
Blowers Samuel	Clark Samuel	Darrs Jeptha
Bogart Cornelms	Clearwater Mathew	Davies Jeptha
Bogart John	Cleary Luke	Davis John
Bogert Jacob	Clow John Gotlip	Davis Joseph
Boing Peleg	Clowes John Gotlip	Davis William
Bont Ephriam	Cloyde Daniel	Davison Barnabas
Bouton Daniel	Clute John B.	Daws Jeptha
Bradner Benoni	Coal Moses	Day Aron
Briggs Caspares	Codmer Ishmael	Dayton John
Brinck Peter	Codner George	Decker Francis
Brinck Solomon	Codney William	De Lancy Abraham
Broadstreat John	Cohoone Elexander	Delaney Abraham
Brooks Jeremiah	Coldwell John	Delimarter Benjamin
Brower Eldrick	Cole Henry	Demsey Thomas
Brown Jeremiah	Coleman James	Dennis John
Brown John	Colford Matthew	Deveraux Joseph
Brown Lackey	Compton David	Dickison Judathan
Brown Malchi	Concklin Nathan	Dinnings Ezra
Brown Samuel	Condradt Henry	Dixon Andrew
Brown William	Conklin Henry	Dixon Thomas
Buel Siras	Conklin John	Dodge Andrew
Bulice Peter	Conklin Matthias	Dolittle Timothy
Bur Daniel	Conner William	Doty Isaac
Burcham Henry	Cook Zebulon	Doty Shadewick
Burdick Gideon	Cool Peter	Dubois David
Burgant Lambert	Cooper Ede	Dubois Jacob
Burgarth Lambert	Cooper Henry	Ducy Samuel
Burgess Stephen	Cooper John	Dunbar Amos
Burhans Abraham	Cordigal Abraham	Dunham Samuel
Burlison Fearnot	Cordman Joseph	Dunning David
Burns William	Cornelius John	Durgey Fidias
Burris Charles	Cornwell William	Dykman William
But Daniel	Cotterell Abis	Earls Daniel
Butler Joseph	Cowden John	Edwards Thomas
Cace Zenes	Cowen William	Eivs Phelise
Cadmen Joseph	Crafford Thomas	Elder Joseph
Campbell John	Crane James	Ellison James
Campbell Robert	Craven John	Ellison Jeremiah
Canton David	Crist Christian	Ellison Samuel

Ellison Thomas	Griffin Ebenezer	Howes Seth
Engals George	Griffin Joseph	Hubberd Joseph
Evans Joseph	Griswold David	Hudler Solomon
Everitt Jacob	Guy John	Hudson Richard
Everitt John	Guy Timothy	Hugan John
Felter Peter	Hadley Isaac	Hull Nathan
Fish Abner	Hadley Joseph	Humphrey Emry
Fish William	Hagaman Nicholas	Hunt Daniel
Fitch Elisha	Hall Christian	Hunter Moses
Fleeman Solomon	Hall William	Hutt John
Flemin Forton	Halleck Jeffrey	Huyck Nicholas
Flin Thomas	Hanmore Jabia	Hyatt Elias
Fogus Christian	Hanlon Rufus	Hyms Frederick
Foot Simeon	Harden Joseph	Irvine Henry
Foster John	Harrington John	Jackson John
Foster Jonathan	Harris Eliphalet	Jacobie Bastian
Francis John	Harris Henry	Jermin James
Freel Peter	Harris William	Jimison Thomas
French John	Havens Thomas	Johnson John
French Samuel	Hay William	Johnson Peter
Fuller Benjamin	Hayet Elias	Jones Abraham
Funck Christian	Hazard Joshua	Jones Isaac
Funck Jacob	Head Joseph	Jones Jonas
Gage Alden	Heath Winslow	Jones Joseph
Gardiner Isaac	Heathway Jon'a	Jones William
Gardiner Samuel	Heirs Phelix	Joy Amos
Garrison Joseph	Hender Joseph	June Abraham
Gates Samuel	Henderson Alexander	Kent Thomas
Gault Alexander	Hendrickson John	King Jacob
Gearvey Francis	Hennion John	King John
Gernea Benjamin	Henry Robert	Knap Benjamin
Gibbs David	Herrick Joseph	Knap Ephraim
Gibbs Isaac	Herris Henry	Koomer Aaron
Gifford Joseph	Herron Eliot	Krum Benjamin
Gilberts Jesper	High William	Lafaver Noah
Giles Samuel	Hobart Joseph	Landus Ebenezer
Gill William	Hochtaling John	Langdon Benjamin
Gilson Zachariah	Hodge Daniel	Langler James
Goff Boswell	Hodge John	Lathrop Ebenezer
Gold Elijah	Hodgeson George	Lathrop Lebbus
Goodhue Joseph	Hoghtaling John	Lawrence George
Goold Pearl	Hoghtaling Tennis	Lawson Matthew
Goss Oliver	Hollister Smith	Lee Jonathan
Gould Jesse	Hollobard Jesse	Leeman Archibald
Gould William	Holmes Jeddediah	Lefoy Abraham
Graft Philip	Homer Joshua	Leggitt Lue
Graham William	Hopkins Robert	Lemon Archabald
Graves Josiah	Horton Jeremiah	Lemon John
Green James	Horton Samuel	Leroy Daniel
Green John	House Cornelius	Leroy Robert
Greer Joseph	House Seth	Letts Abraham
Grenie Benjamin	Hover Philex	Lewis Isaac
Griffen Joseph	Howard Enos	Lewis James

Linerd Henry
Lint Elias
Little Stephen
Little William
Litts Abraham
Livingston Richard
Lothrop Lebious
Luckey James
Lucks Johannis
Luddington Elisha
Luff Nicholas
Luick Andrew
Luicks Abraham
Luicks Johannis
Lull Nathen
Lummes Andrew
Lyons Amaziah
McCarty Hugh
McCoy James
McCoy John
McDaniel Cornelius
McDonold Edward
McEune Cornelius
McFarling Andrew
McGee James
McInsbry Thomas
McKee Thomas
McNutt Alexander
McPherson Daniel
McRobert John
McWilliams James
Maaterstock John
Maclos William
Magee John
Magey Peter
Mandovel Mathew
Mapes Henry
Mapes James
Marsh Samuel
Martin Thomas
Masters William
Maybee Peter
Mead Eli
Mead Isaac
Meebe Peter
Mege Peter
Merrit Abraham
Merrit Amos
Merrit Ebenezer
Millard Nathaniel
Miller Amos
Miller Henry
Miller John

Miller William
Millet Jonathan
Milor Samuel
Milspaugh Cristia
Mires John
Montanye John
Montonya John
Moor John
Moore Joseph
Mores Hezekiah
Morgan David
Morris Duncan
Morris Ebenezer
Morrison Adward
Morrison Duncan
Morrison Hugh
Morrison Jonathan
Moser Joseph
Moses Joseph
Moss Isaac
Mott Jacob
Mott Robert
Mount Samuel
Muller Amos
Murphy Thomas
Mynderse Abraham
Mynderse Harman
Nelson Absolom
Newkirk Mindert
Nichols Jonas
Nickles William
Nimham Isaac
Notingham Thomas
Nowe Lewis
Odie Jonathan
Onderdonk Isaac
Onderdonk Thomas
Osterhout Henry
Ostrander Henry
Ostrander John
Overpaw John
Ovett Isaac
Palmer John
Pareols Peter
Parks Daniel
Parks Oliver
Paroch Peter
Parsons Peter
Partial John
Patterson Asay
Peets Michel
Penneld Isaac
Penil Moses

Perkney Lewis
Persell Peter
Perslow Henry
Phelps Eliiah
Philhama Jurden
Philip David
Philips David
Pike Jarvis
Pinfield Isaac
Pinkne Lewis
Pitt Ephraim
Plough Henry
Pollard David
Pool William
Porch Andrew
Prince Kimbell
Quackenbos James
Radly Jacob
Radly John
Raniad Naniad
Rannels Benjamin
Ray Raysal
Read Frederick
Read Leonard
Reed Frederick
Reed Leonard
Reeves Nathaniel
Ressman Henry
Rice Jonas
Rice Samuel
Rice Seth
Rich William
Richmond Josiah
Rider William
Rightenbergh Addam
Rindas John
Rinders John
Rines John
Ripinbalk Adam
Riser Isaac
Rises John
Robberts John W.
Robert John M.
Robertson James
Robins Daniel
Robinson Charles
Robinson Ezra
Robinson Jesse
Robinson Peter
Robison Hector
Rogen Michael
Roger Michael
Rogers Daniel

Rogers Michael	Slut John	Tornure James
Rogers Rubin	Sluyter Cornelius	Trout Adam
Romer Aaron	Smally Rubin	Valentine Peter
Roose James	Smith Daniel	Valleau Stephen
Rosa Abraham	Smith Garret	Vanatten Aron
Rosa John	Smith Henry	Van Benschoten Hannan
Rose James	Smith James	Van Bura George
Rosman Henery	Smith John	Van Buren George
Rowland John	Smith Prusia	Van Burgh John
Rowley Jabish	Smith Samuel	Van Bury George
Rumsey Jesse	Smith Solomon	Van Dalsen James
Runnels Benjamin	Snyder William	Van Dalson John
Runnels John	Snyder Willis	Vandeburgh John
Runnels Silas	Spananburgh Jacob	Vandenburgh Abraham
Rynarde John	Speed Henry	Van Derbelt Dirk
Rynder James	Sprague John	Van Houten Abraham
Rynders Jacob	Spreag John	Van Houten John
Safford Jonathan	Stanton Benjamin	Van Neder Henry
Salbury Gedion	Stanton Rufus	Van Noder Peter
Saterly Joseph	Starns William	Van Schaick Roger
Scanlon Matthias	Stevens David	Van Sicklen Cornelius
Schanklin Jeremiah	Stevens Elijah	Van Sickler Cornelius
Schoolcraft Peter	Stevens Solomon	Van Stenbergh John
Schoonhover Thomis	Stevens Stephen	Van Tasel Abraham
Schoonmaker Edward	Stevens William	Van Tassel Cornelius
Scofield Abner	Steward John	Van Tuye John
Scott Alexander	Steward Solomon	Van Urder Hendrick
Scott John	Stewart Samuel	Van Urder Peter
Scott William	Still Robert	Van Valer James
Scutt Solomon	Stocom William	Van Valkenburg Thomas
Seabree John	Stoddard John	Van Valkenburgh Gershom
Seabury John, Jr.	Stone Selvester	Van Valkenburgh Harma
Seamons John	Stoneburner David	Van Voarhast John
Sears Alliten	Stoner Henry	Van Yevern Jonathan
Sears John	Stopplebean Peter	Vanzandt John
Sebrew John	Storms Isaac	Viele Johanes
Seward John	Strader Jost	Vredenburgh Abraham
Sharp John	Sutling Ambres	Walsworth Gilbert
Sharp John, Jr.	Swart Benjamin	Ward Josiah
Shaver Adam	Swart William	Ward Moses
Shaw Henry	Taulman Jacob	Warner Ebenezer
Shell Adam	Taulman Peter	Warren Benjamin
Sherwood Daniel	Taulman William	Way John
Shout John	Taylor David	Webb Joseph
Shower Adam	Taylor James	Webers John
Shulp John	Teil Andrew	Webster Milo
Shurt John	Terneure James	Welds Calven
Shurts John	Terry Benjamin	Well Joshua
Simmons John	Thomas Caleb	Wells James
Simmons Reuben	Thomas Ephraim	Wentworth James
Simpson Robert	Tice John	Westervelt Casparus
Skinner John	Tigner Jonathan	Wharry Robert
Slouter Willam	Tirl Andrew	Whitcom John

Whitcomb Ezra
White William
Willard Abel
Williams Gilbert
Williams Job
Williams Nathan
Willis William
Wilson John
Wilthouse Aaron

Wilthouse John
Witney David
Wixon David
Wood Isaac
Wood Jacob
Wood James
Wood John
Wood Moses
Wood Robert

Wood Timothy
Woodard Ephraim
Wooding Rubin
Woodward Ephraim
Woolcut Justis
Yorus Benjamin
Younge George

The Levies--(Pawling)

COLONEL ALBERT PAWLING
MAJOR THOMAS DEWITT
MAJOR ELIAS VAN BUNSCHOTEN
ADJUTANT CORNELIUS DUBOIS
ADJUTANT JOHN ELSWORTH
QUARTER MASTER EDWARD CONNOR
PAY MASTER JOHN VAN DEUSEN
SURGEON JOHN SMEDES
SURGEON PETER VAN DER LYN
CAPT. BROWN
" JOHN BURNET
" CHRISTOPHER CODWIS
" LEVI DEWITT
" WILLIAM FAULKNER
" JOHN A. HERDENBORGH
" ROBERT HUNTER
" JOHN ENGLISH
" JOHN L. HARDENBERGH
" MARTIN HOMMEL
" JOSHUA T. JANSEN
LIEUT. RICHARD LAWRENCE
" JOHN McBRIDE
" WILLIAM MOSIER
" WILLIAM NOTTINGHAM
" JAMES OAKLEY
" JOHN OSTRANDER
" THOMAS OSTRANDER
" ALDERT ROOSA
" HENDRICUS TEERPENNING
" NATHANIEL TUCKER
" HENRY VAN HOEVENBERGH
" MOSES YEOMANS
ENSIGN DANIEL FRAIR

" JONATHAN LAWRENCE
" GILBERT J. LIVINGSTON
" ONDERDONK
" HENRY PAWLING
" JONATHAN PEARSEE
" RICHARD SACKETT
CAPT. ABRAHAM VAN AKEN
" DERICK WESBROOK
" ABRAHAM WESTFALL
" DANIEL WILLIAMS
" ROBERT WOOD
LIEUT. CORNELIUS ACKERMAM
" TIMOTHY COLEMAN
" JOHN J. DUBOIS
LIEUT. MICHAEL DYCKMAN

ENLISTED MEN

Acker Henry
Ackerman John
Ackerson Cornelius

Adriance Theodorus
Agins James
Airs Felix

Albertson Richard
Allen Abenezer
Allen John

Allison Isaac
Allison Samuel
Alsdarph Philip
Amberman Dirck
Anderson George
Anderson John
Andrews John
Anson James
Anthony John
Armstrong Archibald
Arnel William
Arnold William
Aspenno Anthony
Averet Timothy
Averts Timothy
Avery Henry
Avery Nehemiah
Ayers Thomas
Baily Moses
Baker Coenradt
Baker Judah
Baker Richard
Baker William
Ball William
Ballard John
Bames William
Bames William, Jr.
Bamp Sherry
Bancker Frederick
Barber Elisha
Barber Joseph
Bark George
Barnes William
Barnes William, Jr.
Barnet John
Barns John
Baroon Anthony
Barret John
Barrick George
Barrow Daniel
Bartlet Levi
Bartley Jacob
Base Daniel
Bass Daniel
Bassemer John
Basset Ceasar
Bayard John
Beam William
Bedford Cornelius
Bedford Jonas
Benjamins David
Bennet Mitchel
Berger Jacob

Berger Wouter
Besemer Michael
Bevier Coenradt
Bishop John
Bishop Levi
Bishup John
Black Abraham
Black Lewis
Bloom Oaky
Bloomer Joseph
Bocrum Nicholas
Bocrum William
Bodley William
Boerum Nicholas
Boerum William
Bogue John
Bohannar James
Bouton Samuel
Bouton Timothy
Bovies David
Bowker Silas
Bowker Silas, Jr.
Bradlee Nathan
Bradly Ephraim
Bradly Nathaniel
Bramor Anthony
Braur Robert
Brawn Eldrick
Brink Adam
Brink Cornelius
Brink Cornelius, Jr.
Brink Jacob, Jr
Brink John
Brink John C.
Brinkerhon Henry
Brodhead Henry
Brodhead William
Brook Thomas
Brooks John
Brooks Mickel
Brower Eldrick
Brower Henry
Brower Teunes
Brown Asa
Brown Henry
Brown John
Brown Malachi
Brown Moses
Brown Peter
Brown Samuel
Brown Zephaniah
Bruce Robert
Brush David

Brush Eliakim
Brush Isaac
Bruton Arthur
Budd Frederick
Bunker Solomon
Bunker Thomas
Burger Zachariah
Burgus James
Burhance Terrick
Burhans Cherck
Burhans Isaac
Burhans John
Burhans Therk
Burl Thomas
Burl Zachariah
Burnett John
Burns Edward
Burns William
Burt Christopher
Burwell James
Bush Henry
Bush Peter
Butler John
Byard John
Callagham Thomas
Calwell Arthur
Camble James
Camble John
Cammel William
Cantfield Amos
Cantine John, Jr.
Card Hugh
Carrier Andrew
Carney Barnabas
Carpenter Nehemiah
Carpenter Nicolaes
Carte William
Carter Luke
Case Enos
Case William
Case Zenos
Cassady Nicholas
Catterlon Nathaniel
Cawin Daniel
Chamber Cornelius
Chamberland Jacob
Chambers Jacobus
Chambers John
Chambers Joseph
Chapman Daniel
Chapman Stephen
Chapman Uriah
Chase Ebenezer

Chase Gedeliah
Chatneld Caleb
Chatterdon Nathaniel
Chris Matthew
Chrispel John
Christ Thomas
Christian Cornelius
Church John
Churchell Jonas
Churchell William
Claerwater John
Claerwater Matthew
Claerwater Petrus
Clark John
Clark Samuel
Clawter John
Cleland William
Clerk John
Coddington Benjamin
Coddington Levi
Cole Simon P.
Collamar Ebenezar
Collin William
Collins John
Colwall Arture
Combs Michel
Concklin John
Concklin Samuel
Coningham William
Connon Peter
Connor Daniel
Connor James
Connor William
Conway Cornelius
Conway John
Cook Benjamin
Cook David
Cook Dines
Cook Durias
Cook Nathan
Cool Simon P.
Coon John
Coone John
Cooper Henry
Cooper James
Cooper John
Coragell Abraham
Cornelius John
Cornell Benjamin
Corregle Abraham
Cottenden Levi
Courgell Abraham
Cowen Thomas

Cox Benjamin
Cox John B.
Cox William
Craft Thomas
Crandall Luke
Crandle Luce
Crane James
Crane William
Cree Joseph
Crispel Abraham
Crispel Elisha
Crispel Hendrick
Crispel Jacob
Crispel John, Jr.
Crist Matthias
Critsinger John
Croft James
Cronk Timothy
Crosby Enoch
Crossman Michael
Crover George
Crowel Joel
Crumb Benjamin
Crumb John
Cuddeback Peter
Culp Johannis
Cunnigham John
Cunningham Abel
Cunningham Henry
Cunningham James
Cunningham William
Curen Portrick
Curtis Jeptha
Daily Robert
Dains Abraham
Dalway Andrew
Darby George
Daton Frederick
Davis Andrew
Davis Benjamin
Davis Daniel
Davis Frederick
Davis Samuel
Davis Valentine
Davis William
Davis William, Jr.
Day Jonathan
Dean Abraham
Deane Samuel
Decker John
Decker John, Jr.
Decker Moses
Docker Noah

Decker Uriah
Decker Urias
Degroot Joseph
Delameter John
Delana Dennis
Delaney Dennis
Demond Isaac
Demon Peter
Dempsey Thomas
Denton Joseph
Depare Andries
Depuy John
Deveny Archibald
Devis Andrew
Devour Abraham
Dewitt Abraham
Dewitt Cornelius
Dewitt Cornelius 0.
Dewitt Jacob
De Witt Jacobus
Dewitt James
Dewitt John, Jr.
De Witt Levi
Dewitt Tony
Dewitt William
Dickson Andrew
Dimick Samuel
Dingah Elijah
Divany Archibald
Divine Archibald
Dixon Hezekiah
Docker Jacob
Dodge Stephen
Dolson Jacob
Dolway Jeremiah
Dowty Elias
Doxy Stephen
Drake Gilbert
Draper John
Dubois David, Jr.
Dubois Gerrit
Dubois Isaac
Dubois John
Dumond Cornelius
Dumond Egenas
Dumond Isaac
Dumond Peter
Dunbar Amos
Dunbar William
Dunlap William
Dunneven Daniel
Dunning David
Dutcher Barnes

Dutcher Henry
Dutcher Rockliff
Dutcher Rulef
Dykman Benjamin
Eckert Henry
Eganor John
Eggenaar Johannis
Eggenaer Jacobus
Elit David
Ellison Isaac
Ellison Samuel
Eliot Thomas
Elsworth Henry
Elsworth John
Emrich John
Emrich Peter
Emrich Fitter
English George
English William
Ennis Cornelius
Ennis Peter
Ennis William
Ennist James
Ensley Simeon
Ettinge Thomas
Everitt Jacob
Everts Ambrus
Everts Timothy
Every Henry
Every Nehemiah
Eygenaar John
Farguson Guilbert
Faulkner John
Faulkner William
Fawster Samuel
Fawter Samuel
Felter Peter
Ferguson Gilbert
Ferress John
Ferris Alexander
Ferns Ezra
Ferris Gedion
Ferris James
Ferris John
Ferris Samuel
Ferris Sylvenus
Fice John
Fierce Jonathan
Fieris Coenradt
Fiero Abraham
Fiero Peter
Finch Fawster
Finch Reuben

Finch Samuel
Finn Ezra
Flinn David
Flinn David
Flyn Philip
Fogurson John
Folknear John
Foot John
Ford Asher
Ford Esha
Forgason Gilbert
Foster Benjamin
Foster Samuel
Fouler Joseph
Fowler Moris
Fox Oliver
Fox Samuel
Frair Isaac
France John
Frances William
Franklin George
Frans Adam
Frasher John
Freer John
Freer Peter
Frim Ezra
Fuller David
Fullerton William
Gains Josiah
Galasby David
Galasby John
Gale John
Gardner Samuel
Garlinghouse Joseph
Garmain James
Garnse Samuel
Garrison John
Garrison Jonas
Garvey Frances
Gauf Asel
Gilbert Jesse
Godfray David
Goff John
Gold Walter
Goodspeed Isaac
Graham James
Graham Zachariah
Graton Crora
Greaves Thomas
Green Peter
Greenwall Daniel
Gregory Benjamin
Griffin John

Groenvout Daniel
Gunsales Manuel
Haasbrook George
Hadeley Mosses
Hadly Isaac
Haite Abijah
Hall Benijah, Jr.
Hall Benjamin
Hall Boston
Hall John
Hall Robert
Hallock Joseph
Hallock Moses
Hallock Thomas
Hallot William
Hallsted Richard
Hallsted Samuel
Halmes Jeremiah
Handay Manassa
Hanmer Geabes
Hanmore Jabash
Hanmore Moses
Hannions John
Hardenbcrgh Jacob
Harden Thomas
Harp Abraham
Harp Henry
Harris Thomas
Hart William
Hausbruck Joshua
Hawkens Stephen
Hawking Thomas
Hawkins Thomas
Haws William
Hays Jesse
Hays Nathaniel
Head Briton
Heaton William
Hedgee Evert
Hedger Evert
Hedgers Samuel
Heermanse Edward
Height Richard
Helm Daniel
Henderson Bamp
Hennion John
Herring Hercules
Herrington Reuben
Herris Henry
Herris Noah
Hicks John
Higby Jacob
Hill Nathan

Hillhouse John	Jones David	Lewis Felix
Hines James	Jones Isaac	Lewis Gilbert
Hocks Jonathan	Jones James	Lewis Jabesh
Hodge Ralph	Jones Jeremiah	Lewis James
Hodges Israel	Jones Simeon	Lewis Robert
Holmes John	Jordan Michael	Light Josiah
Holstead Thomas	Josillin Zebediah	Linch Lawrence
Homans John	Karr William	Lines Michel
Homer Francis	Keator Cornelius	Lint Isaac
Hommel Abraham	Keator John	Lions Abel
Hommel Hermanus	Keator William	Lions Barny
Hood John	Kelley Patrick	Little Frances
Hoornbeck Cornelius	Kelly Isaac	Litts David
Hoornbeek Benjamin	Ketcham John	Lockwood Isaac
Hoornbeek Ephraim	Kickfer William	Lockwood Moses
Hopkins Thomas	Killam Silas	Lockwood Timothy
Hopper John	Killey David	London Edon
Horton Samuel	Killey Denniss	Lonts John
Hoskis Bennony	King William	Louie Albert
House Cornelius	Kittle Henry	Loun John
House William	Klyn John	Low John
Howe Timothy	Knap Nathaniel	Lucky George
Howel Isaiah	Konstable Gerrit	Lucky Samuel
Hummel Abraham	Kostable William	Luke John
Hunter John	Krom Henry	Lutts Coenradt
Hunter Robert	Krom Simon	Lyons Abel
Hurton William	Krom Simon C.	McCallan Thomas
Hutchens Essel	Krom Benjamin	McCann James
Hutchins Asa	Krom John	McClane John
Hutchins Ezekiel	Krum William	McCloud Alexander
Hutton William	Kuykendall William	McClure William
Hyatt Eleven	Lain William	McCollagham Thomas
Hyatt Elias	Laine Samuel	McCollan Thomas
Hyne. Philip	Lake John	McCollom James
Hynpagh Peter	Lake Joshua	McCollum James
Ingles George	Langendyck Cornelius	McCrany William
Inson Richard	Langyear William	McDannel Daniel
Ives Ephraim	Lanson John	McDonald Daniel
Jack Esquire	Lanson William	McFitzgerald Christopher
Jackling Freman	Lattemore Rogers	Mc Gee John
Jackson Hannibal	Lawfavour John	McGee Samuel
Jay Augustus	Lawrence Joseph	McGuire Daniel
Jayne Matthias	Lawson George	McGuire Hugh
Jean Matthew	Lawson Matthew	Mack Johannis
Jermaine James	Lawson Samuel	Mackey Alexander
Jinson Richard	Leasure Samuel	Mackey Jesse
Johnson Andrew	Lee Zepthe	Mackey John
Johnson Andrew, Jr.	Lefoy Abraham	McKloud Alexander
Johnson Benjamin (col'd)	Legget William	McMaster John
Johnson Jacob	Leinson John	McMickel John
Johnston William	Leinson William	McName William
Jones Asa	Lent Hercules	McNamel John
Jones Benjamin	Lent James	McNarno William

McNeally Patrick	More Daniel	Osborn John
McSwainy Daniel	More Thomas	Osterhoudt Tounis
McWherter James	Morrel John	Osterhout Elias
Madris James	Morris John	Osterhout Ezekiel
Magie John	Morris Robert	Osterhout Henry
Matony John	Morrison Robert	Osterhout Peter
Mapes Bethuel	Mosher Seth	Osterhout Teunes, Jr.
Mapes Henry	Mosure Abner	Ostrander Jacobus
Mapes Stephen	Mountanie Peter	Ostrander Moss
Marcle Johannis	Mowris Petrus	Ostrander Teunes
Mark Johannis	Mowris Samuel	Ostrant Aldert
Markle John	Mullen Patrick	Ottarris William
Martial James	Muller John	Otter John
Martin Archibald	Murphy Robert	Oumerman Derick
Masten Daniel	Murphy Thomas	Ousterhout Hermanus
Masten Joseph	Myer Jacob	Owens Benjamin
Masters Dannial	Myer John	Owens David
Maston Matthew	Myer Peter	Owens John
Matthew James	Myer Philip	Pain Ceazar
Mead Ebenezer	Myer William	Palmatier William
Mead Joseph	Myers Abraham	Palmer Aaron
Mead Marshall	Myers Benjamin	Palmerton Thomas
Mead Mortiat	Myers Jacob	Palmeteer John
Mead Moses	Myers John	Pargret Samuel
Means Charles	Myers Philip	Parker James
Merckle Jacob	Myers William	Parks Samuel
Merkle John	Nairon James	Parrish John
Merrinan Titus	Nathan Reace	Parshal David
Merrit Ebenezer	Nearing James	Pass Jonathan
Meyr Abraham	Nelson John	Patterson Ezecal
Meyr Teunes	Newkerk Benjamin	Patterson Israel
Meyrs Abraham, Jr.	Newkerk Isaac	Patterson James
Meyrs Henry	Newkerk Jacob	Pattison Michel
Michels Joseph	Newkerk John	Pattison Thomas
Milburn John	Newman Jonathan	Pawling John
Miller Abraham	Nicolaes John	Peltze Evert
Miller Arra	Niven William	Penbrook William
Miller Ezra	Niver William	Penear John
Miller George	Northroup Eli	Peresonus Jacobus
Miller Jacobus	Nostrand George	Pergret Samuel
Miller John	Nothingham Thomas	Peterson John
Miller Joseph	Oaheley Thomas	Phelps David
Mills Jonathan	Oakley Thomas	Philips Samuel
Mills Samuel	O'Bradly Daniel	Plass Freeman
Mills Solomon	Obrien Morgon	Ploegh Hendrick
Minnin Thomas	Ochmoody Jacobus	Polhamus Daniel
Mitchell Joseph	Oddle Abiather	Pool William
Money Absalom	Odie Jonathan	Popple William
Money John	O'Ferl Michel	Porch Andrew
Montanie Peter	Oldfield George	Post Cornelius
Montanier Peter	Oliver Thomas	Post Hendrick
Moore Daniel	Oosterhoudt Ezekiel	Post Henry
Moore Thomas	Opherl Michel	Post Isaac

Post Jacobus	Rosekrans Dirck	Shurter Casparus
Post Martin	Ross Aron	Sillisbury John
Post Samuel	Ross Finly	Silsby Elijah
Presler Abraham	Rote Christian	Simmins John
Pudney James	Rowland Luke	Simmons Benjamin
Purdy John	Rumsey Jesse	Simmons Cornelius
Quick George	Rumsey Nathan	Simmons Enoch
Quick Jacob	Rundel Elnathan	Simons John
Quick John	Rundle Abraham	Skoonmaker John E.
Ransom Harry	Rundle David	Slator David
Ransom Henry	Rundle Syras	Slator John
Ray Daniel	Ryan John	Slator William
Raymonts Sands	Ryder Benjamin	Sleighter John
Read Samuel	Ryder John	Stint Harculas
Read William	Rynus John	Slutt John
Reed James	Sacket Prime	Sluyter Abraham
Regnaw Isaac	Sackett Richard	Sluyter Nicholas
Relyea John	Sadlor John	Sluyter William
Relyea Simeon	St. Clair George	Smedes John
Relyea Simon	St. John Adam	Smith Gerritt
Reton Peter	St. John Joseph	Smith James
Reves Elisha	St. Johns Joseph	Smith Jeremiah
Rice John	Sammons Cornelius	Smith John
Richard Nathaniel	Sammons Jacob	Smith Jonas
Richards Exrah	Sammons Thomas	Smith Joseph
Ritenbergh George	Saxton John	Smith Timothy
Robbison Isaac	Schoonmaker John	Smith Zacheriah
Robbison William	Schoonmaker Martin	Snyder Abraham
Roberson Jesse	Schutt Christian	Snyder Christian
Robertson John	Schutt Frederick	Snyder Elias
Robinson William	Schutt Solomon	Snyder George
Robison James	Scoffield Ceazar	Snyder Henry
Rodgers James	Scoffield Moses	Snyder Jacob
Roff Aaron	Scofield Elisha	Soleven John
Rogers James	Scoonover Joseph	Southard Henry
Rogers John	Scutt Solomon	Southard John
Rogers Joseph	Secaus Jonas	Spanenbergh Jacob
Romer Aaron	Secor Jonas	Spark Robert
Romsey Jesse	Sergeant Jame	Sparks Abraham
Roosa Abraham	Shampmeday Andrew	Sparks Robert
Roosa Aldert	Sharer Robert	Sparling John
Roosa Evert	Shaver John	Squoral Daniel
Roosa Jacob	Shaw James	Squrrel Daniel
Roosa Johannis	Shields William	Stagg Adam
Roosa John	Shiely Coenradt	Stagh Benjamin
Roosa Richard	Shoecraft Jacob	Stanley Joseph
Roosa William	Shoecraft John	Staples Nathan
Roosekrans Jacobus	Short Henry	Stater David
Rordon Pordick	Short John	Stephens John
Rose Jacob	Short Peter	Steward Charles
Rose James	Shulp John	Stewart John
Rose Richard	Shuls John	Sticks John
Rosekrans Cornelius	Shultz John	Stillwill James

Stingro Solomon
Stockbridge John
Stone John
Storm Abraham
Strong John
Stryker Abraham
Stuart John
Sturdivent David
Sulevan John
Sultiven William
Sumans Jacob
Suthard John
Sutton William
Swaar Jacob
Swart William
Swartwout Cornelius
Swoonover Benjamin
Taning Henry
Tannor Zophar
Tarpenning Jacob
Tarring Henry
Taylor Elijah
Taylor Ely
Taylor Henry
Teerpenning Jacob
Teerpenning Lawrence
Teerpeny Abraham
Tennor Zophar
Ter Bush Henry
Ter Bush Joseph
Terry Benjamin
Terwileger James P.
Terwileger Martin
Terwileger Wilhelmes
Terwilleger Aaron V.
Terwilleger Abraham
Terwilleger Jacobus
Terwilleger Peter V.
Tharp Matthew
Thompkins Lawrence
Thompson Abijah
Thompson Jedediah
Thompson Jediah
Thompson Jesiah
Thompson Joel
Thompson Joshua
Thompson Obijah
Thomson Thomas
Thornton William
Thurston Jason
Tibbies Robert
Tibbies Solomon
Tice Henry

Tice John
Tillsey Job
Tillton Peter
Tilson Timothy
Tip William
Tompkins Jonathan
Tonkry Nicholas
Toundsend Garerdus
Travis Philip
Travis Salvenus
Trawilligar James P.
Triddle Esquire
Trim Ezra
Trumper Nicholas
Trusdle Samuel
Turk John
Tuttle James
Twaghtman John
Tyler Charles
Tyler William
Umberman Dirck
Upright George
Valentine Peter
Van Aken Nathan
Van Amburgh Jeremiah
Van Anker Nathan
Van Asdell John
Van Auken Elias
Van Benschoten Jacob
Van Bunschoten Solomon
Van Cleaf Michel
Van Cleak Michael
Van Clerk Michael
Van Debogart John
Van De Bogart Peter
Van De Hoet Matthias
Vandemark Ezekiel
Vandemark Solomon
Van Demerk Jacob
Vandemerke John
Vanden Merk George
Van Denmerk Joseph
Van Der Hoof Mathia
Vanderhoof Matthew
Van Dermerk Ezekiel
Vangalder Andrew
Van Garden Jacobus
Van Gerder Andries
Van Heenbergh Abraham
Van Hoevenbergh Eggo
Van Houten John
Van Kamp Abraham
Vankay Cornales

Van Keuren Philip
Van Keuren Tjerck
Van Kleeck Michael B.
Van Leuven Christian
Van Leuven Zachariah
Vanorder Peter
Van Osdell John
Van Pelt John
Van Scorte Abraham
Van Steenbergh John
Van Steenbergh Peter
Van Urden Peter
Van Wagene Daniel
Van Wagenen Jonathan
Van Wart John
Van Wort Goret
Vearing James
Venwer Martin
Vocke Gudfry
Vocke Henry
Vurgin John
Waggoner Tobias
Waily Thomas
Waley Thomas
Wandle Henry
Ward Josiah
Ward Solomon
Ward Thomas C.
Ward William
Waterbury James
Weed Jonathan
Weeks James
Weeks Obediah
Weisenfelt George
Welch William
Weldon James
Wells Princean
Wellsworth Gilbert
Wenigar Samuel
Wentfield Simon
Wesbrook Abraham
Westfall Levi
Weston Joseph
Wheat Amos
Wheeler Timothy
White John
White Nathan
White Tone
Whitney Jacob
Whitney Justus
Whitney Seth
Whony Daniel
Wherry Daniel

Whorry John
Wicks Phinehas
Wiley Thomas
Wilcox Isaac
Willems Dage
Williams Abraham
Williams Gilbert
Williams James
Williams John
Williams Reace
Williams William
Willis Henry
Willis James
Willis John

Willis Thomas
Wilson John
Winegar Samuel
Winfield Abraham
Winfield Elias
Winfield Simon
Winkells John
Winn Peter
Winne John
Winney John
Winney Peter
Winniger Samuel
Wispier John
Wittaker Edward

Wood John
Wood Jonah
Wood Jonas
Wood William
Woodworth Daniel
Woolcot William
Woolf Peter
Worden Barnard
Wyley Thomas
Yeaple Hanicle
Yeaple Jacob
York John
Young George

The Levies-(Graham)

COLONEL MORRIS GRAHAM
LIEUT. COL. BENJAMIN BIRDSALL
LIEUT. COL. HENRY LIVINGSTON
MAJOR ANDREW HILL
MAJOR MELANCTON LLOYD WOOLSEY
ADJUTANT THEODORUS BAILEY
ADJUTANT JELLIS A. FONDA
ADJUTANT JOHN OSTRANDER
QUARTER MASTER DAVID HUNT
QUARTER MASTER EDEN HUNT
PAY MASTER JAMES MAGEE
SURGEON PETER OSBORN
CAPT. ELIJAH BOSTWICK
" LEMUEL CONKLIN
" JOHN HESMANSEE
" SILAS HUESTED
" JACOB JOHN LANSING
" JAMES MAGEE
" MALCOMB

" CHRISTOPHER MULLER
" WILLIAM PEARCE
CAPT. REQUA
" JOHN M. SACKETT
" ADIEL SHERWOOD
" ISRAEL VEAL
" DANIEL WILLIAMS
" JAMES WILSON
" JOHN WILSON
LIEUT. WILLIAM BLOODGOOD
" JOHN CALENDER
LIEUT. MICHAEL DYCKMAN
" ANDREW P. HEERMANSEE
" JACOB HOCHSTRASSER
" JACOB J. HURMANCE
" DANIEL LEROY
" ROBERT H. LIVINGSTON
" JEREMIAH MULLER
" JOHN ODLE

Additional Names on State Treasurer's Pay Books
Lieut. George Harsen, Lieut. Jacob H. Hermansee

Enlisted Men

Abrams John
Adams Noah
Alser Amiel
Anders William
Anderson John
Andreas John
Andrews Isaac
Andries Jacob
Antis William
Allans William

Ayres Thomas
Babcock Benjamin
Babcock David
Bacon James
Bailey David
Bailey Richard
Bailey Timothy
Baker Conrad
Baker Thomas
Baker Storm

Barber William
Barkman John
Barner Joseph
Bames Jacob
Barnes James
Barnhart Christopher
Bamhurst Christopher
Bartholimew Dewalt
Becker Adam
Becker Philip

Becker Storm	Clary Luke	Degolder John
Becker William	Clous John Gotlip	DeGraff Jesse
Beebe Constant	Cloyd Daniel	Delong Elias
Beekman Henry	Clute John	Dickerson Judathan
Bell John	Clute John P.	Dodge Daniel
Bell Robert	Coats Zebulon	Dolittle Timothy
Benchotten Herman	Codman Joseph	Doty Isaac
Bennet Joseph	Codney William	Doty Shadwick
Berger William	Codwiss Christopher	Doughty Isaac
Birkman John	Cohoone Alexander	Dubois Jacob
Black Henry	Cole Henry	Dunbar Amos
" Black Jack "	Cole Moses	Earle Joseph
Black Robert	Coleman John	Elsworth John
Blackman Joel	Conklin Matthew	Evans Joseph
Blackmore Joel	Connelly Jacob	Everouth John
Bloodgood William	Conradt Henry	Felbush Jesse
Blyn Simonn	Cook James	Fish William
Bont Ephraim	Cook Zebulon	Fisk William
Boyd Peleg	Cool Peter	Flack James
Brannon Abraham	Cooper Eden	Fogus Christian
Briggs Stephen	Cooper Obadiah	Foster John
Brink Peter	Coopper John	Francis John
Brink Solomon	Cotral Abis	Frayer John
Brooks Jeremiah	Covenhoven Francis	French John
Brown Cornelius	Covenhoven William	French Joseph
Brown John	Crane James	Fryer John F.
Brown Samuel	Crapo Peter	Funk Christopher
Bugarth Lambert	Crist Abraham	Gardinier Samuel
Burch John	Crist Christian	Gates Simon
Burgarth Lamber	Crist Matthew	Gault Alexander
Burhans Abraham	Crou Peter	Gibson David
Burr Daniel	Cry John	Gilbert John W.
Burris Charles	Cudberth Benjamin	Gold Elijah
Bussing John	Cully David	Goodhew Joseph
Bussing William	Cunningham John	Goss Oliver
Cadman Joseph	Curby John	Gould Elijah
Cady David	Currington Enoch	Gould William
Calender John	Curtis Joel	Graft Philip
Cameron David	Curtis Joseph	Graves Nodiah
Campble William	Daniels Jacob	Graves Timothy
Canady Henry	Darling Samuel	Gray Thomas
Cansa James	Darrow Arnasias	Green James
Cantine Moses	Darrow Ammerias	Green Silas
Carolina Joseph	Darrow Daniel	Griffen William
Carpenter Uriah	Davies John	Griffith W.
Case William	Davies Joseph	Griswould David
Chapman Amos	Davies William	Griswould Miles
Chapman Heerman	Davis John	Groat John
Chard Bears	Day John	Groot Hezekiah
Chism Peter	Dayton John	Gurman Benjamin
Church James	Decker Francis	Hadley Jacob
Church Samuel	DeCline Leonard	Hadley Joseph
Clarwater Matthew	DeCullier James	Hagedorn John

Hagedom Samuel
Hagerman William
Haguman W.
Hall Benijah
Hall Christopher
Hall William
Hampaugh Peter
Hams William
Harrington Abraham
Harrington Isaac
Harrington John
Harrington Zachariah
Harris Elphalet
Harris Noah
Harsin George
Hawns Thomas
Heath Stephen
Hendrickson John
Herring Solomon
Hickman Michael
Hilton Jonathan
Hiltzinger Michael
Hinkley Gershom
Hodge Daniel
Hodgeson George
Hoghtaling John
Hoghtaling Teunis
Hollabard Jesse
Hollister Samuel
Hollister Smith
Homer Joshua
Homes Jedediah
Hopping David
Horton Samuel
Hover Philex
Howard Enos
Huberson Benjamin
Hudson George
Hughan John
Hugom John
Huick Nicholas
Hukman Michael
Hunt Daniel
Hurlbut Jesse
Hutchinson Benjamin
Hutt John
Huyck Nicholas
Hyms Frederick
Ingles George
Irvine Henry
Isdawy James
Jacobie Bastian
Johnson Elijah

Johnson Shubal
Johnson Peter
Jonck Jacob
Jones William
Joy Amos
Joy Joseph
Kelso Benjamin
Kempel John
King John
Krum Benjamin
Lamont Archy
Landus Ebenezer
Lamed Henry
Lawyer Lambert
Leaman Archibald
Lee Jonathan
Lee William
Lefever Noah
Legget Lue
Lemon Archibald
Lemon John
Lewis Christopher
Lewis Hendrick
Lewis Jacob
Lewis Reuben
Little Stephen
Little William
Livingston Richard
Lothrop Ebenezer
Louck Henry
Low John
Luce Israel
Ludington Elisha
Luiks Abraham
Luiks Andrew
Luiks Johannis
Lull Nathan
Lumas Andrew
Lummes Andrew
Luyck John
Lyons Amaziah
McCay James
McCoy James
McCoy John
McDonald Edward
McEwen Cornelius
McIntosh Andrew
McIntosh John
McIntosh John, Jr.
McKee Thomas
McKennie Joseph
McKinney Joseph
Marrett John

Mandevile Matthew
Mandevill Matthew
Mann Solomon
Mapes Henry
Mapes James
March Marchus
Marselus Alexander
Marsh Samuel
Mayall Joseph
Mayfield John
Mead Eli
Mead Isaac
Merrit Jeremiah
Merritt Ebenezer
Miles William
Miller Christopher
Miller Henry
Miller Jeremiah
Miller John
Mindersick Frederick
Modevel Matthew
Moffat John
Moloy Thomas
Monies John
Montanye John
Moore Ephraim
Moores Hezekiah
Moot Robert
Morrell William
Morris Ebenezer
Morrison Adward
Morrison Edward
Moshier Nicholas
Mosuce Nicholas
Mott Joseph
Mott Robert
Mount Samuel
Mudge Ebenezer
Murfey Thomas
Myers John
Myndersa Frederick
Mynderse Herman
Myndersenck Frederick
Mynheer John
Nelson Absolom
Nichols John
Nichols Thomas
Nichols William
Norton Stephen
Notingham Thomas
Osborn Peter
Ostrander Henry
Ostrander William

Palmer Amasiah
Palmer John
Parcells Peter
Parks Timothy
Partridge John
Patterson Asa
Pawling Cornelius
Peak Garret
Penfield Isaac
Perslow Henry
Philip David
Pike Jarvis
Pinfeild Isaac
Plum John
Plum John M.
Pratt Robert
Price David
Prince Kemple
Proper Peter
Quick Abraham
Radly Jacob
Radly John
Rawley Jabez
Renard William
Reply Hezekiah
Rice William
Richmond Abijah
Richmond James
Rider John
Rider William
Robberts John
Roberts John
Robertson William
Robins Daniel
Robins Ezra
Robins Timothy
Robinson Ezra
Robinson Hector
Robinson Peter
Robinson William
Rogers Michael
Rogers Reuben
Romer Aaron
Romney John
Rosa John
Rossman Henry
Rowland John
Rowley Jabish
Rubison William
Rumney John
Rumsey Jesse
Rynard John
Rynders John

Rynders William
St. Anthony
Salisbury Gideon
Salisbury Joseph
Salyea Henry
Saunders Wait
Saxton Gershom
Scantling Jeremiah
Schaick Jonathan
Schoolcraft Peter
Schoonmaker Edward
Scott William
Seward John
Shader Jost
Shaver Adam
Shaver John
Shell Adam
Shiels James
Shoefelt William
Shuffalt William
Shuffalts John
Shurts John
Shutts John
Skinner Solomon
Slater James
Slocum William
Slowter Cornelius
Smally Ruben
Smith Daniel
Smith James
Smith Michael
Smith Nicholas
Smith Peter
Smith Richard
Smith Samuel
Snyder William
Speed Henry
Spinenbergh Jacob
Spitcer Aaron
Spitzer Aaron
Springsteen Jeremiah
Stafford Jonathan
Stalker William
Stansel Nicholas
Stephens William
Stevens David
Steward John
Still Robert
Stopplebean Peter
Strader Jost
Stuart John
Stubrack Barant
Sturdevant Isaac

Sullivan David
Swart Benjamin
Talman Jacob
Taylor James
Taylor Joseph
Teal Andrew
Terry Benjamin
Terry Norton
Thomas Caleb
Thomkins Lawrence
Thompson John
Tigncr Jonathan
Tinneger George
Tolbush Jesse
Tollman Thomas
Treat Woodbridge
Tripp Anthony
Truesdale Thomas
Trusdall William
Valentine Richard
Valleau Stephen
Van Aernam Abraham
Vanaton Aaron
Van Banchoten Heerman
Van Buren George
Vanderbergh John
Vanderbiit D. K.
Van Houten Abraham
Van Ness David
Vanorden Henry
Vanorden Peter
Van Tassel Abraham
Vantile John, Jr.
Van Tuyle John
Van Valkenburgh Gershom
Van Valkenburgh Harma
Van Valkenburgh John
Van Valkenburgh Lucas
Van Vradenburgh Peter
Van Zandt John
Vermillie Jacob
Victory John
Vischer Bastian H.
Vredenburgh Abraham
Vredenburgh Peter
Vredinburgh William
Wadsworth John
Waggonet Hermonias
Wait George
Walcott Justice
Waldron William
Wallace Benjamin
Walsworth G.

Wanson John
Ward Charles
Ward Christopher
Ward Josiah
Wares Christopher
Wason James
Wason John
Wasson James
Waters David
Webbers John
Wentworth James
Westfall Abraham

Westhead Edward
Whitcom John
Whitcomb Ezra
Whitcomb John
White William
Wilkie Augustus
Williams David
Williams Thomas
Williams William
Williamson James
Wilson Jesse
Wilson John

Wilthouse John
Winters John
Wixon David
Wolfe Anthony
Wood James
Wooding Rubin
Woodward Ephraim
Woolcot Justice
Woolsey M.
Wynances John
Young George
Youngs William

The Levies--Independent Corps of 1,000 Men
(Raised under Act 33, passed March 13, 1779)

Lieut. Rial Bingham.

The Line and the Levies -- (Not Identified)

The following men (according to the certificates of the muster-masters) served either in the Line or the Levies, having been hired by the several classes under the Land Bounty Rights; but, there is nothing in the Land Bounty Rights to indicate in which regiment of the Line or the Levies they served. Their regiments, however, are indicated elsewhere.

Colonel Fred Weisenfels; Major Elias Van Benschoten; Capt. Joseph Harrison; Capt. Jonathan Pearsee; Capt. Henry Pawling; Lieut. John Ostrander.

Enlisted Men.

Barlow Joseph
Brush David
Buckhout James
Clark Benjamin
Clark John
Clark Samuel
Collins John
Concklin Samuel
Constable Garret
Cook Darius
Cook John
Cornelius John
Cowen Thomas
Cry John
Davis John
Davis William
Day Aaron
Delaney Dennis
De Witt William
Douglass James
Doxey Stephen
Dubois Cornelius

Dubois John
Dumond Cornelius
Dutcher Henry
Elsworth John
Elsworth William, Sr.
Elsworth William, Jr.
Ennis Peter
Fiero Abraham
Finch John
Foot John
Foot Simeon
Fowler George
Garrison John
Gee Moses
Gildersleeve Joseph
Green James
Griffin John
Hall Robert
Hardenberg John L.
Harington William
Harris Henry

Harris William
Havens Thomas
Helmer John
Hicks John
Hood John
Horton Thomas
Hosier Thomas
Johnson John
Johnson Josiah
Johnston Benjamin
Jones David
King John
King William
Lane Jeremiah
Lane William
Lee Jonathan
Livingston Richard
Low John
Lusk Jacob
McArthur Alexander
McCoy Daniel

Mc Coy John
Martin Thomas
Miles William
Miller Andrew
Miller George
Miller James
Miller Peter
Milligan Robert
Moore William
More John
Murphy Thomas
Myers Abraham
Myers David
Odle Jonathan
Osterhout Henry
Owens Isaac
Perigo Usual
Perry David
Plough Henry
Price John

Pudney Thorn
Richardson William
Robertson William
Robins Daniel
Robison James
Romer Aaron
Rowley Seth
Sluyter Cornelius
Sluyter Jacob
Smith Isaac
Smith John
Smith Lemuel
Smith William
Smith Zachariah
Southard Henry, Jr.
Speed Henry
Stephens John
Stevens John
Steward John
Stewart Charles

Stewart John
Taylor John
Thompson James
Thompson John
Todd Adam
Van Buren George
Vandemark Cornelius
Vanderlyn Peter
Van Dermark Cornelius
Vandyke Cornelius
Welch John
Wells Peter
White James
White John
Wilson William
Windfield Simon
Wolff Samuel
Wood Robert
Young Henry

THE LINE

First Regiment (Van Schaick)

COLONEL GOOSE VAN SCHAICK
LIEUT. COL. CORNELIUS VAN DYCK
MAJOR JOHN GRAHAM
MAJOR BENJAMIN LEDYARD
MAJOR JOSEPH McCRACKEN
ADJUTANT JOHN BRODGDEN
ADJUTANT JOHN L. HARDENBERGH
ADJUTANT PETER BENJAMIN TEARSE
ADJUTANT JACOB H. WENDELL
ADJUTANT JOHN H. WENDELL
QUARTER MASTER HENRY VAN WOERT
PAY MASTER ABRAHAM TEN EYCK
PAY MASTER JEREMIAH VAN RENSSELAER
CHAPLAIN SOLOMON FRELIGH
SURGEON DANIEL BUDD
SURGEON WILLIAM MEAD
SURGEON DANIEL MENEMA
SURGEON CALEB SWEET
CAPT. JOHN C. TEN BROECK
" DAVID VAN NESS
" JAMES VAN RENSSELAER
" NICHOLAS VAN RENSSELAER
" ABRAHAM A. VAN WYCK
" RICHARD VARICK
" JOHN WANDLE
" JOHN H. WENDELL
" JOHN WILEY

" JOB WRIGHT
" GUY YOUNG
CAPT AARON AORSON
" LEONARD BLEEKER
" WILLIAM BROWN
" JACOB CHEESMAN
" WILLIAM CODE
" JOHN COPP
" ROBERT EDMOMSTON
" ANDREW FINCK, JR.
" S. GILBERT
" WILLIAM GOFORTH
" JOHN GRAHAM
" JAMES GREGG
" JAMES GRIGG
" BENJAMIN HICKS
" CORNELIUS T. JANSEN
" JOHN JOHNSON
" DAVID LYON
" ROBERT McKEAN
" MOSES MARTIN
" DANIEL MILLS
" CHARLES PARSONS
" JOHN QUACKENBOS
" BARENT STAATS SALISBURY
" GEORGE SYTEZ
" GEORGE SYTVIS
" HENRY TEABOUT

LIEUT. JOSIAH BAGLEY
" ABRAHAM B. BANCKER
" JOHN BARNS
" GERAURD BECKMAN
" VICTOR BICKER
" WILLIAM BLOODGOOD
" BENJAMIN BOGARDUS
" ABRAHAM E. BRASHER
" JAMES CLARK
" JOB COOK
" HENRY DEFFENDORFF
" DANIEL DENNESTOK
" JOHN DENNEY
" HOLTON DUNHAM
LIEUT. HENRY SWARTWOUT
" PETER B. TEARSE
" JOHN C. TEN BROECK
" ABRAHAM TEN EYCK
" SAMUEL THORN
" PETER VAN BUNSCHOTEN
" NANNING VAN DERHIDEN
" CORNELIUS VAN DYCK
" ARONDT VAN HOOK
" JOHN VAN NESS
" BARTHOLOMEW J. VAN VALKENBURGH
" TOBIAS VAN VEGHTEN
" ISAAC VAN WERT
" HENRY VAN WOERT
" PETER VERGEREAN
" GOEB'T H. VONWAGNER
" PETER ISAAC VOSBURGH
LIEUT. WILLIAM A. FORBES
" JOHN FURMAN
" DANIEL GAUS
" BENJAMIN GILBERT
" ABRAHAM HARDENBERGH
" NATHANIEL HENRY
" EBENEZER HILLS
" JOHN HOOGHEIR
" JOHN HOUSTON
" SAMUEL LEWIS
" RANALD T. MCDOUGALL
" PETER MAGEE
" CHRISTOPHER MILLER
" WILLIAM MOULTON
" CHRISTOPHER MULLER

" EDWARD NICOLS
" DIGBY ODLUM
" JAMES WILLIAM PAYNE
" BENJAMIN PELTON
" JONATHAN PIERCY
" MICHAEL RYAN
" WILHELM RYCKMAN
" BARENT STAATS SALSBURY
" WILLIAM SCUDDER
" ADIEL SHERWOOD
" EPHRAIM SNOW
" JOHN WILLIAM WATKIN
" JACOB H. WENDELL
ENSIGN LUTHER BISSEL
" WILLIAM BLOODGOOD
" JONATHAN BROWN
" ALEXANDER CLINTON
" WILLIAM W. DEPEYSTER
" JAMES FAIRLY
" DOUW J. FONDA
" JOHN FONDA
" DOUW FONDEY
" THEADOSIA FOWLER
" BENJAMIN GILBERT
" THOMAS HAIGHT
" BENJAMIN HERRING
" THOMAS HICKS
" NICHOLAS KETTLE
" JACOB I. KLOCK
ENSIGN GARRET G. LANSING
" GILBERT R. LIVINGSTON
" JOHN McCLUNG
" JOHN MARSH
" JAMES MOORE
" JOSEPH MORRELL
" JEREMIAH C. MULLER
" ELIAS PALMER
" GEORGE PALMER
" JOSEPH PUTMAN
" CORNELIUS C. ROOSEVELT
" WILHELM RYCKMAN
" ADAM TEN BROECK
" JEREMIAH VAN RENSSELAER
" JOHN WALDRON
" JOHN PERKINS WENDELL
" SAMUEL YOUNG

ENLISTED MEN

Abbee Samuel
Abenather Jiles
Able Hendrick

Able John
Acker Albert
Acker Conrad

Ackerson Jacob
Ackinson James
Aoldland Francis

127

Ackler John
Ackley Joel
Acklin Francis
Adaar Alexander
Adams Emanuel
Adams James
Adams John
Adams Matthew
Adams Samuel
Adams Thomas
Adams William
Adamy Henry
Addams Albertus
Adier Alexander
Africa Cask
Agard Joseph
Agard Judah
Agard Noah
Aim George
Aitkins Andrew
Akens Moses
Algoyer Bastian
Alhiser George
Alkinkrack John
Allen Amissy
Allen John
Allen Jonathan
Allen Richard
Allen Samuel
Althiser George
Altiser Jeremiah
Amarr John
Amerman Jam
Ammermam Obadiah
Amory John
Anderson Cornelius
Anderson David
Anderson Durias
Anderson Samuel
Anderson William P
Anson Lockward
Anthony John
Anthony Peter
Appart John
Arlow John
Armstrong Adam
Armstrong Archibald
Armstrong John
Armstrong Thomas
Artwick Cristian
Artwick Lawrence
Ash Henry
Atkinson James

Auston Lockward
Babbat Reuben
Babbitt John
Babcock Elias
Babtist John
Bacchus George
Bacchus John
Backer Christopher
Backhorn Jacob
Bacon Thomson
Badger Joshua
Badinger Philip
Bacchus George
Bacchus John
Bagley David
Bailey John
Bailis Elias
Baily Joseph
Baise James
Baker Benjamin
Baker Christopher
Baker Elnathan
Baker Hendrick
Baker Henry
Baker Ichabod
Baker John
Baker Joseph
Baldwin Cornelius
Baldwin David
Ball Joseph
Ball Robert
Ballantine William
Ballard Benone
Baman Trueman
Bambridge Charles
Bangle John
Banks Benjamin
Bannon Edward
Baptiste John
Barclay John
Bardeen Robert
Barker Stephen
Barman Ebenezer
Barnes Henry
Barnes Patrick
Barnhart John
Barret John
Barret William
Barrett Walter
Barrit James
Barron John
Barry John
Barse Isaiah

Bartholomew Daniel
Bartow Lasha
Basharow John
Basiel Michael
Bass Henry
Bassaroon John
Bassell Richard
Bates Conrad
Bates Justice
Batis Conradt
Battersby Robert
Battic John
Bauman Lemuel
Bawn Samuel
Baxter Lockwood
Baxter William
Baylis John
Beadle Moses
Bealor Jacob
Bealor Joseph
Beard Jam
Bears David
Beckweth Jedediah
Beddinger Phillip
Bedner Johan Christian
Beeby Ezra
Beedle John
Beedle Moses
Beekman John
Beidell Thomas
Bell John
Bell Robert
Beneway Ezekiel
Benford George
Beng William
Benham James
Bennet Charles
Bennet Henry
Bennett William
Bennitt James
Bermingham James
Berrnerd Samuel
Berryhill John
Berve Jacob
Berwist John
Bevans Benjamin
Beven Benjamin
Bevie Jacob
Bevins Jacob
Bice Henry
Bice Peter
Biggraft Georgre
Biller Michael

Billington Elias
Bingham Abisha
Birch Isaiah
Bishop James
Bishop John
Blaar Jacob
Black Archibald
Black David
Black John
Black Peter
Blair Kelso
Blanch James
Blanchard Ephraim
Blancher Ephraim
Blanck Cornelius
Blatner John
Blayer John
Blie Christian
Blie Daniel
Blie John C.
Bliss Samuel
Blom Albart
Bloom Albert
Bloom John
Blowers Ephraim
Blue Daniel
Blum Albert
Boere J.
Bogardus Hendrick
Bogart Gilbert
Bogart John
Boice James
Boice John
Bolton James
Bolton John
Bolton Matthew
Bolton William Livingston
Bombreys George
Bonnell Nathaniel
Bonnell Simeon
Booker John
Boom Frederick
Boom John
Boom Nicholas
Boon John
Borgordes David
Bornhart John
Boss Joseph
Bouch William
Bourguin John James
Bourk John
Bourns John
Bouse Henry

Bouse James
Bouse Peter
Bouy William
Bovie Jacob
Bovie Mathew
Bowen John
Bowen Wessel
Bower George
Bowman Albert
Boyce James
Boyce John
Boyd George
Boyd Jonah
Boyd Jonathen
Boyd William
Boyer Godlep
Boyle Philip
Brader Andrew
Brading John
Bradley James
Bradshaw William
Bradt James
Brady Thomas
Bragin John
Braidey Richard
Brand Henry
Brand Isaac
Brandoes George
Brant Christian
Brant Christopher
Brasher Henry
Brass Abraham
Brass John
Bray Thomas
Breadinbaker Baltes
Bredenbaker W.
Brend Isaac
Brewton Bartholomew
Briggs John
Brighton John
Britlingar Frederick
Broadbrook Edward
Bromagham Thomas
Bromley John
Bromley Simon
Bromley William
Broughton Bartholomew
Brown Charles F.
Brown David
Brown Elisha
Brown Evert
Brown Francis
Brown George

Brown Isaac
Brown James
Brown James, 2d
Brown John
Brown Joseph
Brown Nathaniel
Brown Nicholas
Brown Thomas
Brown Thomas B.
Brownan Samuel
Browne Nicholas
Bruce Benjamin
Bruch David
Bruin Moses
Bruless Elias
Brumbly John
Brumbly William
Brumley John
Brumley Simon
Brumley William
Brunck Casper
Bruster Benjamin
Bruter Arthur
Bruton Bartholomew
Bryan John
Bryan Paul O.
Buckett John
Buckhout James
Buel Abel
Buel Ezra
Buis James
Bulger John
Bullack Archibald
Bullion William
Burch Isaiah
Burch Philip
Burch Samuel
Burck Edmund
Burgess Michael
Burk John
Burk Patrick
Burkdoff John
Burkstaff Peter
Burn Daniel
Burn David
Burnes Barney
Burnes Henry
Burnham William
Burns Frederick
Burns Robert
Burr William
Burrough Nathan
Burrough Thomas

Burton Bartholomew
Burve Matthew
Burvis Thomas
Bush John
Bushland Patrick
Butler John
Buttler Thomas
Button Thomas
Buyford Henry
Buys James
Buzer Fetter
Byerd Godfrey
Byington David
Cable Jacob
Cable Zabulon
Cahel Robert
Cahill Cornelius
Cahill John
Cain Abel
Cain Henry
Caldwell Mathew
Caldwell Philip
Callichan John
Cambell Robert
Camell George
Cameron Daniel
Cameron Hugh
Campbell Archibald
Campbell Burdee
Campbell Canute
Campbell Duncan
Campbell George
Campbell Hugh
Campbell James
Campbell John
Campble Burdock
Campble Kenneth
Canada John
Canal John
Cane Henry
Canely Patrick
Canfield Dennis
Canfield Thomas
Canfield Timothy
Cannon Thomas
Canter Jonas
Cappurnal Adam
Carmack William
Carman Abraham
Carman Hendrick
Carman Joseph
Carman Samuel
Carman Thomas

Carman Willet
Carmichael John
Carr Dan
Carr William
Carter Jeremiah
Carter Rubin
Case Joseph
Casey James
Casey John
Casey Robert
Cashel R.
Cassedy Edward
Casselman Christian
Castelman Christophal
Casterline Hiram
Catch John
Cater William
Catline Bradley
Cator William
Catterling Matthias
Causton John
Celia John
Chace Robert
Chadwine Lewis
Chambers Leonard
Chanels John
Chapey Stephen
Charles Christian
Charlsworth John M.
Charters James
Chase Jacob
Chase John
Chase Robert
Chasey Stephen
Chasley Peter
Chatfield David
Chatfield Samuel
Chatnell Christopher
Chatterton Joseph
Chattin William
Chilner Christopher
Christainsa Peter
Christian Charles
Christian Zachariah
Churchill Stephen
Cidney Rodolph
Clapper Peter
Clark Benjamin
Clark John
Clark Ransome
Clark William
Clarke Anthony
Clement Nicholas

CLements Jacob
Clinton Joseph
Clopper Peter
Clough Benjamin
Coakly John
Cockley John
Codwise George P.
Cogden John
Collard Abraham
Collard Edward
Collins James
Collins Joseph
Colwell Philip
Commadine Nicholas
Condo William
Connelly John
Conoway William
Cook John, Sr.
Cook John, Jr.
Cooper John
Cooper Thomas
Copeland William
Copernoll Adam
Corigal John
Cornelius Hendrick
Cornwall Caleb
Corter John
Coster John
Cotter James
Countz Adam
Cousin Matthew
Cousins Matthew
Cowdry Benjamin
Cox Charles
Craig John
Crak Godlip
Cranck John
Crandle Godfrey
Crank John
Crantz Mark
Crapow Peter
Crawford Samuel
Crickenboom Johannes
Cronkhite John
Cronkhite Patrick
Crosson Samuel
Crouse Albert
Crouse Elbert
Crowder Anthony
Crowfoot Samuel
Cummins Cornelius
Cummins John
Curry Thomas

Daily Nathan
Dalton Benjamin
Dalton John
Daniel George
Daniels Henry
Daniels Thomas
Darling Ephraim
Darling Moses
Daugherty William
Davenport James
David Isaac
Davidson William
Davis Cornelius
Davis Daniel
Davis David
Davis Evan
Davis John
Davis Richard
Dawler George
Dawson Daniel
Day Aaron
Day William
Dean Henry
Dean James
Dean Samuel
Dean William
Debbedy Brent
Debois John
Debois Lewis
Debrouce John
De Camp Matthias
Decker John
Decker John H.
De Clark Abraham
Deforest Abraham
Defrance John H.
Defreest Abraham
De Freest Henry
Degrushe Ellas
Delamater John
Delong Daniel
Delong Ezekiel
Demont Joseph
Demount HenJost
Dennis John
Dennison Daniel
Denniston Daniel
De Pew John
De Roshea Anthony
Derotter George
De Statsmarn Jean
De Vaults Peter
Devenport Daniel

Devenport John
Devinport Thomas
Devrance Henry
Dewit Aaron
Deyo Hugh
Dickens William
Dickson James
Dickson John
Dimmuck Samuel
Dingman Abraham
Dingman Adam
Dingman Gerrardus
Dingman John
Dobbs William
Dodge Alexander
Doghorthy Mark
Doleway Andrew
Dolton Frederick
Donaghy Patrick
Donally John
Donnelly James
Donoven John
Dority Francis
Dorn John
Dorrity William
Dorson Daniel
Dorum Stephen
Doty Isaac
Dougall Thomas
Doughaty John
Dougherty Charles
Dougherty William
Doughty Elias
Doughty John
Douglass George
Douglass James
Douglass Jonas
Douglass William
Dowler George
Downing Andrew
Downing Richard
Downs Patrick
Drincks Andrew
Drum Jacob
Duboise Lewis
Duff David
Dulhagin Frederick
Duncan George
Duncan James
Duncan John
Duncomb Dennis
Dunford Wells
Dunham Andres

Dunham Stephen
Dunham Sylvanus
Dunhom Iseral
Dunlap James
Dunlap John
Dunn Joseph
Dunnavin Daniel
Dunning Jacob
Dunning Jesse
Dunning Michael
Dunnivan John
Dunscomb Edward
Durgen Patrick
Durham Stephen
Durkir Mathew
Dutcher Benjamin
Dutcher Bernard
Dutcher David
Dutcher Derrick
Dutcher Henry
Dyckman Joseph
Dyke John
Dyke Joseph
Eagins Joshua
Earnestpier Joh
Earvin James
Easterly Thomas
Easton Henry
Eaton George
Echler John
Ecker Lambart
Ecklar John
Edds Joseph
Edes Joseph
Edgerly John
Edmans Matthew
Eggens Joshua
Eggs Samuel
Eison Aaron
Ekons Samuel
Eldridge Jonathan
Eldridge Joseph
Eligon Abraham
Eligon John
Elliott Francis
Elliott John
Ellis Benjamin
Ellis Daniel
Ellis William
Elliss Thomas
Elverson William
Elverston Edward
Elviston William

Elwiston Edward
Elwiston William
Emingway Samuel
Emrich Hendrick
Ennis Henry
Erven James
Erwin Andrew
Erwin James
Essmond John
Euerhite John
Evans Joseph
Evans Patrick
Everan Martin
Eveults Stephen D.
Ewing Benjamin
Eyres William
Fairchild Jesse
Falter Augustus
Fargerson James
Farguson William
Farrel Garret
Farrol John
Fauck Jacob
Fealay John
Feishler George
Felly Augustus
Felte Augustus
Fergueson John
Ferguson Israel
Ferguson James
Ferguson Robert
Ferguson William
Ferrell John
Ferris John
Ferry John
Fichter George
Field Patrick
Filty Augustus
Finch Jonathan
Finn Thomas
Finney John
Firkins James
Fisher George
Fitch Caleb
Fitzgerald John
Fitzgibbons William
Fleming Michael
Fletcher James
Flick Martin
Fling Henry
Fling Thomas
Flinn Andrew
Flinn John

Flint Jonathan
Flood Francis
Floods Alexander
Florince Thomas
Flyhearty Stephen
Flynn John
Fonna Anthony
Foor John C.
Forbes Alexander
Forbush Alexander
Forbush Bartholomew
Forbush Jacob
Force David
Ford John
Ford Timothy
Foreman Christian
Forgason Hazekiel
Forguson James
Forneyea John
Foster James
Foster John
Foster William
Fothergill Hugh
Fothingill Hugh
Foulks Robert
Foulstrow Henry
Foushee Pedro
Fowler James
Fowlstroh Henry
Fox Philip
Foy David
Foy Edmond
Foy Edward
Foy Patrick
Fradenbergh Petter
France Conrad
Franck Jacob
Fraser Jeremiah
Fravel Henry
Frazer Duncan
Frazer Jeremy
Frazer John
Frazier Jeremiah
Frazier Simeon
Frederick John
Fredinburgh Isaac
Fredinburgh Matthew
Fredinburgh Peter
Fredrick John
Freehart Lewis
Freeland John
Freeman Elisha
Freeman Obadiah

Freeman Stephen
Freeman Thomas
French Jacob
French Joseph
Freyenschiner George
Friday Conrad
Friensiner George
Frilick Joseph
Frinck Elisha
Frisbee Edward
Frost Edmund
Frost Samuel
Fry Christopher
Frye Peter
Fullen Michael
Fullerton John
Fulmer George
Fulton Francis
Funna Anthony
Furman Gabriel
Fyingling John
Gadge John
Gaites Michael
Galaspy William
Galbreath Richard
Gallaway James
Gallaway John
Gamble Thomas
Gankins Philip
Ganoshow Peter
Gantly Peter
Gardener Andrew
Gardener Peter
Gardenier Samuel
Gardineer Gilbert
Gardineer Peter
Gardner Jacob
Gardner Levy
Gardner Peter
Gardner Thoffias
Gardner William
Garrat Samuel
Garret James
Garrison Abraham
Garrison Hartshorn
Garrison Peter
Garter Henry
Gasper Peter
Gates Michael
Geabs Addem
Geers Benjamin
Genung Benjamin
Geonovoly Samuel

George Robert
Germain Isaac
Gibbs Eliakim
Gibbs Simeon
Gibson Thomas
Gifford William
Gilaspy William
Gilbert John C.
Gilbert Samuel
Gill James
Gilmor William
Ginnings Solomon
Ginnis Peter
Glasbey William
Gleeson Thomas
Glen Robert
Glenney William
Godington William
Godwin William
Goff Isaac
Goff Joseph
Goldar William
Goodale Benjamin
Goodcourage John
Goodwin William
Goolsmith Jeremiah
Gordenear John
Gorman Patrick
Gorman Richard
Gouss Jacob
Grace James
Grady Thomas
Graham Robert
Grant Allen
Grant Benone
Grant Jacob
Graw James
Gray Eliphalet
Gray James
Gray John
Gray Philip
Green Boswart
Green Charles
Green Peter
Green Silas
Green Timothy
Gregg Thomas
Griffon Benjamil
Griffiths Barney
Grimes Samuel
Grimseley William
Grite William
Groote William

Gross John
Grote William
Groundhart George
Guilleeo John
Gundellow John
Guth John G.
Guthrie Abram
Gutlich Christian Ernest
Haburn William
Hadger Robert
Hadley Bishop
Hadlock James
Hagarty John
Hagerman Nicholas
Haily John
Haise Thomas
Hait Joseph
Hale John
Halinbeck Aaron
Halinbeck Casper
Hall Charles
Hall G.
Hall James
Hall Simon
Hall William
Hallebrant John
Halmer Leaord
Ham Thomas
Haman John F.
Hamilton James
Hamilton William
Hamlet Richard
Hamilton George
Hammon Daniel
Hanimond Daniel
Hand David
Handell John
Handerson Samuel
Handley Thomas
Hanford Obadiah
Hanion Ede
Hankey John
Hanley John
Hannawell John
Harman Jacob
Harpear William
Harrious Hendrick
Harris David
Harris George
Harris Hendrick
Harris Michael
Harris Thomaa
Harris William

Harris Zachariah
Harrison Levi
Harrison Philip
Harriss Richard
Hart Thomas
Harter Adam
Hartigh John
Hartiwick Christian
Harvey William
Harway John
Hasan John
Hattis Thomas
Hauff John
Haven John
Havens Joseph
Hawel Aaron
Hawes Joseph
Hawke John Wain
Hawkins Isaac
Hawkins John
Haycock John
Haydon Hosea
Hayes Thomas
Haynes Thomas
Hays Stephen
Hays William
Hazard Raymond
Heard David
Heathcrock David
Heavens Joseph
Hedgers Dayton
Height Stephen
Heller Nicholas
Helmer Anyost
Helmer John
Helmer John, Jr.
Helmer John Dedrick
Helmer John Jost
Helmer Philip
Helmer Richard
Helmes H.
Helts Frederick
Hemingway Samuel
Hemminway Isaac
Hender Frederick
Henderson Elisha
Henderson Patrick
Henderson Samuel
Henderson William
Hendrickson Cornelius
Hendry David
Henford Obadiah
Henkey John

Henly David
Henning John C.
Herd Joseph
Herter Adam
Hervey William
Hews James
Heyer Jacob
Hicklin William
Hiddy James
Hide Thomas
Hier Jacob
Higbey Samuel
Higby John
Higgins Archibald
Higgins Samuel
Higgins Thomas
Hildredth Elijah
Hill Ebenezer
Hill Henry
Hill John
Hill Nicholas
Hill Samuel
Hilton William
Hilts Frederick
Hines Thomas
Hines William
Hipe Jacob
Hitchcock James
Hoaksly James
Hoareford Jesse
Hodge Abraham
Hodge David
Hodge James
Hodge Stephen
Hodges David
Hofman Aaron
Hofman Andrew
Hogan Patrick
Hogan Roger
Hogle John
Holbert Aaron
Hollay Samuel
Holley Benjamin
Holms David
Honeywell John
Hooper Jacob R.
Hooper Robert R.
Hope Thomas
Hopkins Samuel
Hopkins William
Hopp Abraham
Hoppell John
Hopping Ebraham

Hoppole John
Horner George
Horsford Jesse
Horsmer George
Horton Thomas
Hosford Ithamer
Hosier Thomas
Hoskins Thomas
Houff John
Hous John
House Christian
House Jacob
House John
Howard Randal
Howard William
Howell Aaron
Hoyt Thomas
Hubbard Adam
Hubbard Caleb
Hubbell Isaac
Hudson Bernard
Hudson John
Hudson William
Huff Abraham
Huff John
Huff William
Huffman Aaron
Huffman Andrew
Huffsteder Christian
Hufnegal Christian
Huges James
Hughes John
Hughes Joseph
Hughes Michael
Hughes Thomas
Hulbert Aaron
Hull David
Hull William
Humphreys David
Hungerford Daniel
Hunter Jonathan
Hurd Elijah
Hurley Anthony
Hurley Arthur
Hurligh John
Hurtock John
Huston John
Huston Silvenis
Hutcheons Edward
Hutchins Jedidiah
Hutchins John
Hutt John
Hutton Andrew

Hutton Robert
Huxley James
Hyatt Abraham
Hyde Thomas
Hyer Alexander
Hyer Jacob
Hyme Conradt
Hynes Thomas
Hyre Jacob
Indian Stepny
Ingersol John
Ingoson John
Isaacs Isaac
Jabely Jacob
Jackson Archibald
Jackson Francis
Jacobs John
Jacobus John
Jamison Alexander
Jarvice Joseph
Jenks Thomas
Jennings Luke
Jennings Solomon
John Francis
John Jeremiah
Johnson Abraham
Johnson David
Johnson Josiah
Johnson Nicholas
Johnson Shubael
Johnson William
Johnston John
Johson Nicholas
Jolly Richard
Jolly William
Jones David
Jones Edward
Jones Evan
Jones Ezra
Jones Jacob
Jones James
Jones Simon
Jones Thomas
Jones William
Jonsons William
Jonston Edward
Jonston James
Jordan Robert
Jordon Thomas
Joseph Peter
Joseph Reuben
Juell John
Kablem Reuben

Kady John
Kallam Reuben
Kanely Patrick
Karnes Georee
Karr Mark
Kater James
Kater Wilhelimu
Keady Daniel
Kearish Frederick
Keef Arthur
Keef William
Keelen Icabud
Keeler John
Kefelty Felte
Kelch John
Kelch Nicholas
Keller John
Keller Nicholas
Kelly David
Kelly Hugh
Kelly Patrick
Kelly Philip
Kelme Lemuel Jones
Kelsh John
Kelsh Nicholas
Kelts C.
Keltz Nicholas
Kendrick Thomas
Kener Christian
Kennedy Robert
Kent Jacob
Kepple John
Kerby Thomas
Kerfer Henry
Kerk George
Kerr Abner
Kerr Anthony
Kerr Henry
Kerr James
Kerr Mark
Ketch John
Kets Conradt
Kett Richard
Keyser Henry
Keyser John
Kidd Alexander
Kiddy James
Kiddy John
Kilburn Zacheus
Killer John
Killer Nicholas
Killip Alexander
Kils John

Kilts Conradt
Kimon Robert
Kincaid William
King John
King William
Kingsland Nathaniel
Kinler Nicholas
Kinter Nicholas
Kirby Thomas
Kirk George
Kirkland William
Kitchel Matthew
Kller John
Knap Aaron
Knap Mathew
Knight John
Korl George
Korl Saverines
Krak Godlip
Kronkhite John
Kronkhite Patrick
Kunnian Benjamin
Kyser Henry
Lackey Hugh
Ladd Joseph
Lafferty John
Lafling John
La Lancit John
Lamb Joseph
Lambert Abraham
Lambert John
Lambson Thomas
Lampier Francis
Lander Edward
Landon Benjamin
Lane Thomas
Lang James
Lanpher John
Lansing Gerrit
Lasher Jacob
Latemore Roger
Lathers Ezekiel
Laughlin Barnard
Laverty John
Lavey John
Lawell Abraham
Lawn George
Lawrence Isaac
Lawrence Jacob
Lawrence Mathew
Laybagh Abraham
Leaplink John
Leuthier Ezekiel

Lecky Hugh
Lee Daniel
Lee David
Lee Robert
Lees Martin
Left John
Lemon Alexander
Lenny Philip
Lent Hercules
Lent Moses
Leonard Robert
Leonard Thomas
Leroy Henry
Lestor Thomas
Lestrange Samuel
Letahers Ezekiel
Lewee John
Lewes Lockert
Lewey John
Lewis Henry
Lewis James
Lewis John
Lewis Joseph
Lewis Lockard
Lewis Peter
Lewis William
Lewman Peter
Lewy John
Light James
Light Lemuel
Lighthall Abraham
Lighthall James
Lighthall John
Lighthall Lancaster
Lighthart Daniel
Limbaker John
Linch Owen
Linch William
Lindsey Abraham
Linegar John
Liniger John
Link Henry
Linn Aaron
Linsey Abraham
Lint Philip
List John
Littall A.
Littlejone John
Lock Philip
Lockhart Hugh
Locksul John
Lockwood Anson
Loft John

Logan Thomas
Loik Philip
Loman Peter
Lombaker John
Long Andrew
Long Elias D.
Longley John
Lonkes Nicholas
Loomes Peter
Loosie Jacob
Louckas Petter
Loucks Andrew
Loucks John
Loucks Jost
Loucks Matthew
Loudon William
Loughren Hugh
Louis John
Loux Hendrick
Love Davis
Lovejoy John
Low James
Low John
Lowdor William
Lower Henry
Lower Jacob
Lowman Peter
Lucherd Fredirick
Lucum John
Ludlow David
Ludlow Samuel
Lugar Christ
Luse Robert
Lusk Michel
Luthar John
Lyby John
Lynch James
Lynch Michael
Lynch Owen
Lynch William
Lyney John
Lyon Ebenezer
Lyon Joseph
Lyons James
Lysle John
Lytle William
McAlpin William
McArthur Duncan
McArthur John
McCally Hugh
McCann Mich
McCarrol Joseph
McCarthy Daniel

McCarty Dennis
McCauley James
McCawley Hugh
McCevers James
McChesnay William
McChesney John
McClane Daniel
McClaughlin Bernard
McClean Anthony
McClean John
McCloud Daniel
McClough Joseph
McClure Moses
McCollough Andrew
McColly Hugh
McColm Samuel
McColum Ruben
McComin John
McConnel Hugh
McConnel William
McConnoly Hugh
McCord William
McCormac Bryan
McCormic John
McCormick James
McCoy Alexander
McCoy George
McCoy James
McCoy William
McCracken William
McCullom Samuel
McDaniel Daniel
McDaniel Michael
McDavitt Henry
McDermot Cornelius
McDonald Daniel
McDonald Donald
McDonald Hugh
McDonald James
McDonald John
McDonald Michael
McDonald William
McDonnell James
McDormet Cornelius
McDormot Henry
McDougall James
McDougall John
McDowal Ben
McDugle William
McElroy James
McEntosch John
McFall Paul
McFarland Hosea

McFarland John
McFarlin Hosser
McFarlin John
McFarling Thomas
McGaryhee Edward
McGauchee Edward
McGee James
McGerrihe Edward
McGinis Daniel
McGinly James
McGinnis John
McGinnis Stephen
McGlaughlin John
McGraw John
McGreggor Daniel
McGriger John
McGuigan Michael
McGurchy Edward
McIntire Bernard
McIntire Phinias
McIntire Thomas
McIntosh John
Mackarell Joseph
McKay Alexander
Mackay Alexander
McKay Alexander A.
McKay John A. A.
McKay William
McKeel Michael
McKellop Alexander
McKenney John
McKenny James
McKenzie Malcom
McKewn James
Mackey John A.
McKillip Alexander
McKinley Archibald
McKneal John
McKown James
McLain Anthony
McLane John
McLaughlin Bernard
McLaughlin John
McMaham Michael
McManes Hugh
McManus William
McMasters Alexander
McMickell John
McNeal John
McNeil John
McQuarter William
McQuin Philip
McRannels Owen

McWilliam James
Madison Samuel
Mafit John
Mahan Patrick
Mahon John
Maitor John
Maker Solomon
Mallad Andrew
Malone John
Manchester Elias
Manes Isaac
Mansey Nathan
Manuel Andrew
Mapes Phineas
Mara Patrick
Marche Anthony
Marcle Henry
Marines George
Marjason Frederick
Markee John
Marony Alexander
Marony Florence
Marricle Anthony
Marricle Henry
Marricle Samuel
Marsden Humphrey
Marselis Garret
Marsh Ephraim
Marsh John
Marshal Simeon
Marshall Robert
Marshall Thomas
Marstes Jonathan
Martin John
Martler Peter
Marull Henry
Masden Humphrey
Mash Ephraim
Mason George
Masters Jonathan
Master George Peter
Mathews James
Matrat Fransis
Matrat Gidion
Maxwell Cornelius
May Henry
Mazure Christian
Mead John
Measal Peter
Medcalf William
Meeker Solomon
Meeker Uzel
Mcgun James

Meggs Seth
Mellon Charles
Melony John
Mennen Robert
Meradeth Peter
Merral John
Merricle Henry
Merrill John
Merrit Stephen
Merselus Garret
Messenger Uriah
Michells Thomas
Mike John
Miles John
Millar John
Millard Daniel
Miller Alexander
Miller Casper
Miller Daniel
Miller David
Miller Henry
Miller Nicholas
Miller Peter
Miller Thomas
Millner Thomas
Mills Alexander
Mills John
Mineck Henry
Miner Moses
Ming Edward
Mingas Morris
Mingas Moses
Minick Barnhart
Mipe John
Mitchel Ensign
Mitchel Joseph
Mitchell Edward
Mitchell George
Mitchell Hugh
Mitchell James
Mitchell Penant
Mitchell Vinant
Molay John
Molter Peter
Momenday David
Monday William
Money Ambisct
Monger Benjamin
Monger Bouten
Montgomery James
Mooney William
Moore Abraham
Moore Frederick

Moore John
Moore Marcus
Moore Philip
Moore Pliny
Moore Richard
Moore Robert
Moore Thomas
Moore William
Moorewise Daniel
More Jacob
More Martin
More Thomas
Morey Thomas
Morgan James
Morgan John
Moroney Florence
Morrell William
Morris Edmund
Morris Harvey M.
Morris Isaac
Morris James
Morrison Edward
Morrison Hugh
Morrisson Richard
Morrow Andrew
Mosher Hezekiah
Mosher Nicholas
Moss Daniel
Moss Ebenezer
Moss Isaac
Moss Stephen
Mott Samuel
Mott Thomas
Mountanye Jacobus
Mounts Richard
Muche Johannis
Mulford Ezekiel
Mulholland James
Mullen John
Muller Peter
Mulligen Philip
Mulony William
Multer Peter
Mumford James
Muncey Nathaniel
Munday David
Munroe Alexander
Munrose Elijah
Munsey Nathaniel
Murey Bartley
Murphey Daniel
Murphy Edward
Murray Bartly

Murray George
Murray James
Murray William
Musta Mathew
Mutry James
Mutter Peter
Myers Frederick
Myers Henry
Myres Jacob
Nafee Garret
Nagle Fradrick
Narley Mathus
Neal Jeremiah
Nebby Michael
Neilson Allen
Nellson Allen
Nelme Lemuel Jones
Nelson John
Nesbit Joseph
Newman William
Newtown Jonathan
Nicholls George
Nickason Ellphas
Niel John
Niet Thomas
Nisbit Joseph
Norse Goorope
Northon Henry
Northwear George
Norton George
Norton Henry
Norton John
Notewear George
Nott Samuel
Nottingham Thomas
Notz Jacob
Nutter William
Oar William
O'Brian Andrew
Obrine Cornelius
O'Bryan John
O'Bryan Thomas
O'Cain Jeremiah
Odie Joshua
Odie Richard
O'Donaghy Patrick
O'Farrel Michael
Ogden Daniel
Ohlin Henry G.
Olen Henry G.
Olendorf Leonard
Olendorph Samuel
Oliphant William

Olmsted Nehemiah
Ondekirk Myndert
O'Neil Charles
O'Neil James
Onele John
Ootesohoudt Peter P.
Orr Baltis
Orr William
Osburn Aaron
Osmur John
Osterhout Isaac
Ostrander Peter William
Otter Isaac
Oudeskirk Myndert
Owens Daniel
Owens Terence
Owens Uriah
Paddock John
Padrow Dennis
Painter Edward
Painter Frederick
Palmer Jabish
Palmeteer Isaac
Pangborn Beeby
Pangborn Noah
Pangborn Samuel
Pangburn Jonathan
Park Timothy
Parker Edward
Parker Elisha
Parker Isaac
Parker James
Parker John
Parker Nathaniel
Parker Richard
Parker Richard Jr.
Parker Richard J.
Parkhoof Frederick
Parks John
Parry Richard
Paterson James
Paterson Thomas
Pathen Ebenezer
Patrick Robert
Pattan Edward
Patterson Edward
Patterson James
Patterson John
Patterson Joseph
Patterson William
Paul Arthur
Paul William
Payne Richard

Peak William
Pearse John
Peas Nathaniel
Pease Conrad
Pease Hanyost
Pease John
Peck William
Peen John
Peers John
Pell John
Perau John
Perigo Usal
Perkhoff Frederick
Perkins James
Perkins Joseph
Perry William
Perse John
Peters John
Petry Jacob
Pettit Samuel
Pettit William
Phelps Israel
Phelps Jonathan
Phillip Wouter
Phillips William
Philpsa Christian
Pickering Richard
Pier John Ernest
Piggle Henry
Pilgrett Henry
Pinkney Jonathan
Piper Lewis
Pippinger Abraham
Pitter William
Plainer John
Platto Thomas
Plimley Henry
Plough Dennis
Plowman Christopher
Plumley Henry
Poff George
Porter Elisha
Porter Nathaniel
Potter Samuel
Poulson Michael
Povey Joseph
Pratt Charles
Preble Samuel
Preston Benjamin
Preston Jonathan
Preston Othniel
Prett Jacob
Price Adam

Price James	Reed Joseph	Rooker Joseph
Prime Michael	Reed Nathaniel	Roomer William
Primley Henry	Reed Thomas	Roosa Albert
Prindle Jotham	Reemer George	Roppolt George
Prine William	Rees Martinis	Rose Albert
Proctor Robert	Reily Thomas	Rose Andrew
Proper Frederick	Relay Lewis	Rose John
Prossor Philip	Rendolf Nathaniel	Rose Samuel
Prouth Degory	Rennix William	Rositer Charles
Pudney Thorn	Reonalds Isaac	Rosman Coenraedt
Pudny Francis	Requig Jacob	Rosman Frederick
Putman David	Retchey Charles	Rosman Philip
Quackenbos Cornelius	Revelea Eselea L.	Ross Simeon
Quackenbush Jacob	Revelea Lewis	Rossiter Charles
Quackenbush John	Rex James	Rotchery James
Quain Peter	Reyning Jacob	Rourk Mathew
Queen Christopher	Reynolds Abijah	Row Anthony
Quin Patrick	Richards Peter	Row James
Quinn William	Richards Samuel	Row Stephen
Rabal George	Richards Simon	Rowland Daniel
Race Charles	Richardson Isaac	Rowley Timothy
Radenbergh Peter	Richardson Robert	Ruckerstice John
Ragan William	Rickhow Abraham	Rudall William
Rains John	Ricmond Semion	Rude William
Rair John	Rider George	Rudolph Christian
Raljie David	Ridout David	Rudolph Christopher
Raljie John	Riemer Johan George	Ruland Thomas
Ramsey Adam	Riley James	Rumpass George
Rancier John	Rinder Christian	Runals James
Randell Henry	Risdall William	Rundle Henry
Randle Henry	Ritcherds Simon	Runian Benjamin
Randle Thomas	Ritchie Charles	Runnions Benjamin
Randolph Christopher	Ritter Moses	Russell James
Rankens James	Rivers Joseph	Russell John
Rankin James	Rivet Samuel	Russell Joseph
Rankins Daniel	Robennire Christian	Ryan Daniel
Rankins Thomas	Robert Jacob	Ryan Dennis
Ransier John	Roberts Thomas	Ryan J.
Ransur John	Robertson Richard	Ryan Robert
Ransur William	Robertson Ronert	Ryan Thomas
Rappolt George	Robertson William	Ryder George
Ravelia Lewis	Robins Aaron	Rynax William
Ray James	Robins John	Rynder Christian
Ray Michael	Robinson James	Rynders James
Read James	Robinson John	Rynders John
Reany David	Robinson Richard	Rynhart George
Rear John	Robisson Robert	Ryring Jacob
Rearden Thimothy	Rochery James	Sager John
Redding Frances	Rockwell Simeon	Sager Stotts
Redwood Prince	Rodman Joseph	Sailer Zacheus
Reece Martin	Rogers Allen	Sailor Jacob
Reed James	Role Samuel	St. Lawrence George
Reed John	Rood William	Salisbury Gasper

Salisbury John
Salisbury Joseph
Salley Andrew
Salmond William
Salsbery Joseph
Salsbury Cornelius V.
Saltsman Jane D.
Saltsman John
Saltsroan Peter
Salyer Zacheus
Sanders Robert
Sangh Peter
Santford John
Saultas Solomon
Saunders Robert
Savage Richard
Saxberry William
Sayer Robert
Scheehan Jeremiah
Schellenbergh George
Schoolcraft John
Schoolcreft Lawrence
Schreeder John J.
Schriner Lodewick
Schriver Peter
Schryver Christyan
Schultz John
Scofield Silvenus
Scott Edward
Scovill Silvenus
Screeder John J.
Scrivenor Zadock
Scriver Christopher
Seabrin Frederick
Seager John
Seager Staats
Seager Thomas
Seamore Henry
Scandlin James
Seeger John
Seely Ephraim
Seevey Joseph
Seggar John
Selfridge John
Selfridge William
Selyca Lewis
Semore Henry
Service Philip
Servis Daniel
Servis Philip
Sessinger Nicolas
Setler Andrew
Sevain Thomas

Sevey Joseph
Sexbury William
Shade John
Shankland Andrew
Shannon Thomas
Sharer James
Sharerer Lodewak
Sharlock John
Sharon John
Sharp Cornelius
Sharp John
Sharp Lewis
Sharp Thomas
Shaver Henry
Shearman Jesse
Shearman Peter
Sheely John
Shell George
Sheldon Joseph
Shelenbergh George
Shell Christopher
Shell Elisha
Shell George
Shell William
Shelly Cyrus
Shely John
Shepherd True
Sheppard Henry
Sheppard Thomas
Sherdeur Abraham
Sherlocke John
Sherman John
Sherman Peter
Sherriden James
Sherriden Richard
Sherwood Samuel
Shields Daniel
Shiels John
Shiffington John
Shilly Cyrus
Shipman John
Shirts Henry
Shirts John
Shirts Nathis
Shirts Peter
Showers Adam
Shrum Jacob
Shuetts John
Shufelt George
Shule J.
Shultze John
Shurtz Henry
Shuts John

Shutts Peter
Sickel John
Sickels Abraham
Sickels Zackariah
Sidsor Michael
Siles Christopher
Simmons John
Simmons Philip
Simmons Polter
Simpkins Gideon
Simpson James
Sinclair William
Sinnct John
Skeehan Jeremiah
Skellenbergh George
Skiffington John
Slate William
Slater Nicholas
Slighter Nicholas
Slingerlandt Peter
Sloane Hugh
Sluiter Jonas
Sluiter Nicholas
Slump Martin
Sluyter Jacob
Slyter James
Small George
Smalley Timothy
Smith Archibald
Smith Conraedt
Smith David
Smith Duncan
Smith Elihu
Smith George
Smith Isaac
Smith Jacob
Smith James
Smith John
Smith Joseph
Smith Robert
Smith Stephen
Smith Thomas
Smith William
Snell Zeley
Snyder Jacob
Solyer Zaecheus
Soper John
Soper Richard
Sorning Adam
Souls Thomas
Southerland Daniel
Sox Jacob
Spaperd Didimew

Sparick Christian
Spear Henry Frederick
Spears Jonathan
Speigler Henry
Sperick Christian
Spinne Daniel
Spirick Christian
Spray John
Spring Benjamin
Spur John
Squire Jonathan
Srader Christian
Staal Gorlegh
Stader Christian
Stagg Jasper
Stagg John
Stalker Malcome
Stall Charles
Stall Garlock
Stalsman John D.
Stanly Daniel
Stansbury William
Stanton Elijah
Stanton John
Starling Levi
Starr George
Stauder Christian
Steed Johannes
Steen William
Steinly John
Stephens Abraham
Stephens William
Stephenson John
Stering Adam
Stevens Abraham
Stewart Charles
Stewart Joshua
Stiles Moses
Stiller John
Stilt David
Stivers Caleb
Stock Charles
Stock George
Stockham Isaac
Stoddard Ichabud
Stokes John
Stone John
Storing Adam
Storm James
Stout John
Stoutenger George
Stoutenger John
Stover George

Stover Nechi
Stratton Husey
Strawder Christian
Strobridge James
Stryker Elias
Stump John
Stump Martin
Sturdivant Samuel
Sturgess Isaa
Stymeson Robert
Sudder Benjamin
Sudlow Samuel
Sulfridge William
Sullivan Cornelius
Sutherland Daniel
Sutton Benjamin
Sutton James
Swales John Commons
Swan Joshua
Swaney Daniel
Swartwout Cornelius
Swartwout Henry
Swartwout Simon
Swayer Lambart
Swigar Paul
Syle Christopher
Tably Jacob
Tabor Edward
Tagget Robert
Talbot William
Talmadg John
Tare Godfry
Tarrey Nathaniel
Taylor Edmund
Taylor George
Taylor William
Temple Joseph
Tenneray Zopher
Tepperwine Christian
Terry Nathaniel
Tharp David
Tharp Peter
Tharp Thomas
Thomas Edmund
Thomas Ezekiel
Thomas John
Thompson Alexander
Thompson Andrew
Thompson James
Thompson John
Thompson John (2)
Thompson William
Thorn Peter

Thorp Richard
Thurner William
Tiercy John
Tilsey John
Tipperwine Christian
Titsworth Thomas
Titus John
Tobin Edward
Tobley Jacob
Tolbard William
Tolbert William
Tombs John
Tombs Stephen
Tomkins Abraham
Tomkins Edward
Tomkins Israel
Tool John
Toorel Roger
Torbin Edward
Totton Samuel
Townley Joshua
Trigleth Richard
Tully Samuel
Turnbull William
Turner John
Turner Samuel
Tuttle Joel
Uens William
Uthest John
Utter Gilbert
Valence William
Valentine William
Van Allen John
Van Alstin Abraham
Van Amborough Abraham
Van Amburgh Abraham
Van Atler Joseph
Van Atta John
Van Atta Joseph
Van Benthuysen Martin
Van Beuren George
Van Blarcum Jacobus
Van Blarcum James
Van Bluck John
Van Bonhagel John C. B.
Van Buran George
Van Cleef Lawrence
Van Debal Jacob
Van De Bogart Gysbert
Van Debogert James
Van Denbergh Daniel
Vanderboc Jacob
Vanderbogart Nicholas

Van Derbow Jacob
Van Derhoof Cornelius
Vanderhyden Adam
Vanderhyden Derrick
Vanderhyden Gersham
Vanderwerker Jacob
Van Derwerker James
Van Derwerkin Martin
Van Deshider Adam
Van Deusen Abraham
Van Devore John
Vande Water Cornelius
Vandueus William
Van Dyck Peter
Van Dyck Peter T.
Van Etten Jacob
Van Etten John
Van Etten Joseph
Van Everin Martin
Vangothnet Joseph
Van Hauren Cornelius
Van Hoaft John
Van Hook Isaac I.
Van Houton John
Van Kleeck Henry
Van Kleeck James
Van Loan Nicholas
Van Ness Cornelius
Van Netten Joseph
Van Orden Albert
Van Order Charles
Van Salisbury Cornelius
Van Size John
Van sly Martin
Van Slyck Martin
Van Snell John
Vantassel Cornelius
Van Teveren Martin
Van Tine John
Van Valkinburg Lambert
Van Vleet Andrew
Van Vleit Abraham
Van Vorst Christian
Van Vorst John
Van Winkel Symon
Van Zile William
Varian John
Veal Jeremiah
Vedder Aaron
Very George
Viele Andrew G.
Viesell Nicholas
Vinegar Samuel

Vonck Peter
Vonck William
Vradenbergh Isaac
Vradenburgh William
Vredenbergh Matthew
Vredenbergh Peter
W--- Rubin
Waddle William
Wadkins Thomas
Waggerman Emanuel
Waggerman George
Wagoner Frederick
Walch Thomas
Waldron Barent
Wale Patrick
Walker Matthew
Wall Patrick
Wallace Daniel
Wallace William
Wallacer Christian
Wallicer Christopher
Wallis James
Walsh Edward
Walsh John
Walter Jacob
Walter Martin
Walters David
Walton Jacob
Walton John
Wan Thomas
Wandell Jacob
Wandell John
Ward Daniel
Ward David
Ward Jesse
Ward John
Ward Josia
Warder Thomas
Waring Benjamin
Waring Michael
Warmoed Christian
Warmood Mathias
Warmoth Christian
Warner Christian
Warner Michael
Warren Edward
Wart Benjamin
Waters Sterling
Waters William
Watkins Benjamin
Watson Joseph
Watson Major
Watson Thomas

Waugh Samuel
Way John
Weasell Nicholas
Weatherstine John
Weaver Adam
Weaver Christian
Weaver George
Weaver Henry
Weaver Michael
Weaver Nicholas
Webb Samuel
Webber Adam
Webber George
Webber William
Webbers James
Wederick Michael
Wederwax William
Wedge Stephen
Weed Abijah
Weed Ezra
Weekes Abraham
Weeks Jacob
Weeks Micajah
Weeler Robert
Weghan Conrad
Wegman John
Weighlien Mathias
Weiscover Jacob
Weiss Lewis
Weken Conrad
Welch Henry
Welch John
Welch Nicholas
Welch Richard
Welch Thomas
Weldon Jeremiah
Wells John
Welsh Joseph
Welsh William
Wemp Barent
Wemple Barent
Wemple Barent H.
Wendell Jacob
Wendell John
Wendell John H.
Wendle Addem
Wesels Evert
West Stephen
Wessell Nicholas
West Williston
Westfield Andrew
Weston James
Wetherick George

Wetherick Michael	Williams William	Wormoet Christian
Wey John	Williamson John	Wormwood Christian
Weyland Mathew	Willice John	Wormwood Matthias
Wezil Nicholas	Willis James	Wrather Thomas
Whalen Richard	Wills John	Wright Benjamin
Whaler John	Wilmot Leonard	Wright Edward
Whaley Michael	Wilmoth Francis	Wright John
Whalin Walter	Wilsey William	Wright Robert
Whay John	Wilson James	Wright Samuel
Whealen Richard	Wilson John	Wuine William
Whealon Walter	Wilson Josia	Wyatt John
Wheeler Henry	Wilson Michael	Wybert Frederick
Wheeler Isaac	Wilson Robert	Wychaline Matthew
Wheeler John	Wilson Samuel	Wyfenbach Henry
Wheeler Robert	Wilson William	Wysehover Jacob
Wheeler Samuel	Winblow Edward	Yengling John F.
Whiswick George	Windeler Mathew	Yeomans Isaac
White Ely	Windford Henry	Yets James
White James	Windsor John	Yonkins George
White Joseph	Winn Joseph	Young Christopher
Whiteside William	Winn Peter	Young Ebenezer
Whitley John	Winne Killijan	Young John
Whitley William	Wisenbeck Henry	Zambert Abraham
Wibert John	Witham William	Zeager Thomas
Wichland Mathias	Witherick George	Zeaster Michael
Wick James	Witherick Michael	Zerrener Lodewick
Wifenbach Henry	Wolf Michael	Zundell George
Wiggins William	Wolkens Benjamin	Zyrances Christopher
Wilcox Abner	Wood James	Zyranius Christopher
Wiley Alexander	Wood Peter	
Wilkenson Thomas	Wood Samuel	
Wilkinson James	Woodcock Peter	
Wilkinson Robert	Wooderd Titus	
Wilks John	Woodroff Ephrim	
Willagan David	Woodroff Matthias	
Willes John	Woodroff William	
Willet John	Woodruff Daniel	
Williams Charles	Woodworth Reuben	
Williams John	Wooley Abraham	
Williams Robert	Worden Nathan	
Williams Solomon	Worder Thomas	
Williams Uriah	Wormley Jacob	

THE LINE - SECOND REGIMENT

The Line-Second Regiment

COLONEL PHILIP VAN CORTLAND	MAJOR PETER SCHUYLER
LIEUT. COL. ROBERT COCHRAN	ADJUTANT JOHN L. HARDENBERGH
LIEUT. COL. PETER REGNIER	QUARTER MASTER WILLIAM COLBREATH
LIEUT. COL. FREDERICK WEISSENFELS	QUARTER MASTER LEVI DE WITT
MAJOR NICHOLAS FISH	PAY MASTER MICHAEL CONNOLLY

PAY MASTER ROBERT PROVOOST, JR.
CHAPLAIN ISRAEL EVANS

SURGEON EBENEZER HAVILAND
SURGEON DANIEL MENEMA

CAPT. HEZEKIAH BALDWIN
" SAMUEL T. BELL
" ELISHA BENEDICT
" JAMES BLEADEY
" MICHAEL CONNOLLY
" HENRY DuBOIS
" THEODOSIUS FOWLER
" ABNER FRENCH
" ABRAHAM FRENCH
" CHARLES GRAHAM
" JOHN GRAHAM
" JONATHAN HALLETT
" JOHN F. HAMTRAMCK
" JAMES JOHNSTON
" EDWARD LOUNSBERY
" THOMAS MACHIN
" ELIHU MARSHALL

LIEUT. ROSWELL BEEBE
" FREDERICK BEEKMAN
" TJERCK BEEKMAN
" CALEB C. BRUSTER
" BENJAMIN CHITTENDEN
" MATTHIAS CLARK
" JEREMIAH CLARKE
" CHRISTOPHER CODWISE
" WILLIAM COLBREATH
" MICHAEL CONNOLLY
" DANIEL DENISTON
" SAMUEL DODGE, JR.
" JAMES FAIRLIE
" ANDREW FINCK, JR.
" JOSEPH FRELICK
" WILLIAM GLENNY
" ELEAZER GRANT

LIEUT. BARNABUS OWENS
" CHARLES PARSONS
" NATHANIEL ROWLEY
" ISAAC SHERWOOD
" ISRAEL SPENCER
" SAMUEL TALMADGE
" RUDOLPH VAN HOVENBERGH
" RUDOLPH VAN HOWENBARGH
" NICHOLAS VAN RANSELEAR
" TUNIS VAN WAGENEN
" ISAAC VAN WOERT
" MICHAEL WEBSELL
" CHARLES F. WEISSENFELS

" DANIEL MILLS
" CHARLES NUKERK
" HENRY PAWLING
" SAMUEL PELL
" BENJAMIN PELTON
" JOEL PRATT
" ABRAHAM RICKAR
" ISRAEL SMITH
" BARENT TENEYCK
" THOMAS THOMPSON
" HENRY VANDERBURGH
" BENJAMIN WALKER
" ANDREW WHITE
" GEORGE WHITE
" JACOB WRIGHT
" CHRISTOPHER P. YATES
" LIEUT. JACOB BAMPER

" DORICK HANSEN
" JOHN L. HARDENBERGH
" THOMAS HUNT
" CHRISTOPHER HUTTON
" GEORGE JOHNSON
" JAMES JOHNSON
" JOHN KEYSER, JR.
" GIDEON KING
" JOHN G. LANSINGH
" GILBERT J. LIVINGSTONE
" JOHN McCLAUGHRY
" WILLIAM McCUNE
" WILLIAM MOULTON
" JARVES MUDGE
" WILLIAM MUNDAY
" CHARLES NEWKIRK
" WILLIAM NOTTINGHAM

" ANDREW WHELEY
" ROBERT WOOD
" EPHRAIM WOODRUFF
ENSIGN JOHN BROWN
" NEHEMIAH CARPENTER
" SAMUEL DODGE
" PETER DOLSON
" STEPHEN GRIFFIN
" THOMAS HAIGHT
" JOSEPH HARPER
" LEWIS R. MORRIS
" RICHARD MOUNT
" WILLIAM PETERS

" ROBERT PROVOOST, JR.

" THOMAS READ

" DIRCK SCHUYLER

" BARNABUS SWARTWOUT

" BARTHOLOMEW VAN DERBURGH

" EPHRAIM WOODRUF

ENLISTED MEN

Ackerman William	Bachus Jacob	Bartoe Morres
Ackey Adnijah	Bacon Penial	Barworth James
Ackley Jacob	Badleis John	Basamer Jacobus
Ackley James	Bagle Silas	Basan Daniel
Acurman William	Bailey James	Basemer Michael
Adams Noah	Bailey Joseph	Basemore John
Adams Peleg	Baily Ebenezer	Bason Daniel
Adamy Henry	Baker Benjamin	Batersby Robert
Addems John	Baker Elijah	Bates Zephaniah
AdkinAndrew	Baker Judah	Baxter Lockwood
Aimes Hugh	Baker Pearce	Bay John
Ainsworth Henry	Baker Samuel	Bayles James
Albright Jacob	Baldon Zuriel	Baylie Ebenezer
Albright John	Ball Shadrick	Baylis John
Alexander Jonathan	Bangel John	Bayson Daniel
Alger George	Banks Benjamin	Beach Amos
Allen William	Baragar Walter	Beach Asa
Allison John	Barans Glean	Beagle Silas
Allison Robert	Barber Benjamin	Beaker Judah
Alport John	Barber John	Beatch Amos
Amerman Derrick	Barber Stephen	Beats Zepheniah
Ames Ashel	Barber William	Becannon Samuel
Ames Levi	Bardeen Robert	Becker Henry
Ammerman James	Bare Jacob	Beebe Bonerges
Ammermon Cornelius	Barker Jonathan	Beebe Burnagus
Anderson Alexander	Barkeus William	Beebe Rodrick
Anderson Samuel	Barkin William	Beech Amos
Andress Thomas	Barlow Joseph	Beely Joseph
Andrews Isaac	Barnam Samuel	Beets James
Anthony John Francis	Barnes Richard	Beevins Christ
Arkenburgh Henry	Barnheart David	Beggs Jonathan
Armstrong Archibald	Barns Abijah	Begraft Thomas
Armstrong Benjamin	Barns Elisha	Bell James
Armstrong John	Barns James	Bell Matthew
Armstrong Jonathan	Barnum Samuel	Belnap Asa
Arnold Oliver	Barrager Walter	Benedick Ambris
Ashly Aaron	Barren John	Benedict Ambrose
Asquith John	Barrett Michael	Benjaman Jonathan
Asten Benjamin	Barrett Peter	Benjamen Samuel
Asten Holmes	Barrian John	Benjamin Ebenezer
Asten Jeremiah	Barrit Bartholamy	Benjamin Jonathan
Asten Martin	Barrit Ephram	Benjamin Samuel
Astin John	Barritt Oliver	Benn Daniel
Avary Nicholas	Bartholemee John	Bennedict Caleb
Avery Nicholas	Bartholomew John	Bennet Jabin
Ayer Nathaniel	Bartlet Lemuel	Bennett Jacob
Babcock Garsham	Bartoe Jonas	Bennett James

Bennett Samuel
Bennit Joshua
Bennitt Jeremiah
Bennitt John
Bennitt Timothy
Benson Thomas
Benson William
Benten Arthur
Bentty George
Berger Walter
Berlow Joseph
Berrian John
Berry William
Besemer Jacobus
Betts James
Bettys William
Bevens Christopher
Bevens John
Biddle William
Bigham James
Bill Ezariah
Bingham Abijah
Birch John
Bismer Michael
Black David
Black Jacob
Blackney John
Blake Felove
Blakely John
Blinn Simeon
Bloose John
Blossome Peter
Boardman Ephraim
Bockers Jacob
Bodley Andrew
Bogardas Peter
Bogardis Abrahai
Bogardus David
Bogart Myndert
Bogge John
Boice Jeremiah
Boice Peter
Boice Simon
Boils James
Boldrige Daniel
Bolen Michael
Boleton George
Bolton John
Bolton Jonatha
Boman Albart
Boman Luke
Bonett Joseph
Bonus James

Booker John
Bordman Andrew
Borrill Zachariah
Bose Peter
Bosweek James
Boswick Edward
Bostwith James
Boswith William
Bournan Luke
Bovie John
Bowan Charles
Bowman Lewis
Boyd George
Boyles James
Bradain John
Bradner Andrew
Bradner Benoni
Brady Lewis
Braett Andrew
Brandt John
Brann Samuel
Breaden John
Bream Baltus
Bredinbaker Baltis
Brett James
Brewer Jeremiah
Brewer Samuel
Brewton Arthur
Briant John
Briant Thomas
Bridges James
Briggs Daniel
Brigs Jonathan
Brinck Cornelius
Brinton David
Britt James
Broadt Andrew
Brockway Russell
Brooke Thomas
Brooker Walter
Brooks Joseph
Brooks Thomas
Brotherton John
Brott Andrew
Brower William
Brown Benjamin
Brown David
Brown Joel
Brown John
Brown Jonas
Brown Joseph
Brown Justice
Brown Samuel

Brown Thomas
Browne Frances
Bruhard Nathaniel
Brush Eliakim
Brush Selah
Brust Martin
Brutan Arthur
Buchanan Samuel
Buck Enoch
Buckanon Samuel
Buckhoud William
Buckhout John
Budine Francis
Bunce Abraham
Bunce Daniel
Bunt Lodwick
Bunting Thomas
Burch John
Burchard Nathaniel
Burdick Elisha
Burdick Gideon
Burdick Henry
Burdick Moses
Burge Michael
Burges Archibald
Burgess James
Burke John
Burke Thomas
Burket John
Burline Lewis
Burn Henry
Burnett Ebenezer
Burnett John
Burnham William
Burnhert David
Burns James
Burns Michael
Burns Robert
Burrows Thomas
Bursh Eliakim
Burton Arthur
Burwell Zechariah
Busby William
Busen John
Bush John
Bussing John
Cabalson Michael
Cable George
Cady John
Cady Lemuel
Cady Palmer
Cahoone Hyman
Cahoone Joseph

146

Cairley Joseph
Calkin Simon
Callegan John
Cambec James
Cambell Andrew
Cambell William
Cammoran Daniel
Camp Asa
Camp Elias
Campbell Andrew
Campbell John
Campbell William
Campble John
Canby James
Cane William
Canfield Samuel
Canklin Daniel
Cargel Isaac
Carll David
Carly Joseph
Carman John
Carrigan William
Carrill David
Carson James
Carter James
Carter John
Cartwright Henry Abraham
Casaday Peter
Casady Edward
Casselman Richard
Castor Adam
Catherling Matthew
Cavender Moses
Caviller Moses
Cazard Richard
Certain James
Certer Philip
Chainny Ware
Chalenor Christopher
Chamberlin Girdon
Chamberlin Wyatt
Champlain James
Champlan Edward
Chance Christian
Chania Wire
Chapman Asa
Chapman Charles
Chapman Joseph
Chapman Josiah
Chapple Benjamin
Charlesworth John M.
Charters James
Chase Caleb

Chase Jacob
Chase Lett
Chatfield David
Chavalier John
Chelson Beriah
Cherrey John
Cherwood Nemiah
Chesshier Neamiah
Christeen Peter
Christian John
Christian Peter
Christman Nicholas
Christoper Andries
Christopher Andrew
Christy John
Church David
Church Reuben
Clark Abijah
Clark David
Clark John
Clarwater Martin
Clause Christopher
Claxton George
Cleark John
Cleveland Jonas
Cleveland Josiah
Clewater Martin
Cliff Joseph
Cline Jacob
Close Samuel
Closser Christopher
Clumpha William
Coal David
Cobler Conrad
Cockle George
Coe Philip
Coefield James
Cogdon John
Cohoon Himan
Cokely John
Coldwell William
Cole Abraham
Cole David
Cole Frances
Cole Henry
Cole John
Cole Moses
Cole Philip
Cole Samuel
Cole Tunis
Collin John
Collings Alber
Collings John

Collins Edward
Collins John
Collins William
Combs John
Combs Peter
Commons Patrick
Conaway John
Conckim John
Concklin Joseph
Condon David
Conkling Daniel
Conn William
Conner Daniel
Conner Patrick
Conner William
Connite Conrod
Connolly James
Connor Edward
Connor James
Constable Garrett
Contryman John F.
Conway Cornelius
Cook George
Cook Sapines
Cooke Hyman
Cooke Nicholas
Cool George
Cool Rufe
Coombs Peter
Coon Jacob
Coon Peter
Coon Timothy
Coon William
Coony George
Cooper John
Copelin William
Corkins Simon
Cornel Joseph
Cornelison John
Cornelius John
Cornwall Joseph
Corter John
Cortney Francis
Cortor Philip
Corwin George
Corwine Gersham
Cosier Hezekiah
Costeloe James
Costerhoudt Peter
Costerly James
Cottrill Richard
Countriman Jacobus
Courter Philip

Courtney Francis
Covet Philip
Cowen Thomas
Cox Charles
Cox John
Cox Robert
Cox Simon
Cozard Richard
Craft Jacob
Craft James
Craft Nathaniel
Craigen Peter
Crain William
Crandle Henry
Crandle William
Crandle Willson
Crandle Wright
Crane John
Crankhite Abraham
Craton Thomas
Crawfoot Zachariah
Crisple Abraham
Cristenon Benjamin
Cristiansy John
Crofoot Samuel
Croft James
Crofts Jacob
Crook William
Crosman Daniel
Cross John
Crowin Silas
Crugor William
Crum William
Crumb Christopher
Crumb John
Culbertson William
Cully Charles
Cummin Benjamin
Cummings John
Cummins Ebenezer
Cummins John
Cuningham James
Cuningham Shubal
Cunningham Archibald
Cunningham Henry
Currin Samuel
Curry James
Curtes Caleb
Curvain Edward
Curwin Gersham
Curwine Edward
Cushan John
Dailey Israel

Dalton Frederick
Da nford Prince
Danford Wells
Danielson Isaac
Danielson Thomas
Danilson Peter
Dannils George
Danniston Thomas
Darby Asa
Darby Charles
Darmot Richard
Darrow Christopher
Darrow George
Darrow Jedediah
Daton Ezekiel
Daugherty John
Davee Isaac
Davee John
Davenport Humphrey
Davenport John
David Isaac
David Jonathan
Davle Isaac
Davie John
Davie Oliver
Davis Anderson
Davis Andrus
Davis Benjamin
Davis Chapman
Davis David
Davis Ezra
Davis Herman
Davis Hugh
Davis John
Davis Joshua
Davis Patrick
Davis Peter
Davis Richard
Davis Samuel
Davison Andrew
Daviss Richard
Davisson James
Davisson John
Day Aron
Dayton Benjamin
Dayton Bennit
Dean Benjamin
Dean James
Deane Isaac
Decker Christopher
Decker Martin
Decker Michael
Deen Henry

Deffendorff Henry
Defoe George
Defoe John
Degrusen Elias
Deharsh Philip
Dekerson Abraham
Demerist Nicholas
Deming Simeon
Demitt Joseph
Demond Moses
Demond William
Demshee Anthony
Denney Peter
Dennis John
Dennis Mydert
Denniston Thomas
Denton Preston
Depew Abraham
Depew Cornelius
Depew Francis
Depew Henry
Depew John
De Pont Bostion
Dermott Richard
Derry James
Derusia Anthony
Devanport Jonathan
Devore Abraham
Dewey Elieha
Dewitt Benjamin
DeWitt John
DeWitt Peter, Sr.
DeWitt Peter, Jr.
Dexter Jonathan
Dickens James
Dickenson Daniel
Dickerson David
Dickeson Abraham
Dickins Peter
Dickins Thomas
Dickinson James
Dickinson Varsil
Dickson Robert
Dimmick Perms
Dimminick Samuel
Dimmis John
Dimmuck Benjamin
Dimon Moses
Dimond William
Dobson John
Dodge Richard
Dolloway Jeremiah
Dolph Moses

Dolton Frederick	Eliot Henry	Fits Gerral Thomas
Dolton Thomas	Eliott Archabald	Fitzgerald Michael
Donalds George	Elkingburgh Peter	Fitzgerald Thomas
Donaldson Isaac	Elliot Francis	Fitzjearls William
Donnalds John	Elliott John	Flagg Ebenezer
Donnaldson Peter	Ellis Jacob	Flansbury Daniel
Dority William	Ellis John	Fleming Jacob
Doty John	Ellison John	Fleming William
Doty Samuel	Elsworth John	Fling Thomas
Doughty Elias	Elvingstone Edward	Flint Nathan
Doughty Peter	Ennest Peter	Flood Francis
Douglas George	Ennis David	Flummin Francis
Douglass James	Ennis Peter	Follerd John
Douly Elias	Enris David	Foot Joseph
Douw Volkert	Epton Benjamin	Forbush Nicholas
Dow Vulker	Ergenbrech John	Force Timothy
Downing Andrew	Erwin John	Ford Benjamin
Doxey Stephen	Esmond John	Ford George
Drake Asel	Evans Thomas	Ford Timothy
Drennin Hamilton	Evins John	Fordon John
Drew George	Evins Moses	Forganson James
Drew Oliver	Factor John	Forgerson Samuel
Drummond David	Fairchild Abner	Forguson James
Drummond Griger	Fairchilds Ephraim	Forster Nathaniel
Dubois John	Fall Robert	Forster William
Dudley Simon	Fanford Obadiah	Fosburgh Jacob
Duguid John	Farrel Garret	Foster Benoni
Dunbar William	Farrington Robert	Foster John
Duncan James	Fashee David	Foster Nathaniel
Duncan Thomas	Featherly John	Fouler Cornelius
Dunivan John	Featherly Thomas	Fowler George
Dunlap Andrew	Fellows Moses	Fowler Michael
Dunlap James	Felt Solomon	Foy Patrick
Dunn Alexander	Felton Lewis	Foyer Thomas
Duran Francis	Fenton Amos	Fradenbourgh Mathew
Dutcher Barnett	Ferdon John	Framer Michael
Dutcher Barrick	Ferguson Samuel	Francis John
Dwyre Thomas	Ferris John	Francisco Henry
Dybol Hezekiah	Ferris John, Jr.	Francisco John
Dybol Zachariah	Ferry Charles	Frank Henry
Eagleston John	Fetherly John	Franks Michal
Eaglestone James	Fetherly Thomas	Frazier John
Earl William	Fields Philip	Frear Peter
Easterly Thomas	Fiero Abram	Frebush Mathew
Eastwood Daniel	Finch Jonathan	Fredrick Johannes
Eavens John	Finck Hanjost	Freeland John
Edwards William	Fine Andrew	Freeman Nathaniel
Edwords Edward	Finel Edward	Freer Peter
Egans Elijah	Finton Amos	Fremain Jonathan
Eggbert Daniel	Fish Caleb	Freman Jonathan
Eggers Elijah	Fish Moses	Fremire Micheal
Egleston Eli	Fish Sebra	Fretter John
Elder Joseph	Fishee David	Frimiah Mitch

149

Frimier John	Goff Ashbel	Grogan John
Frost Edmond	Goff Oliver	Grograin John
Froth James	Gold John	Guile Joseph
Fuller Daniel	Golding Thomas	Guillion John
Fuller Josiah	Goldsmith Ezra	Haburn William
Fulton Alexander	Goodall James	Hackley Ezekial
Fulton John	Goodfellow Moses	Hadley Joseph
Fulvia Thomas	Goodin George	Hadlock James
Gabine John	Goodwin Abraham	Haight Ceaser
Gage Richard	Goodwin George	Haight Thomas K
Gall John	Gordon Abraham	Halenbeck Jacob
Garbine John	Gorham Jabus	Hall, David
Gardener John	Gorman Patrick	Hall Israel
Gardinier Andries	Got William	Hall John
Gardner Andrew	Gould Asa	Hall Lynos
Gardner Benoni	Gould John	Hall William
Gardner Jacob	Graham John	Hallack Jeffera
Gardner James	Grahams Andrew	Hallett Richard
Gardner Jesse	Grahams Moses	Hallick Jeffery
Gardnier Clark	Granger John	Halnbeck Henry
Gareheart Matthew	Graves Jedediah	Halsapel Zachariah
Garmin James	Graves Joseph	Halsey Abraham
Garrlson Abraham	Graves Lewis	Halsey John
Garrison Hartshorn	Gray John, Jr.	Halsey Thomas
Garrison John	Gray Thomas	Hambleton William
Garrison William	Gready Thomas	Hamelin Adam
Garvey Francis	Green Beriah	Hamilton Patrick
Gaudt Benjamin	Green Clark	Hamlin Adam
Gay Edward	Green John	Hammer William
Gee David	Green Peter	Hamon John
Gee Ezekiel	Green Silas	Handley James
Gee John	Greenwood John	Hanes John
Gee Moses	Gregg David	Hanford Jeremiah
George Joshua	Greswill Miles	Hanley James
Gerard Benjamin	Grey Nicholas	Hanyon Garret
Germin James	Grey Silas	Harding Henry
Gibbons John	Grey Thomas	Haris Moses
Gibson John	Griffen Hezekiah	Harmanse Edward
Gilaspie James	Griffeth Abraham	Harper James
Gilbert John	Griffeth Jeremiah	Harper William
Gilbert Seth	Griffeths Abraham	Harrington Anthony
Gilbert William	Griffin Aaron	Harrington Ebenezer
Gilchrist William	Griffin Benjamin	Harrington James
Gilder Ebenezer	Griffin James	Harris Cato
Gildersleeve Joseph	Griffin John	Harris David
Gilderslivis Joseph	Griffin Joseph	Harris George
Giles Richard	Griffin Joshua	Harris Henry
Gimblet Peter	Griffis Abraham	Harris John
Ginnings John	Griffiths Joshua	Harris Moses
Girle Thomas	Griffitts Samuel	Harris Richard
Glaspy James	Griggs Jeremiah	Harris William
Glexton George	Grill Thomas	Harrison Joseph
Glover Thomas	Grisal Jabus	Hart Daniel

Harty Christopher
Hasbrook George
Hasbrouck David
Hassum John
Hatchins William
Havens Isaac
Havens William
Havilish Michael
Hawk George
Hawkey Henry
Hawkey Richard
Hawkins John
Hawkins Zopher
Hawley Benjamin
Hawley Samuel
Hawley Zadock
Hay James
Hayes John
Hays John
Hays Nathaniel
Hazerd James
Heath Josiah
Heavens Peter
Heavlish Michael
Hebmore John
Helmer John
Henderson Samuel
Henderson William
Henjcricklick Johan
Henneysee John
Henry Wells
Henson Nathaniel
Heppel Adam
Herington Isaac
Hermans Edward
Herring Jacob
Herrington Benjamin
Hessum John
Hewet Benjamin
Hewett Edmond
Hewit Arthur
Hibbard James
Hibbirdt John
Hicks Jacob
Hicks Joseph
Hicks Lewis
Hiet Henry
Higby Samuel
Higgins Archibald
Higgins Jonathan
Higgins Thomas
Higher Alexander
Higley Rozel

Higley Seth
Hill Aza
Hill Elijiah
Hill Solomon
Hill Thomas
Hill William
Himilan Adam
Hines John
Hitchcock John
Hitchcok Samuel
Hix Joseph
Hofford Elijah
Hofford Jesse
Hogan John
Holcomb Beriah
Holcomb Mathew
Holdridge Amasa
Holdridge John
Holdridge Richard
Hole James
Holkens James
Hollenbeeck Jacob
Holly Samuel
Holmes John
Holmes Obadiah
Holmes Stephen
Holmes Thomas
Holms Daniel
Holms Ezekiah
Holms John
Holms Thomas
Holsapple Zacharias
Holtzer John
Hope Thomas
Hopkins Noah
Hopper John
Hopper Peter
Horan Phanten
Hornebeak Ephereham
Horsford Joseph
Horton Christopher
Horton Isaac
Horton Thomas
Horton William
Hoser Thomas
Hosford Joseph
Hosier Hendrick
Hoskins Thomas
Hoskins William
Hosmer John
Hotskiss William
Hough John
Houghboom Jacob

Houns Zepheniah
House Anthony
House Henry
House Laphariah
Housworth Michael
Howe John
Howe Zephaniah
Howell George
Howell Lemuel
Howell Seth
Howes Zephaniah
Howley Zadak
Hoyt Ceaser
Hubbert John
Hudler Nicholas
Hudsal Nicholas
Hughson Nathaniel
Hull Seth
Hull William
Humphries Alexander
Humphry Alexander
Humphry James
Humphry John
Hunt David
Hunt Joshua
Hunt Prince
Hunt William
Hunter James
Hunthley Thomas
Huntley Bethuel
Huntley Thomas
Hurd Elijah
Hurly James
Hutly Thomas
Hutsal Nicholas
Hutton Christopher
Huyks Joseph
Hyatt Abraham
Hyatt Alphen
Hyatt Alpheus
Hyatt Alvan
Hyatt Henry
Hyatt Minah
Innes Peter
Irwin John
Ivorey Jacobus
Ivorey James
Jabine John
Jabwain John
Jackson Francis
Jackson Micael
Jackson Thomas
Jackson William

Jacobs John
James Ebenezer
James Joyce
James William
Jansen Robert
Jansing Robert
Jaquist John
Jarvis Nathaniel
Jeffers John
Jeffriss John
Jett Michael
Jinkins Philip
Jinson Robert
Joce David
Johns Jacob
Johns Samuel
Johnson Daniel
Johnson David
Johnson Elisha
Johnson James
Johnson Justus
Johnson Moses
Johnson Peter
Johnson Prince
Johnson Richar
Johnson Thomas
Johnson William
Johnston James
Johnston Josiah
Johnston Robert
Johnston Samuel
Joice David
Jones David
Jones Ebenezer
Jones Evan
Jones Ezekiel
Jones Ezra
Jones Griffin
Jones Ivens
Jones Jacob
Jones John
Jones Joseph
Jones Peter
Jones Ruben
Jones Samuel
Jones Seth
Jones Thomas
Jore David
Joyce James
Jupter Silas
Kably Michael
Kader Adam
Kader John

Kanneday John
Kartwright Henry
Katcham Joseph
Keating Robert
Kedar Adam
Kedar John
Keddar Stephan
Keeler Frederick
Keeth John
Kelley Robert
Kelly Barny
Kelly Coenrod
Kelly Edmund
Kelly John
Kelly Joshua
Kelly Moris
Kelly Peter
Kelly Robert
Kelly Silvinus
Kelsey Benjamin
Kelsey Ebenezer
Kelson Phineas
Kennady James
Kennedy John
Kennion William
Kenny Charles
Kent Isaac
Kenyon William
Kershaw John
Kertrem Jesse
Ketcham Joseph
Ketchem John
Killey Silveney
Kind William
King John
King Philip
King Reuben
King William
Kinkade William
Kinnaday John
Kinnen William
Kinner Jonathan
Kinney Charles
Kinney James
Kinny Roger
Kinsham Frederick
Kinyon William
Kipp Abraham
Kipp Amos
Kipp James
Kipp Moses
Kirn Michael
Kirn William

Kisard Richard
Kitcham Abraham
Kitcham Joseph
Knap Caleb
Knapp Benjamin
Knapp Caleb
Knapp Daniel
Knapp Isaac
Knapp James
Knapping Jeremiah
Knickabocker Andrew
Kniffen Amos
Knight William
Knights Lucias
Knikaboker Herman
Knoutz John
Koel Henry
Kole Philip
Konklin Joseph
Koole Teunis
Krane William
Kress John
Krom Christopher
Krook William
Krous Jacob
Kyser Edward
Kyser Joseph
Lacey Philip
Lain John
Lakely John B.
Lalefferty Stephen
Lamb Arthur
Lamb John
Lamb Pomp
Lambert David
Lambert John
Lambertson Simon
Lane Jeremiah
Lane John
Lane William
Langdon Benjamin
Langin William
Lannee Philip
Larabee Elias
Larey Cady
Lavett John
Lawder Edward
Lawn George
Lawrance George S.
Lawrence Benjamin
Lawrence Jacob
Lawson Christopher
Lawyer Christopher

Layer Christopher	Lovette John	McFall Pawl
Layton William	Lovjoy Nathan	McFarling Hosier
Learey Cadey	Low John	Mc farling William
Leary John	Lowry John	McGinny James
Leather William	Luca John	McGlaughtin Neal
Leek Johan Hangerick	Ludlum Daniel	McGomery John
Lee Daniel	Ludlum John	McGowen Jeremiah
Lee Ephraim	Luis James	McGraw James
Lee William	Lummess Write	McGregory Daniel
Lenny Philip	Lush John	McGunney James
Lent Abram	Lusk John	McIntyer Alexander
Lent Elias	Lutz Coonradt	McKarney Stephen
Lent Henry	Lyons David	McKeal Adam
Lent Jacob	Lyons Hosea	McKee William
Leonard Edward	Lyons Michael	McKelle Adam
Leppard John	Lyonson William	McKenny Charles
Lepper John	McAllister William	McKenny James
Lester John	McAntiere Alexander	McKenny John
Le Strange Samuel	McArthur John	McKerney Stephen
Letty William	Mc bane Giles	McKillip Archibald
Levy Jacob	McBride Wiliiam	McKillip Daniel
Lewis James	McCalley Alexander	McKim John
Lewis Jesse	McCarney Stephen	McKinney Charles
Lewis Leonard	McCartee Phelex	McLeal Charles
Lewis Nathan	McCartney Isaac	McLean John
Lewis Richard	McCarty Isaac	McLean Neal
Lewis William	McCarty James	McMannus Robert
Light John	McCarty John	McMaster James
Light Lemuel	McCharlesworth John	McMiching John
Like Henry	McCine David	McMurdy James
Linch William	McClean John	McNamee Charles
Lindon James	McCIean Neal	McNeal Adam
Linney Philip	McClosky Peter	McNeal Charles
Lint Elias	McClure William	McNeil John
Lister John	McCollum John	McPeak Dennis
Livingston Jacob	McCoomick John	McRenemee Charles
Loader Daniel	McCoy Daniel	McSine Daniel
Loader William	McCray John	Mad Calf William
Lobby John	McDaniel John	M-ah Josiah
Loder Samuel	McDaniel Michael	Mahu Peter
Lofberry Isaac	McDaniel Randle	Malay James
Loins Hosea	McDanold Ronald	Mallory Jonathan N.
Lomus Jacob	McDole John	Man Michael
Loofborrow Isaac	McDonald James	Manning Stephen
Lord Benjamin	McDonald John	Manrose Elijah
Lord Timothy	McDonald Michael	Manross Jesse
Lossey Jacob	McDonald Peter	Mantanyia Peter
Lothorp Icabod	McDonald Raynold	Marble Ephraim
Louchee Jacob	McDonald Roland	Marian Francis
Loucks Peter	McDonall Patrick	Marlin J.
Lounsberry John	McDowel John	Marling Isaac
Lousbarry John	McDugle Daniel	Marly John
Love Michael	McFyers Daniel	Marshall Peter

Marshall Robert
Martin Alexander
Martin Thomas
Martling Isaac
Marvin Mathew
Mason Thomas
Masson Thomas
Masters Daniel
Masthers James
Mastin Daniel
Mathers James
Matherson August
Matthews James
Maxim Adonijah
May Daniel
May Hendrick
Mayhew Peter
Mead Jehiel
Mead Nathan
Meaner Ichabod
Meddock John
Meggs Seth
Megriger Daniel
Melcher Paulis
Menrony Florens
Merchall Robert
Merewise Jacob
Merrian Francis
Merritt Jeremiah
Mervin Mathew
Messer William
Metcalf William
Methers James
Michel Edward
Michel George
Milden Daniel
Mildridge Thomas
Miller Benjamin
Miller David
Miller Elisha
Miller Jacob
Miller James
Miller John
Miller Josiah
Mills Andrew
Mills Samuel
Milton John
Mingo Marting
Minks John
Mitchel Ensign
Mitchel James
Mitchel Joseph
Mitchell Martin

Mitchell Richard
Mitchell Samuel
Mitchil David
Moffet William
Moke Gerardus
Molatt Ishmil
Molloy John
Monday James
Mondon John
Monger Joseph
Montayne Peter
Montgomery Hugh
Montgomery James
Moon Matthew
Moony William
Moor Charles
Moor Zebulon
Moore Charles
Moore Thomas
Moorley Abner
Moot Henry
Moot Noah
More John
Morewise Jacob
Morgan Joseph
Morgan Stiff
Morgan William
Morloy James
Morphet William
Morrel John
Morrele Isaac
Morrell Isaac
Morrell Robert
Morrill John
Morris John
Morris Matthew
Morrisson David
Moss David
Mott Isaac
Mott Noah
Mount Henry
Mtt Soon John
Mudg Abraham
Mullen William
Mullerner Moses
Mutlin John
Mullin William
Mulliner Moses
Mumford James
Munday James
Munden John
Munro Alexander
Munrose Elijah

Murdock Moses
Murray Isaac
Murray Nathan
Murray William
Mute William
Myer Moses
Myers David
Naidler Nicholas
Narnil John
Neas George
Nebor Michael
Neeby Michael
Newcom John
Newcomb James
Newcomb Kinner
Newcomb Thomas
Newkerk Myndert
Newman Joseph
Newton William
Nicholas John
Nicholas Thomas
Nicholls Stephen
Nichols Asa
Nichols Thomas
Nichorson Thomas
Nickells Stephen
Nickerson Archibald
Nickerson J.
Nickerson Thomas
Nickolls John
Night William
Noble Gabriel
Noeys William
Nois William
Norstrand John
Norton George
Norton Isaac
Norton William
Norve Lewis
Nothingham Thomas
Noty Jacob
Nowe Lewis
Nowel Lewis
Nowell Thomas
Nunk Henry
Oakly John
Oakly Jonathan
Oathout Tilman
Obrien John
Occerman Elijah
Occurman William
Ockerman William
Odel William

Ogden David
Ogden John
Ogdon John
Oliver Drew
Olmstead John
Olmsted Nehemiah
Omberman Cornelius
O'Niel John
Oosterhoudt Cornelius
Oothoudt Tilman
Orr Daniel
Orvis Gersham
Orvis Waighstill
Osburn Nathaniel
Osterhout Gilbert
Osterhout Henry
Ostrander Adam
Ousterhout Peter
Outhout Silvester
Owen Abel
Owen Daniel
Owen Mowberry
Owens Isaac
Owens Moses
Oxten John
Padder John
Padrick John
Pain Daniel
Palmer Jonathan
Palmeter John
Palmitear John
Palmitier Joseph
Pangbourn William
Pangburn John
Papping Daniel
Par Matthias
Pardy Silas
Parish Cyprian
Parker Ebenezer
Parker Edward
Parker James
Parker Samuel
Parks John
Parry John
Parsons Elisha
Parsonus James
Patterson Hezekiah
Patterson John
Pattison Michael
Pavy John
Payner Peter
Peck John
Pedder John

Peeler Jacob
Peirce Joseph
Pellam Francis
Pemberton Thomas
Penear Peter
Penny Jonathan
Perigo Usual
Perry William
Peters John
Peterson Barnabas
Petterson John
Pettet Samuel
Pew Abraham
Pew Francis
Pew Henry
Pew John
Phelps Ebenezer
Phelps Israel
Phenix Matthew
Philiph David
Philiph Joshua
Philips David
Philips Joshua
Philips Samuel
Philps Ebenezer
Pichtol Henry
Pike John
Pinear Peter
Pitcher Jonathan
Pixley John
Pixly Squire
Plapper Christian
Plaugh Niceholes
Plough Dennis
Plum Stephen
Plummer Ezra
Pocknett John
Pocknot John
Poinear Peter
Pollard Thomas
Polman Salter
Post Conelius
Post Henry
Potter Isaac
Potter Samuel
Powell Elisha
Powell Sam
Powell Seth
Powell Stephen
Powell Thomas
Powers Charles
Pratt Chalker
Pratt William

Preston Jonathan
Price James
Prichard Thomas
Prime Kimble
Prince Campbell
Prince Kemble
Prior Abner
Pritchard Eleanathan
Pritchard Isaac
Proston Isaac
Pudney James
Pudney Thorn
Pulaman Salter
Pulis John
Pullman Salter
Pumpshin Daniel
Putman Salter
Putman William
Putnam Jonas
Putney James
Quawkenboss Jacob
Quick Cornelius
Quick Jacob
Quinn Thomas
Rabby Michael
Rady James
Ramond Seth
Ramson Henry
Ramson Jacob
Ramson James
Randall Henry
Randel Henry
Randel John
Randels Joseph
Rano Symon
Ransom Jacob
Ransom James
Rapp George
Ray Isaac
Ray James
Rayley James
Raynold John
Read Brian
Read William
Readey James
Realey James
Redman John
Reed Brian
Reed John
Reed Joseph
Reed Nathaniel
Reid John
Remsen Jacobus

Rennells James
Reno Simeon
Reston William
Reuben Moses
Rexford Samuel
Reyder John
Reynolds Eliphalet
Reynolds John
Reynolds Joseph
Reynolds Timothy
Rhodes John
Rhodes Joseph
Ribley Michael
Rich Henry
Richard Gilbert
Richard Philip
Richards Ezra
Richards Gilbert
Richards Philip
Richardson Bezilla
Riche Henry
Richman John
Richmond Benjamin
Richmond John
Rickey Jeremiah
Rider John
Riggs Daniel
Righley Joseph
Riley James
Riley Sylvester
Risten William
Ritter Moses
Roach William
Roads Joseph
Robards Caleb
Robarts Jonathan
Robarts Warren
Roberson John
Roberson Robert
Roberts Caleb
Roberts James
Roberts Jonathan
Robins Daniel
Robinson Edmund
Robinson George
Robinson Issacher
Robinson James
Robinson John
Robinson Stephen
Robinson William
Robley Michael
Rock Hezekiah
Rock Samuel

Rocks William
Roe Lyman
Roomer Benjamin
Roosa Aaron
Roosa Abraham
Roosa Jacob
Roosa Jonathan
Root Joseph
Rosa Jacob
Ros Abraham
Ros Andrew
Ros Jacob
Ros James
Ros John
Ros Peter
Ross John
Ross Joseph
Row Antonio
Rowey Daniel
Royal Peter
Rudulph Henry
Ruff Adam
Rugar John
Runnel Able
Runnell Eliphalet
Runnells Stephen
Runnels Eliphalet
Runnolds Timothy
Runo Simeon
Russel Jonathan
Russel Thomas
Russell James
Russell William
Russle Jonathan
Russle Thomas
Ryan John
Ryder John
Sackett Benjamin
Saddler John
St. John Tedious
St. Lawrence George
Sarnmons Cornelius
Sammons Ephrehan
Sammons George
Sampson Isaac
Sanders John
Sanders Robert
Sandford Daniel
Sandford John
Sargason William
Sartin James
Saunders John
Sawyer Jonathan

Saxton Ebenezer
Scaitts James
Schaits James
Scheyer Jacob
Schoomaker Henry
Schoonmaker Henry
Schriver Jacob
Schutt Frederick
Schutt Timothy
Scilkirck James
Scott Edward
Scott James
Scott John
Scott Timothy
Scott William
Scriver Peter
Scuitts James
Sculthorp John
Sealy Joseph
Sears Francis
Sedore John
Seeds George
Seemore Abraham
Seers Moses
Seeton Wiilard
Selkirk James
Sellers Michael
Semore Abraham
Scrine James
Serjantson William
Sertain James
Service Philip
Service Richard
Servis Richard
Seton Wiilard
Sevis Francis
Seymor Thomas
Shafer George
Shall George
Shance Christian
Shannan Robert
Shants Christian
Sharewood Neamiah
Sharp Hendrick
Shatler John
Shavalier John
Shaw David
Shaw Ichabod
Shaw James
Shaw Michael
Shaw Richard
Shaw Rubin
Shaw William

Shearman Michael
Sheer Abraham
Sheerman Jesse
Shehan Maurice
Shennon Thomas
Shepherd Isaac
Sherewood Abraham
Sherewood Nathan
Sherwood James
Sherwood M.
Sherwood Nathan
Sherwood Nehemiah
Shett Peter
Shiping William
Shippen William
Shoecraft John
Shoemaker Daniel
Shoemaker David
Shomaker Henry
Shorwood Nathan
Shouthard John
Shove Frederick
Shucraft John
Shuter John
Sikles Zacharias
Silkirk James
Silsby David
Simmons John
Simmons Joshua
Simmons Michael
Simons Joshua
Simons Martin
Simpkins Jeremiah
Simson John
Sinnot Pat
Sitz Nicholas
Sixby John
Sixby Nicholas
Skaits James
Skinner Isaac
Skinner Josiah
Skinner Thomas
Skutt Frederick
Slate Ezlk
Slippey David
Sloan Stephen
Slouter John
Slover Isaac
Slowter Andrew
Slowter Ephraim
Slowter Evert
Slowter John
Slutt Peter

Sluyter Andrew
Sluyter Evert
Small Benjamin
Smallee Thomas
Smally Isaiah
Smally Thomas
Smily Thomas
Smith Archibald
Smith Baltzer
Smith Benjamin
Smith Caleb
Smith Christopher
Smith David
Smith Ebert B.
Smith Elihu
Smith Ezekiel
Smith George
Smith Gersham
Smith Henry
Smith Isaac
Smith James
Smith Jered
Smith Jesse
Smith John
Smith Joseph
Smith Lemuel
Smith Moses
Smith Peter
Smith Richard
Smith Samuel
Smith Senior
Smith Shorten
Smith Solomon
Smith William
Smyth Elijah
Smyth Richard
Snedecker Moses
Snedicar James
Sniduar James
Sniffen Amos
Sniffen Nehemiah
Snow John
Snowden John
Sohake Jonathan
Solyer Zacheus
Soucer Henry
Southard Harvey
Southard Henry
Southend John
Southerd John
Southerland William
Spece John
Speed George

Spencer Asa
Spencer David
Spencer Jabez
Spencer John
Spencer Samuel
Spicor Jacob
Spiers Joseph
Spilsbery Jacob
Sprague John
Sprigs Lazarus
Spring Ephraim
Spring Henry
Springstead Casparis
Springsted Abraham
Springsted Harmaumes
Springsteen Abraham
Springsteen Christopher
Springsteen George
Springsteen Harmance
Squirell Jacob
Staats Silvester
Stagg John
Stanbery Elijah
Stanciel William
Standford John
Stanford Daniel
Stansbury William
Stanton Benjamin
Stark Amos
Steel James
Steel John
Steenberg Peter
Stenbarreger Theodore
Stephen Nathan
Stephens Hendrick
Stephens Nathaniel
Sternbergh, David
Stevens John
Stevens Philip
Stevenson John
Steves Philip
Stewart John
Sthephens Henry
Stilefen John
Stillwell Thomas
Stilwell James
Stine William
Stinebrinner David
Stivers Philip
Stives Caleb
Stocker William
Stoner John
Stoner Nicholas

Storms John	Thornton James	Utter Gilbart
Stratton William	Thorrington James	Utter Isaac
Strawbridge Absolom	Thump Frederick	Vacter Nicholas
Streat Samuel	Tice John	Valentine Obadiah
Street Samuel	Tiemans Jonathan	Vallance Zachariah
Stringham Henry	Timberman Henry	Vallean Stephen
Stump John	Tire John	Van Atten Jacobus
Sturdeman Samuel	Titsworth Thomas	Van Cleack Henry
Stursburgh David	Titus Jonathan	Van Cleack Peter
Sucanox Daniel	Tobias John	Vandavore John
Succanox Peter	Todd Adam	Van de bogort Mindert
Sullivan Dennis	Todd John	Van De Burgh Mathew
Summers Hugh	Todd Thadeous	Van Demarker John
Surgeson William	Tode Adam	Van demerk Cornelius
Surs Francis	Tompkins Nathaniel	Vandermark David
Suthard Henry	Touttell Joel	Vandermark Zachariah
Sutler John	Towey David	Vander Marken Cornelius
Sweep Jacob	Townsond Samuel	Vandihider Adam
Sweet Reuben	Trautt Michael	Van Gelder Mathew
Sweet Samuel	Traverse Jacob	Van Gilder Isaac
Swift John	Traves Uriah	Van Gordes John I.
Symen Martin	Travis Abraham	Van Hoosen Garret
Symkins Jeremiah	Travis Scott	Van Hoozan Jacob
Symons Ephraim	Travis Uriah	Van Horn John
Symons Willitt	Treeman Jonathan	Van Kleek Henry
Syrine James	Treet Richard	Van Ness Cornelius
Tabor Thomas	Tremins Abner	Vannetten Jacobus
Talliday John	Trere P.	Van Nornam Isaac
Talmage Joseph	Trewelliger John	Van North John
Tapping Daniel	Trewileger Jacob	Vannute Charles
Tatcher Samuel	Trewillagar Ary Van Etten	Van Oman Isaac
Taylor Edward	Trimier Michael	Van Orman Isaac
Taylor John	Triming Abner	Vansaunt John
Teatsworth Thomas	Trimmings Jonathan	Van Sice Joseph
Templar Thomas	Trout Adam	Vantosels Cornelius
Ten Eyck John	Trout Michael	Van Tyne Isaac
Ten Eyck Joseph	Trowbridge Absalom	Van Valkenburgh Francis
Terwilleger James	Truewilleger James	Van Vlack George
Tharp Richard	Tubbs Cyrus	Van Volkingburgh Francis
Thomas Henry	Tuck John	Van Vordenbargh Thomas
Thomas James	Tucker Joshua	Vany Vinson
Thomas John	Tulva Thomas	Varian John
Thomas William	Tumans Peter	Varnill John
Thompson Benjamin	Tummons Abner	Varron John
Thompson James	Turnar Peter	Vaughan William
Thompson John	Turner William	Veley Andrew G.
Thompson Timothy	Tuthhill Joel	Venice John
Thomson Daniel	Tuthill William	Venus John
Thomson Elias	Tutle Solomon	Venute Charles
Thomson Joshua	Tuttle Abnerlin	Vermiller Peter
Thomson Stanley	Tylar Ezra	Verny Vincent
Thomson William	Underdunk Titus	Verritty Gilbert
Thomus Henry	Upright Michael	Vincent Joseph

Virnute Charles	Weed Abijah	Wildy Edward
Volingtine Richard	Weed Ezra	Wiley Edward
Volkingburgh Francis	Weeks Abraham	Wilkelow John
Vredenburgh Thomas	Weeks James	Wilkerson Joseph
Vulvia Thomas	Weeks Melatiah	Wilkerson Samuel
Waggoner Henry	Weemire Frederick	Willard Abel
Waldrom John	Weesmiller Henry	Willcox Aron
Waldrum Joseph	Welch John	Willcox John
Waldrum William	Welsh Edward	Willer Amos
Wales Timothy	Wendell Harmanus	Willess Thomas
Walker Edward	Wendle John	Willey Edward
Walker Israel	Wentworth John	Williams Charles
Walker John	West Jacob	Williams Francis
Walker Justus	West John	Williams John
Walker Matthias	Westervelt David	Williams Thomas
Walker Samuel	Wever John	Williamson James
Wall Patrick	Weyemiller Hendrick	Willkox John
Walles James	Wheeler Amos	Willmot John
Walner Abram	Wheeler Daniel	Willsey Isaac
Wandell John	Wheeler Joshua	Willson Abraham
Wanute Charles	Wheeler Peter	Willson Jacob
Wapshear Simon	Wheeler Richard	Willson John
Ward Abijah	Wheeler Samuel	Willson Thomas
Ward James	Wheeler Timothy	Willson William
Ward Robert	Wheelor John	Willy Samuel
Ward Thomas	Wheler William	Wilson Archibald
Ward Zadock	Wheller Richard	Wilson Samuel
Warden Thomas	Whiley Edward	Winchell John
Wareing Michael	Whipple Nathan	Winters John
Waring Benjamin	White Anthony	Winthrop William
Warner Edmoud	White Ephraim	Wire Jerimiah
Warner William	White Henry	Wisenfelts George
Warren Francis	White John	Wissenfels John
Warren John	White Paul	Wolf Hendrick
Warren Nathaniel	White Peter	Wolf James
Warren William	White Philip	Wolf Samuel
Washborn Abel	White William	Wood Jacob
Waterman Henry	Whitehead John	Wood James
Waterman James H.	Whitehead William	Wood John
Waterman John	Whitford Joseph	Wood Joseph
Waterman Samuel	Whitham Joseph	Wood William
Watkins Benjamin	Whitney Ezekiel	Woodmore Cornelius
Watson Richard	Whitney Jacob	Woodward Benedict
Waymire Frederick	Whittemore Cornelius	Woolcutt Justus
Weaver David	Whittmore Benjamin	Wordan Nathan
Weaver John	Whyley Simeon	Worden Thomas
Webb John	Wickham Stephen	Worry John
Webb Nathaniel	Wicklow John	Wright Barrick
Webb Samuel	Wilber Ichabod	Wright Ephram
Webster Daniel	Wilber Josiah	Wright John
Webster Thomas	Wilbur Jacob	Wright Uriah
Weckham Stephen	Wilbur Joseph	Wygant Tibias
Wedge Benjamin	Wilcox John	Yale Nathaniel

Yarington William
Yates John
Yauness John
Yeomans Eleazer
Yeomans Jeremiah

Yewmans Eleazer
Yewmans Jeremiah
Yomis Jacob
Yones John
Youmans Jeremiah

Young John
Younkin George
Zamens Ephreham
Zellers Michael

The Line, Third Regiment

COLONEL JAMES CLINTON
COLONEL PETER GANSEVORT
LIEUTENANT COLONEL JAMES BRUYN
MAJOR ROBERT COCHRAN
MAJOR JAMES ROSEKRANCE
ADJUTANT CHRISTOPHER HUTTON
ADJUTANT GEORGE SYTZ

QUARTER MASTER NEHEMIAH CARPENTER
QUARTER MASTER PRENTICE BOWEN
QUARTER MASTER THOMAS WILLIAMS, JR.
PAY MASTER JEREMIAH VAN RENSSELAER
SURGEON HUNLOKE WOODRUFF
SURGEON'S MATE JOHN ELLIOT, JR

CAPT. AARON AORSON
" ANDREW BILLINGS
" LEONARD BLEEKER
" JACOBUS S. BRUYN
" EZRA BUELL
" EZEKIEL COOPER
" DANIEL DENTON
" THOMAS DE WITT
" LEWIS DUBOYS
" I. GREGG
" JAMES GREGG
" JOHN GRENELL
" DANIEL GRIPPING
" ELIAS HASBROUCK

" JOHN HULBERT
" JAMES HUMPHREY
" CORNELIUS J. JANSEN
" ROBERT JOHNSTON
" GEORGE LIGHT
" JOHN NICOLSON
" ABRAHAM SWARTWOUT
" GEORGE SYTEZ
" HENRY TEABOUT
" HENRY TIEBOUT
" ELIAS VAN BUNSCHOTEN
LIEUT. JOSIAH BAGLEY
" JOHN BALL

LIEUT. PETER DEBOIS BEVIER
" BENJAMIN BOGARDUS
" ISAAC BOGART
" PRENTICE BOWEN
" WILLIAM COLEBREATH
" PHILIP CONINE
" NATHANIEL CONKLIN
" HENRY DEFENDORFF
" BALTHAZER DEHART
" GEORGE DENNISON
" GEORGE I. DENNISTON
" DAVID DUBOIS
" WILLIAM HAVENS
" JOHN HUNTER
" CHRISTOPHER HUTTON
" GEORGE HAMILTON JACKSON
" CORNELIUS T. JANSEN
" ALEXANDER KETCHAK
" PETER KOGGEN
" ANDREW LAWRENCE

" SAMUEL LEWIS
" GILBERT R. LIVINGSTON
" GEORGE LYTZE
" THOMAS McCLELLAN
" PETER MAGEE
" WILLIAM MARTIN
" BENJAMIN MARVIN
LIEUT. NATHANIEL NORTON
" THOMAS OSTRANDER
" ALBERT PAWLING
" SAMUEL SMITH
" GARRET STAATS
" LEVI STOCKWELL
" WILLIAM TAPP
" HENRY VANDERBURG
" NANKING VANDERHYDEN
" THOMAS WARMER
" JOHN WELCH
" MOSES YEOMANS

ENSIGN AMENT ALDERT
" JOHN BURHANCE
" ALEXANDER CLINTON
" DOUW FONDA
" DOUW I. FONDA
" BENJAMIN HERRING
" GARRIT G. LANSING

" SAMUEL LEWIS
" PETER MAGEE
"JOSEPH MORRILL
" MATTHEW POTAN
" JOHN SPOOR
" JEREMIAH VAN RENSSELAER

ENLISTED MEN

Aartwick Lawrence	Atkins Henry	Bates Joseph
Abbey Lemuel	Austin David	Batman William
Abbey Samuel	Avrey Humphrey	Batnar Paul
Acker Albert	Babbet Reuben	Bearvert John
Acker Conrad	Babbit John	Beckhorn Jeremiah
Ackerman David	Babcock David	Bedle Moses
Ackerman Edar	Bagley David	Beedle John
Ackerson Benjamin	Bailey Joseph	Beegle Thomas
Ackerson John	Bailey Wilkey	Beekman John
Ackerson Thomas	Baily Leonard	Beenns Stephen
Ackley Joel	Bakehorn Jacob	Begle Moses
Adams Ephraim	Bakehorn Jeremiah	Beidle John
Adams Stephen	Baker Bartholomew	Belknap John
Adams William	Baker Daniel	Belknap William
Adamy Henry	Baker Ichabod	Benjamin Daniel
Ade Lester	Baker John	Bennet -- s
Ademy Henry	Baker Joseph	Bennett Charles
Adley Peter	Baker Pars	Bennett Henry
Alderman Ephraim	Baker Thomas	Bennett Jeremiah
Allen Thomas	Balding Jesse	Benson Thomas
Allison John, Sr.	Ballas Elezer	Berdan John
Allison John, Jr.	Banchralt John	Berry Charles
Allison Peter	Banker John	Berry James
Allison Richard	Banker Thomas	Berton George
Allison Thomas	Banks Benjamin	Berwart John
Alone Christian	Baptist John	Beurum John
Ambler Nathan	Bardu Elias	Bickford James
Ambler Nathaniel	Barker Stephen	Bishop John
Ammermon Obadiah	Barkhoff Frederick	Bishop Levi
Anderson Ezekiel	Barnes Henry	Black John
Anderson George	Barnes Stephen	Blacker John
Anderson William	Barnhum Samuel	Blancher William
Andrews Benjamin	Barns Henry	Blanck Cornelius
Anning Daniel	Barns James	Blank Cornelius
Anthony Francis	Barret Michael	Blauvalt Abram
Anthony George	Barrett William	Blekwell Gerret
Anthony John	Barrey Charles	Blowers Ephraim
Anthony Peter	Barrit William	Blowers George
Apart John	Barton Rober	Bogard Martha
Appart John	Barton Robert	Bogardus Lewis
Armstrong John	Barwolf Christian	Bogart John
Artwick Lawrence	Bass Henry	Bohall Paul
Ash Henry	Basset Cornelius	Bont Thomas
Ashley Aaron	Basset Joseph	Dony William

Booth Henry
Bordon John
Boreman James
Bound Rodman
Bourk Edmond
Bourk John
Bovie Nicholas
Bower Jeremiah
Boyce James
Boyce John
Boyce John P.
Boyd Robert
Bradley Cornelius
Bradley Richard
Bradt Christopher
Brady George
Brady Richard
Brandt Edward
Brannen Abraham
Brannon Timothy
Brant Christian
Brant E.
Brass John
Bray William
Brenck Peter
Brewster Benjamin
Brewster William
Briggs John
Brink Robert
Brisbee James
Brocket Moses
Bromley Simon
Brondow Frederick
Brown Charles Fred
Brown Daniel
Brown David
Brown Henry
Brown Isaac
Brown John
Brown John F.
Brown Jonathan
Brown Peter
Brown Richard
Brown Robert
Brown Samuel
Brown Thomas Clark
Brown William
Bryant John
Bryant Melancthon
Bryent Thomas
Buckstaff Peter
Buis James
Bulson Cornelius

Bunce Edmund
Bunce Jesse
Bunskolen Solomon
Buoy William
Burch Philip
Burch Sabins
Burden John
Burgess Michael
Burgun Oliver
Burhans Edward
Burhans John
Burhans Samuel
Burjes Peter
Burk Edmund
Burk John
Burkdorf John
Burke Edmond
Burke John
Burns John
Burrell Zachariah
Burris John
Burroughs John
Burton George
Bushell Joseph
Buskirk Garret
Butler Richard
Butnar Paul
Buyce James
Buyer Godfrey
Buyford Henry
Byer Godfrey
Cable Andrew
Cain Edward
Cain John
Caldwell William
Calf John
Callam Reuben
Cambell Kenneth
Cameran Hugh
Campbell Duncan
Canfield Timothy
Canter Jonas
Carle John
Carll Lemuel
Carman Abraham
Carmical Blakney
Carmichel Peter
Carpenter Moses
Carpenter Samuel
Carr Norris
Carragill John
Carsad Richard
Carsday N.

Cartell John
Casady Luke
Case George
Case Joseph
Cashaday Nicholas
Casler Joseph
Cassells Eliphalet
Cavenough John
Cavin Thomas
Cazard Richard
Certain James
Chaddock Nathaniel
Chaddock Sylvanus
Chambers Francis
Chambers Henry
Chambers Jacobus
Chapel Benjamin
Chase George
Chase John
Chase Robert
Chasee Stephen
Chatfield Lewis
Chatfield William
Chickens Thomas
Christman Nicholas
Chulwell Thomas
Clanchy Daniel
Clansy Daniel
CLark Anthony
Clark Jeremiah
Clark John
Clarke Benjamin
Clarwater Jeremiah
Clemens John
Clement Nicholas
Clerk Benjamin
Clerk Martin
Cline Franses
Clinton Joseph
Clock Jonathan
Closs John
Coad William
Codgdon John
Coe John D.
Cole Francis
Cole Garet
Cole Thomas
Collins James
Collins Joseph
Collins William
Colman Timothy
Commadine Nicholas
Commedin Nicholas

Conckling John
Conckling Selah
Conckling Thomas
Conckling Timothy
Conden Philip
Condon David
Cone John
Conet John
Conklin Joseph
Conklin Nathaniel
Conklin Samuel
Conklin Silvanus
Conkling David
Conkling Jacob
Conkling Jonathan
Conkling Thomas
Connolly Hugh
Connaway John
Connoway Cornelius
Conolice John
Conro Darling
Constable Garret
Cook Burnit
Cook George
Cook Jonathan
Cook Samuel
Cook Thomas
Coon James
Coonet John
Cooper Abram
Cooper John
Cooper John, Jr.
Cooper John C.
Cooper Zebulon, Jr.
Cordise George Frederick
Cordwise George
Cormical Blackney
Cornwall Caleb
Cornwall John
Cornwall Joseph
Cornwell Silvanus
Corrigal John
Corter John
Corwin Jonathan
Corwin Nathan
Corwin Thomas
Cousins Mathew
Cowdrey Benjamin
Cowen James
Cozens Matthew
Crambary Francis
Cramberry Francis
Crandell Luke

Crandle Luke
Creamer John
Creaton Thomas
Crekenborne Johannis
Crickenboom John
Crispell Anthony
Cristman Nicholas
Cristy John
Crosshar Samuel
Crossman Abner
Crossman Simeon
Cunningham Charles
Curoday Nicholas
Curry Samuel
Curtis George F.
Curtis John
Darby Asa
Darby John
Davenport Thomas
David Henry
Davin Richard
Davis Chapman
Davis Gilbard
Davis John
Davis Matthew
Davis Nathan
Davis Samuel
Davis William
Dawson Daniel
Dawson Richard
Dayton Samuel
Dayton Samuel, Jr.
Dean Edward
Dean Joseph
Dean Samuel
Debois Jacobus
Debois Johannis
De Bois John I.
De Clark Abraham
Deffendorf Henry
Deforest Henry
Dejo Hugh
Delamarter John
Delamater John
Demont Joseph
Dempsey Mark
Dempster John
Denn Thomas
Dennis John
Denny Samuel
Deratt John
Devan Cornelius
De Vaults Peter

Devaults Stephen
Devee Henry
Devee William
Devenport Thomas
De Witt Benjamin
Dewitt Jacob
Deyo Hugh
Deyo Hugh H.
Dickerson Jeremiah
Dillinge John
Dobb John
Dobbins Thomas
Dodge Alexander
Dodge Henry
Dodge Zachariah
Dods Zachariah
Doherty Thomas
Douden John
Doughty Isaac
Douglass William
Dowlar George
Downs James
Dreyer Frederick
Driskelt Cornelius
Dumond Joseph
Dumont John
Dunlap James
Dunlap Thomas
Dunn Stephen
Dunnivan Anthony
Dupee Abraham
Eager James
Eagins Joshua
Early Samuel
Easton Henry
Edes Joseph
Edgarly John
Egans Joshua
Eggs Samuel
Elleback Emanuel
Ellen Jesse
Elliot Francis
Elliot John
Elliot John, Jr.
Ellon Jesse
Ellot Archabel
Elmendorph Petrus
Elmendorph Petrus, Jr.
Elsworth Peter
Elting Thomas
Emica John G.
English Joshua
English Samuel

Ennis Henry
Ennist Cornelius
Erwin James
Evans Joseph
Everhart John
Everhile John P.
Everstine Francis
Fairchild Jesse
Farrington David
Fausdick Samuel
Fero Andris
Ferran Cornelle
Ferreigh John
Ferry Omer
Fersha Dennis
Fetzerman Barnet
Field James
Finch Charles
Finton Peter
Fitzerman Barna
Fletcher James
Fling Henry
Flynn John
Fokes Robert
Foot Johan Caspar
Forbes Alexander
Force David
Foren James
Forguson Robert
Forman Gabriel
Forr John C.
Fosdick Samuel
Foster Daniel
Foster James
Foster Thomas
Fothergill Hugh
Fountain John
Fowler Jabez
Fowles James
France Coonradt
Frayer Thomas
Frazier John
Frear Solomon, Jr.
Frederick John
Freeland John
French Coonradt
Freyer J.
Freyer Thomas
Friday Coonradt
Fryer Robert
Fulton Francis
Fulton William
Funna Anthony

Furman Gabriel
Furne Francis
Gadge John
Gahan John
Gail John
Gain Francis
Gains Christian
Gake Samuel
Gall John
Gardenier Samuel
Gardineer Samuel
Gardiner Andrew
Gardiner Jeremiah
Garnet John
Garrell John
Garrison Abraham
Garret Benjamin
Garvey David
Gates John
Gattes David
Gee Thomas
Geege John
Gelston William
Geraghty Bartholomew
Gibson Andrew
Giers Benjamin
Gifford William
Gilbert Samuel
Gildersleaves Philip
Gildersleeve Finch
Gildersleeve Richard
Gillaspy James
Gillaspy James J.
Gillaspy William
Gillaspy William, Jr.
Gilmore Robert
Glen Robert
Glenn George
Goldsmith William
Goodcourage John
Gould John
Grace James
Graham Andrew
Gray John
Gray Robert
Green William
Gregg Thomas
Griffes James
Griffing James
Grimsly William
Grite William
Groot William
Groseman Frederick

Grote William
Grummon Joseph
Haburn William
Hadley Bishop
Haight Abraham
Haight Thomas
Hall John
Hallet Moses
Halsey Matthew
Halsey Matthew, Jr.
Halsey William Rogers
Haman Daniel
Haman James P
Haman John F.
Hamilton William
Hand Daniel
Handen John
Hanney James
Happle Adam
Hardenbergh Henderik
Hardenbergh Leonard
Harder Adam
Harlow Robart
Harriot J.
Harriot Thomas
Harris George, Jr.
Harriss Silas
Hart Andrew
Hart Gilbert
Hart Thomas
Harter Adam
Harvey William
Hasbrouck John, Jr
Hatch Timothy
Hatton Jacob
Haven Isaac
Havens Daniel
Havens Joseph
Haycock John
Hebbard Abel
Hedges Elias
Height Abraham
Hellit Francis
Hender Frederick
Henderson Elisha
Henderson Patrick
Henry Michael
Herrald Henry
Herteel John
Hevington William
Hewit Benjamin
Heyer Alexander
Hickey John

Hicks Jacob
Hide Thomas
Hievnard Hendrick
Higby Daniel
Higgans Jonathan
Higher Garrit
Hile Coonrad
Hill David
Hill Eliphelet
Hill Henry
Hill John
Hill Nicholas
Hoffman David
Hogan Patrick
Hoghtaling William
Holbert Aaron
Holley Benjamin
Home Casper
Hone William
Honeywell John
Hooper Jacob R.
Hooper Robert R.
Hopkins Stephen A.
Hopp Abraham
Hopping Henry
Hopping Joseph
Horton Isaac
House John
Houser Andrew
Houstman George
Houxly James
How John
Howard James
Howel Samuel
Howell Aaron
Howell Edward
Howell Lemuel
Howell Stephen
Hubbard Rosel
Hudson John
Huff Robert
Huffner Hendrick
Huggans James
Huit Daniel
Hulbert Aaron
Hull Nathaniel, Jr.
Hull Samuel
Hully Arthur
Hulser John
Hungerforth Daniel
Hunt Benjamin
Hunt Guilead
Hunter Jonathan

Hunter Thomas
Hurley Arthur
Hurley James
Hutson John, Jr.
Huxley James
Huxley John
Hyer Alexander
Hyer Garret
Hyet Joseph
Hyle Coonrad
Hyne Hartman
Hynes Hendrick
Isaacs Isaac
Jackson Archibald
Jackson Francis
Jagger Abraham
Jansen Frederick
Jeffrey John
Jenkin Ennis
Jennings Elnathan
Jessup Zebulon
Jinnings Hazakiah
Jinnings Jonathan
Johnson Edward
Johnson Daniel
Johnson John
Johnston Daniel
Jones David
Jones Elicom
Jones Jeremiah
Jones Joseph
Jones Nathaniel
Jones Seth
Jones Shadrick
Jones Thomas
Jones William
Kallam Reuben
Karr Mark
Kater James
Keator Petrus
Keator Wilhelmus
Keener Christian
Keener Christopher
Keisbergh Christian
Kellam Reuben
Kelley Patrick
Kelley Robert
Kelley Thomas
Kellion Coonradt
Kelly John
Kelsey Benjamin
Kenny John
Kent Thomas

Ketcham Daniel
Ketcham Philip
Keyser Abraham
King Aaron
King Jeremiah
King Joel
King John
King Jonathan
Kinney Jese
Kinny Charles
Kip Mathew
Kip Moses
Kirk Joseph
Kitcham John
Kitcham Samuel
Klaerwater Daniel
Klock J.
Knapp Benjamin
Knapp Elijah
Knapp Jeremiah
Knapp William
Knapping Jeremiah
Koile David
Kortreght Silvester
Krack Godlieb
Krak Godlip
Krom Benjamin, Jr.
Kysinger Philip
Ladd Joseph
Lafter John
Lalancet John
Lambart Davi
Lambert Abraham
Lambert John
Lambert Moses
Lampyer Francis
Langdon Ananias
Lansing Evert
Laport John
Laroy John, Jr.
Lattamore Thomas
Lawrence Benjamin
Lawson George
Lawyer William
Leach John
Leaster Michael
Lee James
Lee Thomas
Leek Abraham
Lees Martin
Leiencet James
Lemmon Alexander
Lemon Alexander

Lennington Thomas	McAnanny John	Maker Nathaniel
Lennox Samuel	McAuley Robert	Maker Solomon
Lent Harculous	McBride James	Mallow Thomas
Lent Moses	McBride John	Mane Matthew
Leonard Henry	McCart James	Mantanye Jacobus
Leonard Robert	McCarty Dennis	Manuel Isaac
Lepling John	McCay Alexander	Marsten James
Lewis Lockart	McClanning John	Marvin Elihew
Lewis Peter	McClean John	Marvin Matthew
Lewis Richard	McConnelly Hugh	Marvin Moses
Lewis Thomas	McCord William	Marvin Seath
Lewis Zadock	McCormick James	Mason James
Lighthall James	McCormick Thomas	Masten Daniel
Lighthall Lancaster	McCoy Alexander	Masten James
Limbaker John	McCoy James	Mathers John
Lipling John	McCutcheon Thomas	Mathews Peter
Little Peter	McDaniel James	Matleg Caleb
Little William	McDaniel John	Matleg Daniel
Littlejohn John	McDermot Cornelius	Matlock Caleb
Loader Daniel	McDonald Alexander	Maxwell Cornelius
Lockert Lewis	McDonald Daniel	Maxwell William
Loins Michael	McDonald Donald	Mayberry Richard
Looper Abraham	McDormit Cornelius	Maybus Leonard
Looper Amos	McDougal Alexander	Meeker John
Loose P.	McEwan Duncan	Meeker Nathaniel
Loosee Paul	McFarland John	Meeker Solomon
Loper David	McGinnis John	Megere James
Losey Paul	McGlaghlin William	Melcher Paul
Losing Peter	McGown Archibald	Mellow Thomas
Lossing Lowrence	McGraw Alexander	Melshire Paul
Loucks Hendrick	McGuin Abraham	Mence Christopher
Louden William	McGuire Abraham	Merrick Seth
Louks Hendrick	McGuire James	Merricle Samuel
Lourey Alexander	McIntire Phineas	Mershall William
Loux Hendrick	McIntosh John	Middagh George
Loux Nicholas	McKenzie John	Miers Jacob
Love Davis	McKenzie Neal	Miles John
Lovely Francis	Mackey Thomas	Miller David
Low Jacob G.	McKim John	Miller Henry
Lowcey Paul	McKneel John	Miller Jacob
Lowdon William	McKown James	Miller John, Jr.
Lowman Peter	McKown John	Miller Levi
Loyal Edward	McLaughlin William	Miller Ludwick
Lucy Eleazer	McMaster Alexander	Miller Nathan
Ludlam George	McMichael John	Miller Peter
Ludlam Stephen	McNeal Henry	Miller Zephaniah
Ludlum Daniel	McNeal John	Miller William
Lusk Francis	McQuin Philip	Milles John
Luther John	McVay John	Mills David
Lutner James	Madden Owen	Mills Henry
Lyon Asa	Mahan Patrick	Mills Nathaniel
Lyon John	Mahanne Cain	Milspaugh Mathias
Lyon Joseph	Maines Mathew	Minick Barnhart

Minick Hendrick
Minie Christopher, Jr.
Minnen Robert
Minroo George
Mitchell Robert
Mixer Daniel
Moloy William
Monrow Alexander
Montcrief Charles
Moor Frederick
Moor John
Moor Robert
Moor Samuel
Moore Frederick
Moore John
Moore Thomas
Morcraft William
Morewise Jacob
Morgin David
Morris Edmond
Morrison Daniel
Morrison Richard
Morrison Thomas
Morriston Richard
Morrow Patrick
Mosher John
Mosier Hugh
Mosure Ruben
Mott Henry
Mott Jacob
Mott Joseph
Mott Samuel
Mott Thomas
Mowris Daniel
Mulholand James
Mullon John
Munro Alexander Jr.
Murphey Peter
Murray Bartley
Murray James
Murray William
Mute William
Myer Frederick
Myers Frederick
Myers Jacob
Myrick Seth
Nangle Frederick
Neilson Allen
Nelson Allen
Nelson Caleb
Nemiah John Henry
Nemire John Henry
Nevels John

Newbergh John
Newman William
Newton William
Nichols Simon
Nicous Robert
Nicols Joseph
Nicolson Jonathan
Nicolson Thomas
Noble Cornelius
Norris Isaac
North John
Northrop Ebenezer S.
Nortrap Moses
Nostrant Isaac
Nostrant John
Nostrant Luke
Nottingham William
Nyx Cornelius
Oakes Ephraim
Oakes John
Obrient John
O'Connoley James
Odle Tomkins
Ohlen Henry G.
Oldham John
Olendorph Leonard
Oliphant William
Oliver Thomas
Olmendurff Leonard
Oneal John
Oosterhoudt Isaac
Orr Baltis
Orsborn Ezekel
Osborn Aaron
Osborn Cornelius
Osborn Josiah
Osterhout Isaac
Osterhout Peter
Ostrander Peter
Ostrander Peter William
Owen Daniel
Owens Daniel
Owens Thomas
Owens Uriah
Paddock Levy
Pain Jonathan
Pain Paul
Painter Edward
Palfreman William
Palmateer Isaac
Palpeman William
Parker Daniel
Parker Edmund

Parker Edward
Parker Timothy
Parkhoff Frederick
Parks Ebenezer
Parks Jonah
Parks Timothy
Parks William
Parshel James
Parson Isaac
Patterson James
Patterson John
Patterson William
Pease Nathaniel
Peirson Isaac
Peirson John
Pelgrit Hendrick
Pells Henry
Peltz Hendrick
Peltz Henry
Peresonias Jacobus
Perkhoff Frederick
Perkoff Hendrick
Perksmith Englars
Perchase Joseph
Peters John
Peters Simon
Peterson John
Phenix Robert
Phillips William
Pillgret Hendrick
Pillow John
Pinckney Jonathan
Pinkney Jonathan
Pinton Peter
Piny Edward
Piper Lewis
Pitt Abraham
Pittman John
Pixty Eli
Plato Thomas
Platto Thomas
Plough Jochiam
Plough Samuel
Plumsted Nathaniel
Post Cornelius
Post Richard
Poulson Michael
Powlson Michael
Pratt Chalker
Pratt John
Preston Benjamin
Preston Othaniel
Price Adam

Price Benjamin
Price Robert
Prince Joseph
Prindle Joseph
Prouth Degory
Putney Joseph
Quackenboss Benjamin
Queen Christopher
Quigley George
Rahea Denie
Ralje David
Randell Henry
Randle Henry
Ranger Samuel
Rannels Abijah
Ray William
Read James
Record Wilmot
Reed Garret
Reed Samuel
Reeves Daniel
Rendal Henry
Renne Coral
Rennix William
Rergtmire Conradt
Reynard John
Reynolds John
Reynolds Michael
Rice Samuel
Richardson Alexander
Rider George
Riely Charles
Riley John
Rilya David
Rinder Christian
Ripenbergh Adam
Risdale William
Roads Noah
Roberts Warren
Robinson Andrew
Robinson George
Robinson James
Robinson John
Robinson Richard
Rocaster John
Rodgers Samuel
Rogers James, Jr.
Rogers Stephen
Romer William
Romine John
Roos Lemuel
Roosa Jacob
Root George

Rosa Aaron
Rosa Aldert
Rose Albert
Rose Thomas
Ross John
Rotheart George J.
Rouse Thomas
Rowley Seth
Rowley Thomas
Ruland Thomas
Rumler Thomas
Rump Henry
Ruskill Marlain
Russell Joseph
Russell Oliver
Rutan Peter
Ryan Patrick
Ryan Robert
Ryley Patrick
Rynard John
Rynder Christian
Rynder Christopher
S-- Ephriham
St. Johns Noah
Sammons Matthew
Sandford Benjamin
Sapin Thomas
Sassin Thomas
Sax Jacob
Sayre James
Sayre Joshua
Schreeder John Joachim
Schruder John J.
Schryver Christopher
Schultz John
Scott Andrew
Scott John
Scott Timothy
Scott William
Scriber Christian
Scriber Peter
Scudder Alexander
Scudder Edmund
Seaberry John
Seaman Daniel
Seaman Isaac
Seaman J.
Seaman Micha
Seamans Ephraim
Seamans Isaac
Searles Thomas
Searls Thomas
Secor Isaac

Secor James
Seely Silvanus
Seevey Joseph
Semall Anthony
Serals Thomas
Sevey James
Seyley Coenradt
Shade Adam
Shades Adam
Sharriner Lodwick
Shatter Hussey
Shaw John
Shawl John
Shay John
Shearwood James
Sheets James
Sheffield Robert
Shell Christian
Shell Christopher
Shell George
Sherlocke John
Sherriden Richard
Sherril Abraham
Sherril Jeremiah
Sherrow James
Sherwood Elijah
Sherwood Seymour
Shields Daniel
Shields James
Shift George
Shires Jacob
Shirlock John
Shirts Peter
Shirts Samuel
Shoecraft Joho.
Short Jacob
Shriner Lodewick
Shriver Lodewick
Shultz John
Shurky Thomas
Sickels Abraham
Sickles Abraham
Simkins Gideon
Simons Moses
Simpkins Gedion
Simwell Anthony
Skiffington John
Slaughter Isaac
Slead Joseph
Slone Thomas
Sluyter Jacob
Sly Samuel
Slyter James

Smider Christejan
Smith Alexander
Smith Archibald
Smith Daniel
Smith David
Smith Duncan
Smith George
Smith Hezekiah
Smith Hugh
Smith Isaac
Smith Jeremiah
Smith Joel
Smith John
Smith Josiah
Smith Nathaniel
Smith Peter
Smith Petrus, Jr.
Smith Solomon
Smith Thaddeus
Smith Wait
Sommers Hugh
Sox Jacob
Sparling John
Spear John
Speer John
Speigler Frederick
Speigler Hendrick
Spensor Joseph
Spensor Mathias
Spiegler Hendrick
Staats Silvester
Stag Jasper
Stagg John
Stalker William
Stanbury Elijah
Star Eli
Starling Levy
Steenbergh Abraham
Steeples Nathan
Stephen Samuel
Stephens Abraham
Stephens John
Stephens Reilef
Stephenson Samuel
Sterling Levi
Stevens Eliphelet
Stevens John
Stevens Samuel
Stewart Samuel
Still James
Stilwill James
Stimas Isaac
Stimwell Anthony

Stitt James
Stodgden Robert
Stokes Alexander
Storer Nehemiah
Stout James
Strickling Samuel
Stuart John
Stump Charles
Sturges Isaac
Sullivan Dennis
Sullivan John
Sumurch Henry
Sutherland Daniel
Sutherland James
Sutler Samuel
Swan Peter
Swartwout Cornelius
Sweeny Roger
Talladay John
Tallerday Stephen
Talmadge Elisha
Tammond Peter
Tarry Daniel
Tarry David
Taylor Alexander
Taylor Thomas
Teachout William
Temount Joseph
Tenure James
Ter Bush John
Terry Samuel
Terwelleger Benjamin
Terwelleger James
Thomas John
Thompson Elias
Thompson John
Thompson Joshua
Thomson Benjamin
Thorp Thomas, Sr.
Thorp Thomas, Jr.
Tisdell William
Tisdit William
Tobin Edward
Todd Jonathan
Toll Roger
Tomkins Abraham
Tompkins Abraham
Tompkins Thomas
Tompson John
Tone Andrew
Tool Roger
Topping Daniel
Town Timothy

Townshand Richard
Trait Abel
Troop George
Trull John
Truman Jonathan
Tubee John
Tuley John
Turner Alexander
Turner John
Turner Richard
Tuthil Azariah
Tuttle Henry
Tuttle Stephen
Twisle John
Umphrey Evins
Umphrey John
Upright George
Upright James
Upright Nathan
Utest John
Vader Samuel
Vail Jeremiah
Vail John
Vail Micah
Vail Peter
Valentine Joseph
Valentine Peter
Van Ambergh Abraham
Van Amboro Abraham
Van Atta John
Van Benscoter Elias
Van Blarcum James
Van Blaricum James
Van Blazicum James
Van Bunhagele John C. Benj.
Van Bunhagle Benjamin
Vancamp Abram
Van Cleef Lawrence
Vandemark Cornelius
Van Den Bogart Esoyas
Vandenburgh Jacob
Van Der Burgh Henry
Van Der Burgh Jacob
Van Derhyden Adam
VanDerhyden Derrick
Van Derhyden Gershom
Vandervoort James
Van Der Warken Martin
Van Deusen Abraham
Van devoort James
Van Every David
Van Gasbeek Thomas

Van hour Rineas
Van Kleak James
Van Kleeck Moses
Van Kleek James
Van Klief Laurence
Van Loan Peter
Van Nosdal Cornelius
Van Nosdall John
Van Ordan Charles
Vansail Egbert
Van Schank Anthony
Van Sickle Ferdinand
Van Sise John
Van Sise Joseph
Van Stenburgh Jeremiah
Vantine Isaac
Van Wagoner John
Varner Henry
Varriken Johannes
Vary George
Vasey George
Vaults Peter
Veal John
Veeder Samuel
Verling Andrew M.
Vessels Joseph
Vonck William
Vradenburg William
Vredenburgh William
Wade Bernard
Waddle William
Wagerman Emanuel
Wagerman George
Waggerman Emanuel
Waggerman George
Wains William
Waiter Thomas
Walby Roger
Wall Patrick
Wallace James
Wallace John
Wallis John
Walter Coonradt
Wandle John
Ward Daniel
Ward Thomas
Warden Nathan
Waring Benjamin
Warnor Martin
Warren Edward
Warren Francis
Warring Benjamin
Wass John

Watkins Elijah
Watson Joseph
Watson Richard
Watson William
Way John
Weasels Joseph
Weathersline John
Weaver Christian
Weaver Christopher
Weaver George
Weaver Henry
Weaver Johannis
Weaver Richard
Webb Daniel
Weed David
Weeks Andrew
Weeks Jacob
Weeks Jonathan
Weeks Obediah
Weken Conrad
Welch John
Welch Richard
Welch Thomas
Welden Robert
Weldon Jeremiah
Wells John
Wells Peter
Wesell Joseph
Wetherstine John
Wey John
Weychouer Jacob
Weyfenback Hendrick
Weyherner Jacob
Weyschouer Jacob
Wharry David
Wharry Evins
Whay John
Whiley John
White Joseph
White Thomas
Whitham William
Whitman John
Whitter Ezra
Wilbur Esau
Wiggins Thomas
Wiley John
Wilkinson Robert
Willer Charles
Willes James
Willes Thomas
Willett Francis
Williams Abraham
Williams Arthur

Williams Ebenezer
Williams George
Williams John
Williams Robert
Williams Solomon
Williamson John
Willis John
Willis Thomas
Wills John
Wilsey William
Wilsie William
Wilson John
Wilson Robert
Wilson Thomas
Winchester Amariah
Windover John
Wise Gutlip
Withem William
Witmozier Henry
Witt Christopher
Wood Eliphelet
Wood Gilbert
Wood John
Wood Jonathan
Wood Silas
Wood Thomas
Wood Timothy
Woodworth Joshua
Wooley Jared
Worden Nathan
Worden Nathaniel
Wordenton Mathew
Wright Abraham
Wright Edward
Wright Samuel
Wybert Frederick
Wyfenback Henry
Wynins William
Wyschover Jacob
Yarington William
Yates James
Yengle John F.
Yeoman Moses
Yeomans Isaac
Youmans William
Young Daniel
Young Isaac
Young John
Youngs Israel
Youngs John
Youngs Nathan
Zagart Christian

Zanno Frederick   Zeaster Michael

The Line - Fourth Regiment

COLONEL JAMES HOLMES
COLONEL HENRY B. LIVINGSTON
LIEUT. COL. PIERRE REGNIER
LIEUT. COL. FREDERICK WEISSENFELS
LIEUT. COL. FREDERICK WIESSENFELS
MAJOR JOHN DAVIS
MAJOR BENJAMIN LEDYARD
MAJOR JOSEPH McCRACKEN
ADJUTANT PETER SACKET
ADJUTANT SAMUEL TALLMADGE
ADJUTANT JOHN TUTHILL

QUARTER MASTER JAMES BARRETT
QUARTER MASTER NEMEMIAH CARPENTER
QUARTER MASTER GELSTON
QUARTER MASTER JOB MULFORD
QUARTER MASTER PETER VONK
PAYMASTER JOHN FRANKS
CHAPLAIN JOHN P. TESTARD
SURGEON CALEB SWEET
SURGEON JOHN FRANCIS VACHE
SURGEON JOHN F. VASHER
SURGEON JOHN FRANCIS VASHER

CAPT. JOSEPH BENEDICT
" JOHN DAVIS
" HENRY DODGE
" EDWARD DUNSCOMB
" PETER ELSWORTH
" THEODORUS FOWLER
" SILAS GRAY
" RUFUS HERRICK
" AMBROSE HORTON
" WILLIAM JACKSON
" BENJAMIN MARVIN
" DANIEL MILLS
" NATHANIEL NORTON
" DAVID PALMER
" JONATHAN PEARSEE
" JONATHAN PERRY
" JONATHAN PLATT
" ----------REEVE
" DANIEL ROE
" JAMES ROSEKRANS
" SAMUEL SACKET
" ISRAEL SMITH
" NATHAN STRONG
" NATHANIEL STRONG
" JONATHAN TITUS
" BENJAMIN WALKER
" NATHANIEL WOODARD
LIEUT. WILLIAM B. ALGER
" JAMES BARRETT
" CORNELIUS BECKER
" -------------BENJAMIN

LIEUT. ABRAHAM RIKER
" ISAAC A. ROSA

LIEUT. LEONARD BLEECKER
" GOULD BOUGHTEN
" HENRY BREWSTER
" --------BRUSH
" MANNING BULL
" PETER BUNSHOTEN
" EDWARD CONKLIN
" SYLVANUS CONKLING
" WILLIAM CRANE
" DAVID DAN
" DANIEL E. DENISTON
" DANIEL DENNISTON
" HENRY DODGE
" JAMES DOW
" PETER ELSWORTH
" PETER C. ELSWORTH
" WILLIAM ELSWORTH
" THEDOSIOUS FOWLER
" JOSEPH FRILICK
" CHARLES GRAHAM
" WILLIAM HAVENS
" THOMAS HUNT
" ELIJAH HUNTER
" ABRAHAM HYATT
" JOHN LAWRENCE
" THOMAS LEE
" JOHN LLOYD
" WILLIAM MATTHEWMAN
" MILES OAKLEY
" ISAAC PADDOCK
" SAMUEL TREDWELL PELL

" --------SAYER
" GEORGE SMITH

" ISAAC SPRINGER
" GILBERT STRANG
" JACOB THOMAS
" JESSE THOMPSON
" DANIEL TOPPING
" WILLIAM TROOP
" ROBERT TROUP
" AZARIAH TUTHILL
" JOHN VAN ANTWERP
" PETER VAN BUNSCHOTEN
" RUDOLPH VAN HOEVENBARGH

" ISAAC VANWART

" ROSWELL WILCOCKS
"------------YOUNGH
ENSIGN JOHN BARR
" CALEB BRUISTER
" SIMON CREGIER
" SIMON CRYGIER
" SAMUEL DODGE
" JOSEPH FROILICK
" STEPHEN GRIFFIN
" JOSEPH MORRILL
" JOHN PUNDERSON
" SAMUEL TALMADGE
" EPHRAIM WOODRUFF

ENLISTED MEN

Acker Jacob	Baker Benjamin	Beebe Bonarges
Acker Jacob	Baker Elijah	Beedle William
Ackerson C.	Baker Henry	Beel Matthew
Adams Daniel	Baker John	Bellamy Silas
Adams Ebenezer	Bakcr Joshua	Benedict Ambrose
Adams James	Baker Pierce	Benjamin David
Adams Jesse	Balding Jehlal	Benjamin Stephen
Adams Major	Balding Nathaniel	Bennadict Benjamin
Adorns Samuel	Baley Jonathan	Bennadict Nathan
Adurns Thomas	Baley Leonard	Bennadict Peter
Allen Samuel	Ball Samuel	Bennet James
Allison Richard	Banker Jacob	Bennet William
Allport John	Banker William	Bennett Jacob
Alport John	Baptist John	Bennett Timothy
Amberman Cornelius	Barber Reuben	Benschoten Elias
Ambler Benjamin	Baremore Edward	Bentley William
Ambler Stephen	Barkens William	Bergordus Peter
Ammerman Cornelius	Barker Jonathan	Berrnard Samuel
Anderson James	Barlow Nathan	Berry Charles
Andress Joseph	Barnhart David	Berry Jabez
Anson James	Barnhart Jeremiah	Berry James
Anthoney Simon	Barns Glean	Berry John
Antone John	Barns John	Bertley Andrew
Armstrong Jonathan	Barns Peter	Betson Thomas
Ashford Nathaniel	Barrows James	Betts Nehemiah
Ashley William	Barry Charles	Bingham Abisha
Aston Benoni	Bartley Andrew	Bishop Ebenezer
Atkins Robert	Barto John	Black David
Atwater John	Bartoe Morris	Black Richard
Austin Holmes	Basely Cornelias	Black William
Austin Lockwood	Bassett William	Blank Jasper
Avery Nehemiah	Bayless Richard	Blaze Christopher
Avout Philip	Bayley Daniel	Blendberry Elijah
Aymes Francis	Beaty Hugh	Blonck J.
Backcus Jacob	Bebee Benorger	Blonk Jesper
Bailey Elias	Becker Peter	Bockus Jacob
Baker Anthony	Beckwith Silas	Bodley Andrew

Bogardus Henry
Bogg John
Bogurdus Nung.
Boice James
Boiles James
Boncher William
Bond John
Bonker William
Boughton Moses
Boughton Simeon
Bourne William
Bouten Samuel
Bouton Joseph
Bouton Joseph, Jr.
Bower
Bowers Isaac
Bowers James
Bowman Bacchus
Bowne Rodman
Boyles James
Bradt John
Brady John
Bragame John
Brainerd Ruben
Braney Lowring
Brant John
Brant William
Brewer Jeremiah
Brewland Johiel
Briggs Jacob
Briggs Jeremiah
Brock Robert
Brooks Daniel
Brooks Jediah
Brooks John
Brooks Robert
Brooks Thomas
Brown David
Brown Deliverance
Brown Eliphelet
Brown Hubbard
Brown John
Brown Joseph
Brown Samuel
Brown Stephen
Brown William
Brown Zephaniah
Brundage Nathan
Brunson Samuel
Brush Selah
Brush Simeon F.
Brustier Daniell
Bruton Arthur

Bryon Thomas
Buchannan Samuel
Buckingham Stephen
Buckleman Henry
Budd John
Budin Francis
Budine Francis
Bump Joseph
Bunday Jeremiah
Bunker William
Burch Jonathan
Burch Henry
Burd Jeremiah
Burdick Elisha
Burges Stephen
Burgess Archibold
Burget Millbury
Burhans Fjerrick
Burhans John
Burhans Thirh
Burhans Yerick
Burkstaff David
Burnet Ebenezer
Burnet Squire
Burnham William
Burnhart David
Burns David
Burns Edward
Burr Daniell
Burrance John
Burnt William
Burrows James
Burrows Samuel
Bush Simon T.
Bussing John
Bustee Peter
Camby James
Cammeron Alexander
Camp Asa
Campbell Andrew
Campbell Jacob
Campbell James
Campbell John
Canaday John
Canady James
Canby James
Canfield Amon
Canneld Daniel
Cankhert Henry
Carby Richard
Carll
Carney Barny
Carney William

Carny Thomas
Carpenter James
Carr Anthony
Carr James
Carrey John
Carrion Green
Case Ichabod
Casey James
Cashan William
Cashin William
Cato
Cato Tunis
Cavins Partrick
Chapman Daniel
Chappel Benjamin
Chappel Benjamin, Jr.
Charlesworth John Miles
Chase Isaac
Chatterton James
Cherry John
Chesley John
Chevalier John
Chinander John
Christee J.
Christen Peter
Cisco Dick
Clackson George
Clark Barnabas
Clark Cornelius
Clark David
Clark Ephraim
Clark James
Clark John
Ciark Joseph, Jr.
Clark Peter
Clarke Joshua
Clements John
Cliff Joseph
Clift Joseph
Close Christopher
Closs Peter
Closser Christopher
Coats Joseph
Coe Benjamin
Cole Aaron
Cole Abraham
Cole Barnabas
Cole Oliver
Cole William
Coleman Samuel
Collins Edward
Collins John
Colly Henry

Colver Joseph
Colvin James
Conden Philip
Conington Joseph
Conkling Daniel
Conkling Edward
Conkling Nathan
Conkling William
Conkright Henry
Conn William
Conner Joseph
Connerly Dennis
Connoly James
Connor James
Connor John
Connor Patrick
Connor Timothy
Constable Garret
Converse Samuel
Cook
Cook Alexander
Cook Darias
Cook George
Cook Moses
Cook Nathan
Cook Nathaniel
Cook Obadiah
Coon Jacob
Coon Peter
Cooper David
Cooper John
Copinger Walter
Coppenger John
Corkangs Eli
Cornell Caleb
Cornwall Caleb
Cornwell Thomas
Cortright Henry
Corwine Edward
Corwine Gersham
Cossington John
Cottrell Richard
Couchoover William
Couray Michael
Cowan Isaac
Cox John
Cox Simon
Cozard Richard
Craft Nathaniel
Craig John
Crane Josiah
Crannell Isaac
Crawford John

Crawford Thomas
Cregear John
Crissler John
Cristie William
Cronch James
Cronk Hendrick
Cronk Timothy
Crosby Enock
Crosby Isaac
Crosby Thomas
Crosman Dan
Cross John
Crossman Daniel
Crowfot Nehemiah
Cummers Jonathan
Cunningham Archibald
Cunningham Henry
Cunningham John
Cunningham Shubal
Curaw Michael
Curby John
Cure William
Curry Elijah
Curry Michael
Cursor Tunis
Curtis Naniad
Curtis Niard
Curtis Solomon
Curwin Edward
Curwin Gersham
Curwine Gersham
Cuzard Richard
Daggett Mahew
Dale Richard
Daley John
Dalton Walter
Dan Abijab
Dan Jonathan
Danavan Peter
Daniels John
Dannolds John
David Isaac
Davids William
Davies Chapman
Davies Joseph
Davis Caleb
Davis Chapman
Davis Henry
Davis John
Davis Joseph
Davis Joshua
Davis Patrick
Davis Peter

Davis Richard
Davis Thomas
Davison John
Dawson John
Day Aaron
Day Isaac
Day Jonathan
Day Lewis
Dayley John
Dayton Bennet
Dayton Samuel
Dayton Samuel, Jr.
D'Bushe Anthony
Dean Abram
Deaton Frederick
Decker George
Decker Jacobus
Decker James B.
Decker John
Decker Jonathan
Decker Michael
Decker Yerry
Deen Isaac
Deen John
Deen William
DeFrees Ebenzer
De Frees, Reuben
Delaney Dennis
Demerest John
Demerest Nicholas
Demorest John
Demott Peter
Deniereft Nicholas
Dennis Mydert
Dennison Thomas
Denniss Miner
Denniston Thomas
Denny Peter
Depont Bosteon
Depue George
Derby Thomas
De Rusha Anthony
Desert John
Dew Francis
Dick Henry
Dick Thomas
Dickerson Abraham
Dickerson Benjamin
Dickerson David
Dickerson Jeduthan
Dickerson John
Dickson Andrew
Dickson Gabriel

Dickson Nathan
Dickson Richard
Dickson William
Dieson John
Dieson Nathan
Dimond Jonathan
Dodge Samuel, Jr.
Dodge Stephen
Dole John M.
Dollaway Andrew
Dolph Jonathan
Donnalds John
Dose Richard
Doty John
Dougherty Mark
Doughty Elias
Doughty George
Dowd Isaac
Downing Andrew
Doxey Stephen
Doyle Hugh
Doyle John
Drake Benoni
Drean Patrick
Drenning Hamilton
Duall Samuel
Ducher Adam
Duff Peter
Duguid John
Dunbar William
Duncan Thomas
Dunk Henry
Dunmore Caesar
Dunnavan John
Dunnavun Peter
Dunnivan John
Dunscomb Edward
Dupont Bosteon
Duran Francis
Dutcher Bornt
Dutcher John
Dwire Simon
Eaddy James
Earl John
Easton Henry
Eastwood Benjamin
Edgit George
Edwards David
Egberts John
Elker Emmer
Elliot John
Elliot John, Jr.
Elliott Archibald

Ellis John
Ellison Isaac
Ellison Richard
Ellison Thomas
Elsworth Ezekel
Elsworth John
English John
Ennis Peter
Ephram Ebenezer
Epton Benjamin
Erwin John
Esmond Isiah
Esmond James
Essmond John
Evalt Philip
Evens William
Everit Francis
Every Nehemiah
Fairly William
Fansher John
Fardon Samuel
Farrier Thomas
Fegan Timothy
Ferbush Simon
Ferdon A.
Ferdon Thomas
Ferdone Samuel
Ferguson Samuel
Ferris John
Ferris Jonah
Ferris Joseph
Ferris Ludowick
Ferris Samuel
Fichett Abraham
Filer Thomas
Finch Eliatham
Finch Einathan
Finch William
Finton Amos
Fish Ebner
Fisher James
Fitch James
Fitzgerald Christ'r
Flemming Patrick
Fletcher Lawrence
Flinn John
Flood Cilas
Forbush Alexander
Ford William
Forgison Jeremiah
Forsey Josh.
Fosburgh Peter
Fosdick Samuel

Foster John
Foster Nathaniel
Foster Vincent
Foster William
Fountain Stephen
Fowler Philip
Foy Edward
Fralick John
Francis John
Franke Michel
Franke Peter
Franks Michael
Frasier Jeremiah
Frayer Simon
Fredenbergh James
Freeman Nathaniel
Freeman Robert
Fross Stephen
Frye Benjamin
Fuller Josiah
Fulve Thomas
Furdon Thomas
Furman Samuel
Galasby James
Gantly Patrick
Gardner Jesse
Gardon Andrew
Garrisson Abraham
Garrisson Peter
Gates Nathaniel
Gee David
Gee Ezekiel
Gee John
Geers Benjamin
Gibbons John
Gibson John
Gibson Robert
Gilchrist William
Gillaspy James
Gillcrist John
Gillcrist William
Gillet Joseph
Glover Thomas
Gold William
Golden Isaiah
Golden Thomas
Goldsmith Ezra
Goldsmith John
Goodin George
Goodspeed Hosia
Goodwin George
Gordon William
Gorman Richard

Gosper John
Gosper Peter
Graham Alexander
Graham John
Granger John
Graves Josiah
Graves Seldon
Gray Benjamin
Gray James
Gray Samuel
Greatman John
Green Ebenezer
Green James
Greer David
Gregeer John
Gregory Jehiel
Gregory John
Grey Robert
Griffen Barney
Griffin Benjamin
Grinnel Amasa
Grumman Ephrain
Guin Michael
Guy Edward
Guyre Luke
Haight Jager
Hains Joseph
Hains Saunders
Halenbeek Abraham
Hall Isaac
Hall James
Hallet Jonathan
Halsey Abraham
Halsey Ethan
Halsey Job
Halsey Stephen
Halsey Thomas
Hambleton John
Hammon Chason
Hammon Isaac
Hand Joseph
Hanley James
Hanmore Jabez
Hannah James
Hannevan Rice
Hanries William
Happer John
Hardy David
Harmancy John
Harner Nicholas
Harper William
Harris Abijah
Harris Cilas

Harris David
Harris Evans
Harris Moses
Harris William
Harris Zach
Hartness Andrew
Hartnys Andrew
Hartshorne John
Harvey David
Hatt Frederick
Haukins Samuel
Hawkins David
Hawkins Noah
Hawkins Zachariah
Hawkins Zopher
Haynes Joseph
Hazard James
Heartness Andrew
Hedges Nathan
Helmer John
Henderson Alexander
Hennesey John
Henry David
Hermance John
Hermans Edward
Hermansee Edward
Herrick Amos
Herrick Samuel
Herrick William
Herrington John
Hicks Jacob
Higby Samuel
Higgins Moses
High Benjamin
Hike John
Hill Asse
Hill Thomas
Hill William
Himes Joseph
Hinkley Thomas
Hissam John
Hitchcock John
Hodges Joseph
Hoff Bastian
Hoff Henry H.
Hoff William
Hogarty Bernard
Hoit Job
Hoit Silvanus
Holloway Joseph
Holly John
Holly Samuel
Holmes Asa

Holmes Becker
Holmes Daniel, Jr.
Holmes James
Holmes John
Holmes Nathan
Holmes Thomas
Homan John
Hooker John
Hopkins Eli
Hopkins James
Hopper John
Hopper Samuel
Horsford Ithamer
Horton David
Horton Frederick
Hosport Samuel
House Jacob
House Zachariah
How Libeous
Howe John
Howe Silas
Howell
Howell George
Howell Jehiel
Howell Seth
Hoyt Thomas, Jr.
Hubbard
Hubbard Abel
Hubbard John
Hubbard Ezekiel
Huber Jacob
Hubert John
Hudman Charles
Hudson
Huff William
Huffman John
Hufman Gabriel
Hughes John
Hughson William
Humphrey John
Humphrey Samuel
Hunt David
Hunt Solomon
Hunt Theophilus
Hunter Benjamin
Hunter Ezekiel
Hunter Jonathan
Huson William
Hutchings Gabriel
Hyatt Abraham
Hymes Joseph
Hyser Henry
Ice Daniel

Impson Elias
Impson Robert
Indian Thomas
Ingalls Elihu
Inglish John
Israel Aaron
Jacklin Samuel
Jackson Thomas
Jamerson William
James Ebenezer
James Richard
Jane Jotham
Jarman David
Jarvis Nathaniel
Jarvis Thomas
Jay David
Jay John
Jeffries John
Jeyne William
Jillet Joseph
Jillon P.
Johns Silas
Johns Thomas
Johnson David
Johnson Isaac
Johnson James
Johnson John
Johnson Joseph
Johnson Samuel
Johnson Uriah
Johnson William
Johnston Benjamin
Johnston Samuel
Jones David
Jones Evans
Jones Jacob
Jones James
Jones John
Jones Squire
Jones Thomas
Joy Samuel
June Stephen
Kader Adam
Kader John
Keaffer William
Keder Stephen
Keefe Arthur
Keefer William
Keeler David
Keeler Ebenezer
Kelley Dennis
Kelley Isaac
Kelley Robert

Kelly Maurice
Kelly Morris
Kelly Robert
Kennedy John
Kenner Jonathan
Kenney Charles
Kenney Jese
Kenny Charles
Ketcham John
Ketcham Samuel
Keynon Robert
Kiff John
Kilsey John
King William
Kinner Jonathan
Kinney Charles
Kinney Elijah
Kuffen James
Ladoo John
Ladow John
Lamb Isaac
Lamb Joshua
Lambert Cornelius
Lambert Joseph
Lane Jeremiah
Lansing John
Larabie Elias
Laraby Elisha
Lashier Abraham
Latham John
Lawrence John
Lawrence Uriah
Lawrence W.
Leak J.
Leawrance Richard
Lee James
Lee Japath
Lee Seth
Lee William
Lent Hendnck
Lent Jacob
Leonard David
Leonard Edward
Leopard John
Lepper John
Leveraga Samuel
Leverage William
Levey Jacob
Lewis Henry
Lewis Jabez
Lewis Samuel
Lhommedieu Mulford
Light John

Light Lemuel
Liley John
Linch John
Linch Laurence
Lines Hosea
Link Henry
Lion Hosea
Liscomb Isaac
Liscomb Samuel
Little William
Livingston Dick
Livingston Richard
Lloyd James
Loanis John
Lock John
Lockwood Azariah
Lockwood Hezekiah
Lockwood Israel
Lockwood Jonathan
Lockwood Nathan
Lockwood Reuben
Lodovick Peter
Loeson Laurance
Longworth Isaac
Looper James
Loper Abraham
Love John
Love William
Lovejoy Andrew
Lovelis George
Lovelis Jeremiah
Lownsberry Nathaniel
Lowree William
Ludlum Daniel
Ludlum John
Lufberry Jonathan
Lupton
Lusee E.
Lusk Jacob
Lusk Michael
Lusk William
Lwinas Herry
Mabee Tobias
McAlester William
Macaulay Charles
McCaffety James
McCarty Dennis
McCauley Charles
McCharlesworth John
McClain John
McClarien David
McClean Neal
McClow Joseph

McColister William
McCollem John
McCollum Malcom
McColum John
McCracken John
McCullough Andrew
McDaniel John
McDole John
McDoll John
McDonald John
McDonald Michael
McDougall D.
McDowal William
McDowel John
McElley John
McEntach William
McEvers John
McFairley William
McFall David
McGilles Hugh
McGllorl Fergus
McGowin Duncan
McGready James
McIntosh William
McKee Michael
McKiel Adam
Mackrill Richard
McLain Hugh
McMannus William
McMicken Ebenezer
McNeal Charles
McNeil Charles
McNeil Thomas
McOlister Alexander
McPherson Lawrence
McWhorster John
Mahane Patrick
Mahone James
Mahony Cornelius
Main Robert
Makraback Dyke
Maloy John
Mapes John
Marchant Able
Mark G.
Marks Aholiab
Marling Deliverance
Marr James
Marray Warren
Marsh Benjamin
Marshal Amon
Marshall James
Martin Archibald

Martin James
Martin Michael
Martin Samuel
Marvin Stephan
Mason Francis
Mason Thomas
Masson Francis
Masters Jonathan
Matthews Henry
Mattison Aaron
Maxwell Cornelius
Mead David
Meaker Daniel
Medler Christian
Medler Christopher
Meed Ezekeel
Meeker Uzual
Meesy Benjamin
Merrill Joseph
Merrit Ebenezer
Merrit Luke
Merry Benjamin
Metzger John
Midler Christ'r
Millar John
Miller Benjamin
Miller Frederick
Miller George
Miller Jack
Miller Jesse
Miller John
Miller Justus
Miller Lewis
Miller Peleg
Miller Peter
Miller William
Miller Zephaniah
Milles Jesse
Mills Andrew
Mills James
Mingos Haronimus
Mink Johannes
Minks John
Mires John
Mitchel George
Mitchel Samuel
Mitchel William
Mitchell James
Money William
Moody James
Moody John
Mooney William
Moore Frederick

Moore John
Moore Joseph
Moore Robert
Moore Thomas
More Martin
More Robert
More Thomas
Moreign Alex
Morpeth William
Morrel James
Morrel Jesse
Morrel John
Morrell William
Morris Edward
Morris Robert
Morrison Duncan
Morse John
Mosher John
Moss David
Moulton Cato
Moulton Josiah
Moulton William
Mount Thomas
Mow James
Mucklow Joseph
Mulford Samuel
Mulliner Moses
Munday James
Munn Benjamin
Munroe Peter
Murfe John
Murn Muhel
Murphy Daniel
Murphy James
Myer Christ'r Grind't
Myers David
Myers Zach
Nail Henry
Neal Henry
Neder John
Neelson W.
Neilson Thomas
Nelson Thomas
Neves W.
Newman Abraham
Newman Jeremiah
Newman Joshua
Newman N.
Nichols James
Nickols Isaac
Nicols Simon
Nipper John
Nogert John

Norstrandt James
Norton Abel
Norton Calvin
Norton George
Norton Sible
Nostrander James
Nostrant George
Notingham Lewis
Nucom Thomas
O'Brien James
O'Brion Paul
Ogden David
Ogden John
Ogden Jonathan
Ogilsvie John
Ogstrander Peter
O'Kie A.
Olden Daniel
Onderdunck Abraham
O'Neal Thomas
Orr William
Orsor Abraham
Orsor Edward
Osborn Abraham
Osborne Henry
Osburn D.
Osterout Gilbert
Ostrander Henry
Ostrander James
Ostrander Peter
Owen Moses
Owens Ameziah
Owens Elisha
Owens Terrence
Pain Silas
Palmer Amaziah
Palmer Isaac
Palmer James
Palmer Jonathan
Palmer Silas
Palmiteir John
Pangbourn John
Pangbourn William
Pangburn John
Pangburn William
Pardy Nathaniel
Parent Nathaniel
Parisoneous J.
Park John
Park Robert
Parker Ebenezer
Parker Joseph
Parks John

Parks William
Parsells Matthew
Parshall James
Parsons Charles
Paterson Simon
Paul Joseph
Peck Nathan
Peirce Thomas
Peirson
Pell John
Pembrook W.
Pemderson John
Pendle Jonathan
Pennear Peter
Penney John
Pennoyer Jesse
Penoyer Israel
Penton Amos
Perkins Thomas
Perlee Edmond
Perry David
Pershall James
Persons John
Peterson Simeon
Pettit Abraham
Pettit Daniel
Pettit Samuel
Phillips David
Phillips Jonathan
Pickle Henry
Pickle John Henry
Pierce Thomas
Pierson
Piggs Richard
Pinyard William
Place Christopher
Place James
Plank Nicholas
Plass Michel
Plaus Peter
Plimley William
Plosser Peter
Plumb Stephen
Poimer Peter
Polamater John
Pollard Thomas
Polly Hugh
Pond Samuel
Post
Post Samuel
Potter George
Potter William
Poular John

Powel Vinson
Presher Abraham
Presher William
Preston Benjamin
Pride J.
Prim Azariah
Prime Peter
Primm Peter
Prior Abner William
Putman William
Quant Henry
Quinded David
Quinn Thomas
Racket
Racket Noah
Raigins William
Raimond Benjamin
Rainey Jeremiah
Ramis James
Randall Nathaniel
Randle Moses
Randle Seith
Raney John
Ransier George
Ray Charles
Raymond James
Raynor Ichabod
Reader Jacob
Reed George
Reed James
Reed John
Reeve Luther
Reeves Israel
Reives Nathaniel
Renny Jesse
Reymond Isaac
Reynolds Briggs
Reynolds David
Reynolds Ebenezer
Reynolds Eli
Reynolds James
Reynolds John
Reynolds Timothy
Rice Ezekiel
Rice Samuel
Rich Henry
Richards David
Richards John
Riggs Daniel
Ritchie Alexander
Ritchie Isaac
Roader Jacob
Roads Jacob

Roberds Edmun
Roberts Amos
Roberts John
Robertson James
Robins Evans
Robinson Andrew
Robinson D.
Robinson James
Robinson Matthias
Robinson Peter
Rockwell Ebenezer
Rodgers Own
Roe John
Roe Lemon
Roe Silleman
Roe Simon
Rofft Aaron
Rogers John, Sr.
Rogers John, Jr.
Rogers Owen
Rogers William
Romer Benjamin
Romer Peter
Roome Benjamin
Roomer Hendrick
Rose Andrew
Rose Jonathan
Rosman Adam
Rosman Henry
Rosman Philip
Ross Aaron
Ross Nathaniel
Ross William
Rossell Thomas
Rough Conrade
Row John
Row Simon
Rowland Phillip
Rowland Thomas
Ruland Jehiel
Rundle David
Runnels Abijah
Runnels Joseph
Russell Jonathan
Russigue Abraham
Russle W.
Sage Allen
Sagor John
St. Lawrence George
Salmon
Salmon Absalom
Salyer Zaccheus
Sanderson James

Sandford Daniel
Sandford John
Sanford Daniel
Sattally Richard
Saxton Gilbert
Sayrs Nathaniel
Scantling Jeremiah
Scales James
Schofield Samuel
Schofield Silas
Schofield Smith
Schouten Henry
Schouten John
Schriver Jacob N.
Schut Frederick
Schut James
Schut Tennis
Scott Alexander
Scott Elijah
Scott Henry
Scott James
Scott John
Scott William
Scoulen H.
Scriver Christian
Scriver Henry
Scutt William
Sealey Joseph
Seaman Moses
Seaton Rufus
Seeds George
Seers Joseph
Seward John
Shannon Robert
Shatton David
Shaw John
Shaw Michael
Shaw Peleg
Shay M.
Shea Philip
Shear Lodiwick
Shelp Joseph
Sherkeys J.
Sherwood Micajah
Shevalier John
Sibbio Thomas
Sickler Coonradt
Sickler Mitthias
Sicknar Jacob
Simmons Caleb
Simmons E.
Simmons John
Simmons Joshua

Simmons Samuel
Sinnott Patrick
Sisco Dick
Sisco Philip
Sitzer Barant
Size Gilbert V.
Slason Stephen
Slosson Amos
Slutt A.
Slutt M.
Slutt W.
Sly William
Smally Timothy
Smith Benjamin
Smith Caleb
Smith David
Smith Ebenezer B.
Smith Ebner B.
Smith Ezekiel
Smith Gersham
Smith Gideon
Smith Isaac
Smith James
Smith John
Smith Joseph
Smith Josiah
Smith Moses
Smith Nathan
Smith Nathaniel
Smith Obediah
Smith R.
Smith Samuel
Smith Solomon
Smith Thaddeus
Smith William
Snadiker Moses
Snedeker Moses
Snowden John
Snyder Peter
Southerland James
Speed George
Speed Henry
Spicer Jacob
Sprage Alexander
Spring Nathaniel
Springer Isaac
Springston Jacob
Squire Jacob
Squirrell Jacob
Stagg Adam
Stagg John
Stalker S.
Standish Amos

Stanford John	Taylor William	Turner Joseph
Stanley Daniel	Teatter John	Turrel Jones
Staples Nathan	Teller J.	Tuthill James
Stebins Lewis	Ter Boss J.	Tuttle Moses
Steen William	Terboss Simon	Tyler Shuble
Steenborgh Peter	Terbush C.	Underdunk T.
Steeples Nathan	Terbush Simon	Unter Josiah
Stephans Jessee	Terry Elijah	Upton Benjamin
Stephens John	Terry James	Utley Ase
Stephens Justice	Terry Samuel	Utter Joseph
Stephens Thomas	Thaire J.	Utter William
Stewart John	Thomas G.	Vail Thomas
Still James	Thomas John	Vallentine Gab'r
Still John	Thomas Richard	Valts Coonrod
Stitt John	Thompson Benjamin	Van Allen J.
Stokes William	Thompson Elias	Vanarter James
Stone Asa	Thompson James	Van Benscoten Elias
Stone David	Thompson John	Vandebogart John
Storms Abraham	Thompson Richard	Van Debogart Minard
Stratten Samuel	Thompson William	Van DeBogart Myndert
Streat H.	Thomson Zebulon	Vandemark G.
Streat W.	Thorp Peter	Vandervort Jacob
Stringham Henry	Tice John	Vandevour John
Strong John	Tice Joseph	Vandusen Peter
Strong William	Tieman Peter	Van Etten Peter
Stuard John	Tinkler Henry	Van Gelder Isaac
Sturdifent Jonathan	Titus Isaac	Vanhoosen Rinier
Suckinut John	Titus James	Van Hooser Rynier
Suffrin George	Titus Jonathan	Van Horn John
Suitt William	Tompkins Edward	Van Houten John
Sullivan James	Tompkins Nathaniel	Van Hoven Ryner
Swan Robert	Tool John	Vanlene R.
Swartwout Henry	Topping Daniel	Vanline J.
Swartwout John	Town Jacob	Van North John
Swartwout William	Townsend Absolom	Vanoore Philip
Sweed William	Toy Samuel	Van Size Gilbert
Sweet Amos	Traver Francis	Van Steenbergh Peter
Sweet Benoni	Traver Nicholas	Vantassell Isaac
Sweet George	Travess Jacob	Van tassell John
Sweet John	Travess Silvanus	Van Volkenborgh Fran
Sweet John, Jr.	Travis Robert	Van Wicklen Fredrick
Sweet Nathan	Trewilleger J.	Vanworma Cornelius
Sweet Robert	Trim Azariah	Vanna Vincent
Swift Ambrose	Trowbridge James	Venier Peter
Talmadge John	Tubbs Stephen	Vise Daniel
Talmage Joseph	Tubee John	Voh Peter
Tappen Daniel	Tucker John	Vonck Henry
Tappen N.	Tucker Joshua	Vredenburgh James
Tarrent Thomas	Tucker Samuel	Wade Elia
Tattenton Jeptha	Tum David	Wait Christopher
Taylor Jasper	Tuman David	Walker Edward
Taylor Joseph	Tuman Peter	Walker Mathew
Taylor Oliver	Tuman Peter, Jr.	Walker Matthias

Wall John
Wallace Benjamin
Wallice Uriah
Waner Killean
Ward Abijah
Ward Jadoc
Ward Robert
Ward Zedock
Warden Bernard
Waring Newman
Warner Martin
Warson Thomas
Washburn Joel
Waterbury Ely
Watkins William
Watson Thomas
Watson William
Wattaker Edward
Wattles William
Weaver John
Webb Ebenezer
Webb Silvanus
Webster Joseph
Weed Abijah
Weed Gilbert
Weed John Drew
Weed Nathan
Weed S.
Weeks James
Weeks John
Weeks Jonathan, Jr.
Weeks Macejah
Weiss Daniel
Welch Elijah
Welch Ephraim
Welch Henry
Welch Isaac
Welch James
Welch John
Welch Joseph
Welch Luke
Welch Thomas
Welch William
Wells Calvin
Wells Elijah

Wells P.
Wells William
Wentworth James
West Ase
West Jacob
West Joseph
West William
Westfall Levi
Whaley Samuel
Whaley Timothy
Wheeler James
Wheeler John
Wheeler S.
Wheeler Thomas
Whipple Nathan
White Ephraim
White George
White Henry
White John
White Samuel Curran
White Stephen
White Thomas
Whitehead Aaron
Whitehead Isaiah
Whitehead William
Whitman John
Whitney Jacob
Wickham Stephen
Wicks James
Wicks Jonathan
Wiggins William
Wilcout W.
Wildley Edward
Wiley Edward
Wilkinson Robert
Wilks Willis
Williams Aaron
Williams Abiah
Williams Adam
Williams Charles
Williams David
Williams John
Williams Peter
Wllliamson James
Willis Abraham

Willis David
Willis W.
Wills J.
Wilsee H.
Wilson John
Wilson Michael
Wilson Nathaniel
Wilson Samuel
Wilson W.
Wilson Walter
Wiltice Joseph
Winass Silas
Winchall Samuel
Winchell James
Witteker Edward
Wood Jacob
Wood John
Wood Matthew
Wood Nathan
Wood Samuel
Wood William
Wood Zopher
Woodruff David
Woodruff Jeremiah
Woodruff Joshua
Woodruff William
Word Abijah
Worden Darious
Worden James
Wordin Shubel
Worpeth William
Wright John
Wyer Jeremiah
Yarrington William
Yeoman Eliezer
Youmans Eleazer
Youmans Jonas
Youmens Jones
Young Isaac
Young John
Young Thomas
Yurks Harmanus
Zedmond Bartho'w

THE LINE - FIFTH REGIMENT

COLONEL LEWIS DUBOYS
LIEUT. COL. JAMES S. BRUYN
LIEUT. COL. MARINUS WILLETT
MAJOR SAMUEL LOGAN

ADJUTANT JAMES BETTS
Q'R MASTER NEHEMIAH CARPENTER
QUARTER MASTER OLIVER GLEANE
QUARTER MASTER FRANCIS HANMOR

QUARTER MASTER FRANCIS HANNER
QUARTER MASTER JAMES JOHNSTON
PAY MASTER SAMUEL TOWNSEND
CHAPLAIN JOHN GANO
SURGEON SAMUEL COOKE
SURGEON EBENEZER HUTCHINS
SURGEON'S MATE EBENEZER HUTCHINSON
SURGEON'S MATE ROBERT MORRISEN
CAPT. PHILIP DUBOYS BEVIER
" HENRY DODGE
" DAVID DUBOIS
" HENRY S. DUBOIS
" HENRY GODWIN
" SILAS GRAY
" JOHN HAMTRAMCK
" JOHN F. HAMTRAMIK
" AMOS HUTCHINGS
" JOHN JOHNSTON
" THOMAS LEE
" ALEXANDER McARTHUR
" JAMES ROSAKRANS
" JACOB ROSEKRANS
" JAMES STEWART
" HENRY H. VANDERBURGH
LIEUT. DANIEL BIRDSALL
LIEUT. THOMAS BRINCKLE
" JOHN BURNIT
" MICHAEL CONNOLLY
" HENRY DODGE

" SAMUEL DODGE, JR.
" SAMUEL ENGLISH
" JOHN FUSMAN
" FRANCIS HANMER
" SAMUEL INGUSH
" PATTIN JACKSON
" DANIEL LAWRANCE
" ABRAHAM LEGGET
" ALEXANDER McARTHUR
" JOHN McCLAUGHREY
" EBENEZER MOTT
" THOMAS NICHOLSON
" HENRY PAWLING
LIEUT. SOLOMON TEMPLETON
" HENRY SWARTOUT
" HENRY I. VAN DER BURGH
" HENRY W. VAN DER BURGH
ENSIGN BANKAR
" ASAHEL BERRY
" NEHEMIAH CARPENTER
" ALEXANDER FURMAN
" FRANCIS HANMER
" JAMES JOHNSTON
" ABRAHAM LEGET
" JOHN McCLAUGHRY
" HENRY SWARTWOUT
" BARTHOLOMEW VAN DEN BURGH
" EDWARD WEAVER

ENLISTED MEN

Abebin John
Aberson Stephen
Abritt John
Ackerson Cornelius
Ackler Jacob
Ackly Jonathan
Ackor Cornelius
Adams Ephrem
Addoms Peleg
Aggins James
Aires Thomas
Akeley Jacob
Akerson Cornelius
Albertson Stephen
Albright John
Alderson Stephen
Aldridge Jacob
Allin Jasper
Allson John
Amberman James

Amerman James
Amerman Obadiah
Anderson Joseph
Andrews Joab
Arkens John
Arston Holmes
Astin John
Austen Holmes
Austin Holmes
Avary Nicholas
Avery Richard
Babcock Abraham
Babcock Elisha
Babcock John
Bailey J.
Bailey Jonathan
Bailys Jonathan
Baker Samuel
Baker William
Baley Jonathan
Banager Walter
Bancker Nathaniel
Barkins William
Darlow Jonas

Barnam Samuel
Barriger Walter
Barritt John
Barry Elisha
Bartlet Samuel
Bartlit Lemuel
Bartow Jonas
Battersby John
Bayles Jonathan
Beach Amos
Beam William
Beard William
Beeck Amos
Benedic Ambrose
Benedict Ambrose
Benjamin Samuel
Benker Lawrence
Bently William
Berkins William
Berry Elisha
Bertlet Lemuel
Betts James, Jr.
Bevins Crispamur
Bevins David

Bevins Francis
Bishop Ezekiel
Bishop James
Bishop William
Blancher William
Blaws John
Bloomer William
Blosom Sol'n
Boge John
Bold Daniel
Boid Samuel
Bolton George
Bonker Bethuel
Bonker John
Bonker Laurence
Bonker Nathaniel
Bonker Solomon
Bonker William
Bonkers Lawrence
Boulton George
Boulton Joseph
Bowers Joel
Boyce Thomas
Boyd George
Boyd Robert
Boyd Samuel
Boyde Samuel
Branen Adam
Branen Reuben
Briant Matthew
Briggs Jeremiah
Brink Adam
Brocket Moses
Brockway Russell
Broker Walter
Brooker Walter
Brooks Joseph
Brown John
Brush Eliakim
Buckbe Josiah
Bugby Josiah
Bunday Jeremiah
Bundy Jeremiah
Buoyd Daniel
Burdge Michael
Burdick Elisha
Burgee Michael
Burhans Samuel
Burnett Ebenezer
Buttles Sebra
Cain John
Caldwell Arthur
Campbell George

Canit Cunradt
Carden James
Carely Joseph
Carley John
Carley Joseph
Carn Mathias
Carr William
Carrigan Daniel
Carrigan William
Case Joseph
Casner Michael
Cass Joseph
Chace Caleb
Chamberlain John
Chandler Jonathan
Channy Richard
Chapman Lemuel
Chatfield Jonathan
Chedestar Benjamin
Cheshier Nehemiah
Cheshire Nehemiah
Cheshley John
Chesser Nehemiah
Chrispell Thomas
Christey John
Christian Peter
Christie John
Christy John
Chyser Nehemiah
Claring J. M.
Clark Benjamin
Clark John
Clark Martin
Clark William
Clarwater John
Clarwater Mart
Clarwattor Martinus
Clay Thomas
Cline Jacob
Cline John
Clinton John
Cocksure Joseph
Coe Philip
Coennight Cunradt
Coil Thomas
Coleman John
Colp John
Combes John
Concklin John
Concklin Samuel
Concklin Thomas
Coningham Moses
Conite Conrad

Connelly Henry
Connight Conrad
Connolly Henry
Cook Isaac
Cook Jacob
Cook Samuel
Cook William
Cooke David
Cooke Thomas
Coombe John
Coombe Peter
Coombes Samue
Cooper Abraham
Cooper Richard
Cornelias John
Cornelius John
Cornwale Joseph
Corren Samuel
Cosgrove John
Cost Martin
Couren Samuel
Cox Thomas
Craft Jacob
Craw Ebenezer
Crawford Asia
Crawford Thomas
Crispell Thomas
Croft Jacob
Crosby Lemuel
Crullin Jeremiah
Crum Hermanus
Crum Jacob
Crumb John
Cullin Jeremiah
Culp John
Cummins Ebenezer
Cummins Elezar
Cumpton Obadiah
Cunningham Moses
Curren Samuel
Curtis Ebenezar
Cutting Francis
Daily James
Daker Christopher
Daker Martinus
Dalency Abraham
Damm Frederick
Danford Prince
Danielson Isaac
Dannelson Isaac
Darlin Ezra
Darling Ezra
Darling John

Davis David
Davis Hezekiah
Davis Jacob
Davis James
Davis John
Davis Samuel
Decker Christopher
Decker Martin
Decker Martinus
Deknight Jos'h
Delamarter John
Delavan Francis
Delevan Frs
Demark Gisbert V.
Deneger George
Denilson Isaac
Denton Amos
Deority William
Depuie Elias
Diamond Moses
Diamond William
Dibble Hezekiah
Dickenson Lewis
Dickenson Versal
Dikeson Gideon
Dillimater John
Dimick Daniel
Dimon William
Dimond Moses
Dimond William
Dodge Richard
Donalson Isaac
Doty Daniel
Douglas William
Douty James
Dow Volker
Dow Volkert
Drake Francis
Dubois Nathaniel
Duglas William
Duigion Patrick
Dunford Wells
Dunlap J
Dunlap James
Dunn Jeremiah
Durgeon Patrick
Eackley Jacob
Eaton Ephraim
Eazor James
Edwards David
Edwards Gilbert
Eggbert Daniel
Elicer John

Ellis Jacob
Ellis Joseph
Ellison John
Every Nicholas
Factor John
Fairin John
Fardon Abraham
Felix Philip
Felton Peter
Ferclon Abraham
Ferdon Abraham
Ferdon John
Fergeson James
Ferguson James
Ferrin John
Filex Philip
Fitmore Silas
Finn Thomas
Fish Sebra
Fitzgerald Thomas
Fitzgerallaid Thomas
Fitzgibbons James
Fitzseaman Barnard
Flannigan Daniel
Fluno John
Flyn John
Forgason Samuel
Forrest Robert
Foster Gilbert
Foster Jerem
Foster William
Fowler Michael
Freazer Lewis
Frier John
Frimyer John
Fullin John
Fulton John
Furlongh Cornelius
Galasby James
Galaspie James
Ganes Francis
Gardeneer Andrew
Gardineer Andries
Gardner Samuel
Garrison Abraham
Garrison Samuel
Gates John
Gearderman Henry
Gee John
Gee Moses
Geraldeman Henry
Geroldaman Henry
Gibbins John

Gibbon John
Gilbert Seth
Gillaspy Robert
Gilmore Daniel
Givans Samuel
Glason Joseph
Gleason Joseph
Gleen Caleb
Godwin Abraham
Godwin David
Goldin William
Golligan Charles
Gones Griffin
Gones Joseph
Goodspead Gideon
Goodwin Abraham
Goolden Lewi
Goslin J.
Gosline Samuel
Gragg Hezekiah
Graham Zachariah
Gray John
Gray Samuel
Grayham John
Greadey Thomas
Gready Thomas
Greeg David
Green Sutten
Gregg David
Gregg Hezekiah
Grifeth Jeremiah
Griffin Benjamin
Griffin Joshua
Guardner James
Guilbert Seth
Guion Michael
Gwen Michael
Hack George
Hackerson William
Hains John
Hallet William
Hallett George
Hallett Solomon
Hallick Jonathan
Halmore Philip
Hanbaragh Abraham
Hanes John
Hankely Thomas
Hankerson William
Hanky Henry
Hanly D.
Hanly David
Hannah James

Hannoh James
Hartwell Thomas
Harty Christopher
Harwood John
Hasbrook George
Hassbrook George
Hauss Simon
Havens Peter
Hawhey Richard
Hawkey Henry
Hawkey Richard
Hearter Christopher
Hendereks Wansor
Hendrickson John
Hendrikson John
Henkerson W.
Hennekey Manuel
Hesom John
Hessam John
Hews Henry
Hews William
Higby Elnathan
Higgins Samuel
Hill Joshua
Hinkley Thomas
Hipp Abraham
Hoisel Nathaniel
Holester Nathaniel
Holet George
Holet N
Hollet Solomon
Hollet William
Holley John
Hollister Nathaniel
Holloway James
Holmes Peter
Holms Jesse
Hoper Samuel
Hopper Peter
Hornbeck Henry
Hortain Silas
Hosuer John
House Henry
Houzer John
Howal Lemuel
Howel Samuel
Howell George
Howell Lemuel
Howkey Henry
Howse Henry
Hozier J.
Huchins Ebinezar
Hughs William

Hull Samuel
Humphre Alexander
Humphrey Alexander
Humphrey James
Humphrey Samuel
Hunt David
Hunt John
Hunt Joshua
Hunter Ezekiel
Hunter James
Hunton John
Hutchinson Ebenezer
Ingram Thomas
Ireland Amos
Jackson Robert
Jackson William
James John
Jay Moses
Jee John
Jenkings Thomas
Jewett Caleb
Johnes Seth
Johns Griffin
Johnson Abraham
Johnson Alexander
Johnson Daniel
Johnson John
Johnson Joseph
Johnson Michael
Johnson Prince
Johnston Abraham
Johnston Daniel
Johnston John
Jones Griffin
Jones Joseph
Jones Robert
Jones Thomas
Joory John
Joory William
Juit Caleb
Kain John
Keef Con
Keeller James
Keesley Paul
Keller James
Kelley James
Kelly Joshua
Kemble Isaac
Kempton Obadiah
Kendrick Thomas
Kennedy Dennis
Kent Thomas
Kepp Abraham

Ketcham John
Keyser John
Kiepp Conn
Kieseer Andrew
Kiesley Paul
Kinsley James
Kip Archibald
Kirberger Philip
Kiser John
Kizer Andrew
Kizer John
Knaap Aaron
Kniffen Amos
Kniffin Nehemiah
Kniver William
Kolb John
Konover Godfry
Kroat John
Kysar Andrew
Lain William
Lake Joshua
Lander Daniel
Lander Ebenezer
Landers Ebenezer
Lane William
Langdon Samuel
Laraway Isaac
Latemor Benjamin
Lates Jems
Latimore Benjamin
Latimore Roger
Lattimore Roger
Laurence William
Lawrance Isaac
Lawrance Jacob
Lawrence Benjamin
Lawrence Jacob
Lawrence William, Jr.
Leak Joshua
Lenington Thomas
Lent Enos
Lent Isaac
Leonard Silas
Letts Evert
Levan Francis
Lewis Henry
Litz Evert
Lockwood John
Lockwood Josiah
Lodar Daniel
Longyear Andries
Longyear Jacob
Lounsbury John

Lovitt John	Mericale Jacob	Nostrant Isaac
Lucey Eleazer	Merkle James	Nowell Lemuel
Lusee Eleazer	Merrit John	Nukemb Kenner
Lust Francis	Metcalf William	Numan Jonathan
Lutter Cuff	Michelvany Phillip	Oakey Abraham
McAfee John	Milagen Robert	Oakley Jonathan
McAnany John	Milard John	Oakly Jonathan
McArthur John	Miligan Robert	Oliphant William
McArthur Thomas	Millar Elisha	Olive Love
McCarty John	Millard Henry	Orr Daniel
McCarty Thomas	Millegan Robert	Osben Daniel
McClannon John	Miller Elijah	Osborn Casar
McClarning John	Miller John	Osburn Daniel
McClean John	Mills Johnam	Osterhout Peter
McClure Moses	Minama Benjamin	Ostrander Henry
McCollester Walter	Mineael Jacob	Otter Nathan
McCorn Edward	Mitchall James	Outhouse Israel
McDermot Francis	Mitchell Joseph	Owens David
McDonald James	Moncref Charles	Pake John
McDonald John	Montanyee James	Palmerton Thomas
McDonald Thomas	Montieth James	Paresonus James
McDougal Dougal	Moonay William	Parisonieer James
McDugal Dugle	Mooney Absolom	Parker Elisha
McGraw James	Mooney William	Paronnus James
McIntosh John	Moor John	Paterson Thomas
McKee John	Moore Jacob	Paterson William
McKeny Michael	Mordoch Archibald	Patks Jonah
McKey Joseph	More John	Patks William
McKey William	Morewise Jacob	Patrick Robert
Mackey William	Morgan Joseph	Patterson James
McKinsley James	Moris Archibald	Paul William
McKown Duncan	Morrison Daniel	Paulding Henry
McKown James	Morrow Patrick	Paulis John
McLean John	Morry Patrick	Peck John
McNeal John	Mott John	Peek John
McVany Philip	Muckelvany Philip	Pembrook William
Mappes Stephen	Mullan William	Penney Jonathan
Mark George	Mullen William	Pepper John
Markel James	Mungomery John	Personus James
Markes George	Munteith James	Peterson Alexander
Marks Holiab	Murfy Edward	Pewits John
Marron P.	Negroe William	Phenix Robert
Marsh Thomas	Neilson William	Philips David
Marshall Robert	Nelson Thomas	Philips Joshua
Marthis Peter	Nelson William	Plank Henry
Mash Thomas	Newcomb Kinner	Plough Henry
Mastis Joseph	Newman Jonathan	Plumb Samuel
Maston Joseph	Nicholas John	Post Zebulon
Matany James	Nicholls John	Pudney James
Mathews Justus	Nichols Stephen	Prague Seth
Mathews Peter	Niver William	Prebell Joseph
Matthews John	North J. V.	Preyer Jasper
Menema Benjamin	Norton Silas	Priam Michal

Pribbell Joseph
Price John
Pride James
Prime Michael
Pryer Jasper
Pudney James
Puller John
Pullis John
Purdy David
Quan Ephraim
Quick Abraham
Race Ephraim
Ralny Jeremiah
Ramsen Henry
Ramsey Jonas
Ramson Jacob
Ramson James
Randle Mathias
Ransom Henry
Ransom Jacob
Ransom James
Rea Benjamin
Read John
Reed John
Reeder Joseph
Rhoades John
Rhoads John
Rhoads Joseph
Rhodes Cornelius
Richard Philip
Richards Gilbert
Richards Phil
Richardson Alexander
Richey John
Richmond Josiah
Ricker Jeremiah
Ricky Jeremiah
Riden Timothy
Riding Timothy
Ried John
Rieston William
Rillaman Jacob
Rippley John
Ristin William
Riston William
Ritter Jacob
Ritterman Jacob
Roase Jonathan
Robertson Daniel
Robertson James
Robeson George
Robeson Robert
Robinson Alexander

Robinson Benjamin
Robinson George
Robinson James
Robinson Robert
Robison James
Robison Thomas
Ronols John
Roose Jacob
Roose Jonathan
Rosakvance Caeser
Rose Jonathan
Rosekrance Depue
Rosekrans James
Rosekrants Dupie
Ross Charles
Ross John
Rubenger Philip
Rultrege Jacob
Rumsey Jonas
Rundle Able
Ruple William
Rusell Thomas
Russel Thomas
Russell Hugh
Russell James
Russell Thomas
Russell William
Russle William
Ruston William
Rylie Silvester
St. John
Sampson Isaac
Samson Isaac
Sandford William
Satterly John
Schoonmaker Coffey
Schoonmaker Henry
Schriver Jacob
Scouten Hendrick
Scouton Henry
Scudder John
Seaman Ephraim
Seamor Abraham
Sears Francis
Secars John
Seimour Abraham
Serine Jacob
Shafer George
Shapher George
Sharkey Thomas
Shaw James
Shaw Moses
Shaw Reuben

Shaw Solomon
Shay Martin
Shear Abraham
Shenedon Nehemiah
Sherkey Thomas
Sherve Andries
Sherwood Nehemiah
Shirkey Thomas
Simkins Jeremiah
Simmons Ephraim
Simmons Ezekiel
Simmons Isaac
Simpson James
Sinkins Jeremiah
Size Abram
Skinnor Jonathan
Slaven James
Slick Stephen
Slocan Jonathan
Slouyter Evert
Slouyter John
Slutt Abraham
Slutt Marvel
Slutt William
Sluyter Evert
Sluyter John
Slyter John
Smalley Thomas
Smawly Thomas
Smedus John
Smith Abner
Smith Abraham
Smith David, Sr.
Smith David, Jr.
Smith Henry
Smith James
Smith Jesse
Smith John
Smith Joseph
Smith Lem Mosier
Smith Reuben
Smith Samuel
Smith Stephen
Smith Thomas
Snyder Peter
Soil William
Southerd John
Speenbergh Joseph
Sprage Seth
Springstead Harman
Springsted George
Springsted Harmanus
Springsted Isaac

Springsteel William	Terwillegar Jacobus	Van Demarken Gysbert
Springsteen George	Terwillegen James	Van De Merk Gysbert
Springston John	Thaier John	Vanderbarak Cornelius
Spunbergh Joseph	Thayer John	Van Der Mark Cornelius
Stalk Seth	Thomas George	Van Der Merk Cornelius
Stalker Seth	Thomas James	Van De Water Augustines
Stanly John	Thomas John	Van Gelder Jacob
Stanly Thomas	Thompson Elias	Van Gelder Matthew
Stansbury Elijah	Thompson James	Van Hoosen Garrit
Starenbargh Elijah	Thomson Arch'l	Van Huson Garret
Steak Stephen	Thonsen Sam	Van Hyning Andrew
Steel Daniel	Thorington James	Van Ness Cornelius
Steel James	Thorn Benjamin	Vannort Joseph
Steel John	Thorn Obadiah	Van North Joseph
Stell James	Thornton James	Van Nosdall John
Stephen Richard	Tillton Peter	Van Orden Albert
Stephens John	Tinagar George	Vanosdal Jacobus
Stevens James	Tinker Joshua	Van Tine Francis
Stolker Seth	Titus James	Van Tine Isaac
Storm John	Tobious Jacob	Van Tine John
Storms John	Toffet Peter	Vantine Robert
Straight Henry	Tomilson Benjamin	Van Tyne Isaac
Straight William	Tompkins Edmond	Vaney Vincent
Streat William	Tompkins Elijah	Vasborough Samuel
Streats Henry	Tonge George	Vasburgh Jacob
Street Abraham	Tonsen Sam'l	Vasburgh Lawrence
Stump John	Tophop Peter	Venote Joseph
Suthard John	Topper Nathan	Veny Vincent
Sutlif John	Townsbury John	Vermiller Peter
Sweep Jacob	Townsend Absalom	Vermilyea Peter
Sweete Robert	Townsend Samuel	Vincent Joseph
Swinton Henry	Travers Scot	Waddle Robert
Swiss Jacob	Traverse Abraham	Walcott William
Talliday John	Traverse Scott	Walker Samuel
Talliday Stephen	Travis Abraham	Wall James
Taloday Solomon	Trewilliger William	Wandle John
Talowday John	Tryon John	Ward Josiah
Taphap Peter	Tucker Joshua	Warren Edward
Tappen Nathan	Tupper Nathan	Wasson James
Tapper Nathan	Turner Francis	Watson Levi
Tar Boss Isaack	Tyne Francis V.	Weaver William
Taylor Elijah	Ulter Nathan	Webber Ichabod
Teknight Jos'h	Underdunck Titus	Weed Samuel
Tellent Edward	Utter Gilbert	Weedd Samuel
Teller James	Utter Isaac, Sr.	Weeker Obediah
Teller James T.	Uutter Gilbert	Weeks Malatiah
Ten Eyck Joseph	Vactor John	Welch Edward
Tenigar George	Vallary John	Weldin James
Tenyke Joseph	Van Amburgh Abraham	Wells John
Ter Boss Cornelius	Vanasdol Jacobus	Wells Peter
Terboss Isaac	Van Asdoll John	Wells Robert
Ter Bush Cornelius	Vanate Joseph	Wells Thomas
Ter Bush Isaac	Vandel John	Welsh Edward

Welsh John
Wemiah Frederick
Wemiers Frederick
Wendall John
Wendle John
West Jacob
West John
Western John
Wever Johanniele
Whaly Benjamin
Wharry David
Wheler Stephen
Wheller Samuel
Wheller Timothy
Wheller William
Whelor Stephen
White Peter
Whitehead John
Whitehead William
Wilboe Jacob
Wilbore Jacob
Wilcout William
Wilkinson Thomas
Will John
Willes William

William Richard
William Wheeler
Williams Ebenezer
Williams Isaac
Williams Richard
Williams Wynerd
Willis John
Willis Thomas
Willis William
Williss William
Wills Peter
Willson Abraham
Willson John
Wilsey Henry
Wilsie Henry
Wimore Frederick
Winchester Danford
Wollcott William
Wood James
Wood Timothy
Woodard John
Woolsey Henry
Worner Edward
Wright Abraham
Wriston William

Wryton William
Yearns Epharim
Yomans Benjamin
Yomans John
Yomans Stephen
Youmans Isaac
Young John
Youngs Henry

The Line - Additional Regiment (Battalion)

COLONEL JAMES LIVINGSTON
LIEUT. COL. RICHARD LIVINGSTON

ADJUTANT JOHN BATEMAN
PAY MASTER JOHN P. D. TEN EYCK

CAPT. DIRCK HANSON
" TIMOTHY HUGHES
" ABRAHAM LIVINGSTON
" AUGUSTIN LOSEAUX
" JAMES ROBICHAUX
" JOHN D. P. TEN EYCK
" PETER VAN RENSSELAER
CAPT. ANTHONY WELP
" ROBERT WRIGHT
LIEUT. JOHN BATEMAN

" WILLIAM BELKNAP
" JOHN BLACKLEY
" FRANCIS BRINDLEY
" ISAAC NICHOLS
LIEUT. THOMAS NICOLSON
" PETER J. VOSBURGH
" WILLIAM WALLACE
" ANTHONY WELP
ENSIGN JOHN GATES
" JOHN HUBBART

Ademy Peter
Anderson Alexander
Anderson James
Barret Peter
Bason Daniel
Beford Anthony
Belford Anthony
Birch John
Bouy William

Bowman Luke
Brock Francis
Brock Nathaniel
Brown Nathaniel
Brusoe Leonard
Bunt Lodewick
Burns John
Burrows Thomas
Burton Arthur

Campbell William
Canuter John
Chance Christopher
Clark John
Clark Joseph
Cogdon John
Collard Abraham
Conden Philip
Conely Dennis

Cook Nicholas
Cooper Abraham
Craghoot John
Crumb John
Cummins John
Elkenburgh Peter
Falconer William
Feagan William
Flinn John
Frazier John
Frymire Michael
Garvy David
Gilbert Joel
Gilbert John
Godwin Henry
Gould Thomas
Griffiths Howel
Halfpenny Patrick
Harold Henry
Harper James
Herald Henry
Hickman Thomas
Holsapple Zachariah
Horan Phanton
Horn Phanten
Howell J.
Howell Joel
Hoyet Henry
Hyett Henry
Jacobs John
Keeler Frederick
Kelly Dennis
Kelsey Benjamin
Ketcham David
Lachry John
Laframboise Jacque
Lawader William
Lewis Isaac
Like Henry
Little Benjamin

Livingston Jacob
Loder William
Lord Benjamin
Lord Jonathan
Lowder William
Loyal Edward
Ludlow William
McCord Alexander
McDonald Peter
McFall Patrick
McGinney James
McGraw Patrick
McPeak Dennis
Mall Alexander
Mallack D.
Malls A.
Martin Almerinus
Matlack Daniel
Matthews P.
Matthewson Angus
Moke Gerardus
Moore William
Morewise Jacob
Munden John
Murphy Peter
Nagle James
Nathan Reace
Newel Edward
Nicolson Andrew
Oharra Cain
Paterson Hezekiah
Plogh F.
Plough Teunis
Powel Thomas
Powers James
Quin Owen
Ready John
Redman John
Rice John
Richardson William

Robertson John
Robinson Edmond
Robinson John
Sadler John
Selkirk James
Sheperd James
Silkirk James
Smallin Jacob
Smith Archibald
Smith John
Smith John Conrad
Spring Henry
Springer William
Steel Joseph
Stener Nicholas
Stoner John
Stoner Nicholas
Swayer Lambert
Swift John
Taylor Ebenezer
Thompson John
Thompson Prime
Thompson Thomas
Tice John
Todd John
Tripp Charles
Valence Zachariah
Van Valkenburgh Fra
Vosburgh Peter
Vroman Peter
Waggoner John H.
Ward Thomas
Warren William
Weaver David
Webster Thomas
Welch William
White Peter
Williams James
Willmot John
Winham Aaron

THE LINE - ADDITIONAL CORPS (GREEN MOUNTAIN BOYS)

The Line - Additional Corps (Green Mountain Boys)

[These muster-rolls are recorded as " Major Brown's Detachment," and that detachment is mentioned as in " General Arnold's Regiment." (The only mention of General Arnold found in our records.) The fact that the "Green Mountain Boys" were at Quebec in 1776; that this detachment was also at Quebec in 1776; that two of the officers on these rolls- Captain and Commissary Elijah Babcock and Captain Robert Cochran-are identical in name and rank with those on a list handed to the Provincial Congress of New York by Ethan Allen and Seth Warner, on July 4, 1775, as officers for the Green Mountain Boys; and the further fact that none of the men are recorded in any other place, or with any other organization, all confirm the belief that the soldiers on its rolls herewith were a part of that historic band.]

COLONEL ETHAN ALLEN
COLONEL SETH WARNER
MAJOR JOHN BROWN
ADJUTANT WILLIAM SATTERLEE
QUARTERMASTER JONATHAN CAPRON
QUARTER MASTER SAMUEL McCLUND
CAPT. AND COM. ELIJAH BABCOCK
" GIDEON BROWNSON
" ROBERT COCHRAN
" GOODRICH
" HOPKINS
" CHARLES NELSON

LIEUT. PALMERLY ALLEN
" MICHAEL DUNNING
" JAMES GOULD
" EBENEZER HYDE
" WILLIAM LIGHTHALL
" DAVID PIXLEY

LIEUT. WALTER SWITZ
" ELISHAMA TOZER
" EBENEZER WALBRIDGE
" SETH WHEELER
ENSIGN BENONI GRANT
" WILLIAM LIGHTHALL

Abbot William	Burris John	Dickey Elias
Alden Felix	Burris Matthew	Doud Jesse
Allen Abraham	Burroughs Matthew	Dressen Jonathan
Allen Amos	Cannada John	Drew Samuel
Allen Samuel	Capee George	Dunlap Samuel
Ames David	Capern Thomas	Dunn Duncan
Andress Jeremiah	Capron Jonathan	Eastman Nathaniel
Andrews Moses	Carley Abraham	Eives Jonah
Averil Ebenezer	Caswell Eliphalet	Erwine David
Averill Robert	Chadock Jonas	Fellows William
Bamur J.	Chamberlin Joseph	Fitch Jonathan
Barker Alexander	Chambers Henry	Fletcher John
Barkley Robert	Chesley James	Flood Moses
Barlow Samuel	Chipman Jessey	Flood Timothy
Beach Samuel	Church John	Fone Timothy
Beamen Jery	Clark Isaac	Foot Jennor
Beder John	Clark Jessey	Force Timothy
Begar Alexander	Clarke James	Freeman Ellas
Beltheh Stephen	Cobb John	Freeman John
Bennet Isaac	Cochran Samuel	Freeman Moody
Bennet Nathan	Collins William	Freeman Richard
Bheartwick John	Colter Joseph	French John
Bishop Enos	Comstock Aaron	Fuller Elijah
Black Primas	Connely John	Fuller William
Blackmon Epheram	Corbit Eldad	Gamble James
Blanchard Abner	Cross John	Garvin Epheram
Blanchard Azriel	Cross Uriah	Gibson James
Blodget Elijah	Cummins Benjamin	Gilbert Elisha
Boeron M.	Curtis David	Goodcourage John
Boggess Thomas	Curtis Timothy	Gordon Alexander
Borow Mathew	David Abel	Grant Benoni
Brown John	Davis Abel	Grapes Phillpo
Buck Isaac	Dernim Asa	Gray John
Burk Jonathan	Dernim Reubin	Griswell Benjamin

Halet John
Hand Ira
Hand Oliver
Hardy James
Hasleton John
Hastens Jonathan
Hawley Ichabod
Haws Edward
Heart John
Heath Benjamin
Henderson David
Heniman Leonard
Heniman Moses
Holmes Orsamus
House Jonathan
Hulburt William
Huntington Jery
Huntley Benjamin
Hutchins Asa
Jewet Jedediah
Johnson Jehial
Jonston Edin
Jonston John
Jurdon Jonathan
Kelley Abraham
Kelley John
Kellog Joseph
Kellom Samuel
Kentfield George
King Reuben
King Thomas
Klein Adonijah
Lapish John
Lee Jonathan
Libbey Joseph
Lighthall William
Locheron John
London
Luttington John
Luttington Moses
McConnel Jonathan
Magee William
Magrager Duncan
Malery David
Mallarce Nathaniel
Matthewson A.
Meloy J.
Messer Abiel
Michel Samuel
Millege John
Miller Robert
Milroy John
Moores Ezra

Morris John
Moss Timothy
Nayson Benjamin
Nayson Edward
Nolds E.
Olcott William
Olford Alexander
Ovits James
Owen Daniel
Owen Silvanus
Pain Francis
Park J.
Parker Amasa
Pasavile John
Patee Zephniah
Patterson George
Paul Robert
Philbrook Eliphalet
Piper Thomas
Powers Nicholas
Prindle Joel
Prose Benjamin
Putnam Asaph
Putnam Ephron
Quackenbush Gerardus
Quackenbush Jacobus
Quin Michel
Renolds John
Richards Edward
Richardson Jonathan
Ripney John
Robertson John
Robinson Peter
Rowe Abner
Rowley Samuel
Rush George
Sanborn John
Saxston George
Serjeant Samuel
Shavalee Joseph
Shepherd David
Simpson William
Smith Abraham
Smith Benjamin Young
Smith Eliphelet
Smith John
Sopers William
Spencer Jesse
Spring Thomas
Squires James
Stannard Libeus
Sterling Archibald
Steven Isaac

Stevens John
Stewart John
Stickney Ezekiel
Stockwell Jacob
Stow Seth
Stuart Samuel
Sturges David
Styles Eli
Sullingham Henry
Thomas John
Thurstininlis Ward
Trouax John
Trowbridge Stephen
Turner Nicholas
Umpsted Israel
Van De Bogart Charles
Van Gelder John
Van Gelder Jonathan
Van Vorst Jelles D.
Van Wagenen Evert
Vine Ebenezer
Vine Robert
Vine Solomon
Wakley Stephen
Walker Jonathan
Wallis Samuel
Waters John
Watkins Daniel
Welch David
Wells James
Whiston John
Wiley David
Willen Amos
Williams Nehemiah
Young John
Young Joseph

The Line - Additional Corps

COLONEL MOSES HAZEN
SURGEON NICHOLAS SCHUYLER
LIEUT. PALMER CADY
LIEUT. ANDREW LEE

ENLISTED MEN

Averil Ebenezer
Blake James
Blake John
Bardewin John
Boardwin John
Boardwine John
Burr Nathaniel
Casey John
Hannigan Joseph
Hole James
Kanallie John
Kanallie Patrick

Knelly John
Lary John
Lufberry Abraham
Marling Deliverance
Mead Duncan
Nichols Richard
O'Hara James
Palmenteer William
Parks John
Paterson Jonathan
Paterson William
Pattersons Jonathan

Poircon James
Pierson John
Ryan James
Storm Abraham
Torrey Samuel
Torry Samuel
Tory Samuel
Travis Silvanus
Van Zile Egbert
Welch William

The Line - Artillery, Second Regiment

COLONEL JOHN LAMB
MAJOR SEBASTIAN BAUMAN
ADJUTANT JAMES BRADFORD
Q'R MASTER HENRY CUNNINGHAM
Q'R MASTER WILLIAM STRACHAN
PAY MASTER JOHN DUTTON CRIMSHEIR
PAY MASTER ISAAC GUION
PAY MASTER WILLIAM STRACHAN
SURGEON'S MATE NORDICA HALE
CAPT. THOMAS THEODORE BLISS
" JONATHAN BROWN
" JOHN DOUGHTY
(BRIGADE INSP.)
" GEORGE FLEMING
" JAMES LEES
" SAMUEL LOCKWOOD
" THOMAS MACHIN
" SAMUEL MANSFIELD
" THOMAS MATCHIN
" ANDREW MOODY
" GERSHOM MOTT
" PETER NESTEL
" ANDREW PORTER
" JACOB REED

" JOSEPH SAVAGE
" JONAS SIMOND
" WILLIAM STEVENS
" CORNELIUS SWARTWOUT
" JOSEPH THOMAS
" THOMAS THOMPSON
" ROBERT WALKER
" JEREMIAH WOOL
CAPT. LIEUT. EDWARD ARCHIBALD
" CALEB BREWSTER
" ISAAC GUION
" ELISHA HARVEY
" BAXTER HOW
" JOHN MILES
" JOHN WALDRON
" HENRY WARING
" ISAIAH WOOL
LIEUT. STEPHEN ALLING
" JONAS ADAMS
" PETER AUSPACH
" JAMES BRADFORD
" CALEB BREWSTER
" JAMES BREWSTER
" ROBERT BURNET

" JOHN BURNSIDES
" JOHN CAMPBELL
" WILLIAM CEBRA
" ALEXANDER CLINTON
" HENRY CUNNINGHAM
" HENRY DEMLER
" EPHRAIM FENNO
" ISAAC FISK
" CHILLION FORD
" JAMES GILES
" ISAAC GUION
LIEUT. OLIVER LAURENCE
" GEORGE LEAYCRAFT
" WILLIAM LEAYCRAFT
" ROBERT H. LIVINGSTON
" TIMOTHY MIX
" WILLIAM MORRIS
" PETER NESTEL
" JACOB REED
" JOHN REEDE
" JOHN SHAW

" ISAAC SMITH
" JOHN SMITH
" WILLIAM STRACHAN
" WILLIAM STRAHAN
" CORNELIUS SWARTWOUT
" PETER TAPPIN
" ALEXANDER THOMPSON
" ISAIAH THOMPSON
" JOHN RUTHERFORD TROOP
" JOHN WALDON
" SAMUEL WHITING
" HENRY A. WILLIAMS
" PETER WOODARD

ENLISTED MEN

Abanathy Giles	Bon Barnes	Coltman William
Allen George	Bon Joseph	Connor John
Alley William	Bonnell John	Cook John
Ames Simeon	Brewster Samuel, Jr.	Cook Michael
Anderson John	Brocket Moses	Corbin David
Aris Francis James	Brower Daniel	Costly John
Arvin James	Brown James	Cox John Luke
Ashfield John	Brown Richard	Coyse Peter
Ashton Joseph	Bruster Samuel	Crawford Thomas
Atwell Peter	Buchanan John	Crudock William
Bacon William	Buchanan William	Crudunk William
Badgerow Francis	Bunn Barnes	Crumb John
Bagley Azor	Bunn Joshua	Crumb Richard
Bailes James	Burges John	Curtiss Andrew
Bailey John	Burroughs Samuel	Daily Robert
Bailey Moses	Byington John	Dalzell George
Ball Allen	Callaghan Thomas	Dart Abiel
Bard Robert	Campbell Daniel	David Hugh
Barns Solomen	Campbell Ephraim	Day John
Bauman Samuel	Carpenter George	Day Thomas
Beard Robert	Cashel Thomas	Deacon Joseph
Bennet Richard	Cashen William	Dean Joseph
Bennet William	Chatterdon Nathaniel	Deane John
Bennett Jacob	Chitsey Banjamin	DeGroot Henry
Bennet John	Chittendon Jared	DeLong Joseph
Berwick Marmaduke	Christy John	Dennis John
Berwick Robart	Clark Anthony	Dennison Prince
Betters John	Clark Martin	Devo Francis
Betts John Wilson	Coen Daniel	DeWitt John
Bishop Joshua	Coleman John	Dixon George

Done Thomas
Doughty John
Douglass John
Dumas Pierre
Dunlap James
Eastwood Amos
English Robert
Farrington James
Fenton Jotham
Fenton Peter
Fisher Bartholomew
Fisher John
Fisk Isaac
Flagley John
Ford Isaac
Francis Philip
Fredrickson John
Garigues John
Gaus Stephen
Geesen Matthew
Gillet Benjamin
Ginson Richard
Goble Joseph
Godwin Joseph
Goe Thomas
Graham William
Graves Joseph
Green Morris
Grob John
Gross Peter
Guillaume Martain
Hackney William
Hackny Joseph
Hallock Joseph
Hammon James
Hammon T.
Hanmer David
Harwood Thomas
Haskins Benony
Hayes Samuel
Hean Frederick
Helm Charles W.
Hesse Henry
Heusted Nathaniel
Holland Shelly
Hopkins Gardner
Houck Henry
Houston Nathaniel
Hutchenson Nathan
Hutchins John
Hyatt Alvan
Irvin James
Johnson John

Johnson Samuel
Johnson William
Johnston Benjamin
Jones John
Jones Thomas
Keaughy Matthew
Kelly John
Kenny John
Kerney Thomas
Kill Christopher
King Adam
Kitchel Matthew
Laflieur John
Lafonton Phineas
LaSalle Jacque
Latta Moses
Lawrence Alexander
Lewis, Charles
Lindsey Hugh
Linit Jacob
Lint James
Lock John
Lockwood Silas
Loger Christopher
Lovlet Francis
Lucas Jonathan
Ludibock John
McCay Alexander
McClue William
McCoy Daniel
McCullough John
McCune Richard
McDonald John
McDonol Anninias
McFarlin Andrew
McKay Alexander
McKinney William
Mc Lean Allen
McTarling James
Mansfield Thomas
Martin John
Mason Francis
Mason James
Mason John
Mead Richard
Meales Matthew
Merritt William
Midgley Joseph
Mielon Francis
Miller Philip
Millot Ferreal
Millspaugh William
Milspaugh John

Mitchell David
Moor Daniel
Moor Francis
Morancy Joseph
Morrison Thomas
Murphy John
Mussey John
Neel John
Nelson Thomas
Nestall Peter
Nestell George
Nestell Martin
Newton Peter
Nichols William
Nistle Peter
Norris James
Norton Jedediah
Oliver Thomas
Parnet Claude Joseph
Parsons Samuel
Patton James
Paxton Edward
Peed Daniel
Pell Philip
Phraner William
Pilltord William
Poalk John
Poole William
Powell William
Preston J.
Prindle Enos Jones
Raymond Francis
Relay Henry
Richardson Robert
Rickhorn Abraham
Riddle John
Robinson David
Robinson Issachar
Rodes Richard
Roe John
Roef Michael
Rollins William
Roop Michael
Ross Findley
Rucar Daniel
Ruff David
Russell Solomon
Ryder Frederick
Savage Richard
Seely Lewis
Sharp Thomas
Shearer James
Sheehan Thomas

Shelly William
Sherwood Andrew
Simons Robert
Slauson John
Smith John
Smith William
Smith Zacheriah
Sommers Ferral
Spranger Henry
Stagg Cornelius
Stephens William
Steymest Gasper
Storms John
Sullivan John
Summers Ferrol
Sutton Thomas
Swift Willard
Tackor Stephen
Telfor William
Thomas Joseph
Thompson Thaddeus
Thompson William
Tompkins Lawrence
Torry David

Travis Silvanus
Tuthill Joel
Vanderhoff Cornelius
Vanderooh Benjamin
Van Emburgh Joseph
Vangarder James
Vangemund Frederick
Van Kleech Michael
Van Schaick Samuel
Villeroy John Nicholas
Vix James
Wandell Adam
Ward Samuel
Weaks David
Weaks John
Webb William
Welsh Richard
Weltch John
Wendell Jacob
Whaly Michael
Whigham R.
White John
Whitney Seth
Wilson Isaac

Wilson William
Winins Silas
Winter Thomas
Wirth Christopher
Wise William
Withwall William
Woodruff Samuel
Wormwood Peter
Yeanor Anthony

THE LINE--ARTILLERY, Third Regiment

Enlisted Man
Hepworth Daniel

The Line-Provincial Artillery (Capt. Alexander Hamilton's Train) CAPT. ALEXANDER HAMILTON LIEUT. JOHN BANE, LIEUT. MARTIN JOHNSON, CAPT. LIEUT. JAMES MOORE, LIEUT. JAMES GILLILAND

Enlisted Men

Barber Robert
Barry Lawrence
Bowers Michael
Brooks Joseph
Brown Joseph
Burrage Robert
Cairns John
Campbell Andrew
Chamberlin Uriah
Child Joseph
Crawford Uriah
Deasy James
Delaney Thomas
Dely Henry
Douglass William

Farguson Lawrence
Finton Robert
Forbes James
Gallaway James
Garland George
Gilbert William I.
Griffiths John
Hackett William
Haight Joseph
Hammond John
Harwood Thomas
Henry James
Hervey John
Hyer John
Johnson Isaac

Johnson Martin
King Adam
King Jacob
Lawler Martin
Lewis Thomas
Lilly James
Lockhart William
McGeers James
McKinny John
Magee James
Martin John
Mason Joseph
Miller David
Norris Stephen
Oharro Mathew

Pilling John
Putt John Christopher
Remsen Aris
Robins Aaron
Robins Valentine
Ryan Lewis

Ryan Thomas
Saler John
Sawers Isaac
Scott William
Smith Samuel
Stakes John

Taylor Richard
Taylor Thomas
Thompson Thomas
Thurston Samuel
Wan Lawrence
Wood John

The Line--Artillery Regiments (Not Identified)

LIEUT. COL. EBENEZER STEVENS
QUARTER MASTER THOMAS GEE
SURGEON GERRET TUNISON
CAPT. EPHRIAM FENNO
LIEUT. WILLIAM PENNINGTON
ENSIGN BENJAMIN HERRING
CAPT. ISAAC HUBBELL

Ackerman William
Aiken James
Ailing Ichabod
Alvoid Thomas, JR.
Alvoid Thomas G.
Ash Henry
Baker William
Bancker James
Bare Edward
Barns Abraham
Barrager John
Barret William
Barton Robert
Beaver Edward
Bennet Joseph
Biles Thomas
Bishop Gavriel
Bishop Levi
Bishop Nathaniel
Boyd James
Bracket Cornelius
Bremer Anthony
Bright James
Brooks Samuel L.
Brown John
Buchez Peter
Burhans John
Burwick John
Bush Conradt
Cable Samuel
Caeley Peter
Cahil John
Campion Matthias
Cann John

Casey James
Chapin Leonard
Christian Michael
Clark George
Clark John
Clarke George
Clarke John
Cochran Thomas
Cohoon David
Cole Benjamin
Coleman Israel
Collier Richard
Colman Israel
Compton Matthias
Cooper Isaac
Cornwall David
Cornwall William
Cottelle Philip
Crab Abijah
Craft Henry
Craly Peter
Culler Henry
Cunningham John
Cunningham William
Cutler Henry
Davids John
Davis Henry
Davis Richard
Davis William
Dayton Ephraim
Dayton Frederick
Dean Ashbell
Dean Benjamin
Decker John

DeGroot John
DeMott William
Dickson James
Dill Nicholas
Diskill Nathaniel
Dolton John
Doty Isaac
Dowling Andrew
Drake William
Dutcher Abraham
Dyckman Richard
Ferris Peter
Fletcher David
Fletcher John
Foot Isaac
Foster John
Fryor Charles
Fuller Peter
Gardner Benoni
Gardner Thomas
Garnet John
Garrison Peter
Garrison Thomas
Gauler Samuel
Gillaspye Joseph
Goble John
Gorham Joseph
Gortly William
Green Samuel
Griffith Thomas
Hagerty Enos
Hague Cornelius
Hains William
Halstead Joseph

Hanley Joseph
Hanmore Moses
Harden Oliver
Harding Oliver
Hardy Benjamin
Hardy Richard
Hardy Robert
Harriot Israel
Harris Henry
Harris James
Hart William
Hartwick John
Hastings Ebenezer
Hetty Coenradt
Hibberd Samuel
Hicks Jacob
Higgens Nathaniel
Higgins Thomas
Hill Edmond E.
Hill Obadiah
Hinkley Joshua
Hitchcock Brampton
Hoff David
Holland John H.
Holstead Joseph
Horner Francis
House Cornelius
Hunt John
Jacobs Able
Jacobs Uriah
Johnson David
Johnson Jacob
Karp Thomas
Kating Thomas
Kelton Thomas
Ketchum Joshua
Kier Teunis
King George
Kip Peter
Knap Samuel
Lackie James
Laden Ambrois
Laverick Gabriel
Lawson Jacob
Leach Christopher
Lee Jeptha
Lee Joseph
Leester Guy
Lemmon William
Lewis James
Lines Ebenezer
Little James
Loring Benjamin

Losier Oliver
Lounsberry Nathan
Lozier Oliver
Luddow Ambrose
McBride James
McBride William
McClean Donald
McCloud John
McDonald James
McGinnes Arthur
Mack Bazall
McKenzie John
McKew John
McKillips Abraham
McLean Allen
Mc Lean Daniel
McLean John
Mallet John
Malone John
Malony Daniel
Marius Jacob
Mead Jonathan
Medler Christopher
Miles Elnathan
Miller Samuel
Mix Stephen
Moffat Alexander
Moor James
Morris Robert
Mortimor James
Mulineaux William
Myer Abraham
Nelson John
Nevit John
Newel James
Nicholas Eli
Nielson John
Orcut John
Osborn Jeremiah
Osman John
Pangburn Samuel
Paris Anthony
Parker Edmond
Parker Jackson
Patterson John
Pembrook David
Pembrook David Jr.
Pembrook James
Perkins John
Pettice David
Pettit Jabez
Pierpoint John
Pittee David

Policy Hugh
Pratt John
Prebble Samuel
Preston Thomas
Price Elijah
Price Nathaniel
Purdy James
Quackenboss Benjamin
Randel Jeremiah
Randle Jeremiah
Ray Caleb
Reckhow Abraham
Rein John
Reins John
Revera John
Reverce John
Riply David
Rissley David
Robertson William
Robeson John
Robinson John
Roe Michael
Ross John
Rudolph David
Ruff Jonathan
Rukhouse Abraham
Rumblow Thomas
Rumsey Nathaniel
Rundolph David
Russel John
Ryan John
St. Clair George
Salmon William
Sanders Robert
Schultz Christopher
Sheerman Edmond
Shell Elisha
Shells Elisha
Slack James
Slater John
Slates John
Smith Daniel
Smith James
Smith Jeremiah
Smith Joseph
Smith Nicholas
Smith Thomas
Smith Wait
Smith Weight
Sommers Samuel
Squire Jonathan
Squire Samuel
States Peter

Stephens Theodore	Todd Yale	Whitemore James
Stockbridge John	Travis Joseph	Whitmore Amos
Stocker Seth	Utter John	Wilcocks Elias
Stymets Isaac	Varial Joseph	Wilcox John
Sunderland John	Vermilyee John	Williams Isaac
Swan William	Vermylyea John	Williams Richard
Sweney Edmond	Wakelee Samuel	Wilsey Jacob
Taylor John	Warner Thomas	Wilson David
Temple Ebenezer	Webb Amos	Wilson Elijah
Terboss Isaac	Webb Gideon	Wittmore James
Thacher Stephen	Weed John	Wood Jesse
Tharpe John	Wessels Hercules	Young Alexander
Thomas John	Wessels John	Young Peter
Thorn Daniel	Wheeler William	Yurks John
Thornton William	White James	Yurkse John
Thorp Thomas	White Jonathan	

The Line--Cavalry, Second Regiment, Light Dragoons

COLONEL SHELDON, ADJUTANT THOMAS F. JACKSON, LIEUT. THOMAS F. JACKSON

ENLISTED MEN

Cooley Samuel, Fraser Simon, Jorden James, Winn John

The Line--Cavalry, Fourth Regiment, Light Dragoons

COLONEL MOYLAN, CAPT. ANTHONY POST, CAPT. LIEUT. PETER TAALMAN, SUPT. EBENEZER YOUNG, CAPT. JOHN SHEPHERD, LIEUT. EZEKIEL SAMPSON

The Line--Cavalry Regiments (Not Identified)

Capt. Jeromimus Hoogland, Lieut. John Stakes

Enlisted Men

Buskhout John, Coe John, Cooper Joseph, Cox John
Cronk Garret Gurnee Stephen, Hogland John, Jacobs Cornelius
Jacobson Cornelius, Kronck Gerret, Slauson Ebenezer, Slauson Nathaniel
Van Huysen John, Willis Benjamin, Wood Ebenezer, Wood Samuel

Brothers In Arms, A Time of Terror, Part Three

The Line—Artificers (Builders)

Lieutenant Colonel Luther Baldwin, Capt. Peter Mills, Lieut. Jotham Wright, Lieut. John Morris Foght

ENLISTED MEN

Carter Luke, Cary Elihu, Clary James, Cole John, Conklin John, Dean Ezra, Dean Moses, Dean Solomon, Dill John, Emson Henry, Gilson Hezekiah, Goldsmith Jeremiah, Hosier John, Lasly John, Seamons Silvanus, Slot Daniel, Taylor William, Thomas Aaron, Thomas Joseph, Thompson Robert, Tyler Timothy

---

The Line--Artificers (Not Identified)

ENLISTED MEN

Dolphan Thomas, Harrison Thomas, Strickland Jonathan

The Line--Miners & Sappers (Not Identified) (Dug trenches, etc.)

Capt. James Gilliland, Capt. Jonathan Lawrence, Capt. Lieut. James Gilliand

---

The Line/Levies, Not identified

The following men (according to the certificates of the muster-masters) served either in the Line or the Levies, having been hired by the several classes under the Land Bounty Rights; but there is nothing to indicate in which regiment of the Line or the Levies they served.

Lieut. Abraham Ten Eyck

Enlisted Men

Abbett Nathan	Ashman Samuel	Balys Richard
Acker Joseph	Aspenwall Eleazor	Bancker Francis Mesnard
Ackerman John William	Atwell Peter	Barker Jared
Akains Aron	Atwood Jabes	Barker John
Allen Jesse	Austin Philip	Barker Levy
Allin Ainisa	Avery Daniel	Barker Solomon, Jr.
Amery Nathaniel	Avery William	Barker Zenas
Ames Simeon	Ayres Robert	Barnet Simon
Andress John	Babcock Jonathan	Barns William
Andrews Zenas	Babcock Newman	Bateman Henry
Angle William	Baker Albert	Baulding Aaron
Armstrong John	Baker John F.	Bayley Moses

Becker Abraham
Becker Christian
Becker Storm A.
Becker William A.
Beckforth Daved
Been George
Benley Henry
Bennet Nathan
Berden Samuel
Besemer Casper
Besimer Johannes
Betts John Wilson
Bevier Simon
Birchard Nathaniel
Bishop John
Black Cato
Black Cesar
Black Walter
Bleakley Nicolas
Blin Seth
Blodjet Abel
Blodjet John
Bloom Peter Clow
Bogards Henry
Bogart Cornelius, Jr.
Boice Abraham
Boon William
Boonsteel Henry
Booth David
Bostwick Salmon
Bouk Peter
Bouley Benjamin
Bovier David J.
Bowen William
Branen Michal
Brewer Cornelius, Jr
Brewer Jacob
Brodhead Henry
Brodhead Thomas
Brown John
Bruer William
Buchannen William
Buckley Andrew
Bulsen Henry
Bumpus Frederick
Burgert Milbery
Burget Lambert
Burgis Stephen
Burnham Josiah
Bush Asahel
Butler Timothy
Calkins Mathew
Cambell Ephraim

Cammell John
Campbell David
Campbell John
Carl David
Carpenter Phillip
Carpenter Prosper
Carpenter William
Carter Henry
Caster William
Castle William
Castler John
Castor William
Cater Zacharias
Catlind Timothy
Cato Prince
Ceasar B.
Center Jonathan
Chambers Cornelius
Chambers William
Chandlar Isaac
Chapman Benjamin
Charhart Jacob
Chase Gideon
Chase Jonathan
Chatterden Nathanie
Christianse John
Christie Robert
Clapp James
Clarke Elias
Clow George
Clupsattle Andrew
Coats Christopher
Cocksing James
Codman John
Cogdin Timothy
Coins Ebenezer
Coldgrove John
Cole Benjamin
Colts Christopher
Conro William
Cooper Joseph
Corris Lawrence
Coulter Thomas
Covert John
Crans Christopher
Crippen Thaddeus
Crispell John I.
Crum Richard
Cruster Leonard
Culver David
Cusick George
Dailey Silas
Dake John

Darbeshire James
Dark Abial
Davice John
Davis Elias
Davis Jack
Dayton Joseph
Dealey Joseph
Defendorff John
Deforeest Isaac
Degollier James
Degrote Joseph
Degrusha Elias
Dolanay John
Delenow Nathan
Deming Asial
Denmik Samuel
Dennis Joseph
Devee Isaac
Devine John
De Witt Egbert W.
De Witt Jacob J.
De Witt Thomas
De Witt William A.
Deyo Elias
Dibble Nathan
Dicason John
"Dick" (mulatto)
Dick Henry
Dickason Lodwick
Dickinson John B.
Dickson Marshall
Dileno Nathan
Dilliber John
Dollaueay Andrew
Dotey William
Downing John
Drum Peter
Du Bois John J.
Dulittle David
Dumond John H.
Dun Oliver
Dunnifor Daniel
Eaghler Frederick
Eaton Elijah
Edsalt Richard
Eldon John
Elliot Gideon
Elliott Christopher
Elmendoph Jacob
Elmer Daniel
Elwood Peter
Ernst Frederick
Evans Samuel

Evens Edward
Eygenaar Jacobus
Ezelyn James
Falkenburgh Adam
Falkenburgh Hermon
Falkenburgh Joseph
Fellows Abiel
Files Philip
Finch Silvanius
Finn Henry
Fisher Darius
Flagg John
Flensberg Antoney
Fonday Jacob G.
Foot Darius
Ford Isaac
Forgeson Calip
Fox Charles
Fox Nathaniel
Fradenburgh Thomas
Frammire Daved
France Jacob
France Sontuck
Frances Phillip
Francis Hendrick
Frankling Nathan
Freeland Robert
Friddle Esquire
Frisbee Thomas
Fynos Antona
Gardiner Nicholas A.
Garnreck William
Gerret James
Gilbert Augustus
Gillet Lemuel
Gillospie David
Gineguint Joseph
Givens Thomas
Goes Nicholas
Golden William
Goodridge Abner
Gorsline James
Granbey Richard
Grass George
Graves Mark
Green Asahel
Green Asia
Green Peter (negro)
Griffin Reuben
Grissel Elijah, Jr.
Hainer Coenrad
Halley
Halsted James

Hamlin Amos
Hamlin Asa
Hanes Caleb, Jr.
Hann Coenraedt
Hannahs George
Harbes Michael
Hardenbarrick Lewis
Hardwick Christian
Harmance John Christian
Hatch Samuel
Hawes John
Hawkins Ruben
Haytt Milter
Header Stephen
Henderickson Peter
Henry Joel
Herrad Thomas
Hess Christian
Hitchman John
Hochstrosscr Baltus
Hollenbeeck Henry
Hollit William
Holslander Adam
Hoisted James
Hooker Gilbert
Hopkins Daniel
Hopkins Stephen
Hosford Samuel
How Titus
Hubbel Richard
Hubble Gershum
Hubble Richard
Hull Abraham
Hummel Johannes
Hummel Johannes, Jr.
Husted Jonathan
Hutchason Jeremiah
Hutchenson Nathan
Hutches John
Ingham George
Inglish George
Jansan Matthew H.
Jansen John T.
Jansen Mathew
"Jeffrie" (Indian)
Jewel John
Johnson Isaac
Johnston David
Kellogg Stephen
Kentor Richard
Kerner Andrew
Kernocker Andrew
Kesler Nicholas

Kimberley John
Kimberly John
King Isaac
King James
Kinkead Crownidge
Kip John
Knapp Abraham
Knout Jacob
Lanes Frederick
Lanphier John
Lansingh Hendrick
Lassing George
Laurence William
Lawraway Isaac
Learns Ira
Lee Benjamin
Lephard John
Lepper Wiand
Lewis Elijah
Lewis Elisa
Lewry Batut
Liddle Charles
Lock John
Lotts Jacob
Lous Michael
Lous Michael, Jr.
Lous William
Louw Abraham D.
Lowne Johanis
Lucy Bartis
Lutts John, Jr.
McArthur Charles
McCallum John
McClean Hector
McDanold Annanias
McDuffee Angus
McElwain William
McKee Thomas, Jr.
McVandoore Mink (negro)
Maines James
Marble Sampson
Martial William
Mastin James
Matancomin Benjamin
Matthews Jabez
Mayer David
Mead Silas
Merile Jacob
Merriam Hezekiah
Mezener John
Misern John
Moon Abraham
Morgan Skiff

Morris Jacob

Morriston Lewis

Mowett James

Murray Jack (negro)

Murry John

Myer Cornelius

Myres John

Myres John, Jr.

Naunauneeknauk David

Naunaunontonke Jacob

Nehamiah John Henry

Nellass Robart

Nestel George

Nicols Siles

Nimham Aaron

Nimham Daniel

Nimham John

Ninham Isaac

Noble Caleb

Norton William, Jr.

Notonksion William

Nottingham Gaston

Nottingham Thomas

Null Christian

Oasten Phillip

Olds Gilbert

Ouderkerk John

Owen Jonathan

Owen Joseph

Owen Thaddeus

Owens James

Owens John Dans

Pain David

Pain Thomas

Palmer Joseph

Palmetier William

Parham William

Parks David

Parr Moses

Passage Joseph

Patchin Walter

Peck Adonijah

Peek Moses

Penbrook William

Perry Daniel

Pettit Jacob

Phillips Amasa

Phillips Isrel

Phillips John

Pickerd Adolph

Pitterson Oliver

Pixley Clark

Ploegh Hendrick H.

Plough Hendrick, Jr.

Plough Nichlas

Plumb Amariah

Plumb Caleb

Post Hendrick, Jr.

Prime Samuel, Jr.

Pudney Richard

Purdy Jesse

Ransom Barzeal

Ransom James

Reinhart William

Reis John

Rennels Isaac, Jr.

Renner George

Reugg Benjamin

Rhodes Richard

Richardson Josiah

Ridder Frederick

Ripenberiger George

Robertson Levy

Robertson Peter

Robinson Levi

Robison Jacobus

Rogers Hugh

Roney John

Root Denison

Rote Henry

Rote Thomas

Rovenworoous William

Rowley Timothy

Runnels Daniel

Russ Nathan

St. John Gideon

Schell Fredrick

Scheller John

Schutt Abraham

Scofield Silvanus

Scrinert Stephen

Scudder Ezekiel

Seaver John

Semons Whelemos

Senequin Joseph

Sewall Reuben

Shades Adam

Shanhenhekuk Moses

Shaver Henry, Jr.

Shaw James M.

Shepard Horace

Shepard Rufus

Shepherd Joel

Shide Fetter

Shiller John

Silkworth William

Smalley Ruben

Smawley Josiah

Smith Bill

Smith Boltis

Smith Edward

Smith Levi

Sparks James

Spicer Nathan, Jr.

Spoor Nicholas

Sprage John

Staten Livy

Sternmen Samuel

Stillwell Henry

Stillwill Henry

Stokes William

Strong Elias

Strong Warham

Sturdavant Zar

Sturtevant Consider

Sumerland Martin

Swart Thomas

Swetland Ambre

Swift Williard

Tarbush Joseph

Taunaku Cornelius

Taylor Spencer

Taylor Walter

Ten Eyck Barent I.

Terwilleger Joshua

Terwilliger William

Tewilleger Peter

Thompson Prime

Throl Rufus

Thursting Daniel

Thurston Joel

Thuston Daniel

Titus (negro)

Tobacco Cobus

Toles Amos, Jr.

Tom

Tomkina Lowrence

Tooles Amos

Townsend James

Treat Ashbel

Trim Israel

Trowbridge John

Trumble Elijah

Tubbs Ichabod

Turner Semor

Tuttle Ezekiel

Tygert Peter

Tyier Ebenezer

Upright John George

Utterman James
Valkenburgh Abraham L.
Van Atta James
Van Bergen David
Van Bergen Peter
Van Bergen Thomas
Van Dycke Arent
Van Ever Martin
Van Evern Garret
Van Sclyke Tobyes
Van Steenbergh John G.
Van Steenburgh Abraham
Van Vleckren George
Van Vleit Aire
Van Voorhis Stephen
Vaughn Richard
Veeder Peter H.
Vosburgh Mark
Wachen Willem
Wadron James
Walter Seth
Watts Thomas
Wautuhyunnaut John
Weading Thomas

Weaver Lowden
Weisenfels John
Welch Ebenezar
Wenompee Isaac
Weston Samuel
Wharry Daniel
Wheatman Benjamin
Whitman Jeremiah
Wickem Danel
Wilgelow Jacob
Wilkeson John
Willeber Gideon
Willey Jonathan
William John
Williamson Nathan
Windfield Abraham
Winegar Henry
Wines Jeremiah
Winne Casper
Winne John J.
Winter Peter
Woodbridge Thomas
Woodcock John
Wooderth Thomas

Woolcot Joseph
Wormut John
Wright Charles
Yearnton Anthony
Yong Matthew
York Daniel
Young Barney
Young Jacob
Young James
Young Johanes
Young John Doctor
Youngs Christ
Youngs Samuel

NAVAL SERVICE

Privateers

Capt. Anthony Rugers
Capt. Samuel Tudor

Sloop "Camden"
Capt. Robert Castle

Frigate "Congress"
Capt. Thomas Grenell
Capt. William Rogers
Lt. Capt. Mar. Victor Bicker, Jr.
Capt. William Mercier

Sloop "Hudson"
Pay Master Henry Benton

Sloop "James"
Capt. Richard Puller

Sloop "Montgomery
Capt. William Mercier
Capt. William Rogers

1st Lieut. Theunis Thew
2d Lieut. John Leaycraft

Sloop "Nancy"
(Formerly the "Charlotte")
Capt. John Harrison

Sloop "Patty"
Capt. Christopher Leffingwell

Sloop "Polly"
Capt. Matthew Van Alstyne
Capt. Christopher Leffingwell
Master Squire Geer

Schooner "General Putnam"
(Formerly the "Betsey")
Capt. Thomas Cregier
Capt. William Mercier
1st Lieut. Thomas Quigley
2d Lieut. David Walker

Master Eleakim Littell
Surg. John Boyd

Sloop "Schuyler"
Capt. James Smith

Sloop "Sally"
Capt. Wilkie Dodge

ENLISTED MEN

Allen Ebenezer
Anthony Benjamin
Armstrong Jonathan
Baker Lionel S.
Baker Lionel S., Jr.
Barkiss Thomas
Barres Timothy
Basset Henry
Beebe Eliphelet
Bell William
Billett John
Bolay Joseph
Bricket John
Bryan Henry
Burns Timothy
Burress James
Butler Thomas
Cambell Archible
Chichester James
Clinton James
Conklang Ebenezer
Conklin Richard
Conkling Titus
Cook James
Damerell Peter
Darcy Augustine
Davies Nathaniel
Davis Ebenezer
Davis Josiah
Denton Stephen
Donaldson Frederick
Donaldson Souevin
Donaldson Subbrinc
Dorsey Augustus
French Cornelius
Fritchet Isaac
Ghit Abraham
Glldersleeve Richard
Goodale Jonathan
Griffis John
Griffith John

Hardy John
Hazon Ezokiol
Hencock Thomas
Hyeat Abraham
Jackson John
Jamison Robert
Kellay Robert
Ketcham Solomond
Knight Burchard
Knight Richard
Lahy Morgan
Latley Morgan
Laurance Nathaniel
Leayted William
Licit William
Lomberd Thomas
McDonald Alexander
McDonald Duncom
McGray John
Markins Thomas
May Elias
Morrell Benjamin
Morrell Jacob
Myer John
Negro Andrew
Noblit John
Parcels John
Parsons Zachariah
Peters Thomas
Platt Daniel
Powel William
Purkinss Thomas
Purkiss Thomas
Purwagnor Solomon
Radley William
Read Thomas
Reeve Elias
Reeve Elisha
Richard John
Roberds Elias

Rogers Jacob
Rogers Joshua
Rosman Samuel
Ruland Thomas
Shaards Thomas
Shelle George
Shells George
Shine John
Shourds Joseph
Simmonds Solomond
Smith Ebenezer
Smith Nathaniel
Steele Thomas
Stelle Thomas
Still Thomas
Swing Peter
Tarbosh Isaac
Taylor John
Taylor William
Ten Eyck Grancy
Ter Boss Isaac
Thayer John
Thines John
Thomas John
Titus Timothy
Tolkenton Joseph
Trail John
Turner Samuel
Waer Joseph
Waistcoat
Weekes Isaac
Weeks Ebenetus
Westcott Jabel
White James
Willasey William
Wood Elias
Wood Eliphelet
Woodruff Benjamin
Wyer John

Sundry persons whose service is evidenced by Manuscripts on file in the Conptroller's Office, but whose names are not found on the papers of any of the regular organizations. (I think some of these names are very familiar and the writer of the previous statement would know where they served, such as Horatio Gates, John Burgoyne, John Frey, Nicholas Herkimer, Major Ross and Peter Gansevoort! Some even served in the enemy camp.)

Allen Herman	Dutcher William	Hawley Seth
Allen Jacamiah	Ealil Peter	Heath W. Maj. Gen.
Alvoid Thomas	Evens Joseph	Hebbard John
Archibald Edward	Evets Milds	Hendry Robert
Bacon Thomas	Faleday John	Herkimer Hendick, Capt.
Baliman J., Lt.	Farster John	Herkimer Nicholas, Brig. Gen.
Ball John Gunel, Capt.	Fenno Ephraim, Capt Lt.	Hesser Martin
Bamhart John	Fey George	Hick Jacob
Bates James	Fick Isaac	Hill Lemuel
Bean John	Fine Jacob S.	Hodnet Richard
Beemus Jotham	Fine John	Hoffmans Aaron
Benedict Jesse	Fish Nicholas, Brig. Maj.	Holdridg Abraham
Benedict Joseph, Capt.	Fitch William	Hoogeboom Peter
Benson Benjamin	Flamming Francis	Hopkins, Col.
Benson Sampson	Folard John	Horner John
Betts John	Follard John	House Peter A.
Betts William	Forman John	Huff Joseph
Bevier Edward	Fothergill Hugh	Huks Benjamin
Bloom Elbert	Frair John	Humphrey Cornelius, Col.
Bodily Andrew	Frans Coenradt	Hyet Henry
Boist Jacob J.	Frasier Duncan	Hyle James
Bowne Benjamin, Maj.	Freebush Matthew	Hynder Elijah
Bradley Stephen B., Col.	Freer Thomas	Hyre Alexander
Braems C.	Freming Abner	Hyres Abraham
Breemer Anthony	Frey John, Brig. Maj.	Ivoris John
Breising Henry	Freyer Charles	Jackson Jesse
Bronck Job	Fullon John	Jen David
Brons Daniel	Fustin Benjamin	Johnson Col.
Brooks James	Gansevoort Peter, Brig. Gen.	Johnston William, Capt. Lt.
Brown, Col.	Gates Horatio, Maj. Gen.	Kaghaatsko Nicholas
Buck Conrad	Gilchrist Adam, Asst. Com. Gen.	Kahehtotow Cornelius
Burgoyne John, Gen.	Gildersleeve F., Lt.	Kakthtotow Cornelius
Cadey Palmer, Lt.	Gillikins James	Kane Thomas
Chaney Isaac	Gincks Thomas	Kantwh Nicholas
Chapen Zadoc	Graves Jedidiah	Kayatshe Nicholas
Claughry John, Ens.	Greene Clark	Keife Arthur
Coen Mark, Jr.	Griffen Joshua	Kelar Frederick
Colver Jonathan	Griffeth Thomas	Ketman Christopher
Covetins Moses	Griffith Nathan	Keyser Edward
Crane John, Adjt.	Griffiths Anthony	Kip Garret
Cudner John, Lt.	Grossvenor, Col. Dy. Adjt. Gen.	Kniskern Jacob
Decker Gerard	Hammon James	Kranck Henry
Dickingson Charles	Hanky John	Kyte Thomas
Dickson Thomas	Hansen David	Laddow Ambrose
Doid Abraham	Harrison James	Ladew Abraham
Dorian John		Ladieu Capt.
Dunavan John		Laferty John

Lancks George
Lang S.
Lansing Jacob John Judge
Advocate
Laulding William
Leech Christopher
Livingston Wm. S., Lt. Col.
Loder Peter
Luck John
Lundelton, Capt.
Lush Stephen, Maj.
Lyben John
Mabee Abraham
McCay
McClean
McDermet Corneliut
Mc Gown Andrew
McKay
McKenny Charles, Jr.
Mc Lean
Mahew Peter
Maitis John
Mane Richard
Mangus Mowris
Maricle Samuel
Marrener William
Marsh Ephraim, Jr.
Marton Ephrim
Masters Alexander
Mattoom John
Maynard Israel
Mead Louis
Menbeth James
Merony Alexander
Merrin, Capt.
Meyer Moses
Miller William O.
Minderse, Capt.
Mingos Morril
Mody Andrew
Morrel Isaac
Morrill William
Morris, Gen.
Morse Ephraim, Capt.
Myer John Henry
Napp Isaac
Nehemire John Henry
Neilson Ele
Nellis Henry, Jr.
Nellis Robert
Neviam James
Nicholas, Col.
Nichols Eli

Nichols Giusham
Nicoll Isaac, Col.
Nicoll James, Col.
Nostrunt Cornelius
Olaavighton John
Ousterhout Frederick
Oustrander Henry
Oviatt Ebenezer
Palfrey William, Pay Mr. Gen.
Palmer Joshua
Pares Anthony
Park Daniel
Paulden Levi
Paulding Levy
Pecavin, Col.
Peck Hiel
Peir John Ernest
Pennear William
Petitt Thomas
Pettie Abel
Phelton Lewis
Piers John
Platt Benoni
Platt Nicholas
Poyton James
Puller Wendall, Jr.
Putnam Israel, Gen.
Quin Thomas
Rakikotow Cornelius
Rase Cornelius
Raymond Seth
Remsen Abraham
Reeves Paul
Reyley James
Reynolds Nathan, Lt.
Reynolds Nathaniel, Jr.
Richey Jeremiah
Richie Charles
Ritzma Rudolphus
Robarts Ezekiel
Robert John
Ross Maj. (Commanding the
Royalist troops in the
expedition of Oct. 1781.)
Rundell Richard
Ruse Abraham
Rutgers Henry, Dy. Mu. Mr.
Gen.
Sarabey Elias
Schahan Jeremiah
Schance Jeremiah
Schutt Abraham H.
Schutt Andrus

Schutt Hendrick, Jr.
Schutt Isaac
Sexton Ebenezer
Sherman Edmond
Sheuden Richard
Shott Lieorge
Shuvalier Elias
Slawson Edward
Slowter Nicholas
Springsteen Altje
Squire Ezra
Stagg John, Lt.
Stevens Benjamin
Stewart Solomon
Stymets Isaac
Sutton Burrall
Swart Evert W.
Swartwout Cornelius,Capt. Lt.
Swartwout Jacobus, Gen.
Tail Andrew
Tallar John William
Tarbush John
Terbus Isaac
Thompson, Ens.
Thompson Stanley
Thorn William
Torrey, Capt.
Travis Carmon J.
Tripp Henry
Tummings Jonathan
Uttes Gilbert
Vanamburg Joseph
Van Benthuysen James
Van Benthuysen Obadiah
Van Buren Matthew, Lt
Vanburen Matthew
Van der Heyden David
Vanderpool Malget
Vandevoort Paulus
Van Etten Peter, Jr.
Van Gasbeck Peter, M
Van Ingen Dirk, Surg.
Vansalisbury John
Van Valkenburgh Baren
Van Vleet Abraham
Varial Joseph
Variel Joseph
Vosburgh Richard
Wandley Abraham
Ward Stephen
Warner Zebulon
Washburn Robert
Washington George, Gen.

Commander-in-chief
Way Benjamin
Webb Samuel B., Gen.
Wedrick Jacob
Weimire Frederick
Wells Michael
Westcott Annanias
Whalen Walter
Wickelow John
Wickham Thomas
Wigglesworth, Col.

Wilbur Joseph
Wilburt Jacob
Wilcocks William
Williams Daniel, Guide
Williams Gilbert J.
Wire Will
Witon Elijah
Wittbeck Peter, Jr.
Wittmarsh Ezra
Woodard Philip
Woodbeck Abraham

Woodbeck Henry
Woods Phineas
Woolcut Claudius
Woolcut Peter
Woolver John
Worner Abram
Yingling John F.
Zarenious Christopher
Zerrener Lodewick

The following lists of regiments were taken from:

New York In The Revolution as Colony and State
by James A. Roberts, Comptroller
Compiled by Frederic G. Mather
Second Edition 1898

The Militia
Albany County Militia--First Regiment
COLONEL ABRAHAM CUYLER
COLONEL JACOB LANSING, JR.
MAJOR JOHN PRICE

MAJOR HARMANUS WANDELL
ADJUTANT HENRY VAN VEGHTEN
QUARTER MASTER GERRIT RYCKMAN

CAPT. ISAAC DE FOREST
" GARRET GROESBECK
" WILLIAM HUNN
" JACOB T. LANSING
" NICHOLAS MARSELIUS
" JACOB ROSEBOOM
" ABRAHAM YATES
LIEUT. NICHOLAS BLEEKER

LIEUT. JOHN CUDERKIRK
" CONRADT GANSEVOORT
" WILLIAM GROESBECK
" HENRY HOGAN
" THOMAS HUN
" ISAAC LANSING
" ABRAHAM SCHUYLER
" JOHN SCOTT

LIEUT. GERRIT VAN SCHAICK
" JOHN A. WENDELL
ENSIGN WILLIAM BLOODGOOD
" JOHN BOGART
" JOHN FONDA, JR.
" JACOB HOGHSTRASSER
" ABRAHAM A. LANSING

Bentheunn I. V.
Brooks Jonathan
Campbell Archibald
Croser John
Davis John
Douw Peter W.
Eights M.
Ellis John
Evertsen Barnabas
Fonda Jacobus

Fryer Isaac
Green James
Hansen Benjamin
Harsen Francis
Hilton Jacob R.
Hilton Jonathan
Hoggstrasser Jacob
Hoogkirk M.
Hunn Thomas
Hyer William
Lansing Henry

Marselis John
Myers John
Nisbey Christopher
Peterson Isaac
Pruyh Christopher
Pruyn Jacob
Pruyn Reynier
Redliff John
Ryckman Garret

Schuyler Dirk
Van Gowan Ryener
Van Sante Ryheart
Van Wie William
Wandelaer John D.
Wermer Cornelius
Wilkinsin John

Albany County Militia--Second Regiment

COLONEL ABRAHAM WEMPLE
MAJOR ABRAHAM SWITS
MAJOR MYNDERT M. WEMPLE
ADJUTANT JOHN VAN DRUSSEN
QUARTER MASTER GERRITT G. LANSING
QUARTER MASTER MYDERT WEMPLE

CAPT. THOMAS B. BANCKER
" JELLIS FONDA
" JOHN MYNDERSE
" ABRAHAM OOTHOUT
" JACOB SCHERMERHORN
(COMPANY EXEMPTS)
" JOHN VAN PETTEN
" JESSE VAN SLYCK
" GERRIT S. VEEDER
" THOMAS WASSON
LIEUT. NICHOLAS BARHEYDT

LIEUT. JELLIS A. FONDA
" WILLIAM MOORE
" JACOBUS PEEK

" JOHN ROSEBOOM
" JACOB SULLIVAN
" JOHN THORNTON
" DANIEL TOLL
" ANDRIES VAN PETTEN
" CORNELIUS A. VAN SLYCK
" PHILIP D. VAN VORST
" ARENT S. VEDDER
" FRANCIS VEDDER

LIEUT. PHILIP VEDDER
" GERRITT S. VEEDER, JR.
" WALTER VROMAN
" LAWRENCE VROOMAM
" MYNDERT. A. WEMPLE

" JELLIS YATES
" NICHOLAS YATES
ENSIGN TEUNIS SWART
" ABRAHAM J. TRAUX
" CORNELIUS Z. VAN SANT-
VOORD
" MYNDERT R. WEMPLE

ADDITIONAL NAMES ON STATE TREASURER'S PAY BOOKS

LIEUT. ROBERT ALEXANDER; LIEUT. JOHN B. VROOMAN; ENSIGN FRAM'R SCHERMERHORN; LIEUT. JOHN B. VROOMAN; ENSIGN ALEXANDER CRAWFORD; LIEUT. ROBERT McMICHAEL

Alexander Alexander
Alexander Robert
Alexander Sandy
Alison William
Ament Evert
Arkson Gerret

Atlass Lent
Aylworth Abraham
Baker Garrit
Balie Jacob
Barheydt Cornelius
Barheydt Jacob

Barheydt John
Barheydt Lewis
Barhout Cornelius
Barhout John
Barhydt Tunes
Barhyt James

Barop John
Barope Andrew
Barope Thomas
Bartley Daniel
Bartlie Micel
Basteanse John
Basteyan John
Bastien John
Bayrop John
Beath Jelles
Beath Roberth
Beath Thomas
Becker Gerret
Berherdt Lewis
Berhydt Tunes
Bersleder Jacob
Bertie Mykel
Bete Thomas
Beth Jelles
Beth Robert
Betts Robert R.
Boice Abraham
Boice James
Bond Richard
Bot Samuel S.
Bovee Nicholas
Bovie Abraham
Bovie Isaac
Bovie Israel
Bowman Frederick
Boyce Abraham
Bradford James
Bradt Aaron A.
Bradt Anthony D.
Bradt Aphrieam
Bradt Arent A.
Bradt Arent S.
Bradt Aron
Bradt Charles
Bradt Cornelius
Bradt Elias
Bradt Ephraim
Bradt Gerret
Bradt Jacobus
Bradt Jacobus A.
Bradt Jacobus S.
Bradt John
Bradt John S.
Bradt Mindart
Bradt Samuel
Bradt Samuel S.
Bragham John
Braghom Joseph

Braghom Symon
Brat Arent S.
Brath Aphreim
Braun Abraham
Breat Antony
Brewer Henry
Broadford James
Broghom John
Broghom Symon
Brouwen Hendrick
Brower Ritchart
Brown Abraham
Burns Arent
Burns David
Buys Abraham
Buys James
Cam Barrent
Caine Peter William
Caine Warrant
Campbell Daniel
Canaday John, Jr.
Carl Henry
Carl William
Cartright Henry, Jr.
Cartright John
Carty Henry, Jr.
Cassedo John
Catlet Thomas
Caurl Henry
Caurl John
Caurl William
Celder Abraham
Cessler Thomas
Challon Alexander
Channel John
Channel Thomas
Channon Alexander
Channon Robert
Channon Thomas
Charlo John
Charlo William
Charloe Handrick
Charloe Handrick, Jr.
Charls Henry
Charls Tobias
Christeanse Asswerus
Christianse Isaac
Cilker William
Cittle Daniel
Cittle David
Cittle John
Clark Henry A.
Clark Matthew

Clement Arent
Clement Eldert
Clement Johannes
Clement John
Clement Peter
Clut Jacob
Clut John F.
Clute Bartholomew
Clute Daniel
Clute Frederick
Clute Jacob
Clute Jacob P.
Clute John
Clute John B.
Clute John Curtis
Clute Isaac
Clute Peter
Clute Petrus
Combs John
Commons John
Condey Adam
Connor Simon
Consale Manuel
Consalus David
Consaul David
Consaul Manual
Corl John
Corneel Wessel
Cornue Daniel
Cornue Wassel
Covie William
Craneford Joseph
Crawford John
Crawford Joseph
Cristeionse Isaac
Cronshorn John
Cummings John
Cunde Adam
Cuyler John
Daves Abraham
Davis Abraham
Davis John
De Evart John
De Garmo Thewes
Degelen James
Degeler James, Jr.
Degollian Joseph
De Graaf Jesse D.
De Graf Connels
De Graff Abraham
De Graff Andrew
De Graff Jesse
De Graff John

De Graff John N.
De Graff John N., Jr.
De Graff Simon
De Graff William
Degrauf Symon
De Grave John N.
De Gullia James
De Gullia James, Jr.
De Gullie Joseph
Dellemont Abraham
Dellemont Hendrick
Dilleno Hendrik
Dorn Abraham
Dorne John
Douw Abraham
Duncan John, Jr.
Eemqie John
Elkson Samuel
Ellice James
Elsworth Abraham
Ement Eldert
Ennie William
Ensil Bertram
Erkson Garret
Erkson Henry
Erkson William
Falbush Andrew
Falbush Jonas
Farlies Caleb
Farly Caleb
Feldhousen John
Fermain John
Ferman John
Flansbury William
Folger Benjamin
Folger Thomas
Folgier Thomas
Fonda Jelles P.
Fort John
Fort John D.
Foulger Thomas
Frank David
Fransway John
French David
Gardner William
Glen Isack
Glen Jacob
Glen John
Glen John S.
Gorden Charles
Gorden Robert
Gorder William
Gordon Joseph

Gordon William
Grag Andrew
Grag James
Gregg Andrew
Groat Abraham
Groat Abraham C.
Groat Andrew
Groat Cornelius
Groat Simon
Groot Amos
Groot Simon
Groot Simon C.
Grot Abraham
Grot Abraham A.
Grot Cornelius
Grote Abraham C.
Hackney George
Hagadorn Harmanus
Hall John
Hall John W.
Hall Nicholas
Hall William
Hanna Alexander
Hannon Alexander
Hare Peter
Harnel Samuel
Harner Samuel
Hars Peter
Harsey William
Harsford John
Hase Dockter
Heddrington Joseph
Hedget Abraham
Hedrengton Joseph
Helmer Henyost
Hendrick Peter
Henry John
Hoopole George
Horsford John
House John George
House Peter
Hughan John
Hydenburgh Sybrant
Jettle Ezra
Jonsing Abraham
Kaneday John
Kaneday Samuel
Kannady Alexander
Kannel John C.
Kees John
Kelder Abraham
Kennedy John
Kennedy Samuel

Kinsley Joseph
Lambert John
Lansing Abraham G.
Lansing Cornelius
Lansing John C.
Lansing John G.
Lansing Gerrit
Lansingh John
Lansingh John C.
Lewes William
Lewis John
Lighthall Abraham
Lighthall Abraham W.
Lighthall George
Lighthall Nicholas
Littel Thomas
Little David
Little John Duncan
Lonpart Jacob
Lonsing Abraham
Luypart Jacob
Lythall Abraham
Lythall Abraham W.
Lythall William
Lytle David
Maap John
Mab Robert
Mabee Cornelius
Mabee John
Mabee John, Jr.
Mabee Peter
Mabie Albert
Mabie Arent
Mabie Cornelius
Mabie John
Mabie John J.
Mabie Patrick
Mabie Peter
Mabis Aron
Maby Cornelius
McBane John
McCallome James
McCanel Alexander
McCartes John
McCarty John
McCarty William
McCew James
McCnut Samuel
McColm James
McDarmont James
McDarmouth James
McDermid James
McDougall Duncan

McEarley John
McFarlin Andrew
McFarlind Andrew
McFerling John
McGeneris Robert
McGinnis Robert
McIntyre William
McKie Samuel
McMarlin William
McMartin William
McMichael Alexander
McMichael Daniel
McMichall James
McMichen Peter
McMickel James
McMickl Danil
McNutt Samuel
McQuean James
McQuier James
Mailes Charles
Main William
Mannen Edward
Mannon John
Marcle Dirk
Markle Matthew
Marrikell William
Marseles John
Marselis Ahasweras
Marselius John
Marselus Gilrt
Martin Charles
Maseles John
Masten Robert
Mayston Robert
Meals Charles
Mebie Juiter
Meebie Albert
Melb John
Mercer Alexander
Mercker William
Merical Dirick
Merseles Egsbert
Merseles Henry
Merselius Arent
Merselius Gysbert
Merselius John
Merselous Hendrick
Merselous John
Merselus Alexander
Mils Chris
Mitchals Hugh
Moass John
Moor James

Moore John
Moore William
Morrell Thomas
Muller Jacob, Jr.
Mulray John
Murry John
Mynderse John
Mynderse John R.
Mynderse Laurence
Mynderse Harmen
Nanning John
Neally Matthew
Neard Christopher
Neiger John
Nixon Josse
Ogden John
Ouderkerk Arent
Passage George
Passage George, Jr.
Patterson Thomas
Patteson Oliver
Peak Jesse
Peck Arent
Peck Cornelius
Peck Daniel
Peck Henry
Peck Jacobus
Peck James J.
Peck Jesse
Peck John
Peck Lewes
Peckburn John
Peeck Arent
Peeck Christopher
Peeck Cornelius
Peeck Cornelius C.
Peeck Harmanus
Peeck Harmanus H.
Peeck Harmanus J.
Peeck Henry H.
Peeck Jacobus
Peeck Jacobus H.
Peeck John
Peeck John J.
Peeck Joseph
Peeck Lewis
Peek Christopher
Peek Daniel
Peek Jacobus Vedder
Peek James J.
Peek Joseph
Peek Lewis
Peeke John J.

Peterson Harmanus
Peterson Herman
Petterson Charles
Petterson Oliver
Petterson Thomas
Philips Thomas
Pruyn Samuel
Putman Aaron
Putman Arent
Putman Arent L.
Putman Aron L.
Putman Cornelius
Putman Cornelius I.
Putman John
Quack Gradus
Quackenbos Genardous
Quackenbos John
Reis John
Reldert Jakop
Renx Anddro
Reyley Jacobus
Rise John
Robison John
Rosa Isaac
Rosa John T.
Rose Elias
Rose John
Ryckman Cournelus
Rykman Cornelius
Rylie Jacobus
Rylie Philip
Rynex Andrew
Rynex John
Rynis John
Rynix Richard
Sacie David
St. John Tedius
Sanders John
Sawer James
Scanger Thomas
Schemhorn Garret
Schermerhoorn Simen
Schermerhorn Andrew
Schermerhorn Andries
Schermerhorn Aurent
Schermerhorn Barnardus
Schermerhorn Bartholomew
Schermerhorn Henry J.
Schermerhorn Jacob
Schermerhorn Jacob J.
Schermerhorn John
Schermerhorn John J.
Schermerhorn Nicholas

Schermerhorn Reijer
Schermerhorn Richard
Schermerhorn Ryer
Schermerhorn Rykert
Schermerhorn Symon
Schuyler Reuben
Seacy Wilhelmus
Shallon Alexander
Shannon John
Shannon William
Shelling Alexander
Shellow Alexander
Shennon Thomas
Shutes Christian
Sickel Phylip F'c
Simonds Reuben
Smealle John
Smeth John
Smilie John
Smith Adam
Smith Robert
Speck Abraham
Speck Tobyas
Speek Tobias
Spitcher Gerrtt
Spitser Arent
Spitser Aron
Spitser Gerret
Staley George
Staly Jacob
Standly John
Stealee George
Stealy Henry
Steeley Matthew
Steers Peter
Stenerd Daniel
Stevens John
Steward Daniel
Steward David
Steward George
Steward James
Steward John
Stewart Daniel
Stewart John
Steylee Jacob
Steylee Matthew
Stirs Peer
Stuart James
Susie Abraham
Susie David
Sullivan Charles
Sullivan Jacob
Swart Jacobus

Swart James
Swart Nicholaas
Swits Henry
Swits Jacob
Swits Jacob, Jr.
Swits Jacob A.
Swits Jacob J.
Swords Thomas
Symons Ruben
Tall Charles
Taus Davis
Tauses David
Taylor Solomon
Taylor Walter
Teller Jacobus
Teller John, Jr.
Teller William
Ten Eyck Jacob
Ten Eyck Myndert S.
Ter Willigen Solomon
Terwilliger Isaac
Terwilliger Jacobus
Terwilliger Solomon
Thaneday John
Thompson John
Thomson John
Thomson Peter
Thorn Samuel
Thornton James
Thornton Thomat
Times Michel
Toll Charles
Toll John
Tortle Selmon
Truax Abraham
Truax Abraham J.
Truax Abraham P.
Truax Caleb
Truax John
Truax John P.
Trumbull John
Turnbull John
Turs Peurs
Turtell Israel
Tutle Ezra
Tuttle Ezerial
Tuttle Solomon
Tyros Michael
Vadder Peter H.
Vagner Andrew
Van Antwerp Garret
Van Antwerp Peter
Van Antwerp Peter A.

Van Antwerp Simon
Van Antwerp Simon J.
Van Antwerpe John
Van Benthuysen Peter
Van De Bogert Joseph
Van De Bogert Nicholas
Van De Graff Abraham N.
Van De Graff John
Van Derhyden Daniel
Van Derhyden David
Van Derhyder Daniel
Van Derhyder David
Van Der Valgen Petrus
Van Der Volger Cornelius
Van Dresen Peter
Van Driesen Peter
Van Duyck Cornelius H.
Van Dyck Cornelius
Van Dyck Cornelius N.
Van Dyck Henry
Van Dyck Henry H.
Van Dyck Henry I.
Van Eps John
Van Eps John B.
Van Eps John J.
Van Fran Richard
Van Guyseling Peter
Van Guysling Cornelius
Van Guysling Jacob
Van Ingan John Vicher
Van Inge John
Van Ingen Joseph
Van Leph William
Van Nes Gerret
Van Patten Frederick D.
Van Pette Adam
Van Pette Frederick
Van Pette Frederick D.
Van Pette Jan
Van Pette Nicolas
Van Pette Philip
Van Petten Adam
Van Petten Arent N.
Van Petten Fradrick
Van Petten Frederick
Van Petten Frederick S.
Van Petten Hendrik
Van Petten Henry
Van Petten Nicholas
Van Petten Nicholas A.
Van Petten Nicholas H.
Van Petten Nicholas R.
Van Petten Nicholas S.

Van Petten Philip
Van Petten Simon
Van Petten Simon F.
Van Pitten Andrew
Van Schaick Gerret
Van Sice Abraham
Van Sice Cornelius
Van Sice Gysbert
Van Sice Isaac
Van Sice Jacobus
Van Sice John
Van Slyck Aaron
Van Slyck Adrian
Van Slyck Andrew
Van Slyck Anthony
Van Slyck Cornelius
Van Slyck Cornelius A.
Van Slyck Cornelius P.
Van Slyck Harmanus
Van Slyck Harmanus N.
Van Slyck Peter
Van Veeder Peter
Van Vlak Benjamin
Van Voghter Anthony
Van Vorst Jellis
Van Vorst John D.
Van Vorst Peter
Van Vranken Dirk
Van Vranken Maus
Van Vranken Maus M.
Van Vranken Nicholas
Van Vranken Nicolas N.
Van Vranken Richard
Van Vranken Rykert
Veader Cornelius
Veader Nicholas
Veader Peter S.
Veader Thelmes
Vealy Philip
Vedder Albert
Vedder Albert A.
Vedder Alexander
Vedder Arent
Vedder Arent A.
Vedder Arent T.
Vedder Barrent
Vedder Cornelius
Vedder Francis
Vedder Frederick

Vedder Harmanis
Vedder John
Vedder John B.
Vedder Nicholas
Vedder Nicoleas
Vedder Peter
Vedder Seymon H.
Vedder Simon
Veder Nicolas
Veder Halimis
Veder Wilhilmus
Veeder Barent
Veeder Cornelius
Veeder Gerret
Veeder Gerret S.
Veeder Helmut S.
Veeder John
Veeder John B.
Veeder Nicolas
Veeder Peter H.
Veeder Peter S.
Veeder Peter T.
Veeder Simon B.
Veeder Simon H.
Veeder Wilhelmus
Vilen Phillip
Visger John
Visger John, Jr.
Visher John, Jr.
Vlack John
Vreene Alexander
Vrooman Adam
Vrooman Adam H.
Vrooman Adam S.
Vrooman Arent
Vrooman Aron
Vrooman David
Vrooman Hendrick
Vrooman Henry
Vrooman Jacob A.
Vrooman Jacob I.
Vrooman Jacob J.
Vrooman John B.
Vrooman John J.
Vrooman John T.
Vrooman Simon
Vrooman Simon J.
Wagenman Michel
Wagner Michael

Wagner Nicolas
Waller Robert
Wallrad
Walrat Jacob
Wandner Richard
Wandry John B.
Ward Christopher
Warner Richard
Wassalse Harman
Watson Alexander
Weaton Robert
Weaton Ruben
Weist Coonrad
Weller Frederick
Weller Robert
Wemple John
Wemple John J.
Wemple John T.
Wemple Mindert R.
Wemple Myndert
Wendell Ahasuerus
Wendle John B.
Wessel Arent
Wesselse Arent
Wesselse Aron
West Coonrad
Whiley John
White William
Wiely John
Willeger Solomon T.
Williams Cornelius
Williams Jacob
Windelby John B.
Wood John
Yanter Henry
Yates Abraham
Yates Abraham J.
Yates John
Yates Nicolas
Yeats Abraham
Young Calvin
Young Fred
Young Frederick
Young Seth
Younter Henry

Albany County Militia--Third Regiment

COLONEL PHILIP P. SCHUYLER; ADJUTANT JOHN P. QUACKENBOSS; LIEUT. COL. BARENT I. STAATS; Q'R MASTER CHRISTOPHER LANSING; MAJOR ABRAHAM D. FONDA

CAPT. JOHN GROOT
" JARIVAN HOGAN
" HOOKS
" JACOB J. LANSING
" LEVINIS F. LANSINGH
" HENRY OSTROM
" TEUNIS A. SUNGERLAND
" JACOB VAN ARNUM
" JOHN A. VAN WIE
" ABRAHAM VEEDER
" BASTIAN T. VICHER
LIEUT. JOHN AKER

LIEUT. MATTHEW FLANSBURGH
" WILLIAM FLANSBURGH
" GERRITT R. GERRITSEE
" WENDEL HILDENBRAND
" EPHRAIM HUDSON
" TIMOTHY HUTTON
" JACOB LANSING
" JOHN LEONARD
" BARENT MEYNDERSE
" PETER S. SCHUYLER
" ISAAC V. VAN AERNAN

" ISAAC VAN ARNUM
LIEUT. LEVI VAN AUKEN
" GERRIT VAN DEN BERGS, JR.
" GEORGE WAGONER
" JACOB WEEVER
" LEVINUS WINNE
" CHRISTIAN A. YATES
ENSIGN ADAM DEITS
" DIRK HEEMSTRAAT
" WILLIAM TILLMAN
" JOHN VAN ARNUM

ADDITIONAL NAMES ON STATE ON STATE TREASURER'S PAY BOOKS

MAJOR JOHN PRICE
LIEUT. JACOB SCHERMERHORN
LIEUT. AUREY VAN WIE
CAPT. DERICK VAN ARNUM
LIEUT. EDWARD THOMAS
ENSIGN JOHN SHAVER
ENSIGN JOHN H. VAN WIE
LIEUT. DERICK DE FOREST
LIEUT. TEUNIS VAN DE BERGH
LIEUT. HENRY OSTRANDER

ENLISTED MEN

Algate Thomas
Allet William
Angus James
Annold Elisha
Anthony Israel
Anthony John
Aonhoudt Christean
Appel Hennrich
Arnhoudt John
Arrenson
Backer Lowick
Backer Philip
Balner Caunnuad
Bancker Garret
Banks Arthur
Bard Francis
Bartt John
Bauch Nicolas

Bauman Andrus
Beard Francis
Beaver Edward
Becker Adam
Becker Gerret
Becker Henry
Becker John
Bell Stephen
Bender Christian
Berkley Michael
Bever Thomas
Bevins Benjamin
Bevits Benjamin
Bishop Joseph
Bloomendall John
Bogeart Christopher
Boger Peter
Bonkle John

Boom Abraham
Bovis Ride
Bowman Andrew
Bradt Adrian
Bradt Daniel A.
Bradt Gerret
Bradt Hendrick
Bradt John
Bradt Peter
Bramblee William
Bratt John T.
Brower John
Browers Richard
Browne Richard
Bruier Richard
Bulman Jacob
Bulsen Gerardus
Bulsen Henry

Bulsen John
Bulsin Benjamin
Burger John
Burnside John
Burnside William
Calwell John
Cammel Harmanus
Carman Frederick
Carr Joseph
Carr William
Casbert John
Chestney John
Chestney William
Church Jacob
Clase John
Claver Nicholas
Clute Fradrick
Clute Gradus
Clute Jacob
Clute John
Clute Nicholas
Clyne Nicholas
Coenie William
Collance Cornelius
Cooper Obediah
Corking Ese
Corsbort John
Coss Cunrat
Cougneed Peter
Covenhoven Samuel
Craney Philip
Crannel Martha
Crannel Nicholas
Crannell William Winslow
Crannell Martin
Cullan Cornelius
Cunniger John
Cuyler Abraham
Daner Moses
Dannals Jacob
De Forest Dirck
De Forest Jesse
Detap John
Delong David
De Voe John
Dewever Abraham
Douglas John
Dygert George
Dygert William, Jr.
Ecker Dennis
Effner Joseph
Ellicks Frederick
Erchard Edward

Everse John
Eversy Evert
Evertsen Evert
Faro Chritien
Faro Henry
Faro Patris
Featherly John
Feddely Philip
Flansburgh David
Flansburgh Denal
Flansburgh John
Flansburgh Peter
Fonda Jacob D.
Foster Jacop
Fradenbergh Isaac
France Cristiffel
France Jacop
Frasner Lefvenes
Frat John
Frats Casper
Frats Nicholas
Frederick Matthew
Freeman John
Friet Michel
Fryer John
Gardinier Hendrick
Gauns Frederick
Goewey Andrew
Goewey Barent
Goewey Garret
Goewey Solomon
Grass Mikele
Groat John
Groesbeck Anthony
Groesbeck Gilbert
Groesbeck Gysbert
Groesbeck Peter W.
Groesbeeck John
Groot Abraham
Groot Derick
Groot Isaac
Gunsal Peter
Gunsalis John
Guree Philip
Hallenbeck Jacob
Hamilton James
Hanse Jacob
Harbeck John
Heamstreadt Dirck
Heemstraet Jacob
Heemstraet John
Heemstrat Isaac
Heemstrat Philip

Heermans Israel
Heldenbrand Wendel
Hemstraat William
Heverlin John
Hickman John
Hilten Peter
Hockstrasser Baltis
Hockstrasser Jacob
Hockstrasser Paul
Hogeboom John
Hogeboom Samuel
Hoghtaling Storm
Horn John
Hoyer George Fred
Huick Henry
Hundermont Henry
Huppol France
Jacobson Evert
Jenkins John
Johnson George
Johnson John
Johnson William
Jolly James
Kane William
Kerker Henry
Kerker Jacob
Kerner Frederick
Kerner Jacob
Klem Joseph
Lagrang Isaac
Lagrange Christian
Lagrange Jacob
Lansing Christopher
Lansing Henry J.
Lansing Jacob I.
Lansingh Jacob H.
Lansingh Jacob J.
Laraway Isaac
Laraway Levinus
Latta William
Leekwa Lodewick
Leelman Jacob
Leverse Douw
Leverse Mattew
Leversy Lebinis
Levey Michael
Lewis Rober
Little Henry
Little John
Long Adam
Loop Coenrad
Lotteridge William
Luke Solomon

McAdam Hugh
McChasney Hugh
McChesney John
McChesney Joseph
McGee John
McHisnay Joseph
Machisne Henry
Machisne Joseph
Mackey Alexander
Maersel Gerret M.
Man Jacob
Mareel Michael
Marinus George
Marinus Jeremiah
Marinus William
Markel Michael
Matcher Lodewick
Meyer Percival
Miller Jacob
Miller Jeremiah
Miller John
Miller Samuel
Milwain Thomas
Minchal Isaac
Minkler Esaaccoh
Mitchel John M.
Moak Jacob
Moak John
Morrell John
Muir William
Muller Jacob
Muller John
Murphy John
Murry Thomas
Myers Andries
Myers Philip
Mysener John
Newman Charles
Newman Henry
Nicoll Francis
O'Brian Levis
O'Brian Lodowick
Ochenback Peter
Oliver John
Olver John
Onck Jacob
Onger Frederick
Oothout Henry
Oothout Volkert
Orlep Willin
Orlog William
Orlogh Frederick
Orlope Fradrick

Orlope Henry
Ostrander Teunis
Ostrom John
Ostrom Ruliph
Oudercark Isac
Ouderkerk Jacob
Ouderkerk John
Ouderkerk Peter
Ouderkerk Peter P.
Ouderkirk Tackle
Oudeskerk Andrew
Outnhok John
Oxburger John
Page Samuel
Painter Philip
Pall James
Parkele Jacob
Parker Jacob
Parkle Jacob
Parkly Michael
Pass Christopher
Pass Lodwick
Passinger Andrew
Peers Christian
Pells Gerret
Peterson John
Phero Christopher
Philips James
Philips John
Philips Joseph
Platt Alaxander
Ponhall Adam
Post Richard
Quack Frederick
Quack Isaac
Quack Jacob
Quackenbos Adrian
Quackenbush Garret
Quackenbuss Peter
Quanth Fradrick
Radley John
Radliff Peter
Raff Cristiffel
Rankel John C.
Reeder John
Reese George
Reese Philip
Relyea Peter
Remsy Hendrick
Restyne John
Reyla Jacob
Roff Frederick
Roff John

Roman Peter
Rose John
Ross John
Rouble Hendrick
Rucel John
Ruff John
Runcel Handric
Runchal John
Ruso Frederick
Saltes James
Salts Benjamin
Scharp Coenrad
Scheefer John
Scheefer Peter
Schiley William
Schnyder Lutwig
Schoolcraft John
Schoolcraft John, Jr.
Schoolcraft Lawrence
Schuyler Peter
Schuyler Philip
Schuyler Reuben
Scraper George
Seeger John S.
Seeger Peter
Severs John
Shaver Jost
Shaver Peter
Shaw John
Shell Philip
Shelly William
Shuck Zacherias
Shutter Jacob
Simson Henry
Sitterling Henry
Sitterling Jacob
Sitterling John
Sitterly Jacob
Sixbee John
Slater Robert
Slingerland Isaac
Slingerland Jacob
Slingerland Peter
Smith John
Smith John, Jr.
Smith Martis
Smith Wilhelmus
Snyder William
Sommon Nicholas
Soud John
Sparback Martinus
Spawn Jocham
Springer Benjamin

Springer Dennis
Stansel Nicholas
Still Francis
Stoop Francis
Summers Nicholas
Swart George
Syber Jacob
Syble Jacob
Syble Martinus
Taylor James
Taylor Joseph
Teachout Jacob
Tid Samuel
Tilleback Hendrick
Tillman John, Jr.
Tilman Derick
Tingue John
Tisler George
Toll Simon
Truax Abraham
Truax Christian
Truax Isaac
Truax Isaac, Jr.
Truax John
Tucker William
Tymer Peter
Valkenburgh Jacob
Van Acker John
Van Aernam Abraham G.
Van Aernam Johannis
Van Aernem Jacob
Van Aernem Johen W.
Van Alen John
Van Arnam Abraham
Van Arnem Evert
Van Arnem William
Van Auken Henry
Van Auken Levy
Vande Lende Peter
Van Den Berger Cornelius
Vandenbergh Abraham
Van Denbergh Burger
Van Denbergh Cornelius
Van Den Bergh Cornelius W.
Van Den Bergh Evert
Van Denbergh John
Van Denbergh Levinus

Van Denbergh Winant
Vandenbergh Winant E.
Vanderzee Albert
Vanderzee Albertus
Vanderzee Cornelis
Van Deusen Arent
Van Duesen Matthew
Van Dyck David
Vanetten William
Van Ness John
Van Olenda Jacob
Van Patten Nicoless
Van Pette John
Van Petten Frederick
Van Petten Peter
Van Schaick Gerit G.
Van Sice Cornelius
Van Veghten Philip
Van Viet Auc
Van Wie Casparus
Van Wie Peter
Van Woert John
Van Woert Rutgert
Van Woord John
Van Wort Jacob
Van Zandt John
Veeder Lucas W.
Venolinda Petris
Verplanck Abraham
Vicar John
Vichter Andries
Vinc John
Vischer Gerret
Vlaat Henry
Volok John
Voorhuse John
Vosburgh Abraham
Vosburgh Garret
Vosburgh Jacob
Vredenburgh Isaac
Vroman Adam
Vroman Cornelius
Vrooman Arent
Vrooman Hanry
Vrooman Isaac A.
Vrooman Jacob
Vrooman Nicholas

Wagner Johann
Waldrom Cornelius
Walls Frederick
Walls Teunis
Wands James
Wands John
Ward Andrew
Ward Benjamin
Ward Edward
Ward John
Ward Moses
Ward Richard
Warmer Peter
Warren William
Watson Zelots
Waults Frederick
Weaver John
Weever Hendrick
Welder William
Wells Teunis
Wemple Aaron
Wemple Arent A.
Westfael Petrus
Wilder William
Williams Petrus
Willson William
Winchel
Winne Anthony
Witbeck Abraham
Witbeck Casparut
Witbeck John
Witbeck John L.
Witbeck Samuel
Witbeeck Wouter
Witeman Jacob
Witterker Thomas
Woormer Fradrick
Wormer Arent
Wormwood John
Wyley William
Wynkoop John
Yates John G.
Ylsebee Niecholas
Ylsbee Niecholas
Young Henry

Albany County Militia -- Fourth Regiment

COLONEL KILLAN VAN RENSSELAER; MAJOR CORNELIUS VAN BUREN; LIEUT. COL. JOHN H. BEECKMAN; ADJUTANT JOHN E. LANSING; MAJOR JACOB C. SCHERMERHORN; QUARTER MASTER JACOB STAATS

CAPT. ANTHONY BRIES
" JAMES DENNISON
" JONATHAN NILES
" STEPHEN NILES
" JOHN OSTERHOUT
" DANIEL SCHERMERHORN
" JOHN W. SCHERMERHORN
" NICHOLAS STAATS
" LAWRENCE TOWNSEND
" ICHABOD TURNER
" ROBERT WOODWORTH
LIEUT. BETHNEL BARNUM
" OLIVER BENTLEY

LIEUT. WILLIAM CORNING
" JOEL DEASE
" ZACHARIA HERRINGTON
" ALEXANDER HUBBS
" DAVID HUSTED
" JAMES JONES
" OBEDIAH LANSING
" HOSEA MOFFET
" JOHN MOON
" SILAS MOREY
" JONATHAN NILES
" JOHN OSTRANDER
" SETH PERRY

LIEUT. REUBEN ROWLY
" JACOB SCHERMERHORN
" WILLIAM SEATON
" SAMUEL SHAW
" PHILIP STAATS
" JACOB VAN VALKENBURGH
" HARPERT WHITBECK
ENSIGN EBENEZER JUDD
" JOHN POTTER
" ISAAC SHELDON
" JOHN J. STAATS
" PETER TEN EYCK
" MARTIN VAN BUREN

Abrahams Anthony
Acker Jury
Agnew William
Allen John
Andrews Amos
Andris Amos
Armstrong John
Arnold David
Arnold Stephen
Arnold William
Astyer Isaac
Aursen Thomas
Austin Stephen
Auston Isaac
Avery Abel
Aylsworth George
Babcock David
Babcock Elisha
Babcock Enoch
Babcock John
Babcock Silas
Babcock Silas, Jr.
Babett John
Backer Ichabod
Backer John
Badcock Jonathan
Baker David
Baley George
Barber Edward
Barheyd Elisha
Barhite Walter
Barnum Israel
Barnum Jabus
Barnum William
Bartel William
Bartle Andries

Bateman Reuben
Baurhite Jacob
Beats Jesse
Becker Adam
Becraft Abraham
Becroft William
Begal Samuel
Begel John
Bell John
Benn John
Bennem Peter
Bennet Ezra
Bennet Jesse
Bently Benjamin
Bently Joseph
Bently Joshua
Bently Oliver
Bently Samuel
Berry Elisha
Berry Samuel
Bigelow Joseph
Bissle William
Boos Jeremiah
Brain Moses
Bresea Hendrick
Brest William
Briesee William
Briggs Christopher
Bristol Abraham
Bristol Daniel
Bristol John
Bristoll Abraham, Jr.
Broadhook John
Brocks Joshua
Brockway Consider
Brockway Justus

Brockway Richard
Brockway Yestus
Brodhacker Bartley
Bronner Peter
Brotherton John
Brotherton Micasah
Brotherton Zopher
Brown Caleb
Brown Isaac
Brown Jesse
Brown Jonathan
Brown John
Brown Nehemiah
Brown Peter
Brown Robert
Brown Samuel
Brown Thomas
Brown Timothy
Bruce Benjamin
Bump Reuben
Bunt Evert
Bunt Mindert
Bunt Peter
Burguss Thomas
Burwell William
Bush Daniel
Bush John
Butler Jonathan
Butler Zachariah
Cabels Zebulon
Cain Isaiah
Cals Zebulon
Canter John
Carmichael John
Carpenter Jack
Carpenter Samuel

Carpenter Walter
Carr Charls
Case Joseph
Cates Zebulon
Caveneer John
Center Richard
Chapman Josiah
Charmichel John
Chatfield Cornelius
Chesley Simon
Church James
Clark Caleb
Clark Cary
Clark Thomas
Claw Laurance
Clegrove James
Coale Peter
Coats Joseph
Coats Thomas
Cole James
Cole Joseph
Cole Royal
Colgrove James
Coll Moses
Colom Joshua
Comens Ebenezer
Cone Ichabod
Cone John
Conick Jonathan
Connor Alexander
Cook Isaac
Cook Joseph
Cook Levi
Cook Richard
Coon James
Coon Nathan
Cooper Obadiah
Corey Benjamin
Corey John
Crain Edmund
Crandal Luke
Crowley Jonathan
Cudney William
Cummins Philip
Cunniggnas William
Curtice Thomas
Dachsteter Pieter
Daley Ebenezer
Daverix Elisha
Delano Thomas
Deliton Benjamin
Denison Daniel
Denison Ebenezer

Denord Humpfrey
Deveraux Elisha
Deverix Jonathan
Deverixe Joseph
Deveruex Theadeus
Dey Amos
Dickerson Ichabod
Dimons Henry
Dockstader Peter
Doty John
Dow John D. P.
Ducker David
Dumer Abraham
Dye Amos
Dye John
Dymen Abraham
Earing Samuel
Egberts Anthony
Egberts Benjamin
Egberts Martin
Ehring John
Elsworth George
Eltinge Abraham
Eltinge Henry
Eltinge John
Faakes Isaac
Falensby Jacobus
Falensby John
Farrington Robert
Ferguson Benjamin
Ferguson Jermiah
Filkin Henry
Filkins Abraham
Filkins James
Filkins Johanes
Fisk Joseph
Fisk William
Flagelland Joseph
Folmsbee Jacobas
Folmsbey Jeroen
Fonda John
Fosc Consider
Fox Consider
Fox William
Freeman John
Frezone John
Fullomsbe John
Gains Francis
Gardenier Henry
Gardinear Nicholas
Gardiner Robert
Gardinier Nicolas H.
Gardner Benjamin

Gardner Benjamin, Jr,
Gardner Bennone
Gardner Howland
Gardner Simeon
Gates Jered
Gates John
Gates Nathan
Gates Nathaniel
Gates Simon
Geyer John George
Ghoes Henry
Gorton Peleg
Gray James
Green Ambrose
Green Daniel
Green David
Greene Obadiah
Greenfield Archibald
Greenfield Bethuel
Greenfield James
Greenfield Benjamin
Greenman Preserved
Griffis Abner
Gyer John
Hacks James
Hakes Nathan
Halcomb Beriah
Halenbeck Casper
Hall Benoni
Hall Gardner
Hall George
Hall George William
Hall Gustner
Hall Peter
Hall Rowland
Hall William
Hall Yestus
Hamblin Samuel
Handerson John
Hanks Benjamin
Hanks John
Hansen Dirck
Harrington William
Harrington Zachariah
Harrintan Benjamin
Harrintan James
Harris Ahaze
Harris Benjamin
Harris Ephraim
Harris Ezekiel
Harris James
Harris John
Harris Joseph

Harris Nicholas
Hase Nathan
Haus Benjamin
Henckley Gersham
Henry Ephraim
Herdick Peter
Herdick William
Herdick William, Jr.
Hergher Gothlick
Herington John
Herrick Johannus
Herrington Abraham
Herrington Benjamin
Herrington Isaac
Herrington James
Herrington Nathaniel
Hewit Edmund
Hewit James
Hewit Oliver
Hicks George
Hicks Thomas
Hill Ebenezer
Hill Samuel
Hinckley Gershom, Jr.
Hindersass John Georg
Hinkley Paul
Hoard David
Hoard George
Hoard Isaac
Hoard Nathan
Hoard Samuel
Hoard Simeon
Hobusen Henry
Hocksey Frederick
Hocksey William
Hoems Solomon
Hogeboom Dirck
Hogg John
Holland James
Hollenbeck Michel
Holmes Abraham
Homes Abraham
Honckley Gershom
Hoose Peter
Hopkins Frederick
Hopkins Noah
Horton Lemuel
Horton Levy
Houck William J.
Howard Benjamin
Howard Janthon
Howard John
Howard Josiah

Howard Nathan
Hoyt John
Hunter Jonathan
Huyck Hanry
Huyck Hendrick
Huyck Nicholas
Huyck William
Hyms Solomon
Ingels James
Ingels Samuel
Janse Roelif
Joens William
Jones Amos
Jones Henry
Jones James
Jones Roger
Joslen William
Keeffe Daniel
Kerker Yedlocfc
Kilsey Ebenezer
Kittel John
Kittle Nicholas
Knap Ebenezer
Knap Henry
Knoulton Elijah
Knowlton Ephraim
Knowlton Robert
Lamb David
Lamphear Amos
Landers Jabez
Landers Jesse
Lansen William
Laurence William
Lawrence John
Letese James, Jr.
Levy John
Lewis John
Littar James
Little Stephen
Lobdele Sylvanus
Loce Peter
Lodawick Henry
Lodewick John
Loesey Peter
Low John
Lower Casper
Lower Michael
Lumis Daniel
McCalif Nicholas
McGan Peter
McGibbons Peter
McKown James
McMullan Hugh

McMullen Daniel
Magee John
Malleson Timothy
Malloy Thomas
Maloy John
Mane Henry
Mane Jeremiah
Manger Lawrence
Manyer Laurence
Marinus George
Marinus Jeremiah
Marinus Jury
Marinuc William
Mark Isaac
Marks Comfort
Marks Ebenezer
Marks Joseph
Martin James
Michel Nicholaos
Mickel Jurian
Middleton Benjamin
Miers John
Miles Jeremiah
Miller Jeremiah
Miller John
Miner Amos
Mobyor Timothy
Moker Conraud
Moll Isaa
Moll Jecobas
Moll Mindart
Moll Walter
Moon Bennony
Moon Jeremiah
Moon John
Mott Jeremiah
Muller John
Muller Nicolas
Myers Jeremiah
Mynderse Frederick
Myors John
Nelson Jonathan
Newman Isaac
Newton Abner
Nichals Caleb
Nicholas David
Nichols Benjamin
Nichols Simeon
Nichols Sisson
Nickle Nicholas
Niles Robert
Nolton Abner
Northrup Daniel

Northrup Needham
Northrup Nicholas
Northrupt Joseph
Odeal Jonas
Odel Gersham
Odel Simon
Odell David
Odell William
O'Niel Charls
Ostrander Adam
Ostrander Andrew
Ostrander Gerret
Ostrander Henry
Ostrander Isaac
Ostrander Jonathan
Ostrander Peter
Ovensants Philip
Palmer Gideon
Palmetier Thomas
Pan Moses
Parker Timothy
Partrick Robert
Partrick Robert, Jr.
Pater Elisha
Patrick Matthew
Pearce Levi
Pease Abner
Pease George
Perce Joel
Perie Benjamin
Perry Josiah
Phillips Anthony
Pike Ezra
Pool Anthony
Pool Garit G.
Pool Garret
Pool George Jurian
Pool Henry
Pool James
Pool John
Pool Matthew
Potter Rowland
Price Elijah
Proper James
Proper Peter
Queen Henry
Queen Owen
Race Daniel
Reynolds Henry
Reynolds Joseph
Robenson Benjamin
Robinson Isak
Rogars Joseph

Romien Abraham
Ronald Henry
Ronals Henry
Root Asahel
Rose Ary
Rose Belts
Rose Daniel
Rose John
Rose Nathaniel
Rose Ore
Rose Wiat
Rous Jacob
Rouse Baltus
Rouse Frederick
Rowley Timothy
Ryckman Frederick
Ryckman Gerret
Ryley Sylvester
Sackett Benjamin
Sackett John
Salsbury Harmanus
Salsbury Joseph
Salsbury Laurance
Salsbury Lucas
Salyea Henry
Satin Ease
Schemehorn Jacob H.
Schermehorn Cornelius
Schermehorn Jacob I.
Schermehorn Samuel
Schermerhorn Jacob
Schermerhorn Jacob I.
Schermerhorn Luke
Schermerhorn Philip
Scholl Johan Jost
Seamen Harmenit
Seaton William
Sebie William
Seeger Edward
Sennet Isaac
Seton Willard
Sharp Eliakim
Sharp Solomon
Shaw Anthony
Shaw Comfort
Shaw James M.
Shaw Jeremiah
Shelden George
Shelden William
Shelly John
Sherman Jinker
Shever Hendrick
Sholl John Jost

Shortenburgh Jury Jacob
Shouse Jacob
Shovers Gorge
Shovers William
Shower William
Skinner John
Sliter William
Slyter James
Smith Reuben
Spencer Nicholas
Spoor Henry
Spoor Isaac
Spoor Jeroen
Sprague David
Sprague George
Spring Ephraim
Springsteen Benjamin
Springsteen William
Springteen Jacob
Sprong David
Sprong Epraim
Sprong John
Staats Barent
Staats John
Stall Peter
Stephens Jered
Stephens William
Stewart Eliphlet
Stoul Peter
Sullivan David
Swain John
Sweet Samuel
Sweeting Lewis
Sweeting Nathaniel
Taber Harmen
Taber Havens
Taber Record
Taber Benjamin
Tabor William
Taller Ebeneser
Tanner Abel
Taylor John
Thomas Benjamin
Thomas Israel
Thomas William
Tibbits Jona
Tift Edmond
Tippet Jonathan
Tolmans Thomas
Townsend James
Trim Walter
Turck John
Turk Thomas

Turk Hendrick
Turner Lamuel
Udall John
Udall William
Valentine Benjamin
Valk Isaac
Valk John J.
Valk Matthew
Valkenburgh Dirck
Valkenburgh Jacob
Valkenburgh Jacob N.
Valkenburgh Jacobus
Valkenburgh John
Vallentine Richard
Van Bura Martin B.
Van Buren Abraham
Van Buren Cornelius
Van Buren Harmanus
Van Buren Hendrick
Van Buren John
Van Buren Maas
Van Buren Martin
Van Buren Martin C.
Van Buren Martin P.
Van Buren Peter M.
Van Buren Tobias
Van Buren Tobias H.
Van Buren William
Van Den Bergh Abraham
Van Den Bergh Barent
Vanden Bergh Cornelius
Van Den Bergh Garret
Van Den Bergh John
Van Denbergh P.
Vanden Bergh Volkert
Van Der Pool John
Van Derpool Melkert
Van Dobow Jacob
Van Dueson Christopher
Van Dusen Harpert
Van Hoesan Harman
Van Hoesen Mundert

Van Hoesen Rynier
Van Huzon Coonrad
Van Iveren Barent
Van Ostrander John
Van Rensselaer James
Van Salsbury Cornelius
Van Valcenburgh Lambart
Van Valckenburgh Matthew
Van Valkenburgh Abraham
Van Valkenburgh Jochim
Van Valkenburgh Matthew
Van Valkenburgh Nicholes
Van Valkenburgh Peter
Van Veghten Volckert
Vinhagen John
Vinhagen Martin
Vinigar Asahel
Vischer John
Vosburgh Matthew
Wald Joseph
Wandel Garit
Wardon Moses
Wardon Nathaniel
Waye Josiah
Wells Ebenezer
Wells Nathaniel
Wendee Garrit
Wenslor Abraham
Wessel Luke
Wessels Andries
West Jonathan
Westcot Joseph
White John
White Nathaniel
Whiteman Benjamin
Whiteman Benoni
Widbeck Abraham
Wiley Primus
Williams John
Willson John
Willson Robert
Winegar Ashbell

Wingerd Peter
Witbeck Harper
Witbeck John
Witbeck Jonathan
Witbeck Martin C.
Witbeck Thomas
Witbeck William
Witebeck Leonard
Witeman George
With Evert
Wolcott Luke
Wood Barney
Wood Job
Woodard Abijah
Woolcot Joseph
Woolcot Justis
Worden William
Worner Joseph
Wylie John
Wyngaert Peter
Yates Evert
Yoels Thomas
Young John
Young Thomas
Zu Stralsnnd Fillib

Albany County Militia--Fifth Regiment

COLONEL GERRIT G. VAN DEN BERGH; MAJOR BARENT STAATS; COLONEL HENRY QUACKENBOS; MAJOR CONERAT TEN EYCK; LIEUT. COL. VOLKERT VEEDER
Capt. George Hogan; Capt. Philip Luke; Capt. Teunis Slingerland; Capt. John Van Wie; Capt. William Winnie; Lieut. John De Voe; Lieut. Thomas Esmay; Lieut. William Flensburgh; Lieut. Jurian Hogan; Lieut. Ephrim Hudson; Lieut. John Leonard; Ensign Ezra Clevelend; Ensign Henry Shafer; Ensign Cornelius Van Den Zer.

ENLISTED MEN

Aernout Jacob
Albragh John
Allenbrach John
Arnhoadt John
Basinger Andrew
Becker Gerrit
Becker Walter
Bradt Anthony
Bradt Peter B.
Bratt Adrian
Burhans John
Conger Reuben
Conger Uzziah
Devoe John
Esmay Thomas
Flansburg Matthew
Flensburg Daniel
Flensburg William
Fuller Gershom
Haswell Joseph
Heller Jacob

Hillebrandt John
Hooghtaling James
Hungerford Elisha
Johnson John
Joost Benjamin
Luke Solomon
Moke Francis
Moke John
Ogenpact Benjamin
Oliver John
Oosterhout Henry
Ostrander Henry
Palmetier John
Pangburn Richard
Pangburn William
Post Benjamin
Salsbury Joseph
Schoenmaker John
Seeger Gerrit I.
Seeger Gerrit S.
Seger John

Shater Charles
Shaver Hendrick
Taylor James
Taylor Lucas
Van Aernam Isaac
Van Buren Moses
Van Deusen Matthew
Van Etten Benjamin
Van Etten William
Van Wie Andries
Van Wie Gerrit
Van Wie Isaac
Van Wie John H.
Viele Jacob
Viele Simon
Winne David
Wyncoop Evert

Albany County Militia--Sixth Regiment

COLONEL STEPHEN JOHN SCHUYLER; ADJUTANT JACOB VAN ALSTYN;
LIEUT. COL. HENRY K. VAN RENSSELAER; Q'R MASTER MATTHEW VAN ALSTYN;
SURGEON WILLIAM PETRY;
ASST. PAY MASTER JONATHAN BURRALL

CAPT. CALEB BENTLEY
" ISAAC DOGERT
" ISAAC DE FOREST
" JACOB DE FOREST
" JACOB DE FREEST
" HENRY DENKER
" HENRY H. GARDENIER
" LEVI HOKWELL
" DAVID HUSTED
" JAMES HUSTED
" JOHN LANDMAN
" CORNELIUS LANSING

CAPT. AUGUSTEN ODFII
" BENJAMIN RANDALL
" GEORGE SCHARP
" SAMUEL SHAW
" CHRISTOPHER TILLMAN
" ANTHONY VAN SCHAICK
(COMPANY EXEMPTS)
LIEUT. GEORGE BENINGER
" JOHN CRANNY
" JOHN FONDA
" JOHN P. FONDA
" CHARLES GREENE

LICUT. DAVID HUGHSTEAD
" ANDREW MILLER
" JAMES ODLE
" DAVID RANDALL
" JOHN RILEY
" MARTINUS SCHARP
" LODWICK SNYDER
" RYNIER VAN IVEREN
ENSIGN PHILIP HENRICK
" CORNELIUS VAN DEUSEN

ADDITIONAL NAMES ON STATE TREASURER'S PAY BOOKS

LIEUT. JONAS BALL
" BENJAMIN BLIDTH
" BENJAMIN ELLIOTT

" DANIEL GRAY
" JAMES GRAY
" DANIEL HULL
" HEZEKIAH HULL

" HUGH MCMANUS
" STEPHEN RANDALL
" MATTHEW SCHARP
" JONATHAN SEAVER

" NANNING VAN DER HEYDER
" JOHN WILKESON
ENSIGN JOHN CLARK

" JAMES GREEN
" JEREMIAH GRIFFITH
" JAMES PADGET

" THOMAS PALMER
" JOSHUA WARDEN

ENLISTED MEN

Adams Elijah
Anderson Alexander
Armstrong Robert
Aursen Thomas
Baardt Andries
Baerdt Andries, Jr.
Bailey Elisha
Baker Ebenasar
Baker Elleton
Barber James
Beninger David
Beninger Jacob
Beninger John
Beninger Phillip
Beninger Zachariah
Bennet Owen
Bennit Ephraim
Benson John
Beringer John
Beringer Zachariah
Berkman John
Berringer David
Berringer Jacob
Bloemendal John
Boyd George
Boyde William
Briggs Joseph
Brust Jacob
Brust Matthew
Bumbar Ruben
Burchim Henry
Butler Jonathan
Cammel Henry
Campbel James
Cancker Peter
Canter Jonas
Carner John
Carner Philip
Coenraedt Frederick
Colehamer Andrew
Colehammer Christian
Colehammer George
Concklin John
Coon Abraham
Coon James
Coon Nathan

Coon William
Cooper Christian
Cooper Christopher
Cooper Peter
Cooper William
Crandell Lute
Crennel William
Cuyler Jacob
Deforeest Jesse
De Freest David P.
De Freest John
De Freest Peter
De Freest Phillip
Dick Henry
Dick Nicholas
Dirck Anthony
Dox Samuel
Drum Andrew
Dunbar William
Eastwood John
Eight Abraham
Elmondorph Jacob
Evens James
Evertsen Evert
Feller Jacob
Feller Nicholas
Feller Zacharia
Fonda Douwe
Fonda Isaac
Fonda Jacobus
Frear Hughen
Frelich Jacob
Fisher Christopher
Gasevoort Coenrat
Goewy John
Grauberger Daniel
Greene John
Greene Luke
Griswold Jabes
Habzinger Carl
Haner John
Haner Philip, Jr.
Haner Wilhelmus
Hansen Benjamin
Harsen Francis
Harwick Phillip

Henneker Emanuel
Henner John
Henselpeck Coenr't
Herway David
Herwey Coenraet
Herwick Coenraat
Herwick Yoost
Heyner Philip, Jr.
Heyner Wilhelmus
Hogel Edward
Hogil Jacob
Hogil Nicholas
Hoogstrasser Jacob
Hull Daniel
Hull Hezekiah
Huntsekker George
Jackson Ephraim
Johnson Thomas
Kanker Peter
Killy John
Kip Benjamin
Krockhyte John
Kuhn Peter
Lansing Cornelius
Lansing Thomas
Lappies William
Leap John
Lent John
Lewis Phineas
Liverse Levinus
Lones Adam
Lones Bastian
Maley John
Martin Thomas
Marvin Matthew
Mattison David
Meyer Henry
Miller Barent
Miller Herman
Miller Hendrick
Miller John
Milton Henry
Milton John
Morrison William
Myer Cornelis
Myers Henry

Near Carel
Near Charles
Near John
Neher Charles
Nestle Christian
Norton Christophel
Norton William
Ostrande Hendrick
Ostrande Isaac
Ostrande John
Ostroom Ruloff
Paddock Henry
Paddock Job
Parker Andrew
Peck Abraham
Peeck Gerrit
Perker Andrew
Philip Michael
Plass Henry
Possasy Henry
Pruyn John
Pruyn Rynier
Pugit James
Randal Matthew
Robertson Abraham
Rogers George
Sabin Stephen
Saris Thomas
Saxton Ebenezer

Schermerhorn Jacob
Scott David
Sharp George
Sharp Peter
Shaver John
Sickles Zacharia
Smith Michael
Smitt Jacob G.
Snyder Gotlib
Snyder Jacob
Springer Jacob
Still John
Strunk Hendrick
Strunk Hendrick, Jr.
Sweet Godfrey
Thomas Israel
Valintine Jacob
Valk Abraham
Van Aelsteyn John
Van Aelsteyn Matthew
Van Buren Cornelius
Van Buren Leonard
Vande Bergh Gerrit
Vanden Bergh Gilbert
Vanden Bergh Gysbert
Vanden Bergh Jacob
Van Den Bergh Matthew
Vanden Bergh Matthew C.
Vanden Bergh Rynier

Vanden Bergh Titus
Vanden Bergh Volkert
Vander Heyden John
Van Der Heyden Matthew
Van Deursen Frederick
Van Duusen Hendrick
Van Etten Benjamin
Van Hoesen Henry
Van Ivere Cornelius
Van Ivere Gysbert
Van vere Jacob
Van vere Martynis
Van vere Reynier
Van veren Jacob
Van veren Martinus
Van Valck Abraham
Veeder John
Visscher Nanning
Vosburgh Myndert
Walter John
Wendell Jacob H.
Wendell John
Willig Phillip
Willoughby William
Winne Killian
Witbeck Peter
Wool Robert
Yates Joseph
Young Jacob

Albany County Militia--Seventh Regiment

COLONEL ABRAHAM J. VAN ALSTINE; MAJOR ISAAC GOES; LIEUT. COL. PHILIP VAN ALSTINE; SURGEON EZEKEL THOMAS; MAJOR HARMAN VAN BUREN

" HERMAN VOSBURG

CAPT. CHAPMAN
" BURGER CLAW
" AARON OSTRANDER
" JOHN PHILIP
" JOHN SMITH
" GERSHOM TRUESDEL
" ABRAHAM VAN BUREN
" ISAAC P. VAN BURGH
" EVERT VOSBURGH

LIEUT. JONATHAN CHAPMAN
" PETER HUEGENNIN
" FELTER LANDT
" JACOBUS MCNEAL
" REUBEN MURRAY
" EDWARD PAINTER
" MATTHIAS TAYLOR
" ABRAHAM VAN ALLEN
" JOHN VAN ALSTYNE

" JOHN J. VAN ALSTYNE
LIEUT. PETER J. VOSBURGH
" WILLIAM VOSBURGH
" PHILIP WOLFROM
ENSIGN JOHN GOES
" BURGER T. HUYCK
" GEORGE LONG
" HENRY STEVER
" JOHN VAN BUREN
" JACOBUS VAN NESS

ENLISTED MEN

Baches John
Baily Stephen
Baily Timothy

Bawney John
Bell John A. Lem
Bensk Rudolph

Berry William
Berry William, Jr.
Blanchar Ahiathar

Blanchard Abraham
Bresec Jellis
Brewer Abraham
Bullis William
Bumham Mashall
Burton Josiah
Calder Hendrick
Canniff William
Carn John
Cecil Richard
Chapman Amos
Chapman Asa
Chapman David
Chapman Ezekiel
Chapman Ezra
Chapman Noah
Claw Andrew
Coenraut Nicholas
Cole Gerard
Cook John
Cornelisan John
Cornelus John
Cramphin Balsan
Crippen Reuben
Crocker Amos
Curtis Ebenezer
Curtiss David
Curtiss Joseph
Davis Dennis
Davis George
Delamattor Benjamin
Delametter Jacob
Deyor Peter
Dingman Casper
Dingman Isaac
Dingman Jacob
Dobs Daniel
Dorn Abraham
Ealon Elijah
Earl Moses
Earl William, Jr.
Eldridge Joseph
Elkenbragh John
Elkinbrach John
Feeley John
Feely John
Ferguson Jacob
Folmer Zemtus
Fols Conrat
French John
Fuller David
Gardaneer Peter H.
Gardner Godfrey

Goes Derick
Goes Ephraim
Goes John, Jr.
Goes Laurence
Goes Michael
Goes Tobias
Gould Jesse
Graper Ruben
Graves John
Graves Richard
Green Augustus
Gwin Oren
Haak Christopher
Hall Justice
Hamblin Seth
Hamblin Zaccheus
Hancy Fradrick
Hare Daniel
Hark Daniel
Hawk Christopher
Herder John
Herrick George
Hoffman George
Hogan William
Hoyer George
Hrkiman George
Hubbard David
Huguenin David
Humphry Ezra
Huyck Burger D.
Huyck Burger I.
Huyck John, Jr.
Huyck John A.
Ittick George L.
Itting Conrat
Jenkins Anthony
Johnson Isaac
Johnson John
Johnson Peter
Joslin Henry
Kane William
Kelder Hendrick
Kinne Jesse
Kittle John
Kittle Nicholas
Knapp Isaac
Lister Frederick
Luny William
Lusk Jacob
Lusk Michael
Lusk William
McFail Patrick
Mc Michael James

McPhaile Patrick
Mans John J.
Marsail John
Marshall Enos
Miller Casper
Miller John
Miller Jonathan
Mitchel James
Mitchel James, Jr.
Moet Coenradt
Moet Johannis
Molony John
Montgomery Alexander
Moore John A.
Moot Conrath
Moot Johannis
Morey Elisha
Morey Elisha, Jr.
Morey Samuel
Moshier Jonathan
Mott Henry
Mott Jeremiah
Mudge Michael
Muller John J.
O'Briant Cornelius
Olthousen Nicholas
O'Neal James
O'Neil John
Paine Daniel
Painter Thomas
Pearsee Isaac
Peersye Isaac
Peterson Benjamin
Peterson Philip
Pew John
Philip Pelnis
Philip Peter
Proper Frederick
Quithot Stephen
Randal Nathaniel
Rees Benjamin
Richmon George
Richmond Conrad
Richmond Simeon
Robertson George
Robinson George
Robison Jeremiah
Root Asahel
Root David
Rowland Samuel
Rowse Coenradt
Ryan Edward
Ryan William

Salisbury Sylvester
Sally John
Sally Thomas
Salsbury John
San Moses
Saunders Isaac
Scharaly Peter
Scharp Jacob
Scharp John
Scharp Laurence P.
Scott John
Scott William
Sebring Lewis
Seley John
Seller Frederick
Sharp John
Sharp Lawrence
Sharsa Daniel
Shutts John
Sisson Richard
Smith Asa
Smith Christian
Smith John
Smith Joseph
Smith Samuel
Snyder Peter
Snyder Simon
Staats Abraham
Staats Abraham J.
Staats Abraham T.
Staats Jacob
Staats John
Staats John Jr.
Statts Abraham
Stever Jacob
Stoplebeen Johannes
Suthard Thomas
Thomas Caleb
Thomas Jacob
Trusdeil Hiel

Trusdell Richard
Trusduil Iseel
Utly Jeremiah
Van Aelstyn Thomas
Van Alen Abraham
Van Alen Dirck
Van Alen Cornelius
Van Alen Gilbert
Van Alen Henry
Van Alen John E.
Van Alen Peter
Van Alstine Abraham
Van Alstyne Leonard
Van Beuren John
Van Buren Cornelius
Van Buren Ephraim I.
Van Buren Ephraim T.
Van Buren Francis
Van Buren Tobias
Vanderpoel Andrew
Van Derpoel Andries
Vanderpoel Jacobus
Van Deusen Peter
Van Dusen John
Van Hoesen Jacob
Van Hoesen Jacob J.
Van Hoesen John
Van Nass Adam
Van Ness David
Van Slyck Dirick
Van Slyck Peter
Van Valkenburgh Bartholomew
Van Valkenburgh Bartholomew T.
Van Valkenburgh Claudius
Van Valkenburgh Jacob
Van Valkenburgh Jacobus
Van Valkenburgh Joachim
Van Valkenburgh Joachim J.
Van Valkenburgh John

Van Valkenburgh Lambert
Van Valkenburgh Lawrance
Van Valkenburgh Peter I.
Van Valkenburgh Peter J.
Vosburg Matthew
Vosburg William
Vosburgh Abraham
Vosburgh David
Vosburgh Joachim
Vosburgh Peter A.
Vratenburgh John
Vredenbergh John
Wever George
Wheeler Samuel
White Henry
Whitwood Charles
Whitwood Cornelius
Whitwood Samuel
Wickham Warren
Wilsey Jacob
Wilson Andrew
Wilson Dirick
Wilson Richard
Wiltse Jacob
Wingand James
Wingardt Jacobus
Witbeck Andrew
Witbeck Andrew, Jr.
Witbeck Andris
Wolf George
Wolf Peter
Wolfram John Tice
Wolfrem Philip
Wolfrom Mathise
Wright Arl
Wright Daniel
Wyngart Jacobus
Wynkoop Peter
Yeralewyn John
Young Frederic

Albany County Militia--Eighth Regiment

Colonel Robert Van Rensselaer
Lieut. Col. Barent I. Staats
Lieut. Col. Henry J. Van Rensselaer
Lieut. Col. Asa Waterman
Major Richard Esseltyne
Major John McKinstry
Major Henry Van Rensselaer

Quarter Master John Fisher

CAPT. EBENEZER CADY
" JOSEPH ELLIOTT
" JONAH GRAVES
" ABNER HAWLEY
" NATHAN HENDRICK
" CORNELIUS HOGEBOOM
" MICHAEL HORTON
" CASPER HUYCK
" GIDEON KING
" JEREMIAH JOHANNES
MULLER
" JOHN OSTERHOUDT
" WILHELMUS PHILIP
" JACOB PHILLIP
" HENRY PLATNER
" JOHN PRICE
" DIEL ROCKEFELLER

CAPT. JACOB VAN ALLEN
" ISAAC VOSBURGH
LIEUT. SAMUEL ALLIN
" THOMAS BROWN
" PETER A. FONDA
" GERRITT GROOSEBECK
" JAMES HOGEBOOM
" RICHARD HOGEBOOM
" CHARLES McARTHUR
" DAVID McKINSTRY
" NATHANIEL MIGKELL
" NATHANIEL MILLS
" JOACHIM MULLER
" GEORGE PHILLIPS
" EDWARD REXFORD
" JONATHAN REYNOLDS
" PETER ROCKEFELLER

LIEUT. NATHANIEL ROWLEY
" CASPARUS SCHULT
" JOHN SCOTT
" GOSAH VAN BEURIN
ENSIGN LEANARD DACKER
" ESA HOLMES
" SIMON LOTHROP
" SAMUEL OLMSTED
" MAURICE ROWLEY
" JOHN SHUTTS
" ADAM TEN BROECK
" MYNDERT VANDERBOGERT
" GERRITT W. VAN SCHAIK
" PETER VAN VALKENBURGH
" JAMES WINGARD

NAMED AS OFFICERS, BUT NO RANK GIVEN

PETER GROAT; JOHANNIS SHULDT; PETER WEISSMAN; JACOB PHILLIP, JR.; JOHANNIS SHULT; PETER WIESSMER

ENLISTED MEN

Acker David
Adams Daniel
Adams Noah
Adsit John
Akins Aaron
Akins James
Akins Samuel
Allen Jonathan
Allen Timothy
Alsworth William
Andreas Spira
Andrew Sperry
Anneling John
Aring Samuel
Armerly John
Ashley Peter
Ashton Peter
Atwaters Benjamin
Atwaters Jeames
Atwood Timothy
Austin Peter
Babeck Charles
Baker Andrew
Baker John, Jr.
Baker Jonathan
Baker Samuel

Bamhower Andries
Bantley Samuel
Bantley Thomas
Barker James
Barnet Tyman
Barringer Peter
Barrit Jonathan
Bartle Henry
Bartle John
Bartle Peter
Bartle Peter, Jr.
Bartle Philip
Bartle Philip H.
Bartley John
Bay John
Bayley Asher
Beach Michel
Becker Aarent
Becker Cornelius
Becker John
Beeraft William
Beeroft Jonathan
Begraft Abraham
Begraft George
Begraft Jonathan
Begraft Thomas

Begraft Thomas, Jr.
Benjamin Daniel
Benjamins Ebenzar
Benn George
Bennum Cornelius
Bentin Doctor
Berger Henry
Best Benjamin
Bibbins John
Boent Evert, Jr.
Boent Jacob
Boent Jacob, Jr.
Boent Matties
Boent Mindert
Boent Peter
Boerst Jorst
Boerst Jorst, Jr.
Bonestail David
Bonestail David, Jr.
Bonestail Frederick
Bonestail Peter
Bostwick Edward
Braun Johan Christ
Bresee Cornelius
Bresee Gabriel
Bresee Nicholas

Brooks Joshua, Jr.
Broon Edward
Browen Jurry
Brower Abraham
Brower David
Brower George
Brower Peter
Brown Amos
Brown John
Bryan John
Buebee Constant
Bunt Ephraim
Bunt Peter
Burgart Hendrick
Burgat Hendrick
Burger Peter
Burghart Henry
Burghart Jeremiah
Burnett Peter
Burns Nathan
Bursen Daniel
Bush John
Cable Johan George
Cacoll James
Cadman George
Cady David
Camer Jacob
Campbell John
Caner George
Caring Carel
Carlett William
Carrey Thomas
Carter Jacob
Carter Jacob, Jr.
Carvel John
Casper Fetter
Caul Jacob
Cavel Hendrick
Cavel Peter
Cayry Thomas
Champion Job
Chapman Stephen
Chatsy Joseph
Churchill Stephen
Clapper Fredrick
Clapper George
Clapper Henry
Clapper John
Clapper Peter
Clapper William
Clark Abram
Clark David
Clark John

Cleaveland Ezechael
Cleveland Lemuel
Clinchman Christopher
Coal Andrew, Jr.
Cohoon Joseph
Cole Hesparis
Cole Isaac
Cole John
Cole Peter
Colley David
Colley Matthew
Colley Thomas
Colman John
Concklin Jacob
Conklin Isaac
Constaver Phillip David
Conyne Casparus
Cool John
Cool Peter
Cool Peter, Jr.
Cool William
Coon Samuel
Coons Adam
Coons Jacob
Coons John
Coons John, Jr.
Corlett William
Cotton John
Coventry William
Cowle Andres
Cowle Thoda
Cramer Lawrance
Crepes Hendrick
Criselar Henry
Criselar John
Crousious Christian
Crowsioni Johanny
Cudney William
Culley Thomas
Cully David
Cyser John
Dacker Broer
Danvor Daniel
Darling David
Darling Jesup
Darrow Jedidiah
Davis Amos
Davis Daniel
Davis George
Davis Jacobus
Davis William
Day Aron
Deal Laurence

Decker Abraham
Decker Broer
Decker Christopher
Decker George G.
Decker Hendrick
Decker Hendrick B.
Decker Johannis
Decker Jores
Decker Jores J.
Dederick Frederic
Dedrick Christian
Dedrick Johannes
Dedrick Peter
De Lamater Gloride
Delamater Jacobus
De Lamater Jeremiah
Delamater Jeremyes
De Lamatter Dirck
Delamatter Jeremiah J.
Delematter James
Deming Daniel
Denions William
Dennis Ezechael
Denneger Mathew
De Pew Elias
Derring Adam
De Yeae Jacobus
De Yeae Jacobus, Jr.
De Yeae Richard
Dicker Francis
Dickson Walter
Didemer George
Didemore John
Dinghmanse William
Dingmansa Dolves P.
Dingmanse Adolfus
Dingmanse Adolfus, Jr.
Dingmanse Andsiel
Dingmanse Hendrick
Dingmanse Johannis
Dingmanse Johannis, Jr.
Dingmanse Peter
Dirck William
Dixson William
D'Lamater Glonde
Docker Jores H.
Doty Isaac
Doty Joseph
Doty Samuel
Dox Peter
Droel John Hendrick
Duff Jonathan
Dutcher Henry

Dutcher Rulef
Dyckman Sampson
Earl Joseph
Eckker David
Edwards Abel
Edwards Samuel
Egelston Benjamin
Egers George
Egins Aaron
Egins James
Ellas Jacob
Elling Abraham
Elliot John
Elliot Peter
Ellison David
Ellison William
Elswort Runs
Elting James
Elting John
Emrich Adam
Emrich Frances
Emrigh Adam
Emrigh Francis
Emrigh George
Emrigh Matties
Enderson Jacob
Enderson John
Enderson Peter
Ergie James
Esselstine Gabriel
Esselstyne Abraham
Esselstyne Andries
Esselstyne Coenradt
Esselstyne Isaac
Esselstyne Jacob
Esselstyne Jacob, Jr.
Esselstyne Richard
Ettinge Abraham
Ettinge John
Everts John
Everts John, Jr.
Evertson Thomas
Fairchild Stephen
Feith Conrath
Ferris Timothy
Filka Stephen
Finger John
Finkle John
Finney Isaac
Fisher Frederick
Flaus Peter
Fonda Abraham
Fonda Cornelius

Fonda Douw
Fonda Jacobus
Fonda Jeremiah
Fonda Lawrence
Fonda Peter A.
Foot John
Fortal John
Fox Jonathan
Frayer Abraham
Frayer Isaac
Frayer John
French John
Frogran John
Fryer Isaac T.
Funday Cornelius
Gaal Jacob
Gardiner James
Gardiner Jeroan
Gardiner William
Garrison John
Gaul Jacob
Good Joseph
Goes Ephraim
Goes Mattise R.
Gordon William
Gott John
Graadt Hendrick
Graadt John
Graadt Wilhelmus
Graadts Peter
Graff Isaac
Graudt Hyron
Grautt Hendrick
Grautt John
Grautt Peter
Grautt Wilhelmus
Graves Noadiah
Graves Seldon
Green Ebenezer
Green Thomas
Green Thomas, Jr.
Green William
Grihdelmyer Christian
Grindlemyer Christopher
Griswold Jabez
Groat John N.
Groat Hendrick
Groat Henry, Jr.
Groat Huron
Groat Hyrone
Groat John
Groat Peter
Groat Wilhelmus

Haber Johannes
Haddick William
Hagadorn Christopher
Hagedorn John
Hagedorn Jonas
Hagedorn Peter
Hagedorn Joseph
Hale Daniel
Halenbeck Andries
Halenbeck Dirck
Halenbeck Hendrick
Halenbeck Jacob
Halenbeck Jeroan
Halenbeck John J.
Halenbeck John R.
Halenbeck John W.
Halenbeck John William
Halenbeck Matties
Halenbeck Matties, Jr.
Halenbeck Michael
Halenbeck Robert
Halenbeck Samuel
Halenbeck William
Hall Matthew
Hallenback John
Haltsapple Johannis
Haner Christopher
Haner Jacob
Hanner Peter
Harder Adam
Harder Jacob P.
Harder Michal
Harder Peter
Harlow Eliab
Harman Rowse
Harmance Hendrick
Hartick Garrit
Hartick Joneton
Harvy John
Hatch William
Hauver Antren
Haver Andres
Haver Andrew
Haver Christian
Hawkins Daniel
Hawley James
Hawley William
Hawley Zadok
Hayner Peter
Heermanse Hendrick
Hegaman John
Heirmanse Jacob
Heldredg Richard, Jr.

Hellicas Baltus
Hellicas Christian
Hellicas Frederick
Hellicas Lodewick
Helm Jonas
Helm Peter
Helm Peter. Jr.
Helmer Johan Jost
Hendricks John
Hendrye Benjamin
Henry Jacob
Herder Adam
Herder Benjamin
Herder George
Herder Jacob
Herder Jacob, Jr.
Herder Jacob H.
Herder Jacob J.
Herder Jacob P.
Herder John
Herder Jores
Herder Michael J.
Herder Michel
Herder Michel. Jr.
Herder Nicholas
Herder Peter
Herdick Abraham
Herdick Francis, Jr.
Herdick Franck
Herdick Gerrit
Herdick Jacob
Herdick Jacob F.
Herdick Jeroan
Herdick John
Herdick John F.
Herdick Jonathan
Herdick Justice
Herdick Peter
Herdick Peter, Jr.
Herdick William
Herdick William, Jr.
Herdick William L.
Hermance Andres
Hermance Jacob
Hess Michel
Heydenbergh Sybrant
Heydorn Christopher
Heyser Hendrick
Heyser Hendrick, Jr.
Hight Stephen
Higley Daniel
Hilten Jacob W.
Hines Sander

Hnye Charles
Hoff William, Jr.
Hoffman Jacob
Hoffman Johan Nicoll
Hoffman Michel
Hogeboom Bartholomew
Hogeboom Cornelius
Hogeboom James
Hogeboom Jeremiah
Hogeboom Johannis
Hogeboom Peter
Hogeboom Stephen
Hogeboom Tobyas
Hoghtaling Henry
Hoghtaling Jacob
Holcomb Zephaniah
Holembick Matthias
Hollenbeck Samual
Holliday Henry
Holmes Asa
Holms Jedediah
Holsappel William
Holsapple Johannis
Holsapple Johannis, Jr.
Holsapple John
Holsapple William
Holtsapple John, Jr.
Hopp Thomas
Horton William
Hough Zephamah
Houghtaling Dirck
How Samuel
Howard Enos
Hubbard William
Huffman Augustus
Huffman Jacob
Huguenin David
Huick Marten
Huller Simon
Hultsapple Johannis, Jr.
Hultsapple William
Huston Daniel
Huyck Casper
Huyck Johannis
Jackson Isaac
Jackson James
Jackson Robert
Jacobs John
Jager Hendrick
Jennes David
Jolley Henry
Jorean William
Jubb Negro

Jurdon William
Keble John Jurey
Keble Peter
Kelder Hendrick
Kelder Jost
Kelder William
Kelley Daniel
Kells Hendrick
Kelts John
Ketchum Jonathan
Ketchum Stephen
Kettil Daniel
Killey Daniel
Killmore Phillip
Kilmore George
Kilmore, George 375
Kilmore Hendrick
King Conrade
King Charles
Kittle John
Kline Anthony
Kline Henry
Kool Gerret
Krath Wilhelmus
Krisler Hendrick
Laap Andries
Laap George
Laap Thomas
Land George
Land Jeremi
Land Jeremiah F.
Landt Frederick
Landt George
Landt Jeremiah
Landt Johannis
Landt Johannis, Jr.
Landt Johannis L.
Landt John, Jr.
Landt Lawrence
Lant Jurry
Larvey Elisha
Larvy William
Lasher John
Lee Ephraim
Lee Israel
Legges James
Legges Tobyas
Legit Tobies
Lemon William
Lewis Abraham
Lewis Peter
Link William
Loomis Androw

Loop Bastian
Loop Christian
Loop Martin
Loop Peter
Lothrop Josiah
Lott John
Lovejoy Andrew
Lovejoy Benjamin
Ludlow Henry
Ludlow Henry, Jr.
Ludlow William H.
Lych Barent
McCall Robert
McCulley Alexander
McDonald
McFale Henry
McFall Robert
McGee James
McGinnis Jacob
McGoraghey John
McMollin Charles
Madfall Neal
Maier Abraham
Mandiville Matthew
Mannol Docter
Mantle Frances
Mantle Wynant
Marchell Danel
Marhill Daniel
Marte Nicholas
Marten Nicolaes
Martin William
Maul Friedrick
Maul John
Meerit Amos
Meggs Seth
Melius Anthony
Merrit Stephen
Merrit Thomas
Mesick Fite
Mesick Hendrick
Mesick Henry J.
Mesick Jacob J.
Mesick John
Mesick John J.
Mesick Peter
Mesick Peter J.
Mesick Thomas
Meyer Frederick
Michel Henry
Michel Jacob
Michels Anthony
Mighel William

Miles Anthony
Milham John
Miller Andries
Miller Christopher
Miller Dirck
Miller Frederick
Miller Jacob A.
Miller Jeremiah
Miller Jeremiah C.
Miller Jeremiah J.
Miller Peter
Miller Samuel
Miller Samuel A.
Miller Stephen
Miller William
Millet William A.
Mongomry Eshable
Monnal George
Montgomery Ezekiel
Moon David
Moon Paul
Moon Richard
Moore Paul
Morris John
Morris Judg
Morris Nicholas
Morris Richard
Morris Robert
Mory Elisha
Moul Fraderick
Moul John, Jr.
Moull Jacob
Moull Johannis
Mowal Frederick
Mowal Johannis
Mowal Johannis, Jr.
Mowel Jacob
Mowel John, Jr.
Moyer Fradrick
Moyer Hendrick
Mudge Ebenezer
Muller Christopher
Muller Cornelius
Muller Cornelius C.
Muller Cornelius C. S.
Muller Cornelius H.
Muller Cornelius J.
Muller Cornelius Johannis
Muller Cornelius R.
Muller Cornelius S.
Muller Dirck
Muller Fretireck
Muller Henry

Muller Hessen
Muller Jacob
Muller Jacob, Jr.
Muller Jacob C.
Muller Jeremiah
Muller Jeremiah C.
Muller Jeremiah C. S.
Muller Jeremiah J.
Muller Jeremiah T.
Muller Jeremiah W., Jr.
Muller Jeremy C.
Muller Jocham
Muller Johannis
Muller Johannis C.
Muller Killian
Muller Peter
Muller Stephen
Muller Stephen C.
Muller Stephen H.
Muller Stephen I.
Muller Stephen J.
Muller William
Muller William C.
Mullory Jeremiah Johs
Mun Paulies
Munsee Daniel
Murgethroydt Joseph
Murphey Samuel
Myer Henry
Naile John
Neer Charles
Neer Henry
Neer Jacob
Neer John
New Peter
New Simeon
Nicoll Nicholas
Nooney Thompson
Noyes John
Nuan Frederick
Oostrander Cornelius
Oostrander Hendrick
Oostrander Jacobus
Osterhout John
Ostrande Arent
Ostrande Hendrick
Ostrande Hendrick, Sr.
Ostrande Jacobus
Ostrande Philip
Ostrande Wilhelmus
Ostrander Aron
Ostrander Hendrick
Ostrander Henry, Jr.

Ostrander Wilhelmus
Pabody U. Briggs
Palmer John
Palmer Stephen
Pardee Silas
Patchen Zebulon
Patrick James
Patrick Thomas
Patterson Jacob
Patterson James
Patterson John (Doctor)
Patterson John
Patterson Richard
Paulding Nehamiah
Payn Daniel
Petterson Benjamin
Phelps John
Philip Adam
Philip Christian
Philip David
Philip George
Philip Hendrick W.
Philip John H.
Philip William
Philip William, Jr.
Philips Adam
Philips Christian
Philips Ebenezer
Phillip Christean
Phillip Hendrick
Phillip Hendrick H.
Phillip Jacob
Phillip Jacob, Jr.
Phillip Jacob H.
Phillip Wilhelmus
Phinney Isaac
Pichtell Jacob
Pichtell Thomas
Pichtell Thomas, Jr.
Pierce John
Pike William
Pitcher Isaac
Plank Michael
Plass Coenradt
Plass Johannis
Platner Hendrick
Platner Jacob
Plunt David
Plunt Henry
Plunt John
Pratt Bill
Pratt Robert
Pratt William

Preston Isaac
Price Timothy
Raadt Andries
Raadt Coenradt
Raadt Hendrick
Raadt Philip
Race Ephraim
Race Henry
Raes Jonathan
Ran Johannis
Rament William
Rath Coenradt
Raudt Andries
Raudt Hendrick
Raut Adam
Raut Andrew
Raut Conrad
Raut Philip
Raymond William
Ree Daniel
Rees Hendrick
Rees Hendrick, Jr.
Rees John
Rees Jonas
Rees Jonathan
Rees Jonathan, Jr.
Rees Jonathan H.
Rees Jonathan J.
Rees Jonathan W.
Rees Philip
Rees Thomas
Rees William
Relgen Jonathan
Reynolds Lewis
Richardson Joseph
Rifenberger Hendrick
Ring Coenradt
Risedorph Jacob
Robbins Thomas
Robbins William
Roberson John D.R
Roberts Peter
Robins Henry
Rocbaugh Robart
Rodman Thoms
Roe Ebenezer
Rogers Othaniel
Rolf John
Rome William
Rooreback Robert
Rorapaugh Robert
Roseboom Barent
Rosman Bastean

Rosman George, Jr.
Rous Harman
Row Hendrick
Row John
Row William
Rowland John, Jr.
Rowley John
Russell Dirck
Russman George
Russman Jurrey
Russman Sebastian
Ryne Lawrence
Rysen John
Salback Jacob
Salback Johannes
Salsberry Johannis
Sarring Amos
Saxton James
Scerrin Amos
Scharp Lawrance
Schermerhorn John
Schermerhorn John, Jr.
Schermerhorn William
Schoenmaker Hendrick Jr.
Schoenmaker Henry
Scholtus Hendrick
Schoudt Coenradt
Schudt Peter
Schult Henrich
Scism Peter
Scott James
Scott William
Segar David
Shafer Philip
Sharp Cornelous
Sharp Jacob
Sharp Johannis
Sharp Johannis, Jr.
Sharp Nicholas
Sharts Andres
Sharts Johannes
Sharts Juriah
Sharts Nicholas
Sharts Nicholas, Jr.
Shaver Adam
Shaver Peter
Shaver Phillip
Sheaver Henry
Shephard James
Shephard Jonathan
Shirts Jurry
Shirts Nicholas

Shirts Nicholas, Jr.
Shoemaker Godfree
Shoemaker Hendrick
Sholt Hendrick
Sholt Hendrick, Jr.
Showerman Andres
Shufelt Jeremiah
Shufelt Henry
Shufelt Peter
Shuldt Hendrick
Shuldt Hendrick, Jr.
Shuldt Johannis
Shult Johannis
Shurts Abraham
Shurts David
Shurts Nicholas, Jr.
Shurts Uriah
Shuts Abraham
Shuts David
Shuts Simon
Silkey James
Silvernagel Peter
Simon Jacob
Simson James
Simson Robert
Skinkle Henry, Jr.
Skinkle Henry I.
Skinkle Jacob
Skinkle Jonas
Skinner Josiah
Smart John
Smith Benjamin
Smith Christopher
Smith Coenraedt
Smith Coham Adam
Smith Derick
Smith Dirck
Smith Francis
Smith George
Smith George, Jr.
Smith George A.
Smith George Adam
Smith George P.
Smith Henry
Smith Henry P.
Smith Jacob P.
Smith Jered
Smith Jeremiah
Smith Jeremiah C.
Smith Jerry
Smith Johannis
Smith Johannis C.
Smith John

Smith John G.
Smith John P.
Smith Peter
Smith Peter A.
Smith Peter Adam
Smith Peter Johannis
Smith Philip
Smith Richard
Smith Timothy
Smith Tuenes G.
Smith Tunis
Smith Tunis P.
Smith William
Snook John
Snook Martinus
Snyder Coenradt
Snyder George
Snyder Henry
Snyder Hendrick
Snyder Peter
Snyder Peter, Jr.
Snyder William
Snyder William H.
Sours Peter
Sower Uldrick
Spanord Anthony
Spencer Samuel
Spencer Samuel, Jr.
Spoor Cornelius
Squire Jesse
Stalker Embrew
Stalker John
Stalker Joseph
Stanze William
Stark James
Stever Henry
Stolp Gerlough
Stolp Peter
Stoppelbean George Adam
Stoppelben Faltin
Stopplebean Jacob
Stopplebean Jacob, Jr.
Stopplebeen George A.
Stopplebeen Hendrick
Stopplebeen Hendrick, Jr.
Stopplebeen Michael
Stopplebeen Michel H.
Stopplebeen Nicholas
Stopplebeen Peter
Stopplebeen Valentine
Storm John
Strickland William
Stuppelban Jacob

Stuppelban Nichol
Stuppelbean Nichol
Stuppleban Jacob
Stupplebean Hendrick
Sufelt George
Sufelt George, Jr.
Tallmage John
Talmage Elisha
Teater George
Tedmore John
Ten Broeck Anthony
Ten Broeck Henry L.
Ten Broeck Jeremiah
Ten Broeck John
Ten Broeck John Jeremiah
Vande Water Michael
Ten Broeck Peter
Ten Broeck Peter B.
Ten Broeck Samuel J.
Ten Broeck Samuel Jeremiah
Ten Broeck Samuel John
Ten Eyck Barent
Thompson Alexander
Thompson John
Tickner Benjamin
Tileman Abraham
Tittemood John
Tittiman Abraham
Toby Seth
Tolley Dyer
Tolley Johan F.
Tran John, Jr.
Treat Teas
Treat Theaus
Trier Isaac T.
Tripp Anthony
Trull John
Tunecliff John
Tunecliff William
Turner Gilbert
Turner Gysbert
Tuttle William Y.
Utley David
Vallance Zachariah
Van Alen Adam
Van Alen John
Van Alstyne William
Van Back Nicholas
Van Beuren George
Van Beuren Peter
Van Bregen Peter
Van Deboe Jacob
Van De Bogert Michael

Vandekar Dirrick
Vandekar Joghem
Vandekar Solomon
Van Der Kar Dirck
Van Der Kar Jacob
Van Der Kar Jocham
Van Der Kar Johannis
Van Der Kar Nicholas
Van Deusen Abraham
Van Deusen Adam
Van Deusen Cornelius
Van Deusen Glonde
Van Deusen Glouds
Van Deusen Jacob
Van Deusen Johannis
Van Deusen Johannis J.
Van Deusen John I.
Van Deusen Mattawe M.
Van Deusen Matthew
Van Deusen Robert
Van Deusen Tobyas
Vandusen Barent
Van Dusen Henry
Van Dusen Malacher
Van Dusen Martin
Van Epps Evert
Van Hoesen Abraham
Van Hoesen Albertus
Van Hoesen Burry
Van Hoesen Cornelius J.
Van Hoesen Cornelius N.
Van Hoesen Gerrit G.
Van Hoesen Hendrick
Van Hoesen Jacob
Van Hoesen Jacob, Jr.
Van Hoesen Jacob C.
Van Hoesen Jacob F.
Van Hoesen Jacob I.
Van Hoesen Jacob J.
Van Hoesen Jacob
Van Hoesen Jacob Jurry
Van Hoesen Jacob L.
Van Hoesen Johannis
Van Hoesen Johannis C.
Van Hoesen Johannis J.
Van Hoesen Johannis Janse
Van Hoesen John
Van Hoesen John Hoes
Van Hoesen John Hoes,
Jr.
Van Hoesen John Jacabse
Van Hoesen John Joseph
Van Hoesen John Jurry

Van Hoesen Justice
Van Hoesen Nicholas
Van Hoesen Peter
Van Huesen Cornelius
Van Ness William
Van Ness William, Jr.
Van Renselaer Killyaen
Van Rensselaer Henry
Van Rensselaer John R.
Van Rensselaer Peter
Van Rensselaer Robert
Van Rensselaer William
Van Salsbergh Cornelius
Van Salsbergh Lukas
Van Valkenburgh Abraham
Van Valkenburgh Bartholomew
Van Valkenburgh Bartly
Van Valkenburgh Matties
Van Valkenburgh William
Van Valkencis John
Van Valkeneer Justice
Van Valkeneer Peter
Van Wagenaer Gerrit
Vasbarry Peter
Venson Abraham
Vischer Bastian H.
Vonck Peter
Vosburgh Abraham
Vosburgh Dirck
Vosburgh Evart
Vosburgh Isaac
Vosburgh Isaac P.
Vosburgh Jacob
Vosburgh Jacob, Jr.
Vosburgh Jacob D.
Vosburgh Jacob P.
Vosburgh Jacobus
Vosburgh Peter
Vosburgh Matthew
Vredenburgh Isaac
Vredenburgh Jacobus
Wadsworth John
Wagenaer Carel
Wagenear Jacob
Wagenear John
Wagner Peter
Ward Jacob
Warne Peter
Warne Richard
Warner Peter
Warner Richard
Wattles Samuel
Waymar John

Weager Henry
Weager Jacob
Weager Philip
Weissman Peter
Wemple Walter
Wendell Garrit
West Benjamin
West William
White Benjamin
White, John, Jr.
White Jurry
White Peter
White Uriah
White William
Wiessmer Peter
Wiessmer Peter, Jr.
Wiley Alexander
Williams Williams
Willcocks Simeon
Willcox Nathaniel
Williams Thomas
Wilsey Cornelius
Wilsey Cornelius, Jr.
Wilsey Henry
Wilsey Jacob
Wilsey Jeames
Wilsey Thomas
Wilton Jacob W.
Wiltse Henry
Wiltse Thomas
Wineradt George
Wise Michel
Witbeck Hendrick
Witbeck Jacob
Witbeck John
Witbeck Lukas
Witbeck Thomas
Witlow John Hartick
Wood James
Wood John
Wood John, Jr.
Wood William
Woodard Asa
Wyat Peter
Yager Hendrick
Yates Peter W.
Yates Robert
Yorker Jacob
Young Calvin
Young Philip
Young William
Zanegall Robert W.

Albany County Militia--Ninth Regiment
Colonel Peter Van Ness; Major Jacob Ford

Capt. Bartholomew Barrett	Lieut. Daniel Barnes	Lieut. Jonathan Pitcher
" Jonah Graves	" Abner Kellogg	" Eleazer Spencer
" Josiah Graves	" Charles McArthur	" Abel Whalen
" Abner Hawley	" David McKinstry	" Daniel Wilson
" Joshua Whitney	" Nathaniel Mead	Ensign Stephen Graves
Lieut. Benjamin Allen	" Amaziah Phillips	" Pheniheas Rice

Additional Names on State Treasurer's Pay Books

Lieut. Col. David Pratt	Lieut. Will Ove
Capt. Joseph Allen Tanner	" John Reynolds
Lieut. Caleb Clark	Ensign John Crippen
" Thomas Hatch	" James Delong
Lieut. Charles McKinstry	
" Thomas McKinstry	

Enlisted Men

Ackley James	Chaimberlin Gurden	Freamon Jonathan
Adset John	Childendon Benjamin	Freeman Daniel
Adsit Samuel	Chittendon Benjamin	Gardner John
Andreas Ebenezer	Cisel Peleg	Goff Oliver
Andress Ebenezer	Cleaveland Oliver	Gold Jonathan
Andrews Elisha	Cohoon Joseph	Gould Elijah
Bagley Asher	Colver Ebenezer	Gould Jonathan
Barret Ebenezer	Crippen John	Graves Increase
Barret Eleazer	Crippen Roswel	Graves Soldon
Barrows Ebenezer	Culver Ebenezer	Green Thomas
Benjamin	Darner Christopher	Green William
Blackman Joel	Darrow Ammerus	Griswell John
Bont Matthias	Darrow Christopher	Griswold David
Borghordt Lambert	Davis Andrew	Hacket Joseph
Bower Daniel	Day David	Hall Benijah
Brown Benjamin	Deen Gains	Hamblin Jesse
Bunhas Charles	Denison Christopher	Harris Eliphalet
Bunt Ephraim	Devonport Jonathan	Hatch Thomas
Bunt Matthias	Dibble Henerey	Hawkins Daniel
Burgert Hennerey	Dolittle Timothy	Hawley Daniel
Burget Johoicam	Doolittle Hackaliah	Hawley Zadok
Cadman John	Dudley Simeon	Hewit Arthur
Cadman Joseph	Earle Benjamin	Hollister Smith
Carrier Amos	Elmer	Horsford Ithamer
Casterrar John	Foot Samuel	House Thomas
Castor John	Foster John	Howes Thomas
Chamberlain Benjamin	Frask James	Huit Arthur

Huntly William
Hurlbert Jesse
Jackson James
Joal Ebenezer
Johnson Thomas
Johnston Abner
Keeney Roger
Ketcham Jesse
Killogh Benjamin
Lawrane Judah M.
Lawrence Joseph
Leanord John
Lee Joel
Liment Archibald, Jr.
Limont John
Lothrop Ebenezer
Lovejoy Andrew
McArthur John
McKever James
Malleray Samuel
Martin Robert
Meaker Robert
Mirit Amos
Mortain Robert
Mudge Ruben
Nicols Eliachim
Palmer John
Palmer Stephen
Palmitier Benjamin
Palmmer Gilbert
Palmmer James
Parks Samuel
Penfield Isaac
Phelps Jonah

Pottor Gideon
Pratt Samuel
Rea Hugh
Reiss Matt
Reynolds Jonathan
Richinson Joseph
Richmond Edward
Robbins Daniel
Robinson Hector
Rodman Joseph
Rodman Thornas
Roldman Joseph
Root Joshua
Root Moses
Root Nicholas
Rowland John
Rowland John, Jr.
Rowley Jabesh
Salsbury -idion
Saxton Ebenezer
Scoot Matt
Shepherd Jonathan
Smith Eli
Smith Elijah
Snyder William
Sole Ebenezer
Spalding John
Spalding Nehemiah
Spalding Samuel
Speer Cornelius
Spencer Amos
Spencer Asa
Spencer David
Spencer Eleazer

Spencer Eliphas
Spencer John
Spencer Matthias
Spencer Phineas
Spencer Samuel
Spencer Tuneas
Stark Amos
Stuart John
Taylor David
Taylor James
Teeckner Benjamin
Thomlinson Lemuel
Tickner Benjamin
Tickner Jonathan
Tilman Jacob
Titus Silas
Tyler Ebenezer
Valcomburgh Johoicam
Van Hoesen Francis
Van Valcomburey George
Vawn Edward
Vawn Richard
Virgin Asa
Walch Thomas
Welch Jonathan
West Samuel
White Johoicam
White William
Wise Samuel
Witmore Reuben
Woodin Rubin
Wrolen John

Albany County Militia--Tenth Regiment

Colonel Morris Graham; Adjutant Philip Rockefeller; Colonel Henry Livingston; Qr. Mr. Christian Van Valkenburgh; Major Dirck Jansen; Surgeon Thomas Thompson; Major Samuel Ten Broeck

Capt. Joseph Elliott
" Adam Husradt
" Conrad Kline
" Henry Pulver
" Diell Rockefeller
" Dirck Rockefeller
" Jacob F. Shaver
" John Shaver
" Philip Smith
Lieut. John Best
" William Casper

" Jacob Hagedorn
" Bartle Hendricks
" Henry Irvine
" John McArthur
" Nicholas Power
Lieut. William Rockefeller
" Jacob Roschman
" Harmanes Ross
" Casparus Schultz
" Charles Shaver
" John Shuts

" Johannes Staat
" Johannes Stall
" Peter Van De Bogart
" Henry Will
Ensign Leonard Dacker

" Asa Holmes
" Philip Knickerbacker
" Marx Kun
" Colin McDonald

Additional Names on State Treasurer's Pay Books

Lieut. Wandel Pulver; Ensign John Herder; Ensign James Rovinson; Lieut. Adam Segendorph; Ensign Bastian Lesher

Enlisted Men

Adams Baily	Clum Adam, Jr.	Delamater Abraham
Andon Casper	Clum Hendrick	Dick Henry
Angle William	Coale Johannis	Dick Paulus
Astin Jacob	Coale Peter	Dicker Charles C.
Attwood Timothy	Coens William	Diness Philip
Bain Casparues	Coitrs John, Jr.	Diness Yerry
Baker John	Cole Isaac	Dings Jacob
Barganer Peter	Cole John	Dings John
Barnet John	Cole Peter	Dings Stutfle
Barnet Simon	Comb Samuel, Jr.	Dolph John
Bartley Simon	Concklin Elisha	Donnolly William
Basseroom John	Concklin John	Dougherty Cornelius
Batts Johannes	Conradt Johannes	Dounatty William
Bearsh John	Coombe Samuel	Douy Cornelius
Becker Jacob	Coon Adam	Dubois Abraham
Ben James	Coons Peter	Dunsbach Philip
Berringer Peter	Coons Philip	Egelston Benjamin
Best Benjamin	Cork John, Jr.	Elkenbraugh Jacob
Best Hendrick	Corol Michael	Elkenbrugh Philip
Best Peter	Cotman Conradt	Elliott Michael
Biest William	Crammer William	Engell George
Bitser Wilhelmus	Cun Samuel	Erkenbergh Fite
Blass Michael	Cund Hendrick	Fox Jonathan
Blass Peter M.	Cunn Adam	Frasier William
Blass William	Cunx William	Frits William
Bless Hendrick	Cunx William H.	Funck Christian
Bower Nicholas, Jr.	Currey William	Funck Jacob
Bownen Hendrick	Curry John	Funck Peter
Bruiree Johannis N.	Dacker John C.	Gardner James
Bruise John F.	Danels Thomis	Gardner John
By Phenber Jacobus	Dannilty William	Gobobe John
Cain Paul H.	Decker Abraham	Graves Bort
Campbell John	Decker Benjamin	Haber Johannos
Campbell Martin	Decker Conradt	Hagadom Jacob
Capes Martin	Decker George	Hagedoom William
Casper Christian	Decker Isaac	Hagedorn William
Casper Christopher	Decker Jacob	Halter John
Cleeveland Lemuel	Decker Jacob C.	Halter John, Jr.
Cline Anthony	Decker John	Halter Michael
Clum Adam	Decker Lawrence I.	Halter Peter

Hatter John
Hatter Michael
Hatter Peter
Haver Christian
Haver Johannis
Haver Peter
Heiser Petrus
Herder John
Herder Michel
Herder Petrus
Herder Philip
Heyser Henry
Heyser Jacob, Sr.
Heyser Jacob, Jr.
Heyser Peter
Hofs William
Horck John, Jr.
Houshapple Zacharias
Houward Adam
Hunt Palathia
Hus Casper
Hyck Abraham
Hyck John B.
Imik Johannis
Jacobs Bastian
Janes David
Jorgh Michael
Kain Paul H.
Keephart Caleb
Kline Jacob
Kline Peter
Lape Jurry
Lape Thomas
Lasher Conradt B.
Lasher G. B.
Lasher Garret
Lasher Garret, Jr
Lasher Johannis
Lasher Johannis, Jr.
Lasher Johannis J.
Lasher Philip
Lasher William
Laubay Carl
Laubay Jacob
Lawrence John
Lawrence Peter
Lemnery Solomon
Lesher Bastian
Loomis John
Lynch Peter
McArthur Arthur
McArthur John P.
McClean Hector

McIntire John
MacFall Hendrick
MacFall Neal
MacFall Patrick
McFall Robert
McGill John
Mayer Johannis
Merky Max
Meyer Friderick
Miller Jonas
Miller Matthew
Minklar Jacob
Moor Peter
Moor Philip
Mower Barent
Nash John
Needen John
Nott John
Ostrander Benjamin
Ostrander John
Parish John
Parve Daniel
Petri Cunrath
Petrie Conrad C.
Phillips Christian, Jr
Phillips Christopher
Phillips Christopher, Jr.
Phillips John
Phillips Peter
Plass Peter
Plass Peter M.
Polver Jacob
Post William, Jr.
Pulver Wandel
Purden Edward
Quackenbos Daniel
Quackenbos Garret
Race Benjamin
Race Ephraim
Radclift John
Rath Adam
Renolds Lusia
Ringsdorph Phillip
Risdorf George
Robertson James
Robinson James
Rockefeller Diell, Jr.
Rockefeller Simeon
Rose Andrew A.
Rosman Samuel
Rossman Adam
Roth Adam
Russ Hermanns

Russ Samuel
Ruth Adam
Ruyans Philip
Ryfenbergh Adam
Salback Jacob
Salback Johannis
Salback Philip
Salbagh Thomas
Schmit Petrus
Schmit Zacherias
Schnnyder Ludwig
Schut Isaac
Schut Solomon
Schut William
Scutt William
Sebo Harry
Segendorph Adam
Sharp Peter
Shaver John
Shaver Peter
Shefter Johannis
Shefter Nicholas
Shiffer Johannis
Shipperly Barnet
Sholtis Philip
Sholts Barent
Shudes Henry
Shultis Barent
Shultis Davis
Shultis Henry
Shuts Adam
Shuts Johannes W.
Shuts Peter
Simon Battis
Simons William
Sipperly Barnet
Sisam John
Skuts John A.
Slos John
Smith James
Smith Johannis
Smith Joseph
Smith Peter
Smith Philar
Smith Samuel
Smith Zachariah
Snook Conrad
Snyder Conrad
Snyder Conrad, Jr.
Snyder George
Snyder Samuel
Snyder William
Snickerm Philin

Spickerman John
Spilman Conrad
Stahl Johann Henrich
State Benjamin
Stimon Baltis
Strader Jost
Stribel Ulrich
Temple James
Ten Brook Wessel
Ten Eyck Abraham
Ten Eyck Jacob
Ten Eyck John, Jr.
Ten Eyck John B.
Thomas Johannis
Thompson Abisha
Thompson George
Trater Joseph
Trever Peterus
Tunsback Philip
Turner Gilbert

Valkenburgh Christian
Van De Bogart Arent
Van De Bogart James
Van De Bogart Michael
Van De Bogen Peter
Vande Waters Hynis
Van De Waters Michael
Van Dusen George
Van Dusen Robert
Vonck Christian
Vonck Jacob
Vonck Peter
Vosburgh Jacob
Vosburgh Lawrence
Vosburgh Peter
Washburn John
Washburn Martinus
Waters Michael
Weeks Andrew
Whitimast Zachariah

Whitman Izra
Whitmore Stutfel
Widbeck Jacob
Wiest John
Will Chistian
Will Christopher
Will Herik
Willas Henry
Witeree Phillip
Witmore Philip
Yager Philip
Yager Wandle
Young Zacharias
Yunck William
Yunck Zachariah
Zeber Petrus
Zent Wissell
Zimmerman Henry

Albany County Militia Eleventh Regiment

Colonel Anthony Van Bergen; Lieut. Col. Cornelius Dubois; Pay Master Benjamin Dubois
Capt. Benjamin Dubois; Capt. Thomas Houghtaling; Capt. Myndert Van Schaick; Capt. John A. Whitbeck; Lieut. Anthony Abeel; Lieut. Abram Overpagh; Lieut. John Persons; Lieut. Francis Salisbury; Lieut. Wessel Salisbury; Lieut. Jacob Van Veghten; Ensign James Bogardus
Additional Names on State Treasurer's Pay Books
Lieut. Jochem Tryon; Lieut. Henry Van Bergen; Ensign Peter Bronk; Ensign Christian Meyer; Ensign John C. Schack; Ensign Peter Van Bergen
(No enlisted men found)

Albany County Militia--Twelfth Regiment

Colonel Jacobus Van Schoonhoven; Lieutenant Colonel James Gordon; Major Andrew Mitchell; Major Ezekiel Taylor; Adjutant Joseph Cook; Adjutant David Rumsey; Quarter Master Simon Fort; Quarter Master Hugh Peoples; Surgeon John Cuerden

Capt. Benjamin Aylsworth
Capt. Tyrannis Collins
Capt. Thomas Hicks
Capt. David Rumsey
Capt. Elias Steenbergh
Capt. Joshua Taylor
Capt. John Van Den Bergh
Capt. Nanning Vischer
Capt. Stephen White

Lieut. Hendrick Bonter
Lieut. Thomas Brown
Lieut. John Corey
Lieut. Stephen Sherwood
Lieut. Samuel Ten Broeck
Lieut. Nicholas Vanderkar
Lieut. John Van Vrancken
Lieut. Nicholas Van Vrancken
Lieut. Nathaniel Weed

Lieut. Epenetus White
Lieut. Benjamin Wood
Ensign Caleb Benedict
Ensign Christian Bonter
Ensign Michael De Groff
Ensign Samuel Dox
Ensign Nathan Raymond
Ensign Maas Van Vrancken
Ensign William Walderon

Enlisted Men

Adams Edward
Armstrong Daniel
Arnol John
Arson Thomas
Ashley Alden
Baily Timothy
Ball Flamon
Ball John
Ball Stephen
Banter John
Barber Solomon
Barheck James
Barne Samuel
Barnes Benoni
Barnes James
Barns Thomas
Barns William
Barnum Thomas
Barter Joseph
Bealy Timothy
Benedict Elias
Benedict Elisha
Benedict Elisha, Jr.
Benedict Felix
Benedict Ryer
Benedict Uriah
Betteys Jeremiah
Betteys William
Bigford Samuel
Bourn William
Bogardus Scheboleth
Bohanner Robert
Boskerk Martin
Bradshaw William
Bratt Aaront
Bratt Dirck
Bravon Thomas
Brewer Jery
Brooks Joseph
Brown Valintin
Bruer Jeremiah
Bruss Jeremiah
Bryant John
Buchanan Ebenezer
Buckingham Ebenezer
Burk John
Cabel John
Callogg Eliphalet
Camble Harmanus
Cannel Christian
Canniff Isaac
Carey John
Chambers Daniel

Chard Barce
Chatman Josiah
Chestney John
Christee John
Christiaan Cornelius
Christianse Cornelius
Chrtiyonse Cornelius
Cilberth John
Clinton John
Clute Dirick
Clate Gerardus
Clute Gerardus.Jr.
Clute Gerret
Clute Gerret D.
Clute Jacob
Clute Jacob G.
Cole Azor
Cole John
Collins Manasah
Concklin James
Concklin Thomas
Conlin Jacob
Connel John
Conner John
Cook John
Corpe Joseph
Corpe Nathaniel
Crawford John
Craydenwiser Henry
Creamer Christopher
Creamer Hendrick
Creamer Jury
Creps Peter
Crydenwiser Henry
Cunee John
Cuner John
Cunie Ephraim
Curdon John
Dais John
Davis John
Degraff Abraham
Degrave Michael
DeGroat Elias
DeGroat Henry
DeGroat Nicholas
Degroff Michael
Degroff Simon
Delong Daniel
Delong David
Delong Ezekiel
Demilt Isaac
Devoct Abraham
Devoe Dirick

Devoe Isaac, Jr.
Devoe John
Devoe John R.
Devoe Martinus
Devoe Samuel
Devoe William
Doppe Johannis
Doty Philip
Douglass Jonathan
Dox Isaac
Dox John
Drett John
Drett John, Jr.
Dunning Jesse
Efner Henry
Efner John
Efner Wilhelmus
Eldred Robert
Eldridge Robert
Elsworth George
Evans Ebenezer
Evens Nathan
Fairchild Matthew
Filmer John
Fitch John
Flynn John
Fonda Isaac H.
Fonda Isaac I.
Fonda John H.
Forgison Peter
Fort Daniel
Fort Nicholas
Fort Nicholas, Jr.
Foster William
Fowlar John
Fracikle Philip
Fraisier John
Frayzer John
Fulington James
Fullerton James
Fullmer Jacob
Fulmer Johannis
Fulwieser Abraham
Gardner George
Garremo Samuel
Goreham Jabez
Green Daniel
Gregory Uriah
Grigg John
Griggs
Griggs Abraham
Griggs Evert
Griggs John

Griswould John
Groom James
Grooms David
Grooms William
Groot Claus
Groot Cornelius
Groot Derick A.
Groot Derick C.
Groot Jesse
Groot Nicholas
Haens James
Hagedorn Henry
Hagedorn Peter
Hagerman Adrian
Hagerman Nicholas
Hall Levy
Halstead Timothy
Hart Nicholas
Hatt Jacob
Hawkins
Hawkins Arthur
Heagley Seth
Heemstrat David
Heemstrat Dirick
Hiat Roger
Hicks Samuel
Higby Flemin
Higby John
Higby Lewis
Hollister Josiah
Hollister Lazarus
Holmes Caleb
Hooper John
Hooper Stephen
How David
How Isaac
How Jesse
Hubbell Jabez
Hubble Abijah
Hull David
Hunter David
Isdle John
James Henry
James Nathaniel
Jengins Edmon
Jennings Jesse
Jinnin Edmund
Kanedy John
Kanedy Thomas
Kellogg Azor
Kellogg Eliphalet, Jr.
Kennedy George
Kennedy Robert

Kennedy Thomas
Lake Benjamin
Lansing Henry
Lansing Isaac
Lansingh Garrit T.
Lattemore Francis
Lattemore John
Laverse Anthony
Leverse Levenus
Luik George
Mab John
Mab Thomas
McChesney John
McClean Cornelius
McCoy Charls
McCoy William
McCray Samuel
McCready David
McCrear Samuel
McCue Samuel
McDonalds Michael
McIntosh John
McKnight John
McKnight Thomas
McNeil Archibald
McNeil William
Mahannan Robert
Main William
Mastin George
Maston George
Matthews Clark
Mead Zachariah
Merrick Stephen
Middlebrook Michael
Miller Christopher
Miller Jacob
Miller James
Miller Jeremiah
Miller John
Miller Joshua
Mirick Abel
Mitchel Robert
Moe Abraham
Moe Husted
Moe Jacob
Moon Jacob
Moon William
Morehouse George
Mosier Joseph
Mourehouse Joseph
Muckle John
Munn Israel
Murry James

Names Abraham
Nash Azor
Nash John
Nash Samuel
Nesler Conrad
Nesler John
Northrop Thadeus
Northrop Wilson
Northrup Thadeus
Novell James
Olmsted Daniel
Owen Epenetus
Owens Abernatus
Page Samuel
Palmer Amaziah
Palmer Beriah
Palmerton Joshua
Palmeteer William
Palmeter Joshua
Palmetier Isaac
Patchin Jabez
Patchin Samuel
Patchin Squire
Patchin Zachariah
Patterson Adam
Pearse James
Pearse John
Pearse Richard
Peebles Hugh
Peirson John
Philmore Sirus
Prevoct Reech
Prevost Alexander
Putman John
Quackenbush Jacob
Quackinbush Gradus
Reeve William
Rhen William
Rice William
Roff Philip
Root Asa
Root Stephen
Rose John
Rossel Rosel
Rue Joseph, Jr.
Rumney John G.
Rumsey David
Saupers David
Schaaf Henrich
Schonter Hugh
Schoonhoven James
Schouten Darrick
Schouter Jacob

Schouter Johanis
Schut
Schutt Alexander
Scott James
Scranton Marchen
Scribner Aaron
Scribner Thadeus
Sears Sunderland
Seeley John
Seeley Stephen
Seely Nehemiah
Seever Sunderland
Sharp Philip
Shear Matthias
Shere John
Shere Peter
Sherred James
Sherwood James
Shouten Jacob
Shuter William
Sign John
Sines John
Siney Peter
Sinix Peter
Smith Abijah
Smith Benijah
Smith Elias
Smith Elijah
Smith Henry
Smith John
Smith Lewis
Smith Moses
Snodye William
Sooprs David
Sprag Elisha
Sprage Ebenezer, Jr.
Sprage John
Sprague Elijah
Sprague John
Steenbergh James
Steenbergh John
Steenbergh Peter
Sutton James
Taylor John
Teachout Isaac
Teathout Jacob
Teathout Nicholaes

Teathout William
Thalhimer Peter
Todd Robert
Tooper William
Traver Francis
Tymensia Aldert
Vallentine Gabriel
Van Aelstine Daniel
Van Camp Simeon
VanDenBergh Cornelius
VandenBergh Gerrit
VandenBergh Neeklaes
VanDenBergh Nicholas C.
VanDenBergh Peter
VanDenBergh Rutgert
VanDenKar Abraham
VanDenKar Arent
VanDenKar Derick
VanDenKar Hendrick
VandenKar Nicholas
VanDenWerken Barent
VanDenWerken Francis
VanDenWerken Gradus
VanDenWerken John J.
VanDenWorker Albert
VanDerhyden Abraham
Vanderwerken John
VanDe Werke John A.
Van Ness Cherck
Van Ness William
Van O'Linde Daniel
Van Schaick Goose
Van Schoonhoven Hendrick
Van Vleck Tunis
Van Vrancke Jacob
Van Vrancken Claus
Van Vrancken Evert
Van Vrancken James
Van Vrancken John
Van Vranken Abraham
Van Vranken Adam
Van Vranken Cornelius
Van Vranken Dirick
Van Vranken Gerrit
Van Vranken Isaac
Van Vranken Nicholas
Van Vranken Rykert

Van Vranken Samuel
Van Vranken Woub
Vedder Corset
Vedder Harman
Vedder Harmanus
Vedder Jacob
Vensen John
Vischer Eldert
Vincent Jeremiah
Vischer Teunis
Wait Oliver
Walderon Evert
Walderon Gerit
Walderon Peter
Ward William
Watrous Edward A.
Way Daniel
Way David
Weaver Edward
Weaver Josias
Weed Bill
Weed Phineas
Weed William
Weight Abner
Welden Timothy
Wellden Abraham
White Epenetus
White John
White Jonas
White Nathaniel
Wilde William
Williams David
Williams Fradrick
Williams John
Williamson William
Wilsee Jacob
Wilsee John
Witey William
Wood Elijah
Wood Enoch
Wood John
Wooding Timity
Wooley Daniel
Wooley Jonathan
Wyley Stephen
Young John

Albany County Militia--Thirteenth Regiment

Colonel John McCrea; Colonel Cornelius Van Veghten; Major Daniel Dickinson; Major Jacob G. Van Schaick;
Adjutant Elisha Andrus; Quarter Master Michael Beadle

Capt. Holton Dunham
Capt. Michael Dunning
Capt. John Thompson
Capt. Peter Van Wort
Capt. Peter Winnie
Capt. Ephriam Woodworth
Lieut. Ashbel Andruss
Lieut. Abel Balnap
Lieut. Stephen Benedict
Lieut. John Davis
Lieut. Isaac Doty
Lieut. Hezekiah Dunham
Lieut. Benjamin Guile
Lieut. Philipp Rogers, Jr.
Lieut. Samuel Sheldon
Lieut. James Storm
Lieut. Joshua Wheeler
Ensign Isaac D. Fonda
Ensign William Green
Ensign Nathaniel Grommon
Ensign Richard Hilton
Ensign John Hunter
Ensign John Mahoney
Ensign Joseph Row
Ensign Benjamin Sheldon
Ensign Gerritt Van Buren
Ensign Reuben Wright

Additional Names on State Treasurer's Pay Books
Lieut. Jabez Gage; Ensign Jacob D. Fonda

Enlisted Men

Abbet David	Anthony Stephen	Beadlestone Henry
Abeel James	Archer David	Beams Jeremiah
Abeel William	Armstrong John	Becker Peter
Ackerman David	Armstrong Thomas	Bedle Thomas
Ackerman Isaac	Arnold Abemelick	Beltar John
Ackerman James	Arnold John	Bemus William
Ackerman Robert	Ashman Samuel	Bennet Bildad
Airl Nathaniel	Austin Phinehas	Benson Bildad
Albert White	Babcock Job	Benson Elihu
Allen James	Babcock Jonathan	Benson Job
Andress John	Badcock Nehemiah	Benson John
Andress Nathaniel	Baker Edey	Bently Benedict
Andrus Ephraim	Baldwin Alexander	Bently Thomas
Andrus John, Jr.	Banter John	Bidwell Daniel
Andrus Joseph	Barber Simeon	Bidwell David, Jr.
Andrus Nathaniel	Barden Abraham	Bidwell Jacob
Andruss Ashbel, Jr.	Beadle Daniel	Bise William
Andruss Deliverance	Beadle Joseph	Bitcler Henery
Andruss Titus	Beadle Michael	Black William
Anthony Richard	Beadle Thomas, Jr.	Blanding John

Bowdish Henery
Bowdish Gideon
Bowler Simeon
Bradshaw William
Briggs Abraham
Brisbee Samuel
Brisben James
Brisbin William
Brown Benjamin
Brown Joel
Brown Luther
Brownell Benjamin
Bryan Samuel, Jr.
Buck John
Buck Peregreen
Burden Abraham
Burllinggame Silas
Bush Benjamin
Button Elezer
Cady Zebulon
Calvert John
Campbell Daniel
Campbell Samuel
Campbell Solomon
Cans Joseph
Carpenter Barnet
Carpenter Barney
Carpenter Benjamin
Carpenter John
Carpenter Warren
Carr Joseph
Case Alexander
Case Joseph
Coffin Bartlet
Collins Elber
Conklin Nathaniel
Couton Simeon
Chamberlin Joseph
Chapman Ezekiel
Chapman Noah
Chapman Samuel
Chatfield Jesse
Chidester Daniel
Chidester Nathan
Child Increase
Christionse Cornelius
Clapp Lemuel
Clement Peter
Clute Ephrama
Clute Evert
Clute Gradus
Cobb Ebenezer
Cole Abraham

Collins Benjamin
Collins William
Colvert James
Colvert John
Comstock Peter
Conklen Samuel
Conkling John
Cook Nathaniel
Coon Jeremiah
Cooper William
Coppe Nathaniel
Cornell Paul
Corps Nathaniel
Crandall Jeremiah
Crawford John
Crowel James
Culvert James
Cuningham James
Daly David
Daly Samuel
Davis Ebenezer
Davis John
Davis John, 3d
Davis Nathan
Dean Henry
Dean Jabez
Dennis Humphrey
Dennis William
Devoe Jacob
Dickenson Zebulon
Dickerson Joseph
Dickerson Zebulon
Dickinson Joseph
Dickinson Samuel
Dumbolton John
Dun Henry
Dunham Elijah
Dunham Hezekiah
Dunham Samuel
Dunham Silvenus
Dunham Solomon
Dunning Ebenezer
Dunning James
Dunning Jesse
Dunning Lewis
Dunning Linus
Dutcher John
Dutcher John D.
Dwelly Abner
Dwelly Abner, Jr.
Dyer Ezra
Eddy Zephiniah
Edmond Robert

Edmond Samuel
Edmonds Matthew
Edwards Abel
Edwards Timothy
Fellows John
Finch Samuel
Finel Edward
Fish Abner
Fish Benjamin
Fish Ephraim
Fish Joshua
Fish Pardon
Fisher Henry
Flyn Patrick
Ford Asher
Ford Thomas
Ford William
Foster Jonathan
Foster Thomas
Foster William
Freeman Elijah
Freeman Elisha
Freeman Gideon
Freeman James
Freeman Stephen
Frisbe William
Fuller Nathaniel
Fuller Varsel
Fullington Alexander
Gage Jabish
Gage Jesse
Gates Stephen
Gay Timothy
Gay William
Gecocks Thomas
Gifford William
Gregory David
Gregory Reuben
Griffith William
Griggs Simon
Grommon John
Guile Amos
Guilc Daniel
Guy Timothy
Hagerty William
Hairns John
Halbert White
Hall Sylvester
Hammond Benjamin
Hammond Jonathan
Hammond Paul
Hammond William
Harsha Hugh

Hart Isaac
Hart Jeremy
Hasel Conrad
Hasel Counwast
Havens John
Havens Peleg
Hawk George
Hawkins Adone
Hawkins Edward
Herrington Nathaniel
Hewit Asa
Hibbert Elisha
Higgins Thomas
Hilton Jonathan
Hilton Peter
Hilton Richard
Hitchcock Stephen
Holmes Caleb
Holms Samuel
Hooper Stephen
Howard Jesse
Hubbell Nehamiah
Hull David
Hull Eliphalet
Hull Seth
Hull Setton
Hunt George
Hunt Thomas
Hunter John
Hunter Robert
Hunter Samuel
Huper Stephen
Hurst Thomas
Husted Edward
Hutton Jonathan
Ingensle Daniel
Ingersoll Daniel
Ingersoll Jesse
Ingersoll Philip
Inman Abraham
Inman Benjamin
Inman Ezekiel
Inman Michael
Jackson Andrew
Jakedays George
James Henry
James Robert
Jaqueways George
Jefferies Thomas
Jefferson Thomas
Johnson John
Johnston Peter
Jones Stephen

Jordan Peter
Keeler Isaac
Keeler Isaiah
Knowlton John
Koon Jeremiah
Kose Daniel
Laing John
Lampher Levi
Lansing Garret
Lansing Garret G.
Laranes Gideon
Lawrence Gideon
Lent Abraham
Lent Hendrick
Lent Jacob
Lightheart Barney
Lilly Abner
McBride John
McBride John, Jr.
McCarthy Moses
McCouchan Andrew
McGee William
McKillip William
Mahauney Gacob
Mahoney Jacob
Manserd Simeon
Mansfield Thomas
Marshall Abraham
Marshall Simeon
Marvins Jared
Merrick Thomas
Mervin Gerard
Millard Robert
Millerd Edy
Millerd Eleazer
Millerd Jadidiah
Millerd Nathaniel
Milligan Robert
Mills Timothy
Mires Stephen
Mirick Thomas
Moony Thomas
Moor Hose
Moore Alpheas
Moore Charles
Moore Gideon
Moore Phinheas
Moore Reuben
Moorey Gideon
Morey Thomas
Mosher David
Moss Simeon
Mulligan Robert

Munger Benjamin
Munger Philip
Munger Samuel
Munger Timothy
Neilson John
Newell Asa
Newell Ebenezer
Newland Israel
Newland Joseph
Newland Rial
Newman Benjamin
Norton Samuel
Norton James
Norton William
O'Ferrel Amherst
Palmer Jerard
Palmer John
Palmer Othniel
Palmer Tand
Parke Daniel
Parke Jehiel
Parks Amasiah
Parsons Henry
Patrick Ebenezer
Patrick Joshua
Patrick Robert
Patrick William
Patrick William, Jr.
Patten Jonahan
Pattson Thomas
Pebe Simeon
Perkins Christopher
Perkins Oliver
Persons Henry
Pery John
Peters Matthew
Pettes Matthew
Pharis Levi
Phelps Elisha
Phillips Shadrick
Potten Rowland
Potter Alien
Potter Jonathan
Potter Nathaniel
Potter Simeon
Potter Thomas
Prince Jonathan
Prindle Joel
Purchase Thomas
Purdy Ebenezer
Randle Elias
Rankle John
Ray John

Ray Roswell	Sayles Stephen	Toms John
Ray Zachariah	Scidmore Abner	Toms Stephen
Raynolds George	Scidmore Hoppar	Trip Thomas
Reagle Daniel	Scidmore John	Tripp Caleb
Redder Evert D.	Scidmore Solomon	Tripp David
Reed Elias	Sea Abraham	Tripp Everett
Reeve William	Sea David	Tripp Job
Reis John	Sea Harmanus	Tripp Peleg
Reis John, Jr.	Sealey Joseph	Tripp William
Reynolds Benoni	Sears Abraham	Tuttle Abijah
Reynolds Elias	Sears Samuel	Tuttle Jabez
Reynolds George	Sexton Garshen	Tuttle John
Reynolds John	Seymour William	Tuttle Mizah
Rice John	Sheffield Christopher	Tyler Shubel
Rice John, Jr.	Sheffield Nathan	Valintine Peter
Richmond Benjamin	Sheldon Benjamin	Van Amburgh Matthew
Ridder George	Sheldon John	Van Arnum Abraham
Riddle George	Sheldon Samuel	Van Buren Hendrick
Roads John	Shephard Nathaniel	Van Buren Martin
Roads William	Sherman Henry	Van dike Dirick
Robards Ezekiel	Shipman Timothy	Vandelinda Daniel
Robards Purchase	Slocum Elezer	Vandelindar Gerardus
Robards William	Slocum Joseph	Van Den Bergh Garret
Robenson Isachar	Smith Daniel	Vandenbergh Wynant
Roberts Isaac	Smith Elisha	Vanderwarker Isaac
Robertson Robert	Smith Thomas	Vanderwarker Marta
Robins William	Snider Mark	Van Dick Dirick
Robinson Charles	Spike Daniel	Van Hasen Matthew
Robison Charles	Springer Richard	Van Hyning Henry
Rockwell Simeon	Stafford Amos	Van Schaick Hendrick
Rods William	Stafford Samuel	Vinhagen Martin
Rogers Daniel	Staklen Ebenezer	Vroman William
Rogers Jac'b	Stevens Ebenezer	Walls Tunis
Rogers Joseph	Stevens Joseph	Washburn Daniel
Ronnels Elias	Stevens Peter	Washburn Joel
Ronnels Thomas	Stevens Samuel	Watson Cyprian
Root Asa	Stewart Samuel	Watson James
Root Denison	Stiles Reuben	Watts Thomas
Root Stephen	Stiltes Isrell	Weatherhead Edmund
Ross Benjamin	Storm David	Webster Elihu
Ross Daniel	Storm Isaac	Weeks Daniel
Ruger Frances	Storm Isaac, Jr.	Weeks William
Ruger Joseph	Storm James	Welch Daniel
Ruger Moscs	Strang Gabriel	Wells James
Ryan Christopher	Strickland Ebenezer	Wendel Abraham
Sasson Thomas	Strong Gabril	Wetsel Christian
Saxton Gershom	Studmore Zopher	Wheler Ephraim
Sayles Ahab	Taylor Israel	Wheler Joshua
Sayles Ezekiel	Thompson John	Whipple Erick
Sayles Jacob	Thornton John	Whipple Esek
Sayles John	Tifft Stanton	White Albert
Sayles Mordeui	Tombs James	White Rufus
Sayles Silvanus	Toms James	White James

Whitehead Thomas
Whitehock Stephen
Wicks William
Willcocks Tyle
Willcox Francis
Willcox Gilbert
Willcox Tyler
Willes Ezekiel
Willes Hezekiah

Willes Reuben
Willes Thomas
Williams John
Williams Joseph
Williams Robert
Williams William
Williams William, Jr.
Willse James
Wiltsey James

Wiltsey John
Wiltsey Gardus
Woodbeck Thomas
Woodworth Amos
Woodworth Reuben
Wright Reuben
Young Daniel

Albany County Militia--Fourtheenth Regiment
Colonel John Knickerbacker; Colonel Peter Yates; Lieut. Col. John Van Rensselaer; Adjutant Jacob Van Valkenbergh

Capt. John Abbet
Capt. Gerritt Tunnes Bradt
Capt. Thomas Brown
Capt. Matthew De Garmo
Capt. James Hadlock
Capt. Daniel Hobble
Capt. Hendrick Mandeville
Capt. Cornelius Vandenburgh
Capt. Henry Van Der Hoff
Capt. Cornelius Wiltse
Capt. Jacob Yates
Capt. Peter Yates
Lieut. Joel Abbott

Lieut. William Brack
Lieut. John B. Bratt
Lieut. Matthew Brewer
Lieut. Richard Davenport
Lieut. Jacob De Garno
Lieut. Eldart Fonda
Lieut. Nathaniel Ford
Lieut. Jacob Fort
Lieut. Joseph Hallstead
Lieut. Jacob Haulenbeck
Lieut. Ignas Kip
Lieut Peter Martin
Lieut. John Palmer

Lieut. Nathaniel Rowley
Lieut. Jesse Toll
Lieut. John Van Antwerp
Lieut. Abner Van Name
Lieut. Jacob Van Nass
Lieut. Jacob Van Wormer
Ensign Joseph Gifford
Ensign Simeon Van Darosh
Ensign Simon Vandercock
Ensign Derick T. Van Veghten
Ensign John Van Wormer

Additional Names on State Treasurer's Pay Books
Qr. Mr. Stephen Viele; Lieut. Henry Brace; Lieut. John Harden; Lieut. John Van Wormer; Lieut. Gamaliel Wells

Enlisted Men

Acker Solomon
Adams John
Adkins Thomas
Agan James
Agan John
Aller Abraham
Aller John
Aller Peter
Anthony Bartholomew
Anthony Ellabart
Antony Borthmeues
Armstrong Nathan
Arnold
Arnold Ebenezer
Arnold Elisha
Asten William
Attlar Abraham
Babcock Joshua
Bacon Abel
Bacon Penuel

Bacon Phinehas
Bacon Winthrop
Bacor Herrington
Bagges James
Baker John
Baker Lemuel
Barnet Moses
Barnhart Frederick
Barnhart Jost
Bartel Increas
Bartholomew Philip
Basset Seth
Bates William
Bayelas John
Benedict Aaron
Benedict Isaac
Benedict James
Benedict Joseph
Beniway John
Bennet Amos

Bennet Banger
Bennet Jonathan
Bennet Richard
Bennet Robeson
Bennet Robinson
Bennet William
Bennidick Aaron
Benson Abel
Benson Elias
Benson Elnathan
Benson Joel
Benway John
Benway Peter
Bernhert Frudarick
Bernhert Henry
Bernhert Joseph
Besset Seth
Bethewel
Beyce Tohide
Bikker Nicholas

Blair John, Jr.
Blakesley James
Bleecker John J.
Blowers Abiel
Bouse Jonathan
Bouse Nicholas
Bovee Jacob
Bovee Jacob, Jr.
Bovee Peter
Bovie John
Bowdish John
Boyce Jehoiada
Boyce Millerd
Bratt Daniel
Bratt Nicholas
Brice Henry
Brown Charles
Brown David
Brown Henry
Brown Hezekkah
Brown Jonathan
Brues Henry
Bump Ichabod
Bump James
Bump Jezebud
Bunda Elijah
Bunda Nathaniel
Bunda Simeon
Bunday Ashble
Bundy Elisha
Bundy Simeon
Burroughs Benjamin
Burroughs James
Burtch Richard
Buschart Conrad
Bush Conratt
Bush Guilbard
Bush John
Cadey Zebulon
Caldwell Robert
Camp Nicholas
Carey Lemuel
Carey Seth
Carpenter Jeremiah
Carpenter Josiah
Case James
Chace Lemuel
Champ Nicholas
Chappell Samuel
Chard Abraham
Chase Abraham
Cheney William
Chezel John

Chitteson Elisha
Ciberly Barent
Clark Israel
Clark John
Clark Jonathan
Coal John
Cole James
Cole John
Coll James
Comenengs Josiah
Commins Francis
Commins Isaiah
Commons Josiah
Connell Edward
Cook Henry F.
Coone William
Couey John
Couly John
Covell James
Covey John
Cox John
Crandle Samuel
Crawbarrak Peter
Crittenton Zebulon
Cronk Cornelius
Cronk Francis
Cronk Stephen
Cronkheit Cornelius
Cronkhite Abraham
Cronkhite Aury
Cronkhite James
Cronkhite Stephen
Cronkhite Tunes
Cross Daniel
Cuttinton Jediah
Darrow James
Daught John
Davenport Peter
Degarimo Matthew
Delano Nathan
Delong Jacob
Delong Nicholas
Demaray Samuel
Demoray David
Demoray Davis
Demoree Nicholas
Denton Nathaniel
Devenport Jacob
Dewitt Benjamin
Dewy Isaiah
Doty Jacob
Doty Ormond
Doty Peter

Douglas Thomas
Downson Ichabod
Dunham Elijah
Dunham Ephraim
Dunham Charles
Dunning Ephraim
Dutcher John
Dutcher Lawrence
Dyer Ezra
Earl David
Eastwood Benjamin
Eastwood Benjamin, Jr
Eastwood Daniel
Eastwood Nathaniel
Echard Solomon
Eckert Peter
Eckert Peter, Jr.
Eckert Solomon
Elliot Daniel
Engrum Humphrey
Evins Samuel
Eycleshymer Peter
Fake Gorg
Finch Ebenezer
Fish Abraham
Fisher Abraham
Fisher Adam
Fisher Christian
Fisher George
Fisher Jacob
Fisher Jeremiah
Follet John
Fonda Abraham
Fonda Eldart
Ford Jacob
Ford John
Ford John James
Fort Abraham
Fort Abraham J.
Fort John
Fort John Isaac
Fort John J. B.
Fort Lewis
Fowler Levy
Fox Nathaniel
Fradenburce John
Francisco Abraham
Francisco Cornelous
Francisco Derick
Francisco Dick
Francisco Henry
Francisco Jeremiah
Francisco John

Francisco John J.
Francisco Levy
Francisco Michael
Francisco Richard
Francisco Thomas
Fredenburgh Abraham
Freeman Isaac
Frier Nicholas
Fuller Daniel
Fuller Jonathan
Fuller Timothy
Gallipser William
Gallup Rufus
Gallup William
Garrison Abraham
Garrison John
Gifford Benjamin
Gifford Gershom, Jr.
Gifford Giddon
Giles Gilbert
Gillet Beriah
Glass William
Goesbeck Nicholas W.
Golding Benjamin
Golding Jesse
Graves Russel
Grawborgar Peter
Greer Chard
Griffeth Aaron
Griswold David
Griswold Jabez
Griswold Josiah
Griswould Ephraim
Groesbeck Herman
Groesbeck Nicholas
Groesbeck Nicholas W.
Groesbeck Peter
Groesbeck Peter, Jr.
Groesbeck Peter W.
Groff John
Grommon Jacob
Groot Derick
Grousbeck Peter
Growsback Daniel
Grusback Nicholauser, Jr.
Grusebake Nicholis
Grusebeck Hugh
Grusebeck Jacob
Grusebeck William
Guernsey William
Hadlack Samuel
Hadlock Jonathan
Halenbeck Henry

Haling William
Hall William
Hallen William
Hallenbeck Daniel, Jr.
Halley Daniel
Halley Joseph
Halsted Thomas
Handerson Edward
Hanyon Garret
Harden John
Harold William
Hayle Francis
Haynes Pardon
Helling William, Jr.
Henderson Edward
Henewell Rice
Heninger Henry V.
Henney Charls
Hicks Daniel
Hicks Thomas
Hill John
Hill John, Jr.
Hill William
Hix William
Hodges Benjamin
Hodges Ezekiel
Hodges Ezekiel, Jr.
Hodges Isaac
Hodges John
Hodlat Samuel
Hogale Abraham
Hogel John
Hogges Daniel
Hogins Benjamin
Hogle Frencis
Holley Daniel
Holsted Ezekiel
Holsted Thomas
Honeywell Rice
Hooper William
Hopkins Joel
Hornback Deniel
Hose John
House John
Howard Matthew
Hubbil Matthew
Hubble Daniel
Hubble Ithemer
Huble Jonathan
Humphry Evans
Humphry James
Hunt Amasa
Hunt Emery

Huss John
Husting James
Huston James
Huyck Peter
Hynis Benjamin
Ingram Humphrey, Jr.
Isacks Samuel
Ively John
Jadwin Joseph
Johnson John
Johnson Josiah
Kannedy Josiah
Karr Jonathan
Ketcham Daniel
Ketcham Jonas
Ketcham Samuel
Ketchum Abijah
Ketchum James
Kiff John
Kip Lodewick
Kitchum Daniel
Kittchim William
Klein Joseph
Kogh Hezekiah
Lake Garet
Lamb John
Lampmen Peter
Lamser Isaac
Lanard Isaac
Lanard Thomas
Lang Joseph D.
Langunan Abraham
Lansing Henry
Latham David
Lee John
Lempmen Abrm.
Lennard Isack
Lennard Tomes
Lent Abraham
Lent Philip
Lenuell Robert
Lomis Jacob
Lomis Job
Loveless Benjamin
Loveless Elisha
Loveless Jeremiah
Lucas John
Luke James
Lyon George
Lyones James
McClave William
McGowan James
McKay William

McNeal Neal	Ostrander Johntise	Richerdson Isaac
Mace William	Ostrander Peter	Richeson Thomas
Manderis Hendrick	Overocker Adam	Rickard Conrod
Mandeville John	Overocker George	Rickart John
Marrick Abel	Overocker Jacob	Robins Evens
Marroy William	Overocker Michel	Roman Peter
Marsh Ephraim	Paddock Levi	Root Josiah
Marsh John	Paddok Job	Rose Benjamin
Marsh William	Page Amos	Rose Cornelius
Marshel Elihu	Palmer David	Rose John
Marthis Henry	Palmer Fenner	Rosefalt Jacob
Martin Henry	Palmer Garsham	Rouse Jacob
Martin Jeremiah	Palmer Nathan	Rouse John
Martin Joseph	Palmer Nathaniel	Rouse Jonathan
Martin Nathan	Paree David	Rouse Nicholas
Martin Peter	Parker Caleb	Rowland Oliver
Martin Thomas	Parker Jonathan	Rowland Samuel
Mash John	Parse Benjamin	Ruger Gideon
Mash William	Patterson Robert	Ryon John
Masters William	Pattis William	Samboorn Nathaniel
Matthews Henery	Pattson William	Sammons Jacob
May John William	Pearce Levi	Scheley Martin
Mead Nehemiah	Perce David	Schryer Nicholas
Mead Noah	Perry Absalom	Scot Stephen
Meads Joseph	Peter Felix	Scott Benjamin
Mendeveil John	Pierce Benjamin	Scott Thomas
Merrel Morris	Pierce David	Scribner Abel
Merrill Moses	Pierce Norris	Scribner Abel, Jr.
Merrit Moses	Porter Felix	Scribner John
Mervin John	Powell Jonathan	Scribner Samuel
Millard Stephen	Powell Richard	Scribner Zadok
Milliman John, Jr.	Powell Thomas	Scutt Abraham
Monrow Nathan	Powell William	Seal John
Mullory William	Price John	Sealy Matthew
Mumford Robson	Price John, Jr.	Seperley Barned
Munro Samuel	Price Jonathan	Sharp John
Munson Titus	Price Samuel	Sharp Peter
Murpey Thomas	Purdy Peter	Shaw Comfort
Near George	Quackenbus Harman	Shaw Daniel
Nelson John	Quackenbush Gose	Shaw Nathaniel
Newcomb James	Rager Gabral	Shearer William
Nicklison Israel	Ramer Frederick	Shearman Caleb
Nickoll Asa	Raniser Christian	Shele Martin
Nokes John	Ray William	Shepard Israel
Nye Seth	Rehern Joseph	Shepard William
Oakley Stephen	Renler Lawrence	Sipperley Jacob
Odel Gershom	Reynolds Jeremiah	Sisson John
Oderkerk Frederick	Riar George	Slatry Patrick
Oketey Stephen	Rice John	Slauter Patrick
Oller Peter	Rice Seth	Slip William
Omsted Gidian	Richardson James	Sly Elisha
Ostrander Abraham	Richenson James	Sly John
Ostrander John	Richenson William	Smith Benjamin

Smith Simeon	Van Derhook Isaac	Wandell John
Smith William	Van Der Werken Martin	Weatherwax Alexander
Sneider Johannes	Van Groesbeck Johans	Weatherwax David
Snyder Christopher	Van Grosbeck Wouter	Weatherwax Martin
Snyder Jacob	Van Hyning Hendrick	Weatherwax Peter
Snyder John	Van Name Aaron	Wederwax Alexander
Sordam Samuel	Van Nest Jacob	Weeb Jonethan
Spaulding Elijah	Van Nest John	Weeler Jonathan
Stark Asel	Van Nest Soromer	Wells George
Stark Christopher	Van Norton Henry	West Willrston
Stark Christopher, Jr.	Vansent John	Wetzel George
Start Asahel	Van Sirdam Samuel	Wheeler Jonathan
Start Christopher	Van Sordam Andris	Wheeler Richard
Start William	Van Sordam Lowrans	Whitford Caleb
Stephens James	Van Sordam Tunis	Wightman Edward
Stephens William	Van Vactan James	Wilfort Goleps
Stilwill John	Van Vaghten Herman	Wilkins Obadiah
Stilwill Samuel	Van Valkenburgh Jacob	Williams Asher
Stinson William	Van Vorees Garritt	Williams Azael
Strovel John	Van Wormer Henry	Williams John
Supphen Abraham	Van Wormer John	Williams Thomas
Surdam Samuel	Vele Tunas	Williams Thomas F.
Sweet Amos	Velie Cyprian	Williams Thomas P.
Sweet William	Viele Abraham	Williamson James
Teachout Jacob	Viele John	Willsen Ebenezer
Tensler James	Viele John T.	Wiltse Francis
Thompson Israel	Viele Lewis	Wiltse Martin
Tibbit George	Viele Lodervecus	Winchel
Tinseller John	Viele Peter	Winchel Jeremiah
Tinslar John	Viele Stephen	Winne Gerret
Toll Charles H.	Vinigar Adam	Wintworth Alpheus
Toll Jesse	Vissdue Eldert	Witerley William
Toll Simon	Voorhees Caret	Witherwax Johannes
Tusslar John	Vradenburgh Jacobes	Withtord Ciltip
Tyler Samuel	Vradenburgh John	Wittick Abraham
Van Allen Henry	Vroman Adam	Wood Nathaniel
Van Allen Manuel	Vrudenburgh Abr'm	Wool James
Van Antwerp Lewis	Wait Benjamin	Wright Alexander
Van Antwerp Simon	Wait John	Wuller Jonethen
Van Arnon Lewis	Wait William	Yates Abraham
Van Arnum Luke	Walderon Cornelius	Yates James
Van Buren Marthen	Walderon Gerit	Yeats Peter
Van Buskerk Peter	Walderum Garret	York Daniel
Vancark Peter	Waldo John, Sr.	Young David
Vandenbergh Philip	Waldo John, Jr.	Young John
Vandenbergh Winant C.	Wallis Elijah	Young Manuel
Van Der Cook Cournelius	Wallis Elisha	Younglove Samuel
Van Der Cook Michel	Wallis Nathaniel	
Vanderhof Jacob	Wallis Nehemiah	
Van Derhoof Gilbard	Wallis Timothy	

Albany County Militia--Fifteenth Regiment

Colonel Peter Vroman; Lieutenant Colonel Peter Ziele; Major Jost Becker; Major Thomas Ekesen, Jr.; Adjutant Lawrence Schoolcraft; Quarter Master Peter Vall; Quarter Master Jacob Winney

Capt. Storm Becker	Lieut. Jacob Borst	Lieut. Martin Vroman
Capt. Christian Brown	Lieut. John Dietz	Lieut. Martinus Ziele
Capt. William Deitz	Lieut. Cornelius Feeck	Ensign Isaac Becker
Capt. Alexander Harper	Lieut. Peter Heager	Ensign John L. Bellinger
Capt. Jacob Heger	Lieut. Johannes J. Lawyer	Ensign John Brown
Capt. Dirk Miller	Lieut. John Myers	Ensign John Enders
Capt. George Richtmyer	Leiut. Jacob Snyder	Ensign Jacob Lawyer
Capt. Christian Strubrach	Lieut. Peter Snyder	Ensign Peter Swart
Capt. Teunis Vroman	Lieut. Peter Snyder, Jr.	Ensign Peter Van Antwerp
Lieut. John Bauck	Lieut. John Thornton	Ensign Nicholas Warner
Lieut. Henry Borst	Lieut. Ephraim Vroman	

Enlisted Men

Acker George	Becker Johannis K.	Brown Adam
Ackerson Thomas	Becker John A.	Brown Adam, Jr.
Backer Albartus	Becker John Alb.	Brown John
Baker Johannis	Becker John Gert	Brown Migel
Ball Matthew	Becker John J.	Brown Joseph
Barnes Joseph	Becker Nicholas	Bruer Peter
Barnhart Philip	Becker Storm	Burst Peter
Bartholomew Tabald	Becker Storm A.	Burst Philip
Bauch Christian	Becker William	Burst Martines
Bauch Cornelius	Beik Martines	Cachey Hugh
Bauch David	Beiker John P.	Cadogan Barne
Bauch Henrich	Beker Abraham	Caghey Andrew
Bauch Jacob	Belinger Johannest	Caghey Andris
Bauch John	Bellinger Marcus	Caghey Hugh
Bauch Nicholas	Bellinger Marcus, Jr.	Cannady John
Bauch Peter	Bereamp Benjamin	Christian
Bauch Thomas	Berg Abraham	Coenrad Henry
Bauch William W.	Bergh Philip	Coenrad Henry, Jr.
Bauck Johannes	Bevam Benjamin	Coleman Thomas
Bauck Lawrence	Boon Richard	Cornelisen Cornelius
Bauck Nicholas W.	Borst Baltus	Cortney William
Bauck William	Borst Jacob	Cowley Jonathan
Beacker George	Borst Johannes	Cramer Charles
Becker Abraham	Borst John, Jr.	Criscoll Jacob
Becker Adam	Borst Joost	Daley Nathan
Becker Albartus	Borst Joseph J.	Dannea Lewis
Becker Bill	Borst Jost	Dietz Johan Jost
Becker Coenraed	Borst Migel	Dietz William
Becker David	Borst Peter	Dominick John
Becker Fredrick	Borst Philip	Ecker Jost
Becker Garrit	Borst Martines	Eckerson Cornelius
Becker George	Borst John	Eckerson John
Becker Harmanus	Brant Michel	Eckerson Teunis
Becker Hendrick	Brantner Anthony	Eckerson Tunis, Jr.
Becker Jacob	Braun William	Egars Julius
Becker Johannes	Brewer Peter	Enders Jacob

Enders Johannes
Enders Peter
Enders William
Evans Joseph
Fakes Piter
Falk Jacobus
Feeck Jacob
Feeck Nicholas
Feek Johanes
Ferguson John
Finck Peter
Finck William
Forster George
Forster Jacob
Frymer George
Frymer Johannes
Frymier David
Frymier John
Frymier Michael
Gerlock Nicholas
Granatier Jacob
Granatier John
Grans Michael
Hagar Handrick
Hagar Joseph
Hagedorn Adam
Hagedorn Bartholomew
Hagedorn Dirck
Hagedorn Samuel
Hager John
Hagetorn John
Hatzel George
Hauck Henrich
Heager Peter
Heger Adam
Henry William
Herron James
Herron James, Jr.
Herron Robert
Hills Christopher
Hills George
Hilsinger Jacob
Hilsinger John
Hilsinger Michael
Hitsinger Peter
Hilts Steffel, Jr.
Hiltsinger Michal
Hitzman Hendrick
Hoftrasser Jacob
Howell Vanson
Huiver Felix
Humphrey Benjamin
Humphrey John

Humphry James
Humphry John
Ingolt Johannes
Jansen Johannis
Jansen Joseph
Janson Hendrick
Jessey Juas
Kanidy John
Kayser Abraham
Kayser Johannes
King Leonard
Knieskern Jacob
Knieskern Johannes
Kniskern Hendrick P.
Kniskern Henry
Kniskern Peter
Kniskern Tunis
Koenig Johannis
Koenig Migel
Koenig Stoffel
Koening Leonard
Krieler Baltus
Kriselor John
Krisler John
Lamb William
Laucks Andreas
Lawyer Abraham
Lawyer David
Lawyer Jacob
Lawyer Johannes L.
Lawyer Lambert
Lawyer Lawrence
Lawyer Nicholas
Lawyer Peter
Leek William
Long Nicholas
Loucks Jeremiah
Low John
McCoy John
McCoy John, 1st.
McCoy, John 2d
McKay John, 1st.
McKay John, 2d.
McKee Samuel
McLout Alexander
Mahalean Hugh
Mann Jacob
Mann Peter, Jr.
Mann William
Marinas Jerremy
Mattice Abraham
Mattice Coenraed
Mattice Elias

Mattice Frederick
Mattice George
Mattice Henrich
Mattice John
Mattice John, Jr.
Mattice John H.
Mattice Joost
Mattice Nicholas
Mattice Nicholas F.
Merckel Jacob
Merckel John
Merckel Philip
Merckel Nicholas
Mercker Henrich
Merenis George
Morrow James
Muller Dirik
Munie Jacob
Murphy Timothy
Nitzley Gerret
Nott John
Otto Frantz
Otto Gottlieb
Pain John
Pasolee Gya
Patchin Isaac
Patterson Thomas
Perree Daniel
Price Daniel
Reinhardt George
Reinhardt Mattice
Reinhardt William
Resue John
Richter John
Richter Nicholas
Richtmeyer Christian
Richtmeyer Jacob
Richtmeyer Jonn George
Rickart George
Rickert Johannes
Rickert Marcus
Rickert Nicholas
Right John
Right Thomas
Ritter Andrene
Ritter Christian
Ritter John
Ronyon Samuel
Rorick Bearney
Rorigh Kasper
Roth Thomas
Salge Henrich
Schaefer Johannis T.

Schaefer Lamport
Schaefer Marckus, Jr.
Schafer Adam
Schafer Jacob
Schafer Johannes
Schafer John
Schefer Christian
Schefer Debald
Schefer Denes
Schefer Hendrick
Schefer John
Schefer Joost
Schefer Peter
Schefer Peter, Jr.
Schefer Marcus
Schefer Tenes, Jr.
Schell Christian
Schell Jacob F.
Schell Jost
Schneyder Lutwig
Scholman George
Schoolcraft Jacob
Schoolcraft William
Schulcrafft Peter
Schuyler John
Schuyler Simon
Shaver Henry
Shell Adam
Shelmidine Richard
Sidney Peter
Singer
Sitney William
Sitnich Jost
Sitnig Henrich
Slaughter Nicholas
Sluyder Nicholas
Snyder George
Snyder Henry
Snyder Jacob, Jr.
Snyder John

Snyder John, Jr.
Snyder Philip
Snyder William
Sternberg Jacob
Sternberger Abraham
Sternberger Lambert
Sternberger Lambert, Jr
Strubach Barend
Sternbergh David
Stynbrenner Benjamin
Sutherly Ankis
Swart Lawrence
Swart Thunes
Tenery Sever
Thornton Thomas
Tufts Zachariah
Turner James
Valck John
Valconburgh Joacum
Valkenburgh Adam
Valkenburgh Joost
Van Allen Philip
Van Antwarp John
Van Antwarp Peter
Van Bremer Thomas
Van Denbergh Daniel
Van Dyck Cornelius
Van Dyck Jacob
Van Dyck John
Van Gelten Antreas
Van Lone Jacobus
Van Sice Joseph
Van Sisen Joseph
Van Slyck Peter
Van Valkenburgh Har-
manus
Vroman Adam
Vroman Adam J.
Vroman Barent
Vroman Bartholomew

Vroman Isaac, Jr.
Vroman Johan
Vroman Jonas
Vroman Martinas
Vroman Peter
Vroman Peter A.
Vroman Peter C.
Vroman Peter J.
Vroman Simon
Vrooman Samuel
Waldaway Henry
Weaver Christian
Weaver Henry
Webber Christian
Wenn John
Werner Christopher
Werner George
Werner George, Jr.
Werner Joost
Werner Joost, Jr.
Werth Henrich
Werth Johannes
Wever Henry, Jr.
Wholebur John, Jr.
Wileber John
Williams Elias
Winn John
Young William
Zart John
Zeck Nicholas
Zeh David
Zeh Jost
Ziegraft Jacob
Ziellie Peter, Jr.
Zimer William
Zimmer Adam
Zimmer George
Zimmer Jacob
Zimmer Peter

Albany County Militia--Sixteenth Regiment

Colonel John Blair; Colonel Lewis Van Woert; Major James Ashton; Adjutant John McClong; Adjutant Joseph
Younglove; Quarter Master Joseph Younglove

Capt. William Brown
Capt. Cornelius Doty
Capt. George Gilmore
Capt. Elias Golden
Capt. Samuel Hodges
Capt. John McKillip

Capt. John Pattis
Capt. John Pettit
Capt. Joseph Wells
Capt. John Whiteside
Capt. William Woodworth
Lieut. James Bolton

Lieut. Admiral Burtch
Lieut. Samuel Clark
Lieut. Jonathan French
Lieut. Daniel Heath
Lieut. William Powell
Lieut. Nathan Smith

Lieut. Andrew Thomson
Lieut. Benjamin Tiffany
Lieut. Gerrit Van Nass
Lieut. Thomas Whiteside

Lieut. Gershom Woodworth
Lieut. Abraham Wright
Ensign Solomon King
Ensign Henry Loop

Ensign James Morrison
Ensign Isaac Perine
Ensign Archibald Robinson
Ensign Hugh Thompson

Additional names on state treasurer's pay books
Lieut. Joab Green; Ensign Richard Robinson

Enlisted Men

Allen Caleb
Allen David
Allen James
Allen John
Allen Stephen
Allis William
Almey John
Armstrong Nathan
Ashton Thomas
Astin Parvis
Aston Johen
Aurner Richard
Austin Davis
Austin John
Babcock Johen
Backer John
Backer Martin
Baker David
Baker Marlines
Baker Peter
Bane Benjamin
Barber James
Bartt Henry
Beach Thomas
Beavon Jacob
Beebe Nathaniel
Bell Martin
Belmore Stephen
Bennet Jonathan
Berry Bowlen
Berry Ephraim
Bills Elisha
Black James
Black Robert
Blaer Johen
Blair Robert
Blake James
Blower William
Blowers Charles
Blowers Samuel
Boice Benjamin
Boice Henry

Bolton Alexander
Botchen Peter
Bowman Robert
Boyce Millerd
Brace Robert
Bratt John
Brayton Joseph
Brayton Matthew
Brewer Elias
Briggs Josiah
Bright Johenson
Britman Johnson
Brower Elias
Brown David
Brown Samuel
Browning Blackmon
Bruar Hanrey
Buchanan Patrick
Buck Amos
Bump Aaron
Bump Moses
Bur Aaron
Burch Amas
Burch Beverley
Burch Ichabod
Burch Richard
Burch Thomes
Burt Henry, Jr.
Burtch Beverly
Burtch Jenelus
Buscek Marting
Bushark Martin
Buskark Dirick
Buskark John
Butten Peter
Buttey Zebulon
Caldwell Joseph
Canada Thomas
Canady James
Carey Seth
Chase Daniel
Chase Phinehas

Chase Samuel
Clarey Luke
Clark John
Clobright Christopher
Cole Barnabas
Collins John
Collins Julius
Colter James
Conner John
Cook Ichabud
Cooper John
Cooper William
Core Johen
Corey Jonathan
Cornel Joseph
Cotnel Heber
Cottell Eber
Coudin James
Coudin James S.
Coulter Alexander
Coulter James
Covell James
Covell Jonathan
Covell Joseph
Cowan Alexander
Cowan James
Cowan Robert
Cowan William
Crosman Daniel
Crowel Seth
Culver Bezaliel
Culver Nathan
Dack Charles
Dantum William
Datter Benjamin
Davis Squire
Deake Charles
Deake Charles, Jr.
Deming Samuel
Dennis Samuel
Dounlap John
Dunham Joseph

Dunlap William	Harman William	Lewis Robert
Dutcher Solomon	Harren Ellet	Lewis Ruben
Earll Daniel, Jr.	Harren Johen	Locke Nicholas
Earll Robert	Hart Daniel	Locke Nicholas, Jr.
Easterwood Abel	Hathaway John	Loop Martin
Edgar William	Hay William	Lucas David
Edie James	Heath Daniel	Lucas Nathaniel
Eldred James	Heath Daniel, Jr.	Luke Clary
Eldred Thomas	Heath Elijah	McAuley William
Eldridge James	Heath Joseph	McChenry John
Eldridge Thomas	Heath Samuel	McClaughry Richard
Ellis Daniel	Heath Simeon	McDonald Edward
Ellis William	Heath Stephen	McKie James
Esvet David	Heath Timothy	McKilip Thomas
Fisher Amos	Heath Windslow	McWaters James
Fisher William	Henry Joseph	Magee James
Foort Daniel	Herman Lemuel	Manley John
Forde Thomas	Hill Thomas	Mead Aron
Fort Johen	Hodge Solomon	Menter Robert
Fort Peter	Hodges Curtis	Meser John
Forth Daniel	Hodges Daniel	Millar James
Fowler George	Hodges Joshua	Millar Robert
Fowler Isaac	Hodges Samuel	Miller John
Fowler Johen	Hogel Cornelius	Mires John
Fowler Morrel	Hogel Peter	Moger Nicholas
French David	Hoges Carter	Morel Jonathan
Fuller John	Hoges Daniel	Morrel John
Gaffin Jemes	Hoges Ezekiel	Morrison James
Galaway Thomas	Hoges Isaac	Morrison John
Giffert Gedion	Holland John	Morrison Samuel
Gillmore George	Hond Thomas	Mosher Daniel
Gillmore James	Hosken Joseph	Mosher Hezekiah
Gilmore William	Houghtaling Jacob	Mosher Jabez
Golden Elias	Hunt Elven	Mosher Jabez, Jr.
Golden John	Hunt Thomas	Mosher Nicholas
Goldihe William	Hurly Elisha	Moshier David
Gould William Deak	Irvine James	Mushet William
Gray David	Irwin James	Nobles John
Gray Hugh	Jaquez Thoma	Norton David
Gray William	Johnson Edon	Norton Joneton
Green Bowen	Johnson William	Odel Jonas
Green John	Keittle Benjeman	Omsted Judson
Green Thomas	King Hezekiah	Onderlee Johen
Greene Job	King Israel	Oviatt Isaac
Grene Benjamin	Lake Abraham	Palmer Jeremiah
Grene Jeremiah	Lake Christopher	Paterson Robert
Groat Henry A.	Lake Henry	Paterson William
Groat Henry D.	Lake Henry, Jr.	Patterson Adam
Haeth Aleyh	Lake Nicholas	Pattson Adam
Hall Burges	Lake Nicholas, Jr.	Perry Aaron
Hall Thomas	Lampkin Thomas	Perry John
Hammond William	Lastwood Abel	Perry Rowlen
Hannan William	Lewie Christopher	Peters Andrew

Peters Joseph
Pettes Asa
Petteye Asa
Pettit Micajah
Phelps Timothy
Philips Francis
Pickla Clark
Porter Elijah
Potter Samuel
Pottice Assa
Powel William
Powers John
Preston David
Preston John
Preston Samuel
Preston William
Prince David
Prince Job
Quckanbus Tuenes
Rice David
Rickely Clark
Robertson Archibald
Robertson William
Robinson William
Rodgers Hugh
Rodgers James
Rolo James
Rolo Walter
Rose John
Ross John
Ross Walter
Rotch James
Roth Benjamin
Roughling James
Rutty Zebulon
Santesal Abraham
Schoolcraft Adam
Schoolcraft Christian
Schoolcraft Christopher
Schoten Johen
Schoulcraft Cobus
Scott John
Scott Steven
Scribner Abel
Scribner Samuel
Seeley David
Seeley Ebenezer
Seelye David
Sefridge Edward
Selfridge John
Selfridge Oliver
Serdam Tunels
Shaaff William

Shaf Henry
Shaf William
Shaff John
Shairman Batchelor
Shairman Shubael
Shan Joseph
Sharman Shubel
Sharp Andrew
Sharp Cornelius
Sharp Johen
Sharp Peter
Sharp Richard
Shauff John
Shaw Daniel
Shearman Back
Shearman Batchelor
Shepman Ezekiel
Sherman Johen
Sherman Lemuel
Shipman Daniel
Shipman Elisha
Shrman Henry
Skelly Alexander
Skelly Welyoum
Small James
Smit Benjamin
Smith Caleb
Smith Henry
Smith Roggerd
Spalden Ellijha
Sprague Gibson
Sprague Solomon
Steel Thomas
Stephens William
Stevens Matthew
Stewart James
Still Thomas
Stock Godfrey
Summers Robert
Sweet David
Symers Robert
Tallman Jonathan
Tallman William
Tanner Joseph
Taruble Judah
Telfer George
Terry Nathaniel
Thomas Robert
Thomson William
Toot Daniel
Trable Judah
Valintine Joseph
Valintine Stephen

Vallantine Alexander
Vanduse Abraham
Van Duzer Abraham
Van Duzer John
Van Sandam Anthony
Van Tassell Abraham
Van Tessel Cornelius
Vantessel Hanrey
Volentine John
Vollentine Joseph
Wadsworth Elisha
Waldo David
Waldo Jonathan
Waldo Joneton, Jr.
Wallis Benjamin
Ward Alihu
Ward Joneton
Warner James
Waters James M.
Webb Johen
Weir John
Weir Robert
Welch Henry
Weller Amos
Wells Austin
Wells Daniel
Wells Edmon, Jr.
Wells Henry
Wells Shelar
Wells Timothy
Welsh Morto
Weltch Murty
West Benjamin
Whaling James
Wheeler Jacob
Wheeler Samuel
Whiteside Detten
Whiteside Thomas
Whitsid Edward
Wier James
Wilcox David
Willar Amos
Wilson Nathan
Wilson Samuel
Wing Benjamin
Wing David
Woodard Joseph
Woodworth Caleb
Woodworth Gershom
Woodworth Josiah
Woolsworth William
Worden Nathaniel
Wright Caleb

Wright Samuel   Younglove David

Albany County Militia--Seventeenth Regiment

Colonel William B. Whiting; Quarter Master Andrew Hunter; Lieutenant Colonel Asa Waterman; Quarter Master John Waterman; Major Martin Beebe; Surgeon Patrick Hamilton; Adjutant Jonathan Warner.

Capt. Elijah Bostwick	Capt. Godeon King	Lieut. Thomas Hurlburt
Capt. Ebenezer Cady	Capt. Isaac Peabody	Lieut. Moses Jones
Capt. John Davis	Capt. John Salisbury	Lieut. Ezra Murray
Capt. Elisha Gilbert	Capt. Jacob Vosburgh	Lieut. Edward Wheeler
Capt. Daniel Herrick	Lieut. Samuel Bailey	
Capt. Aaron Kellogg	Lieut. William Hollenbach	

Additional Names on State Treasurer's Pay Books

Lieut. Peter Barker	Lieut. Reuben Rowley	Ensign Nathaniel Colver
Lieut. Ebenezer Benjamin	Lieut. Elijah Skinner	Ensign Samuel Darby
Lieut. John Calender	Lieut. Policarpus Smith	Ensign Asa Doty
Lieut. Asahel Gray	Lieut. Samuel Thompson	Ensign Benjamin Ford
Lieut. Nathan Herrick	Lieut. Josiah Warner	Ensign Jeremiah Hubbard
Lieut. Ezra Lee	Lieut. William Warner	Ensign Samuel Jones
Lieut. James Phelps	Ensign Benjamin Andrus	Ensign Samuel Russell
Lieut. Samuel Rexford	Ensign Elijah Cady	Ensign Henry Walter

Enlisted Men

Beebe Hosea	Hamlin Peras
Chapman Jonathan	Jackson Thophilas
Chapman Samuel	Orton Thomas
Foster William	Root David
Graves John	Volentine Stephen

Albany County Militia, Independent Company

Capt. Petrus Van Gaasbeck

Enlisted Men

Bartell Philip A.	Blass Michael	Decker Leonard
Berringer Petrus	Blass William	Dick Paul
Best Benjamin	Combs Samuel, Jr.	Finger Coenraedt
Best Johannis, Jr.	Decker Andries	Freer Simon
Best Jury, Jr.	Decker Benjamin	Ham Jacob
Best Peter	Decker Jacobus	Hendricks Bartell
Best Wilh's	Decker James	Hop Thomas
Blass Hendrick P	Decker James B're	Meyer Fredrick

Miller Jacob
Post Samuel
Post Wilhelmis
Power Jacob, Jr.
Power Nicholas, Jr.
Proper Fredrick, Jr.
Rosman Coenraedt I.

Shaver Peter
Shuts Ian
Shuts Johannis H.
Smith William H.
Snyder Lodewyck
Spikeman Frederick
Stael Hendrick, Jr.

Stael Johannis
Stiever John
Vader Samuel
VanDeWater August
Vonck Jacob
Wheeler William

The Continental Army

The Continental Army of the Revolution
From: Magazine of American History
Vol. VII December 1881, No. 6

It has been sometimes a subject of reproach that in the earlier belligerent movements of the war of the American Revolution, no troops from New York took part; that Ticonderoga and Crown Point were captured without her co-operation; that the British were besieged in Boston without her aid, and that even a year later her delegates in the Continental Congress were without instructions upon the final vote upon the Declaration of Independence. If, however, the people of this state were slow to resort to arms, it was not from any indifference, because no colony had been more intensely agitated by the great questions of the day. The political situation of New York was, however peculiar. This was due to the manner in which it had come under English domination.

By the laws of England two classes of colonies were recognized, viz.: 1st, Settled or Discovered colonies, and 2d, Conquered or Crown colonies. To the first class of Settled or Discovered colonies belonged all of the original thirteen United American Colonies except New York, which belonged to the latter class. The peculiar characteristic of these Settled or Discovered colonies was that when unoccupied land had been taken possession of in the name of the Crown of England, and afterwards colonized an settled upon by English subjects, the Common Law of England became their inheritance, and also all the rights and liberties as against the prerogative of the Crown, which they would have enjoyed in England; such as, no taxation without representation; freedom of speech, and later, of the press; the right of trial by an impartial jury of their peers from the vicinage, after indictment by a local grand jury, and other rights not necessary here to be enumerated. In addition to the character of Settled or Discovered colonies which the other twelve United American Colonies possessed, many of them—particularly in New England—had received special chartered right and privileges, confirmed under the Great Seal of England with considerable formality.

On the other hand, in a Conquered or Crown Colony, except so far as rights were secured by any terms of capitulation, the power of the sovereign was absolute. The conquered were at the mercy of the conqueror, and although they might preserve their laws and their institutions for the time, the Sovereign in Council had absolute power to alter those laws in any way he might deem proper, and in short, in the language of the late Lord Chief-Justice of England, they might "be dealt with legislatively and authoritatively as the Sovereign might please." Such was the condition of the Colony or Province of New York, and although the Charter of Liberties and Privileges, passed on the 30th October, 1683, secured to its people an appearance at least of a privilege to participate in the government nevertheless, after James II ascended the throne, Governor Dongan was instructed, on the 29th May, 1686 to declare the Bill of Privileges under which the Assembly existed "repealed, determined, and made void," and the sole power of legislation transferred to the Governor and Council.

William and Mary and Queen Anne successively resisted the application and demands of the representatives of the people of the province of New York; and until the final contest in the Revolution, a political struggle was maintained with greater or less intensity. The removal of Chief Justice Morris without cause in 1733, and the appointment of James DeLancey as Chief Justice; the trial and acquittal of John Peter Zenger in 1735, and assertion of the liberty of the press; the refusal of the New York Assembly in 1762 to grant any salary to Chief Justice Benjamin Prat, because he was commissioned "during His Majesty's pleasure'" the appointment by that body of a

Committee of Correspondence with the other colonies in 1764; the subsequent organization of the "Sons of Liberty," and local resistance to the Stamp Act; the conflict between citizens and soldiers in John Street, New York, in January, 1770 and the resolves of the New York Assembly in 1768, 1774 and 1775, were all incidents of this struggle for exclusive internal parliamentary liberty.

In the New England Colonies the Whigs rested firmly on their rights as Englishman in "Settled Colonies," and on their chartered privileges. Their political opponents, therefore, were comparatively few, and held opinions as to the rights of Crown and Parliament founded largely in sentiment and regard for the mother country.

In New York, the Whig party in demanding the same rights that were claimed by the Whigs of New England, were to a considerable extent revolutionary, although they were prompted by the same spirit that gave Magna Carta and the Petition and Bill of Rights to England. On the other hand, the Royalists or Tory party in New York had good English precedents for their adhesion to the Crown.

Each party in New York, therefore, had legal grounds for the support of its political claims. The line of demarcation was less distinct, political feelings became more embittered, and as a consequence, when overt acts of war took place, a large number of the able bodied citizens of the province of New York engaged in the contest on one side or the other. Family influence also contributed to the intensity of party feeling, as was shown in the struggles of the De Lancey's and Livingston's and their respective family and political adherents for political supremacy. The events which finally brought into existence the New York Provincial Congress, which met on the 22d May 1775, will not here be touched upon.

On the 28th June 1775, the New York Continental Line of the American Revolution was organized under the resolves of the Provincial Congress. It consisted of four regiments of infantry and one company of artillery, viz.: The 1st (or New York) Regiment of which Alexander McDougall became Colonel, Rudolphus Ritzema, Lieutenant-Colonel, and Herman Zedwitz, Major; the 2d (or Albany) Regiment of which Goose Van Schaick became Colonel, Peter Yates, Lieutenant-Colonel, and Peter Gansevoort, Jr., Major; the 3d (or Ulster) Regiment of which James Clinton became Colonel, Edward Fleming, Lieutenant-Colonel and Cornelius D. Wynkoop Major, the 4th (or Dutchess) Regiment of which James Holmes became Colonel, Philip Van Cortlandt, Lieutenant-Colonel and Barnabas Tuthill Major; lastly the Company of Artillery, of which John Lamb became Captain, which was raised in New York City.

Already the Continental Congress had appointed Philip Schuyler to be Major General and Richard Montgomery to be Brigadier-General, and the New York Continentals stepped forward to take their places in the military history of their country. Unfortunately the period for which these regiments were enlisted was short, and as a consequence, the services of the New York Continental Line prior to 1777 can be discovered only by patient inquiry. All four regiments, and also Lamb's Artillery Company served in the Canada campaign of 1775-6 under Montgomery and in the operations which resulted in the capture of the forts at St. Johns and Chamblee. In the middle of November, General Montgomery entered Montreal, and immediately began to reorganize his army for the winter campaign. The six months for which the New Yorkers had enlisted expired with that month, but, in the language recorded by one of their officers in his diary, "the Yorkers in general resolved to see an end to the campaign." Accordingly a large number of them re-enlisted to the 15th April 1776 and accompanied General Montgomery to Quebec. In the siege and during the assault of that place, where their commanding general fell, the New Yorkers bore a conspicuous part, and a number were killed, wounded and taken prisoners. Lamb's artillery company was almost destroyed, and he himself dangerously wounded and captured.

On the 15th April 1776 at headquarters before Quebec, Brigadier-General David Wooster, who had succeeded to the command of the besieging forces, arranged a number of the officers of the New York Line into a regiment of which John Nicholson, Major of the Third New York (James Clinton's) was made Colonel, and Frederick Von Weisenfels, of the same regiment, Lieut.-Colonel, and a sufficient number of the New York rank and file were re-enlisted to complete the regiment. The remainder, comprising the fragments of McDougall's, VanSchaick's, Clinton's and Holmes' regiments, returned home.

Congress had in the previous month provided for raising four New York regiments (8th and 24th March, 1776), viz.: 1st New York, Colonel Alexander McDougall and Lieut.-Colonel H. G. Zedwitz; 2d New York, Colonel James Clinton and Lieut.-Colonel H.B. Livingston; 3d New York, Colonel Rudolphus Ritzema and Lieut.-Colonel Frederick Von Weisenfels; 4th New York, Colonel Cornelius D. Wynkoop and Lieut.-Colonel P. Van Cortlandt.

The New York Convention also provided for raising a new Continental regiment for Colonel Van Schaick, making five New York continental regiments for 1776 in addition to the regiment formed at Quebec under Colonel John Nicholson, which completed its service with the Northern Army. Colonel Van Schaick's regiment, on the 20th June 1776 was stationed in detachments at various posts between Half-Moon and Crown Point, while Colonel Wynkoop's was at Ticonderoga. Their subsequent service was wholly under General Schuyler.

When it became apparent early in 1776 that New York City was to be the objective point of Sir William Howe's new operations, measures were taken to fortify and garrison it. Among the troops assigned to this duty were the 1st, 2d and 3d New York Regiments of McDougall, Clinton and Ritzema. On the 9th August 1776 McDougall and Clinton were promoted to be Brigadier-Generals.

In the Battle of Long Island (August 1776) the New York Continental Line was not engaged, nor in the action at Harlem Heights although present. The 2d New York (late Clinton's) was sent into Connecticut, to Saybrook on special service. The 1st and 3d New York were in the battle of White Plains, and were conspicuous for their valor. Indeed, the principal part of that action was borne by McDougall's brigade, to which they belonged, and by the Delaware regiment. Chatterton's Hill, where the brunt of the action was fought, has become a historic locality.

Referring in his memoirs to the conduct of these troops, the accomplished Brigadier-General Rufus Putnam, then Chief Engineer on the ground says: "The British in their advance were twice repulsed; at length, however their numbers were increased, so that they were able to turn our right flank. We lost many men, but from information afterwards received there was reason to believe they lost many more than we. The rail and stone fence, behind which our troops were posted, proved as fatal to the British as the rail fence and grass hung on it did at Charleston, the 17th of June 1775.

In this battle the 3d New York (Ritzema's) suffered the most. Its Colonel, however was not on the field, and Lieut.-Colonel Weisenfels led the regiment. In the retreat through the Jerseys the 1st and 3d New York formed part of General Lee's division which subsequently joined Washington and were in the surprise and capture of the Hessians at Trenton. They were in the brigade under Colonel Sargent, from the 11th December 1776. Immediately after this brilliant action these New York regiments were ordered home to reorganize "for the war," their terms of enlistment having expired.

At last Congress awakened to the fact that the war must be carried on with *regular* troops, and not be an undisciplined, expensive and not always reliable militia levy. Accordingly on the 16th September 1776, that body declared that the quota of New York on the Continental establishment should consist of four regiments of infantry.

One the 15th October, 1776, the New York Convention appointed committees to visit respectively the army in the Northern Department under Major-General Schuyler, and the main Continental army under General Washington in order to obtain from the General officers the characters of the New York officers then in Continental service. Lewis Graham was the chairman of the committee which at once visited the main army, and James Duane the chairman of the committee which went northward. At this time New York had a number of volunteer and militia regiments in actual service; and the committees extended their inquiries also to these in order to obtain recommendations. The principal among these volunteer and militia regiments were the 1st New York Volunteers, under Colonel John Lasher, of New York City, which was in the lines at the battle of Long Island. Also, Col. William Malcom's, Col. Samuel Drake's and Col. Cornelius Humfrey's, all of Brig.-General John Morin Scott's Brigade; also, Col. Isaac Nicholls', Col. Thomas Thomas', Col. James Swartwout's, Col. Levi Paulding's, and Col. Morris Graham's, of Brig.-General George Clinton's Brigade. General Washington himself, and also Generals Schuyler, George and James Clinton, McDougall, and John Morin Scott made carefully considered recommendations.

The full Committee of Arrangements of the New York Convention met in Fishkill on the 15th day of November 1776, and after hearing the reports of the respective sub-committees on their return from the main and northern armies, began to consider the characters and merits of all the persons recommended for commissions in the reorganized New York Continental Line. There were many meritorious officers whose services were deemed necessary to the state. Some of these who remained in Canada when the terms of service of their old regiments had expired, had obtained exceptionally high rank, which caused much difficulty and considerable heart-burn in arranging them and their former superiors in the new Line. The papers of the Committee in the Secretary of State's office, in Albany, show the difficulties it had to contend with and the care taken in making selections. Thoroughly patriotic and earnest in the American cause, they came to the conclusion that New York could contribute one more regiment of infantry than called for by Congress, and they accordingly so recommended and proceeded to act on that basis, which was approved.

On the 21st November 1776 the officers of the first four New York Continental regiments were announced, and soon afterwards, on the 14th December, those of the fifth regiment. Colonel Goose Van Schaick was assigned to the 1st regiment, Colonel Philip Van Cortlandt, who had succeeded Ritzema as Colonel, was assigned to the 2d regiment, Colonel Peter Gansevoort, Jr., late Lieut.-Colonel of Van Schaick's regiment, was promoted to the 3d regiment, Colonel Henry Beekman Livingston, late Lieut.-Colonel of James Clinton's was promoted to the 4th regiment, Colonel Lewis Dubois, lately appointed a Colonel by Congress, was assigned to the 5th regiment.

Thus at last, after nearly two years of war, the New York Continental Line was permanently formed and engaged in the service of the United States until peace and independence should be secured. The military history of these regiments can now be briefly chronicled: Of the 1st, Colonel Goose Van Schaick personally deserves a passing notice, because at the close of the Revolution, he was, by date of commission, the senior colonel in the Continental service. A native of Albany, where he was born in 1737 he became a lieutenant at the age of nineteen in the expedition against Crown Point; promoted to a captaincy in 1758, in the New York regiment under Lieut.-Col. Isaac Corse, he took part in the expeditions against Forts Frontenac and Niagara, and in 1759 was made Major in Colonel Johnson's New York regiment. In March 1762, he became Lieut. Colonel of the 1st New York Regiment, and in the battle of Ticonderoga was severely wounded in the face by a blow with the butt of a French musket. Shortly after his assignment to the 1st New York Continentals in November 1776 he was successful in recruiting his regiment, which was first stationed at Fort George and in the Spring of 1777 was ordered to Cherry Valley to protect the inhabitants against incursions by the Indians; and thence, in May to Saratoga companies being detached to Fort

Edward and Fort Ann, and to Fort Dayton on the German Flats. Here the 1st New York remained during the stirring events of the Burgoyne Invasion and then marched to join the main army under General Washington and passed the memorable winter of 1777-08 at Valley Forge. In General Orders of General Washington dated Army Headquarters, Valley Forge, 31st May 1778, the regiment was temporarily assigned to the place of the 8th Pennsylvania Continentals, in the Second Pennsylvania Brigade, in the division under Major General Mifflin, and pursued Sir Henry Clinton across the Jerseys, participating in the battle of Monmouth. Thence the main army marched to the Hudson River, crossed at King's Ferry, near Stony Point, and moved down to White Plains. There on the 22d July 1778 in General Orders, his Excellency General Washington, as his soldiers and Congress always officially termed him, formed the New York Continental brigade under Brigadier-General James Clinton, composed of the 1st New York (Van Schaick's) 2d New York (Van Cortlandt's), 4th new York (Henry B. Livingston's), 5th New York (Lewis Dubois'). Thenceforward, to the end of the war there was always a New York Continental Brigade, which as we shall see, by its perfect discipline, good conduct and gallantry in action, attracted the favorable notice of the continental officers from other states, and of the officers of the French Army.

In the fall of 1778 the 1st New York was sent to the Northern Department, and on the 1st December was stationed at Fort Schuyler, with detachments in Albany and at Saratoga (now Schuylerville). On the 18th April 1779, one battalion of the regiment and one battalion of the 3rd New York were sent under Colonel Van Schaick against the Onondaga settlements near Salina, which were destroyed, and the expedition, after six days absence, returned to Fort Schuyler. Here the regimental headquarters remained, with detachments at Schenectady, Albany and Saratoga, until the 1st January 1781, when the 3d Regiment (Gansevoort's) was incorporated with it, and the New York Continental line of infantry was reduced to two regiments, under Colonel VanSchaick and Van Cortlandt, for the remainder of the war, pursuant to the resolutions of Congress of the 3d and 21st October, 1780. The further history of the 1st New York is identical with that of the 2d New York, as they thenceforward served continuously together, and as the 1st January 1781, was the time when all the continental regiments of each ctate line were incorporated and consolidated, this date forms a good point at which to leave the 1st New York in order to narrate the previous history of the remaining four regiments of VanCortlandt, Gansevoort, Henry B. Livingston and Dubois.

The record of services of the 2d New York, under Colonel Philip VanCortlandt is to be found in considerable detail in the autobiography of that distinguished officer, in the New York Genealogical and Biographical Record for July 1874 (Vol. V. p. 123) and in The Magazine for American History for May 1878 (Vol. II p. 278). It will not be dwelt upon here. Briefly the 2d, after being recruited and organized "for the war," took post in May, 1777 at Peekskill in McDougall's Brigade in the command of Major-General Israel Putnam, and after outpost service in Westchester county, near the British lines, was withdrawn and marched to Fishkill, where it embarked in sloops for Albany in August 1777 and soon joining Major-General Gates, was ordered to march to the relief of Fort Stanwix (or Schuyler), but had occasion to go no further than Schenectady. The 2d New York was in the battles of Stillwater and Saratoga, and at Lieut.-General John Burgoyne's surrender, and then marched southward and joined General Washington at White Marsh. It served at Valley Forge, was in the battle of Monmouth, and in July marched to White Plains, and then went to the frontier in Ulster county until April, 1779, when it marched to Fort Penn, and thence through the wilderness to Wilkes-Barre, where it joined Major-General John Sullivan's historic expedition against the Five Nations, and was in the action at Newtown. After the close of this expedition, the regiment marched via Easton in Pennsylvania, Sussex, Warwick and Pompton to Morristown, New Jersey, where it was quartered in tents during the remarkably severe winter of 1779-80, and did not get into log huts until the snow was deep on the ground. In the spring the regiment marched to Fort Edward, in the Northern Department and thence in November 1780 to Schenectady via Albany, where the rank and file were quartered in the barracks, and the officers billeted in private houses. This was the station of the regiment on the 1st January, 1781, when the 4th New York (late H. B. Livingston's, but then under Lieutenant-Colonel Commandant Baron Frederick Van Weisenfels) and the 5th New York (late Lewis Dubois', under Lieutenant-Colonel Commandant Marinus Willett), were incorporated with it, and the junior supernumerary officers honorably retired with the promise of seven years' half-pay.

The 3d New York (Colonel Peter Gansevoort, Jr.) after its organization and recruitment was stationed at Fort Schuyler (old Fort Stanwix) in 1777 and defended that work during the memorable siege by Brigadier-General Barry St. Leger, in which the successful sortie was made for which the thanks of Congress was given (Res. 4, Oct., 1777). A detachment was on duty at Albany from December 1778 to May 1779 and in June the whole regiment assembled at Canajoharie and formed part of Brigadier-General James Clinton's brigade, which joined Major-General Sullivan in the expedition against the five hostile tribes of the Six Nations. Colonel Gansevoort's regiment afterwards joined the main army at Morristown, New Jersey, where it remained during the winter of 1779-80, and was, in the earlier operations of the year 1780, under General Washington, after which it took post in the Highlands of the Hudson in July 1780 and subsequently proceeded to Fort Edward, where the regiment was incorporated with the 1st on the 1st January 1781.

The 4th New York (Col. Henry B. Livingston) had the most eventful history of any of the New York regiments. Just after its organization, it was in the defense of Peekskill, 23 March 1777; then in August with the 2d New York, joined Major-General Gates, participated in the battles of Stillwater and Saratoga, and was at Burgoyne's surrender. It then marched to the South, and was at White Marsh under General Washington on the 2d December 1777 and during that terrible winter in huts at Valley Forge. On the 14th May 1778 as the regiment was sickly, General Washington ordered its commanding officer to apply for tents and "remove the men from their huts." Taking part in the battle of Monmouth, it did good service. It was sent after the army reached White Plains, under the Marquis de Lafayette to Rhode Island, where it was present at the siege of Newport and subsequent battle of Rhode Island which Lafayette characterized as one of the best fought actions of the Revolution. Returning in the fall of 1778 to the Hudson, it marched to Albany and rejoined Brigadier-General James Clinton and was in the movement via Otsego Lake, down the Susquehanna to join Major-General Sullivan, and was in the expedition against the Five Nations and at the action at Newtown. Subsequently the regiment rejoined the main army in the winter camp at Morristown, 1779-80; was in the Highlands of the Hudson in the following summer, and then proceeded to Fort Schuyler, where it was incorporated with the 2d New York (Van Cortlandt) on the 1st January 1781.

The 5th New York Continental Infantry (Colonel Lewis Dubois) was an unfortunate though gallant regiment. After its organization and recruitment in the winter and spring of 1778-9 it was stationed at Forts Montgomery and Clinton on Poploopen's Kill opposite Anthony's Nose on the Hudson. Here it participated in the gallant defense of those forts under Governor George Clinton and his brother, Brigadier-General James Clinton on the 6th October 1777 and lost heavily. In the final successful assault of the British forces under Sir Henry Clinton at sundown, a considerable portion of the regiment became prisoners of war, including the Lieutenant-Colonel, Major, Quartermaster, one Captain, seven Lieutenants and three Ensigns. A battalion of the regiment managed to escape in the darkness of the night, and was on duty during the winter in the Highlands and at Newburgh and Peekskill, until the fall of 1778, when it proceeded to Albany and Schenectady, and formed part of Brigadier-General James Clinton's brigade, which joined General Sullivan in his Indian expedition. At its conclusion the regiment marched to Morristown, New Jersey, for the winter of 1779-80. It's subsequent history is identical with that of the 2d New York, until its incorporation with it on the 1st January 1781, in the Mohawk valley. From this date the history of the 1st New York (VanSchaick) and 2d New York (Van Cortlandt), constituting the newly arranged New York Line, is one and the same.

In June 1781, while French and American Armies were in Westchester County making threatening demonstrations against New York City, General Washington sent orders for these two regiments to join him. Accordingly the detachments at Fort Plain, Stone Arabia, Johnstown, Schoharie, Fort Herkimer, Fort Dayton, etc., were called in and assembled at Schenectady and Albany and the two regiments in a few days proceeded to Stoney Point via the Hudson River, where they encamped during those movements of the allied armies before New York which deceived Sir Henry Clinton as to their real objective point. Each regiment had a light infantry company of selected men. These two companies were detached on the 31st July and with two companies of New York Levies, formed into a battalion under Lieutenant-Colonel Alexander Hamilton, late an Aid-de-camp to Washington.

On the morning of the 19th August 1781 the American and French Armies paraded at Philipsbourg, and pioneers were sent forward to clear the road to Kingsbridge; but to the surprise of the troops, they themselves were faced about and marched rapidly to King's Ferry, and as soon as possible crossed to Haverstraw. Soon the truth broke upon the minds of the Allies. Their great commander had outwitted Sir Henry Clinton, and they were marching south to attack Earl Cornwallis.

In this historic march General Washington in General Orders dated Springfield, New Jersey, 28th August 1781 organized a light division under Major-General Benjamin Lincoln, which contained the choicest American regiments in the expedition. This division consisted of the light infantry on the right under the accomplished Colonel Alexander Scammel of the 1st New Hampshire Continentals, who lost his life before Yorktown; the two New York Regiments on the left under Brigadier-General James Clinton, and the two New Jersey regiments and the Rhode Island Continental Regiment in the center. As to the siege of Yorktown and the gallant conduct of the New York Light Infantry under Alexander Hamilton, in the assault of the advanced redoubt in front of the American right, on the night of the 14th October, or of the conduct of Colonel Lamb's Artillery Regiment, it is not necessary therefore than to refer. On returning north, the New York and New Jersey Regiments escorted 1,700 British troops as far as Fredericksburgh, Virginia.

Brevet Brigadier-General Van Cortlandt in his autobiography has given an interesting instance of the depreciation of the continental currency in which his regiment was paid, by noting that at Hanover Court House he was given his choice of paying, for a bowl of apple toddy, five hundred dollars in continental money or one dollar in silver. Marching through Alexandria, Georgetown, Bladensburgh, Baltimore, Philadelphia and Trenton, the New York Infantry went into camp for the winter at Pompton, New Jersey, and built themselves huts. Here General Washington and his wife visited them and remained from Saturday evening until Monday morning. The condition of the New York Infantry at this time is well illustrated in the General Orders of General Washington from Army Headquarters, Newburgh, 20th May 1782 in which referring to the last inspection made of the army, he said: The Commander-in-Chief "cannot, however, conceal this pleasure he receives from finding the two regiments of New York in the best order possible, by the report of the Inspector-General, which also concurred with his own observations."

On the 4th June 1782, the New York Regiments were again inspected by Inspector-General Baron de Steuben, and reported as being "in excellent order." This report General Washington announced in General Orders to the army from his Headquarters, Newburgh, on the following day.

On the 28th August he placed these regiments as a brigade in the division of Major-General Horatio Gates of the main army.

But little more remains to be said of the New York Infantry. In the autumn maneuvers at Verplanck's Point, they attracted particular attention by their steadiness and discipline. Indeed, at this time the American Infantry, veterans in war, had acquired under Baron de Steuben's remarkable training, a degree of military proficiency which made them the equal if not the superior of the best disciplined regiment of Europe. In the winter of 1783, under a previous resolution of Congress (7th August 1782) a further reduction and incorporation of Continental regiments was decreed. From this the New York Line was spared, as the quota of New York was kept complete by the exertions of Governor George Clinton. In January the two regiments marched to their last post in the vicinity of New Windsor and built huts on the road leading to Little Britain. In May 1783 the Society of the Cincinnati was formed at the cantonment, and on the 6th June the New York officers became members.

As the terms of re-enlistment of their rank and file were "for the war," the two regiments were furloughed on the 8th June 1783; the men proceeded to their homes, and on the 3d November 1783 were finally honorably discharged the service. Colonels Van Schaick and Van Cortlandt were each brevetted Brigadier-Generals on the 30th September 1783. The musical instruments of the Band of the 2d New York, and the colors of the two regiments, were taken to Poughkeepsie and there presented to Governor Clinton by Colonel Van Cortlandt, and it would be interesting to trace the history of these honored flags. In this connection it is deserving inquiry as to what has become of the flags captured during the Revolutionary War. None are known to exist, either of those taken at the Hessian surrender at Trenton, or at Burgoyne's surrender at Fort Hardy, while of the twenty-eight flags taken at Yorktown, but six are deposited in the chapel of the United States Military Academy at West Point.

I shall not enter into any statement as to the earlier uniforms of the New York Infantry, my paper on the Uniforms of the American Army, published fully covers this subject; it is enough to state that in October 1779 General Washington under the authority given him by Congress, prescribed for the new York Line the following uniform, viz.: Black cocked hats, edged with white binding, black cockade or rosette, and black plume; coats to be of dark blue faced with buff; but in August 1782, the facing was changed to red, buttons and lining to white, white worsted shoulder knots, white cross belts, white under dress and black half gaiters.

I have now chronicled the services of the New York Continental Line proper. It is not, however, to be understood that New York furnished no other forces to the American cause. On the contrary, for reasons already stated, political feelings were so intense that at one time or another very nearly every able-bodied man in this state took up arms on one side or the other.

On the 23d December 1776 Congress alarmed by the retreat through the Jerseys and dwindling away of the army, vested General Washington with quasi dictatorial powers, and authorized him to raise, on Continental establishment, sixteen "additional" regiments of infantry, three regiments of artillery, and four regiments of cavalry. These were separate and distinct from regiments called for from the states. General Washington appointed the officers, whereupon Congress commissioned them, and the men were recruited irrespective of state lines. Accordingly a large number of men were enlisted in New York State, not only in these regiments, but in the two Canadian Regiments raised in like manner. Quite a number also enlisted in New England Regiments, in consequence of the large bounties offered. The following named regiments were largely recruited in New York, viz.: 1st Canadian Continental Infantry, Colonel James Livingston; 2d Canadian Continental Infantry, Colonel Moses Hazen; additional Continental Infantry (Vermont), Colonel Seth Warner; additional Continental Infantry (Connecticut and Rhode Island), Colonel S. B.

Webb; additional Continental Infantry (New York and New Jersey), Colonel Oliver Spencer; 2d Regiment Corps of Artillery (New York Artillery), Colonel John Lamb; 3d Regiment Corps of Artillery, Colonel John Crane; 2d Regiment Continental Cavalry, Colonel Elisha Sheldon; 4th Regiment Continental Cavalry, Colonel Stephen Moylan; 2d Battalion Continental Partizan Legion, Lieutenant-Colonel Henry Lee.

After a time the New Yorkers in these regiments were duly credited to the state and acknowledged by it. The 2d Regiment of the Continental Corps of Artillery, under Colonel John Lamb, was particularly a New York regiment, nearly all of its companies having been raised in that state, and after 1782 it was frequently called the "New York Artillery Regiment," because it was placed on New York's quota, although originally raised by General Washington himself. The history of this regiment is interesting, but can only be briefly alluded to here. We have seen that in June 1775 New York raised an Artillery Company under Captain John Lamb which went to Canada and did gallant service in the siege of and assault on Quebec under Montgomery. Leaving New York City in August 1775 with 70 enlisted men, this company by actual field casualties was reduced by the return made in the lines before Quebec on the 30th March 1776 to 31 rank and file under Captain-Lieutenant John Wool. Upon the expiration of their enlistments, this company disappeared as a living unit of organization. Several of its officers, however were promoted and appointed subsequently in Colonel Lamb's Regiment the 2d Artillery and one, a Lieutenant in the company now to be noticed. The senior company in this regiment was organized quite a year before the regiment itself was authorized, pursuant to a resolution passed by the New York Provincial Convention in New York City on Sunday the 6th January 1776 for the defense of the Colony and to guard its records. The sabaltern (meaning junior officers) officers were speedily appointed. Alexander McDougall, then Colonel of the 1st New York Infantry, recommended Alexander Hamilton, then a student in Kings College for the Captaincy. After an examination by a board of officers, he was accordingly commissioned Captain of the "New York Provincial Company of Artillery" on the 14th March 1776. Already a few men had been enlisted for one year, but Hamilton, with that political sagacity for which he became distinguished saw that what was then in progress was to be a long and arduous one, and he accordingly directed his subalterns to recruit for the war. These instructions were not fully complied with, although over a third of the 95 rank and file recruited under authority of the New York Convention were thus enlisted. This fact is more remarkable as the continental forces for this year were raised on short enlistments, which generally expired in December, at the most critical period of the contest. During the retreat through the Jerseys General Washington was left with but the skeleton of an army, which remained in service at his urgent solicitation for a few additional days, until their places could be supplied by militia and troops newly raised. Hamilton's Company after the arrival of the American army in New York City from the siege of Boston was, while in the city, temporarily attached to Colonel Henry Knox's Regiment of Massachusetts Continental Artillery, which however, had been raised for one year only. During the battle of Long Island the company was sent across the East river and did good service. Present during the action at Harlem Heights, it subsequently specially distinguished itself in the Battle of White Plains, where it was attached to General McDougall's Brigade. In the retreat through the Jerseys it marched with the rear guard, and at New Brunswick engaged in a sharp artillery duel across the Raritan River with a company of the royal artillery which was in the van of Cornwallis' pursuit. At Trenton, Assunpink Bridge and Princeton, the company did such good service, and displayed such discipline and steadiness under fire as to attract the particular attention of Washington to its youthful commander, who was then only in his 20th year. After the army went into winter quarters at Morristown, the great chief offered Captain Hamilton the commission of Lieutenant-Colonel and Aid-de-camp on his staff. This flattering offer was accepted on the 1st

March 1777. Meanwhile after independence had been declared, the style of the company had been changed to that of "The New York State Company of Artillery." On the 6th March 1777, Lieutenant-Colonel Hamilton from Morristown wrote to the New York State Convention informing it of the condition of his late company and asking that it might be permanently transferred to the service of the United States. On the 17th March 1777, the Committee of the New York Provincial Convention from Kingston replied and authorized the transfer and it still remains in that service.

General Washington immediately promoted Captain-Lieutenant John Doughty of a New Jersey Artillery Company, who was a graduate of Kings (Columbia) College, to its command to date 1st March 1777 and assigned it to the new 2d Regiment of Artillery (Colonel John Lamb). Captain Doughty distinguished himself in service, was brevetted Major the 30th September 1783, and when all the rest of the Continental army of the Revolution was mustered out, was specially retained in service with his company. Later when Congress on the 20th October 1786 found it necessary to raise enough artillery companies on the peace establishment for a battalion, Captain and Brevet-Major Doughty was promoted to be Major of the battalion, and the old 1st Lieutenant of the company, James Bradford was promoted to its Captaincy. In the disastrous defeat of St. Clair on the 4th November 1791 the old Alexander Hamilton-Doughty Company suffered severely and its Captain, Bradford, was killed. In the following spring, at Fort Washington, now Cincinnati, Ohio, this company and another company of the battalion, which had been raised in 1784 and was then on duty with it, were incorporated. Each had about 35 men as each had suffered heavily in St. Clair's defeat. There were enough officers and non-commissioned officers left in each to raise the joint company to the full compliment. Twice afterwards, before 1822, the company met with like recruitment by incorporation. The living unit of organization however, remained. Its daily roll calls and drum beats or bugle calls continued, and from the day when Captain Alexander Hamilton first paraded his company in the present City Hall Park in New York City to the present time, the United States has had the services of a continuous and organized body of artillery soldiers in the unit of artillery organization, now known as Battery F, 4th Regiment, United States Artillery, which has under late orders for artillery changes, recently changed station from Washington Territory to Fort Warren, Boston Harbor, Mass. On its battery Guidon may property be inscribed: New York, 12th July 1776 (affair with the British ships of war): Long Island; Harlem Heights; Pelham Manor 18th October 1776; White Plains; New Brunswick; Trenton; Assunpink; Princeton; Brandywine; Germantown; Monmouth; Springfield; Yorktown; Wayne's victory over the Miami Indians in 1794; Battle of New Orleans under Andrew Jackson 1815; and all the principal actions under Major-General Winfield Scott in 1847, namely, the siege of Vera Cruz, Cerro Gordo, Contreras, Chapultepec and City of Mexico. In the late war of the rebellion it likewise "served in many actions" namely: Winchester, Va. 25th May 1862; Cedar Mountain, Va., 9th August 1862; Antietam, Md 17th September 1862; Chancellorsville, Va., 2d to 4th May 1863; Gettysburg, Pa. 1st to 3d July 1863.

One other artillery company was raised by the New York Provincial Congress on the 16th March 1776 in New York City under Captain Sebastian Bauman, for actual continental service. It also was assigned to Colonel Lamb's regiment of artillery when that regiment was raised on the 1st January 1777 and disappeared with the honorable discharge on the 20th June 1784 of all of that regiment, except the Alexander Hamilton company of artillery.

This is in brief, the record of the New York Line. The names of its general officers, Schuyler, McDougall, Montgomery, George Clinton and James Clinton, occupy a prominent place in the history of the War of the Revolution. Our country owes its independence principally to the military exertions of the New England states and of New York, New Jersey and Maryland with the assistance of foreign powers. The efforts of Pennsylvania although respectable, were not as great, after the revolt of her Continental Line, as her resources warranted. Delaware exerted herself to raise one regiment, but after a portion of it was captured at the siege of Charleston, S.C., in 1780, she could not keep in the field more than about two companies. The amount of military service rendered to the cause after 1778, by the great states of Virginia, North and South Carolina and Georgia was in no comparison whatever to their respective abilities.

By the resolution of Congress of 26th February 1778 Virginia was required to have fifteen regiments and North Carolina nine, but in May 1778 (29th) Congress provided for the supernumerary officers of the North Carolina line to go home to recruit. Only three infantry regiments remained of this latter state's line under General Washington and when they were sent southward and captured at Charleston in May 1780, her efforts, except with one small regiment and hastily levied militia, practically ceased.

In Virginia, the fifteen regiments called for by Congress in May 1778 were consolidated into eleven in September of that year. In the following year the quota of this state was reduced by Congress to this number, and three small regiments were sent to Charleston and captured there. In the fall of 1779 the enlistments of most of the Virginia Line expired and the state never had more than enough men for two respectable regiments of Continental infantry in service, although its quota was eight. When, therefore, Major General Gates needed the services of "regulars," Virginia and North Carolina could give him only militia hastily levied, as supports to the two gallant Maryland Continental brigades. History tells us that in the battle of Camden, which prostrated the power of the United States in the South, the Virginia and North Carolina militia at the first advance of the British, threw down their loaded arms and fled in the utmost consternation from an advantageous position. They subsequently measurably redeemed their character for steadiness under fire at Guilford Court House and Eutaw Spring. New York on the other hand, never failed to respond when called upon, and in addition to her excellent and reliable Continental Line, turned out at one time or another, all her able-bodied militia.

In looking at the composition of the British forces in America in 1782, more than twenty-five American loyalist volunteer regiments or battalions are found enrolled. Of these, the 1st American Regiment or Queen's Rangers, under Lieut. Colonel Simcoe; 2d American Regiment or Volunteers of Ireland, under Lord Rawdon; 3d American Regiment or New York Volunteers under Lieut. Colonel Turnbull; the Prince of Wales American Regiment, under Colonel Mountfort Brown; the Loyal American Regiment under Colonel Beverly Robinson and Brigadier-General Oliver DeLancey's brigade of three regiments, were all, presumably largely recruited in New York City and its vicinity. This fact show the intense earnestness with which the people of New York entered into the war, when once that course was decided upon.

In 1780 Congress reduced the quota of New York, as has already been said, to two regiments of infantry as her fair proportion to the general defense, but directly afterwards Governor Clinton offered to raise two regiment of levies. Congress accepted and on the 28th April 1781, Lieut. Colonel Commandant Marinus Willett and Lieut. Colonel Commandant Frederick Weisenfels who had been previously honorably discharged as supernumeraries, were appointed to the command of these regiments. The two remained in service in addition to the regular New York Continental line until the 25th December 1783 and did excellent service on the frontiers and two companies as light infantry at Yorktown.

When peace came Virginia made haste to get rid of her Continental officers and soldiers by granting them their promised land bounties in Kentucky or in the territory northwest of the Ohio and Virginia thenceforth gradually lost her position among the states of the union in regard to population and growth. Governor Clinton and the authorities of New York with a wisdom beyond praise, retained her honored soldiers within the state, by granting military lands in the territory wrested from the Six Nations and in the tract ceded for a like purpose within her limits without loss of jurisdiction, to Massachusetts, many continental soldiers of that state received land bounties and settled. Possibly nothing aided so much to the development of New York as this action, and it was not long before the state indeed became fully entitled to the name which Washington had bestowed on it, of *the Empire State.*

The Public Papers of George Clinton
(Selections)

Excerpts from <u>Public Papers of George Clinton</u>, published by the State of New York 1899 are valuable for a behind the scenes look at the Revolutionary War.

For a view of the militia, please refer to <u>A Time of Terror</u> page 251. This is a continuation of the subject covered in that article.

Page 112, Volume I

"During the war of the Revolution, however, the pay of United States forces was much more attractive than that allowed State troops, and, in consequence, great difficulty was found in maintaining state quotas, because men preferred to join the National organizations rather than continue their enlistment with the State forces.

In view of all that has come down to us, it is difficult which to admire most, the audacity or courage of the men who undertook this experiment. The problem of breaking away from so powerful a country as England was serious enough in itself, but that seems infinitesimal in importance in comparison with those larger questions, the conduct of the war and the construction of a government should the experiment succeed.

History affords no parallel to the absolute helplessness of the Colonies when the final separation came. Of an army, of a Navy, of leaders to command and funds to maintain armies and navies, of an exchequer, of a system of revenue to secure funds to prosecute the war, the country at large and the States were equally deficient. The civil leaders who suddenly found themselves as arch rebels and nation builders had had no more experience than could be picked up on the hustings or in the local assemblies of the Colonies; the men who came to the front to command troops were alike lacking in military training and military ability, save that here and there was one who had served in the war with France fifteen years before—notably George Washington. A number of them had served in what the late Gen. Gordon Granger would have stigmatized as "rag-tag bob-tail disappearing militia" and had exchanged shots on the frontier, but with the few exceptions noted, none had seen service with large bodies of troops or understood the simplest principles of war.

If this element of weakness prevailed in the line, how much more conspicuous was it in the staff upon which an army relies for food, for comforts, for equipment, for ammunition, for pay, for transportation and for medical supplies.

For a long time the organization of the army was in a pitiable condition. Staff officers were willing and earnest, but willingness could not furnish ability or earnestness supplies. The success of American arms has been due as much to the intelligence as to the bravery of the ranks. Under the vicious contract system he was made to suffer as keenly and as brutally as his descendant in subsequent wars. He knew that many of his superiors were incompetent and that a number were dishonest. He saw supplies and provisions that were to come to him embezzled by officers of high rank. Washington calls attention to the suspicions that furloughs were bestowed upon convalescents who were sent to work upon the farms of the general officer who granted them."

Page 120, Volume I

"One fourth part of the Militia in every county was to consist of minute men, who were ordered "to be ready on the shortest Notice to march to any Place where their Assistance may be required for the Defence of their own or a neighboring Colony." As the minute men were expected to be called into action before the body of the militia were sufficiently trained, it was recommended "that a more particular and diligent attention be paid to their instruction in military discipline."

The grave if not perilous condition of the American Army and the American cause can be best illustrated by extracts from the letter of prominent general officers:

"I have neither boats sufficient," writes Schuyler to Congress, July 21, 1775 from Ticonderoga, "Nor any materials prepared for building them. The stores I ordered from New York are not yet arrived. I have therefore not a nail, no pitch, no oakum and want a variety of articles indispensably necessary which I estimated and delivered to the New York Congress on the 3d. An almost equal scarcity of ammunition exists, no powder having yet come to hand. Not a gun carriage for the few proper guns we have and as yet very little provision. There are now two hundred troops less than by my last return. These are badly, very badly armed, indeed; and one poor armorer to repair their guns."

Public Papers of George Clinton, ed. Hugh Hastings, NY 1900,Vol. IV pp 674-675.

A List of the Inhabitants of Cherry Valley the number in family and number in Each family that is not able to Support them Selves viz.

Taken by James Scott & James Rickey Mar. 27th 1779.

	Number in Family	Not able to Support them Selves
Jeramiah Bakon	8	4
Nathaniel Hamel	4	1
Will'm Dickson	9	3
William Galt	9	7
James Scott	6	5
James Willson	8	6
Will'm Thompson	13	9
Widdow Rebeckah Thompson	6	3
Will'm McConnal	3	2
James Moor 4 prisoners	7	3
Col. Sam. Campbell 6 prisn's		1
Rev'd Wm Johnston	9	4
James Campbell	8	6
Thomas Ramsey	2	1
Will'm McClelon 3 prisoners	6	4
Jonathan Ogdon	8	3
James Mars	4	2
John McCollom	1	1
Alex'r McCollom	10	6
Daniel McCollom	7	4
Wm Hall	1	1
Widow Willson	1	1
Col. Sam Clyde	10	5
Widow Henderson	2	1
Rev'd Sam. Dunlope	2	1

Vol IV pp 721-723

Return of the Distressed Inhabitants who have suffed By the Enemy the Last Summar in Conejohere Destrect, in the County of Tryon, and State of New York.

Chirry Valley

Heads of Families	Number in Each family
Rev'nd Saml. Dunlap	2
Saml. Campbell, Coll.	2
Saml. Clyde	11
Nathanel Hamel	4
Jarimiah Backen	8
Asariah Holobord	1
William Dixon	9
William Galt	9
James Scott	6
James Willson	8
Samuel Ferguson	1
Saml. Warfield	3
Jane McClellan	6
John Campbell, Jun'r	9
James Ramsey	3
Thomas Ramsey	2
James Campbell	9
John Campbell, Sen'r	6
Daniel Ogden	7
Rev'd William Johnston	10
James Moor	3
James McCollom	3
William McConnal	3
William Thompson	12
John Foster	6
Abegill Winston	4
Alex'dr McCollom	8
Hugh Mitchal	3
John Thompson	6
	Total 164

Saml. Clyde, Lt. Coll.
Canejohery, Aprl. Ye 13th 1779.

The above Menchonad Persons heve Lost all there houses, Barns, Green Cattel, Cloos, and mony Except John Campbell, Jun'r., who got all his Stock Seved.

Regurn of Springfield, that was Destroyed By the Enemy Last Summer, in Conejohere Destrict, Tryon County Aprl. Ye 13 1779.

Heads of Fameles	Numb'r in Eich family
George Canouts	8
Isaec Coller	5
William Stansel	9

George Mayer	5
Conrad Picket	10
Henrey Bratt	7
Devett Teygert	4
Adolph Wallrat	4
Isaec Quack	4
John Spallsbere	6
Josiah Heeth	5
Henery Deygert	5
George Bush	4
The widow Davis	4
	Total 80

Return of Woonded Men in Canejohery Destrict that is not abel to help Sellves.

Capt'n James Scott, Jacob Right, Beral Sparkes, John Picket.

The above Menchoned Inhabitants of Springfield Lost all there Personal Property, Except there Clothing; there Buldings was all Burnt, and there Cattel almos Drove of, and there Green and hay, they were not able to Cutt.

Page 210, Volume I

Estimated Population of the Several Colonies.

New Hampshire 100,000
Massachusetts Bay 350,000
Rhode Island 58,000
Connecticut 200,000
New York 200,000
New Jersey 130,000
Pennsylvania 300,000
Delaware 30.000
Maryland 250,000
Virginia 400,000
North Carolina 200,000
South Carolina 200,000
Total 2,418,000

Page 76, Volume VI

List of Prisoners taken in Tryon County

An exact List of the Persons which were taken by the Indians near Fort Plank the 2nd day of August 1780.

Jacob Lamber, 11 yrs, John Frances Lambert age 7yrs 6 mo. Both children of Peter Lambert
Jno. Sever, 8yrs, child of Jno. Sever
Jacob Keller 10 yrs, Son of Solomon Keller
Eve Miller 25 yrs, wife of Theonesius Miller
Catharina Miller 2 yrs, Child of Eve and Theonesius Miller
Mary Shnyder 14 yrs, Rachael Shnyder 9 yrs, daughters of Jacob Shnyder

Christina House 16 yrs, Elizabeth House 11 yrs, belonging to the Widow of Henry House

Elizabeth House 21 yrs, Christina House 4, Jacobus House 9 mo., wife and children of Hanyose House

Eve Meyer 5 yrs, child of Joseph Meyer

Eliz'th Rush Sleyfer 23 yrs, wife of Paulus Rush Sleyfer

Rebacca Schrieber 25 yrs, Eliz'th Schrieber 7 yrs, Ab'm Schrieber 4 yrs, Maria Schrieber 1 yr, wife and children of Stephen Schrieber

Barbara Schneck 37 years, Marg't Schneck 13 yrs, Christina Schnieck 9 mo., wife and child'n of Geo. Schneick

Jacob Eccler 7 yrs. Son of Hen'y Eccler, Jun'r

Mary Lepper 24 yrs, Fred'k Lepper 1 yr., wife and child of Fred'k Lepper

Adam Haverman 10 yrs, son of Jacob Haverman

Cathrina Woolendorf 20 yrs, wife of Danl. Woolendorf

Marg't Lones 24 yrs, Marg't Lones 5 yrs, Martinus Lones 3 yrs, Cathrina Lones 6 ms., wife and children of Jno. Lones

Christina Bettinger 7 yesr, child of Martin Bettinger

Eliz'th Bost 20 yrs

Jacob Brooner 63 yrs, Frena Brooner 13 yrs, father and daughter

Mary Gywitz 17 yrs, daughter of Fred'k Gywitz

Marg't Walls 13 yrs, daughter of Jacob Walls

Maria Eliz'th House 17 yrs, daughter of Her. House

Maria Sitz 7 yrs, daughter of Baltus Sitz

Conrod House 15 yrs, son of Adam House

Conrod Kreemer 13 yrs, son of Godfrey Kreemer

Susanah Mackley 7 yrs, Anna Mackley 3 yrs, children of Phelix and Catharina Mackley

Cathrina Triesleman 30 yrs, Marg't Trieslman 10 yrs, Eliz'th Trieslman 8 yrs, Anna Triesleman 1 yr, wife and children of Christian Trieslman

Geor. Snouts 50 yrs, Jno. Snouts 10 yrs, father and son

Maria Steed 19 yrs, Jno. Steed, wife and child of Jno. Steed

 Jacob Fehling tacken in Palatine District about y 2d of Aug'st 1780. Conrad Lawer & Sohn, tacken the 16 of October 1780.   Daughter of late Jost Davis and a Son of John Kring. Peter Casselman, the later End of July. Henry Riemenschneider, John Nichol Wohlleber, Jacob Aahring and wife, with two Sons and four Daughters. Friedrich Rasbach & wife with a Son. Samuel Ball & wife; Rudolf Furry; John Duer & wife; Jacobus & Gerhard van Sluyk; John Fahrenbos; Jost Klock; Nicolaus Fahrenbos; John Seiffert; Bartle Picker; Adam Furry; John Street with a Son of 12 yrears; John Garter & 1 Son; Jacob Klock; John Keyfer & two Sons (a Captain of Militia); Frederic Windecker's Son; Johannes Helmer; Henry Schafer; Daniel Lapton & 3 or 4 Sons.

Page 79, Volume VI

Destruction of Canajoharie
General Ten Broeck Forwards to Governor Clinton a Report from Colonel Wemple

Albany 3d Aug't 1780, 7 O'Clock P.M.

Sir, the inclosed Copy of a Letter just received from Collo. Wemple will inform you Excellency of the Destruction of greatest part of Canajohary. In Consequence of Major Graham's Letter to Collo. Van Schaick, of which your Excellency has had a Copy I ordered the Albany and

Schenectady Reigment, with on half of General Rensselaer's & the one half of the remainder part of my Brigade (except the four Northen Regiments to Tryon County). The Militia of this City and Schenectady have turned out with alacrity. A very small propoertion of the Remainder has come forward owing in great measure to the season the Harvest just beginning. I can't but lament the Fat of Tryon County, the most opulent part of which (Stone Arabia excepted) is now fallen. I have ordered the Colonels of my Brigade to make Returns your Excellency has desired immediately, which shall be transmitted as soon as they come to Hand. I remain with great Esteem your Excellency's Most Obedient humble Serv't.

Ab'm Ten Broeck.

His Excelency George Clinton

Page 80, Volume VI

Colonel Wemple's Letter
Fort Plank Aug't 2d 1780 7 O'Clock.

Sir, Yesterday I detached two officers & thirty men af mine & Collo. Cuyler's Regt. at the Willigas to wait the arrival af a Convoy af Boats at that place & with the rest af our men we proceeded to Caughnawaga, where we arrived last Evening & at four this morning we began our march & arrived at Caugnawaga opposite to Mr. Frey's about eleven, with an Intentian to halt till they arrived with the Batteaux, which we expect to morrow about noon; immediately after we had cantoned as compact as possible our men, we were alarmed with a heavy smoke between Jahn Abeails & Fort Planck about four miles distant from where we had taken up our Quarters. This immediately was confirmed in the Eye of our whole Body & found the Enemy were bussy employed to burn & destroy.

Instantly I did order both Regiments to be formed & proceed against the Enemy, who were at that time in their full Carear and tho our Numbers were not equal, yet I can assure you I should be void af Justice if I omitted mentianing their Prudence & cool behaviour without Distinction to all Rancks. An altho they had been in full march since early in the morning they came up with such Vigor that the Enemy on our approach gave way & though in sight we had no opportunity to give them Battle they retired in the usual way. Our first Halt was at a Fort erected near Mr. Abeals House. The Inhabitants happy to see us. Directly after we had refreshed the men a few minutes, a Number of Volunteers who were least fateigued joined me with the Field officers of both Regiments to see the Fate of this Fort, which we found as full of sorrowfull we men & Children for their Husbands & Friends which were missing. They had, how ever,not made any Attempt to attack this Place. Such a Scean as we beheld since we left the River, passing dead Bodies of Men & Children most cruelly murdered, is not possible to be described.

I cannot ascertain at present the Number of poor Inhabitants killed and missing but believe the Loss considerable as the People were all at work in the Fields. I have endeavoured to obtain the Strength of the Enemy; the accounts differ so much that I cannot asscertain their Number, but from the many Places they sat on Fire, as in one Instant, & from parties out in a large Circuit of Country collecting & driving off Cattle, I am lead to believe that their Number is not small; our men are much fateigued.

We propose to remain here this Night. In the Morning we shall proceed and act as Circumstances shall turn up & will inform you more particular. Some Persons pretend to say not less then, one hundred dwelling House are burnt; as so on as I can any ways collect the more particular Facts, I shall not hesitate one Moment to let you know.

As to General Rensselaer, I have no other accounts from him but that he left Fort Herkimer on Monday last in the afternoon; he then by the best accounts I have been able to collect, besides the Convoy of Capt. Hicks, with about 50 Head of Cattle & that his party consisted of about five hundred men. I have great Reason to believe he has got safe into Fort Schuyler.

The Enemy began setting Fire & destroying some way near this place & proceeded on to Canajohary near the River burnt their Church, Abeals House & its Neighbourhood & upwards, where they I am lead to believe got sight of us & then retreated. You will please to observe that very great Devestation is committed south west of this place; excuse my Haste & the Distressed Situation & Circumstances & hope will sufficiently appologise. I am, D'r Genl. &c.

[To General Ten Broeck.]   (Copy)

Ab'm Wemple.

Page 88, Volume VI

Fort Plank August ye 8th 1780

Sir, I have herby sent you acount of the fete of our Destrect. On the second Instant Joseph Brant at the head of about four Hundrad and fifty Indens and Tories, Brook in upon our Settlements and Leaid the Best Peart of the District in ashes and kild forten of the Inhabitants that we have found; took betwixt fifty and sixty, mostly weoman and child Prisnors, twelve of them they have sent back; and they kild and drove away upwards of three Hundrad heade of Cattel and Horses big and small. They have burnt fifty three Dweling Houses and as many barns, one Elegent Church, one grist Mill, two small forts, that the wemon flead out of, and have burnt allmost all the farmers wagons and Emplements they had to work with, so that the Suffirers are in a mesirable Condietion.

Nothing left to suport themselves on, but what grean they have groing, and that they are not abel to seve for want of Tools and verry fue to be had here; this affer [affair] hapned at a verry onfourtnat Hour, when all the Militia of the County was Called up to Fort Schuyler, to guard nine Battows about half Loded. It was said the Enemy intended to cut of on ther Pasidge; there was schers [scarce] a man left that was abel to go, that it seems as every thing Conspaird for our Destruction; in this quarter one holl Destrict allmost Destroid and the best Rejmt. of Militia her [here] rendrad [rendered] unabel to help themselves or the Publick; this I refere you to General Renssler for the Truth of.

This spring when we found that we were not liekly to have Eany assistance and we new that we was not abel to withstand the Enemy in oure habetions, went all to woork and bult ourselves forts to live in, which we had nigh Effected and could a have seved our lives and Effects had we got Liberty to a maid use of them, but that could not be; we must all turn out, not that we had Eany thing aginst assisting the general to open the Passidge to Fort Schuylar, but still douptd what hes hapned, when we should be gon, but it was still insisted on there was no danger, which hes proved the greatest Blunder ever was hapned in the County, since the Commensment of the war and Discoridged the Militia, so that to send generals her without men, is just liek sending a man to the woods to chop without an ax. I am sensable had the general had men shuftcent, he woold given general saticsfaction to the Publick and Inhabitants her.

I am, with due Respect, your most Obedent Humble Servent. Saml. Clyde.

To his Excelency, Esqr.

Page 123, Volume VI

Petition from Widows and Orphans Ruined by the Ravages of the Enemy in Tryon County, for Order to Draw Provisions.

To his Excellency George Clinton Esquire, Governor, and Commander in Chief of the State of New-York.

The Humble Petition of Mary Tenis, Catharine Shefein, Elizabeth Browning, Catharine Ringle, Margaret Keller, Mary Clements, Elizabeth Irine, Susannah Ohene, Gertrude Stinewax, and Magdalene Snackein, Widows of New Petersburgh, Kingsland District, in the County of Tryon, and State of New York.

Humbly Sheweth, That your Poor Petitioners are all Widows, who are left with large Families of Children; our husbands are all killed by the Indians, and now lately, the Indians has Burn'd our houses and Barns, and taken away, and Destroy'd, all our Horses and Cows. And your Petitioners dare not venture home, to get our Harvest in. So that we, and our Fatherless Children are reduc'd to Poverty, and must inevitably want, if not reliev'd by your Excellencies Humanity and Bounty.

Your Petitioners, begs leave to acquaint your Excellence, that General Van Rensselaer, ordered all the inhabitants of New Petersburgh to leave the Place, and we are now at Fort Dayton, with scarce anything to subsist ourselves and Children.

Your Petitioners therefore Humbly Prays, that your Excellency will be pleas'd to grant, that we may draw Provision. Or order your poor Petitioners such Relief, as your Excellency out of your abundant Goodness, shall think fit. And your Petitioners, shall ever Pray.
Fort Dayton August 18th 1780.

The number of those Widows, together with their Children, is Forty and four, and all of the Children incapable of earning a Livelihood.

Page 135, Volume VI

A Threatening letter from Joseph Brant.

Sir, I understood that my friend Hendrick Huff & Cool is taken Prisoners near Esopus, I wou'd be glad if you wou'd be so kind as to let those people know that took them, not to use my friends too hard, for if they will use hard or hurt them, I will certainly pay for it, for we have several Rebels in our hands makes me mention this for it would be disagreeable to me, to hurt any Prisoner; therefore, I hope they will not force me. I am , your hu'ble S't
Jos. Brant, Gusuts 11th 1780.
To Coll. Vroman

(Colonel Peter Vroman to Governor Clinton)
A List of the prisoners names who were with Brant on the Dellaware, the 11th of August 1780, and taken the 9th Instant, viz: Ephraim Vroman his two sons Bartholomew and Josias; Simon Vroman his wife and one son Jacob, three Sons of my brother, namly John, Barent and Tuenes all that was left; himself his wife and one son kill'd; John Vroman and his Sons Martines, Thomas Marienes; Abraham Delly and Hendrick Heger.

The names of those fourteen persons was sent by Ephraim Vroman.

Sir John Johnson Reported as Contemplating Antoher Raid Along the Mohawk Valley

My dear Sir, We have just received an Express from Tryon County, from Col. Harper, who mentions that a Man employed by Genl Rensselaer to gett intelligence, informs him that Sir John Johnston has sent a party into Johnstown, to inform the Inhabitants that he is coming on with about 2000 men, and intends making his first stroke at Stone Arabia. That the Inhabitants at Johnsons Bus have baked a Quantity of Bread for the use of Sir John's men. The General intends going immediately to Schernectady to have Scouts continually out.

Genl. Ten Broeck will put the Militia of his Brigade, (at least such a part as may be necessary) under marching Orders, to march at a moment's warning; by the Information, Sir John was to have been at Johnstown yesterday. He will order Col. Harper to Johnsons Bush and if any Bread can be found seize it, and the Persons who have it. His Reason for taking Post at Schenectady, is that in case, there is any thruth in the account that he may collect a force in Person, an Endeavour to confute the designs of the Enemy. The Genl. Would have wrote himself but is gone to confer with Genl. Ten Broeck. I am, S'r Sir, with much Esteem your mo't Obt. Humble Servant.

Lewis R. Morris (Gov'r Clinton)

Page 169, Volume VI
General Robert Van Rensselaer Makes Report of the Situation in the Mohawk Valley

Fort Rensselaer, Sept'r 4th '80.

Dear Gov'r. The Reports of the Enimy Intentions are still vague and uncertain; some say Sir John is coming by the way of Lake Champlain, Brant and Butler from the westward; small parties are frequently seen upon the Frontiers. Last Thursday they attacked the House of one Sheel about three Miles North of Fort Herkimer. The House was bravely defended by the Man, his two sons, and wife; he supposed they killed and wounded fifteen or sixteen of the Enimy. They left one killed and one wounded on the ground; the Prisoner says the party consisted of thirty six British Troops and thirty Indians. Capt'n Allen of the Levies went the next Day in pursuit of them with fourty Men, who was not returned yesterday even'g.

On Satruday last, I sent of Twelve Boats with Provision for Fort Schuyler, Escorted by two hundred Men under the Command of Collo. Brown, of the Massechutsets Levies, which leaves the Frontiers verry thin of Men. I have also sent out a Scout to Unedilla and Ocquage, at which places I am suspicious they make their Rendevouz. I am anxious to hear from your Quarter, and shall esteem it a particular favour to hear from you.

I am, Dear Gov'r, your most obed't humb. Serv't,
Robt. V'n Rensselaer.
His Excellency Governor Clinton

Page 287, Volume VI
For the Relief of Tryon County
Kingston 11th October 1780.

Sir, I have this moment received a Petition dated 8th [6th] Instant subscribed by yourself & other Inhabitants of Tryon County. In Answer to which I am happy in being able to inform you that Legislative Provission is made for calling out a Part of the Militia for a certain Period of the further

Defence of the Frontiers, and Orders are accordingly issued for this Purpose, which I trust will reach you before this can, as they were forwarded some Days since. The Sense of the Members representing the Frotnier Counties were [was] taken as to the number of Men necessary for this Service, & I trust, therefore, the Force ordered to be raised will prove competent. The greatest Fear I have is, that is may not be brought into the Field as early as Exigencies may require. In this Case, I must entreat the best Exertions fo the Militia of Tryon County, until those intended for their Relief can be collected & be assured of every Effort on my Part for your Protection. I am &c.

George Clinton
To Colo. Klock

Page 292, Volume VI

The Outlook for the Mohawk Valley

Albany, Oct'r 13th 1780.

Sir, A very considerable body of the enimy appeared on Tuesday at Fort Ann which was instantly given up by Capt'n Sherwood; they came on to the River and burnt a Number of Houses, about Fort Edward; yesterday they returned towards Lake George. Genl Ten Broeck's Militia above Albany are ordered to Fort Edward.

This Morn'g I have an Express from Fort Schuyler, informing that S'r John, Butler and Brandt with a very large Body were at Oneida. That they had Cannon, Mortars, and Shells with them; an Ind'n Deserted and went into the Fort with this Notice and carried a five Inch Shell with him as an evidence. I have consulted with Genl. Tenbroeck, and he joins in opinion with me, that it is proper to have assistance from you of at least 800 men. I beg, therefore, that you will be pleased to give your orders accordingly; unless we have reinforcements immediately, no doubt but Fort Schuyler and all that remains of the fine Country, the Mohawk River, particularly Stone Arabia will be destroyed. It is also necessary that Cattle and flour come forward not only for your subsistence but for the Troops already here. It is a fact that we have no Beef, nor is there either wheat or flour collected notwithstanding my consent and most pressing Solicitations.

I am perswaded that you will see the propriety of marching the Troops forward instantly; you know little is to be depended on in this Quarter and the Levies are necessarily scattered so that it is impossible to collect any Body of them without leaving some valuable part of the Country exposed.

I have wrote to the Gov'r this Morn'g, but at that time did not imagine the enimy were so formidable.

Yours, very respectfully.

W. Macocmb, Col. Commdt.
To Genl Rensselaer.

Page 302, Volume VI

This one is VERY interesting, it talks about the food supply, namely food on the hoof.

The Enemy Destroys Schoharie, Letter to the Governor.

Dear Sir, The Letter of which the inclosed is Copy was delivered me this Morning. The Express who brought the Letter advises that Colonel Veeder directed him to inform Mr. Glen that 150 of the enemy in Addition to the Number mentioned in his Letter, were in the upper part of Schohary.

I shall in an Hour or two, as nearly as I can estimate, have between 6 & 700 Men; fifteen Head of Cattle intended for Fort Schuyler arrived here yesterday. I have ordered six to be killed this Morning to victual the Troops for two Days, and as I shall in all probability be necessitated to make use of the Rest and want an additional Number, your Excellency will perceive the Necessity of directing the agent of take Measures for replacing those destined for the Fort. The Cattle are extremely small and I am informd will not at an Average neat [net] more than two hundred wt. Per Head.

As I have been disappointed in procuring the Horses & wagons I intended, I shall immediate march to Fort Hunter and upon my Arrival take such Measures as Circumstances will admit of to intercept the enemy's Retreat.

The express who brought Colo. Veeder's Letter says that Major Woolsey sallied from his garrison yesterday and killed five and took 2 of the enemy. The prisoners are British soldiers.

I am, very respectfully, your Excellency's most obed't Servant.

Rbt V'n Rensselaer.

Schenectady Oct'r 18 A.M.

Lower Fort Schohary, Oct'r 17th 1780.

Dear sir, The Enemy have burnt the whole of Schohary; the first fire was discovered about the middle Fort 8 O'Clock this morning; they passed by this post on both sides at 4 O'Clock this afternoon; they took the whole of their booty and moved down to Harmen Stineys; they have fired two swivel shoots thro' the roof of the church. I have sent three scouts to make some discoveries about the middle Fort at different times this day, and none have as yet returned; no express has arrived at this post from either fort; by what we have seen of the Enemy we suppose their force to be between 5 or 600, mostly regulars and Tories.

V. Veeder, Lt. Col. 3 O'Clock at night. The express says there were 150 more of the Enemy at the upper part of Schohary. H. Glen, Esqr.

Page 304, Volume VI

The Governor Writes about his Measures for the Defence of the Frontier

Albany 19 October 1780.

D'r Sir, I wrote you yesterday, since which I have seen your Letter to Genl. Ten Broeck giving an account of the Enemy's appearance near White Creek. They are also at Schohary in very considerable Force, have'g artillery with them; they have completed the Destruction of that Settlement. Thus circumstanced I have been obliged to divide the small Force that could be raised immediately from the lower Parts of this County to oppose the Enemy at Balls Town and Schohary, and as yet it is impossible to do more that detach Colo. Schuyler's Regt. To the assistance of the Militia in your vicinity; this I have directed Genl. Ten Broeck to do and they are to march immediately. Before I left Pokeepsie I wrote Genl. Washington accounts of the Enemy's appearance on our Frontiers & the Capture of Forts Ann & George and pressed the Necessity of Send'g some Troops for our Relief. I am &c.

P.S. I this morn'g wrot to Genl. Washington, repeat'g my Request for Relief and immediately after this is done, I mean to set out for Schenectady, leav'g G. T. Broeck in Command here, with orders to forward you further assistance as soon as a sufficient number of Militia shall come in to render that measure propert. You will immediately order Colo. Stepen Schuyler's Regt. To Saraghtoga, to join the Militia collecting there, and assist in the Protection of the Inhabitants in that Part of the Country ag't the Incursions and Depredatiions of the Enemy.

TO: Genl. Schuyler

Colonel Staats Estimates the Enemy's Strength at One Thousand, Including Two Hundred Indians.

Lower Fort, October 18th 1780.

This moment your Excelency's Letter came to hand; two Prisinors from Sir John's army arivd at the same time, with the following Inteligenc, that Eight O'Clock this morning, Johnson, Butler and Brant, movd with their army from Sidnyes sawmill down the Mohawk Road to the said River, where they where to joyne the Party of the enemy from the Norward, of which their strength by the acco'nt of the Prisoners, is one thousand men, of which where 2 hundred Indians; the Rest Rigular Troops and Torys; another Party of 150 where gone to Katskill; the Posts at this Place are safe.

Barent J. Staats, Lut. Colo.
To his Excelency George Clinton, Esqr.

Page 305, Volume VI

The Enemy Ravaging the Country Near Fort Hunter.

Mohawk River, 6 Miles East of Fort Hunter, Octo'r 18th 1780 6 P.M.

Sir, This Moment General Rensselaer is advised by express, that the enemy are burning the country in the Neighbourhood of Fort Hunter. Their Force could not be ascertained when the Man came away. Genl Rensselaer intends to push on by Moon Light, as soon as he possibly can; perhaps your Excellency may deem it advisable to order the Militia now at Schenedyady to march up, so as to cover our Retreat should we experience a Defeat, which we have, however, no Idea of at present, as the Militia evince not a disposition to engage as pomisses a happy Issue. I have the Honor to be your Excellency's most obed't Serv't.

J. Lansing Jun'r
[To G. C. Governor]

Page 306, Volume VI

The Governor Notifies Washington of the Situation Along the Frontier.

Albany, Octo'r 18th 1780 10 P. M.

Sir, I wrote to your Excellency from Poughkeepsie on Saturday last and communicated to you the accounts which I had then received from this Quarter. The next day I set out for this place and arrived here on Monday. Upon my arrival I found the main Body of the Enemy which appeared in the Northward had returned by the way of Lake George and that part of the Country seemed again to be in a State of Tranquility. Yesterday morning, however, I was informed that a Party had made its appearance at Ballston, and destroyed some Buildings there, and about noon we received accounts that the Enemy were at Schohary and it is now confirmed that they have destroyed the whole of that valuable Settlement. Their Numbers of one Division are computed at about 600 and the account of the other Division is uncertain. They have artillery with them. Major Woolsey who commands. . . of Levies made a Sally from one of the small Forts there and took two Regulars and killed five Savages. By what Route they came, or mean to return, I have not been able to ascertain.

Yesterday morning I ordered Genl. Van Rensselaer with some Troops to Schenectady, with Directions as soon as he could make the proper Discoveries and if his Force should appear competent to march and endeavor to intercept them. By a Letter from Gen. P. Schuyler at Saratoga, I am informed that the Enemy yesterday burnt the Settlement of White Creek in Charlotte County, and the Smoke was discoverable from the Height near his House. The Post at Fort Edward after the Removal of the Stores is evacuated; the Levies who were stationed there having insisted that their Time of Service is expired and Colo. Livingston the Commanding Officer with the other Officers are now on their Return. I have ordered out the whole of the Militia from this part of the State; a considerable part are already in the Field and I shall leave this immediately for Schenectady in order to make the necessary arrangem'ts.

From this State of matters your Excellency will perceive the necessity of sending a Force, if it can possibly be spared, for the Defence of this part of the Country. No Dependence can be placed on the militia's remaining long from Home, and the three months Levies will soon be dismissed, so that without some. . farther Protection, Schenectady and this Place will be our Frontiers.

I received no Intelligence from the Grants, either whether the Enemy have done any mischief there, and whether their militia is turning out for our assistance.

[G. C.]

[To General Washington]

Page 309, Volume VI

WASHINGTON'S GLOOMY OUTLOOK.
Temporary Enlistments Detrimental to the Cause and Expensive, A Catalogue of Evils.

Head Quarters, near Passaic Falls, 18th October 1780.

Sir, In obedience to the orders of Congress, I have the honor to transmit your Excellency the present state of the troops of your Line, by which you will perceive how few men you will have left after the 1st January next. When I inform you also that the troops of the other lines will be in general as much reduced as yours, you will be able to judge how exceedingly weak the army will be at that period, and how essential it is the states should make the most vigorous exertions to replace the discharged men as early as possible.

Congress are now preparing a plan for a new establishment of their army which when finished, they will transmit to the several States with requisitions for their respective Quotas. I have no doubt it will be a primary object with them to have the levies for the War, and this appears to me a point so interesting to our Independence, that I cannot forbear entering into the motives which ought to determine the States without hesitation or alternative to take their measures decisively for that.

I am religiously persuaded that the duration of the War and the greatest part of the misfortunes and perplexities we have hitherto experienced are chiefly to be attributed to the System of temporary inlistments. Had we in the commencement, raised an army for the War, such as was within the reach of the abilities of these States to raise and maintain, we should not have suffered those military Checks which have so frequently shaken our cause, nor should we have incurred such enormous expenditures as have destroyed our paper Currency and with it all public credit. A moderate compact force on a permanent establishment capable of acquiring the discipline essential to military operations would have been able to make head ag't the enemy without comparison better than the throngs of militia which at certain periods have been, not in the field, but in their way to and from the Field; for from that want of perseverance which characterises all militia, and of that coercion which cannot be exercised upon them, it has always been found impracticable to detain the greatest part of them in service even for the term for which they have been called out, and this has been commonly so short, that we have had a great proportion of the time, two *sets* of men to feed and pay, one coming to the army and the other going from it. From this circumstance, and from the extraordinary waste and consumption of provisions, Stores, Camp equipage, arms, Cloathes and every other article incident to irregular troops, it is easy to conceive what an immense increase of public expence has been produced from the source of which I am speaking. I might add the diminution of our agriculture by calling off at critical Seasons the labourers employed in it, as has happened in instances without number. In the enumeration of articles wasted, I mention Cloathes. It may be objected that the terms of engagement of the levies do not include this; but if we want service from the men particularly in the cold Season we are obliged to supply them notwithstanding, and they leave us before the Cloaths are half worn out.

But there are evils still more striking that have befallen us. The intervals between the dismission of one army and the collection of another have more than once threatened us with ruin, which humanly speaking nothing but the supineness or folly of the enemy could have saved us from. How did our cause totter at the close of 76, when with a little more than two thousand men we were driven before the enemy thro' Jersey and obliged to take post on the other side of the Delaware to make shew of covering Philad'a, while in reality nothing was more esy to them with a little enterprise and industry than to make their passage good to that City, and dissipate the remaining force which still kept alive our expiring opposition!

What hindered them from dispersing our little army and giving a fatal blow to our affairs during all the subsequent winter, instead of remaining in a state of torpid inactivity and permitting us to hover about their quarters when we had scarcely troops sufficient to mount the ordinary Guards?

After having lost two Battles and Philadelphia in the following Campaign for want of those numbers and that degree of discipline which we might have acquired by a permanent force in the first instance, in what a cruel and perilous situation did we again find ourselves in the Winter of 77 at Valley Forge, within a day's march of the enemy, with little more than a third of their strength, unable to defend our position, or retreat from it, for want of the means of transportation?

What but the fluctuation of our army enabled the enemy to detach so boldy to the southward in 78 and 79 to take possession of two States, Georgia and South Carolina, while we were obliged here t' be idle spectators af their weakness set at defiance by a Garrisan af six thousand regular troops, accessible every where by a Bridge which nature had formed, but of which we were unable to take advantage from still greater weakness, apprehensive even for our own safety?

How did the same garrison insult the main army of these States the ensuing Spring and threaten the destructian of all our Baggage and Stores, saved by a good cauntenance more than by an ability to defend them? And what will be our situation this winter, our army by the 1st January diminished to a little more than a sufficient Garrison for West Point, the enemy at full liberty to ravage the Country wherever they please, and, leaving a handful of men at New York, to undertake expeditions for the reduction of other States which for want of adequate means of defence will it is much to be dreaded add to the number of their conquests and to the examples of our want of energy and wisdom?

The loss of Canada to the Union and the fate of the brave Montgomery compelled to a rash attempt by the immediate prospect of being left without troops, might be enumerated in the Catalogue of evils that have sprung from this fruitful source. We not only encur these dangers and suffer these losses for want of a constant force equal to our exigencies, but while we labor under this impediment it is impossible there can be any order or economy or system in our finances. If we meet with any severe blow, the great exertions which the mament requires to stop the progres af the misfortune, oblige us to depart from general principles to run into any expence or to adopt any expedient however injurious on a large scale to procure the force and means which the present emergency demands. Every thing is thrown into confusion, and the measures taken to remedy immediate evils perpetuate others. The same is the case if particular conjunctions invite us *to* offensive operations; we find ourselves unprepared, without troops, without magazines, and with little time to provide them. We are obliged to force our resources by the most burthensome methods to answer the end, and after all it is but half answered: the design is announced by the occasional effort, and the enemy have it in their power to counteract and elude the blow. The prices of every thing, men, provisions &c. are raised to a height to which the Revenues of no Government, much less ours, would suffice. It is impossible the people can endure the excessive burthen of bounties for annual drafts and substitutes increasing at every new experiment: whatever it might cost them once for all to procure men for the War would be a cheap bargain.

I am convinced our system of temporary inlistments has prolonged the War and encouraged the enemy to persevere. Baffled while we had an army in the Field, they have been constantly looking forward to the period of its reduction, as the period to our opposition and the season of their successes. They have flattered themselves with more than the event has justified; for they believed when one army expired, we should not be able to raise another: undeceived, however, in this expectation by experience, they still remain convinced, and to me evidently on good Grounds, that we must ultimately sink under a system which increases our expense beyond calculation, enfeebles all our measures, affords the most inviting opportunities to the enemy, and wearies and disgusts the people: This has doubtless had great influence in preventing theiir coming to terms, and will continue to operate in the same way. The debates on the ministerial side have frequently manifested the operation of this motive and it must in the nature of things have had great weight.

The interposition of neutral powers may lead to a negociation this winter. Nothing will tend so much to make the Court of London reasonable as the prospect of a permanent army in this Country, and a spirit of exertion to support it.

'Tis time we should get rid of an error which the experience of all mankind has exploded, and which our own experience has dearly taught us to reject the carrying on a War with militia, which is nearly the same thing, temporary levies against a regular permanent and disciplined force. The Idea is chimerical, and that we have so long persisted in it, is a reflection of the judgment of a nation so enlightened as we are, as well as a strong proof of the empire of prejudice over Reason. If we continue in the infatuation, we shall deserve to lose the object we are contending for.

America has been almost amused out of her liberties. We have frequently heard the behavior of the militia extolled upon one and another occasion, by men who judge only from the surface, by men who had particular views in misrepresenting, by visionary men whose credulity easily swallowed every vague story in support of a favorite Hypothesis. ***I solemnly declare I never was witness to a single instance that can countenane an opinion of militia or raw troops being fit for the real business of fighting. I have found them useful as light parties to skirmish in the Woods, but incapable of making or sustaining a serious attack.*** This firmness is only acquired by habit of discipline and service. I mean not to detract from the merit of the militia. Their zeal and spirit upon a variety of occasions have entitled them to the highest applause; but it is of the greatest importance we should learn to estimate them rightly: we may expect every thing from ones that militia is capable of, but we must not expect from any services for which Regulars alone are fit. The late Battle of Campden is a melancholy comment upon this doctrine. The militia fled at the first fire, and left the Continental troops surrounded on every side and overpowered by numbers to combat for safety instead of Victory. The enemy themselves have witnessed to their Valor.

An ill effect of short inlistments which I have not yet taken notice of, is that the constant fluctuation of their men is one of the sources of disgust to the officers. Just when, by great trouble fatigue and vexation (with which the training of Recruits is attended) they have brought their men to some kind of order; they have the mortification to see them go home, and to know that the drudgery is to recommence the next Campaign. In Regiments so constituted, an officer has neither satisfaction nor credit in his command.

Every motive which can arise from a consideration of our circumstances, either in a domestic or foreign point of view, calls upon us to abandon temporary expedients and substitute something durable, systematic and substantial. This applies as well to our civil administration as to our military establishment. It is as necessary to give Congress, the common Head, sufficient powers to direct the common forces, as it is to raise an army for the War, but I should go out of my province to expatiate on Civil affairs. I cannot forbear adding a few more remarks.

Our finances are in an alarming state of derangement. Public credit is almost arrived at its last stage. The people begin to be dissatisfied with the feeble mode of conducting the War, and with the ineffectual Burthens imposed upon them, which tho' light in comparison with what other nations feel are from their novelty heavy to them. They lose their confidence in Government apace. The army is not only dwindling into nothing, but the discontents of the officers as well as the men have matured to a degree that threatens but too general a renundation of the service, at the end of the Campaign. Since January last we have had registered at Head Quarters more than one hundred and sixty resignations, besides a number of others that never were regularly reported. I speak of the army in this Quarter. We have frequently in the course of this Campaign experienced an extremity of want. Our officers are in general indecently defective in Cloathing. Our men are almost naked, totally unprepared for the inclemency of the approaching season. We have no magazines for the winter; the mode of procuring our supplies is precarious, and all the reports of the officers employed in collecting them are gloomy.

These circumstances conspire to shew the necessity of immediately adopting a plan that will give more energy to Government, more vigor and more satisfaction to the army. Without it we have ever thing to fear. I am persuaded of the suffieiency of our resources if properly directed.

Should the requisitions of Congress by any accident not arrive before the Legislature is about to rise, I beg to recommend that a plan be devised which is likely to be effectual for raising the men that will be required for the War, leaving it to the Executive to apply it to the Quota which Congress will fix. I flatter myself, however, the requisition will arrive in time.

The present Crisis of our affairs appears to me so serious as to call upon me as a good Citizen to offer my sentiments freely for the safety of the Republic. I hope the motive will excuse the liberty I have taken. I have the honor to be, with the highest Respect, Yr. Excellency's most obt. and humble Serv't

Go. Washington.

TO: His Excellency Gov. Clinton.

Page 318, Volume VI

Colonel Livingston Proceeds by the River Road.

Johnstown 1 O'Clock

D'r Sir, I have rec'd your two Letters the one dated four and the other five miles from Fort Hunter. We set out immediately for Colo. Klock's. Capt. Gano is with us, and we have replaced his garrison with the lame men and some unarmed. We shall proceed by the River Route, as we are informed by Capt. Gano that it is impossible to take our waggons the other Road, and we cannot spare a guard sufficient for their security if we send them alone. We have had no Intelligence of the Enemy's movements except thro' your Excellency. I am, with Respect, your Excellency's most obed. ser't

H, B. Livingston.

TO: His Excellency Gov. Clinton.

Colonel Duboys in Pursuit of the Enemy

11 O'Clock.

D'r Coll, We are now as far as Fall Hill Boll's House, in full pursuit of the Enemy, they pass'd this place sum half an hour high; they spoke with some people here, and said that they had 1200 pick'd men and could go where they pleasd; after they pass'd this a smart fireing was heard, supposed to be at the fort as they pass'd the Germain Flatts; I have three more prisners of their party; no Time must be Lost, in pursuing them, Sir John is wounded through the thigh; they Enquired of Esqr. Bell particularly, concerning the strength of Fort Scuyler and their Numbers there; they Left all their Cattle behind them where they Cross'd the River. Esqr. Bell supposed their Numbers to be about 400; they Divided at the Fall Hill one part by Germain Flats the other by Andrus Town. I am, yours sincerely. Lewis Duboys.

TO: Genl. Ranslear.

Page 310, Volume VI

General Van Rensselaer. Close upon the Enemy-Colonel Brown Reported to Have Been Defeated.

Canajoharie opposite Frey's 11 A. M.

Sir, This Morning about nine I arrived so near the Enemy's Rear as to afford me a prospect of engaging them before Noon. They have, however, by the Celerity of their Movements affected their Escape to Stone Arabia, part of which is now in Flames & the whole will probably share the same Fate, before I can posilibly support the distressed Inhabitants. I intend to ford the River immediately and march in quest of them, but harrassed and fatigued as my Force is by a long March, I am apprehensive I shall not be able to pursue them with that Dispatch which is Necessary to overtake them. No Exertion, however, shall be wanting on my part to effect it.

Two prisoners who were brought in at Fort Hunter informed Mr. Cuyler that Sir John intended to return by the way of Crown Point; that he had left his Boats in the Onondaga Lake but had since altered his intended Rout to Crown Point by the way of Stone Arabia. I am, your Excellency's obed't Servant

Robt. Van Rensselaer.

Dubois will join me at Walradth's about a Mile above this. I am this Moment informed that Colonel Brown who with a party opposed the Enemy was defeated. His Loss is not ascertained. The Enemy are it said between 600 & 1000 strong.

TO: His Excellency Gov. Clinton.

Page 320, Volume VI

The Enemy Only a Mile in Van Rensselaer's Advance.

Sir, The Enemy are by the best Intelligence I can collect and from their Burnings about a Mile in Advance of my Brigade. I have about 900 Men including about 50 [?] Indians. I shall pursue with as much Dispatch as is consistent with Safety to the Troops under my Command. I am, your Excellency's obed't Servant,
A Deserter who arrived this afternoon advises that the Enemy's Force does not exceed 500 Men. Mohawk River about 2 Miles above Fort Rensselaer, North Side of the River after 5 P.M.

General Ten Broeck Despatches Expresses to Colonels Van Bergen and Snyder.

Albany, 19th Oct'r [1780] 1 O'Clock in the morning.
Sir. Your Excellency's letter I have Received with the Inclosed note from Lieut. Col. Staats; have wrote to Col. Van Bergen & Col. Snyder the Intelligence it Contains & an Express will go with it Instantly. I have nothing farther from the northward since your Excellency left this, nor from Ballstown; if any Cattle come they will be forwarded Immediately, I will deliver Colo. Hay your message. I Remain, with great Esteem, your Excellency's most Obedient Humble Servant
Ab'm Ten Broeck.
TO: His Excellency, George Clinton, Esq.

Page 321, Volume VI

Cattle and Flour in Transit from Albany to Schenectady.

Albany, 19th Oct'r [1780] 4 O'Clock P. M.
Sir, Mr. Benson's favor of this date, I have Received & have delivered Dr. McCrea's note to Dr. Treat; he is Preparing the necessaries & will send them on Immediately. Thirty head of Cattle & 50 Barrells of Flour are this moment going on to Schinectady. My Exertions shall be used in forwarding on Provisions as fast as they come. I beg your Excellency's Pardon for opening the Inclosed Letter from General Schuyler, I wish I was able to Comply with his Request. I need not tell your Excellency that it is Impossible Considering the weak state of my Body. I shall Continue to do every thing in my Power to forward the Service. I have sent him a Copy of Mr. Benson's letter & have wrote in the most Pressing manner to the Colonel, his Brother, now in his march to Saratoga to Push on & Endeavor to Intercept Sir John if he should Escape Genl. Rensselaer. I Remain, your Excell'cys most Humble Servant
Ab'm Ten Broeck.
P. S. Ab't 150 men of Livingston's militia are now Crossing the Ferry. I shall hurry them on. His Excellency George Clinton.

Colonel Stoutenburgh Ready to Impress Supplies from Pirvate Families

Albany, 19th October, 1780.
D'r Sir, I acknowledg the rec't of your favour of this Date, it affords me great Satisfaction that I am able to inform your Excellency that it is in my Power to comply with your demand of both

Cattle and flour, (without proceeding to an Immediate Impress from private Families,) most of the latter is already on the Road; the Cattle will be sent on from here early tomorrow morning, they consist of 30 head of fine Cattle; if your Excellency thinks it necessary after this Supply to proceed to Impress from Private Families, I stand ready to Execute your Commands; in the mean time, shall wait your Excellency's further orders, while I am with the most Sincere Esteem & Regard, your Excellency's most Obedient Hum. Serv't, Isaac Stoutenburgh.
TO: His Excellency Gov. Clinton.

Page 322, Volume VI

Flour and Cattle Arrive at Fort Herkimer

Fort Harkermer, Saturday 1 O'Clock.

Sir, Col. Livingston is just arrived; he tells me Provisions are coming on, both flour & Cattle. I have Procur'd a Number of baggs & Irnpress'd some good Horses and shall be on as soon as Possible. Col. Hay will be here with more Provitions in about three Hours. I am &c.
J. Dyckman.
TO: Gov'r Clinton.

Colonel Duboys in Pursuit of the Enemy.

Fort Harkerman 1 O'Clock [October. 1780.]
D'r Sir, I am here; pursued the Enemy so close that I prevented them from Burning or Doing the Least Damage to the Inhabitants; from what I can Learn by the Inhabitants, the Enemy is not above four miles in front of us; my men much Fatigned, without Provisions. I must here make a halt, untill I can get some provisions to Refresh them,

The Enemy is very much fatigned, They travelled almost all night, without any Refreshment; they must make a halt.

This moment, I Rec'd Information that the Enemy is at a place Call'd Shoemaker's Land, about four miles from here; Genl. Ransler this moment appears in Sight with the Militia.

The Enemy are Bending their Course for Buck Island. I am your etc.
Lewis Duboys.
P. S. My men have agred to march without eating. I expect to catch them in 3 ours thime.
TO: His Excellency Governor CJinton.

Page 323, Volume VI

List of Ordnance and Stores Captured from Sir John Johnson.
A Return of Ordinance & Stores taken from the British army, Comm'd by Sir John Johnston. Fort Rensselaer Oct'l" 19th 1780:

1 Piece Brass Ordinance 3 pd. with Emplim'ts Comp.; 23 Rounds, Round Shott ftx'd; 10 do Canister; 1 Quadrant; 2

Powder measures; 1 hand Saw; 1 four pd. wt.; 1 half do; 1 Quart'r do; 1 Scale beam; 1 mallet & set; 20 fuses; 1 Seane marlin; 2 Port fires; 1 Cole Chisel; 1 augur; 1 Punch; 1 Seane Quick match; 100 wt. Corn Powder; 1 Drudging box.

Jo. Driskill, Lieut. Artillery.

Page 324, Volume VI

Impress Warrant to Henry Glen and Colonel Wemple

By his Excellency George Clinton, Esquire, Governor of the State of New York &ca. &ca. &ca.

To Colo. Abraham Wemple, & Henry Glen, Esqr. or either of them Greeting.

The Emergency requiring the same, you are hereby authorized & required to impress forty Head of Fat Cattle & Sixty Barrels of Flour, for the Use & Service of the Army for which this shall be your Warrant.

Given at Scheneectady, this 19th October, 1780.

Geo. Clinton.

The Provission impressed is immediately to be forwarded the Troops under my Command.

From: Geo. Clinton.

Sir John Johnson Escapes Again, The Situation in Saratoga County.

Saratoga, Octo: 20th 1780.

Dear Sir, Your Excellency's favor of yesterday morning from Caghnawaga I had the pleasure to receive at five in the after noon. I am happy to learn that Sir John Johnson has been overtaken and put to rout; when your letter arrived, we had about 150 men at Fort Edward and as many more had arrived here about ten in the morning; those at Fort Edward without any beef, and those here with none but what I could furnish them, all my cattle fit for the knife are already killed and I have sent to try and collect some more, but I fear a supply will arrive too late to push a party in pursuit of the enemy who were at Ballstown. I have, however, sent to Fort Edward on the subject, but with little hopes. that any will move from thence; one of the enemies party, who stole into the Country and was taken, informs that Major Carlton intended to remain at Tyconderoga and to push for White Creek as soon as the militia should be retired; the prisoner calls himself an ensign and came from New York in August last. Another villain is gone past here, who. corroborates the account as some tones advice with whom he lodged.

The panic that has siezed the people is incredible; with all my efforts I cannot prevent numbers from deserting their Habitations, and I very much apprehend that the whole will move, unless the militia will remain above until a permanent relieve can be procured. I am D'r Sir, most sincerely your Excellency's Obed: Hu. Serv't

Ph. Schuyler

His Excellency Gov. Clinton &c.

The women and Children whose husbands are gone to Canada still remain here; they will be an intolerable burthen to the Country if they remain in it all winter, I beg your Excellency as soon as you can spare time to turn your attention to their disposition.

Albany, Oct'r 26 1780.

Sir, I have been favored with your Letter of the 20 Inst. We are just returned from the Pursuit of Sir John, tho unfortunately without that complete Success, which I informed you we had

Reason to expect after the Engagem't at Canajoharie. There are, however, ab't 40 Prisoners and the Enemy have lost their Baggage & artillery; this action also stopt them in their Devastation & obliged to fly with precipitation.

Colo. Gansevoort's Regt. has marched to your Frontier; this I doubt not will give you immediate Protection and a Proportion of the Levies will be ordered to that Part of the Country as soon as they are raised.

The necessary Passports for the women & Children you mention, shall be made out immediately, after I am furnished with their Names and the steps taken prescribed by the Law made for that Purpose.

[G. C.]

TO: [General Philip Schuyler.]

Page 329, Volume VI

Colonel Klock Directed to Call Out Tryon County Militia.
Colonel Bellinger to Send 20 Men of His Regiment to Fort Dayton and 20 to Fort Herkimer.

Fort Renselaer, Oct. 23d, 1780.

Sir, The late Invasion of the Enemy has delayed the raising of the Troops which were intended to relieve the Levies in this County; and it will be some days hence before any Troops can be collected for the Defence of the several Posts on the River; you will, therefore, order out from the County Militia such number of men to those Posts as the Officer commanding the Department shall require, and you may be assured they will be relieved as soon as possible. I am &c.

[G. C.]

To Col. Klock, commanding the militia in Tryon County.

Fort Herkemer, Octo. 23d 1780.

To Colo. Bellinger;

Sir, Until Troops can be raised for the Defence of the County, it is necessary that the Militia be detached to hold the Frontier posts. You will, therefore, order Twenty men of your Regiment into Fort Dayton, and the same number into Fort Herkemer, this day. There will be officers left at those Posts to direct the 'Dnty, and your men will be releived as soon as possible. I am &c.

G. C.]

Page 345, Volume VI

The Governor Informs James Duane of the Devastation Along the Mohawk Valley.

Pokeepsie, Oct'r 29th 1780.

Dear Sir, I returned late last Evening from Tryon County & have only time at present, by Mr. Ray who just stop'd here on his way to Phila., to acknowledge the Receipt of your Letter by Mr. Knolton, who arrived the Even'g before I left home. Colo. Benson informs me of the receipt of another Letter from you by Mr. which was forwarded to me at Albany; but which as I returned by water I have not yet received.

I must refer you to the enclosed Paper for an acc't of our and the Enemy's Proceed'gs on the Frontiers as far as it respects men: but I have the mortification to inform you, that for want of a permanent & adequate force & before a suff't body of the militia could be assembled to prevent it, the whole of the valuable Settlem't of Schoharie & a part of the Settlem't of Balls Town & almost the whole of the Intermediate Country on both sides of the Mohawk River from Fort Hunter to Fort Rensselaer at the upper end of Cannojoharie, including the settlement of Stone Arabia are burnt & laid waste; on a moderate Computation we have lost at least 150,000 bush'ls of wheat besides other Grain & forage & 200 Dwellings. Schenectady may now be said to become the limits of our western Frontier, the first Object worth a new Enterprize.

I am not surprized at the Conduct of Congress with respect to our dispute with the People on the Grants; for upwards of a year past it has appeared to me that they were encouraged & supported in their Revolt & that Delay was studied to strengthen their opposition. There were many, however, who firmly believed that Congress would take up the matter & decide upon it & enforce their Decision agreable to their Resolutions of June last. The Evasion of it and the encouragement afforded to the Revolters has given universal Disgust to all Ranks of People, & in confidence I cannot but inform you that the most sensible among us begin to be of a premeditated intention to make a sacrifice of this State to answer the political views of others & of Interested Individuals, & I should not be surprised, tho' I may be mistaken, if these Jealousies should so far prevail as that at the next meeting of the Legislature, our Delegation should be withdrawn & the Resources of the State which have hitherto so lavishly been afforded to the Continent, be withheld for our own Defence.

Yourself, Mr. Floyd, Mr: Scott, Mr. L'Hommedieu & Genl. McDougall are appointed Delegates for the ensuing year & by the next Convenient opportunity your Commission will be transmitted. I have the honor to be &c.
Geo Clinton.

P. S. I lodged at Colo. Livingston's the night before last & I have the Pleasure of inform'g you that Mrs. Duane & the family are well.
The honble. James Duane, Esqr.

Since writing the above, I am informed, tho' not otticially, that a Detachm't of Sixty men who were ordered to march from the Garrison of Fort Schuyler to hang on the enemy's flank in their Retreat, unfortunately before they discovered the Enemy, fell in with their main body & the whole of them two E'xcepted, are made Prisoners. I am in, great Hopes, however, that this Account is not true as the Orders given to the Party by Maj'r Hughes was couched in the most cautious Terms; they were to proceed with the greatest Circumspection & not to hazard any Thing that might endanger their Retreat.

Page 351, Volume VI

THE LATEST RAID OF THE ENEMY.
Severe Losses Incurred--Governor Clinton Forwards a Detailed Report to the Commander-in-Chief.

Pokeepsie, Oct'r 30th 1780.

Dear Sir, My last Letter was dated at Albany & communicated the disagreable Intelligence of the Destruction of Schoharie & Part of Balls Town; ab't 12 miles No. E't of Schenectady, since which I have not been able to write to your Excellency. As I then proposed, I immediately left Albany in order to take the necessary measures for check'g further Incursions of the Enemy. On my arrival at Schenectady I was advised that the diff't Parties of the Enemy at Schoharie & Balls Town had left those Places; the former moving towards the Mohawk River & the latter shaping their course towards Sacondaga. Genl. Van Rensselaer who had arrived at Schenectady before me at the head of ab't four or five hundred Militia & with orders to act according to Emergencies on receiving this Intelligence, immediately moved up the River in hopes of being able to gain their Front, but this proved impracticable as their route was much shorter & their Troops more enured to march'g;. they reached the River at the confluence of the Schoharie Kill ab't six miles ahead of him, & recommenced in that fertile Country their Devastations by burn'g the Houses & with marks of the greatest barbarity, destroy'g every Thing in their way.

Under these Circumstances I was exceedingly perplexed. The militia under Genl. Rensselaer were inferior in number to that of the Enemy. The few I had wth me were too far in the rear to sustain them & not much could be expected from the militia of the Country, through which the Enemy passed, their whole attention being engaged in the preservation of their Families & the Levies were necessarily very much dispersed at the diff't Posts to cover the frontier Settlements ag't the Incursions of small Parties. Genl. Rensselaer, however, continued to move on & being soon after joined by Colo. D'uBois with between 3 & 400 Levies & 60 of the Oneida Indians, pursued the Enemy with vigor; he came up with them and attacked them at Fox Mills (26 miles from where the Enemy first struck the River) about Sun set. After a considerable Resistance they gave way & fled w'th Precipitation, leaving behind them their Baggage, Provisions & a brass three Pounder with its ammunition.

The night came on too soon for us to avail ourselves of all the advantages which we had Reason to promise ourselves from this action. The Enemy took advantage of passing the River at a Ford a little above where they again collected & renewed their march up the River with great celerity & it became necessary for our Troops, who had marched upw'ds of 30 miles without halting, to retire from the ground to refresh themselves. The Pursuit was, however, renewed early in the morning & the Enemy so closely pushed as to prevent their doing any farther mischief.

The morning after the action, I arrived with the militia under my immediate Command: but they were so beat out with fatigue, having marched at least 50 miles in less than 24 Hours, as to be unable to proceed any farther. I, therefore, left them & put myself at the head of the advanced Troops & continued the pursuit till within ab't 15 miles of Oneida, & if we cou'd possibly have procured Provission to have enabled us to have persisted one or two Days longer, there is little Doubt but we might have succeeded at least so far as to have scattered their main Body & made many Prisoners, but there was no supplies, but such as I was obliged to take from the Inhabitants on our Route & these was inadequate & the Collection of them attended with Delay, nor could the Pack Horses with the small Quantities procured in this disagreeable manner, overtake us in so rapid a march through a perfect wilderness. I was, therefore, obliged tho' reluctantly to return, most of the Troops having been near two Days utterly destitute & unable to proceed. Sir John, Brandt & Butler, immediately after the action at Fox Mills, left their Troops & with a Party of Indians on Horseback, struck across the Country & went towards Oneida, taking their wounded with them. We discovered where they joined their main body again near the waters of the Susquehanna ab't six miles on this side where we quitted the pursuit Brandt was wounded through the foot.

The Enemy's Force under Sir John, from the best account I have been able to collect, amounted to 750 picked Troops from the 10th & 34th British Regts, Hessian Yaugers, Sir John's Corps, Butler's Rangers & Brandt's Corps of Indians & Tories & the Party that appeared at Balls-Town, of ab't 200 chiefly British & by some acc'ts it appears they intend'd to form a junction Johns Town. In the diff't Skirmishes, a considerable number of the Enemy were killed; the exact amount I am not able to ascertain. We have taken ab't 40 Prisoners, recovered most of those they had taken from us at Schoharie & other Places, with the negroes, Cattle & Plunder. Our principal Loss is Colo. Brown of the Bay Levies; he by false Intellignce, was led into the fire of the whole body of the Enemy, & fell with 39 of his & the militia & Levies of this State & two made Prisoners.

The account I formerly transmitted your Excellency respecting the Enemy to the northw'd was as far as I have since been able to learn, nearly true. The little Post & garrison of Fort Ann appear to me to have been surrendered thro' Treachery or Cowardice. Capt. Chipman the command'g officer of Fort George, having on the first alarm sent out his whole garrison (supposing the Enemy to consist of only ab't 30 Indians & Tories only) except 14 men, obtained a very honorable Capitulation before he could be induced to surrender.

The Losses we have sustained by these diff't Incursions of the Enemy will be most severely felt; they have destroyed on a moderate Computation, 200 Dwellings & 150,000 bushels of wheat with a proportion of other grain & forage. The Enemy to the northw'd continue in the neighborhood of Crown Point & the Inhabitants in consequence of their apprehensions of Danger are removing from the northern Parts of the State. Colo. Gansevoort by the advice of Genl. Ten Broeck marched to cover that part of the Country & Colo. Weissenfels march'd to Schenectady where his Regt. will continue to escort a suff't supply of Provisions to Fort Schuyler, a very inconsiderable Part of which is as yet provided & unless particular a.ttention is paid to this Business (as the Season for water Transportation in the course of a month will be over & it will be impossible to forw'd it by Land), the Post must in the course of the winter be abandoned.

The Levies incorporated in this Regt. whose Times expire ab't the middle of December, were immediately to march to Fort Herkimer to keep open the communication of Fort Schuyler with the Country. This Regim't with the others of this State are so exceed'gly destitute in point of Clothing (notwithstand'g every attempt of the state to supply them) that I could have wished some other Regt. better provided ag't the severe Climate had been ordered to garrison that Post especially as I find from this consideration & because the Troops of this State conceive it a hardship constantly to garrison it, this Duty is become extremely disagreable to them.

I forgot to mention that when we arrived at Fort Herkeimer, a Letter was dispatched to Major Hughs commdg. at Fort Schuyler, giving him an acc't of the Force & Route of the Enemy & of their Boats lying at Onondaga Lake, that he might, if he found it consistent with the safety of his garrison, send out a small Party to annoy the Enemy on their march. By his Letter to Colo. Malcom, I find he dispatched a Party of sixty men for this Purpose, with orders to use the utmost precaution ag't surprise or any thing that might prevent their returning to the Fort. Since my Return from Albany, a Report prevails that this Party were ambushed by the Enemy & defeate: but from Major Hugh's cautious orders & as I have no official acc'ts, I do not credit it. I have the Honor &c.
[G. C.]
P. S. The Enemy bro't with them two brass mortars for 4 ¾ shells which they concealed on their Route from Schoharie. From some discoveries we are in hopes of find'g them.
[To General Washington.]

Page 422, Volume VI

The Govemor Directs General Clinton to Abolish, Suttlers-Prisoner
McGinnis Ordered, Liberated-Spy Van Driessen.

Pokeepsie 20th Nov'r 1780.

D'r Sir, I Two Days since received your Letter of the 12th Instant. I apprehended great Difficulties (from what I experienced myself) in procuring a Competency of Provission for the

Northern Department, &, therefore, pressed Colo. Hay & his Assistance to use every possible Exertion to collect the necessary Supplies in Season & the more effectually to enable him, granted an Impress Warrant authorizing him to seize to the ammount of the Deficiencies of the assessments in the Different Districts. This was giving every assistance in my Power & fully complying with my Promise to the Com'r in Chief. Colo. Hay now informs me that a sufficient Number of Cattle are now on their Way to you & that he has promising Prospects of being able to afford you a competent Supply of Flour.

I am informed that the public Service is much Injured by a Number of Idle Persons becoming Suttlers in the different small Posts on the Mohawk River & the Morals of the Inhabitants who have fled into them for safety, debauched. I have to request, therefore, that you will issue your orders possitively prohibitting the Practice in future. There is a certain McGinnis in Albany gaol, confined in Consequence of the Sentence of Court Martial, whom I promised in Consideration of his executing the two Spies lately convicted at Albany, to liberate. I thought the Sheriff woud of Course have discharged him, but I am informed this is not the case. I request, therefore, you will order him to be released and Vandriesen to be further reprieved until the first of February next. I have no news. Your Family were well the last I heard of them. I am with great Regard, yours affectionately [G. C.]

The Grass Hopper came down with Colo. Malcom, but none of the ammunition or Stores taken with it. The Colo. Tells me they were plundered; cant we find out by whom that they may be punished.

TO: Genl. Clinton

Note: General James Clinton was Governor George Clinton's Brother

Page 449, Volume VI

Colonel Clyde's Tales of Disaster, Including the Enlistment of His Apprentice.

May it please your Excellency, About ten days ago Lieut. Smith, of Capt. Brown's Company of Artillery, Enlisted an apprentice Lad of mine named James Simons, who was bound to me by his father, & had two years and Seven months to Serve; he was in the Seven months Service at Fort Schuyler; as soon as I was Inform'd that the Lad had Inlisted I follow'd him to Albany but unfortunately arrived a few hours after the Company had Sailed for West Point, by which I was prevented of obtaining any Redress, if I was Intituled to it; my Circumstances will not permit me to follow any farther. I, however, have taken the liberty of Representing this affair to your Excellency, & flatter myself that if in your power, afford me the Relief I am Intituled to.

The whole of my Personal property was destroy'd at Cherry Valley; a Crop I had Raised on the Mohawk River is again Burnt by the Enemy; the taken of a person from me who was & could be usefull to me is an additional distress to which I was not Intituled.

If my apprentice could be annex'd to one of the Regiments of this State and the County of Tryon Credited for a man so that I might Receive a Compensation, I should be much better satisfied than at present Your Excellency Interposition in this affair will much oblidge your most obed't Humble Servant.

Saml Clyde.

Albany, 30th Nov'r 1780.

TO: Gov. Clinton.

Page 525, Volume VI

General James Clinton Places Colonel Cochran in Command of Fort Schuyler

Albany, Dec'r 27th '80

Dear Sir, Your lettor of the 21st inst. Was handed me by the Viscount DeNoailles, with similar Letters from His Exc'y Genl Washington. I have been as attentive to them as Circumstances would admit.

I have directed Lt. Col. Cochran to take Command of Fort Schuyler, where I have this day sent fifty Barrels of Flower, being all that I could collect. Col. Weissenfiels is impatient to be relieved. I wish to know the Determiniation of Col. Bevier and Major Logan as well as that of several other officers in Confinement because our arrangement will remain incompleat until that is known.

Capt'n Norton will have the honor to hand you this and to take your orders. I am, Dear Sir, yours Affectionately. James Clinton.
TO: Gov. Clinton

Page 551, Volume VI.

Colonel Samuel Clyde's Regiment in a Demoralized Condition.

Courish Bush, Jan'y ye 6th 1781.

Dear Sir, I Rec'd an act of the Legislature for Raising of men during the war for this State and your Orders for Putting the same into Execution last week, and this day I Rec'd youre ordars for Proloingen the Time till Fabuary nixt; liek an ordar to Pay in all fines and Peneltes from delinquet Clesses to the Trishre; how the men will be Raised I cannot tell; the Inhabitants, are to distresed; it wiLL be verry hard and mony they have not got; and as to fines and Penelties on delinquet Clesses, i have non in the Rej'mt; last Spring I detioned Twelve men to the seven months Leves which was one for every Clees I had, and when Cougbnawago was Destroid in the Spring, many of oure Inhabitants moved out of the Destriect, and in the Summer I Delivred Eighten men more to the three months Leves, aLL good men, which makes Thirty in all out of this Litlel Rej'mt, and what Remened was ablidged to be allmost Constant on Duty, exceept about five weeks in Hervest time, and offen to find there own Provision which hes ben the Case for this two years Past, and without eany Payor Rewat'd, for there Time that by the Destress of the Enemy and the hard usege from the State, the Inhabitants are allmost in Desper. I have but two Companys that I can say hes escaeped the Revenge of the Enemy, and one of them was abJidged to join Sir John's Pearty last fall, which seved them.

But I hop if the Militia up here are to have eany Pay or Reward for there Serves dun, that they could have it; it woold Releve many that are in Destress, and be a mens of Incoridging of them to do there Duty, for the futter we have dun every thing in oure Powr for the generall good, but now we, are not abele to help our sellves. I hop that we may be Concidred in our Present Circumstance.

I should be verry glead if I could no when you woold be in Albany for to see you about those that joind with Sir John's Pearty last fall. But my Present Circomstance will not alow me to go eany farther. From your most Obedant Humbl Serv'nt.

Saml. Clyde
To His Excelency George Clinton, Esqr.

Page 660, Volume VI

List of Prisoners Taken in Tryon County

To his Excellency, George Clinton, Esqr. Governor of the State of New York, General and Commander in Chief of all the Militia and Admiral of the name of the same.

The memorial of the Subscribers Humbly Sheweth

That Peter Hansen of Tryon County was taken Prisoner by the Enemy in October or November 1778. That Adam Fonda, Frederick Sammons, Hermanus Terwilliger, Benj'n De Line, Joseph Myers, Barent Hansen and Samuel Kennedy all of Caugnawaga District in Tryon County were also taken by the Enemy in May 1780. As also Cap'n Alex'r Harper, John Hendry, Lieut., Isaac Patchin, William Lamb, Wm. Lamb Jun'r, David Brown, John Brown, Solo'n Brown, Doctor Brown, Esaray Thorp, all of Harpersfield taken the 7th April 1780. Henry Agar, taken from the Brakaben Schohare District. That the above named Persons are now Prisoners in Canada and taken from their own Houses and not in Arms and have left distress'd Families.

Your memorialists humbly pray your Excellency to use your Influence that the said Persons may be Exchang'd and return'd to their Families. And your Memorialists as in Duty Bound shall ever pray.

Zept Batcheller.
February 27th, 1781.

Free Gift Patchin, from Harpersfield, Lap & 4 Sons-RemSneyders Bush Street's Son; Jacob Forbes, Son, Fred'k Wendeter, Son, Barkly Piket, Jun'r, Jacob V. Slyk, Garret V. Slyk, Johannes Helmer, Johannes Garter & 2 Sons, Joseph Newman, Johannis Sauer, Jacob Aker taken 2 April 1780, not taken in Arms.

John Frank from German Flats 8 June, 1778, Laurenc Frank Sep'r 1778, John Heller July 1780, Jacob Faling Aug't 1780, not taken in Arms.

Capt. Markus Dermot, Oct. 1780, Geo. Dockstedder, Do. Nich's Harder, Do. Taken in Arms; Capt. John Kiser March 1780, not in Arms.

Note: Do means same or ditto.

Page 27, Volume VII

Proclamation by Sir John Johnson to People on Mohawk River

The Officers and Soliders of Sir John Johnson's Regt. Present their affectionate and loving wishes to their Friends and Relations on the Mohawk River & earnestly entreat them to assemble themselves & come into Canada or the upper Posts, where under that Gallant leader, they may assist their Countrymen to quell & put an end to the present unnatural Rebellion, in hopes soon to return to their native homes, there to enjoy the happiness they were formerly blessed with under the best of Kings, who is willing to do every thing for his subjects.

May 22nd 1781.

Page 78, Volume VII

Colonel Willett Sends to the Governor a Report, an Affidavit and a Statement Regarding Depredations Near Schoharie

Sir: The enclosed confession of William Sommer, one of the Men who came to me with the Letter I mentioned to your Excellency in my Letter of yesterday, contains such an Exhibition of a long train of horrid Villiany in the Miscreat Inhabitants of Torloch, that I shall send out a party to endeavor to take such of those Wretches as may yet be found in that Settlement, in order to bring them to Justice. But as nothing short of a gallows can be a just reward for their actions, I should be glad to know from you, whether you conceive there will be any Difficulty in bringing them speedily to that punishment, for should not this be the case, I am willing to risk all the consequences in having them hanged myself. I shall send this with an Express who will have directions to see your Excellency in order to procure me an Answer as soon as possible.

Cannot power be given to me to remove the Rascally disaffected Inhabitants from these Frontiers. No attention having been paid to those Orders you formerly sent to the Militia Officers for that purpose, nor do they appear to me to be the proper persons to do this business.

My party is returned from Torloch, but as I had not the Evidence I now have against the Inhabitants of that place before the Party went out, I did not give them orders to secure the Inhabitants. Notwithtanding, the party brought in ninety head of cattle, they left a considerable number with the people, so that I am in hopes they are not yet gone off; I shall, therefore, send out a party in order to take the Inhabitants and bring them to me, as soon as possible. Just at this time I am not able to do this, having very few men and a large party gone to drive some of the Cattle we took at Torloch to Fort Herkimer, for the use of the Troops at that place.

I wish to know what Force I may expect this way and I should be very glad of some directions from you, and be informed how to manage with so small assistance such complicated business as I am engaged in. Above everything, I entreat you try to let us have men that we may beat the Enemy again, and again, should they (as no doubt they will) pay us any more visits. Our late success has, to be sure, been greater than we had a right to hope for, but tho we have been very fortunate this once and Heaven has appeared signally for us, yet let us not forget to keep our Shoulders to the wheel by doing all we can; therefore, once again I ask for help against a future Day, which is perhaps very real, for we are told of Troops being on this way from Bucks Island and from other parts of Canada. Pray give us all the help as well as all the Council you can against such an event.

William Sommer is a Son of one Dominie Sommer, who is it a Minister living at Schohary. He appears intelligent, but is no doubt a great villian; he has made the enclosed discoveries in the hope of procuring forgiveness which I told him would be the case; if his Acc't turned out to be all true and that it does not afterwards appear he has concealed anything he knew. What can become of the remainder of the Levies from Dutchess County and Capt. help among the rest? I am, Sir, Your most obedient & very Humble servant.

P.S. I enclose you a copy of the curious letter which Mr. Sommer in Company with one other Man (who appears to be ignorant of Deviltry that has been carried on in that Quarter) brought to me from Torloch.
Governor Clinton.

AFFIDAVIT OF WILLIAM SOMMER.

Sometime in the Spring of the year 1777, Peter Summer, Jacob Mirch, and Jacob Miller sent a letter with a list of the Names of sundry inhabitants living at Torloch to Joseph Brant, the Indian, informing him that they would come over and join him; that accordingly about the beginning of August twenty Six in number under the Command of Jacob Miller, a Capt. of which number I myself was one, went and joined General St. Ledger whilst he lay before Fort Schuyler; that after continuing there about Five Days, Harmanus Barnhout and myself returned again to Torloch. And that sometime last fall, Jacob Mirch formerly of Torloch, but now with the Enemy, came to Torloch and Informed us that the enemy were a comming down, and that they had passed Fort Schuyler, that they were very strong and Intended to murder every man Woman and child before them, upon which Lieut Conradt Brown, George Riddich, Christopher Riddich, Jacob Hanes, Jun'r, David Frauts, Jacobus Happer, Christian Otman, Jacob Coughman, Robert Aurson, Henry Mirch, George Walker, Ernest Frats, Jacob Hanes, Mathias Mirch, Christopher Fraunce, Jacob Fraunce, Michael Mlrch, Abdries Fichter, Michael Frederick, George Frymin, Michael Bost, Michael Frymi, Jacob Fester and myself, formed ourselves into a Company under the Command of the aforesaid Jacob Mirch, and as soon as Sir John Johnson, who commanded the enemy on an Expedition into those parts at that time, had got down into the Country, we set out in order to join him and marched almost to Schohary, when meeting with Jost Brown, Isaac Vroman, Brassier Cryslar and one, old Jocham, all Inhabitants of Schohary, who told us that Sir John Johnson had left Schohary. We again returned to our homes at Torloch, except George Riddick, Henry Mirch and David Frauts. who went off with the said Jacob Mirch to the Enemy.

Sometime in June last Christopher Riddick wrote to Joseph Brant requesting him to come over with a party and fetch him and several other families (who had sons with the enemy) with their Effects away, but don't know whether any answers have been rec'd to that Letter. Four days before the action of the 10th Inst at Torloch. Henry Mirch who went off to the enemy last Fall, came to Torloch and informed us that Joseph Brant was coming with a strong party of Indians and Tories to Destroy Curry Town, which party arrived on the Borders of Torloch the Day following, where they were furnished with provisions, and on the next day being Sunday, Marched from Torloch lor Curry Town being joined by Lieut. Conrat Brown, Christian Olman, Christopher Riddick, Jacob Hanes, Jun'r, Henry Frauts, Michael Mirch, Jacobus Hopper, Matthias Mirch, Earnest Frets, Andres Fichter, Martis Bowman, Michael Fichter, George Walker, Godleap Bowman, John Summers, Henry Hanes, Frederick Mirch, Henry Loucks, Conrat Hopper, Christian Hanover, John Conradt, Jacob Coughman, Charles Hearwager, Michael Fredericks, Henry Hanes, Jun'r, Jacob Fraunce and myself, all Inbabitants of Torloch and Rynbecks; (we were all painted and equiped like Indians as were al the Tories belonging to the party). We were promised by Joseph Brandt and Barent Fry, the two Commandants of the Indians and Tories, Ten Dollars for every Scalp we took, and that each person who would join them should have fifty acres of land. That early on Monday morning we arrived at Curry Town, and after surrounding the Settlement began to set fire to their Houses and Barns and to drive away their horses & cattle, and that during these transactions I saw two white Children and one Black Child who were killed. After having burnt all the Houses and drove away all the Cattle that could be come at, we returned back as far that night as the Neighborhood of Torloch; the Indians and Tories going to their old Encampment in that Neighborhood together with some of the Inhabitants of Torloch, a few of which went to their own homes that night and joined the Enemy again before Day. About 6 o'clock in the morning the Indians were alarmed by the Hallowing of an Old Woman, and the whole immediately prepared for action and advanced towards the place where they heard the hallowing, and upon their discovering the Enemy, made great shoutings and Fired, but were soon obliged to retreat. They afterwards made several other Stands and tired in the best manner they could, untill finally they were obliged to Run quite off, dispersing and running some one way and some another, baving a great many men killed and Wounded. I myself saw Twenty Five who were killed; the greatest part of which were Indians, and from Reports of others, I was afterwards told they had upwards of Forty Killed and about as many wounded. I counted the Indians before the Battle begun and they were one hundred and Ninety In Number. The Tories amounted to between Ninety and a Hundred. After the action was over and the Enemy gone off, the People who lived at Torloch all went to their Homes And some time in the afternoon of the same day had a meeting at Lieut. Conradt Brown's when it was agreed to send the Letter which we brought here.

Jacob Clock who lately went of from Palatine district was with the Party under the Command of Barent Fry as I was informed.

William Sommer.

Personaliy appeared at Canajohary. this Fifteenth Day of July, One thousand Seven bundred and Eighty One before me William Petrie, Esq'r one of the Justices of the Peace for the County of Tryon, William Sommer, yeoman, living in the settlement called Torloch, and being sworn upon the Holy Evangelist of Almighty God, says that the Accounts contained in this Paper to which he has fixed his name are all strictly true to the best of his knowledge & Belief.
Sworn belore me,   Wm. Petrie, Justice

STATEMENT OF LIEUTENANT BROWN.

The 11th of July 1781.

Honored Sir, this is to give directions of the unlucky accident that is happened in Our Settlement, Sunday last we were all met together in a appointed Place, in order of a meeting to receive the Sacrament by old Domine Summer; we met together about ten o'clock in the forenoon, and in about one half an hour after this there came in two Men which lives in the Settlement which brought us the news that they heard a very hard firing of guns near of our Settlement, by this Alarm our meeting was broke up. Some People run for their Home and some stayed at the Meeting House with the old Minister; and presently we heard two guns fired about a mile from the Meeting House; directly after this there came in a horse with a saddle on belonging to the People which had been in the Meeting. Immediately we sent out a scout of three Men towards we thought where the two guns was fired.

The Scout brought us in the news that they found the tract of a large Party which passed the East Side through the Settlement. After this there came in two Men which lives at the lower end of the Settlement, which told us they went Westward, and that they have murdered Philip Hoffman and his wife, and took away two Horses. Sir, I am your most humble Servant Conradt Brown, Lieut.

Page 170, Volume VII

Colonel Marinus Willett to Governor Clinton Concerning Levies, Defence of the Frontier and new Officers.

Albany 6, Augt. 81

Sir, I expect this letter will be handed to you by the Attorney General. I have had some talk with him about my situation and the need I stand in of some Cash. He promises me to acquaint your Excellency of the substance of my Conversation with him. And he tells me he thinks you are authjorized to order us money on account. If upon examination this should appear to be the case I need say nothing more than I have already said, except that the difficulty of doing almost every kind of business is rendered greater for want of Cash.

The Regiments of Colonels Whiting, Van Ness, Van Alstine and Henry Rensselaer, of Claverack have forwarded the most of their new levies. I have received none from any other Regiments, but am doing all I can to press them in this business. By Governor Hancock's letter you will see how the reinforcements from the Eastward stands. I can hear of none moving this way. Should the necessary orders from the Commander in Chief be not yet forwarded, your Excellency will perceive the propriety of endeavoring to have it done without loss of time.

Colonel Lush will forward to you a list of the Officers appointed to take charge of the new levies. I beg leave to remind your Excellency that Lieutenant Abram A. Fonda, John Low and Bartel Hendricks were received and have done duty in the former levies in the place of some Lieutenants who did not accept of their appointments, but have not yet received Commissions.

Tomorrow of next day I propose to set out for Tryon County When I shall visit every post in the County, make some distribution of the ordance which is at present at Fort Herkemer a part of which ought before this time to have been removed but which has been out of power for want of strength. I am Your Excellencie's most obedient and very humble servant.
TO: His Excellency Governor Clinton.

Page 230, Volume VII

Colonel Willett Reports to the Governor the Presence of a Party of the Enemy
Whom He Vainly Pursued.
Fort Renselaer, 19th Augt. 1781.

Sir, Your Excellencies letter of the 14th Instant was handed to me yesterday evening at the German Flats, where I have been upon the business of removing part of the ordnance and stores from that place agreeable to Instructions for that purpose from General Clinton. I feel for the Inhabitants of Wawarsink who have lost their houses and Cattle. We will endeavor to be in a situation to meet those fellows should they bend their course this way.

E'very day since I left Albany I have been upon the move. The morning after my arrival here from that place a party of one hundred and fifty Indians &c made their appearance six miles above this place on the North side of the river. They burnt two empty houses and barns and three or four stacks of wheat, and made an attack upon the house of Mathew Timmerman, but were forced to quit it, without affecting anything. Upon the appearance of a small Detachment of levies and the assembling of the neighboring Inhabitants they fled shooting a few horses and cattle as they went off. I was two nights and part of three days in pursuit of them. But their flight was too brisk for me, and I lost considerable ground on taking a rout by the advise of my Guides to endeavour to gain their front. So that I was obliged to quit the pursuit, having no prospect of overtaking them. The men worn down with fatigue and quit out of provisions. By a fellow who through lameness had delivered himself a prisoner to one of the Inhabitants, I learnt the strength of the party, and that they came from Buck Island, which place they left the first of this month.

I should be glad to be informed by your Excellency who is to Muster the levies, and be directed into the particular modes necessary to be taken in order to receive their pay.

The returns called for in your letter of the 7th Instant shall be prepared and forwarded as soon as possible. I find much attention and labour necessary in order to procure a supply of provisions.

I have the honor to be your Excellencies most obedient and very humble serv't.
Marinus Willett.

His Excellency Governor Clinton.

P. S. I have just learnt that a sergeant belonging to the levies who had been two weeks in Albany, and was ordered to march this way, was stopped by the sheriff just as he was coming out of town and confined in gaol for Debt. Such Villanous practices as these ought to be stopped if possible. Tiner and such rascals will delight in intriguing in this way.

Page 350, Volume VII

Colonel Willett to Governor Clinton-Difficulties ot Enlisting Three Year Men-Apologizes tor Trespassing Upon the Governor's Time.

Fort Renslaer, 22d Sepr. 1781. Dear Sir, Your favour of the 11th instant was delivered to me two days ago at Johnstown where I have been at the request of the Whigs of the Lower part of the County to enquire who were the proper subjects to be remov'd from those parts agreeable to the Law, for removing the dangerous and disaffected from the frontiers.
I believe there is more arms than is sufficient at Albany to furnish all the three years men with and which are subject to Genl. Starks order. I furnished arms for some of those men when I was last at Albany by Order of Genl. Clinton, and I think there can be little difficulty in procuring Arms for as many Men as are at present engag'd in that service. But Clothing is avery Capital Article, and in my Opinion the most likely means that can be fallen uppon to procure Recruits at present-for the Levies grow bare of Cloth's indeed, and will in general soon be fit for little more than Garrison duty and many of em not for that merely for want of Cloths. If, therefare, it is possible to pracure a speedy supply of Clothing I conceive it will enduce much to encourage men from the Leives to engage in this service.

My Ideas of what in futer will be most effectual in procuring men for the Three Year Service I wauld gladly give your Excellency if I had any that I thought likely to ensure success. But I frankly acknowledge I have no flattering Ideas on this subject. Money and Clothing are in my Opinion the best means af pracuring Soldiers. Hence I conclude something that will make a Show as a Bounty and a Suit af good Cloaths redy to Deliver each Recruit up an his entring into the service, will be as likely means as any to became effectual in this business. Land with speculations in Land may do something but I do not understand that business. All, therefore, that I can say upan the Subject is, that I should be happy in Contributing in this Business if it was in my power, And should men far permanent service be rais'd for the defence of our frontiers and a plan adapted far their Defence that laaks tame as if it wauld answer the Expectation of the publick no man living wauld be readier too Exert himself in this Business then I will, But too serve another Campaign with the embarasments that has hither, and is like to Continue to attend this. I hape will never fall to my lt again.

Prospects from the Sother'd are truly pleasing. May they be Crowned with a Success eaqual to our reasanable expectations. We have receiv'd same formidable threatning in this Quarter. Should the Enemy pay us a serius visit, and we be so fortunate as to procure timely notice We propose to endeavour to speak to them on their way.

I wrot to yaur Excellency some time ago respecting the Mode of Mustring and paying the Levies. It is high Time some person should be Appointed to muster them as I cant see how they are ever to receive their pay until they are Mustered, I whish to have your Excellency's direcktions in this matter as soon as possible.

Thus farr during my Command in this Quarter I have been no small trouble to you, but your Excellency may rely upon it that when I do tresspass upon your time it is with reluctance. My situation has sometimes pointed it out as necessary to be particular and perhaps tedious. I have and still do find obstacles in my way that I did not expect, And am not without apprehension from circumstances that have come within my Observation that I shall have difficultys from other Quarters-that will equal all the moderation I can muster if not more to bear with for the Strange disposition I have found in professed whigs to Assist Tories and the support they may find from Laws which it is not possible to frame for every contingency that may arrive in a County Situate as this is, gives me reason from the present face of Affairs to suppose events not of the moste pleasing nature.

I have just hinted those matters to your Excellency, where I whish to have it lay for the present.

I am with the Greatest respect Your Most Obdt. & Humb. Sert.
Yr. Excellency Governor Clinton.

Page 370, Volume VII

Colonel Willett to Governor Clinton Regarding
News from the Fleet and Deserters.

Fort Renselaer, 2d October 1781.
Dear Sir, Please to accept of my hearty thanks for your favour of the 26th ultimo. by Captain Moody. The Victory obtained by the French over the British Fleet, brightens our Prospects. May it pave the way for our speedy entrance into the long lost Metropolis of this State.

To prevent the affluence of the dissafected from placing them into Offices of Power, I humbly conceive an object worthy the Attention of our Legislature. For events of this nature to take place after we have fought our way into the harbor of peace, Must be truly Mortifying to honest Whigs. May our Legislative Body have wisdom to provide means of security for honest Patriots, and Weapons to punish Villians & Rascals of every denomination.

I feel myself under particular obligations to your Excellency for the attention you have paid to the uninterruption of my present command. Nothing new presents itself in this Quarter at present.

I am endeavouring to prepair Materials to furnish your excellency with the State of my regt. for October. I wish to hear of means being provided to apprehend & punish deserters from the levies after the expiration of their time. Since we have executed the two men for Desertion and transferred one to the regular service, we have had no desertions from this Quarter and that is more than six weeks.

I shall be much obliged to you for directions respecting the Mustering of the levies to enable us to prepair our pay abstracts,
I am your Excellencies most obedient & very humble servt.
His Excellency Govr. Clinton.

Page 443, Volume VII

A Skirmish Near Johnson Hall

Major Ross Overtaken by Colonel Willett Who Drives Him From The Field With Serious Loss.
Schenectady, 26th October 1781. 6 O'Clock P.M.

My Lord, Last night about 10 O'clock I sent of Mr. Van Ingen, a young Gentleman who is my Clerk, to Colo. Willett in order to bring me the particulars, who theis moment returned. The Colo. Had no time to write. He has made a State of what has happened as near as he can recolet, he has been on the place where the Action was, which I herewith inclosed Colo. Wemp with the greatest part of his Regiment and the Albany Militia and about 30 Warriers of the Oneidaians left this in the Morning for Colo. Willett. Colonel Schuyler's Regiment went on this afternoon. I look out for the ammunition which will be forwarded the moment it arrives; please to excuse my writing in great hurry.

I am your Lordships Most Ob. Hum. Servant
H. Glen
To Major Genl. Sterling

Major Ross commanding officer at Bucks Island with about 450 men left that place in Batteaux and proceeded to Oneida lake where they left their boats, some provisions and about 20 lame men to take care of them, and proceeded from thence by the way of Cherry Valley to the Mohawk River, and made their first Appearance at the place opposite to Anthony's Nose from whence they proceeded to Warrens Bush and its Vacinity and destroyed upwards of 20 farm houses with out houses, great quantity of grain and killed two persons; after that they crossed to Mohawk River at a fording place about 20 miles Above this placer and proceeded in Order to Sir William's [Johnson] Hall, where they arrived about one Quarter of an hour before Colo. Willet with his body, who had crossed the river about 6 miles higher and Marched also for the same place. Colo. Willett commenced an Action with the British which was much in his favor, had not some of his troops which covered a field piece gave way, which was the loss of the piece and Ammunition Cart which in a little while after he bravely recovered, the Enemy had, however, striped the Cart of all its Ammunition. The Enemy retreated about 6 miles back into the woods; when the last Account just now comes leaves them; about thirty British have been taken during the Action and in the Morning before the Action commenced yesterday in the Afternoon. Colo. Willet went in persuit of them this morning with a force about equal to their as Account is also come to hand (although not official) that a party is sent from Fort Herkimer to destroy their boats and provisions, there are 7 of the enemy found dead on the field of action this Morning and 3 of ours between thirty & 40 wounded on both sides.

26 October 6 O'clock P.M.
For Major Genl. Lord Sterling.

The Loyalists

CARLETON, Sir Guy, LORD DORCHESTER. British soldier, born in Strabane, Ireland, 3 September, 1724; died in Maidenhead, 10 November, 1808. He greatly distinguished himself at the sieges of Louisburg, Quebec, and Belle Isle, and was wounded at the siege of Havana in 1762. In 1772 he became governor of Quebec, which he defended against the American army in December, 1775. He commanded the army that invaded New York in 1776, and fought a battle against Arnold on Lake Champlain. In 1777, on the nomination of Burgoyne to the command, he threw up his commission, but was appointed the same year lieutenant-general, and in 1781 appointed commander-in-chief in place of Sir Henry Clinton. When peace was concluded in 1783 he returned to England and was raised to the peerage.

HALDIMAND, Sir Frederick, British general, born in the canton of Neuchatel, Switzerland, in October, 1718; died in Yverdun, Switzerland, 5 June, 1791.

British/Canadian/Loyalist Armies

The Indian Department: The Indian Department was once organized to regulate the fur trade between the Indians and the white men but when the unrest began and then spread, the Indian Department in Canada assumed a military role and the officers received military ranks.

Both the Americans and British tried to sway the Native Americans to fight on their side, but because of their love for Sir William Johnson, the British were more successful. Guy Johnson, nephew of Sir William and later his son-in-law who was the superintendent after Sir William's death in 1774, lived in what is now the western part of Amsterdam at Guy Park Manor. Now one must cross railroad tracks to enter the manor.

The role of the Native Americans during the period 1775-1783 was an uneasy one. All parties involved in the war courted them and looked to them for support and feared them as enemies.

The Native Americans were badly split by the conflict of the American Revolution. At first they tried to remain neutral in the white man's war, but were drawn into the war. Only the Oneidas were allies of the Americans and this caused a rift in the Iroquois Confederation. When the war ended the Native Americans departed from their ancestral lands. Even the British surrendered some of their rights and lands in the peace treaty which followed. Rightfully, they felt betrayed by all the white men. Sadly, the Natives who supported the Americans were treated the same as that of those who supported the King; all were driven from their ancestral lands.

Other Native Americans, the former French allies known as the Seven Nations of Canada, of which the remnants of the Huron, the Ojibwa, and the Abeneki, as well as the Catholic Mohawks of Caughnawaga, were natural allies of the British by their physical location and their traditions.

In the main, however, as the war progressed, the far-sighted and conservative diplomats of the First Nations chose to support the cause of a distant British king over the close and voracious, land grabbing rebellion.

The Canadian governement supported several Indian Departments during the Revolution. John Campbell commanded the Department responsible for the Seven Nations of Canada, some Mohawks, and any western Natives brought East in direct support of military expeditions against the rebellious provinces.

Colonel Campbell's Deputy was Captain Alexander Fraser, who was given the Company of Select Marksmen to provide military support to Native warriors in 1776. Many Indian Deparment officers accompanied Capt. Fraser in 1776 and 1777, serving as the links between his regular unit and his Native allies.

After 1777, Fraser continued to work with the Natives while apparently commanding the 34th Foot's Light Company, largely composed of survivors of his Company of Select Marksmen. In 1779, The Indian Department and the Light Company of the 34th were both present at the last Native attempt to stop the Clinton/Sullivan Expedition against the Indians.

The Professional Soldiers: Detachments from two regular regiments served in the "upper posts." These were the 8th and 34th Regiments. Two companies from the 47th also helped build Fort Haldimand on Carleton Island in 1778. One regiment, the Roayl Highland Emigrants, began as a provincial corps. On Decmeber 24, 1778 the two battalions were placed in the regular army as the 84th.

The Provincials: To help subdue the rebellion, Britian raised many Provincial Corps of the British Army in her colonies. They were commonly called Loyalist regiments. These provincials thought of themselves as British Americans, in the ranks were men from every ethnic group living along the frontiers of the north: Huguenot French, Palatines, Swiss, Blacks, Alsatians and Dutch.

King's Royal Regiment of New York: The commander was Sir John Johnson, Sir William's son. Sir John fled from his home in Johnstown with 200 followers in June 1776 even after he had promised not to do so and went straight north through the Adirondack Mountains and arrived in a terrible state, half starved in Montreal. He raised two battalions of provincial corps to wreak havoc on his former neighbors.

Butler's Rangers: John Butler, who was from Caughnawaga or modern day Fonda, was a lieutenant-colonel of a full strength corps. The first action the corps saw was at the Battle of Oriskany. Native Americans also served in this corps including Captain Joseph Brant who served under John and as did John's son, Walter Butler, depending on the campaign.

By 1777 the British realized that overtures to the Indians might win over the Six Nations, and so they sent instructions to Sir Guy Carleton, the Governor and Commander-in-Chief at Quebec, to engage the Indians in an expedition led by Lieutenant Colonel Barry St Leger. St Leger was to command the right wing of an invasion of Upper New York, entering the colony at Oswego and moving down the Mohawk to Albany where he was expected to meet a larger army commanded by General John Burgoyne. This combined army would then make contact with an army moving north from New York City commanded by General Howe. In this manner a three pronged pincer would grasp New York from the rebels and effectively end the war. St. Leger was stopped at Oriskany, Burgoyne surrendered and Generak Howe never left New York City. Thus was halted the great pincer maneuver that was planned to stop the war in the early stages.

Butler moved into the Indian country in the spring of 1778. He held numerous conferences with the Indians and dispatched small expeditions against rebel fortifications. By late June he had mustered a sizeable force of 200 Rangers and 300 Indians and moved against Wyoming Valley (now Wilkes Barre, Pa).

Butler once again moved his Rangers back into the Indian country where they conducted devastating raids against the rebel frontier.

On November 10th after traveling through newly fallen snow, Butler's son, Captain Walter

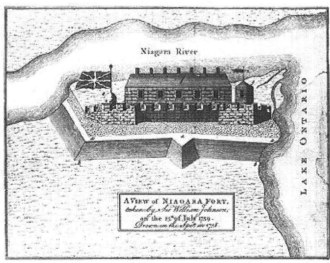

A VIEW of NIAGARA FORT, taken by Sir William Johnson, on the 25th July 1759. Drawn on the spot an 1728.

From a set of plans of forts in America, published by Mary Ann Rocque, London, 1765 (Courtesy, New York Public Library)

Butler, led a punishing raid into the tiny community of Cherry Valley. This terrible raid has left a stain on the history of the corps.

In 1779 the Americans mounted a major offence against Niagara, cutting through the Indian country and destroying almost every Indian village they entered.

At Newtown, on the Chemung River, Butler attempted to defeat and turn back the Americans, but artillery destroyed the confidence of the Indians and his defensive position was soon threatened by flanking forces. Butler ordered a retreat and the Rangers did not engage the rebels again until an ambuscade at the head of Lake Conesus. The trap was prematurely sprung, and Butler was forced to withdraw. Fortunately for Niagara, Sullivan had overextended his supply line, and within days of reaching Niagara he was forced to turn back.

The Rangers conducted a number of expeditions against the rebel frontier throughout the spring and summer of 1780. In the fall, Sir John Johnson was ordered to mount a major thrust into the Mohawk Valley by way of Oswego, and the Rangers were ordered to join him. As a raid, it was extremely successful, and Washington reported to Congress that the destruction would "likely to be attended with the most alarming consequences."

The war began to shift westwards, and one company of Rangers was dispatched to Detroit, and began operations against the Ohio frontier.

After a summer of company sized raids in 1781, Major John Ross was ordered to mount another expedition against the Mohawk. Again, as a raid, it proved successful, but Captain Walter Butler was killed in action while commanding the rear guard at West Canada Creek.

Captain William Caldwell's re-enforced company was in action at Lower and Upper Sandusky in June 1782 and won a significant victory over the American forces. In August, Caldwell's company was again in action at the Blue Licks in Kentucky where the Rangers and Indians were again successful. At the same time, Captain Andrew Bradt's company raided Wheeling, West Virginia, and put the settlement to the torch. This was the last action fought by the Rangers during the Revolution.

Other small units: Detroit Volunteers were French speaking farmers who came from along the Detroit River. The Loyal Foresters, recruited among the frontiersmen in Pennsylvania. Joseph Brant's Volunteers formed a third small unit of whites and natives.

The Native Americans: The Iroquois Confederacy of the Six Nations; Mohawk, Oneida, Cayuga, Onondaga, Tuscarora and Seneca. The only ones to side with the Americans were the Oneidas and this alienated them from the other tribes in the confederacy.

Forts Along The Frontier.

Fort Haldimand (1778 - 1814 ?), near Capt Vincent.

Located on Carleton (Buck's) Island. It was originally a British supply depot since 1775. This was the primary British naval base on Lake Ontario during the American Revolution. Construction was left uncompleted when the war ended in 1783.

It was an extensive stone and

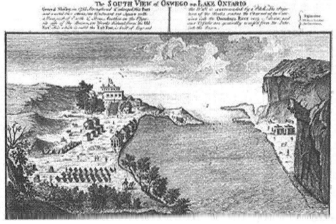

earthwork fort with 30 guns. The Americans took it without a fight in 1812, and then destroyed it. The island was formally annexed by the United States in 1817, the only territory to change hands as a result of the War of 1812. Some earthworks still remain. This is private property.

Fort Oswegatchie *(1760 - 1813), Ogdensburg*

The British fort was built on the site of the French **Fort la Présentation** (1749 - 1760), which was sometimes referred to as **Fort la Galette**. It was a palisaded enclosure with a stone redoubt and five guns. It was attacked and burned by Mohawks in 1749, rebuilt in 1750 as a moated, square earthwork fort with palisades 70 feet to a side, bastions at each corner, a powder house, chapel, barracks, warehouses, and a sawmill. It was captured by the British in 1760. It was attacked by Patriots in 1779. Americans took control in 1796. Garrisoned in 1812, and captured by the British in 1813. A reconstruction is being planned. A redan battery was located on the other side of town in 1812-1813, also captured by the British.

Fort William Augustus *(1760 - unknown), Ogdensburg*

Located three miles downstream from Fort Oswegatchie on Chimney Island (Isle Royale), this was previously French **Fort Lévis** (1759). It was a square log fort with four bastions, barracks, magazines, and officers' quarters, with 35 guns, and garrisoned by 300 men. The French may have also called it **Fort Isle Royale**. This position was regarded as a more strategic location to defend the river. The British attacked and captured the fort, and rebuilt it. In 1814, British **Chimney Island Blockhouse** and a 10-gun battery was built on the lower (northern) end of the island, after Ogdensburg was captured. The island was later obliterated by the St. Lawrence Seaway Project in 1957.

Fort St. Regis *(1755, 1814), St. Regis*

Old Fort Niagara (State Historic Site)
(1726 - 1963), Youngstown

Fort La Salle, a temporary French fort, was first established here in 1669. Attacked and destroyed by Senecas in 1675. **Fort Conti** was then built in 1679 but burned down sometime before 1682. It was composed of two 40-foot square log blockhouses enclosed by a palisade. Next came **Fort Denonville**, or

Fort at Niagara, in 1687, a four-bastioned palisade, but was abandoned in 1688 after supplies ran out. Fort Niagara was next - beginning with the "French Castle" or "House of Peace" in 1726. This structure was unique in that it resembled a French baronial mansion. Its granite walls were four feet thick, and massive arches were incorporated inside to support the rows of cannon on the second floor attic. Extensive fortifications and moats were constructed in 1756. The fort was taken by the British in 1759, and was a major base of operations during the American Revolution. Five additional redoubts and stockades were constructed along the portage road in 1760. The **North** and **South Redoubts** were built in 1766. The Americans took control in 1796. During the War of 1812, Fort Niagara and Fort George, Ontario duked it out in an unusual battle between forts. It was captured by the British again in 1813. In 1815 it was ceded back to the U.S. In 1839, modifications were made, including a new stone wall and postern gate, and new masonry casemates in the north and south walls. In 1841, new construction was started outside the old fort, consisting of barracks, Officers' Quarters, and a Life Saving Station. More buildings were added in the area after 1903, when the fort became a training post. In WWII the fort became a draftee reception center, and a POW camp. The old fort was turned over as a park in 1946. The remainder of the base in 1950 became an Air Force NIKE missile base until 1962.

Fort Ontario *(1755 - 1946*, intermittent), *Oswego*

The first fort was an eight-pointed star-shaped log stockade with a ditch. It was 800 feet in circumference, or 124 feet in diameter with a 14-foot high wall and a moat 18 feet wide and eight feet deep. It was armed with eight cannon and four mortars. It was also known as **Fort of the Six Nations**, or **East Fort**. It was abandoned to the French in 1756, and was then destroyed.

The second fort was built in 1758 and was pentagon-shaped with five bastions. It was deserted by 1770, and in a state of decay by 1776. The fort was burned by the Patriots in 1778. The ruins were occasionally used by the British as a base camp during the American Revolution, until it was regarrisoned in 1782. The defensive works were not rebuilt. The last action of the war occurred here as Patriot forces attempted to assault the fortress in the spring of 1783, only to withdraw upon learning of the Paris Peace Treaty. The fort became American in 1796. The British captured and burned it in 1814. The third fort was built between 1839 and 1844. It was converted and used as a training post and hospital between 1905 and 1946. The outer earthworks were removed during this time. It became a state park in 1949.

Source Material: <u>Loyal She Remains</u> Published by The United Emprie Loyalists' Association of Canada, 1984

Historical Map of the Central Mohawk Valley
by John C. Devendorf (used with permission)

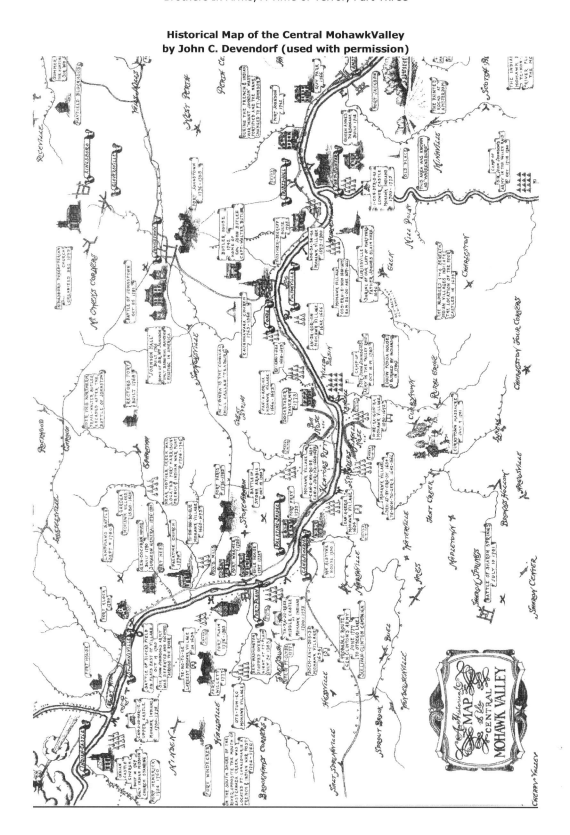

APPENDIX

Witch Hunts

This is the transcript of the trial and conviction of a slave named Gitty who was accused of witchcraft in Tryon County, Town of Palatine, in the area of present day St. Johnsville. This too is part of our past history and deserves a space. The people from the eighteenth century were unable to explain many events and when bad things happened without explanation, they looked for someone who was practicing witchcraft. In this day and age, we know why many things happen, science has explained much to us, but people in the past had no such help.

Tryon County

The examination of Gitty a Negroe Wench the property of Johannes Nellis taken before me Adam Loucks Esq., one of his Majesty's Justices of the Peace for said County relative to burning the barn of her said Master situate in Palatine District in the County reference. This examinant confessed that she on the night of the fifth instant March set fire to the barn of her Master Johannes Nellis. That she went to bed on the night of the said fifth of March that after she had been in bed sometime a man, but whether Black or White she could not tell as it was dark, called to her to get up and set the said Barn on fire upon which she got up took a cole of fire out of the house with her and carried it to the Barn there put it on the Barn floor. After which returned and went to her bed again.

Taken before me this 7th March 1774.
Adam Loucks, Justice.

At a special court held at Johns Town the 11 March 1774, before John Butler, Joseph Claus and Ada Loucks, esqr, Justices one whereof is of the Quorum. The five following principal Freeholders being duly summonded appeared and were sworn
John Thomson
Harmanus Smith
John Fonda
Peter Hanson
James Pennett
The prisoner pleaded not guilty.
Witnesses
Johannes Nellis
Adam Loux
Jacob Klock
??? Negroe Man belonging to Johannes Nellis
James Clow (free Negroe)

At a special court held at Johns Town in and for the County of Tryon this twenty eighth day of March in the year of our Lord one thousand seven hundred and seventy four.
Present
John Butler
Jellis Funda
Joseph Chew
Adam Loucks
Peter Hansen

(All Esquires)

This being Gitty a Negroe Wench belonging to Johannes Nellis, following her burning her master's barn. The prisoner being called pled not guilty.

The following Jurors were seated by Thos. Adams, one of the constables of said county and town.
James Bennet
John Thomson
Hermandus Smith
Peter Hanson
John Funda
Gilbert ?
Nathaniel Hilliard
Andrew Wemple
Wm. B. Bowen
Peter Bowen
John Visher
Christian Sheck
Evidence in behalf of Gitty.
Jun'r Gray
Hend'r Walrat
Jas. Watkins
William Smith?

The jury directed in to court and being called answered and said they find the prisoner guilty and agreeable to said verdict. Sentence was passed that she be carried to the place from whence she came and to be brout from there to the place of execution and there be burnt till she is dead.

Definition of wench (wĕnch)
noun.
1. A young woman or girl, especially a peasant girl.
2. A woman servant.
3. A wanton woman.

A note says that on March 30, 1774, Negress Gitty burnt at Johnstown for firing her master's barn. Slave of Mr. Johannis Nellis of Palatine District. Crime committed 3/5. Costs 22-16-11 (22 pounds, 16 shillings, 11 pence).

Copies of the original documents are on file in the Montgomery County Department of History and Archives in Fonda, NY.

A Witch in Esperence

There is also a story of a witch in Esperance. The lady in question came with her husband from France and settled in Esperance along the Schoharie Creek. The husband died soon after moving to the new home and his wife was left to fend for herself. She managed by raising her chickens and by tending her garden, but kept to herself. Due to her inability to speak English, she was very isolated and misunderstood.

About 1823 some unexplainable things happened to her neighbors and since the cause of the events were unknown, the widow was suspect. A meeting was called in the Stone Church and her death sentence was handed down. She was shot with silver bullets through the window of her cottage while her children were playing next to her. To be sure the witch was gone for good, a stake was pounded through her heart.

From a newspaper clipping on file in the above named Department of History.

Forger and Horse Thief Hung

Until 1836 when Montgomery and Fulton Counties separated, the county seat was in Johnstown and court was of course held at the county court house in Johnstown. In those days, extended hours were the norm for the court, they even held session on Saturdays.

In the year 1787 a case resulted in a conviction and hanging. It was a very different world than the one we occupy today; we deal much lighter with forgers and horse thievies; justice was dealt with a swifter hand.

The People of the State of New York vs. John Wormwood resulted in an indictment and conviction during the trial on a Saturday afternoon, August 18, 1787, for stealing a mare. The said John Wormwood was to be taken to the place of execution on the commons near the court house in Johnstown, and there he was ordered hanged by the neck until he be dead. Further ordered, the Sheriff of the County of Montgomery see this judgement executed on the fifth day of October next between the hours of ten o'clock in the forenoon and two o'clock in the afternoon of the same day.

The other case was tried on Friday November 19, 1790 and it too resulted in a conviction on an indictment for forgery. The said Samuel Cook, was ordered taken to the place of execution and that he be there hanged by the neck until he be dead, and ordered that the Sheriff of the County of Montgomery cause this judgment to be executed on the seventh day of January next between the hours of then o'clock in the forenoon and one of the clock in the afternoon.

From a newspaper clipping on file in the above named Department of History. Paper unknown and date of article unknown.

St. John's Reformed Church Records

St. John's has a tradition going back to the early days of settlement in the valley. The early church was probably a log church which was built at the eastern end of the present day Village of St. Johnsville up on the hill by the old Klock Cemetery. Jeptha Simms mentions the church in this book Frontiersmen of New York.

Volume I, Page 285.

The First Church at St. Johnsville.—"In this connection I should mention the fact that a German Reformed Church was erected at St. Johnsville, then known as "Zimmerman's," in 1770. This structure was built of wood, was of good size, and stood not far from its burying ground, yet to be seen about a mile eastward of the village. It was finished with a sounding board, as were nearly all churches at that period. When erected it was intended also to benefit the Indians in the neighborhood, having seats for them and the slaves of the white citizens. This edifice was demolished about the year 1818, near which time a church was erected to subserve its purposes within the present village. Who first labored in this church I am unable to state. Rev. John Henry Dyslin, a man of good repute, was its pastor form 1790 to 1815, when he died. The Rev. David Devoe was its pastor from 1816 to 1830, during which time the old church was demolished, and the one in the village erected. The second edifice gave place to a new one constructed of brick in 1881."

1725 (when the Palatines first came to the Mohawk Valley) was probably the date of the first wooden church structure, and the second wooden structure was built in 1756. Some say there could not have been a church before the war because there are no records of burning it during the war. Many churches were burned during the war, but the some other churches were not burned. Indian Castle and Fort Herkimer were not burned, for instance. Possibly it was not burned because the troops were already engaged in fighting when they came over the hill toward the church. Here we have another of history's mysteries which seems unable to be resolved from our time. The records which could have solved this riddle probably were burned in the fire at Albany in the early 1900s.

Reverend Dysslin died in 1813, not 1815 as Simms states.

The following records are from 1788-1812, the official time Rev. Dyslin served St. John's Reformed Church. We are sure the dominie began his ministry in 1788, the German church records begin in his handwriting on that date. There is a gap in the records and pages have been torn out of the record book which is most unfortunate.

Book 1

Some of the names begin with a lower case letter. The person who did the copy from the original text in the 1930's typed the names in this manner.

Translation:
Parentes=Parents
Infans=Infant
Testes=Witnesses

von=from (Canajoharie, Palatine, Canadaya Lake [Canada Lake], Caqunewagha or Caugnawaga is the present day Fonda. Danube or Canajoharie Castle is Indian Castle Church.)

VERZEICHNISS DER GETAUFTEN. 1788
Parentes Christoph Fox, von Palatine Catharina Fox, gebohrne Hess 13th Julii Infans. Johann friederich gebohren den 18tn May 1788 Testes friederich Getman Anna Eva Getman
Parentes Garret Van Schleyk, im Canajoharrie Castle Anna Von Schleyk, gebohrne Mebie 10tn Augusti Infans. Elisabeth Testes David P. Schuyler Elisabeth Mebie
Parentes Peter Mersch, im Canajoh: Castle Dorothea Mersch, geb. Mebie 10tn Augusti Infans Stephan Testes Abraham Mebie Rachel fetterli
Parentes Heinrich Hees, im Palatine Catharina Hees, geb: Bellinger 10tn Augusti Infans. Johann Jost Testes. Johannes Krieg Elizabeth Debusin
Parentes Alexander Mieseles, im Palatine Dorothea Mieseles, geb. Walther 17tn Aug: Infans. Johannes Testes. Adam Walther Anna Fox
Parentes Johannes Konnikum, im Canaj. Castle Margaretha Konnikum 17tn Augusti Infans. Johannes Testes Johannes Wendeker Catharina Wendeker

---

Translations. BAPTISMAL REGISTER 1788
Parents Christoph Fox, of Palatine Catharina Fox, born (i. e. maiden name) Hess July 13 Infant Johann Friederick, born Mary 18, 1788 Witnesses Freiderich Getman Anna Eva Getman

Page 4
1788 Parentes Johannes Helmen, von Palatine Magdalena Helmen, geb: Ehle 30n Augusti Infans. Johannes Testes. Johannes Ehle Elisabeth Ehle
Parentes Niclaus Koch Magdalena Koch 31tn Augusti Infans Anna Testes. Salomon Youker Anna Joran
Parentes Johannes Zimmerman 14tn Septembris Infans Elisabeth Testes
Parentes Heinrich Zimmerman, von Schnellenbusch Margaretha Zimmerman, geb. Bellinger 16tn Septembris Infans Magdalena Testes Peter Bellinger Magdalena fehling
Parentes Georg Staring, von Schnellenbusch Anna Staring 20tn Septembris Infans Dorothea Testes Johannes Staring Dorothea Zimmerman
Note. Observe that this record shows the DATE OF BAPTISM in the first column, and that very few dates of birth appear.

Page 5.
1788
Parentes Peter Killsz, von Schnellenbusch Margaretha Killsz 21tn Septembris Infans. Conrad Testes
Parentes Jacob Keller Maria Keller 21tn Septembris Infans Wilhelm Testes
Parentes Datt Kennedy Nancy Kennedy 25tn Septembris Infans. Robert Johnston, gebohren im May 1787 Testes John Johnston Maria Hauss
Parentes Johannes fehling, von Palatine Elisabetha fehling, geb: Schmid 5tn Octobris Infans. Johann Dieterich Testes. Johannes Lauer Maria Schmid
Parentes Isac Von Camp Jannike Van Camp 12tn Octobris Infans. Sara Testes. Moses Von Camp Elisabeth Von Camp
Parentes Georg Rapon, von Palatine Elisabeth Rapon, geb: fehling 25tn Octobris Infans. Anna Testes. Peter Ocher Magdalena fehling
Parentes Philipp Herder, auf German flacht * Catharina Herder, geb: Philips 2tn Novembris Infans. Anna Testes Wilhelm Philips Anna Margaretha Herder
Parentes Johannes Palsli Catharina Palsli 3tn Novembris Infans. Jacob Testes Jacob Hubel Maria Hubel
Translation. * GERMAN FLATTS

Page 6.
1788

Parentes Heinrich Gerber, von Palatine Maria Gerber, geb: Deinman 5tn Novembris Infans. Peter Testes. Peter fox Elisabeth Eigenbrod

Parentes Elias Heid Sara Heid 9tn Novembris Infans. Daniel Testes Justinus

Parentes Niclaus Hauss, im Canajoh. Castle Catharina Hauss, geb: Spon 9tn Novembris Infantes Conrad)Zwillinge Nicolaus) Testes Wilhelm fox Margaretha fox Georg Hahn Catharina Hauss

Parentes Joseph Pikard Magdalena Pikard, geb: fort 16tn Novembris Infans. Andreas Testes. Christian Plotau Catharina fort

Parentes Isaac Ellwood, im Canajoh. Castle Magdalena Ellwood, geb: Schneider 16tn Novembris Infans. Isaac Testes. Jacob Von Ahle Magdalena Sanders

Parentes Jacob C. Klock, von Palatine Anna Klock 23tn Novembris Infans. Elisabeth Testes

Parentes Georg Tyffendorf, von Canajoharrie Catharina Tyffendorf, geb. fox 23tn Novembris Infans. Margaretha Testes Johannes Wendeker Catharina Wendeker

Page 7.
1788
Parentes Philipp fehling, von Palatine Margaretha fehling, geb: Zimmerman 7tn Decembris Infans. Catharina Testes. Wilhelm Zimmerman Catharina Zimmerman

Parentes Georg Hauss, im Canaj. Castle Maria Hauss, geb: Mebie 14tn Decembris Infans. Conrad Testes Bartholomeus Mebie Margaretha freymaurer

Parentes Johannes Hauss Magdalena Hauss, geb: Staring 14tn Decembris Infans. Maria Testes Martin Von Schleyk Maria Von Schleyk

Parentes Nehemiah Hubel Lucredy Hubel 21tn Decembris Infantes John Shubel, gebohren im aprill 1785 Thim, gebohren in august 1786 Testes John Gottlieb Braun Maria Crennel Johannes fehling Anna Glok

Parentes Jacob Keller, von Canajoharrie Magdalena Keller, geb: Nellis 29tn Decembris Infans. Jacob Testes. Johannes Nellis Anna Nellis

Page 8.
1789
Parentes Heinrich Empade, von geisberg Magdalena Empade 4tn Januarii Infans. Jacob Testes Johannes Susanna

Parentes William Nicols, von Schneidersbusch Catharina Nicols, geb: Reay 10tn Januarii Infans. John, gebohren den 12tn May 1788 Testes Simon Nicolls Anna Nicolls

Parentes Jacob gower Hauss, von Schneidersbusch Catharina Hauss, geb: Wendeker 11tn Januarii Infans. Conrad Testes Conrad Pikard Catharina Petri

Parentes Heinrich Scheffer, von Schnellenbusch Anna Scheffer, geb: Schnell 11tn Januarii Infans Magdalena Testes Conrad Zimmerman Magdalena

Parentes Christian Plotau, von Schnellenbusch Catharina Plotau 11tn Januarii Infans. Catharina Testes Gottlieb Braun Catharina Schnell

Parentes Thomas Muscher von Gaissberg Guelia Muscher 11tn Januarii Infans Dines Testes Johannes Bakos Magdalena Bakos

Parentes David Chesti, von Schnellenbusch non Maria Dachi nupti* 11tn Januarii Infans. John Johannes Meyer Catharina Meyer

Parentes John frevel Anna frevel 17tn Januar. Infans Thomas gebohren den 13 May 1788 Testes Thomas Young Maria Lise Young
TRANSLATION: *PARENTS NOT MARRIED

Page 9.
1789
Parentes David Meyer von Canajoh: Castle Anna Meyer, geb: Teygert 18tn Januarii Infans Elisabetha Testes friderich Herder Maria Lise Herder

Parentes Johann Jost Louks, von Canaj: Castle Margaretha Louks, geb: Mebie 1tn februarii Infans. Peter Testes Peter Louks Margaretha Louks

Parentes Peter Hauss, von Gaissberg Anna Hauss, geb: Doreschad 7tn februarii Infans. Maria Testes Adam Scheffer Susanna Scheffer

Parentes Johann Georg Yuker, von Palatine Elisabeth Yuker, geb: Schall 8tn februarii Infans Johannes Testes Niclaus Scheffer Anna Scheffer

Parentes Gottfried Hoe, von Palatine Apollonia Howe, geb: Baxter 8tn februarii Infans. Jacob Testes Jacob Zimmerman Margaretha Baxter

Parentes Michel frank, von Klesberg Catharina frank 8tn februarii Infans. Johan Georg Testes Georg Ocher Elisabeth Ocher

Parentes Johanes flander, von Tillenburg Margaretha flander, geb: Fox 12tn februarii Infans. Jacob Testes Jacob flander Elisabeth fox

Parentes Andreas Palsli, von Palatine Lea Palsli, geb: Pikard 15tn februarii Infans. Maria Testes Jacob Palsli Maria Pikard

Note. Entry No. 7 Johanes Flander. The line over the "n" indicates an "n" omitted. It is the intention in this copy to supply all omissions of this description, but in this particular case it was overlooked by the copyist; therefore the name appears as it was written in the original.

Page 10.
1789
Parentes Peter Weber von German flacht Maria Weber 15tn februarii Infans Elisabeth Testes. Jacob Ibig Elisabeth Weber

Parentes Peter Hellegas, von Palatine Catharina Hellegas geb: Schall 22tn februarii Infans. Jacob Testes Jacob Bellinger Anna fehling

Parentes Dines flander von Palatine Magdalena flander, geb: fox 22tn februarii Infans. Peter Testes Johannas fox Anna fox

Parentes Heinrich flander, von Palatine Magdalena flander, geb: Klok 11tn februarii Infans Elisabeth Testes Georg Wild Dorothea Wild

Parentes John Young, von Canajoharrie Margaretha Young 22tn februarii Infans. Anna Testes Jacob Cordimann Anna Cordimann

Parentes Sebastian Ofenhauser, von Palatine Catharina Ofenhauser 22tn februarii Infans. Anna Catharina Testes Johannes Hess Anna Hess

Parentes Joseph Kesseler, von Palatine Margaretha Kesseler, geb: Braun 23tn februarii Infans Johann friderich Testes friderich Bellinger Catharina Bellinger

Parentes Dieterich Young, von Schneidersbusch Christina Young, geb: Scharmann 25tn februarii Infans. Margaretha gebohren den 25t Jan: 1789 Testes Mr. Paul Hochstrasser Mrs. Margaretha Paris

Page 11.
1789
Parentes Matheus Schall, von Gaiseberg Maria Schall 1tn Martii Infans. Johannes Testes. Johannes Schall Margaretha Schall

Parentes Johann Jost Klock, von Schneidersbusch Maria Klock, geb: Gerlach 1tn Martii Infans. Johannes Testes Johannes Klock Anna Klock

Parentes Jacob J. N. Weber, von German flacht Margaretha Weber 3tn Martii Infans. Abraham Testes John Doleny Gertrud Boom

Parentes Johannes finster, von Neu Deutschland Maria friderika finster 3tn Martii Infans. Georg Testes friderich Ayrer Elisabeth Hofstetter

Parentes Jacob Lenz, von Neu Deutschland Catharina Lenz 3tn Martii Infans. Jacob Testes. Jacob Burcky Anna Burcky

Parentes Michel Wuterich, von New Deutschland Elisabeth Wuterich 3tn Martii Infans. Elisabeth Testes Jacob Lenz Elisabeth Hofstetter

Parentes Jacob Bell, von Germanflacht Elisabeth Bell 9tn Martii Infans. Margaretha Testes Johannes Me ckoms Anna Margaretha Hellmer

Parentes Adam Staring, auf dem lang Chandel Catharina Staring 9tn Martii Infans. Elisabeth Testes friderich Gemmer Catharina Staring

Parentes Johannes Seufer von Schneidersbush Anna Maria Seufer 10tn Martii Infans. Gertrud Testes Georg Louks Gertrud Louks

Page 12.
1789
Parentes RobertG Dreh von Tillenburg Elisabeth Greh, geb: Deyggert 11tn Martii Infans Catharina Testes Jacob frisch Catharina Deyggert
Parentes Heinrich Bellinger von Palatine Anna Eva Bellinger, geb: Counterman 15tn Martii Infans Catharina Testes Michel Bader Catharina Zimmerman
Parentes Levi Odell von Oswago Elisabeth Odell 15tn Martii Infans Margaretha Testes Georg Young Margaretha Wallrath
Parentes Johannes Fink, von Stonearabie Dorothea fink, geb: fox 15tn Martii Infans. Maria gebohren den 15tn febr. 1789 Testes Peter fox Margaretha Hellegas
Parentes Wilhelm feder, von Schneidersbusch Elisabeth feder, geb: Bellinger 20tn Martii Infans. Georg Heinrich Testes Georg Heinrich Bell Catharina Bell
Parentes Johannes Petri, von Schneidersbusch Dorothea Petri 20tn Martii Infans Johann Jost, gebohren den 15tn febr: 1789 Testes Johann Jost Petri Eva Petri
Parentes Johannes Tyffendorf, von Schellenbusch Margaretha Tyffendorf 20tn Martii Infans. Dorothea Testes Georg Tyffendorf Catharina Tyffendorf
Parentes Wilhelm Zimmerman, von Palatine Catharina Zimmerman geb: fehling 22tn Martii Infans Johann Dieterich Testes Dieterich fehling Elisabeth Zimmerman

Pg. 13
1789,
Parentes, Jacob fehling, von Palatine, Anna fehling, geb: fox 22nt Martii, Infans, Peter Testes, Johannes fehling, Elisabeth fehling
Parentes, Jost Klock, von Palatine, Catherina Klock, geb: Krause 22nt Martii, Infans, Heinrich Testes, Heinrick Hees, Catharine Hees
Parentes, friderich Bellinger, von Lang Candel, Magdalena Bellinger, geb: Wollever 25tn Martii, Infans, Catharina Testes, Peter Bellinger, Catharina Scha----*
Parentes, Christoph Schumacher, von Lang Candel, Elisabeth Schumacher 26tn Martii, Infans, Maria Testes, Jacob Schumacher, Maria E. frank
Parentes, friderich Hess, von Lang Candel, Anna Maria Hess, geb: Vollmer 26tn Martii, Infans, Magdalena Testes, Christoph fox, Elisabeth fox
Parentes, Johannes Kesseler , von Lang Candel, Catherina Kesseler 26tn Martii, Infans, Catharina Testes, Conrad Kesseler, Catharina Kesseler
Parentes, Conrad Lauer, von Palatine, Anna Lauer, geb: fehling 1tn April, Infans, Johann Niclaus Testes, John Niclaus Pfost, Elisabeth Pfost
Note, entry No.3. The name of the witness Catharina Scha---? Has been corrected and is illegible: the name may be Schaver.

Pg. 14
Parentes , Jacob Yuker, von Palatine, Magdalena Yuker, geb: Dusler 5tn Aprill, Infans, Maria Testes, Andreas Scheffer, Maria Wallrath
Parentes, Peter P. Schuyler, von Canajoharrie Castle, Catharina Schuyler, geb: Freymaurer 10tn Aprill, Infans, Abraham, gebohren dan 29tn Martii Testes, Abraham Mebie, Margaretha Freymaurer
Parentes, David Mebie, von Canajoharrie Castle, Gertrud Mebie, geb: Freymaurer 10tn Apirll, Infans, Catharina Testes, Joseph Mebie, Catharina Mebie
Note: Some of the pages of the record are too long to transcribe on a single page of the copy. The remainder of such pages have a letter before the page number of the copy, which indicates that the part transcribed on this page is to complete an original page.
Notes for page 19. Omitted there on account of lack of room. Entry No. 1 Infant, Samuel born the 7th December 1782. The last figure of the date is blotted; it may be "1783". Entry No. 4.

Witnesses. Johannes Countermann; Maria, wife Entry No 7. Infant, Elisabeth, born Oct. 11, 1789. Notes for page 20. Omitted there on account of lack of room. Entry No. 1. This entire entry in the original record, is written upside down, by turning the book over. Obviously it is the record of baptism of an illegitimate child. There are a number of other entries following in this record, which were also written upside down by Dominie Dysslin. While the other entries are not as complete in detail as this one, there seems to be every reason to believe, that this was the method adopted by Dominie Dysslin, for recording the baptisms of illegitimate children. On the account of the difficulty in removing carbon sheets from the typewriter, it was not possible to transcribe the "upside down" entries as they appear in the original record.

The translation of entry No. 1 follows: November 19th , was baptised in Yukersbusch, a child called Elisabeth, born November 13, 1789. The mother of the child is Catharina McKieu of Weststeyn, and has declared as father of the child, Ludwig Book living at Weststein. Baptism witnesses were Frederic Ostrot and Elisabeth Ostrot.

Notes for page 25. Entry No. 5. **This entry is written upside down. Entry No. 6. Infants, Maria and Anna. Twins.

Pg. 15

Parentes, Niclaus forbus, von Canajoh. Castle, Sara forbus 13tn Aprill, Infans, Alida Testes, Johannes Meyer, Alida Meyer

Parentes, Wilhelm Bottiger, von Neu Deutechland, Margaretha Bottiger 26tn Aprill, Infans, Johannes Testes, Johannes Bender, Elisabeth Bender

Parentes, Niclaus P. Schuyler, von Canajoh. Castle, Elisabeth Schuyler, geb: Herchimer 28tn Aprill, Infans, Heinrich Testes, Severiras Deyggert, Magdalena Herchimer Testes, Johannes C. Nellis, Della Bellinger 17tn May, Infans, Catharina

Parentes, Georg Lambert, von Cherri velly, Magdalena, geb: Bellinger

Parentes, Johannes Yuker, von Palatine, Anna Yuker 17tn May, Infans, Johnannes Testes, Johannes Scheffer, Elisabeth Schall

Parentes, Jacob Wallrath, von Gaiseberg, Maria Wallrath 17tn May, Infans, Margaretha Testes, Niclaus Dachstetter, Margretha Dachstetter

Parentes, Adam Bersch, von Palatine, Annna Bersch, geb: Eigenbrod 23tn May, Infans, Jacob, geb: dan 5tn May 1789 Testes, Johannes Hess, Maria Eigenbrod

Parentes, Georg Wild, von Palatine, Dorothea Wild, geb: Nelles 24tn May, Infans, franz Daniel Testes, Heinrich Smith, Maria Smith

Pg. 16

Parentes, Jacob Zimmerman, von Palatine, Magdalena Zimmerman, geb: fehling 5tn Julii, Infans, Anna Testes, Johannes fehling, Elisabeth fehling

Parentes, Laurent Rayen, von Gaisberg, Anna Dieter Rayen 5tn Julii, Infans, Cornelis Testes, Johannes Wollever, Catharina Wollever

Parentes, Johannes Meyer, von Schnellenbusch, Catharina Meyer 5tn Julii, Infans, Heinrich Testes, Johannes Meyer , Alida Mebie

Parentes, Peter Bellinger, von Palatine, Elisabeth Bellinger 12tn Julii, Infans, Anna Testes, friderich Bellinger, Catharina Bellinger

Parentes, friderich Wallrath, von Canaj: castle, Catharina Wallrath 19tn Julii, Infans, Elisabeth Testes, Conrad Killsz, Elisabeth Killsz 19tn Julii, baptizatus, Wuster Deken, von Canajoharrie Castle Testes, Heinrich Wollever, ------- Wollever

Parentes, Heinrich Zimmermann, von canajoharrie castle, Elisabeth Zimmerman 2tn Augusti , Infans, Alida Testes, Adam Zimmermann, Dorothea Bischoff

Parentes, Johannes Bakos, von Palatine, Magdalena Bakos 23tn Augustii, Infans, Wilhelm Testes, Johannes Klock, Catharina Klock

Parentes, gnellis C. Bekman, von Palatine, Catharina Bekman, geb: Wallrath 23tn Augusti, Infans, Catharina Testes, Heinrich Bekman, Margaretha Beckman

Pg. 17

Parentes, Georg H(s). Klock, von Palatine, Margaretha Klok, geb: Ofenhauser 26tn Augusti , Infans, Daniel Testes, Daniel Hess, Maria Hess

Parentes, Bartholomeus farbusch, von Canajoharrie Castle, catharina farbusch, geb: forer 6tn Septembris, Infans, Adam Testes, Adam forer, Margretha forer

Parentes, Peter Killsz, von Schnellenbusch, Margretha Killsz, geg: Louks 6tn Septembris, Infans, Anna Margretha Testes, Jost Louks, Catharina Schnell

Parentes, Georg Stahli, vom fald, Dorothea Stahli, geb: Schumacher 13tn 7bris, Infans, Delia Testes, Marx Kesseler , Delia Kesseler

Parentes, Jacob Rima, von Neu Deutschland, Dorothea Rima 13tn 7bris, Infans, Catharina Testes, Georg Rima, Sara Lenzin

Parentes, Johannes Weber, vom fald, Magdalena Weber, geb: Keller 13tn 7bris, Infans, Jacob Testes, Jacob Weber, Elisabeth Meyer

Parentes, Johannes Conr.(s) Klock, von Canajoharrie Castle, Apollonia Klock, geb: Keller 20tn 7bris, Infans, Georg Testes, Warner farbusch, Catharina Klock

Parentes, Ludwig Steinman, von Canajoh: Castle, Catharina Steinman 20tn 7bris, Infans, friderich Testes, friderich bonstetter, Maria Bonstetter

Note. Entries No.1 and No.7. The small (s) probably indicates the possessive and indicates the name of the father of the individual .See also note on page 21.

Pg. 18

Parentes, Ludwig Richard, von Schneidersbusch, Maria Rickard 20tn 7bris, Infans, Anna Testes, Johannes Seufer, Maria Seufer

Parentes, Jacob Krass, von Palatine, Catharina Krass, geb: Hellmer 20tn 7bris, Infans, Georg Testes, Georg Hellmer, Catharina Hess

Parentes, Cornelius Lamberson, von Schneidersbusch, Pally Lamberson 20tn 7bris, Infans, William, gebohren den 4tn Aug 1789 Testes, Jacob G. Klock, Margaretha Klock

Parentes, Georg Herchimer, von Canajoharrie Castle, Maria Herchimer, geb: Louke 29tn 7bris, Infans, Anna Testes, Heinrich Herchimer, Catharina Zimmerman

Parentes, Georg Von Schleyk, von Canaj: Castle, Margretha Von Schleyk, geb: Pikard 11tn 8bris, Infans, Gerret Testes, Gerret Von Schleyk, Anna Von Schleyk

Parentes, ---------, fort von Yukersbusch 13tn 8bris, Infans, Johannes Testes,

Parentes, Georg Adam Smith, von Canaj: Castle, Anna Smith 18tn 8bris, Infans, Rodolph Testes, Joseph Smith, Elisabeth Clerk

Parentes, John Niclaus Christman, Maria Christman 18tn 8bris, Infans, Andreas Testes, Andreas feind, catharina feind

Parentes, Elind Nikerson, Palatine, Margretha Nikerson 18tn 8bris, Infans, Nathanael born 19tn 8brie 1784. Testes, John Rice, Catharina Rice

Note. 7bris - September 8bris- October.

Pg. 19

Parentes, Samuel Jennings, Palatine, Mary Jennings 18tn 8bris, Infans, Samuel born the 7th xbris 1782.

Parentes, Elind Nikerson, Palatine, Margretha Nikerson 18tn 8bris, Infans, John, born 22tn April 1787. Testes, Conrad Klock, Margretha Baxter

Parentes, Elind Nikerson, Palatine, Margretha Nikerson 18tn 8bris, Infans, Elias, born the 8tn April 1789 Testes, Warner farbus, Mary Haus

Parentes, Johannes Dachstetter, Cannajoh: District, Catharina Dachstetter 25tn 8bris, Infans, Elisabeth Testes, Johannes Countermann, Maria, uxer

Parentes, John Enckisch, von Palatine, Anna Enckisch, geb: Klock 28tn 8bris, Infans, Lea Testes, John, Jac: Tyffendorf, Catharina Klock

Parentes, Conrad Killsz, von Canajoh: Castle, Elisabeth Killsz, geb: Cerf 29tn 8bris, Infans, Conrad Testes, Niclaus Killsz, Eva Killsz

Parentes, John Dinis, von Neu Deutschland, Elisabeth Dinis 31tn 8bris, Infans, Elicaboth, nata d

11tn 8bris 1789 Testes, Christoph Strubel, Marie Lise Strubel
Parentes, Christian Warmuth, Canajoh: Castle, Maria Warmuth, geb: Rker 15tn Novembris, Infans,
Christian Testes, Wilhelm Fox, Margretha Fox
Parentes, Conrad Zimmerman, von Schnellenbusch, Magdalena Zimmerman, geb: Schnell 15tn
Novembris, Infans, Maria Testes, John Jost Schnell, Maria Schnell
Note. For translation etc. see page 14

Pg. 20
1789, dan 19tn Novembris warb in Yukersbusch ein Kind getauft nahmens Elisabeth gebohren dn
13 Novbris 1789. Die Muter das kindes ist Catharina Mekieu von Weststeyn. Und hat als Vater des
Kindes anga ge ben dan Ludwig Back wohnhaft su weststein. Taufmeugen waren frederic Ostrot,
Elisabeth Ostrot.
Parentes, Andreas firer, von canajoh: Castle, Anna firer, geb: Aesius 26tn Novembris, Infans, John
Testes, John fehling, Anna Smith
Parentes, Niclaus Von Schleyk, Canajoh: Castle, Elisabeth Von Schleyk, geb: Leder 26tn
Novembris, Infans, Eva Testes, Niclaus Haus, Eva Knieskern
Parentes, Ulric Bader, Yukersbusch, Elisabeth Bader 29tn Novembris, Infans, Ulric, born 15tn
Novembrie 1789 Testes, Jacob Bellinger, Sophia Klok
Parentes, Jacob farbus, von Canajoharrie Castle, Eva farbus, geb: Haus 20tn Decembris, Infans,
Conrad, born 12tn xbris Testes, Conrad Klock, Catharina farbus
Parentes, Johannes Phil (s) Hellmer, von Palatine, Anna Hellmer, geb: Dusler 23tn Decembris,
Infans, Anna Testes, Jacob J. Klock, Anna Klock
Parentes, Alexander Mieseles, von Palatine, Dorothea Mieseles, geb: Walder 25tn Decembris,
Infans, Catharina Testes, Johannes Klock, Catharina Klock
Parentes, Adam Bellinger, von Palatine, Magdalena Bellinger 26tn xbris Infans, Elisabeth Testes,
Peter Bellinger, Elisabeth Zimmerman
Parentes, Johannes Schnell, von Schnellenbusch, Elisabeth Schnell 26tn Decembris, Infans, Johann
Jost Testes, frideric Meyer, Catharina Meyer
Note. For translations, see page 14.

Pg. 21
Parentes, Johannes (Dieter.) fehling, von Patatine, Elisabeth fehling, geb: Schmid 27tn Decembris,
Infans, Matheus Testes, Heinrich Zimmerman, Anna Schmid
Parentes, Heinrich Nellis, von Palatine, Catharina Nellis 27tn Decembris, Infans, Catharina Testes,
John Nellis, Maria Hellmer
Parentes, Jacob (Johannis) Klock, von Palatine, Anna Klock, geb: Klock 27tn Decembris, Infans,
Georg Testes, Jacob Klock, Magdalena Klock
1790
Parentes, Jean Pierre Pouire, von schneidersbusch, Catharina Pouire 1tn Januarii , Infans, Juliane
Testes, Antoine Kaufman, Juliane Kaufman
Parentes, Robert Beyer, von Schneidersbusch, Maria Catharina Beyer 1tn Januarii, Infans,
Catharina Testes, Johannes Beyer, Margretha Beyer
Parentes, Israel Runnels, von Palatine, Dorothea Runnels, geb: Nellee 2tn Januarii, Infans,
Dorothea Testes, John frederic Hess, Catharina Hess
Parentes, friderich Ostrot, von Yukersbusch, Elisabeth Ostrot, geb: Klock 3tn Januarii, Infans, Eva
Testes, Conrad Hellegas, Eva Hellegas
Parentes, Peter Khle, von canaj: Caste, Gadlein Khle 10tn Januarii, Infans, Dorothea Testes, Dally
Mebie, Anthonia Rhle
Notes. Entries No.1 and No.3. The names in parenthesis are as they arrear in the original; they are
the names of the fathers of the individuals.

Pg. 22

Parentes, Adam Wallrath, von Palatine, magdalena Wallrath, geb: Klock 14tn Januarii, Infans, David Testes, Christoph Fox, Catharina Fox

Parentes, Johnannes Preizs, von Palatine, Maria Preizs 14tn Januarii, Infans, David Testes, Jacob G. Klock, Maria Klock

Parentes, Conrad Hellegas, von Palatine, Anna Eva hellegas, geb: Wallrath 14tn Januarii, Infans, Maria Testes, Adam Wallrath, Maria Wallrath

Parentes, Niclaus Scheffer, von Palatine, Anna Scheffer, geb: Schall 17tn Januarii, Infans, Johannes Testes, Peter scheffer, Magdalena Schnell

Parentes, Christian Haus, von Yukersbusch, Christina Haus 17tn Januarii, Infans, Catharina Testes, Heinrich Tillenbach, Catharina Tillenbach

Parentes, Jacob Young, von Canandaya Lake, Eva Young, geb: Knieskern 24tn Januarii, Infans, George. Gebohren d. 18tn December 1789. Testes, Georg Young, Eva Knieskern

Parentes, John Kreninger, von Canaj: Castle, Delia Kreninger 24tn Januarii, Infans, Susanna Testes, John Burger, Susanna Burger

Parentes, John Huber, von Schneidersbush, Gertrud Huber 24tn Januarii, Infans, Anna Testes, Adam Staring, Elisabeth Staring

1790

Pg. 23

Parentes, John Meyer, von Canaj: Castle, Alida Meyer, 24tn Januarii, Infans, Alida, Testes, Urias Reist, Alida Herchimer

Parentes, James Hibey, von Canajoh: District, Anna Ribey geb: Klock, 25tn Januarii, Infans, Catharina, Testes, Jacob Meyer, Catharina Meyer

Parentes, Henry Cranz, von fald, Gertred Cranz, 31tn Januarii, Infans, Marcus, born d 10tn Jan, Testes, Marcus Kesseler, Delia Kesseler

Parentes, John Weber, von der flacht, Maria Weber, 31tn Januarii, Infans, Anna Margretha, Testes, Georg Weber, Margretha Weber

Parentes, James Clarke, von der flacht, Margretha Clarke, 31tn Januarii, Infans, Sara, Testes, John Mayer, Maria Mayer

Parentes, Joseph Mayer, von der flacht, Apollonia Mayer, 1tn Februarii, Infans, Peter, Testes, Peter Bellinger, Elizabeth Bellinger

Parentes, Georg Wallrath, von Canajoh: Castle, Anna Wallrath geb: Leip, ltn Mars, Infans, Heinrich, Testes, Heinrich Dysslin, Ann Margretha Leip

Parentes, Peter Knieskern, von Canajoh: Castle, Lea Knieskern geb : Wendeker, 6tn Mars, Infans, Anna Margretha, Testes, Joh: Georg Hahn, Eva Wendeker

Parentes, Georg Hellmer, von field District, Margaretha Hellmer, 6tn Mars, Infans, Anna, Testes, Joseph Mayer, Catharina Mayer

Pg. 24

Parentes, Christian Hofstetter, von Neu Deutschland, Maria Catharina Hofstetter, 7tn Mars, Infans, Theobald, Testes, Jacob Eyrer, Margretha Eyrer

Parentes, Peter Dachstetter, von Germanflacht, Elisabeth Dachstetter, 7tn Mars, Infans, Elisabeth, Testes, Johannes Dachstetter, Catharina Dachstetter

Parentes, Leonhard Krause, von Palatine, Magdalena Krause geb: Klock, d 11tn Mars, Infans, Leonhard, Testes, Johannes Clas, Gertrud Krause

Parentes, Peter Young, von fort Plain, Elisabeth Young geb: Sever, 14tn Mars, Infans, Jacob, natus den 9tn hujus, Testes, Jacob Young, Maria Young

Parentes, John Thompson, von Palatine, Gertrud Thompson geb: Philipson, 14tn Mars, Infans, Maria, Testes, Heinrich Philips, Minna Philips

Parentes, Wilhelm Heyer von Springfield, Margaretha Heyer, 17tn Mars, Infans, Margaretha, Testes, Franz Paris, Margaretha Deygert

Parentes, Heinrich Zimmerman, von Palatine Town, Margaretha Zimmerman geb: Bellinger, 17tn Mars, Infans, Gertrud, Testes, Jacob Zimmerman, Anna Zimmerman

Parentes, John Wynsi, von Canajoharrie Castle, Rachel Wynsi, 2tn April, Infans, Georg, born the 28tn february 1790, Testes, Georg Haus, Maria Haus
Translation, entry No. 4. Infant, Jacob, born the 9th of the same (March 9, 1790).

Pg. 25
Parentes, Philip fehling, von Palatine, Margretha fehling geb: Zimmerman, 4tn April, Infans, Elisabeth, Testes, Jacob Wallrath, Elisabeth Wallrath
Parentes, David A. Schuyler, Canajoh: Castle, Margretha Schuyler geb: Wollever, 5tn April, Infans, Niclaus, Testes, John Wollever, Catharina Wollever
Parentes, Adam Staring, von field District, Christina Staring geb: Herter, 11tn April, Infans, Maria Elisabeth, Testes, Ludwig Bersch, Margretha Bersch
Parentes, Johannes Kern, von Palatine, Anna Kern, 12tn April, Infans, Wilhelm Jacob, Testes, Wilhelm fink, Eva fink
Mater, Anna Eva Creaney, Canajoh: Castle, 12tn April, **Infans, Georg, Testes, Peter Deygert, Sara Deygert
Parentes, Daniel Hess, von Palatine, Maria Hess geb: Fox, 15tn April, Infans, Maria, et Anna Eva Zwillinge, Adam Bersch, Anna Bersch, Daniel Weber, Catharina Klock
Parentes, Jacob Cristinger, von Canajoharrie, Gertrud Christinger, 18tn April, Infans, John William, Testes, Albert Mebie, Maria Mebie
Parentes, John Hauss, von Canajoharrie, Magdalena Hauss, 18tn April, Infans, Catharina, Testes, Adam Haus, Magdelina Haus
Parentes, Adam Zimmerman, von Canajoharrie, Margretha Zimmerman geb: Matheus, 18tn April, Infans, Elisabeth, Testes, Conrad Matheus, Elisabeth Zimmerman
(For notes etc. see p. 14)

Pg. 26
Mater, Elisabeth Berdrich, von Tillenburg, Pater, John Smith, 23tn April, **Infans, Anna Maria, Testes, Gottlieb Bottiger, Anna Maria Bottiger
Parentes, Christoph Nates, von Gaiseberg, Susanna Naten, 25tn April, Infans, Martinus, Testes, Andreas Smith, Magdalena Smith
Parentes, Georg Oberaker, von Gaiseberg, Johanna Oberaker, 25tn April, Infans, Daniel, Testes, Daniel fort, Anna Nier
Parentes, Conrad Thumm, von Palatine, Anna Thumm, geb: Haus, 1tn May, Infans, Adam, Testes, Adam Thumm, Christina Thumm
Parentes, Peter Moesch, Canajoh: Castle, Dorothea Moesch, geb: Mebie, 2tn, May, Infans, Philipp, Testes, Philipp Scheffer, Maria Mebie
Parentes, Philipp L. Hellmer, von Palatine, Margretha Hellmer, geb: Bellinger, 9tn May, Infans, Catharina, Testes, Jacob J. Klock, Delia Bellinger 9tn May
Parentes, Abraham Herchimer, von Canajoharrie, Dorothea Herchimer, geb: Deygert, 9tn May, Infans, Peter, Testes, Peter Deygert, Sara Deygert
Parentes, Wilhelm fox, von Canajoharrie, Margretha fox, geb: Warmuth, 9tn May, Infans, Johannes, Testes, Peter Knieskern, Lea Knieskern
Notes. Entry No. 1 is written upside down: see notes on p. 14. Mater-Mother: Pater-father A space left for an entry, dated May 9th, but no name ever written in.

Pg. 27
Parentes, John Weytens, Canajoh: Castle, Alida Weytens, 16tn May, Infans, Margaretha, Testes, Niclaus Herchimer, Margretha Herchimer
Parentes, Georg Pickard, Gaiseberg, Maria Pikard, 16tn May, Infans, Magdalena, Testes, John Counterman, Maria Pikard
Parentes, Hunter Quakenboss, Mohacq District, Elisabeth Quackenboss geb: Klock, 23tn May, Infans, Adam, born the 24tn March 1790, Testes, Adam Wallrath, Magdalena Wallrath
Mater, Maria Haus, von Yukersbush, 23tn May, **Infans, William Johnson, Testes, John fehling,

Maria Wallrath

Parentes, Wilhelm Klebsattel, auf dem field, Maria Lise Klebsattel, 29tn May, Infans, Elisabeth, born the 15tn April 1790, Testes, Heinrich frank, Elizabeth Meyer

Parentes, Johann Jost Hess, auf dem field, Elizabeth Hess, 30tn May, Infans, Catharina, Testes, Daniel Petri, Catharina Itig,

Parentes, Johannes Weber, auf dem field, Barbara Weber, 30tn May, Infans, Catharina, Testes, Jacob Weber, Catharina Keller

Parentes, Johannes Auer, von Neu Deutschland, Anna Auer, 30tn May, Infans, Valentin, Testes, Valentin Muller, Anna Maria Muller

Notes. Entry no. 4 written upside down.

Pg. 28

Parentes, Captain John Meyer, auf dem field, Maria Meyer, 30tn May, Infans, Heinrich, Testes, Heinrich frank, Eva frank

Parentes, Garret Von Sleyk, Canajoharrie Castle, Anna Von Sleyk, geb : Mebie, 6tn Junii, Infans, Johann Jost, Testes, David freymaurer, Gladlyn Mebie

Parentes, Heinrich Hess, von Palatine, Catharina Hess, geb: Bellinger, 6tn Junii, Infans, Anna, Testes, John friederich Bellinger, Catharina Bellinger

Parentes, William Wall, von Yukersbusch, Elisabeth Wall, geb: Keller, 13tn Junii, Infans, Johannes, born the 5tn Juny, Testes, Johannes Scheffer, Catharina Joran

Parentes, William Thomson, von Canajoharrie, Rosina Thomson, geb: Wild, 13tn Junii, Infans, Daniel, Testes, Georg Wild, Dorothea Wild

Parentes, Carl Alexander Werner, fort plain, Christina Werner, geb: Crembs, 9tn Junii, Infans, Peter Alexander, Testes, Peter Young, Marie Lise Young

Parentes, _____ Putni, Gaiseberg, Maria Putni, 13tn Junii, Infans, Georg, alt 2 Jahrs., Testes, Georg Preiss, Catharina Preiss

Parentes, Carl Bischof, Palatine District, Maria Bischof, geb: Zimmerman, 13tn Junii, Infans, Maria, Testes, John Zimmerman, Maria Zimmerman

Translation entry No. 7, Infant, George, two years old.

Pg. 29

Parentes, friderich Ritter, von Schneidersbusch, Elizabeth Ritter, 15tn Juny, Infans, Johannes, Testes, Matheus Ritter, Catharina Seufer

Parentes, Heinrich Ansted, von Schneidersbusch, Elizabeth Ansted, 15tn Juny, Infans, Jacob, Testes, Jacob Louks, Catharina Louks

Parentes, Jacob Von Sleyk, von Schneidersbusch, Gertrud Von Sleyk, 15tn Juny, Infans, Catharina, Testes, John Dieterich Petri, Catharina Wendeker

Parentes, Johannes Yuker, von Yukersbusch, Anna Yuker, geb: Ringel, 20tn Juny, Infans, Georg, Testes, Georg Yuker, Elizabeth Yuker

Parentes, Jacob Meyer, von Gorristown, Anna Eva Meyer, 27tn Junii, Infans, Johannes, born the 10tn May 1790, Testes, Michael Bader, Margretha fehling

Parentes, Heinrich Herchimer, von Canajoharrie, Catharina Herchimer, geb: Zimmerman, 27tn Junii, Infans, Anna, Testes, Heinrich Zimmerman, Anna Herchimer

Parentes, Edward Waker, Lake Otsego, Gertrud Waker, 27 tn Junii, Infans, Anna Eva, Testes, Adam Eker, Margretha Eker

Parentes, Peter Wals, von Canajoharrie, Anna Wals, 4tn Julii, Infans, Catharina, Testes, Heinrich Dewi, Catharina Walz

Pg. 30

Parentes, Heinrich H. Fehling, von Palatine, Anna Margretha Fehling, 4tn Julii, Infans, Heinrich, born the 29th Juny 1790, Testes Heinrich Bellinger, Margretha Bellinger

Parentes, John fort, von Gaiseberg, Elisabeth fort, 11tn Julii, Infans, Rachel, born the 5th 9bre 1789, Testes, die Eltern Kinds

Parentes, Jacob Weber, von Enterstown, Gertrud Weber, 18tn Julii, Infans, Peter, Testes, Peter Heyer, Catharina Kass

Parentes, Johannes Dachstetter, German flats, Catharina Dachstetter, 18tn Julii, Infans, Johannes, Testes, Johannes Dachstetter, Anna Bauman

Parentes, Thomas Muscher, Gaiseberg, Gnelia Muscher, 25tn Julii, Infans, Jacob, Testes, Rudolf Tyffendorf, Catharina Tyffendorf

Parentes, Wilhelm Klein, Caqunewagho* District, Maria Klein, 30tn Julii, Infans, Anna, Testes, Jacob Mender, Catharina Mender

Parentes, Peter Wollever, Canajoharrie Castle, Catharina Wollever, 1tn Aug., Infans, Heinrich, Testes, Heinrich Zimmerman, Anna Schnell

Parentes, Daniel Hedok, Palatine Town, Magdalena Hedock, Infans, Daniel) Zwillinge, Maria), Testes, Solomon Yuker, Catharina Klock, Conrad Klock, Elisabeth Joran

Translation, entry No. 2. Rachel, born the 5th November 1789. Witnesses, the parents of the child. Entry No. 6. an improper spelling of Caughnawaga

Pg. 31

Parentes, Peter Eigenbrod, von Palatine, Maria Eigenbrod, 8tn Augusti, Infans, Carl Peter, Testes, Charles Nukerk, Eva M'Dougle

Parentes, friderich Schonolz, Gaiseberg, Elisabeth Schonholz, 8tn Augusti, Infans, Margaretha, Testes, friderich Countermann, Gertrud Counterman

Parentes, Georg Schiff, von fallberg, Christina Schiff, 15tn Augusti, Infans, Alida, Testes, Johannes Meyer, Alida Meyer

Parentes, Thomas Armstrong, Palatine town, Anna Armstrong, 15tn Augusti, Infans, John, Testes, Johannes Meyer, Catharina Meyer

Parentes, Martin Von Sleyk, Canajoharrie, Anna Von Sleyk, 15tn Augusti, Infans, Catharina, Testes, Ebert Vosherk, Catharina Vosberk

Parentes, Matheus Cunning, im fort Plain, Catharina Cunning, geb: Sutz, 17tn Augusti, Infans, Catharina, Testes, Catharina Paris

Parentes, Johannes Hahn, von Palatine, Catharina Hahn, geb: Reuszin, 21tn Augusti, Infans, Johann Georg, born the 14th aug. 90, Testes, Georg Reuter, Anna Reuter

Parentes, Adolph Wallrath, von Palatine, Anna Wallrath geb: Zimmerman, 22tn Augusti, Infans, Margaretha, Testes, John Adam Nelles, Elisabeth Nelles

Parentes, Jacob G. Klock, von Palatine, Maria Klock, 22tn Augusti, Infans, Catharina, Testes, Georg fehling, Catharine fehling

Pg. 32

Parentes, Adam Bauman, von German flats, Barbara Bauman, 5tn 7bris, Infans, Heinrich, born the 22th Julii xx 90, Testes, Heinrich Herter, Anna Bauman

Parentes, Christian Bellinger, von German flats, Barbara Bellinger, 5tn 7bris, Infans, Margretha, Testes, Johan Jost folz, Margretha folz

Parentes, Conrad folz, von German flates, Catharina folz, 5tn 7bris, Infans, Johannes, Testes, Philipp Lenz, Catharina folz

Parentes, Dewald Dieterich, von field District, Margretha Dieterich, 5tn 7bris, Infans, Johannes, Testes, Johannes Connikum, Maria Connikum

Parentes, Michael Mayer, von German flats, Catharina Mayer, 5tn 7bris, Infans, Catharina, Testes, Lorenz Herter, Elisabeth Mayer

Parentes, Joseph Diken, von German flats, Margretha Diken, 5tn 7bris, Infans, Georg, Testes, Georg Cronhart, Elisabeth Muller

Parentes, Georg Tyffendorf, von Scheidersbusch, Catharina Tyffendorf, 5tn 7bris, Infans, Elisabeth, Testes, Johannes Tyffendorf, Margretha Tyffendorf

Parentes, Johannes Riemenschneider, von Schneidersbusch, Eva Riemenschneider, 5tn 7bris, Infans, Adam, Testes, Heinrich*----------, Susanna----------, (*Note. The last names of these witnesses blotted)

Parentes, Christian Baker, von Canajoharrie Castle, Betsy Baker, 8tn 7bris, Infans, Thomas, Testes, John Connikum, Elisabeth Connikum

Pg. 33

1790
Parentes Jacob Klock, von Palentine Anna Eva Klock; 12tn7bris Infans. Maria; Testes Conrad Klock Maria Von Sleyk:
Parentes Leohnard Eggler von Canajoharrie Catharina Eggler; 12tn7bris Infans. Jacob; Testes Jacob Young Eva Young:
Parentes Adam Klock von Palatine Catharina Klock; 12tn7bris Infans. Johannes; Testes Johannes Staring Margaretha Bakos:
Parentes Heinrich Gardner, Canajoharrie Catharina Gardner; 12tn7bris Infans. Johannes; Testes Adam Haber Delia Counterman:
Parentes Niclaus Koch, Palatine Margretha Koch; 19tn7bris Infans. Johannes; Testes Peter Fort Margaretha Baxter:
Parentes Jacob Jac(bs) Klock, Palatine Anna Klock; 25tn7bris Infans. Catharina; Testes Johannes Klock Catharina Klock:
Parentes John Konnikum Margretha Konnikum; 26tn7bris Infans. Rachel; Testes Joh: Niclaus Killsz Eva Killsz:
Parentes Jacob Scheffer, Canajoharrie Angelica Scheffer; 26tn7bris Infans. Jacob; Testes Heinrich Krankheit Anna Krankheit:
Note. Between this and the following page, a leaf has been torn out from the record. It is evident from the fragment remaining, that there was writing upon it. Therefore some twelve or fourteen baptisms, administered in the month of October have disappeared.

Pg. 34

1790
Parentes Jacob Mayer, von fort Schuyler Anna Mayer; 31tn 8bris Infans. Maria Catharina; Testes Heinrich Mayer Maria Hellmer:
Parentes Heinrich Bam, von Canajoharrie Anna Bam; 1tn 9bris Infans. Johannes; Testes Johannes Smith Elizabeth Sander:
Parentes Johann Jost Hellmer, von Palatine Susana Hellmer; 2tn 9bris Infans. Frederic William Steuben; Testes Charles Hukerk Elizabeth Flint:
Parentes Johannes Lauer, von Palatine Magdalena Lauer; 4tn9bris Infans. Anna; Testes Conrad Lauer Anna Lauer:
Parentes Dines flander von Palatine Magdalena flander; 4tnbris Infans Cristoph, born the 13th7bris 1790; Testes Ernst flander Catharina Klock:
Parentes friderich Berger, von Palatine Christina Berger; 5tn9bris Infans. Johannes; Testes Johannes Helmer Anna Hellmer:
Parentes Johannes Schnell, von Schenellenbusch Anna Schnell; 7th9bris Infans. Magdalena; Testes Conrad Zimmerman Magdalena Zimmerman:
Parentes Adam Eigenbrod, von Canajoharrie Ragel Eigenbrod; 14th9bris Infans. Maria; Testes Maria Dewi:

Pg. 35
1790
Parentes David Mayer, von Canajoharrie Castle Anna Mayer, geb: Deyggert; 21tn9bris Infans. Anna; Testes Peter Deyggert Anna Herchimer:
Parentes Joh: Jost Bys, Canajoharrie Castle Barbara Bys; 21tn9bris Infans Catharina: Testes Arnd Braun Catharina Braun:
Parentes Niclaus Haus, von Canajoharrie Catharina Haus, geb: Spon; 21tn9bris Infantes Johannes

et Catharina, gemelli; Testes Johannes Knieskern Elisabeth Ehle, Caspar Ehle Catharina Schenerman:

Parentes Peter Bellinger von Schneidersbusch Elisabeth Bellinger, geb: Zimmerman; 23tn9bris Infans Magdalena; Testes Adam Bellinger Magdalena Bellinger:

Parentes Philipp Fox, von Palatine Catharina Fox; 28tn9bris Infans Johann Jost; Testes Joh: Jost Fox Elisabeth Fox:

Parentes Andreas Palsli, von Palatine Lea Palsli; 12tnXbris Infans Anna; Testes Jacob fehling Anna Fehling:

Parentes Christian Winter von Gaiseberg Sophie Winter; 19tnXbris Infantes Thinkful, born in 8bris 1788, Jannike, born the 7th 9bris 1790; Testes Johannes Counterman Elisabeth Counterman, Jannike Winter:

Parentes Humphry Reist, von Gaiseberg Johanna Reist; 19tnXbris Infans Jacob; Testes Jacob Reist Elisabeth Reist:

Translation, entry 3. 21 Nov.infants. Johannes and Catherine, twins

Pg. 36
1790
Parentes Heinrich Lonks, von Royal Grant Eva louk, geb: Schnell; 24th7bris Infans Johann Jost; Testes Jost Lonke Margretha Lonke

Parentes Rudolf Bersch, von Palatine Margretha Borsch; 25tnXbris Infans Adam, born 21tn Novembris 1790; Testes Georg Bersch Maria Reuter

Parentes James Woodert, von Schuylers Lake Catharina Woodert, geb: Haus; 26tnXbris Infans Angelique; Testes Conrad Haus Angelique Haus

Parentes Heinrich Schmid, von Tillenburg Elisabeth Schmid; 31tnXbris Infans Maria: Testes Peter Schram Maria Hart:

1791
Parentes Johannes Ris, von Palatine Catharina Ris; 1tn Januarii Infans Johann Jost; Testes Rudolf Koch Anna Koch

Parentes Adam Bellinger, von Canajoh: Castle Elisabeth Bellinger; 2th Januarii Infans Johann Jost; Testes Joh: Jost folz Margretha folz:

Parentes John Ony, field District Mary Ony, baptizata codem die: Testes erant Jost Schumacher Bally Schumaker; 7th Januarii Infants Junys, old 8 years John, old 5 years, Robert, old 3 years; Testes Heirich Mayer Anna Eva Mayer, John Mayer Mary Mayer, Andreas Mayer Catharina Mayer

Translation, entry No. 7. Parents John Ony at Field District, Mary Ony; (she) was baptized the same day (jan. 7, 1791): witnesses (for her) were Jost Schumacher and Bally Schumacher

Pg. 37
(1791)
Parentes Johannes frank, filed District Eva frank; 7th Januarii Infans Johannes; Testes John frank Eva Mayer

Notes for page 48 omitted there on account of lack of room.

Entry No. 6 Margretha Ka* The last name blotted; it may be "Kan" or "Karr"

Entry No. 9. ------------ Mayer, Jacob Mayer's widow.

Note for page 53.

Entry No. 6, translation. Witnesses, the parents themselves.

Pg. 38
Parentes Georg Rima, von Neu Deutschland Sara Rima; 9tn Januarii Infans Johannes; Testes Christian Rima Margretha Rima

Parentes Adam Grimm, field District Elisabeth Grimm; 9th Januarii Infans. Anna, born 6th Xbris 1790; Testes John Huber Gertrud Huber

Parentes Johannes Getman, field District Anne Lise Getman; 9th Januarii Infans. Anna Elisabeth;

Testes Peter Getman Anna Getman:

Parentes Johannes Zimmerman, Royal grant Sara Zimmerman; 10th Januarii Infans. Getrud; Testes John Herchimer Gertrud Zimmerman

Parentes Jacob Multer, von Neu Deutschland Maria Multer; 8th Januarii Infans. Elisabeth; Testes Hieronymus Bender Marie Lise Bender

Parentes Johannes fox, von Paletine Maria fox, geb: Clas; 15th Januar: Infans. Peter; Testes Jacob Clas Catharina fox

Parentes Adam Philips, von Palatine Elisabeth Philips; 20th Januarii Infans. Niclaus; Testes Adam Nelles Anna Dumm

Parentes James farbus, von Palatine Margretha farbus; 23th Januarii Infans. James; Testes Jacob Klock Elisabeth nelles

Pg. 39

Parentes Daniel Hart, von Royal Grant Catharina Hart, geb: Garlach; 28th Januarii Infant. Daniel; Testes John Adam Garlach Magdalena Garlach

Parentes Johannes Pikard von Palatine Anna Margretha Pikard; 6th februarii Infans. Peter; Testes Peter *------- Margretha, uxor

Parentes Heirich Gerber von Palatine Maria Gerber; 19th februarii Infans. Marcus; Testes Christopher W. fox Margretha fox

Parentes Jacob Keller von Canajoharrie Magdalena Keller, geb: Nelles; 27th februarii Infans. Elisabeth; Testes Andreas Keller Elisabeth Keller

arentes J. Niclaus Braun, von Palatine Catharina Braun, geb: Drummer; 9th March Infans. Maria; Testes Peter Schnell Maria Schnell

Parentes Melchior folz, junr. German flats Catharina folz; 6th March Infans. Catharina, born the 15th Januarii 91.; Testes Jacob Smith Catharina folz

Parentes Peter Bellinger – Yukersbusch Elisabeth Bellinger; 20th March Infans. Eva; Testes J. fr. Bellinger Eva Bellinger

Parentes Johannes frey, von Tillenburg Adam frey; 23th March Infantes Heirich et Jacob, gemelli; Testes Heirich Haring Anna Haring, Jacob frey Catharina Haring

Note, entry No. 2. *The last name of witness, blotted and illegible.

Pg. 40

Parentes Johannes Krankheit, von Canajoharrie Catharina Krankheit; 27th March Infans. Anna; Testes Johannes Scheffer Anna Scheffer:

Parentes Jost Louks, von Royal Grant Margretha Louks; 27th March Infans. Gertrud, born the 8th d; Testes Heinrich Louks Gertrud Louks:

Parentes Johannes Hellmer, von Palatine Magdalena Hellmer; 27th March Infans. Christina; Testes Heinrich Nelles Christina Nelles:

Parentes Heinrich Kulman, von Palatine Christina Kulman; 30th March Infans. Johann Heinrich; Testes Dieterich Suz Delia fox:

Parentes Georg M. Schmid, von Tillenburg Anna Schmid; 3th April Infans. Maria; Testes Georg Schmid Janike Schmid:

Parentes Heinrich Mayer, von Canajoharrie C. Anna Mayer; 10th April Infans. Abraham; Testes Jacob Wallrath Elisabeth Wallrath:

Parentes Heirich Scheffer, Royal Grant Anna Scheffer; 10th April Infans. Jacob; Testes Johannes Scheffer Margretha Scheffer:

Parentes Johannes hart, Palatine T. Sara Hart; 10th April Infans. Maria; Testes John Markel Elisabeth Markel:

Pg. 41

Parentes Gover Radli, von Palatine Susanna Radli, geb: Clas; 13th Infans Anna Catharina; Testes Jacob Claz Debora Krause:

Parentes Niclaus Bart, Canajoh: Castle Veronica Bart, geb: Mayer; 22th April Infans. Christian;

Testes Catharina Bart:

Parentes John Evenson, Gaiseberg Jannike Evenson; 22th April Infans. Isae; Testes John Keller Elisabeth Keller:

Parentes (Not written in the space for them); 25th April Infantes Samuel, Thomas, Margretha; Testes John Konnikum Margretha Konnikum, Christian Baker Betsi Baker, David Bootman Catharina Bootman:

Parentes Humphrey Deffenburg, Canj: Castle (see note page 72) Maria Deffenburg; 25th April Infans. Johannes; Testes Peter Knieskern Lea Knieskern:

Parentes John Ogny, field District Mary Ogny; 28th April Infans. Margretha; Testes Georg Hellmer Margretha Hellmer:

Parentes Thomas Bell, field District Submiss Bell; 30th April Infans. Augustus, born in Mars 1785; Testes Niclaus Weber Barbara Weber:

Parentes Wilhelm Petri, German flats Margr: Salome Petri; 30th April Infans. Margretha, born the 15th March; Testes Heinrich Herter Catharina Herter:

Pg 42

1791

Parentes Salomon Yuker, Palatine Elisabeth Yuker; 3th May Infans. Rudolf; Testes Adolph Haus Anna Eva Scheffer:

Parentes Jacob Yuker, Palatine Magdalena Yuker; 3th May Infans. Anna; Testes Jacob Dusler Anna Dusler:

Parentes Georg Staring, Schnellenbusch Anna Staring; 8th May Infans. Anna; Testes Adam Zimmerman Maria Von Schleyk:

Parentes Conrad Staring, Royal Grant Margretha Staring; 8th May Infans. Benjamin; Testes Maritn Von Schleyk Maria Von Schleyk:

Parentes Adam Bersch, Palatine Anna Bersch; 8th May Infans. Eva; Testes John Hess Anna Hess:

Parentes Johannes flander, von Tillenburg Margretha flander; 15th May Infans Elisabeth; Testes George flander Delia fox:

Parentes Kneles Bekman Palatine Catharina Bekman; 15th May Infans. Dorothea; Testes Hellmes Schall Dorothea Wallrath:

Parentes Jacob Schnell, Schnellenbush Elsisabeth Schnell; 22th May Infans. Catharina; Testes Peter Wollever Catharina Wollever:

Pg. 43

1791

Parentes Andreas Nelles, Canajoharrie Castle Elisabeth Nelles; 22th May Infans. Heinrich; Testes Peter Deygert Sara Deygert:

Parentes Niclaus Schuyler, Canajoharrie Castle Elisabeth Schuyler; 22th May Infans. Johann Jost; Testes John Herchimer Anna Herchimer:

Parentes Peter Hellegas, Palatine Catharina Hellegas; 28th May Infans Elisabeth; Testes Johannes Wallrath Elisabeth Wallrath:

Parentes Evan Vossberg, Canajoharrie Castle Catharina Vossberg; 28th May Infans. Elisabeth; Testes Johannes Eker Elisabeth Eker:

Parentes Christian Boss, Canajoharrie Elisabeth Boss; 12th Juny Infans Jacob; Testes Jacob Young Eva Young:

Parentes ____ Tillenburg; 15th Juny Infans Jeremias; Testes Georg Reuter _____ Reuter:

Parentes Andreas Michler, von Palatine Anna Michler;15th Juny Infans Jacob; Testes Johannes Hellmer Anna Hellmer:

Parentes Cesar Cox, von Germanflats Catharina Cox; 19th Juny Infans Maria, born the 20th May; Testes Jacob Weber Maria Weber:

Parentes Georg Stahli, von Germanflats Dorothea Stahli; 19th Juny Infans Johannes; Testes John Stahli Catharina Stahli:

Pg. 44

1791

Parentes Heinrich Hart, von Schellenbusch Anna Eva Hart; 26th Juny Infans Maria; Testes Peter Schnell Anna Schnell:

Parentes Rudolf Koch, Palatine town Anna Koch; 3th July Infans Margaretha; Testes Heirich Salzmann Maria Salsman:

Parentes Frederich Klock, Palatine Magdalena Klock; 3th July Infans Anna; Testes Jacob G. Klock Maria Klock:

Parentes Ebenezer Cook, Palatine Elisabeth Cook; 3th July Infans Elisabeth; Testes Salomon Yuker Elisabeth Yuker:

Parentes Friderich Bam, Palatine Elisabeth Bam; 13th July Infans Margretha; Testes John Nelles Maria Hellmer:

Parentes Wilhelm Kusner, Schmeiderbusch Christina Kusner; 17th July Infans Isaac; Testes Christian Pikard Anna Wendeker:

Parentes Andreas Scheffer, Palatine Anna Scheffer; 17th July Infans Johann Friderich; Testes J. Friderich Bellinger Catharina Bellinger:

Parentes Joseph Pikard, Palatine town Magdalena Pikard; 17th July Infans Benjamin; Testes Benjamin Ellwood Elisabeth Ellwood:

Parentes Georg Nihr Gaisberg Elisabeth Nihr; 24th July Infans Catharina; Testes Georg Preiss Catharina Preiss:

Pg. 45

1791

Parentes John Wilks, Gaiseberg Anna Wilks; 31th July Infans Schim; Testes Nicolas Barth Veronica Barth:

Parentes Johannes Lehman, Palatine Catharina Lehmann; 7th August Infans Heinrich; Testes John Eisenach Margretha Crembs:

Parentes Johann Georg Yuker, Palatine Elisabeth Yuker; 7th August Infans Elisabeth; Testes Peter Scheffer Catharina Joran:

Mater Catharina Klock, Jacob's Jun. Tochter; 14th August Infans Jacob, born the 2th Aug; Testes Jacob Klock, Junr. Anna Klock:

Parentes Hermannus Hagedorn, Gaiseberg Margretha Hagedorn; 14th August Infans Heirich; Testes Heirich Walsch Margrctha Finster:

Parentes James ; 14th August Infantes Margretha et Maria, gemelli:

Parentes Michel Kern, Canajoharrie Margretha Kern; 21th August Infans Michel; Testes Robert Gerder Eva _____

Parentes Adam Eker, Canajoharrie Margretha Eker; 21th August Infans Johannes; Testes Johannes Eker Elisabeth Eker:

Note, entry No. 4. Mother, Catharina Klock, daughter of Jacob Klock Junr.

Pg. 46

1791

Parentes Peter Ehle, Canajoharrie Gadlyn Ehle; 21th August Infans David; Testes Peter Deygert Catharina Herchimer:

Parentes frid: Ludwig Scheel, Royal Grant Elisabeth Scheel; 21st August Infans Johann Gottfried; Testes Johann Jost Schnell Susanna Staring:

Parentes Heirich Bam, Canajoharrie Anna Bam; 28th August Infans Catharina; Testes Phillip Bam Catharina Bam:

Parentes Abraham Mebie, Canajoharrie Angelique Mebie; 28th August Infans Cornelius; Testes Cornelius Von Alstyne Catharina Van Alstyne:

Parentes Lebeus Schell, Canajoharrie Maria Schall; 28th August Infans Isaack et Jacob, gemelli; Testes franz Schemel Elizabeth Schemel:

Parentes franz Daschs, Canajoharrie Catharina Dachs; 28th August Infans Maria; Testes Johannes Scheffer Maria Scheffer:

Parentes Johannes Kring, Palatine Elisabeth Kring; 18th 7bris Infans Abraham; Testes Abraham Hess Maria Kring:

Parentes ??eles Krankheit Anna Krankheit; 18th 7bris Infans Anna; Testes Heirich Krankheit Anna Krankheit:

Pg. 47

1791

Parentes Salomon Dieffendorf, of Canajoharrie Christina Dieffendorf; 22th Septbris Infnas Anna; Testis Anna Dieffendorf:

Parentes Peter Schmid, von Tillenburg Jannika Schmid; 24th September Infnas Peter; Testes Abraham Schmid Elisabeth Muller:

Parentes Johannes Muller, von Canajoharrie Elisabeth Muller; 25th September Infans Magdalena; Testes Conrad Muller Christina Muller:

Parentes Christoph Bellinger, field District Anna Bellinger; 2th 8bris Infans Elisabeth, born the 25th Aug: 1791; Testes Peter Bellinger Elisabeth Bellinger:

Parentes Jacob Lenz, field District Maria Catharina Lenz; 2th 8bris Infans Elisabeth, born the 1th Aug: 1791; Testes Michel Wuterich Elisabeth Wuterich:

Parentes Philipp Herter, filed District Catharina Herter; 2th 8bris Infans Cathariona, born the 16tn 7bris 1791; Testes Michel Mayer Catharina Mayer:

Parentes Marx Cranz, field District Catharina Cranz; 2th 8bris Infans Marx, Born the 4th Aug: 1791; Testes Wilhelm Heller Eva Deyggert:

Parentes Johannes Dinis, field District Elisabeth Dinis; 2th 8bris Infnas Eva, posthums, born the 11th 7bris 1791; Testes Heinrich Mayer Eva Sallie:

Parentes Jacob Rima, field District Dorothea Rima; 2th 8bris Infans Ellsabeth, born the 18th July 1791; Testes friderich Rima Elisabeth Mayer:

Pg. 48

1791

Parentes John francis, field Disteict Gertrud francis; 2th 8bris Infans Anna, born the 21th Aug: 1791; Testes Marx Raspach Margretha Mauch:

Parentes Georg Weber, field Distric Margre tha Weber; 2th 8bris Infans Apollon, born the 11th Juny 1791; Testes friderich Rigel Catherina Weber:

Parentes Severinus Deyggert, Canajoharrie Magdalena Deyggert; 2th 8bris Infans Werner; Testes Niclaus Herchimer Margretha Herchimer:

Parentes Ludwig Hikard, Schneidersbusch Maria Rikard; 9th 8bris Infans Conrad, born the 30th Aug 1791; Testes Conrad Rikard:

Parentes Johannes Mayer, Schellenbusch Catharina Mayer; 9th 8bris Infans Elisabeth, born the 23 7bris 1791; Testes Jacob Markel Elisabeth Markel:

Parentes Heirich Huber, Schneiderbusch Elisabeth huber; 9th 8bris Infans Johann Dieterich, born the 20th July 1791; Testes Jacob Keller Margretha Ka*:

Parentes Wilhelm Kilsz, Canajoharrie Eva Killsz; 9th 8bris Infans Niclaus; Testes Niclaus Wendeker Bally Wendeker:

Parentes Harpart Pragel, Schneidersbusch Anna Pragel; 9th 8bris Infans Johannes, born the 15th 7bris 1791; Testes Albert Maldom Anna Eva Klock:

Parentes ____ Mayer, Jacob's sel. Wittwe.; 9th 8bris Infans Isaac; Testes Isaac Ellwood Magdalena Ellwood:

For notes see page 37.

Pg. 49

1791

Parentes Heinrich Nelles, Palatine Catharina Nelles; 16th 8bris Infans Margretha; Testes Johannes Nelles Margretha Klock:

Parentes Georg Lambert, Palatine Magdalena Lambert; 16th 8bris Infans Magdalena, born the 19th

7bris 1791; Testis Magdalena Bellinger:

Parentes Ephraim Keyl, Canajoharrie Cornelia Keyl; 23th 8bris Infans Rachel; Testes John Wils i Rahel Wilsi:

Parentes Neth Hornbeck, Canajoharrie Anna Hornbek; 23th 8bris Infans Jacob; Testes Neth fort Alice fort:

Parentes Andreas fort, Palatine town Margretha fort; 23th 8bris Infans. Andreas; Testes Thomas Muscher Knelia Muscher:

Parentes Arend feinhaupt, Canajoharrie Catharina feinhaupt; 23th 8bris Infans Arendt; Testes Carl Albertin Margretha Albertin:

Parentes Heinrich Petri, Royal Grant Magdalena Petri; 23th 8bris Infans Magdalena; Testes Adam Gerlach Dorothea Zimmerman:

Parentes Johannes Wollever, Royal Grant Catharina Wollever; 23th 8bris Infans. Daniel, mort in April 1792; Testes David Schuyler Margretha Schuyler:

Parentes Jacob farbus, Canajoharrie C. Eva farbus; 23th 8bris Infans Dorothea; Testes Suvel Abee Dorothea Abee:

Translation, entry No. 8. Daniel, died in April 1792

1791

Parentes Georg Wild, Palatine Dorothea Wild; 30th Octobr: Infans Anna; Testes Johannes Nelles Anna Nelles:

Parentes Jacob F. Bellinger, Palatine Sophia Bellinger; 30th Octobr: Infans Catharina; Testes Georg Klock Catharina Klock:

Parentes Jacob Zimmerman, Palatine Magdalena Zimmerman; 30th October: Infans Catharina; Testes Johannes Zimmerman Elisabeth Zimmerman:

Parentes Gottlieb Braun, Palatine Town Anna Braun; 30th Octobr: Infans Sophia; Testes Jacob J. Klock:

Parentes Peter G. Schnell, Schnellenbusch Maria Schnell; 1th Novembris Infans Anna Eva; Testes George Schnell Anna Eva Kilsz:

Parentes Heinrich Herchimer, Canajoharrie C. Catharina Herchimer; 6th Novembris Infans. Gertrud; Testes John Adam Zimmerman Gertrud Herchimer:

Parentes Jacob J. Fehling, Palatine Anna fehling; 6th Novembr: Infans. Elisabeth; Testes Georg Cox Anna fehling:

Parentes John J. fehling Maria fehling; 6th Nobember: Infans. Eva; Testes Conrad Hellegas Anna Eva Hellegas:

Parentes Adam D. Zimmerman, Canajoharrie Margretha Zimmerman; 13th Novembris Infans. Anna; Testes Jacob Matheus Anna Matheus:

1791

Parentes Joh: Adam Smith, Canajoharie C. Anna Smith; 20th Novembr. Infans Eva; Testes Heinrich Rechtmeyer Maria Richmeyer:

Parentes Johannes Haus, Palatine Town Magdalena Haus; 20th Novembr. Infans Anna; Testes Conrad Dumm Anna Dumm:

Parentes **James Johnson, Palatine town **Maria Braun; 20th 9vembris Infans. Elisabeth; Testes Niclaus Braun Elisabeth Braun:

Parentes Wilhelm Zimmerman, Palatine Catharina Zimmerman; 20th Novembris Infans. Peter; Testes Peter Warmuth & his wife:

Parentes Heinrich Bellinger, Palatine Margretha Bellinger; 27th Novembr: Infans. Johannes; Testes Johannes Ehle Delia Ehle:

Parentes Johannes Dusler, Canajoharrie Catharina Dusler; 4th Decembr: Infans. Catharina; Testes Andreas Dusler Catharina Dusler:

Parentes Johannes Krause, Palatine Catharina Kraus; 4th Decembr: Infans. Robert; Testes Simon Nicols Anna Nicols:

Parentes Niclaus Scheffer, Schnellenbusch Anna Scheffer; 25th Xbris Infans. Wilhelm; Testes Wilhelm Schall Anna Eva Scheffer:

Parentes Conrad Pikard, Schneidersbusch Catharina Pikard; 25th Xbris Infans. Maria; Testes Johann Dietrich Petri Maria Pikard:

Note, entry No. 3. Names of parents only written upside down; the rest of the entry written in usual way.

1791

Parentes Heinrich Rikard, Schneidersbusch Catharina Rikard; 25th Xbris Infans. Conrad; Testes Conrad Rikard Elisabeth Rikard:

Parentes Rachel ; 26th Xbris Infans Emanuel; Testes Anna Zimmermann:

1792

Parentes Franz Rascher, Caqunewagha District Martha Rascher, geb: Kleyn; 11th Januarii Infans. Maria, born the 23th Xbr: 1791:

Parentes Jacob Bauman, German Flats Anna Bauman; 15th Januarii Infans. Catharina, born the 29th Xbr: 1791; Testes Jacob Petri Catharina Bauman:

Parentes Lorenz Herter, German flats Catharina Herter; 15th Januarii Infans Lorenz, born the 1th Januarii; Testes Jacob Weber Maria Weber:

Parentes Georg H. Klock, Palatine Margretha Kloack; 16th Januarii Infans. David; Testes Jacob Jb's Klock Catharina H. Klock:

Parentes Johann Nicl. Schnell, Tillenburg Elisabeth Schnell; 21th Januarii Infans. Johannes, born the 12th Jan:; Testes John Schnell Catharina Frey:

Parentes Jacob Joran, Palatine Catharina Joran; 22th Januarii Infans. Elisabeth; Testes Johannes Haus Elisabeth Joran:

1792

Parentes Patrick Kennedy, Palatine Nancy Kennedy 22 Jan: Infans Richard Testes Dianes Helleburg Charlotte Helleburg

Parentes Essyas Nikerson. Canajoh. Betzi Nikerson 29 Jan: Infans Georg Natheus

Parentes John Dougls, Tilleburg Betsi Dougls 29 Januaril Infans James Testes Georg feyl Elisab: feyl

Parentes Johannes Schnell in Palatine Magdalena Schnell 4 Februaril Infans Magdalena Testes Jacob Yuker Magdalena Yuker

Parentes Jacob Young, in Canajoharrie Eva Young 5 Februaril Infans Johannes Testes Johannes Knieskern Eva Young

Parentes Johann Rudolf Schmid, Canajoharrie Catharina Schmid 5 Februaril Infans Daniel Testes Ipsimet

Parentes (note, for trans. See p. 37)

Parentes Jocob Kfring, in Palatine Maria Kring 6 Februaril Infans Johannes Testes Johannes Kring Elizabeth Kring

Parentes John Rye, of Caqunewagha Elizsabeth Rye 9 Februaril Infantes Salomon, 6 years old Jacob, 4 years old John, 18 months old John Mengis Catharina Mengis Testes John Mengis Catharine Kleyn Michael Kiener Margretha Rascher

Parentes Jacob Markel, Royal Grant Anna Elisabeth Markel, geb: Schnel 12 Februaril Infans Henry, born 7 Febr: Testes Henry markel Anna Margretha Markel

Parentes David Mabee - Canajoharrie Castle Gertrud Mabee 12 Februaril Infans Margretha Testes Joh. Jost Louks Margretha Louck

Parentes David Bootman, Canajoharrie C. Catharine Bootman 12 Februaril Infans Magdalena Testes Joh. Georg Kern Magdalena Walther

Parentes Johannes Dechstader, Herkemer County Catharina Dechstader 19 Februaril Infans Peter, born 26 Jany. 1792 Testes Peter Bellinger Elisabeth Bellinger

Parentes Johannes Getman, Herkemer County Anna Lise Getman 19 Februarial Infans John friderich, born 2 Febr 1792 Testes Melchior Vols Anna Margretha Getman

Parentes Wilhelm Deygert, Herkemer County Anna Deygert 19 Februaril Infans Johannes, born 24 Jany 1792 Testes Johannes Boom Margretha Boom .

Parentes Peter Deygert, Herkemer County Elisabeth Deygert 19 Februaril Infans Catharina Testes Casper Deygert Catharina Konnikum

Parentes Heinrich Brickhouse, Herkemer County Catharina Brickhouse 19 Februaril Infans Barbara, born 19 Xbr: 1791 Testes Peter Deygert Barbara Deygert

Parentes John Portus, Herkemer County Portus 20 Februaril Infantes Thomas et William, gemelli Testes Ipsimet

Parentes Translation, entry No. 9, Witnesses, the parents themselves

Parentes Heinrich Frank, Herkemer County Gertrud Frank 20 Februaril Infans Andreas Testes Andreas Mayer Margretha Klebzattel

Parentes Dianes Krankheit, Gaisberg Maria Krankheit 26 Februaril Infans Abraham Testes Johannes Walter Anna Walter

Parentes Albert Mabee, Canajoharrie Castle Marie Mabee 26 Februaril Infans Margretha Testes John Van Driesen Margretha Van Driesen

Parentes John Kreninger, Canajoharrie Castle Gnelia Kreninger 26 Februaril Infans Cathrina Testes John Young Catharina Young

Parentes Peter Mersch, Canajoharrie Castle Doretha Mersch 26 Februaril Infans Elisabeth Testes Georg Schmid Elisabeth Eker

Parentes Adam Wallrath, Palatine Magdalena Wallrath 26 Februaril Infans Daniel Testes Adolph Wallrath Maria Wallrath

Parentes Edouard Negro Slave of John Bellinger in Palatine Margretha 26 Februaril Infans Catharina Testes Georg Cox Sally Macky

Parentes Jacob C. Klock, Palatine Anna Eva Klock 1 Martil Infans Johannes Testes Richard Von Ahle Dorothea Wallrath

Parentes Joh: Jost Bellinger, Palatine Elisabeth Bellinger 4 March Infans Georg Testes Friderich Bellinger Catharina Bellinger

Parentes Jacob Staring, Schenidersbusch Elisabeth Staring 4 March Infans Elisabeth Testes Georg Louks Elisabeth Staring

Parentes Wuster Deken, Canajoharrie Castle Catharina Deken 4 March Infans Margretha Testes Johannes Wellever Catharina Wallever

Parentes Heinrich Flander, Palatine Magdalena Flander 4 March Infans Jacob Testes George Flander Anna Klock

Parentes Jacob Flander, Palatine Catharina Flander 4 March Infans Maria Testes Philip Flander Maria Reuter

Parentes Cornelius Lambes - Palatine District Mary Lambes 10 March Infans John, born 21 gbris 1792 Testes Georg C. Klock Catharina Klock

Parentes Jacob Krankheit, Canajoharrie District Elisabeth Krankheit 11 March Infans Anna Testes James Delom Alidan Delom

Parentes Heinrich Deygert, Canajoharrie Castle Margretha Deygert 11 March Infans Elisabeth, born 8 Mars 1792 Testes Peter Deygert Elisabeth Schuyler

Parentes Heinrich I. Zimmerman, Palatine Elisabeth Zimmerman 14 March Infans Susanna Testes Jacob C. Zimmerman Susanna Zimmerman

Parentes John Enkisch, von Palatine Anna Enkisch 17 March Infans Elisabeth Testes John Kigenbrod Maria Klock

Parentes Robert Creh. Palatine District Elisabeth Creh 18 March Infans Adam Testes Adam Creb Annay Spayer

Parentes Benjamin Ellwood, Palatine Elisabeth Ellwood 18 March Infans Anna Testes Richard Bon Able Catharine Sillenbach

Parentes John Kelly, Canajoharrie Castle Gea Kelly 8 April Infans Angel Testes Conrad Haus Engel Haus

Parentes Niclaus Haus, Canajoharrie Castle Catharine Haus 8 April Infans Jacob Testes Jacob Farbuz Maria Killez

Parentes Joseph Kesseler, Palatine Margretha Kesseler 9 April Infans Jacob Testes Jacob Zimmerman Magdalena Zimmerman

Parentes John I. Nelles, Palatine, Catharina Nelles, geb. Weber; 12tn April Infans Peter; Testes

Peter C. Fox, Nancy Nelles.

Parentes Conrad L. Zimmerman, Palatine Town, Margretha Zimmerman; 13tn April Infans Gertrud; Testes Adam Zimmerman, Gertrud Zimmerman.

Parentes Jacob Christman, Palatine Town, Catharina Christman; 12tn April Infans Margretha; Testes Peter Killsz, Margretha Killsz.

Parentes **William Johnson, Maria Haus; 12tn April Infans **John G.; Testes Peter Killsz, Margretha Killsz.

Parentes Jacob G. Klock, Palatine, Maria Klock; 12tn April Infans Benjamin; Testes Benjamin Ellwood, Elisabeth Ellwood.

Parentes Peter Van Driesen, Palatine, Anna Van Driesen; 20tn April Infans John; Testes John Van Driesen, Margretha Van Driesen.

Parentes Michel Keller, Palatine, Sara Keller; 22th April Infans Elisabeth; Testes Ulric Bader, Elisabeth Bader.

Parentes Wilhelm Wahl, Palatine, Elisabeth Wahl; 29th April Infans Maria; Testes Michel Keller, Sarah Keller.

Parentes Johann Heinrich Vogel, von Tillenburg, Maria Vogel; 6th May Infans Daniel; Testes Daniel Weber, Debora Krause.

Parentes Ludwig Steinman, Canajoharrie, Catharina Steinman (1999 note-Steinman crossed out); 10tn May Infans Rachel; Testes John Wynsi, Rachel Wynsi.

Parentes Georg Eigenbrod, Palatine, Catharina Eigenbrod; 10tn May Infans Peter; Testes Peter Eigenbrod, Elisabeth Smith.

Note, entry No. 2. The names of parents and child, only, are written upside down, in this entry.

Parentes Friderich Knoch, Canajoharrie, Anna Knoch; 13tn May Infans Friderich; Testes Barn. Hudson, Elisabeth Hudson.

Parentes Peter Nelles, Palatine, Catharina Nelles; 13tn May Infans Johannes; Testes John Nelles, Delia Deygert.

Parentes Andreas Palsli, Palatine, Lea Palsli; 20th May Infans Margretha; Testes Heinrich Pikard, Anna Eva Ris.

Parentes Johannes Kern, Palatine, Anna Kern; 22th May Infans Peter; Testes Peter Hellegas, Catharina Hellegas.

Parentes Thomas Muscher, of Canajoharrie, Gnelia Muscher; 27th May Infans Elisabeth; Testes George Yuker, Elisabeth Yuker.

Parentes Gerret Von Sleyk, of Canajoharrie; 28th May Infans Eva; Testes-------.

Parentes Christian Plotau of Palatine, Catharina Plotau; 3Juny Infans Magdalena; Testes Joseph Pikard, Magdalena Pikard.

Parentes Conrad Lauer of Palatine, Anna Lauer; 5th Juny Infans Eva; Testes Jacob Fehling, Anna Fehling.

Parentes Conrad Thumm of Palatine, Anna Thumm; 17th June Infans Jacob; Testes Johannes Hellmer, Magdalena Hellmer.

Parentes Georg G. Klock of Palatine, Catharina Klock; 17th June Infans Eva; Testes Fridrich Bellinger, Catharina Bellinger.

Parentes John Wynsi of Canajoharrie, Rachel Wynsi; 24th June Infans Margretha; Testes Arend Alberti, Margretha Alberti.

Parentes Conrad C. Zimmerman, Schnellenbusch, Margretha Zimmerman; 24th June Infans Catharina; Testes Friderich Raspach, Catharina Raspach.

Parentes Heinrich Gorsten, Schneidersbusch, Susanna Gorsten; 26tn June Infans Adam, born the 4th May; Testes Heinrich Bayer, Margretha Bayer.

Parentes Peter P. Schuyler of Canajoharrie, Catharina Schuyler; 8th July Infans Johann Jost, born the 3d July; Testes Joh. Jost Deygert, Gnelia Deygert.

Parentes Heinrich Krankheit of Canajoharrie; 8th July Infans Maria, born the 24th June; Testes Heinrich Richtmeyer, Maria Richtmeyer.

Parentes Friderich Ritter, Schneidersbusch, Elisabeth Ritter; 12th July Infans Catharina, born the 6th July; Testes Baldus Strauch, Catharina Strauch.

Parentes Georg Bakos, Schneidersbusch, Susanna Bakos; 12th July Infans Georg, born the 8th

July; Testes Georg Edel, Susanna Frank.

Parentes Gover Van Sleyk, Schneidersbusch, Gertrud Van Sleyk; 12th July Infans Friderich, born the 1 July; Testes Friderich Wendeker, Maria Dolder.

Parentes Peter Bellinger, Palatine, Ellisabeth Bellinger; 15th July Infans Margretha, born the 13th July; Testes Andreas Scheffer, Anna Scheffer.

Parentes Peter Schram, Tillenburg, Anna Schram; 15th July Infans Peter, born the 8th July; Testes Leohhard Krause, Magdalena Krause.

Parentes Conrad Killsz, Canajoharrie C., Elisabeth Killsz; 15th July Infans Niclaus, born the 11th July; Testes Niclaus Killsz, Anna Eva Killsz.

Parentes Carl Kern, Canajoharrie C. Margretha Kern; 15th July Infans Catharina; Testes Valentin Wagner, Magdalena Wagner.

Parentes Henry Wallrath, German Flatts, Anna Wallrath; 22th July Infans Johann Jacob, born the 22th June; Testes Peter Bauman, Margretha Gerlach.

Parentes Knelis Hendrekson, Herkemer County, Mary Hendrekson; 22th July Infans Wilhelm, born the 26th June; Testes Gerret Dinman, Catharina Dinman.

Parentes Johannes Dietrs. Fehling, Palatine, Elisabeth Fehling; 29th July Infans Anna; Testes Johannes Smith, Magdalena Fehling.

Parentes Jacob Johs. Klock, Palatine, Anna Klock; 29th July Infans Catharina; Testes John Dieffendorf, Catharina Klock.

Parentes David adon Schuyler, Canajoharrie, Margretha Schuyler; 29th July Infans Lea; Testes Peter Wollever, Catharina Wollever.

Parentes James Wilson, Canajoharrie, Elisabeth; 29th July Infans Eva; Testes Henry Wi*, Anna Mayer.

Parentes Thomas Obynn, Yukersbusch, Magdalena Obynn; 4th August Infans Maria; Testes Joel Haid, Betsi Haid.

Parentes Martin Von Sleyk, Canajoharrie, Anna Von Sleyk; 5th August Infans Niclaus; Testes Niclaus Haus, Catharina Van Alstyne.

Parentes Christian Bellinger, Canajoharrie, Barbara Bellinger; 12th August Infans Barbara; Testes Adam Bellinger, Elisabeth Bellinger.

Parentes James Dannels, Palatine T., Gertrud Dannels; 14th August Infans Bally; Testes Johann Haus, Anna Haus. The name of the male witness has been corrected, and as noted, is illegible; it may possibly be "Winn" or "Wilsy".

Parentes Peter Muscher, Palatine T., Maria Muscher; 14th August Infans Elisabeth; Testes John Rerich, Delia Rerich.

Parentes Albert White, Palatine T., Margretha White; 14th August Infantes Sara, 12 years old; Elisabeth, 4 years old; Maria, 1 year old; Testes James Dannels, Gertrud Dannels; Salomon Yuker, Elisabeth Yuker; Jacob Palsli, Anna Lise Palsli.

Parentes Abraham Arnd, Canajoharrie, Anna Arnd; 19th August Infans Johannes; Testes Adam Zimmerman, Margretha Zimmerman.

Parentes Adolph Wallrath, Palatine, Maria Wallrath; 26th August Infans Adolph Beckman; Testes Cornelis Beckmann, Catharina Beckmann.

Parentes Jacob Scheffer, Canajoharrie, Engel Scheffer; 26th August Infans Magdalena; Testes John Hauss, Magdalena Hauss.

Parentes George Wallrath, Canajoharrie, Anna Wallrath; 2th Sept Infans Daniel; Testes Johann Wallrath, Catharina Wallrath.

Parentes Friderich Josts. Klock, Palatine, Magdalena; 2th Sept Infans Robert; Testes Georg Jbs. Klock, Catharina Klock.

Parentes William Klabsattel, Herkemer County, Marie Lise Klabsattel; 8th Septbris Infans Maria, born the 8th August; Testes Andreas Klabsattel, Marie Klabsattel.

Parentes Jacob Mayer, Herkemer County, Anna Mayer; 8th Septbris Infans Elisabeth, born the 27th Aug.; Testes Jacob Wallrath, Elisabeth Wallrath.

Parentes Christian Sillenbach, Herkemer County, Elisabeth Sillenbach; 9th Septbris Infans Johannes, born the 16th Aug.; Testes Johannes Imhof, Anna Weber.

Parentes Johannes Keller, Herkemer County, Maria Keller; 9th Septbris Infans Margretha, born the

7th Aug.; Testes Peter Ayrer, Margretha Keller.

Parentes Lorenz Frank, Herkemer County, Maria Frank; 9th Septbris Infans Matheus, born the 30th Aug.; Testes Johannes Frank, Eva Frank.

Parentes Elias Muller, Kingsborough, Elisabeth Muller; 10th Septbris Infans Anna; Testes Franz Muller, Anna Schmid.

Parentes Jacob Dieffendorf, Canajoharrie, Elisabeth Dieffendorf; 13th Septbris Infans Cornelius; Testes Cornelis Von Campe, Barbara Von Campe.

Parentes Johann Jost Edel, Palatine District, Maria Edel; 16th Septbris Infans Johann Jost; Testes Heinrich Edel, Anna Bayer.

Parentes Joseph Numen, Palatine District, Elisabeth Numen; 16th Septbris Infans Stephen; Testes Stephan Coming, Debora Coming.

Parentes Niclaus Farbus, Canajoharrie C., Sara Farbus; 16th Septbris Infans Maria; Testes Albert Mabee, Bally Mabee.

Parentes James Dannels, Palatine Town, Gertrud Dannels; 23th 7bris Infantes Richard, 12 years old; John, 4 years old; Testes Friderich Bellinger, Catharina Bellinger; Daniel Enkeson, Anna Enkeson.

Parentes Theobald Thumm, Palatine, Eva Thumm; 23th Septembris Infans Johannes; Testes Adam Thumm, Maria Kringg.

Parentes Georg Dieffendorf, Canajoharrie C., Catharina Dieffendorf; 23th Septembris Infans Anna, born the 20th 7bris; Testes Rudolf Dieffendorf, Anna Fox.

Parentes Frideric Bonstetter, Canajoharrie, Marie Lise Bonstetter; 23th Septbris Infans Eva; Testes Jonas Dillenbach, Eva Knieskern.

Parentes Dines Helleburg, Palatine, Charlotte Helleburg; 26tn 7bris Infans William; Testes Peter Van Driesen, Margaret Haus.

Parentes John Graves, Palatine, ------Graves; 26tn 7bris Infans William, old 12 years; Testes Dines Helleburg, Charlotte Helleburg.

Parentes Graves; 26tn 7bris Infans John, old 4 years; Testes John Graves, ------Graves.

Parentes Johannes Lauer, Palatine, Magdalena Lauer; 6tn Octobris Infans Eva Elisabeth; Testes Dieterich Lauer, Margretha Fehling.

Parentes Dieterich Pilgrim, Palatine, Christina Pilgrim; 11th Octobris Infans Niclaus, born the 6th Octobr; Testes Niclaus Thumm, Elisabeth Thumm.

Parentes Peter M. Ehle, Canajoharrie, Gadlyn Ehle; 14tn Octobris Infans Barnt, born the 17tn Septbris; Testes David Mayer, Anna Mayer.

Parentes Charles Bischop, Palatine, Maria Bischop; 21tn Octobris Infans Anna; Testes Lorenz Zimmerman, Maria Zimmerman.

Parentes Friderich Ostrot. Palatine, Elisabeth Ostrot; 24tn Octobris Infans Elisabeth; Testes Henrich Mayer, Anna Mayer.

Parentes Jacob J. Weber, Herkemer County, Margretha Weber; 28tn Octobris Infans Lorenz, born the 13th 8bris; Testes Lorenz frank, Margretha Weber.

Parentes John Brodhack, Herkemer County, Mary Brodhack; 28tn Octobris Infans Maria; Testes Henry Sallie, Mary Sallie.

Parentes David Ph. Schuyler, Canajoharrie, Helletsy Schuyler; 28tn Octobris Infans Maria; Testes Johannes Schuyler, Maria Smith.

Parentes Johannes Stahli, Royal Grant, Marie Lise Stahli; 11tn Novembris Infans Heinrich; Testes Heinrich Scheffer, Anna Scheffer.

Parentes Heinrich Haus, Canajoharrie, Anna Haus; 11tn Novembr Infans Catharina; Testes Johannes Dusler, Catharina Dusler.

Parentes Dieterich Jbs. Fehling, Palatine, Elisabeth Fehling; 18tn Novembr Infans David; Testes Heinrich Fehling, Anna Zimmerman.

Parentes Isaac Ellwood, Canajoharrie, Magdalena Ellwood; 18tn Novembr Infans Abraham, born the 7th Nov; Testes Peter Knieskern, Lea Knieskern.

Parentes Adam Bellinger, Schneidersbusch, Magdalena Bellinger; 25tn Novbris Infans Magdalena; Testes Marx Bellinger, Margretha Zimmerman.

Parentes Robert Gersten, Palatine District, Eva Gersten; 25tn Novembris Infans Maria; Testes

Henry Gersten, Maria Smith.

Parentes Adam Bellinger, Canajoharrie C., Elisabeth Bellinger; 27tn Novbris Infans Abraham; Testes Christian Bellinger, Barbara Bellinger.

Parentes Johann Jost Klock, Palatine, Dorothea Zimmerman; 4th Decembris Infans Margretha; Testes Heinrich Bekmann, Margretha Bekmann.

Parentes Salomon Yuker, Palatine, Elisabeth Yuker; 9th Decembris Infans Margretha; Testes Jacob Palsli, Margretha Haus.

Parentes Georg Oberaker, Canajoharrie, Jannike Oberaker; 9th Decembris Infans Sara; Testes Kneles Krankheit, Anna Krankheit.

Parentes Philipp Gerlach, Canajoharrie C., Marie Lise Gerlach; 9th Decembris Infans Delia; Testes Johann Eker, Anna Lise Eker.

Parentes David Mayer, Canajoharrie C., Anna Mayer; 9th Decembris Infans Catharina; Testes Johannes Mayer, Alida Mayer.

Parentes John Rice, Palatine, Catharina Rice; 16tn Decembris Infans Maria; Testes Wilhem Wallrath, Margretha Hellegas.

Parentes Philip Hellmer, Palatine, Margretha Hellmer; 16tn Decembris Infans Elisabeth; Testes Peter Young, Marie Lise Young.

Parentes Heinrich Louks, Palatine, Anna Eva Louks; 16tn Decembris Infans Conrad; Testes Conrad Zimmerman, Magdalena Zimmerman.

Parentes Martin Siever, Canajoharrie, Maria Siever; 23tn Decembris Infans Catharina; Testes James Siever, Catharina Siever.

Parentes James Delany, Canajoharrie, Alida Delany; 23tn Decembris Infans Maria; Testes Dines Krankheit, Baly Krankheit.

Mater Maria Hellmer, Canajoharrie; 25tn Decembris Infans Moses, born in July last; Testes Philipp Hellmer, Margretha Hellmer.

Parentes Jacob Snell, Snellenbush, Elisabeth Snell; 30th Decembris Infans Margretha; Testes Jost Snell, Rosina Zimmerman.

Parentes Heinrich Ritter, Sneidersbush, Margretha Ritter; 30th Decembris Infans Margaretha; Testes Johannes Bayer, Margretha Bayer.

Parentes Philipp Muller, Klocksbush, Elisabeth Muller; 30th Decembris Infans Catharina Margretha; Testes Ludwig Mayer, Catharina Mayer.

Parentes Philipp Fehling, Palatine, Margretha Fehling; 30th Decembris Infans Daniel; Testes J. Dieterich Fehling, Elisabeth Fehling.

Parentes Stambrough P. Stancliff, Palatine T., Sybille Stancliff; 30th Decembris Infantes Mary, born the 15th February 1786; Thomas, born the 22nd August 1788; Betsi, born the 8th Octobr 1790; Perry, born the 20th August 1792; Testes J. Jost. Snell, Maria Snell; Johannes Snell, Anna Snell; Johannes Mayer, Catharina Mayer; Conrad Zimmerman, Margretha Zimmerman.

1793

Parentes Marx Dusler, Palatine, Elisabeth Dusler; Jan 1 Infans Catharina; Testes Jost Klock, Maria Kring.

Parentes John Nelles, Palatine, Delia Nelles; 5tn Januarii Infans Margretha; Testes Friderich Bam, Elisabeth Bam.

Parentes Jacob Crass, Palatine, Catharina Crass; 7th Januarii Infans Jacob; Testes Jacob Hellmer, Anna Fox.

Parentes Georg Haus, Canajoharrie C., Maria Haus; 20th Januarii Infans Anna; Testes David Hess, et his Wife.

Parentes Peter Fort, Canajoharrie, Catharina Fort; 20th Januarii Infans Peter; Testes Peter Bakos, Margretha Bakos.

Parentes Georg Stahli, Herkemer County, Dorothea Stahli; 27th Januarii Infans Niclaus, born the 1 Xbris 1792; Testes Niclaus Stahli, Eva Bayer.

Parentes John Doleny, Herkemer County, Elisabeth Doleny; 27th Januarii Infans Elisabeth, born the 21 Xbris 1792; Testes Dieterich Demud, Elisabeth Demud.

Parentes Henry Deygert, Herkemer County, Margretha Deygert; 27th Januarii Infans Maria, born the 19th

Parentes Henry Hees, German Flats, Catharina Hees; 27tn Januarii Infans Magdalena, born the 21 Xbris 1792; Testes John Hees, Eva Hees.

Parentes Georg Weber Junr., Herkemer County, Margretha Weber; 27tn Januarii Infans Maria, born the 11 Xbris 1792; Testes Peter J. N. Weber, Maria Weber.

Parentes Johannes Yuker, Palatine, Anna Yuker; 29tn Januarii Infans Catharina; Testes Friderich Bellinger, Catharina Bellinger.

Parentes Johannes Ougspurger, Canajoharrie, Susanna Ougspurger; 3th Februarii Infans Elisabeth; Testes Georg Nier & his Wife.

Parentes Jacob Nier, Canajoharrie, Catharina Nier; 3th Februarii Infans Johannes; Testes Johannes Ougspurger, Susanna Ougspurger.

Parentes Benjamin Ros, Canajoharrie, Maria Ros; 3th Februarii Infans Susanna; Testes Jonas Krankheit, Maria Krankheit.

Parentes Jacob Joran, Palatine, Catharina Joran; 10th Februarii Infans Eva; Testes Hellmes Schall, Margretha Haus.

Parentes Georg J. Klock, Palatine, Catharina Klock; 10th Februarii Infans Philipp; Testes Philipp Nelles, Elisabeth Nelles.

Parentes James Manson, Herkemer County, Maria Manson; 10th Februarii Infans James, old 7 months; Testes Johann Jost Haus, Elisabeth Gerlach.

Parentes James Woodert, Herkemer County, Catharina Woodert; 10th Februarii Infans Maria; Testes Georg Haus, Mary Lise Haus.

Note for page 74, omitted there on account of lack of room. Entry No. 8.

Humphy Deffenport and Polly (or Maria) Dettenport; compare with entry No. 5, page 41, Humphry Deffenburg.

Parentes Georg A. Smith, Canajoharrie C., Anna Smith; 17tn Februarii Infans Gastina; Testes Heinrich Richtmejer et his Wife.

Parentes Johannes G. Zimmerman, Palatine, Sara Zimmerman; 17tn Februarii Infans Johann Jost; Testes Johann Jost Snel, Margretha Zimmerman.

Parentes Adam C. Haus, Palatine, Magdalena Haus; 17tn Februarii Infans Jacob; Testes Jacob Staring, Elisabeth Staring.

Parentes Peter G. Snel, Palatine, Maria Snel; 17tn Februarii Infans Georg; Testes Jacob Snel, Susanna Killsz.

Parentes Johannes Pickard, Canosserago, Anna Margr. Pickard; 18tn Februarii Infans Adam; Testes Adam Gerlach & his Wife.

Parentes Matheus Ritter, Royal Grant, Anna Eva Ritter; 22tn Februarii Infans Catharina; Testes Adam Klock, Catharina Klock.

Parentes Adam Bersch, Palatine, Anna Bersch; 24tn Februarii Infans Johannes; Testes Wilhelm Nelles, Magdalena Nelles.

Parentes Lorenz H. Herter, Herkemer County, Anna Eva Herter; March 3 Infans Heinrich, born the 25th Febr; Testes Heinrich Herter, Magdal. Frank.

Parentes Jacob J. Weber, Junr., Herkemer County, Margaretha Weber; March 3 Infans Peter, born the 1st Febr; Testes Peter Weber, Junr., Maria Weber

Parentes Heinrich Zimmerman, Palatine Town, Margretha Zimmerman; March 3 Infans Peter; Testes Peter A. Bellinger, Elisabeth Bellinger.

Parentes Johannes Wollever, Palatine Town, Catharina Wollever; March 3 Infans Catharina; Testes John Mayer, Catharina Mayer.

Parentes Jacob Wendeker, Sneidersbush, Maria Wendeker; March 4 Infans Conrad; Testes Wilhelm Killsz, Eva Killsz.

Parentes Peter Muscher, Palatine Town, Mary Lise Muscher; March 17 Infans Gnelia; Testes Peter Scheffer, Elisabeth Rerich.

Parentes Wilhelm Fox, Canajoharrie, Margretha Fox; 21t March Infans Georg; Testes Georg Dieffendorf, Catharina Dieffendorf.

Parentes Peter Wollever, Palatine Town, Catharina Wollever; 1 April Infans Elisabeth; Testes

Johannes Snell, Elisabeth Snell.
Parentes Heinrich Bellinger, Palatine, Anna Eva Bellinger; 7th April Infans Peter; Testes Peter Bellinger, Elisabeth Bellinger.
Parentes Humphry Deffenport, Canajoharrie (See note page 72) Bally Deffenport; 14 April Infans Susanna; Testes Niclaus P. Schuyler, Elisabeth Schuyler.
Parentes Jacob Fr. Bellinger, Yukersbusch, Sophie Bellinger; 21 April Infans Margretha; Testes Heinrich Beckman, Margretha Bekman
Parentes Johannes C. Fox, Palatine, Maria Fox; 21 April Infans Margretha; Testes Daniel Fox, Catharina Fox.
Parentes Robert Bayer, Sneidersbush, Catharina Bayer; 21 April Infans Margretha; Testes Dines Bayer, Margretha Bayer.
Parentes Johannes Haus, Palatine, Anna Haus; 4tn May Infans Heinrich; Testes Heinrich Bellinger, Anna Eva Bellinger.
Parentes John Seckler, Canajoharrie, Anna Seckler; 5tn May Infantes Charlotte, old 2 years; Mary, old 4 months; Testes Conrad Counterman, Margretha Counterman; Adam Bellinger, Elisabeth Bellinger.
Parentes William Hofher, Canajoharrie, Betsi Hofher; 5tn May Infans Jacobine; Testes John Seckler, Anna Seckler.
Parentes Charles Alberti, Canajoharrie, Margretha Alberti; 12tn May Infans Maria; Testes Georg Wallrath, Anna Wallrath.
Parentes Johannes Joh. Bellinger, Palatine, Magdalena Bellinger; 12tn May Infans Johannes; Testes Jacob Fox, Maria Reuter.
Parentes Jacob Mayer, Mohacq District, Anna Eva Mayer;19tn May Infans Adam, born the 21tn Xbris 1792; Testes Johannes Salzberger, Catharina Fehling.
Parentes Georg Rykard, Canajoharrie, Catharine Rykard; 20tn May Infans Samuel; Testes Samuel Krank, Margretha Rykard.
Parentes David Mabee, Canajoharrie, Gertrud Mabee; 20tn May Infans Maria, born the 3 March 1793; Testes Abraham Mabee, Maria Mabee.
Parentes Jacob Farbus, Canajoharrie, Eva Farbus; 26tn May Infans Bartholome; Testes Barthol. Farbus, Catharina Farbus.
Parentes Henry N. Fehling, Palatine, Anna Margretha Fehling; 3th Juny Infans Abraham; Testes Jacob Keller, Magdalena Keller.
Parentes Henry Scheffer, Royal Grant, Anna Scheffer; 9tn Juny Infans Heinrich; Testes Johannes Snell, Anna Snell.
Parentes Heinrich Hart, Royal Grant, Anna Eva Hart; 9tn Juny Infans Catharina; Testes Johannes Hart, Sara Hart.
Parentes Heinrich Hose, Snellenbush, Margretha Hose; 9tn Juny Infans Heinrich; Testes Friderich Snell, Anna Zimmerman.
Parentes Rudolf Koch, Palatine, Anna Koch; 9tn Juny Infans Catharina; Testes Dines Helleburg, Charlotte Helleburg.
Parentes John Preiss, Sneidersbush, Maria Preiss; 10tn July (1999 note-this is probably Juny) Infans Abraham; Testes Joseph Pikard, Anna Eva Pikard.
Parentes Henry P. Deyggert, Canajoharrie, Margretha Deyggert; 16tn Juny Infans Peter; Testes Peter Deyggert, Sara Deyggert.
Parentes Niclaus Barth, Canajoharrie, Verona Barth; 16tn Juny Infans Bernhard; Testes Bernhard Hudson, Elisabeth Hudson.
Parentes Henry Deck, Canajoharrie, Anna Deck; 16tn Juny Infans Wilhelm; Testes Willhelm Zobel, Catharina Zobel.
Parentes John G. Herkemer, Canajoharrie, Bally Herkermer; 16tn Juny Infans Elisabeth; Testes Isaac Raasch, Catharina Herkermer.
Parentes Peter Freeman, Canajoharrie, Rebecca Freeman; 16tn Juny Infans Rebecca; Testes Christian Bellinger, Barbara Bellinger.
Parentes James Dan, Palatine, Gertrud Dan; 23tn Juny Infans Michel; Testes Michel Keller, Sara Keller.

Parentes John Young, Canajoharrie, Margretha Young; 23tn Juny Infans Johann Georg; Testes Georg Dumm eum uxore.

Translation, entry No. 8. Witnesses, Georg Dumm with wife.

Parentes Conrad Counterman, Canajoharrie, Margretha Counterman; 23tn Juny Infans Johann Adam; Testes Adam P. Bellinger, Elisabeth Bellinger.

Parentes Adolph Wallrath, Palatine, Anna Wallrath; 1tn July Infans Jacob; Testes Jacob Zimmerman, Magdalena Zimmerman.

Parentes Gottlieb Braun, Otsego County, Anna Braun; 7th July Infans Benjamin; Testes Johannes Hess, Anna Hess.

Parentes Niclaus Scheffer, Snellenbush, Anna Scheffer; 7th July Infans Margretha; Testes Joh Jost Snell, Margretha Scheffer.

Parentes John Henry Dysslin, Pfarrer der Gemeinde, Anna Dysslin, geb: Klock; 7th July Infans Catharina, born the 2 July; Testes Jacob Klock, Elisabeth Nelles.

Parentes Jacob Christman, Palatine Town, Catharina Christman; 14th July Infans Jacob; Testes Isaac Christman, Maria Snell.

Parentes Andreas Scheffer, Palatine, Anna Scheffer; 21tn July Infans Abraham; Testes Abraham Keller, Elisabeth Keller.

Parentes Georg Counterman, Junr., Canajoharrie, Regina Counterman; 21tn July Infans Margretha; Testes Jacob Counterman, Margretha Counterman.

Translation, entry No. 5. Parents, John Henry Dysslin, Minister of the Congregation; Anna Dysslin, born Klock

Parentes Niclaus P. Schuyler, Canajoharrie, Elisabeth Schuyler; 4th August Infans Margretha, born the 9th June; Testes Niclaus Herkemer, Margretha Herkemer.

Parentes ------; 4th August Infans Gredia Margretha Thomson, 9 years old; Testes Niclaus Herkemer, Margretha Herkemer.

Parentes Joh. Jost Louks, Palatine, Margretha Louks; 11th August Infans David; Testes Jacob Louks, Maria Mabee.

Parentes Johannes Haus, Royal Grant, Magdalena Haus; 11th August Infans Johannes; Testes Johannes Staring, Catharina Von Sleyk.

Parentes Ludwig Rykard, Sneidersbusch, Maria Rykard; 12th August Infans Peter, born the 3d August; Testes Peter Louks, Anna Louks.

Parentes Johannes Rykard, Sneidersbush, Catharina Rykard; 12th August Infans Catharina, born the 5th August; Testes John Puyeux, Catharina Puyeux.

Parentes Johannes Edel, Sneidersbush, Magdalena Edel; 12th August Infans Johannes, born the 6th August; Testes Johannes Petri, Anna Klock.

Parentes Johannes -----, Sneidersbush, Margretha -----; 12th August Infans Adam, born the 5th Juny; Testes Johannes Haus, Magdalena Haus.

Note, entry No. 8. The last names of the parents so blotted as to be almost, if not wholly illegible.

Parentes Johannes Ds. Fehling, Palatine, Elisabeth Fehling; 18tn August Infans Anna Eva; Testes Peter Warmuth, Anna Eva Warmuth.

Parentes Christian Graf, Palatine, Catharina Graf; 18tn August Infans Christian; Testes Christian Graf, Barbara Graf.

Parentes John Cunningham, Canajoharrie, Rebecca Cunningham; 25tn August Infans Elisabeth; Testes Thomas Young, Elisabeth Young.

Parentes Wilhelm Schall, Canajoharrie, Eva Schall; 1 7bris Infans Lea; Testes Peter Knieskern, Lea Knieskern.

Parentes Beat Kern, Palatine, Catharina Kern; 5th 7bris Infans Jacob; Testes Jacob Jb. Klock, Elisabeth Nelles

Parentes Jacob Joh. Farbus, Canajoharrie, Catharina Farbus; 8th 7bris Infantes Niclaus et Martha-- gemelli; Testes Niclaus Farbus, -----Wagoner; Abraham Mabee, Bally Mabee.

Parentes Philipp Fox, Palatine, Catharina Fox; 8th 7bris Infans Anna; Testes Peter Fox, Anna Nelles.

Parentes Johannes Jbs. Fehling, Palatine, Maria Fehling; 13tn 7bris Infans Maria; Testes Jacob Fehling, Maria Fehling.

Parentes Philipp Herter, Herkemer County, Catharina Herter; 15tn 7bris Infans Eva, born the 25th

August 1793; Testes Lorenz Herter, Anna Eva Herter.

Parentes Adam Bauman, Herkemer County, Barbara Bauman; 15th 7bris Infans Peter, born the 6th 7bris; Testes Peter Bellinger, Elisabeth Bellinger.

Parentes -----; 15th 7bris Infans Margaretha, old 4 years; Testes Dewald Rima, Margretha Breitenbucher.

Parentes -----; 21th 7bris Infans Moses; Testes Jacob Wallrath, Catharina Mayer.

Parentes John Knelis, Canajoharrie, Lea Knelis; 22th 7bris Infans Maria; Testes Georg Haus, Maria Haus.

Parentes -----; 26tn 7bris Infans Maria Magdalena; Testes John Henry Dysslin, Anna Dysslin.

Parentes Dines Flander, Palatine, Magdalena Flander; 28tn 7bris Infans Magdalena; Testes Philipp Fehling, Margretha Fehling.

Parentes Peter Van Nihr, Canajoharrie, Catharina Van Nihr; 29th 7bris Infans Peter; Testes Johannes Ehle, Delia Ehle.

Parentes Warner Farbus, Palatine, Marie Lise Farbus; 6th 8bris Infans Niclaus; Testes Niclaus Killsz, Catharina Farbus.

Parentes Albert Blum, Canajoharrie, Anna Eva Blum; 6th 8bris Infans Catharina; Testes Heinrich Lanz, Catharina Lanz.

Parentes Abraham Mabee, Canajoharrie, Anna Mabee; 6th 8bris Infans Albert; Testes Albert Van Driesen, Maria Van Driesen.

Parentes Peter Killsz, Palatine, Margretha Killsz; 6th 8bris Infans Johann Jost; Testes Johann Jost Snell, Maria Snell.

Parentes Johannes Flander, Tillenburg, Margretha Flander; 13th 8bris Infans Johannes; Testes Philipp Flander, Eva Fox.

Parentes Cornelius Beckman, Palatine, Catharina Beckman; 13th 8bris Infans Cornelius William; Testes William Wallrath, Sally Macky.

Parentes Georg Staring, Royal Grant, Anna Staring; 13th 8bris Infans Jacob; Testes Jacob H. Zimmerman, Maria Zimmerman.

Pater William Woswirth, Palatine T.; 20th 8bris Infans Kmartin; Testes Jacob Snell, Anna Zimmerman.

Parentes Heinrich Herkemer, Otsego County, Catharina Herkemer; 22th 8bris Infans Catharina, born the 18th Aug 1793; Testes Jacob Snell, Elisabeth Snell.

Parentes John Macreny, Palatine, Christina Macreny; 22th 8bris Infantes Margretha, born the 27th Novb. 1784; Sally, born the 28th Novbr. 1787; Eva, born the 14th Januar; Testes Peter Ris, Elisabeth Stamm; Andreas Palsli, Lea Palsli.

Parentes Andreas Palsli, Palatine, Lea Palsli; 22th 8bris Infans Niclaus; Testes Niclaus Pikard, Barbara Pikard.

Parentes Christoph Bellinger, Herkemer Town, Anna Bellinger; 3th Novembr Infans Anna, born the 2d 8bris 1793; Testes Henry Wallrath, Anna Wallrath.

Parentes Henry Sallie, Herkemer County, Catharina Sallie; 3th Novembr Infans Margretha, born the 20th 7bris 1793; Testes Adam Sallie, Elisabeth Stahli.

Parentes Peter Lenz, Herkemer, Margretha Lenz; 3d Novembris Infans Catharina, born the 31t 8bris 1793; Testes Peter Rima, Catharina Hochstetter.

Parentes John Cord, Herkemer County, ------; 3d Novembris Infans Betsi, born the 27th 7bris 1793; Testes Henry Frank, Elisabeth Frank.

Mater Betsi Wayer, Herkemer County; 3d Novembris Infans John, born the 1 7bris 1792; Testes Jacob Lenz, Catharina Lenz.

Parentes Heinrich H. Zimmerman, Palatine Town, Apollonia Zimmerman; 4th Novembr Infans Johann Adam, born the 25th 8br 1793; Testes Joh. Adam Zimmerman, Catharina Zimmerman

Parentes Gover Radli, Palatine, Susanna Radli; 10th November Infans Anna; Testes John Clas, Gertrud Clas.

Parentes Ernst Flander, Palatine, Rosina Flander; 10th November Infans Jacob; Testes Henry Smith, Maria Smith.

Parentes Johannes Ehle, Canajoharrie, Delia Ehle; 10th November Infans Johannes; Testes Joh. Georg Hahn, Elisabeth Hahn.

Parentes Joseph Pikard, Palatine, Magdalena Pikard; 17tn November Infans Rudolf; Testes Rudolf Koch, Anna Koch.

Parentes Niclaus Haus, Canajoharrie, Catharina Haus; 17tn Novembr Infans Susanna; Testes John Adam Hahn, Elisabeth Dewi.

Parentes Peter A. Schuyler, Canajoharrie, Catharina Schuyler; 24tn Novembr Infans Anna; Testes Heinrich Keller, Anna Wild.

Parentes Adam Bellinger, Royal Grant, Magdalena Bellinger; 26th Novembr Infans Delia; Testes Wilhelm Veeder, Elisabeth Veeder.

Parentes Peter Van Deursen, Palatine, Anna Van Deursen; 15tn Xbris Infans Johann Jost Schuyler, born the 6t Xbr; Testes Niclaus Schuyler, Elisabeth Schuyler.

Parentes Jacob Kring, Palatine, Maria Kring; 22th Xbris Infans Jacob; Testes Jost Klock, Maria Kring.

Parentes Jost Bellinger, Palatine, Elisabeth Bellinger; 27th Xbris Infantes Heinrich and Johann Adam--gemelli; Testes Heinrich Bellinger & Anna Eva (Bellinger); Jacob Bellinger & Sophie (Bellinger).

Parentes Heinrich L. Zimmerman, Palatine, Elisabeth Zimmerman; 29th Xbris Infans Anna; Testes Isaac Christman, Anna C. Zimmerman.

Parentes Johannes G. Hellmer, Palatine, Magdalena Hellmer; 30th Xbris Infans Gottfried; Testes Anthoni Ehle, Catharina Bersch.

Parentes Wilhelm C. Zimmerman, Palatine, Catharina Zimmerman; 30th Xbris Infans Catharina; Testes Heinrich J. Fehling, Catharina Zimmerman.

1794

Parentes Jacob Moscher, Canajoharrie Town, Gertrud Moscher; 1t January Infans Lorenz, born the 19th 9bris 1793; Testes Lorenz Gross, Maria Gross.

Parentes John Wilx, Canajoharrie, Anna Wilx; 5th January Infans Catharina; Testes Johannes Bart, Catharina Mayer.

Parentes Benjamin Ellwood, Palatine, Elisabeth Ellwood; 5th January Infans Richard; Testes Christian Klock, Elisabeth Staring.

Parentes Johannes Dachstetter, Herkemer County, Catharina Dachstetter; 12th January Infans Niclaus, born the 7th of the Month; Testes Friderich Weber, Catharina Herter.

Parentes Peter Dachstetter, Herkemer County, Elisabeth Dachstetter; 12th January Infans Peter, born the 30 Xbris 1793; Testes Peter Herter, Catharina Herter.

Parentes Peter J. Weber, Herkemer County, Maria Weber; 12th January Infans Marcus, born the 7 8bris 1793; Testes Georg Weber, Margretha Weber.

Parentes Joseph Mayer, Herkemer County, Catharina Mayer; 12th January Infans Daniel; Testes Daniel Petri, Anna Petri.

Parentes Adam Grimm, Herkemer County, Elisabeth Grimm; 12th January Infans Catharina, born the 4th 9bris 1793; Testes Franz Drausch, Barbara Drausch.

Parentes Conrad Staring, Royal Grant, Magdalena Staring; 17th January Infans Magdalena; Testes Valentin Bayer, Margretha Bayer.

Parentes Thomas Muscher, Canajoharrie, Gnelia Muscher; 18th January Infans George; Testes Georg Yuker, Elisabeth Yuker.

Baptizatus; 19tn Jan; Levi Odell, vir adultus in Canajoharrie Castello degens.

Parentes Johannes Mayer, Canajoharrie, Alida Mayer; 19th January Infans Catharina; Testes Georg Rosenkranz, Anna Rosenkranz.

Parentes Adam Franck, Palatine Town, Catharina Frank; 19th January Infans Friderich; Testes Ulrich Bader, Elisabeth Bader.

Parentes Daniel Hess, Otsego County, Maria Hess; 20th January Infans Joseph, born the 2d Aug 1793; Testes Peter Ph. Fox, Margretha C. Fox.

Parentes Peter Bellinger, Palatine, Elisabeth Bellinger; 26th January Infans Maria; Testes Johannes Scheffer, Maria Beckman.

Translation entry No. 5. Baptized, Levi Odell, adult man living in Canajoharie Castle.

Parentes George Wild, Palatine, Dorothea Wild; 26th January Infans Dorothea; Testes Henry

Crembs, Anna Crembs.
Parentes Henry J. Bellinger, Palatine, Margretha Bellinger; 26th January Infans Elisabeth; Testes Jacob Klock, Elisabeth Nelles.
Parentes David Schremling, Otsego County, Susanna Schremmling; 1 February Infans Andreas, born the 19th July 1793; Testes Johannes Keller, Elisabeth Keller.
Parentes Peter Schremmling, Otsego County, Catharina Schremling; 1 February Infans Sara, born the 9th Xbris 1793; Testes Johannes F. Hess, Cathrina Schremling.
Parentes David Freymayer, Palatine Town, Catharina Freymayer; 2d February Infans Gertrud, born the 16th May 1793; Testes Georg Louks, Gertrud Louks.
Parentes Adam D. Zimmerman, Canajoharrie, Margretha Zimmerman; 2d February Infans Maria; Testes Jacob Matheus, Maria Zimmerman.
Parentes Heinrich Gerber, Palatine, Maria Gerber; 2d February Infans Jacob; Testes Jacob G. Fox, Anna W. Fox.
Parentes Heinrich Muscher, Palatine, Levina Muscher; 8th February Infantes Elisabeth, old 2 years; Peter, old 3 weeks; Testes Adolph Hauss, Elisabeth Rerich; Salomon Yuker, Elisabeth Yuker.
Parentes Thomas Obyrn, Palatine, Magdalena Obyrn; 8th February Infans Johannes; Testes Samuel Asch, Catharina Yoran.

Mater Margretha Hauss; 8th February Infans Peter; Testes Benjamin Ellwood, Elisabeth Yoran.
Parentes Joh. Niclaus Thumm, Palatine, Elisabeth Thumm; 9th February Infans Magdalena; Testes Christian Fink, Elisabeth Deyggert.
Parentes Michel Bauter, Palatine, Anna Bauter; 9th February Infans Johannes; Testes Johannes Koch, Barbara Bauter.
Parentes Johannes Hart, Royal Grant, Sara Hart; 9th February Infans Jacob; Testes Heinrich Hart, Anna Eva Hart.
Parentes Adam Eaker, Canajoharrie, Margretha Eaker; 9th February Infantes Elisabeth and Margretha--gemelli; Testes Joh. Jost Snell, Gertrud Snell; Johannes Christman, Anna Eaker.
Parentes Johannes P. Hellmer, Otsego County, Anna Hellmer; 14th February Infans Margretha, born the 17th March 1792; Testes Fridrich Bam, Elisabeth Bam.
Parentes Andreas Michler, Otsego County, Anna Michler; 14th February Infans Philipp, born the 19th Juny 1793; Testes Philipp P. Hellmer, Anna J. Fox.
Parentes James Farbus, Palatine, Margretha Farbus; 14th February Infans Maria, born the 19th January 1794; Testes John C. Nelles, Maria G. Nelles.
Parentes Johann Andreas Dayer, Field District, Catharina Dayer; 16th February Infans Anna Maria Catharina, born the 30th Jan; Testes Valentin Muller, Maria Muller.
Parentes Jacob Mayer, Mohacq District, Anna Eva Mayer; 23th February Infans Magdalena, born the 11 Febr; Testes Jacob H. Fehling, Elisabeth Bauter.
Parentes Johannes S. Snell, Snellenbush, Anna Snell; 23th February Infans Maria; Testes Johannes Stoll, Maria Stoll.
Parentes Jacob Flander, Palatine, Catharina Flander; 23th February Infans Elisbeth; Testes Dines Flander, Magdalena Flander.
Parentes Johann Adam Bellinger, Canajoharrie, Elisabeth Bellinger; 2th March Infans Elisabeth; Testes-----.
Parentes Michel Keller, Palatine, Sara Keller; 2th March Infans Catharina; Testes Lienhard Bam, Catharina Keller.
Parentes Peter Mosch, Canajoharrie, Dorothea Mosch; 2th March Infans Catharina; Testes Niclaus Sternberger, Catharina Sternberger.
Parentes Georg Rabolt, Palatine, Margretha Rabolt; 2th March Infans Elisabeth; Testes Conrad Hellegas, Anna Eva Hellegas.
Parentes Christoph W. Fox, Palatine, Margretha Fox; 13th March Infans Jacob, born the 7th March; Testes Jacob G. Fox, Delia W. Fox.
Parentes Georg Hahn, Canajoharrie, Elisabeth Hahn; 14tn March Infans Johannes Wendeker; Testes Johannes Wendeker, Catharina Wendeker.
Parentes Ulric Bauter, Palatine, Elisabeth Bauter; 16th March Infans Maqdalena, born the 7th

March; Testes Christian Graaf, Catharina Graaf.
END OF CERTIFIED COPY OF VOLUME I. DUTCH REFORMED SAINT JOHN'S CHURCH RECORD.

NOTE
The preceding pages are all that remain of the first volume of the record of the Upper Palatine Church. The book as it now stands, consists of 44 leaves; one leaf in this part of the book has been torn out. The record is bound in parchment, and fully two thirds of the latter part of the book are at present missing, the leaves having been torn out thus opening a gap in the binding, from which the original size of the book can be estimated as having contained about 120 leaves. It is reasonable to suppose that Dominie Dysslin continued to inscribe in this record, the baptisms administered by him up to the time of his death, which occurred in about the month of September in 1812. It is possible that the book may also have contained a Marriage Register.

In view of the fact of this hiatus of over eighteen years in the vital records of this church, particular attention should be given to the remaining pages that appear in this typewritten volume. We have copied a considerable portion of the Treasurer's account book, of St. John's Church. In the lists of subscribers and pew holders, the names of the greater part of Dominie Dysslin's Congregation can be found, as also numerous items of historical interest, to which reference has been made in the introduction. The Treasurer's book is the same size as Dominie Dysslin's record; it is bound in 1/2 calf with paste board sides, cost nine shillings and contains about 200 pages, some of which are blank. It was in use until the year 1873, but only parts of the book have been copied. Some attempt has been made to arrange the items copied in chronological order, as the original record is very much confused. The Trustee's Minutes have been abstracted and not completely copied. Each page as a unit, as it appears in the original is indicated by the dotted lines, thus: -

Book 2

The second book is organized by category, baptisms, marriages, funerals, not by date. So scroll down and you will find some of the older data in there too. Apparently the minister of St. John's administered to a considerable area.

Herkimer, Mongtomery (counties)

Manheim or Menheimor Henhiem, Danube, Minden, Oppenheim (townships or towns).

Records of marriages commenced by the Revd. David Devoe

1816

May 3th Joseph Hart Sally Young Menhiem Montgomery
Sept 29th Jacob Helligas Margreta Thum Oppenheim Montgomery
October 13 Henry P. Kline Cathrien Klock Oppenheim Montgomery
October 23rd Cornelus Van Kamp Caty Defendorf Minden Montgomery

1817

January 2nd Jacob Hart Betsy Baum Menhiem Montgomery
19 Philip Micle Maria Kern Oppenheim Montgomery
27 David Klock Caty Klock Oppenheim Montgomery
March 23rd William Kretsinger Cathrien Fox
April 07 John Waggoner Rebecka Lawyer of Minden & Henhiem Montgomery
April 29 John Osman Caty Klock of Oppenheim Montgomery
June Isaac Williams Anna Defendorf of Minden Montgomery
July 20 Henry Grands Cathrien Grendsorf Columbia Herkemer County
(Sept 14) Lansing Roach Nancy Van alstine Denube Herkemer County
October 20 John W. Coughtry Peggy Ann Duesler Denube Herkemer County
7 December Shull Dunube Nancy Klock Herkemer County

1818

January 3t Frederic Lawyer of Denube Herkimer Caty Stawring Openhiem Montgomery
20 Daniel Waggoner Caty Vanness Denube Herkemer County
(Febr 6) Christiann Sepperman Caty Barns Oppenhiem Montgomery County
13 John Baum Lena Ellwood Denube Herkemer County
26 Simon Vandusen Mary Simmerman Menheim Herkemer County
Febr 26 Joseph P. Nellis Dama Duety Oppenheim Montgomery County
March 08 Benjamin Fox Cathrien Statts Oppenheim Montgomery County
15 Henry Walrath Clarice Loveless Oppenheim Dito
22 Henry Failing Jun Oppenheim Dito Dolly Youker
Sabastisun Kook Oppenheim Montgomery County Betsy Youron Menheim Herkimer County
May 14 Joseph G. Klock Elesebeth Fox both of Oppenheim Montgomery County
(Note at bottom of page for this entry: this was the fourth marriage of...can't read rest)
June 07 Christoffel Klock Elezebeth Dyslin Both of Oppenheim
July 05 Peter Zimmerman Betsy Wise of Menheim Herkemer County
July 06 Daniel Klock of Oppenheim Montgomery County Nancy Defendorf Minden Dito Dito
30 Salomon Ellwood Elizebeth Baum Minden Montgomery
(Sept 21) Chester Brown, Esqr. Attorney of Junius County of Senica Elizebeth Force of Oppenheim, Montgomery County
Novr 25 Ira Abbott Bern Albany County Sophia Dominic Dennube Herkemer
(December 6) John Walrath Lydia Rogers both of Oppenheim
8 Thomas Failing Cathrien Klock Both of Oppenheim
19 John Teppits Menheim Herkemer County Polly Nellis Oppenheim Montgomery County

1819

January 03 James Farbush Maria Anderson Oppenheim Mongomery County
10 Jacob C. Helligas Margaret House Oppenheim Mont
24 Frederic Guitman Margreta Delena Columbia Herkermer
Febr. 14 John Shaffer Maria Denison Both of Oppenheim
18 Silus Hardy of Denhiem (?) Herkemer County Dorothy Failing of Oppenheim Montgomery County
March 09 Robert Nellis Caty Dysslin Oppenheim Montgomery
April 08 Cornelius W. Beekman Sally Stormsboth of Oppenheim Montgomery
11 Abraham Cline Milacent Bedford both of Oppenheim Montgomery
June 27 Salomon Wheler Betsy Terpenny Both of Dennube Herkemer County Cornelius Devoe, Anderithy Gague Married by John C. Toll Oppenheim
July 25 Peter P. Snell of Menheim Herkemer County Maried Caty Elewood of Minden Montgomery County

29 Jacob Failing Jun. Catharien Toll Both of Oppenheim Montgomery County
Sept. 26 David Van Alstine Lidia Terpenny both of Dennube Herkemer County
30 John J. Failing Jun. Oppenheim Montgomery County Cathrien Elewood Minden Montgomery County
October 10 John Woleben Cathrien Jezman Columbia Herkemer County
Novr. 21 Martin Zoe Cobleskill Schoharie County Catharien Sternbergh Denube Herkemer County
28 George Kring Mary Cross Oppenheim Herkemer County
(Decem 7) Peter Bellinger Elizebeth Youker Oppenheim Montgomery

1820

John Wick Pallatine Montgomery County Clarissa Wicks Minden Dito
13 Casper Loib Menheim Herkemer County Polly Elewood Minden Montgomery County
16 John M. Devoe Palantine Polly Klock Minden Montgomery County
20 John F. Bellinger Oppenheim Montgomery Elezebeth Pierce
March 16 Benjamin Vanarlen Maria ZimmermanOppenheim Montgomery County
Note: The Rev. David Devoe was a poor speller; also an indifferent writer. It is hard to distinguish between his "e" and "o", and in many cases the two letters are identical.
April 02 William J. Enders Nancy Leib Married at Menheim Herkemer County
22 Richard Nixon Lena Smith Married at Pallatine Montgomery
May 07 Andrew Gitman Frankford Herkemer County Elezebeth Edict Columbia Herkemer County
8 Revd John Rall Late from Brunswick Irena Lomis Warren Herkemer County
July 09 Jacob Cool Cathriene Baum Oppenheim Montgomery County
Sept. 5 Henry Kring Guity Nillis Oppenheim Montgomery County
(November 26) William Zimmerman Polly Wire Menheim Herkemer County
(December 28) Francis Lighthall Jur Margr?tta Klock Oppenheim Montgomery County

1821

Febr. 6 Daniel Snell Anna Dislin Menheim Herkemer
25 John Borst Sharon Schoharie County Betsey Bellengton Oppenheim Montgomery
March 17 John H. Vedder Cathrien Teharah both of Oppenheim Montgomery County
April 22nd Luis Mushady Menheim Herkemer County Elezebeth Ginnens Openheim Montgomery County
May 20 Daniel Hose Oppenheim Montgomery (Countiest? Betsey House Menheim Herkemer
June 10 Richard Smith Fairfield Elezebeth Markle Menheim Herkemer County
26 John Petrie Menheim Herkemer County Caty House
August 27 Cornelius Kyser Kinston Caty Riece Openheim Montgomery County
John Shall Menheim Caty Wise

1822

Febr. 12 John J. KlockAnna Hillegas both of Oppenheim Montgomery County
Jenury 13 Anthony Walrath Caty Davis Menheim Oppenheim
March 10 George Talbart Perry, of Cayuga; Amanda Herkemer, Dennube Herkemer County
14 Jones Ellwood Peggy Lipe Both of Menheim Herkemer County

1821

Sept. 6 Jacob Bellinger Mary Bellengton both of Oppenheim Montgomery County

1822

June John Shafer Oppenheim Montgomery County Mary Youron Menheim Herkemer County
July 08 Nicholas Zimmerman Christianna Thum Oppenheim
10 Volkert Guitman Peggy Flander Oppenheim
August 05 James Daniels Mahale Lantman Both of Oppenheim
Sept. 22 Simon Dreisback Danub Herkemer County Elizebeth Crous Minden Montgomery
October 20 Ansel Strong Elezebeth Frayer Denube Herkemer
October 27 Paris, Manuel, Phips Nancy Healey Oppenheim Montgomery
Novm 14 Benjamin Klock Thankful House Oppenheim Montgomery
Decembr 26 Christiaun C. House Oppenheim Montgomery Count Cathriene Riese Salsbury Herkemer Co

1823

Benjamin Elebrige Mersellis Cayuga County Nancy Ellwood Minden Montgomery County
Note: There is a possibility that this word is "Eldrige".
January George Putman Elezebeth Klock Oppenheim Montgomery
19 John Hese Jun Nancy Riese Oppenheim Montgomery
(Febr) Joseph Dusler Peggy Spancnabel Oppendeim Montgomery
9 Henry Ostrander Margreta Defendorf Danube Herkemer Co
Adam Snell Menheim Mary Leib Herkemer County
April 03 John Lighthall Polly Crossbee Pallatine
May 15 Daniel Walrath Maria Billinger both of Oppenheim
June 30 Henry Walrath Polly Cambell of Oppenheim
July 27 Christian Guitman Pallatine Mongomery Nancy Thumb Oppenheim
31 Jeremiah Landt Nelly Eliza Ostrander Danube Herkemer
Augt 23 Winga Kelly of Oppenheim Eva Wheeler widow
Sept. 14 Philip Coole Lena Crisman Palatine Montgomery County
21 John Kring Elezebeth Nellis Oppenheim Montgomery
October 12 Peter Vrooman Nancy House Columbia Herkemer Co
Novm 2nd Henry J. WalrathElizebeth Eygabroat Dennube
Decbr 28 Jacob Vedder Mary Daykart Oppenheim

1824

January 25 David Ehle Elisebeth House
27 John Riece Eve Beekman Oppenheim
(Febr 1) Peter Tuesler (d) Lucy Soles Palla ine Montgomery County
24 William Swachamer Maria Failing Oppenheim
March Charles Obyms Nancy Failing Oppenheim
June 27 Jabes Lewis Betsey Young Oppenheim
July 04 John CoolBetsey Baum Oppenheim
6 Christian Walrath Eve Heiring Oppenheim
August 22d Daniel Loadwick Betsey Landtman Oppenheim
October 3rd William McMullin Sally Frayer Danube Herkemer
17 James Green Danube Caty Dominic Herkemer
Novm 25 Jacob Van allen Betsey Unger Oppenheim

1825

January 20 Jsom Simons Eve Jane Vanorden Danube Herkemer Co
(Febr 27) Daniel Klock Polly Devoe Oppenheim Montgomery
March 3rd Henry Hairing Nancy Banker Oppenheim

14 Barnard Cook Amanda Bice Oppenheim
August 14 John Baily Midlefield Caty Boumgart Oppenheim
Novm 10 Jacob Scram Cathrien Groof Oppenheim
18 Abraham Smith Lena Shull Danube Herkemer County
Daniel Borden Cathrien Fuller Oppenheim Montgomery County

1826

January 08 William Ludington Irena Squire Danube Herkemer Co.
28 Daniel D. Walrath Lena Walrath Oppenheim
April 09 James Cambel German Flats Herkermer Co Mary Ellwood Minden Montgomery Co
16 James Klock Marcia Buel Minden Montgomy Co.
30 Christian J. Klock Margaret Walrath Oppenheim Montgomcry
May 04 John J. House Nancy Hofman Oppenheim Montgomery Co.
May 10 David Crouse Maria Lasher Oppenheim M. Co.
June 25 John Dave Danube(Herkemer County Nancy Countriman Herkermer
July 04 Isaac Duesler Elezebeth Loadwic of Oppenheim

1827

January 01 Henry Hese Oppenheim Montgomery Polly Davies Menheim Herkemer
Febr. 18 Christian VedderDorothy Thum Oppenheim Mont. Co.
June 07 Henry Ward Leahr Stanshell Can & Joharie Mont. Co.
August 12 Francis Frederic Elesebeth Bellinger Oppenheim Montgomy Co.
August 25 Charles Klock Julean Buel Minden Montgomery County
July 13 Samuel Bartlet Polly Youron Oppenheim
October 2d Nathan Snell Oppenheim Montgomery Nancy Fox Pallatine

1829

Fbr 8 Ephraim Green Phebe Bigsbee Pallatine Montgomery
1829 Lewis Carnerose Root Montgomery Co. Betsey Reese Oppenheim
May 17 Eber. E.M. ShanteAnn Kathrien Nowls Oppenheim
August 3rd Levi Thum Maria Flander Oppenheim
October 21 Robert Sluyter Ellener Franck Turin Lewis County

1830

January 31 William Hall, a shoemaker, aged 23 years a son of William Hall & Caty Burdick Betsey Heese, aged 21 years a Daughter of Johannes Heese & Elesebeth Bellinger Witness present John Knickebacker & Maria Devoe all of the Town of Oppenheim and known to me, Married at the House of Johannes Heese in the above Town and County of Montgomery.
David Devoe V D.M.

165 Couples
Note. The last marriage was probably recorded at length by Mr. Devoe, on account of a law passed by the Legislature at about this time, which prescribed the form in which marriages should be recorded.

RECORD OF MARRIAGES BY THE REVD. A.H. MYERS

1831 Jany 27th	George F. Bellinger, Cordwainer, Ages 25 yrs of the town of Oppenheim, Nancy Weaver Aged 18 yrs. of Oppenheim Married in St. Johns Ville, Jan. 27th	Witnesses: John R. Myers, Brantingham Lewis Co. N.Y & Hannah Muers, St. Johns Ville
Jan 30th	David H. Shonts, Miller, aged 22 yrs Elizabeth Walrath, aged 21 yrs, both of Oppenheim, Montgomery Co in which town they were married Jan. 30, 1831	Simeon Walrath, Oppenheim Clarissa Walrath, Johnstown.
Feb. 20th	Ethan Barton, Shingle Maker, aged 19, Ephrata. Mary Walrath. spinster, aged 19, Oppenheim. Married in Oppenheim Feby 20th 1831	Thos Edwards, Ephrata, Julia Ann Walrath Manheim.
May 2th	Christopher Nellis, tanner, aged 26 yrs, of Palatine, Montgomery, Co. N.Y. Margaret Myers, spinster, aged 19 yrs, of Oppenheim, Montgomery Co. N.Y. Married by me in Oppenheim, May 12th 1831 A.M. Myers	Richard Beaver& Nancy Nellis both of Palatine, Montgomery Co. N.Y
5/15	Sanford Lee, Teacher, aged 27 yrs, Minden, Lana Klock, spinster, aged 26 yrs, of Oppenheim, in which town they were married.	Solomon Klock & Simon Klock both of Oppenheim.
June 16th	Solomon Klock, farmer, aged 27, of Oppenheim, Elizabeth Bellinger, spinster, aged 22 of Do. Married at the house of John F. Bellinger	Stephen Klock Simon Klock both of Oppenheim.
July 3d	Samuel Frame, farmer, aged 23 yrs. (Manheim) Mary Ann Scott, spinster, aged 22 yrs (Herkimer Co.) Married in St. Johns Ville, Oppenheim July 3d.	Hannah Myers Catherine Blanchard both of Oppenheim.
July 17th	Jonah Kline, farmer, aged 27 yrs. of Oppenheim Catherine Spontnable, spinster aged 19 y. of Ephrata Married at the house of Henry Spontnable, Ephrata.	Josiah Christman Betsey Spontnable
Aug. 14th	Stephen Klock, farmer, aged 19 yrs, of Oppenheim, Anna Bellinger, spinster, aged 19 yrs, of Married in the Parsonage house St. Johns Ville.	Hannah Myers Catherine Blanchard Oppenheim, both of St. Johns Ville.
Sept. 22d	F. Lewis Talyer, Doctor, aged 22 yr. (Daunube, Charlotte Sternberg, aged 20 y. (Herkimer Co) Married in	Abm. Hall Doct. Martinsburg. . Charlotte Macomb, Danube.

Danube, September 22d 1831

Sept 29th	Daniel Eigenbradt, blacksmith, aged 20 yrs. Phebe Helmick, aged 21 yrs, both of Oppenheim Married In St. Johns Ville Sept. 29th 1831.	Betsey Coon . Hannah Myers St. Johns Ville.
Oct. 17th	David Venten, farmer, aged 21 yrs.Mary Quackenbush, aged 17 y. both of Oppenheim in which town they were married Monday evening 17th Oct. 1831.	Benjamin Vedder & his wife of Oppenheim.
1831 Oct. 23	Frederick D. Dockstader, shoemaker, aged 21 yrs of Danube, Herkimer Co. Mary Fox, aged 22 yrs, of Oppenheim Married at the house of Robt. Nellis	Chauncey Nellis Alida Beckmen both of Oppenheim.
Nov. 6th	William Shall, Tailor, aged 29 yrs of Danube Eve Klock, aged 24 yrs of Minden Married in the town of Minden 6th Nov. 1831	Jacob Shall of Danube . Charlotte Elwood, of Minden.
1832 May (20?)	Daniel Failing to Nancy Hess	both of Oppenheim, Monty. Co. N.Y

RECORD OF MARRIAGES BY REV. H. B. STRYKER

1832

December 9 David Flanders, farmer, & Eve Hays, both of Oppenheim, Married on Sabbath Morning at John Hay's in Eukers Bush. Witnesses: John Hays & wife & children.

1833

April 2 Benjamin Booth, Brick Maker, Oppenheim & Mary Thumb, Married at Adam Klock's. Witnesses: Adam Klock & family
May 5 James Best to Mary Getman Married at Thomas Getman's. Witnesses: Thomas Getman & family
May 12 Henry Hays, to Nancy Smith, widow of John Flanders, Married at Parsonage House. Witnesses: Nancy & Jacob Hays, Mrs. Stryker & Caty Tuers.
June 16 Asher Lane to Hannah Scott, Both from Sharon, Married at Fulton Ville. Witnesses: George Bellinger & Lydia Scott
June 27 Adam Smith to Nancy Goodell, From new state Road, married at the Parsonage House. Witnesses: Abrm Veeder, Margt Klock, Volkert Smith & Catharine Smith
July 7 Henry Chrisman to Mary Ann Kiln, Married over the River. Witnesses: John A. Kiln & family.
July 21 Jacob Wasler to Rosina House, Married at the Parsonage House. Witnesses: Mrs. Stryker & family & Elizabeth Lent
June 30 Jacob Harwick to Jans Voorhees, Married at the Parsonage House. Witnesses: Mrs. Stryker

& Elizabeth Lent

June 9 Jacob Stevens, to Sarah Flanders, Married by the Rev. P. Stryker at the House Of Hy Oostrum. Witnesses: Henry Gestrum & his wife, Mr. Hodge & his Wife.

Septr. 10 George Watkins to Helen Caldwell At The House of Dr. B. Caldwell. Witnesses: J. H. Hayes, of Little Falls, James Watkins & David Hillegas.

1833

Sept. 12th Thomas Getman to Nancy Best by H. B. Stryker, at the house of Dr. Best On Turnpike. Witnesses: All the parents, Brothers & Sisters of both parties.

Septr. 19 Stephen Fox to Mary Fox, By P. Stryker, at The House of The Widow of F. Fox Esqr. Witnesses: All the Parents, Also Walter Schram, Francis T. Miller, Peter P. Fox. They were Cousins and Children of Christopher Fox and Frederick Fox Esqr.

Novr. 3 Jacob H. Smith to Hannah Ehle, all of Indian Castle By Rev. P. Stryker at The Parsonage House St. John's Ville. Witnesses: Mr. Zimmerman & Wife & Rev. H. B. Stryker & Family.

1834

January 2d Peter Graves, Farmer, Aged 25 years to Lucy Ann Shears, daughter of S. Shears By Rev. H. B. Stryker at the house of Mr. Smith Shears in Oringe Bush. Witnesses: S. Sheers & family & c. & c.

January 12 Josiah Eigenbrodt, to Belinda Bellinger By Rev. Peter Stryker at The Parsonage House, St. John's Ville. Witnesses: Charles Walrath and Lucinda Bellinger

Jany 15 Isaack Lodowyk, to Julian Klock At The House of Jacob Klock in Oppenheim. Witnesses: Peter C. Noell, Catharine Fox and John Nellis Esqr.

Janny 29 Moses Freer of Danube, to Eliza Graaf of Manheim At the House of John Graaf, Manheim. Witnesses: David Dominick & Nathan Christy.

Februy 18 Christopher Bellinger to Nancy Smith, both of Yukar's Bush. At the Parsonage House, St. John's Ville Witnesses: Mrs. D. Stryker & Miss Eliza Lent.

RECORD OF MARRIAGES BY REV. A. H. Myers

1838

Feb. 25 Christopher Denmark, aged 22, of Palatine to Margaret Fink, aged 17 of Oppenhiem. Witnesses: Levi Nihoff & Mary Bellinger

Feb. 27 Samuel F. Smith of Seneca Falls, Seneca Co. to Maria Cox, of Minden, Monty. Co. Witnesses: L. D. Calkins & Barney Becker

March 6 Joseph W. Hackney of Warren Co. Penn. To Christiana Zimmerman of St. Johnsville. Witnesses: Henry Failing, Theodore Failing & De Witt Failing

March 29 Peter Tymenon, farmer to Margaret Walrath, both of Oppenheim, Married at the Parsonage House. Witnesses: Hannah Myers & Sarah Linford

June 14 Enos Wager, aged 22 yrs. Of Danube to Sophronia Dusler, aged 16 yrs. Of Lasellsville. Witnesses: John Wager & wife.

Oct. 11th David J. Morrison to Rosina Shafer, both of Oppenheim. Witnesses: Solomon Shafer of Oppenheim & Mary J. Boan of Manheim.

Oct. 18 Stornthew Johnson to Alida Baum, both of Oppenheim. Witnesses: Ebenezer Handy & Eunice Johnson, both of Oppenheim.

Oct. 22 Wm. H. Covenhoven to Emaline Veghte, Married in St. Johnsville at the house of D. Bascom. Witnesses: Geo. W. Moore & Sarah Chese, all of Johnstown.

Oct. 24 Leander Fox, of Fort Plain to Barbara Klock, of St. Johnsville. Witnesses: Norman Kimble & Wm. E. Bleecker, both of Fort Plain.

Nov. 30 Jesse Smith of Oppenheim to Catharine Thumb, of St. Johnsville. Witnesses: Doct. J. W. Riggs & Family of St. Johnsville.

Dec. 31 Luther Klock, farmer, of St. Johnsville to Zilpah Ann Tupper, of Oppenheim. Witnesses: John Peck, of Oppenheim & Lucinda Klock of St. Johnsville.

1839

Jany. 3d Peter Hollicass Jr., farmer, of Remsen, Oneida Co. N.Y. to Elizabeth Ausman, of St. Johnsville. Witnesses: John C. Ausman and family, St. Johnsville

Feb. 5 Barnum Ostrom to Ursula E. Fuller, both of Oppenheim, Fulton Co. N.Y. Witnesses: Isaac Dusler & family at whose house they were married.

Feb. 7 Lester H. Sweet to Nancy Failing, both of Oppenheim. Witnesses: Christopher Klock & family, St. Johnsville.

Feby 12 John Hellegass to Elisa Maria Dygert, both of St. Johnsville. Witnesses: Doct. John W. Riggs & Jonas Snell of St. Johnsville.

July 4 Rufus C. Willsey, of Maryland, Otsego Co. to Frances Ellen Failing, St. Johnsville. Witnesses: Peter Klock Esq. & Theodore Failing

July 28 John Strough, Jr. of Manheim, to Dorcas Johnson, of Oppenheim. Witnesses: Mrs. H. Myers & Mrs. Christian Walrath.

Aug. 23 Lawrence L. Timerman to Nancy Timerman, both of Manheim. Witnesses: Jeremiah Wimerman & Martha Timerman, all of Manheim

Sept. 22 William Peterie, of Little Falls, to Eve Youngs, of German Flatts. Witnesses: Jarod Sanders & Mary Gage, both of Little Falls.

Nov. 7 Peter Rose, of Minden, to Maria Cramer, of St. Johnsville. Witnesses: Josiah Zimerman & Jonas Zimerman, both of St. Johnsville.

Nov. 11 Elias Saltsman to Eliza Veght, both of St. Johnsville. Witnesses: Axel Hough & Mrs. Danl. Bascom, both of St. Johnsville.

Nov. 13 Samuel Purdy to Julia Eigenbroadt, both of Palatine. Married at Little Falls, Herkimer Co. Witnesses: Joseph J. Eigenbroadt of Palatine and Mary Catharine Whyland of St. Johnsville.

Nov. 14 Joseph J. Eigenbroadt, of Palatine to Mary Catharine Whyland, of St. Johnsville. Married in St. Johnsville at the house of her father. Witnesses: Samual Purdy & his wife Julia, and Ann Eigenbroadt.

Dec. 17 Anthony Straub to Eve Zimmerman, both of St. Johnsville. Witnesses: David Crouso & Wm. Kretzer, of St. Johnsville.

Dec. 25 James Wilson to Abagail R. Belcher, both of St. Johnsville. Witnesses: Horatio Gardner & Sarah Belcher, both of St. Johnsville.

1840

Jan. 16 Cyrus Baker Jr. to Sarah C. Bigelow, both of Sprakers Basin. Married at the Parsonage House, St. Johnsville. Witnesses: John H. Baker & wife of Little Falls, N.Y.

Jan. 16 Charles Huffman to Lovisa M. Tibbets, both of Oppenheim. Married at the house of John P. Cline, State road. Witnesses: Warren A. Bacon & Sally Tibbets, all of Oppenheim.

Jan. 21 Shadrach Sherman, of Little Falls to Ann Eliza Scott, of Danube. Married at the house of Mr. Hawn, in Minden. Witnesses: John McNeil & Jane Mc Neil, both of Minden.

Feb. 4 Garret H. Timeson, of St. Johnsville, to Maria Countryman, of Palatine. Married at Spraker's Tavern, Palatine. Witnesses: Peter Timeson of St. Johnsville, Joseph Spraker of Palatine.

Feb. 27 George F. Grinnel, of De Witt, Onondaga Co., to Permelia Perkins, of Syracuse, Onondaga Co. Married at the house of Genl. L. Averall, St. Johnsville. Witnesses: Genl. L. Averell & family & a multitude.

April 12 Volkert Smith, aged 24 years, to Sarah Maria Mosher, aged 19, both of Oppenheim. Married at the Parsonage, St. Johnsville. Witnesses: Hannah Myers & Sarah Linford, both of St. Johnsville.

1840

Aug. 19 Soloman Smith, of Fort Plain, to Margaret Failing, of St. Johnsville. Married at the house of Jacob H. Failing. Witnesses: Reubin Failing & Doct. J. W. Riggs, both of St. Johnsville.

Aug. 20 Robert Klock to Catharine Snell, both of Little Falls. Married at the house of Jonas Snell. Witnesses: Jonas Snell & Elizabeth Snell of St. Johnsville.

Sept. 27 David D. Van Slyke, of Minden to Sally Moyer, of Manheim. Married at the parsonage, St. Johnsville, Monty. Co. Witnesses: Nichs. Vn Slyke & Betsey vn Slyke, both of Minden.

Nov. 18 John Pauter to Lucy Abbott, both of St. Johnsville. Married at the house of John William, St. Johnsville. Witnesses: John J. Klock & Eliza Ann Pauter, both of St. Johnsville.

1841

May 16 Solomon Flander to Mary Hase, both of Oppenheim. Married at the house of Peter Hase. Witnesses: Peter Hase Jr. & Jacob Hase, both of Oppenheim.

June 3 Jacob Haring of Sullivan, Madison Co. to Nancy Walrath, of St. Johnsville. Married at the house of Adam J. Walrath. Witnesses: And W. Walrath & Martin Walrath, both of St. Johnsville.

June 8 William D. Cloyes, of Claremont, N.H. to Elizabeth Walker, of St. Johnsville. Married at the house of Luman Bascom. Witnesses: Luman Bascom & family.

June 17 Jeremiah Cox, of Minden to Lucinda Ingersoll, of Oppenheim. Married at the house of her father in Oppenheim. Witnesses: Henry Moyer, of Canajoharie, & Mary Ann Beekman, of Oppenheim.

July 5 William Failing to Catherine Pauter, both of Oppenheim. Married at the Parsonage in St. Johnsville. Witnesses: John H. Youker & Mary Pauter, both of Oppenheim.

Sept. 23 Newton F. Hays, of Earlville, Madison Co. to Anne Leonard, of St. Johnsville. Married at the house of Daniel Leonard, St. Johnsville. Witnesses: Daniel Leonard Jr. & Marcellus Leonard, both of St. Johnsville.

Sept. 30 Garret Miller, of Minden to Perlina Ellen Nellis, of Canajoharie. Married in Canajoharie, near Fort Plain, at the house of Suffrenis Nellis. Witnesses: Jonas Nestell & Sally Langdon, both of Minden.

Oct. 21 Elias Moyer to Margaret Getman, both of Manheim. Married at Saltsmans tavern in St. Johnsville. Witnesses: Moses Timerman & Nancy Moyer, both of Manheim.

Oct. 28 John J. Klock to Eliza Ann Pauter, both of St. Johnsville. Married at the house of Melchior L. Pauter. Witnesses: Jas Klock & Margaret Klock, both of St. Johnsville.

1841

Nov. 18 Samuel Sadler to Louisa Chawgo, both of St. Johnsville. Married at the house of George Chawgo. Witnesses: John Chawgo & Jacob Chawgo, both of St. Johnsville.

Dec. 5 John Henry Dyselin to Lavina Kretser, both of St. Johnsville, Monty. Co. N.Y. Witnesses: George Shoffel & Lucy Ann Williams, both of St. Johnsville.

Dec. 25 William Keeler to Almira Helligass, both of St. Johnsville. Married at the house of Jacob C. Helligass. Witnesses: John P. House & Mary Hase, both of Oppenheim.

1842

Feb. 24 William N. Knieskern, of Danube to Jemima Flander, of St. Johnsville. Married at the house of Peter Flander. Witnesses: Peter Flander & Obadiah Flander, both of St. Johnsville.

Feb. 27 Henry Wiley, of Oppenheim to Mary Ann Klock, daughter of John G. Klock, of St. Johnsville. Married at the Parsonage, St. Johnsville. Witnesses: John D. Robinson, of Oppenheim & Areli Klock, of St. Johnsville.

Mar. 6 John P. Nellis, tailor, of Fort Plain to Sally Tibbets, of Oppenheim. Married at the house of

Nicholas J. Smith, Oppenheim. Witnesses: Christopher Nellis & Gabriel Smith, both of Oppenheim.
Mar. 20 Joseph Vosburgh to Fanny Boyer, both of Little Falls. Married at the inn at Christopher Klock, St. Johnsville. Witnesses: Geo. Bumgardner, T. G. Siely, & Mary Klock, all of St. Johnsville.
May 4 Jacob Sanders Jr. to Anna Maria Moyer, both of Minden. Married at the house of her father in Minden. Witnesses: Joseph Smith & Henry C. Sanders, both of Minden.
May 5 Henry Card to Fanny Philenia Wade, both of St. Johnsville. Married at the house of her father in St. Johnsville. Witnesses: Mortimer Wade & Caroline Crane, both of St. Johnsville.
June 28 Rensselaer Getman, of Ephrata to Elmina Owens, of Danube. Married in Danube at Abm. Owens. Witnesses: James Owens & John Sholl, both of Danube.
June 30 William W. Davis, of Minden to Matilda E. Hase, of Oppenheim. Married at the house of Abraham Hase, Oppenheim. Witnesses: Roswell Carpenter & Jane Hase, both of Oppenheim.
July 5 John Ogsbury, Esq. of Pamela, Jefferson Co. to Maria vn. Deusen, widow of Joseph Cramer, of St. Johnsville. Married at the house of Christian Klock, St. Johnsville. Witnesses: Christian Klock & Lydia Cramer, both of St. Johnsville.
July 5 Peter Garlock, of Canajoharie to Lana Loucks, of Manheim. Married at the house of Loucks, Manheim. Witnesses: Morgan Bidelmen, of Manheim & Catharine Garlock, of Canajoharie.

1842

July 12 Rev. John H. Ackerson to Cornelia K. Orendorff, both of Columbia. Married at the house of Henry S. Orendorff, Columbia. Witness: Mrs. Mary Orendorff, of Columbia.
Sept. 4 Charles P. Smith, of St. Johnsville to Nancy Helligass, of Oppenheim. Witnesses: Jonas Helligass, of Oppenheim & Jas. Henry Lighthall, of St. Johnsville.
Sept. 20 Daniel Ayers, M.D. of Amsterdam to Mrs. Margaret Feeter, widow of Maturin Freeman, of Manheim. Married at the house of Adam Feeter, Manheim. Witnesses: James Feeter, of Little Falls & Adam Feeter, of Manheim.
Sept. 22 Moses Huffman to Caroline Lawton, both of Oppenheim. Married at the Parsonage, St. Johnsville. Witnesses: Hannah Myers & Jane Helen Myers.
Oct. 11 Rev. John Dubois, of Union Village to Miss Sophia Green, of Danube. Married at the house of her father, John L. Green, Danube. Witnesses: Augustus Green & Mary Green, both of Danube.
Nov. 3 Abram Fuller to Catharine Maria Brown, both of St. Johnsville. Married at the house of her father, St. Johnsville. Witnesses: Hiram Brown & Anna Maria Eygenbroad, both of St. Johnsville.
Dec. 15 Dennes N. Smith, painter to Anna Maria Eygenbroad, both of St. Johnsville. Married at the house of Peter W. Saltsman. Witnesses: Chas. W. Webster Esq. & Mary Klock, both of St. Johnsville.
Dec. 15 Sylvester Robinson to Agnes Whyland, both of St. Johnsville. Married at the house of her father Andrew Whyland, St. Johnsville. Witnesses: Hiram Robinson & Mary Bean, both of Oppenheim.
Dec. 22 Obadiah Flander, of St. Johnsville to Elizabeth Hess, of Oppenheim. Married at the Parsonage, 79 persons present at Donation party. Witnesses: Jonas Snell & Fitch Waters, of St. Johnsville.

1843

Jan. 1 Roswell Carpenter to Jane Sophia Hase, both of Oppenheim. Married at the house of her father Abraham Hase, Oppenheim. Witnesses: Jonas House & Phebe Carpenter, both of Oppenheim.
Jan. 2 William Smith, of Little Falls to Ann H. Griggs, of Springfield, Mass. Married at the Parsonage, St. Johnsville. Witnesses: L. F. Pepper, of Little Falls & James Crouse, of St. Johnsville.
Jan. 2 George Crouse, of St. Johnsville to Mary Ann King, of Oppenheim. Married at the house of James Crouse, St. Johnsville. Witnesses: Lewis Averell & Jacob Chawgo, of St. Johnsville.
Jan. 12 Adam VanDriesen to Amarilla J. Smith, both of Oppenheim. Married at the house of Daniel Smith 2d, Oppenheim. Witnesses: James Walrath, of St. Johnsville & David Spontnable, of Minden.

1843

Jan. 16 Thomas Roach, of Utica to Miss Nancy Maria Vroman, of Middleburgh. Married at the house of Ann Day, St. Johnsville. Witnesses: Lansing Markley & his wife Margaret, & Ann Day, of St. Johnsville.

Jan. 25 Bement Parker to Mrs. Mary Ann Suits, both of Canajoharie. Married at the Inn of P. W. Saltsman, St. Johnsville. Witnesses: Orlando S. Richards & Peter Grey, both of Canajoharie.

Mar. 4 Benjamin Saltsman to Elizabeth Gray, both of Palatine. Married at the Parsonage, St. Johnsville. Witnesses: Peter Lampman & Margaret Saltsman, both of St. Johnsville.

May 25 David Hose, tailor to Lydia Cramer, both of St. Johnsville. Married at the house of Christian Klock, St. Johnsville. Witnesses: Geo. Henry Lampman & Jonas Snell, both of St. Johnsville.

Sept. 3 Jonas House, of Oppenheim to Nancy Helligass, of St. Johnsville. Married at the house of Jacob C. Helligass, St. Johnsville. Witnesses: Nathaniel Helligass & Mary Hase, both of St. Johnsville.

Sept. 6 Daniel J. Couch, of Little Falls to Rhoda Burnham, of Newport. Married at the Parsonage, St. Johnsville. Witnesses: Dennis N. Smith & Jane Helen Myers, both of St. Johnsville.

Oct. 18 Deloss Thayer, of St. Johnsville to Elizabeth Knieskern, of Oppenheim. Married at the house of Wm. Knieskern, Oppenheim. Witnesses: De Witt C. Cox & Betsey Quackenbush, both of Minden.

Oct. 19 James VanAlstyne to Adaline Joyce, both of Danube. Married at the house of Mr. Joyce, Danube. Witnesses: John Smith, of Minden & Margaret Crowel, of Herkimer.

Nov. 15 Jacob Hase, farmer to Polly House, both of Oppenheim. Married at the Parsonage, St. Johnsville. Witnesses: Nancy Flander & Dennes N. Smith, both of St. Johnsville.

1844

Feb. 20 William McNeil, of Argyle, Washington Co. to Miss Magdalen Kennedy, of St. Johnsville. Married at the house of Christopher Klock, St. Johnsville. Witnesses: John Henry Klock, of Fort Plain & Barbara Kennedy, of St. Johnsville.

Feb. 25 Joseph K. Chapman to Margaret Klock, both of St. Johnsville. Married at the Parsonage, St. Johnsville. Witnesses: Joel Klock & Rebecca Ann Klock, both of St. Johnsville.

Mar. 10 Daniel Tefft Jr., of St. Johnsville to Mrs. Elizabeth Van Allen (widow of Jacob Van Allen), of Little Falls. Married at the Parsonage, St. Johnsville. Witnesses: Sarah Linford & Theodoric Myers, both of St. Johnsville.

Aug. 11 John N Kring to Assenath Spontnable, both of Oppenheim. Married in the house of Henry Spontnable, near Lassels Ville. Witnesses: Peter Christman & George Dygert, both of Oppenheim.

Sept. 25 Johnathan Thumb to Clorena Hoffman, both of Oppenheim. Married at the house of jervine Hoffman, Oppenheim. Witnesses: Absalom Thumb, of Oppenheim & Sally Hill, of St. Johnsville.

Sept. 29 James W. Walrath to Susan Saltsman, both of St. Johnsville. Married at the house of Jacob Saltsman, St. Johnsville. Witnesses: Andrew Walrath & Stephen Hill, both of St. Johnsville.

Oct. 17 John Peter House, of Oppenheim to Nancy Flander, of St. Johnsville. Married at the Parsonage, St. Johnsville. Witnesses: Dewitt Failing & Mary J. Stickney, both of St. Johnsville.

RECORD OF MARRIAGES BY THE REV. J. KNIESKERN

1845

May 8 Mr. Loadwick to Miss Brown. Married at the Parsonage, St. Johnsville. Witness: Mrs. E. S. Knieskern.

June 10 Mr. Goudermout to Mrs. Chase. Married at the house of Mrs. Scram, St. Johnsville. Witnesses: Peter Scram & Mrs. Scram.

June 26 Peter Bloodough to Friscilla Tansley. Married at the Inn of Mr. Schaffer, Upper St.

Johnsville. Witnesses: Hiram Broodough & Richard Canaday.

Aug. 10 George Berry to Catharine Haise. Married at the house of her father John Haise, Oppenheim. Witnesses: John Haise & family.

Sept. 2 Nehemiah Klock to Almyra Shall. Married at the house of her father Mr. Shall, in Danube, Herkimer Co. Witnesses: David Elwood & Catharine Putman.

Oct. 9 George Adams to Rosette Heely. Married at the house of her father, Anthony Heely, Oppenheim. Witnesses: Dewitt Failing & Janes Butler.

Oct. 10 Sylvester Ritter to Mary Jane Smith. Married at the house of Charles Smith, St. Johnsville. Witnesses: Charles Smith & family.

Dec. 7 Johnathan Mosuro to Mary Snell. Married at the Parsonage, St. Johnsville. Witnesses: Lewis Snell & Cath. Chawgo.

Dec. 24 Henry Wolever to Mary Elwood. Married at the house of her father, Mr. Elwood, Manheim. Witnesses: Geo. Ranson & Eliza Snell.

1846

Jan. 5 Daniel Grouse to (? – no first name given) Crouse. Married at the house of her father, David Crouse, St. Johnsville. Witnesses: C. W. Webster Esq. & Gen. L. Averill.

Jan. 22 Philip Michael to Julian Peck. Married at the house of her mother, Mrs. Peck, Oppenheim. Witnesses: Absalom Thumb & Hannah Thumb.

1846

Jan. 29th Benj. Van Alstine/Betsey Vosburg Married at the house of Mr. Serle, Fort Plain. Witnesses: Wm. Platts, Cath Van Alstine.

Jan. 29th James Smith/Fally Dennis Married at the house of Mr. Searle, Fort Plain. Witnesses: Wm. Platts, Cath Van Alstine.

Feb. 11th Eli Timerman/Abigail M. Green Married at the house of her father, Mr. Green, in Danube. Witnesses: Geo. Timerman, Benj. Timerman.

Feb. 15th Daniel Walrath/Paulina Driesback Married at the house of her sister, Widow Van Volkenburg. Witnesses: Stephen Yates, Esq., Peter A. Timerman. $5.

Feb. 18th Peter W. Putman/Mary Ann Feeter Married at the house of her father, Adam Feeter, Manheim. Witnesses: Geo. Feeter, John Markle. $5.

Feb. 26th Levi Spoar/Nancy Gray Married at the Inn of P. W. Saltsman, St. Johns Ville. Witnesses: Robert Klock, Mr. Baumgart.

March 4th Webster Smith/Abagail Bauder Married at the house of her father, M. Bauder, St. Johns Ville. Witnesses: Jerimiah Walrath, Sarah Jane Bauder.

May 7th Henry P. Sponable/Elizabeth Zimerman Married at the house of her father, Conrad Zimerman, in Minden. Witnesses: Wm. Timerman, Marie Snell.

May 26th John J. Claus/Ann Eliza Crouse Married at the house of her father, John Crouse, in St. Johns Ville. Witnesses: Geo. Crouse, Margaret Flander.

May 28th David Castler/Margaret Lipe Married at the Inn of Mr. Simmons, St. Johns Ville. Witnesses: Robert Phelps, Catharine Castle, All of Fort Plain.

July 4th Valorus Potter/Mary C. Scott Married at the Inn of Mr. Simmons, St. Johns Ville. Witnesses: Mr. Simmons, Miss Crouse.

Sept. 6th Jacob D. Snell/Emily Kilts Married at the house of her father, Lewis Kilts, Manheim. Witnesses: Ephraim Shaffer, Caroline Snell.

Sept. 29th William Feeter/Cath. Eigenbroadt Married at the house of Adam Feeter, Manheim. Witnesses: Steward Lansing, Caroline Markle. $5.

Oct. 21st David Charlesworth/Margaret Saltsman Married at the house of P. W. Saltsman, St. Johns Ville. Witnesses: James Butler, Ch. W. Webster.

1846

Dec. 21st Jeremiah Smith/Mary La Shine Married at the parsonage, St. Johns Ville. Witnesses: A. D. Champny, Geo. H. Williams.

1847

Jan. 7th David Klock/Betsy Snell Married at the house of her father, Jacob F. Snell, Manheim. Witnesses: Geo. Timerman, Doct. Ayres.

Jan. 12th Horace Garlock/Nancy Jeffers Married at the parsonage, St. Johns Ville. Witnesses: Mary Ann Garlock, Emily S. Knieskern.

Jan. 19th Jacob Walrath/Maria Green Married at the house of her father, Lyman Green, Danube. Witnesses: Eli Timerman & wife, Abigail M. Green.

Jan. 21st Peter Zimerman/Mary Haise Married at the parsonage, St. Johns Ville. Witnesses: Geo. Timerman, De Witt Failing.

Jan. 26th Alex Dockstader/Catharine Putman Married at the house of John Shell, Danube. Witnesses: John Shell, Jacob Shell.

Feb. 1st Geo. Whyland/Cath. Jane Winne Married at the house of Christian Shunk, St. Johns Ville. Witnesses: Henry Lintner, Elizabeth Whyland.

Feb. 17th Henry Elwood/Eve Ann Klock Married at the house of her father, J. B. Klock, St. Johns Ville. Witnesses: Sarah Timerman, Mariett Timerman.

March 3rd Walter Hough/Eliza Klock Married at the house of Azel Hough, Esq., St Johns Ville. Witnesses: Azel Hough, Esq. & wife.

May 13th Ogden Croel/Angeline Dyslin Married at the house of her father, St. Johns Ville. Witnesses: James Curran & wife.

June 4th Lansing Wick/Christiana Denmark Married at the house of his father, Minden. Witnesses: Peter Bellinger, Mary Anderson.

July 4th Areli Klock/Polly Klock Married at the parsonage, St. Johns Ville. Witnesses: Mr. Pine, Mrs. E. S. Knieskern.

July 8th Ephraim Shaffer/Rebecca Vedder Married at the house of her father, Oppenheim. Witnesses: Andrew Shaffer, Henry J. R. Failing.

July 13th Doct. Ralph S. Willoughby/Mary Ann Failing Married at the house of her father, St. Johns Ville. Witnesses: Jonas Snell, M. F. Willson$5.00.

NOTE: Carried over to page 351. The record of baptisms commences on original

1847

Oct 21st Jeremiah House/Maria Swackhammer Married at the Rail Road Depot, St. Johns Ville. Witnesses: Levi House, Harriet Shaffer.

Nov. 27th Anson B. Southwick/Margaret Joice Married at the house of Garret Timason, St. Johns Ville. Witnesses: Garret Timason, Mrs. Henry Card.

1848

Jan. 13th Aaron Loucks/Mary Ann Woolever Married at the parsonage, St. Johns Ville. Witnesses: Wm. Merril, Margaret Wolever.

Feb. 3rd Alonzo Hunt/Sarah Dollef Married at the parsonage, St. Johns Ville. Witnesses: Mrs. E. S. Knieskern.

March 2nd Benj. J. Dockstader/Mary Jane Simmons Married at the Inn of Abner Powel, St. Johns Ville. Witnesses: John Simmons, Levi Schram.

March 22nd Chauncy Hyde/Malvina Shaffer Married at the house of John A. Shafer, St. Johns Ville. Witnesses: Geo. Timerman, Jacob Yoran.

April 6th Jacob Haise/Margaret Kring Married at the house of her father, H. Kring, Oppenheim. Witnesses: John N. Kring, Jonah Kline & wife.

April 20th Garret Timeson/Nancy Wagner Married at the house of her father, Stone Arabia. Witnesses: Volkert Wagner, Wm. Nellis.

Sept. 21st Sofirus Snell/Sarah Timerman Married at the house of her father, Geo. Timerman, St.

Johns Ville. Witnesses: James Timerman, Mayrette Timerman. $5.

Sept. 24th John J. Klock/Mary Elias Married at the parsonage, St. Johns Ville. Witnesses: Mrs. E. S. Knieskern.

Sept. 24th Nathaniel Helligas/Margaret Flander Married in the Church at Youkers Bush. Witnesses: -----.

Oct. 4th Cyrus Bean/Emma Shaffer Married at her fathers, Nicholas Shaffer, Oppenheim. Witnesses: Nathan S. Shaffer, Elizabeth Beekman. $5.

Oct. 19th John Leak/-----Walrath Married at the Inn of Mr. Roof, Upper St. Johns Ville. Witnesses: David Dusler,----- Michael.

1849

Jan. 1st Hiram Avery/Eliza Crankshaw Married at the parsonage, St. Johns Ville. Witnesses: Mrs. E. S. Knieskern.

Jan 23rd Reuben Helmer/Eliza Ann Getman Married at the R Road Depot, St. Johns Ville. Witnesses: Manuel Thumb & wife, Mary Ann Thumb.

Jan 25th Nathan House/Ann Eliza Heinaman Married at the parsonage, St. Johns Ville. Witnesses: Nelson House, Eliza House.

Jan. 25th Henry J. Haise/Caty Nellis Married at the parsonage, St. Johns Ville. Witnesses: Mrs. E. S. Knieskern.

Feb. 1st David Baum/Rosina Helligas Married at her father's, Jac. C. Helligas, St. Johns Ville. Witnesses: Christian House, Nathaniel Helligas.

Feb. 1st Dr. D. G. Vaughn/Ruth Ann Kline Married at her father's, K. Kline, Oppenheim. Witnesses: John P. Kline & wife.

Feb. 25th Wm. J. Frank/Cath. Countryman Married at her father's, Thomas Countryman, Minden. Witnesses: Doct. F. B. Etheridge, Charles Kingsbury. $5.

March 8th Jacob H. Haise/Cyrene House Married at the house of her father, John J. House, Oppenheim. Witnesses: Levi House, Anna Haise.

May 15th John M. Moyer/Margaret Ann Klock Married at the house of Mr. Cox, Minden. Witnesses: Jonas Snell, Dr. F. B. Etheridge. $5.

May 24th Elisha Sperry/Mary Elizabeth Young Married at the house of Gen. L. Averill, St. Johns Ville.. Witnesses: Wm. J. Butler, Louisa Van Allen. $5.

June 25th William Klock/Catharine Wagoner Married at the house of her father, Upper St. Johns Ville. Witnesses: Alonzo Waggoner & sisters.

July 4th Nathan S. Shaffer/Elizabeth Beekman Married at the parsonage, St. Johns Ville. Witnesses: Mrs. E. S. Knieskern.

Aug. 30th William J. Higbie/Birrintha Curran Married at her father's, St. Johns Ville. Witnesses: David Helligas, Dr. Ayers.

1849

Sept. 20th George H. Kretser/Rachel Dibley Married at the house of his mother, St. Johns Ville. Witnesses: George Crouse, De Witt Failing.

Sept. 20th Edward Jordan/Elizabeth Kretser Married at the house of her mother, St. Johns Ville. Witnesses: Geo. Crouse, De Witt Failing.

Oct. 11th Robert Nellis/Martha Cramer Married at the house of Christian Klock, St. Johns Ville. Witnesses: Azel Hough, Lewis Snell.

Nov. 15th Samuel Sweet/Cataline Robinson Married at the house of Enoch Snell, St. Johns Ville. Witnesses: Noah Yale, John Elwell.

Nov. 22nd Aaron Warath/Sarah Michael Married at the house of Philip Michael, Oppenheim. Witnesses: David Michael, Lovina Walrath.

Nov. 25th Adison Chrisman/Elizabeth Lampman Married at the house of Benj. Lampman, St. Johns Ville. Witnesses: Jacob Fox, Juliann Lampman.

Dec. 22nd Barny Price/Adelaide West Married at the Inn of A. Powel, St. Johns Ville. Witnesses: Abner Powel & wife.

Dec. 27th John Lasher/Mary Anderson Married at the house of H. W. Anderson, St. Johns Ville. Witnesses: Lewis Snell, Ann Lasher.

1850
Jan. 1st David Quackenboss/Eve Crouse Married at the house of John Crouse, Oppenheim. Witnesses: Daniel Warath, Geo. Crouse.
Jan. 17th James Nellis/Elizabeth Borden Married at the house of Mrs. Borden, St. Johns Ville. Witnesses: John Nellis, Esq., Enoch Snell. $5.
April 11th Henry Johnson/Emaline Green Married at the house of E. Green, St. Johns Ville. Witnesses: Jacob Chawgo, Catharine Beekman.
Aug. 28th Rufus Leipe/Mary C. Klock Married at the house of Mr. Cox, Minden. Witnesses: Wm. J. Butler, Levi Schram. $5.

1850
Sept. 3rd Hobert Sheffer/Julia Stevens Married at the house of Jacob Stevens, St. Johns Ville. Witnesses: Jacob Stevens.
Sept. 10th Peter Helligas/Mary Bauder Married at the house of Joseph Bauder, Manheim. Witnesses: Geo. Timerman, John Lasher.
Sept. 12th Wm. H. Hinaman/Sarah A. Van Allen Married at the house of Peter Van Allen, St. Johns Ville. Witnesses: Noah Beekman, Cath. Beekman.
Sept. 15th Wm. Marselus/Lorette Vedder Married at the parsonage at St. Johns Ville. Witnesses: Mrs. E. S. Knieskern.
Oct. 9th Wm. Mc Cormick/Rebecca Vedder Married at the parsonage at St. Johns Ville. Witnesses: John J. Vedder, Mary Vedder.
Oct. 9th Lewis Snell/Ann Lasher Married at the house of Mrs. Lasher, St. Johns Ville. Witnesses: Mrs. Mary Lasher, Mrs. Pangburn.
Oct. 23rd Melchoir L. Pauter/Eve Zimerman Married at the house of Conrad Zimerman, Minden Witnesses: Christopher Klock & wife.
Dec. 12th Horace Clark/Mary Stevens Married at the parsonage, St. Johns Ville. Witnesses: D. Failing, Wm. H. Saltsman.

Baptism Date 1816 May 3d
Parents: Henry Defendorf, Barbara Sandurs Child: Sandrus was born Apr 24, 1816
Parents: Henry Jeffers, Hanny Ervin Child: Cathrien was born May 3, 1816 Sponsors: Peter Jeffers, Catherine Jeffers
Parents: Johannes Jeffers, Sally Pattoe Child: Coonrod was born Apr. 21, 1816 Sponsors: Conrod Jeffers, Caty Jefers
Parents: Jacob Clause, Lena Eigenbroet Child: John Jacob was born March 16 1816 Sponsors: Jacob J Clock, Mary Loedwick

June
Parents: Jacob E. Snell, Mary Helwick Child: Mary Ann was born May 7, 1816 Sponsors: Francis Snell, Eve Snell
Parents: Jacob Bellinger, Betsy Ingersol Child: Lucinda was born Apr. 16, 1816 Sponsors: Henry Ingleson, Mary Bellinger
Parents: David Goodale, Charity Shefer Child: Sally was born March 18, 1816 Sponsors: Henry Cool, Nancy Shaffer
Parents: Adam Feeter, Mary Kyser Child: William was born may 1, 1816 Sponsors: David Peter, Dolly Feeter
Parents: Henry H. Hayes, Elesebeth Bellinger Child: Frederic was born July 3, 1816 Sponsors: John F. Bellinger, Elesebeth Folse
Parents: Ludwick Eker, Elesebeth Bellinger Child: Caty was born June 30, 1816 Sponsors: David Wollwovor, Rosina Bellinger

Parents: Isaia Nessle, Peggy Altenberg Child: William Henry was born January 22, 1816 Sponsors: William Altenbergh, Elesebeth Altenberg

Parents: Deteric Breeman, Cathrien Rector Child: John was born July 9, 1816 Sponsors: Deterio Braim, Cathrien Hurtic

June 28
Parents: Folton Storie, Margaret Hert Child: John was born Apr, 12, 1816 Sponsors: John Patrie, Caty Petrie

Parents: Cornlius Klock, Elesebeth Fox Child: Cathrien was born Jun 6, 1816 Sponsors: Benjamin Fox, Cathrien Stats

Parents: (None Listed) Child: Allida was born January 29, 1816

Parents: (None Listed) Child: Peggy was born May 19, 1816 Sponsors: Henry Beam, Elesebeth Zimmerman

Parents: (None Listed) Child: Lisa Ann was born May 2 1816 Sponsors: John Defendorf, Elesebeth Wilson

Parents: John H Bellinger, Lena Walrath Child: Eve was born July 14, 1816 Sponsors: Anthony Walrath, Merget House

Parents: Abr. F. Feelech, Margrata Defendorf Child: Francis was born July 27, 1816

1816
October 14
Parents: George J Crouse, Marie Defendorf Child: Caty was born Apr.28, 1816 Sponsors: John Defendorf, Betsy Crouse

Parents: Jacob House, Cathrien Snell Child: Litty was born Augt 15, 1816 Sponsors: Adam House, Lena House

Parents: Gidion Green, Elesebeth Youngs Child: Jerome was born May 14, 1816

Parents: Daniel Ingleson, Betsy Burkdorf Child: Nancy was born May 9, 1816 - 20th

Parents: William P Nellis, Maria Bennit Child: Peter was born Sept. 16, 1816 Sponsors: Jacob J. Klock, Maria Ludewick

Parents: Hesekiah Wheler, Hannah Putman Child: Maria was born October 5, 1816 Sponsors: Issac H Quackenbosh, Cathrien Walrath

Oct 27th
Parents: Joseph Timmerman, Cathrien Timmerman Child: Mary Magdalene was born January 13, 1816 Sponsors: Conrod C. Timmerman, Mary Magdalene

Parents: Johannes Mottice, Nancy Bouck Child: Freceric Aulstine was born Sept. 6, 1816 lives in Middleburgh

Oct 30th
Parents: George Rimsbee, Gene House Child: James was born Sept. 13, 1816 At Middleburg Novm 17

Parents: Peter Timmerman, Lena Garlock Child: Caty was born Octob 24, 1816 Sponsors: Adam Timmerman, Cathrine Snell

Parents: John Snell, Nancy Thum Child: Mary Ann was born October 19, 1816 Sponsors: Henry Louck, Betsy Snell

Parents: Anthony Schyler, Nancy Shell Child: Caty was born August 30, 1816

Parents: Jacob Schut, Anna Veder Child: Lucas was born October 12, 1816 Sponsors: Joseph Petre, Anna Bellinger

Parents: Eliza W. Northrip, Anna Shafer Child: Lucinda was born Octobr 13, 1816 Sponsors: Androw Shafer, Anna Bellinger

Oct 24
Parents: Peter Helligas, Phebe Ingraham Child: Polly was born Novm 3, 1816 Sponsors: Jacob

Walrath Jun., Polly Klock
Parents: Christopher Fox, Nancy Suits Child: Walter was born July 31, 1816 Sponsors: Joseph W. Nellis, Polly Nellis
Parents: Adam A Walrath, Mary Zimmerman Child: Benjamin was born Apr. 22, 1816 Sponsors: Henry Walrath, Caty Clock
Parents: Lodewick Herring, Crate Uker Child: Cathrien was born June 5, 1816 Sponsors: Warner Nellis, Dorathy Uker
Parents: Henry Garlock, Peggy Snell Child: Millondy was born June 25, 1816 Sponsors: Adam Snell, Daliah Garlock
Parents: Cornelius Breese, Lucretia Snuck Child: Nelly was born August 24, 1815
Parents: Henry Burter, Caty Morison Child: Elesebeth was born May 29, 1816

1816
September 24
Parents: Henry Blooda, Hannah Hendrick Child: Lusinda was born August 8, 1816 Sponsors: Jacob P. Snell, Mary Helwick
Parents: Christiaun Walrath, Caty Helligas Child: Polly was born August 30, 1816
Parents: George Cox, Maria Helligas Child: Daniel was born May 19, 1816
Parents: Frederic Zimmerman, Polly Klock Child: Daniel was born May 17,1816 December 21
Parents: Henry Shults, Elesebeth Waggoner Child: Peggy was born Novm 19, 1816

Sept 22
Parents: John C, Zimmerman, Guertry Zimmerman Child: David Sponsors: Conrod C. Zimmerman, Mary Magdelane Snel
Parents: John J. Zimmerman, Mary Baum Child: Ame was born Novm. 14, 1816

Sept 25
Parents: Peter Bellinger, Caty Moyer Child: David was born October 25, 1816 Sponsors: Deobalt Moyer, Margereta Moyer

1817
January 2
Parents: Peter Flander, Margreta Riece Child: Obediah was born Novm 7, 1816

Jan 9
Parents: Abraham Pearce, Anna Lesher Child: Anna was born July 18, 1815

Jan 19
Parents: George Helligas, Betsy Youker Child: Polly was born December 7, 1816 Sponsors: Anthony Walrath, Polly Youker

Jan 26
Parents: Klock

Jan 27
Parents: Joshua Riece, Peggy Markell Child: Jacob was born May16

1815
Febr 3
Parents: George Osterhout, Caty Nellis Child: Hyram was born Decembr 16, 1816 Sponsors: John Bellinger, Betsy Riece

Feb 21
Parents: Daniel Wals, Peggy Thum Child: John was born Febr 20, 1817 Sponsors: John Burger, Lena Hoak

March 9
Parents: John House, Maria Ritter Child: Loisa was born Navm 3, 1816 Sponsors: Luedwic Hart, Barbary Hart
Parents: Adam F Snell, Dilia Garlock Child: Marian was born Febr 22, 1817 Sponsors: Elesebeth Snell, Nicholas Pattie
Parents: Adam Zimmerman, Eve Smith Child: Lusinda was born Febr 10, 1816 Sponsors: Markis Zimmerman, Caty Smith
Parents: Henry Hart, Gurtry House Child: Peter was born Febr 23, 1817 Sponsors: George Hart, Delsy House
Parents: John Lawrence, Elesabeth Miller Child: Caty was born Febr 5, 1812 ----------------------
Child: Betsy was born May12, 1814 --------------------- Child: Amasiah was born June 4, 1816 --------------------------------

 1817
March 9
Parents: John W. Defendorf, Hannah Delong Child: Matilda was born January 25, 1817 Sponsors: GeorgeDefendorf, Cathrien Defendorf
Parents: Levi T. Elder, Mary Goodridge Child: Lusinda was born Apr. 17, 1817

Note: (by original typist) Errors in this record caused by the inability of the recorders to keep the year dates straight, will not be noticed in the notes. Obvious errors will be underscored by the editor; vis. "Apr. 17 1817. I have come to the conclusion that it is a waste of time to analyse errors that bring the date of a child's baptism before its birth. Mr. Devoe is a most flagrant error maker, as to year dates; I have noted about 20 errors of this description to my saying nothing of spelling errors caused by leaaving out or transposing letters. The fact that he was able to leave his spelling of the word "Sponsors" as he first wrote it, without noticing anything wrong with it, is not calculated to inspire confidence as to the accuracy of his record. The most glaring and obvious of his errors, can be easily detected. But the question arises at once, as to how many errors in dates of birth and names of children, has he made that cannot be readily detected? In the year 1806 Mr. Devoe was deficient in his preparatory studies for the Ministry. He was licensed by the Classis of Albany, prior to 1808; but was not ordained until the year 1812. These facts are mentioned here to show that he was not well educated, and had difficulty to comply with the scholarly requirements, before attaining the Ministry.

1817 March 15
Parents: Andrew A. Finck, Deliah Guitman Child: Frederic was born January 8, 1817
Parents: Cornelius Swartwout, Elesebeth Bekman Child: Betsey was born Febr 20, 1817

March 31
Parents: George G. Loucks, Mary Gray Child: Mary Ann was born March 8, 1817 Sponsors: Samuel Gray, Magdalene Gray
Parents: Joseph Adler, Gurty House Child: Jonas was born March 4, 1817 Sponsors: Joseph Adler, Mary Adler
Parents: David Zimmerman, Maria Farbus Child: Coonrod was born March 10, 1817 Sponsors: Coonrod Zimmerman, Mary Magdelene Snell

Apr. 6
Parents: Issac H. Quackenbush, Caty Walrath Child: Andrew David was born Apr 4, 1817 Sponsors: Andrew Walrath, Naomi Walrath

Ap 7
Parents: Jacob J. Zimmerman, Mary Zimmerman Child: Jeremiah was born March 23, 1817
Sponsors: Lorence Zimmerman, Elesebeth Zimerman
Parents: Daniel Shawl, Rachel Smith Child: Garahem was born Nov26, 1817 Sponsors: Gershem Smith, Magdelene Riece

Ap 20
Parents: Michael Schyler Jur., Mary Delong Child: Lovina was born Febr 16, 1817
Parents: Peter Wetherwax, Cathrien Bellinger Child: Marilda was born May11, 1816 Sponsors: Issac Smith, Nancy Billinger
Parents: Jacob Hillegas, Margreta Thum Child: Jonas was born Apr 1817 May 11
Parents: James Van Valkenburgh, Betsy McComes Child: John Taylor was born March 11, 1817

Apr 25
Parents: Adam J. Walrath, Christianna Tusler Child: James William was born Apr 5, 1817 Sponsors: Peter Klock, Betsey Dyslin

June 17
Parents: Harmanus Veedder, Mary Wever Child: Maria was born May 26, 1817

June 22
Parents: John P. Clause, Maria Van buren Child: Jonathan was born May 2, 1817 Sponsors: Peter A. Clause, Guity Van buren
Parents: Daniel Guitman, Delia Zimmerman Child: Frederic was born May 11, 1817 Sponsors: Andrew Finck, Delia Guitman

July 10
Parents: Cornelius C. V. Kamp, Caty Defendorf Child: Eliza was born Jun 31, 1817 Sponsors: Cornelius V. kamp, Barbary Defendorf

July 27 Parents: Jacob Wise, Anna Haber Child: Phillip was born May 25, 1817
Parents: Henry Steward, Sarah Steward Child: Harry was born July 3, 1817

August 3
Parents: Frederick J. Bellinger, Elesebeth Uron Child: Malinda was born July 2, 1817

Aug 11
Parents: John Patrie, Hannah Hart Child: Frederic was born May 11, 1817 Sponsors: Andrew Finck, Delia Guitman
Parents: Phillip Spankebel, Hannah Youker Child: David was born June 113, 1817

1817
August 17
Parents: Jacob Nellis, Polly Parcus Child: Betsy Ann was born December 11, 1817 Sponsors: Rich M. Petrie
Parents: John G. Uker, Cathrien Burter Child: Elesebeth was born July 23, 1817 Sponsors: George Hillegas, Elesebeth Youker
Parents: Nicholas House, Cathriene Spoon Child: Elesebeth was born Jun 13, 1817 Sponsors: Jacob House, Caty Guitman

Sept. 14
Parents: Abraham Shaver, Tyna Clause Child: Lucretia was born August 21, 1817 Sponsors: John Shaver, Cathrien Toll
Sept 16 Parents: Peter Morison, Peggy Burtdurf Child: David was born Apr26, 1817 Sponsors: Henry Burtdurf, Caty Morison

Sept 20
Parents: Samiel Slocum, Anna Hayes Child: Henry was born June 8, 1817 Sponsors: ------, --------
-
Parents: Peter Hase, Maria Daniels Child: Gilbert was born August 22, 1817

Sept 21
Parents: John G. Klock, Guertry Zimmerman Child: Mary Ann was born August 26, 1817 Sponsors: John B. Klock, Eve Zimmerman
Parents: John Mabee, Anna Manck Child: Abraham was born August 26, 1817 Sponsors: Abram Klock, Cathrien Grove
Parents: Kennedy, Klock Child: Richard was born April 26, 1817

Sept 28
Parents: Joseph Leber, Peggy Wolleber Child: Nancy was born May21, 1817 Sponsors: Jacob Wollebar, Nancy Snell
Parents: Richard McKinsley, Deborah Rose Child: Elesebeth was born Sept. 8, 1817
Parents: David Walrath, Elesebeth Forbes Child: James was born August 25, 1817 Sponsors: James Forbes, Margreta Forbes
Parents: Christian Walrath, Maria Hillegas
Parents: _____ Flander, _____ Grove Child: Christiaun
Note. The copyist has ommited a space between entry No. 15 and entry No. 16. Entry No. 15 "Flanders-Grove", takes up as much room as any other in the original, although incomplete.

October 15
Parents: Jacob Hart, Betsy Baum Child: Rosina was born Sept 15, 1817 Sponsors: John Petrie, Barbara Baum
Parents: Jost Klock, Eve Shafer Child: Aron was born Sept. 19, 1817 Sponsors: Frederek Shafer, Anna Failing

Oct 19
Parents: John Osman, Caty Klock Child: Martha was born July 19, 1817 Sponsors: --------, ---------
----

Novm 7
Parents: Robert Ruman, Elesebeth Runion Child: James was born Sep 1817 Sponsors: John J Bellinger, Maria Bignel
- 30 Parents: Jacob Failing, Tooky Child: Ruben was born Sep 1817

1817
December 7
Parents: John Rarick, Cathrien Bellinger Child: John was born Apr 28, 1817 Sponsors: John Hays, Elesebeth Bellinger

Dec 16
Parents: Marcus Sternbergh, Nancy Maybee Child: Adam was born Febr. 15, 1817

Dec 25
Parents: John Vedder, Anna Rizina Zimmerman Child: Maria was born ___ 28, 1817 Sponsors: Richard Vedder, Maria Toll
Parents: Phillip Coon, Maria Spanknebel Child: Christoffel was born July 27, 1817 Sponsors: Johan H. Spanknobel, Hannah Coon

Dec 29
Parents: Daniel McKinsley, Rachel Rose Child: Richard was born Navm 11, 1817
Parents: Samuel Gray Jr., Lena Obeda Child: Levi was born Decm 2, 1817 Sponsors: Jacob Thum, Mary Thum

1818 January 1
Ludwick Ecker, Elesebeth Bellinger Child: Rosina was born Octoner 4, 1817 Sponsors: David Hays, Rosina Bellinger
Parents: Peter Bellinger, Caty Starring Child: Peter was born October 6, 1817

Jan 3
Parents: Henry House, Cornelia Mosure Child: Mary Ann was born January 3, 1818
Parents: Henry P. Cline, Caty Klock Child: George Henry was born Octobr 17, 1817

Jan 18
Parents: Jacob Youker, Elesebeth Spanknabel Child: John Henry was born Octobr 2, 1817
Sponsors: Jacob Failing, Hannah Cox
Parents: Daniel Smith, Betsey Purson Child: Josiah was born June 29, 1817 Sponsors: Joseph Youron, Peggy
Parents: Richard Van aulon, Nancy Zimmerman Child: Jane was born Octobr 12, 1817
Parents: Peter J. Snell, Magdelene Zimmerman Child: Leonard was born Octobr 9, 1817

Jan 21
Parents: John B. Klock Jr., Margrate Klock Child: Levina was born Jun 27, 1817

Jan 31
Parents: Thomas D. Guitman, Elesebeth Scholl Child: Lucinda was born Novm 30, 1817 Sponsors: Joseph Scholl, Elesebeth Scholl

Febr 2
Parents: Coonrod Snell, Margreeta Bellinger Child: Nancy was born Sept. 22, 1817 Sponsors: Sufranus Snell, Eva Fry

Feb 5
Parents: Joseph J. Youron, Anna Swackhammer Child: Sally was born January 6, 1817 Sponsors: Jacob Youron, Sally Pettebone
Parents: Thomas Clark, Lena Young Child: William was born Sept 6, 1817 Sponsors: Christiaun Supperman, Caty Barns

Feb 8
Coonrod Jeffers, Betsy Snell Child: Frederic was born January 25, 1818 Sponsors: Frederic F. Snell, Betsy Snell
Parents: Issac Fry, Margrete Snell Child: Levina was born July 24, 1817 Sponsors: Adam Snell, Delia Snell

1818

Ferb 18

Parents: Frederick H. Bellinger, Elisebeth Bellinger Child: Joseph Frederic was born January 18, 1818 Sponsors: Hannes H. Bellinger, Lena Walrath

Parents: John Yordan, Lena Klock Child: Hannes was born May 13, 1817 Sponsors: Appelone Klock

Parents: John C. Karn, Nancy Boa Child: Elesebeth was born Sept. 21, 1817 Sponsors: John Boa, Elesebeth Boa

Parents: John J. D. Nellis, Elesebeth Klock Child: Cathrien was born October 1, 1817 On his request Receved, on the other side are recorded all his children

All Babtised in ther infancy by differet Ministers Parents: John J. D. Nellis, Elesebeth Klock Child: David was born May 5, 1816 Child: Ruben was born March 30 Child: Barnhard was born August 14, 1810 Child: Elesebeth was born Sept 20, 1012 Child: Nancy was born Febr 22, 1814 Record at the Request of Mr. John J. D. Nellis who wishes to have all his Childrens age on one record. 1818 Febr 26 Parents: Peter Nellis, Caty Fox Child: Eve was born Decembr 5, 1817 Sponsors: William W Fox, Rosena Willis

March 1

Parents: Joseph Walrath, Nancy Dockstader Child: Daniel was born Novr 20, 1817 Sponsors: Daniel Walrath, Caty Zoller

Parents: Lorence Zimmerman, Elesebeth Helmeh Child: Lorence was born Febr. 25, 1818

Parents: John hart, Margreta Child: Ephraim was born Febr 24, 1818 Sponsors: John Young, Mary Young

Parents: John D. Moyer, Margreta Parker Child: Jonas William was born Jun 26, 1817 Sponsors: Jonas Snell, Mary Dyart

March 8

Parents: Petter P. Walrath, Eve Klock Child: Ruben was born Febr 4, 1818

Parents: Adam Duygart, Geny Dusler Child: Christianna was born Jan 16, 1818 Sponsors: Joseph Dusler, Cathrien Dum

Mar 20

Parents: Ludwick Harink, Peggy Youker Child: Peggy was born March 1, 1818 Sponsors: John Bauder, Eve Jaugo

Parents: David Goodale, Charity Shaffer Child: Nancy was born December 7, 1817

Mar 22

Parents: Henry Bloodo, Hannah Nendrick Child: Simeon was born January 18, 1818 April 23

Parents: John Lighthart, Polly Jinnins Child: Samuel was born August 22, 1817

May 10

Parents: Phillip Putman, Christiana Nobels Child: Jacob was born Febr 2, 1818 Sponsors: Jacob Dislin, Betsy Klock

May 11

Parents: Marcus Garber, Elesebeth Defendorf Child: John was born Febr 2, 1818 Sponsors: George Defendorf, Cathrien Fox

May 24

Parents: George B. Snell, Crate Snell Child: Ruben was born Apr. 10, 1818 Sponsors: Abraham nell, Eve Snell

Parents: Henry Zimmerman, Betsy Petrie Child: Anna was born Apr.7

1818 Jun 7
Parents: John Radley, Cathrene Suits Child: Maria was born April 25, 1818 Sponsors: Jacob Schram, Polly Class

(1818) June 7
Parents: John F. Bellinger, Elesebeth Flander Child: Maria was born May15, 1818

June 14
Parents: Henry Garlock, Margreeta Snell Child: (no name entered) was born May13, 1818
Sponsors: Benjan Varslin, Lena Snell

June 16
Parents: Phillip Cramer, Cathrien Hatcock Child: Rebecka was born Apr. 30, 1818 Sponsors: Rebecka Cramer
Parents: Peter Cramer, Peggy Hadcock Child: William was born March 5, 1817

July 4
Parents: John Willson, Susanna Elwood Child: Barbara was born Apr. 27, 1818 Sponsors: Cornelius Van Kamp, Barbara Defendorf

1818 July 5
Parents: John C. Storring, Abbe Cronkreick Child: Matilda was born May16, 1818
Parents: Eliza W. Northrop, Anna Shaver Child: Jonathan was born June 17, 1818
Parents: Issac Nessel, Margreeta Aldenburgh Child: John was born Apr 24, 1818 Sponsors: Henry Adenburgh, Rebecka Johnson
Parents: Melcher Bauder, Sally Swachammer Child: John was born May 30, 1818 Sponsors: John Bauder, Polly Swachammer
Parents: John F Failing, Maria Walrath Child: Lucinda was born May 30, 1818

August 2
Parents: William M. Shafer, Peggy Clauss Child: Rosina was born June 17, 1818 Sponsors: Peter Clauss, Nancy Van atten

Aug 23
Parents: Adam A. Walrath, Mary Zimmerman Child: Manuel was born July 13, 1818
Parents: Peter Radley, Cathrien Docstader Child: Mary Ann was born May 4, 1818 Sponsors: William Radley, Mary Docstader
Parents: Joel Falkner, Margreta Radley Child: James, Decemb 19, 1815
Parents: George Cox, Polly Hillegas Child: Eve was born June 8, 1818

Aug 30
Parents: Peter Flander, Peggy Riece Child: Jemima was born August 11, 1818

Sept. 1
Parents: John C. House, Hannah Bellinger Child: Jonas was born August 30, 1818

Sept 6
Parents: Anthony Geffers, Elesebeth Irvin Child: William was born August 8, 1818
Parents: Jacob Wolever, Caty Crisman Child: Hiram was born August 5, 1818 Sponsors: David Wolever, Eve Crisman

Sept 8
Parents: Issac H. Quackenbush, Caty Walrath Child: Nelly was born Sept. 7, 1818
Parents: Samuel Ginnins, Mary Rice Child: Hyram was born Aprl.1, 1818 Sponsors: Jacob Walrath, Mary Smith Widow

Sept 13
Parents: Andrew Dusler, Christena House Child: Caty Maria was born May 30, 1817 Sponsors: John Duesler, Caty Maria Dusler
Parents: Christopher Hoke, Peggy Jinks Child: William was born July 31, 1818 Sponsors: William Jenks, Hannah Tellepah
Parents: Richard P. Elwood, Betsy Van Kamp Child: Casserce was born May 23rd 1818
Parents: George Devoe, Peggy Ecker Child: John Asxander was born July 11, 1818
Parents: Cornelius Slouter, Maria Wyland Child: Nicholas was born July 27, 1818
Parents: William W Slouter, Caty Van dusen Child: Tyne Elisa was born July 27, 1818
Parents: Joseph Filkins, Peggy Slouter Child: Caty was born August 9, 1818

1818 Sept. 13
Parents: Daniel Sobles, Caty Crisman Child: David Henry was born August 17, 1818 Sponsors: Henry Hilmer, Mary Soble
Parents: Chester Pain, Angelica Veeder Child: Seth Bassett was born March 9, 1818

Sept 20
Parents: Jacob Klock, Sally Conklin Child: Archibald was born Augt 14, 1818

Sept 27
Parents: John B. Klock, Eve Zimmerman Child: Reuben was born Augst 11, 1818
Parents: Henry Walrath, Clarissa Loeless Child: Risina was born Sept. 6, 1818
Parents: Peter A. Zimmerman, Lena Garloch Child: Nancy was born August 29, 1818 Sponsors: Marcus Zimmerman, Nancy Zimmerman
Parents: Daniel Ingelsoll, Betsy Burkdorf Child: Lucinda was born July 28, 1818 October 8
Parents: Joseph Fake, Barbara Willson Child: James Willson was born Sept. 18, 1818 Sponsors: John Willson, Susana Ellwood
Parents: Abraham Fraileh, Margreta Defendorf Child: Lucinda was born August 3, 1818
Parents: Ashbel Loomis, Cathrien Klock Child: Althea was born March 17, 1818 Sponsors: Polly Klock

Sept 10
Parents: Abraham Freeman, Sarah Bellinger Child: Peter was born August 10, 1818

Sept 18
Parents: John Geffers, Sally Platto Child: Salomon was born October 14, 1818 Sponsors: Joseph Rasbeck, Lena his wife
Parents: Simon Van dusen, Mary Zimmerman Child: Guilbert was born 1818

Sept 25
Parents: John Keller, Margreta Rure Child: (no name entered) was born 1818 Novm 1
Parents: William Youker, Clarissa Class Child: Mary Ann was born July 6, 1818 Sponsors: Phillip Spanknable, Hannah his wife

Sept 20
William Finck, Peggy Klinck Child: Daniel was born October 16, 1818

Sept 30
Parents: John C. Zimmerman, Guitty Zimmerman Child: Elizah was born October 29, 1818
Sponsors: David Zimmerman, Mary his wife December 4
Parents: Adam Zimmerman, Nancy Failing Child: William was born Decem 24, 1817
- *0 Parents: Adam F Snell, Delia Garlok Child: Becke was born Decemb 14, 1818 Sponsors:
Frederic F Snell, Becky Shafer
Parents: John H. Zimmerman, Maria Baum Child: Kara was born October 8, 1818
Parents: *eorge Loucks, * ry Gray Child: Caty was born Novm 21, 1818 Sponsors: Leonard
Helmer, Betsey Luis
Note. *Corner of page torn off, and a few letters missing

1819
Date of Baptism - Jan. 1st; Parents Names - Daniel Smith & Betsy Parsons; Childs Name & Date of
Birth - Webster, October 4, 1818
Date of Baptism - Jan. 7th; Parents Names - Christian Supperman & Caty, Barns; Childs Name &
Date of Birth - Levi, Novm. 7, 1818; Sponsors - Dolly Superman
Date of Baptism - Jan. 10; Parents Names - Peter Mosure & Sally Amos; Childs Name & Date of
Birth - Ephraigm, Octobr 13, 1818
Date of Baptism - Jan 11; Parents Names - Coonrad Flander & Elizabeth Nellis; Childs Name & Date
of Birth - Jane, Decem 3, 1818; Sponsors - Joseph P. Nellis & Dama Dua
Date of Baptism - Jan. 26; Parents Names - Isaac Bronner & Mary Hoyer; Childs Name & Date of
Birth - Mary Lisa, Decembr 18, 1818; Sponsors - Maselis Hoyer
Date of Baptism - Jan. 31; Parents Names - Cornelius Klock & Elezebeth Fox; Childs Name & Date
of Birth - Morris, Decembr 18, 1818; Sponsors - Benjamin Klock & Caty Fox
Date of Baptism - Febr. 7; Parents Names - Christiaun A. Walrath & Caty Hillegas; Childs Name &
Date of Birth - Peggy, Jenuary 13, 1819 _____
Date of Baptism - 11 July 1818; Parents Names - Isaac Ellwood & Anna Wilson; Childs Name &
Date of Birth - Elizebeth, May 18, 1818; Sponsors - John Elewood & his wife Polly

Date of Baptism - March 4; Parents Names - Christoffel Klock & Elizebeth Dyselin; Childs Name &
Date of Birth - Barbara, Febr. 25, 1819; Sponsors - Henry Beekman & Anna his wife
Date of Baptism - March 4; Parents Names - Dyar Waterman & Lena Bell; Childs Name & Date of
Birth - Manuel, October 17, 1818; Sponsors - Adam Thumb & Maria his wife
Date of Baptism - March 4; Parents Names - Abraham Pettit & Eve Schram; Childs Name & Date of
Birth - Eve Liza, Sept. 17, 1818; Sponsors - John Schram & Lidia his Daughter
Date of Baptism - March 21; Parents Names - Sabastian Cook & Betsy Youron; Childs Name & Date
of Birth - Mariann, Febr 24, 1819
Date of Baptism - March 21; Parents Names - David Vanslyke & Betsy Hellegas; Childs Name &
Date of Birth - Peter, Febr 1, 1819; Sponsors - George Cox & Mary his wife
Date of Baptism - March 29; Parents Names - Shubel Luis & Lucretia Sisco; Childs Name & Date of
Birth - Dorceus, March 31, 1800 Sponsors - Babtised on a confession of Faith in Jesus
Date of Baptism - Apr. 10; Parents Names - John Ausborn & Caty Klock; Childs Name & Date of
Birth - Benjamin, Feb. 9, 1819
Date of Baptism - Apr. 10; Parents Names - Lodewick Eker & Betsy Bellinger; Childs Name & Date
of Birth - Hannah, March 4, 1819; Sponsors - Daniel Heise & Nancy Bellinger
Date of Baptism - Apr. 30; Parents Names - Henry Zeilley & Nancy Nellis; Childs Name & Date of
Birth - Thomas, Apr. 16, 1819
Date of Baptism - May 9; Parents Names - John G. Youker & Caty Burkdorf; Childs Name & Date of
Birth - Jonas, April 9, 1819
Date of Baptism - May 9; Parents Names - Peter Morrice & Peggy Burkdorf; Childs Name & Date of
Birth - Nancy, Febr 24, 1819
Date of Baptism - May 9; Parents Names - Henry Burkdorf & Caty Morrice; Childs Name & Date of
Birth - Harriet, Febry 4, 1819

Note. Entry No. 8 out of chronological order; year date for rest of page
1819. Entry No. 9, Witnesses. Anna, wife of Henry Beekman, was the widow of Dominie John
Henry Dysalin; see Vol. 1,

1819
Date of Baptism - May 20; Parents Names - John Bauter & Eve Jauge; Childs Name & Date of Birth
James, January 28, 1819
Date of Baptism - May 23; Parents Names - Henry Cool Jun. & Caty Kern; Childs Name & Date of
Birth - Elisa, May 11, 1819; Sponsors - Philip Cool & Maria his wife
Date of Baptism - June 12; Parents Names - Solomon Ellwood & Elesebeth Baum; Childs Name &
Date of Birth - Elesebeth, January 24, 1819
Date of Baptism - June 12; Parents Names - John Baum & Lena Ellwood; Childs Name & Date of
Birth - Catherien, March 25, 1819_____
J. M. Look
on Bapt 1819
Date of Baptism - June 12; Parents Names - Peter Klock & Susanna Feick; Childs Name & Date of
Birth - Peter Feick, May 16, 1819
Date of Baptism - June 12; Parents Names - John H. Bellinger & Lena Walrath; Childs Name & Date
of Birth- Adam, June 5, 1819; Sponsors - Adam A. Walrath, Jun. & Maria Zimmerman
Date of Baptism - June 12; Parents Names - Adam Nestle & Peggy Contraman; Childs Name & Date
of Birth - Sallomon, Aug. 12, 1819 ; Sponsors - Elesebeth Reice
Date of Baptism - June 20; Parents Names - John P. Claus & Mary Van burah; Childs Name & Date
of Birth - David, April 17, 1819
Date of Baptism - June 27; Parents Names - Frederic N. Snell & Elizabeth Snell; Childs Name &
Date of Birth - Hiram, Decembr 17, 1819; Sponsors - Joseph Dusler & Lena Snell
Date of Baptism - July 3rd; Parents Names - Corneuis Devoe & Andertthy Gauge; Childs Name &
Date of Birth - Hannah, June 28, 1819
Date of Baptism - July 14; Parents Names - Jacob J. Wilson & Nelly Quackenbush; Childs Name &
Date of Birth - Nancy, Apr. 28, 1819
Date of Baptism - July 15; Parents Names - Daniel Klock & Nancy Defendorf; > Childs Name &
Date of Birth - Lovina, June 28, 1819; Sponsors- George > Defendorf & Caty his wife
Date of Baptism - July 29; Parents Names - Ebenezer Failing & Hannah Patterson; Childs Name &
Date of Birth - Abagail Jane, June 14, 1817; Sponsors - Jacob J. Failing & his wife Anna Cox
Date of Baptism - July 29; Parents Names - Ebenezer Failing & Hannah Patterson; Childs Name &
Date of Birth - James, April 3, 1818; Sponsors - Nicholas Failing & Polly Youker
Date of Baptism - August 1; Parents Names - Peter Decker & Mary Spencer; > Childs Name & Date
of Birth - Amena, January 29, 1819; Sponsors - Daniel > Spencer & Caty his wife
Date of Baptism - August 1; Parents Names - John G. Klock & Gity Zimmerman; Childs Name &
Date of Birth - Lizeann, Sept. 19, 1819; Sponsors - Christofel Klock & Elezebeth Dislin
Date of Baptism - August 1; Parents Names - Peter N. Schuyler & Nancy Tygart; Childs Name &
Date of Birth - Peggy, July 18, 1819; Sponsors - William Kniskern & wife Peggy Schuyler
Date of Baptism - Novm 21; Parents Names - John Sternbergh & Eve Frayer; Childs Name & Date
of Birth - David, August 1, 1819; Sponsors - David Sternbergh & Elezebeth Freeor
Date of Baptism - Novm 21; Parents Names - Jacob Hellegas & Peggy Dum; Childs Name & Date of
Birth - Benjamin; Sponsors - Benjamin Van alen & Elezebeth Zimmerman
Date of Baptism - Novm 21; Parents Names - John Ausburn & Caty Klock; Childs Name & Date of
Birth - Benjamin, Febr. 9, 1819
Date of Baptism - Novm 21; Parents Names - Lodwick Ecker & Betsy Bellinger; Childs Name & Date
of Birth - Hannah, March 4, 1819; Sponsors - Daniel Hayes & Nancy Bellinger
_____ Page 216.
Note. If Mr. Devoe had written at the top of each page of his record "Remember that you cannot
baptize a child until after its birth!!", it is more than likely that he would have obtained better
results, as to his dates.

1819

Date of Baptism - Octob 23rd; Parents Names - Henry Markell & Nancy Keller; Childs Name & Date of Birth - Elizabeth, Septemb 28, 1819; Sponsors - Jacob J. Keller & Elizabeth Markell

Date of Baptism - November Parents Names - Jacob Hillegas & Peggy Dum; Childs Name & Date of Birth - Benjamin, 1819; Sponsors - Benjamin Van aulen & Betsy Zimmerman

Date of Baptism - Decembr 3; Parents Names - Peter B. Cook & Mary Fox; Childs Name & Date of Birth - Eliza, Octobr 31, 1816; Sponsors - -- Fox & Elizabeth Fox

Date of Baptism - Decembr 3; Parents Names - Peter B. Cook & Mary Fox; Childs Name & Date of Birth - Margreeta, July 9, 1819; Sponsors - Peter Cook & Mary Cook

Date of Baptism - Decembr 20; Parents Names - Henry Hayes & Elezebeth Bellinger; Childs Name & Date of Birth - Jacob, October 24, 1819; Sponsors - Daniel Keller Hayes & Dam

Date of Baptism - Decembr 6 ; Parents Names - Henry Failing Jun. & Nancy Zimmerman; Childs Name & Date of Birth - Mary Ann, Novem 4, 1819; Sponsors - John Adam Failing & Christianna Zimmerman

Date of Baptism - January 24 (1820); Parents Names - David Goodale & Gity Shaver; Childs Name & Date of Birth - Lisa, Novm 5, 1819; Sponsors - Henry Weeder & Betsy Shaver

Date of Baptism - January 24 (1820); Parents Names - Jacob Failing & Catherine Tool; Childs Name & Date of Birth - Simion Toll, Novm 13, 1819

1820

Date of Baptism - Febr 6; Parents Names - John G. Eigebroat & Elezebeth Brown;Childs Name & Date of Birth - Syrus King, Sept 24, 1819; Sponsors - Adam E. Gray & wife Nancy

Date of Baptism - Febr 7; Parents Names - Robert Canida & Lena Klock; Childs Name & Date of Birth - Elezebeth, Sept. 9, 1819; Sponsors - Hyrum Pardee & Mary Billington

Date of Baptism - Febr 8; Parents Names - John W. Hawn & Jemima Smades; Childs Name & Date of Birth - Parmelia, Sept. 12, 1819; Sponsors - George Hawn & Elizabeth his wife

Date of Baptism - Febr 11; Parents Names - Peter Boyd & Lena Devoe; Childs Name & Date of Birth - Peter, April 10, 1819

Date of Baptism - Febr 21; Parents Names - Daniel Hess & Elizebeth Suits; Childs Name & Date of Birth - David, Febr. 24, 1819

Date of Baptism - Febr 27; Parents Names - Adam Dygart & Jane Duslef; Childs Name & Date of Birth - Levi, January 8, 1820

Date of Baptism - March 7; Parents Names - Jacob Manck & Elezebeth Manck; Childs Name & Date of Birth - Sally, October 30, 1819; Sponsors - John J. > Manck & Margretat his wife

Date of Baptism - March 7; Parents Names - John J. Manck & Margreta Gross; Childs Name & Date of Birth - Elezebeth, July 18, 1819; Sponsors - Jacob Manck & his wife Elezebeth

Date of Baptism - March 19; Parents Names - John Mabee & Nancy Monck; Childs Name & Date of Birth - Nancy, March 8, 1820; Sponsors - Jacob Bellinger & Susanna Riece

Date of Baptism - March 19; Parents Names - John Klock & Nancy Noice; Childs Name & Date of Birth - Luther, March 8, 1820; Sponsors - Robert Kanida & wife Lana Klock

Date of Baptism - March 19; Parents Names - Henry House & Cornelia Mosure; Childs Name & Date of Birth - John Peter, Novembr 25, 1819; Sponsors - Polly Mosure

Date of Baptism - March 19; Parents Names - Jacob Higgegas & Peggy House; Childs Name & Date of Birth - Almira, Novm 22; Sponsors - Christiaun House & Eve Hillegas

Date of Baptism - March 19; Parents Names - Henry Peter Klinee & Catheriene Klock; Childs Name & Date of Birth - Waltdr

1820

Date of Baptism - March 25; Parents Names - John Walrath & Anna Shible; Childs Name & Date of Birth - David, Febr 16, 1820; Sponsors - Daniel Walrath & Caty Shible

Date of Baptism - April 2; Parents Names - Jacob Shell Jun. & Elezebeth Deits; Childs Name & Date of Birth - Adelia, Sept. 11, 1820

Date of Baptism - April 3; Parents Names - Abraham Freeman & Sarah Bellinger; Childs Name & Date of Birth - Sally, January 26, 1820

Date of Baptism - April 16; Parents Names - Petor Flander & Margreta Riece; Childs Name & Date of Birth - Gedion, March 6, 1820; Sponsors - John Riece & Eve Beckman

Date of Baptism - April 19; Parents Names - Isaac Quackenbush & Cathariene Walrath; Childs Name & Date of Birth - Eve, April 16, 1820

Date of Baptism - May; Parents Names - George Walrath & Patty Loeless; Childs Name & Date of Birth - Almira, 1820

Date of Baptism - May; Parents Names - Henry Walrath & Clarissa Lovless; Childs Name & Date of Birth - Sylvester, 1820

Date of Baptism - May 14; Parents Names - William Walrath & Margreta Erven; Childs Name & Date of Birth - Elezebeth, March 24, 1820

Date of Baptism - May 14; Parents Names - George Cox & Polly Hillegas; Childs Name & Date of Birth - Lena, January 14, 1820; Sponsors - Lena Quackenbush

Date of Baptism - May 28; Parents Names - Andrew Walrath & Neaome Wilcox

Date of Baptism - May 28; Parents Names - John Rarick & Cathrien Bellinger; Childs Name & Date of Birth - Caty, April 8, 1820; Sponsors - Maria Bellinger

Date of Baptism - June 25; Parents Names - John H. Billinger & Lena Walrath; Childs Name & Date of Birth - David, May 8, 1820; Sponsors - Abraham Walrath & Caty Davise

Date of Baptism - July 8; Parents Names - John Jost Zimmerman & Cathrien Zimmerman; Childs Name & Date of Birth - Luis, December 20, 1819; Sponsors - Jacob J. Zimmerm & Maria Zimmerm

Date of Baptism - July 8; Parents Names - John Jost Zimmerman & Cathrien Zimmerman; Childs Name & Date of Birth - Sally, December 20, 1819; Sponsors - John C. Zimmerman & Guity Zimmerman

Date of Baptism - July 8; Parents Names - Jacob J. Snell & Margreta Zimmerman; Childs Name & Date of Birth - Elezebeth, March 28, 1818, Sponsors - Widow J. Z. & Analiza Zimmerm

Date of Baptism - July 9; Parents Names - Henry Wabell & Maria Kill; Childs Name & Date of Birth - Eliza Maria, October 24, 1819

Date of Baptism - July 9; Parents Names - John Hufman & Nancy Bettleman; Childs Name & Date of Birth - Rutha, Febr 25, 1820; Sponsors - Harmanus Fisher & Caty Davise

Date of Baptism - July 17; Parents Names - John J. Failing Jr. & Cathrien Elwood; Childs Name & Date of Birth - Benjamin Elwood, July 2, 1820

Date of Baptism - July 17; Parents Names - Luis Kills & Polly Kills; Childs Name & Date of Birth - Elmira Maria Emily, March 20, 1820; Sponsors - Adam Kills & wife Elezebeth Nellis

1820

Date of Baptism - July 16; Parents Names - Jacob H. Failing & Charity Te

Date of Baptism - July 16; Parents Names - Jacob H. Failing & Auitty Tooky; Childs Name & Date of Birth - Margreta, June 5, 1820

Date of Baptism - July 30; Parents Names - Chester Pain & Angelina Vedder; Childs Name & Date of Birth - Cornelius, June 19, 1820

Date of Baptism - August 6; Parents Names - Cornelius Devoe & Ann Dorithy Gage; Childs Name & Date of Birth - Madalena, June 20, 1820

Date of Baptism - August 6; Parents Names - James Forbes & Maria Downey; Childs Name & Date of Birth - John Ervin, January 25, 1820

Date of Baptism - Sept. 3d; Parents Names - Coon rod Geffers & Elezebeth Snell; Childs Name & Date of Birth - Lusinda, March 21, 1820; Sponsors - Abr Snell & Caty Geffers

Date of Baptism - Sept. 3d; Parents Names - Daniel Ingelsolo & Elezebeth Burkdorf; Childs Name & Date of Birth - Hyram, May 29, 1820

Date of Baptism - Sept. 17; Parents Names - John Willson & Susanna Ellwood; Childs Name & Date of Birth - Eve, August 16, 1820

Date of Baptism - Sept. 17; Parents Names - Isaac Ellwood & Anna Wilson; Childs Name & Date of Birth - Lene, June 20, 1820; Sponsors - Wide Lena Quackenbush

Date of Baptism - October 8; Parents Names - John B. Klock & Eve Zimmerman; Childs Name & Date of Birth - Hiram, Augus 28, 1820

Date of Baptism - Novm 13; Parents Names - Cornelius W. Beekman & Sally Storms; Childs Name

& Date of Birth - Eliza Cathariene, 1820

Date of Baptism - December 17; Parents Names - Peter Klock & Susannah Feick; Childs Name & Date of Birth - Catherin, October 20, 1820

Date of Baptism - December 23rd; Parents Names - Abraham P. Yates & Cornilea Van everea; Childs Name & Date of Birth - Charles, October 17, 1820

Date of Baptism - December 24; Parents Names - David Heis & Rosna Rosina Billenger; Childs Name & Date of Birth - Jeremiah, October 29, 1820; Sponsors - John Heise & Nancy Bellinger

Date of Baptism - December 24; Parents Names - Jacob Bellinger & Betsy Ingersol; Childs Name & Date of Birth - Nancy, Novembr 15, 1820; Sponsors - John Ingersol & Nancy Riece

Date of Baptism - December 24; Parents Names - Ebenezer Failing & Hannah Paterson; Childs Name & Date of Birth - Mary, Apr. 7, 1820

Date of Baptism - December 24; Parents Names - Ludwick Acer & Elezebeth Bellinger; Childs Name & Date of Birth - Lena, October 20, 1820; Sponsors - William Bellinger & Polly Ingersol

Date of Baptism - December 24; Parents Names - Peter Mosure & Sally Ames; Childs Name & Date of Birth - Sally Maria, June 27, 1820

Date of Baptism - December 24; Parents Names - Nicholas Failing & Mary Youker; Childs Name & Date of Birth - William, April 5, 1820; Sponsors - William Failing & Hannah Cox

Date of Baptism - December 24; Parents Names - Coonrod C. House & Sally Gasset; Childs Name & Date of Birth - Betsy Margrete, May 5, 1820; Sponsors - William Allenburgh & wife Elezebeth

Date of Baptism - December 24; Parents Names - Jacob Best & Gertrude > Crouse; Childs Name & Date of Birth - Catharine, Decembr 3, 1820

1820

Date of Baptism - December 31; Parents Names - Henry G. Walrath & Catheriene Manck; Childs Name & Date of Birth - Mary Ann, Sept. 3, 1920; Sponsors - Abrm Walrath & Mary Leib

Date of Baptism - December 31; Parents Names - Henry Shuls & Elezebeth Waggoner; Childs Name & Date of Birth - David Henry, June 26, 1820; Sponsors - Daniel Shals & Mary Guitman

Date of Baptism - December 31; Parents Names - Jacob Hoes & Leah Shall; Childs Name & Date of Birth - John, Novembr 20, 1820; Sponsors - David Hoes & Polly Snell

1821

Date of Baptism - January 11; Parents Names - Jacob Weber & Margreta Williamson; Childs Name & Date of Birth - Lucretia, April 23, 1820

Date of Baptism - January 11; Parents Names - Philip Piper & Dorothy Schlyea; Childs Name & Date of Birth - Catharien, April 16, 1820

Date of Baptism - January 14; Parents Names - John M. Bauder & Eve Jaugo; Childs Name & Date of Birth - Nathan, May 12, 1820

Date of Baptism - January 14; Parents Names - Frederic H. Bellinger & Elezebeth Klock; Childs Name & Date of Birth - Jonas Frederic, Novembr 7, 1820; Sponsors - Abratham Walrath & Mariah Bellinger

Date of Baptism - Jenuary 14; Parents Names - John F. Bellinger & Elezebeth Bellinger; Childs Name & Date of Birth - Manda, December 23rd, 1820

Date of Baptism - Jenuary 17; Parents Names - Thomas Failing & Caty Klock; Childs Name & Date of Birth - Eve, January 17, 18201

Date of Baptism - Febr 1; Parents Names - David Klock & Caty Klock; Childs Name & Date of Birth - Daniel, August 27, 1820

Date of Baptism - Febr 1; Parents Names - John Simson & Elezebeth Brown; Childs Name & Date of Birth - Eliza Matilda, Novm. 30, 1820

Date of Baptism - Febr 1; Parents Names - Simeon D. Owens & Maria Fishback; Childs Name & Date of Birth - Ira Hamelton, Febr. 6, 1820

Date of Baptism - Febr 24; Parents Names - John D. Flander & Anna Smith; Childs Name & Date of Birth - Solomon, Febr 3, 1821; Sponsors - Peter Smith > & Anna Flander

Date of Baptism - Febr 25; Parents Names - Adam Thumb & Maria Shaver; Childs Name & Date of Birth -Hester, Sept. 18, 1820

Date of Baptism - Febr 25; Parents Names - David Vanslike & Betsy Hillegas; Childs Name & Date of Birth - Betsey, Decembr 19, 1820; Sponsors - William Kniskern & Peggy Shuyler his wife

Date of Baptism - Febr 25; Parents Names - Frederic Katherene Frederic Baumgart & Katheriene Klock; Childs Name & Date of Birth - Martin, Febr 5, 1821

Date of Baptism - March 4; Parents Names - Abraham Hese & Caty Davis; Childs Name & Date of Birth - Jane Suffia, Decembr 30, 1820; Sponsors - Frederic Hese & wife Caty Seger

Date of Baptism - March 11; Parents Names - Peter Youker & Syne Van aulen; Childs Name & Date of Birth - Anna, January 26, 1821; Sponsors - John Youker & Anna his wife

Date of Baptism - March 11; Parents Names - Peter P. Bellinger & Elezebeth Youker; Childs Name & Date of Birth - Hyram, January 6, 1821; Sponsors - Peter Youker & Syna Van aulen

Date of Baptism - March 11; Parents Names - Henry J. Failing & Dolly Youker; Childs Name & Date of Birth - Peggy, Novm 17, 1820; Sponsors - Adam Hellegas & Betsy Hairing

1821

Date of Baptism - March 11; Parents Names - Henry Kline & Caty Klock; Childs Name & Date of Birth - Henryet, Febr 8, 1821; Sponsors - Peter Kline & Deborah his wife

Date of Baptism - March 18; Parents Names - John M. Devoe & Polly Klock; Childs Name & Date of Birth - Matilda, Febr. 8, 1821

Date of Baptism - March 23; Parents Names - Philip Cramer & Cathrien Hecock; Childs Name & Date of Birth - Anna, Decembr 9, 1821; Sponsors- Christian Eigebroet & wife Margrete

Date of Baptism - April 22; Parents Names - Bellenger & Youron

Date of Baptism - April 23rd; Parents Names - Joshua Riece & Anna Margreta Markle; Childs Name & Date of Birth - John Frederic, Sept. 22, 1820

Date of Baptism - April 29; Parents Names - Robert Kenedy & Lena Klock; Childs Name & Date of Birth - Robert, April 22, 1821

Date of Baptism - April 29; Parents Names - Robert Kenedy & Lena Klock; Childs Name & Date of Birth - Mary, April 22, 1821

Date of Baptism - May 10; Parents Names - John Baum & Lena Ellwood; Childs Name & Date of Birth - Benjamin Ward, Jenuary 3, 1821

Date of Baptism - May 22; Parents Names - David Van Alstine & Ledia Tarpenny; Childs Name & Date of Birth - David Benjamin, August 15, 1820

Date of Baptism - May 27; Parents Names - Abraham Mour & Elezebeth France; Childs Name & Date of Birth - Gedeliza, August 1, 1820; Sponsors - Jacob Heer & Charity Mour

Fayett a-Seneca Parents Names - Peter Mour & Magdalena Federley; Childs Name & Date of Birth - Caty Liza, Febr 20, 1821; Sponsors - Coonrod Mour & Elezebeth Bellenger

Fayetta-Seneca Parents Names - Jonas Price & Christianna Mour; Childs Name & Date of Birth - George, Decembr 11, 1820; Sponsors - Joseph Mour & Lena Mour

Fayetta-Seneca Parents Names - Coonrod Mour & Charity Chrisman; Childs Name & Date of Birth - Caty, Sept. 17, 1820; Sponsors - Johannes Crisman & Racel Eigebroat

Fayetta-Seneca Parents Names - Jacob Crim & Christianna Gardner; Childs Name & Date of Birth - Adam, March 18, 1821; Sponsors - Adam Crim & Elezebeth Hover

Date of Baptism - June 3; Parents Names - Daniel Marsh & Nancy Radley; Childs Name & Date of Birth - Suceanna, March 16, 1821; Sponsors - John Radley & Caty his wife

Da te of Baptism - June 5; Parents Names - William N. Shaver & Peggy Claus; Childs Name & Date of Birth - Solomon, April 28, 1821; Sponsors - Abraham Killer & Elezebeth Shaver

Date of Baptism - June 21; Parents Names - Philip Klock & Susannah Dellenbaugh; Childs Name & Date of Birth - Jacob G, May 26, 1821; Sponsors - George J. Klock & wife Catherine Nellis

Date of Baptism - June 21; Parents Names - Peter Vandresen & Dorathy Walrath; Childs Name & Date of Birth - Adam, June 9, 1821

Date of Baptism - June 21; Parents Names - Philip Stauring & Darkus Gardener; Childs Name & Date of Birth - Peter, November 20, 1820

Date of Baptism - June 21; Parents Names - John Vedder & Aurosina Zimmerman; Childs Name & Date of Birth - Josiah, May 24, 1821

Date of Baptism - June 21; Parents Names - William Dusler & Anna Snell; Childs Name & Date of Birth - Julian, May 21, 1821; Sponsors - Peter Smith & Nancy Dayharsh

1821

Date of Baptism - July 1; Parents Names - Jacob D. Flander & Elezebeth Flander; Childs Name & Date of Birth - Magdalene, June 23rd, 1821; Sponsors - John H. Flander & Margreete Flander

Date of Baptism - July 1; Parents Names - Joseph G. Walrath & Anna Dachsteder; Childs Name & Date of Birth - Elezebeth, March 30, 1821; Sponsors - Salmon Cramer & Elezebeth Walrath

Date of Baptism - July 1; Parents Names - Conrod Manck & Maria Mack; Childs Name & Date of Birth - Cornelius, March 1, 1821; Sponsors - Jacob Manck & Elezebeth Monck

Date of Baptism - July 1; Parents Names - Henry Dachstader & Maria Casselman; Childs Name & Date of Birth - Sally, Febr 20, 1821; Sponsors - Abraham Walrath & Cathrien Smith

Date of Baptism - July 1; Parents Names - Frederic J. Bellinger & Anna Merselis; Childs Name & Date of Birth - Eve Cathrien, Febr 4, 1821

Date of Baptism - July 22; Parents Names - James Daniels & Charity Veeder; Childs Name & Date of Birth - Mary, June 30, 1821; Sponsors - Peter Hese & Mary Daniels

Date of Baptism - July 22; Parents Names - John Vedder & Anrozina Zimmerman; Childs Name & Date of Birth - Aron, April 24, 182_

Date of Baptism - July 22; Parents Names - Henry G. Klock & Elezebeth Klock; Childs Name & Date of Birth - Josiah, May 24, 1821; Sponsors - Eriel Bauder & Caty Klock

Date of Baptism - August 2nd; Parents Names - Abraham Walrath; Childs Name & Date of Birth - Hiram, 1821; Sponsors - Daniel Walrath & Eve Hillegas

Date of Baptism - August 2nd; Parents Names - Peter Morison & Margreta Burkdorf; Childs Name & Date of Birth - Julian, May 26, 1821

Date of Baptism - Sept. 19; Parents Names - Joseph Failing & Maria Van alstine; Childs Name & Date of Birth - Augustus Donley, Sept. 12, 1820

Date of Baptism - Sept. 19; Parents Names - Adam Bower & Sally Coonrod; Childs Name & Date of Birth - Henry; August 21, 1819

Date of Baptism - Sept. 19; Parents Names - Adam Bower & Sally Coonrod; hilds Name & Date of Birth - Sally, June 1820

Date of Baptism - Sept. 19; Parents Names - Androw Keller & Betsey Bower; Childs Name & Date of Birth - Calvin Baker, May 20, 1820

Datc of Baptism - Sepl. 19; Parents Names - Urial Bauder & Caty Klock; Childs Name & Date of Birth - Michael, Sept. 30, 1821; Sponsors - Michael U. Bauder & wife Anna

Date of Baptism - Novm. 4; Parents Names - Jacob Youker Jun. & Elezebeth Spanknebel; Childs Name & Date of Birth - Maria, August 9, 1821

Date of Baptism - Novm. 7; Parents Names - George Smith & Elezebeth Suits; Childs Name & Date of Birth - Eliza Maria, May 11, 1821; Sponsors - Philip Cramer & wife Caty

Date of Baptism - Novm. 8; Parents Names - Peter Cramer & Margreta Hadcock; Childs Name & Date of Birth - Albert, June 17, 1821; Sponsors - Rebecca Cramer, widow

Date of Baptism - Novm. 11; Parents Names - Elias Lawton & Hannah House; Childs Name & Date of Birth - Carolina, Sept. 2, 1821; Sponsors - John C. House & Hannah his wife

Date of Baptism - December 2nd; Parents Names - Christoffel Klock & Elizabeth Dislin; Childs Name & Date of Birth - John Henry, October 17, 1821; Sponsors - George J. Klock & Barbara

Date of Baptism - December 2nd; Parents Names - Alber V. Vorhase & Margreet Deniston; Childs Name & Date of Birth - Maria, Sept. 14, 1821; Sponsors - Jacob Schram & Amanda Buckbee
Page 222

Note. Entry No. 15. Date of baptism not Sept. 19, or else year date of birth in wrong.

1821
Children of Westren in Oneida County
Date of Baptism - November; Parents Names - John Waggoner & Sally Van Alstine of Western

Oneida Co.; Childs Name & Date of Birth - Abigal

Date of Baptism - November; Parents Names - John Waggoner & Sally Van Alstine of Western
Oneida Co.; Childs Name & Date of Birth - Richard, January 24, 1817

Date of Baptism - November; Parents Names - John Waggoner & Sally Van Alstine of Western
Oneida Co.; Childs Name & Date of Birth - John Esqinse,
August 18, 1820

Date of Baptism - Noember; Parents Names - Nicholas Riece & Maria Waggoner; Childs Name &
Date of Birth - Malinda, Decembr 24, 1818 _____ of Leray, Jefferson County (no dates
listed)

Parents Names - James J. Murphy & Elezebeth Keyser; Childs Name & Date of Birth - Alexander;
Sponsors - Frederic Crisman & wife Caty

Parents Names - James J. Murphy & Elezebeth Keyser; Childs Name & Date of Birth - Lysander;
Sponsors - Joseph Petrie & wife Dorithy

Parents Names - Jacob Klock & Nancy Cypher; Childs Name & Date of Birth - Jeremlah, Decembr
22, 1820; Sponsors - Henry Ritter & wife Nancy

Parents Names - Allexander V. Brauklin & Caty Knull; Childs Name & Date of Birth - Abraham, July
27, 1820

Parents Names - Peter J. Hoover & Guity Scyper; Childs Name & Date of Birth - Hyram, March 6,
1820

Parents Names - Peter Bloodo & Elezebeth Walrath; Childs Name & Date of Birth - John, October 6,
1820; Sponsors - John Walrath & wife Caty

Parents Names - Frederic Crisman & Caty Snell; Childs Name & Date of Birth - Jacob, March 20,
1821

Parents Names - Richard Hoover & Cathrien Keller; Childs Name & Date of Birth - Amos, Novembr
19, 1821

Parents Names - John Main & Elezebeth Smithson; Childs Name & Date of Birth - George
Washington, May 24, 1821

Parents Names - Daniel Rickert & Permelia Tucker; Childs Name & Date of Birth - Nancy, July 7,
1821; Sponsors - Henry Ritter & wife Nancy Rickert

Parents Names - William J. Young & Rachel Oxburg; Childs Name & Date of Birth - Benjamin,
Novembr 24, 1821

1822

Date of Baptism - January 2nd; Parents Names - Christian A. Walrath & Caty Hilligas; Childs Name
& Date of Birth - Nathaniel, Novm 5, 1821

Date of Baptism - January 2nd; Parents Names - Sabastian Cook & Elezebeth Youron; Childs Name
& Date of Birth - Amos, Sept. 5, 1821

Date of Baptism - January 2nd; Parents Names - William W. Brando & Peggy Van orden; Childs
Name & Date of Birth - William, October 9, 1821

Date of Baptism - Febr; Parents Names - John J. Failing Jun. & Cathrien Elwood; Childs Name &
Date of Birth - Isaiah, January 16, 1822

_____ Parents Names - John Veeder & Rachel Van riper; Childs Name & Date of Birth -
Mary, Jenuary 7, 1820

Note. The lines in the date column, are drawn as they appear in the original record. The date Jan.
2, 1822, probably applies to entry No. 16, (Nathaniel Walrath).

1822

Date of Baptism - Febr; Parents Names - Robert Guilderland & Jane Guilmore; Childs Name & Date
of Birth - James, April 12, 1820

Seneca Count
Town of Fayett

Parents Names - John Van gesen & Sincha Bush; Childs Name & Date of Birth - Ann, Sept. 20,
1820

Parents Names - Jacob Mock & Elezebeth Monck; Childs Name & Date of Birth - Moses, Jenuary 26,

1820; Sponsors - John Mabee & wife Nancy Monck

Date of Baptism - Febr 24; Parents Names - John Monck & Margreeta Cross; Childs Name & Date of Birth - Lusinda, October 8, 1821; Sponsors - Philip Cramer & wife Cathrien Hedcock

Date of Baptism - Feb. 24; Parents Names - Johannes Hess & Elezebeth Bellinger; Childs Name & Date of Birth - Aaron, Febr 17, 1822; Sponsors - Henry H. Hess & wife Elezebeth Bellenger

Page 223

Note. The locality, Fayette Seneca County, applies as well to entry No. 20 (the last on page 73), according to the lines drawn in the date column.

1822

Date of Baptism - March 3rd; Parents Names - Adam P. Bellinger & Betsey Hoover; Childs Name & Date of Birth - George Henry, October 2, 1821; Sponsors - Henry Miller & wife Elesebeth Wolebeon

Date of Baptism - Febr 26; Parents Names - Stephen Hoghtaling & Rabecka Maning; Childs Name & Date of Birth - Elmira, May 13, 1820

Date of Baptism - Febr 26; Parents Names - Isen-lard & Polly Fox

Date of Baptism - Febr 17; Parents Names - Jacob Ausman & Maria Bellinger; > Childs Name & Date of Birth - Crate, Febr 17, 1822; Sponsors - Peter Bellinger & Crate his wife

Date of Baptism - Febr 17; Parents Names - John D. Devoe & Lucina Christy; Childs Name & Date of Birth - Alonzo Christe, July 1, 1821

Date of Baptism - March 30; Parents Names - Charels Devoe & Cathrien Gray; Childs Name & Date of Birth - Edwin, Febr 10, 1822

Date of Baptism - March 30; Parents Names - Abraham Freeman & Sarah Bellinger; Childs Name & Date of Birth - Peggy, Jenuary 11, 1822

Date of Baptism - March 31; Parents Names - Coonrod Jeffers & Elezebeth Snell; Childs Name & Date of Birth - Mary Margret, January 25, 1821; Sponsors - John Snell & Mary Snell

Date of Baptism - April 7; Parents Names - Peter A. Zimmerman & Lena Garloch; Childs Name & Date of Birth - Eli, October 25, 1821; Sponsors - Henry Zimerman & Petey Zimmerman

Date of Baptism - April 7; Parents Names - John Petrie Jr. & Barbara Baum; Childs Name & Date of Birth - Salina, Jenuary 4, 1822; Sponsors - Jacob Baum & Mary Petrie

Date of Baptism - April 8; Parents Names - John H. Bellinger & Lena Walrath; Childs Name & Date of Birth - Daniel, March 25, 1822; Sponsors - Georg Walrath & Patty his wife

Date of Baptism - April 8; Parents Names - Danus Flander Jr. & Catherien Dochsteder; Childs Name & Date of Birth - Elizabeth, April 5, 1822; Sponsors - John F. Bellinger & Elizebeth his wife

Date of Baptism - April 21; Parents Names - John G. Klock & Guitty Zimmerman; Childs Name & Date of Birth - Eli, March 11, 1822

Date of Baptism - May5; Parents Names - James Gark & Nancy Ritter; Childs Name & Date of Birth - Thankful, Febr 14, 1822; Sponsors - Mathew Ritter & wife Anna Leray Penet

Date of Baptism - May 5; Parents Names - Johannes Wies & Catharine Salma, Baumgart; Childs Name & Date of Birth - Jacobes, April 4, 1822 Lowvill

Date of Baptism - May 7; Parents Names - John Opcek & Margreet Hurdick; Childs Name & Date of Birth - John Miller, April 7, 1822

Date of Baptism - May 10; Parents Names - Edward Maning & Elenner Houghtaling; Childs Name & Date of Birth - Elisa, Decembr 30

Date of Baptism - May 18; Parents Names - David Goodale & Charity Shaver; Childs Name & Date of Birth - Jonathon, October 16, 1822; Sponsors - Frederic Shaver & wifeFayetta

Date of Baptism - May 20; Parents Names - John Emerie & Elezebeth Hover; Childs Name & Date of Birth - Mila, May 4, 1822

Page 224.

Note. It is difficult to determine to just which entries, the information in the date column refers. In my opinion, the baptisms administered on May 7 and 10, were performed at Lowville. Thankful Gark was probably baptized at Le Ray. Jacob Wies was baptized on the same day at Penet; this refers to Penet Square, reserved by the Oneida Indians for Peter Penet in the treaty of 1788.

1822

Date of Baptism - May 26; Parents Names - Joseph Youron & Anna Swackhammer; Childs Name & Date of Birth - Mary, Novembr 26, 1821

Date of Baptism - May 26; Parents Names - Jacob P. Snell & Mary Helmick; Childs Name & Date of Birth - Lucina, March 3, 1822

Date of Baptism - May 26; Parents Names - Henry Merselis & Mary Putman; Childs Name & Date of Birth - Delia, March 14, 1822; Sponsors - Jacob Baum & Delia Putman

Date of Baptism - May 27; Parents Names - Peter Flander & Margreeta Riece; Childs Name & Date of Birth - Fenneally, March 18, 1822; Sponsors - Cathriene Fox Widow

Date of Baptism - May 27; Parents Names - Jacob H. Flander & Elezebeth Grove; Childs Name & Date of Birth - Julian, May 7, 1822; Sponsors - Elezebeth Fander

Date of Baptism - June 4; Parents Names - Coonrod Snell & Peggy Bellinger; Childs Name & Date of Birth - Nelson, Febr 20, 1822

Date of Baptism - June 10; Parents Names - Salmon Ellwood & Elezebeth Baum; Childs Name & Date of Birth - Henry, March 21, 1822

Date of Baptism - June 10; Parents Names - Joseph Heese & Anna Nellis; Childs Name & Date of Birth - Hiram, April 8, 1822; Sponsors- Benjamin Nilles & Peggy Riece

Date of Baptism - June 17; Parents Names - Peter Phiper & Dorothy Woleben; Childs Name & Date of Birth - Elezebeth, Febr 24, 1822; Live at Columbia

Date of Baptism - June 21; Parents Names - Isaac Ellwood & Anna Willson; Childs Name & Date of Birth - James Willson, May 9, 1822

Date of Baptism - June 21; Parents Names - Cornelius Groff VanKamp & Caty Defendorf; Childs Name & Date of Birth - Abraham Defendorf, May 27, 1822

Date of Baptism - June 30; Parents Names - Daniel Groff & Eve Failing; Childs Name & Date of Birth - Reuben, May June 20, 1822

Date of Baptism - July 3; Parents Names - Jacob Waggoner & Anna

Date of Baptism - July 3; Parents Names - Jacob Walrath & Anna Waggoner; Childs Name & Date of Birth - William, June 24, 1822

Date of Baptism - July 7; Parents Names - Christoffel Flander & Catherien Flander; Childs Name & Date of Birth - Maria, July 3, 1822

Date of Baptism - July 7; Parents Names - Jacob C. Nellis & Lena Keller; Childs Name & Date of Birth - Christianna, May 29, 1820; Sponsors - Jacob Keller & Nancy Klock

Date of Baptism - July 14; Parents Names - Ebenezer Cox & Anna Keller; Childs Name & Date of Birth - Nancy, May 4, 1820

Date of Baptism - July 19; Parents Names - Ludwick Hairing & Margreta Youker; Childs Name & Date of Birth - Magdalena, June 21, 1822; Sponsors - Jacob Flander & Elezebeth Flander

Date of Baptism - July 21; Parents Names - Henry C. Hart & Eve Bellinger; Childs Name & Date of Birth - Daniel, June 16, 1822; Sponsors - Adam Hillegas & Peggy Hart

Date of Baptism - July 28; Parents Names - Jacob Sholl & Anna Klock; Childs Name & Date of Birth - George, May 16, 1822 Danube

Page 225.

Note. Original page 226 is blank. From here on, a number of pages have been skipped by Mr. Devoe, in order to have the writing on one side of the page only. This was done on account of the fact that the paper absorbed the ink, and the writing came through on the reverse side of the page.

July 28, 1822

Simeon D Owens & wife Maria Fishback child Ira Mason born Decembr 31, 1821

Jacob Dominic & wife Malinda Herkemer child Weidman born Novembr 10, 1821 Sponsors: George Dominic & Caty Weidman

David Van Aulstine & Lidia Tarpenne child Elisha born June 1, 1822

John M. Haun & Jemime Smadis child Henry born January 8, 1822 Sponsors: Matthew Smith & wife Elizabeth

July 30, 1822
Daniel Hess & Elezebeth Suits child Elezebeth born June 22, 1821 Sponsors: David Fox & Elezebeth Klock

August 5, 1822
Abraham Van Alstine & Elezebeth Baut child: Sally born October 15, 1815
Abraham Van Alstine & Elezebeth Baut child: Jane Ann born Octob 30, 1817
Abraham Van Alstine & Elezebeth Baut child: Caty born September 25, 1820

August 6, 1822
John Denmark & Caty Ausman child: Jacob born April 13, 1822 Sponsors: Jacob Fox & Lena his wife

August 7, 1822
Jacob A Walrath & Maria Smith child: Elezebeth born June 16, 1822 Sponsors: Henry A. Walrath & Polly Cambdont
Michael Wever & Gurtruit Frenck child: Peter born Decembr 29, 1816 Sponsors: Tenus Klapsadt & Elezebeth Klapsadt
Columbia Herkemer County
Anson Kables & Margreta Orandorf child: Margretta born Decembr 16, 1816 Sponsor: Margreta Delane widow

August 9, 1822
Nicholas Zimmerman & Christianna Thum child: Joel born August 1, 1822

August 11, 1822
Jacob J. Bellinger & Nancy Flander child: Lovina born June 11, 1822
Peter Nellis & Caty Fox child: Margreta born May 25, 1822 Sponsors: John W. Nellis & Margreta Fox
Abraham Shafer & Carolina Claus child: Walter born May 25, 1822

August 18, 1822
Anthony Schuyler & Nancy Shell child: Mary born April 2, 1821
Aaron Van Antwerp & Catherine House child: (No name listed or dates) Sponsor: Christian & daughter of Capt./

September 1, 1822
John Bauter & Eve Chaugo child: Hyram born June 26, 1822

September 8, 1822
Jacob Crouse & Maria Butler child: Lusinda born July 23, 1822 Sponsors: Philip F. Baum & Elezebeth his wife
Ludwick Ecric & Elezebeth Bellinger child: Sarah born June 17, 1822 Sponsors: John Hese & Sarah Hufman

September 22, 1822
William Comings & Elezebeth Sturbraugh child: Elizebeth Ann born June 12, 1822
Christoffel Fox & Anna Suits child: Seth born June 2, 1822 Sponsors: Seth Nellis & Polly Fox

September 29, 1822
George J. Backus & Barbara Ritter child: George born Sept. 7, 1822 Sponsors: Frederic Ritter & Elizabeth his wife

Johannes Hufman & Anna Bydeman child: Moses born Sept. 27, 1822 Sponsors: Henry H. Hoise & Elizebeth Bellinger

October 6
Henry Baum & Maria Dusler child: Joseph born July 26, 1822 Sponsors: Joseph Kring & Anna Post
Salomon Wheler & Betsy Tarpenny child: Julia born July 18, 1822

October 13
Peter B. Cook & Maria Fox child: Theordore Chapen born May 31, 1822 Sponsors: David Nellis & Nancy Oathout

October 3
Jacob C. Nellis & Magdalena Keller child: Anna Maria born Octobr 26, 1822 Sponsors: Peter C. Fox & wife Anna

October 17
Christian A. Bellinger & Nancy House child: George Henry born Sept. 29, 1822

October 19
Volkert Getman & Peggy Flander child: Hiram born Sept. 21, 1822

October 20
William Kellir & Caty House child: Frederic born August 8, 1822

October 29
Richard Putman & Nancy Shell child: Eve born September 19, 1822 Sponsors: Whilhelmus Shall & wife Eve Kniskern

December 6
Joseph P. Nellis & Dame Deive child: Joshua born October 12, 1822 Sponsors: Warner Nellis & Elezebeth Nellis

December 10
Francis Lighthall & Margreeta Klock child: James Henry born Novm 5, 1822 Sponsors: X Jonas Snell & X 1822 Betsey Klock his wife

December 23
John H. Smith & Jemima Denuse child: Albert born Novm 17, 1822 Sponsors: Moses Keck his wife Elezebeth

December 26
Fairfield
Henry Keller & Christeana Miller child: Levi born Decembr 4, 1822

December 28
David Vanslick & Elezebeth Hillegas child: Adam born Novm 17, 1822 Sponsors: Adam Quackenbush & Margrete Kneskan
Jacob Wilson & Nelly Quackenbush child: Henry born April 16, 1822
Abraham Frailech & Margreta Defendorf child: Josiah born Decembr 4, 1822

Note. Entry No. 14. One might suppose that the cryptic marks made by Mr. Devoe, indicate the death of Jonas Snell in 1822. However, from data secured for the introduction, I am sure that Jonas Snell was alive, at least 60 years later and possibly 60. Elizabeth Klock, his wife, did not die until March 12, 1889.

1823 Baptisms

January 5
Henry Failing Jun. & Hannah Zimmerman child: Dewit born Decembr 1822
Peter Klock & Susanna Feick child: Eliza born Novembr 9, 1822
Androw Walrath & Naome Wilcox child: Cornelius born 1822 Sponsors: ------- Nellis & Betsey
Herring David Walrath & Susanna Bowman child: Aza Walter born Decembr 15, 1822 Sponsors: Daniel Walter & Mary House

January 12
George Hillegas & Betsey Youker child: John Henry born July 26, 1823 Sponsors: Henry G. Klock & Elezebeth Klock
Henry P. Cline & Catherine Klock child: Peter born Novembr 1822

January 19
State Road
Peter Mosure & Sally Amoz child: Emily Jane born October 20, 1822
Leray Jefferson County
William Churchel & Catherine Zimmerman children: Alzade born April 13, 1821 & Aldalina born Novm 22, 1822

January 26
Lowvill Luis County
Androw Shaffer & Margreta Bellinger child: Gedion born October 5, 1822 Sponsors: Daniel Louck & Lena Bellinger

January 28
Henry Burk & Margreta Shaffer child: Mary Margret born July 1, 1822 Sponsor: Henry Shaffer

January 30
Isaac Hessel & Margreta Allenburgh child: Margreta Ann born January 23, 1823 Sponsors: Elezebeth Allenburgh

Febr 8
Anthony Walrath & Caty Davis child: Sary Ann born January 11, 1823

Febr 10
Henry Ausman & Betsey Bellinger child: Rosina born April 15, 1823 Sponsors: Jacob J Youker & Sina Bellinger

March 8
William Cooney & Polly Eigebroet child: Adam born Febr 20, 1823

March 13
Nicholas Failing & Maria Youker child: Mary Magdalena born Febr 19, 1823

Henry Walrath & Clarica Lovless child: Alonzo born Febr 1823 Sponsors: George Walrath & Patty his wife

March 5
Gatersburg
John Simson & Elezebeth Brown child: John Brown born Octobr 1, 1823_

March 16
John J Radley & Caty Suits child: William born January 10, 1823 Sponsors: Christoffel Fox & Anna Suits
Henry Burkdurf & Caty Morice child: Caty born June 19, 1823_

March 16
Jacob C. Hillegas & Margreta House child: Nathaniel born Febr 27, 1823 Sponsors: Adam Walrath & Juliann House
Daniel Defendorf & Peggy Merkle child: Henry
child: Edward born January 2, 1820 Sponsors: John Riece & Nancy Hufman
child: Abraham born 10 March 1822 Sponsor: Nancy Markle

March 26
Androw Bellinger & Caty House child: John Andrew born January 28, 1823 Sponsors: John Docsteder & Nancy his wife
William P. Nellis & Maria Benidic child: Sylvester born September 24, 1822 Sponsor: Betsey Nillis
March 30
Jacob Hillegas & Peggy Thumb child: Nancy born Novembr 11, 1822 Sponsor: Nancy Thum

March 31
Samuel Slocum & Annah Hese child: Samuel born March 28, 1823 Sponsors: Abrm Hese & Wife Caty

May 18
William Crouse & Cathriene Miller child: Aaron born Decembr 14, 1822 Sponsors: David Hilles & Elezebeth Nellis

May 22
John Steering & Peggy Nellis child: Jane born January 13, 1823

May 25
John Shaver & Mary Uron child: Alva born April 31_, 1823

June 1
Abraham Shaut & Caty Gardiner child: John born March 20, 1823 Sponsors: John Gardner & Nancy Shaut
William Snell & Caty Riece child: Mary born Aprl 18, 1823
Abraham Owens & Sally Van Valkenburg child: James Van Valkenburg born March 9, 1823

June 9
John Willson & Susannah Ellwood child: Susannah born October 28, 1823
Philip F. Baum & Elezebeth Handey child: Jacob born May 9, 1823 Sponsors: Jacob F. Baum & Caty Post

June 27
Isaac Quackenbush & Cathrien Walrath child: Elizabeth born June 11, 1823
Jacob Youker & Elezebeth Spanknoble child: Rhua born March 5, 1823
Peter Youker & Risina Van aulen child: Betsey born March 18, 1823

July 12
Nicholas Snyder & Anna Eykeson child: Jacob born March 31, 1823

July 17
Christoffel Flander & Cathrien Flander child: Elick born June 30, 1823

July 26
Henry Klock & Elezebeth Klock child: Hezekiah born July 17, 1823 Sponsors: Thomas Klock &
Nancy Bankde
Robert Keniday & Lena Klock child: Barbara born June 16, 1823

August 3--Root
Cornelius Wessls & Sally Van evera child: Jane Eliza born Febr 18, 1823

August 21--Palatine
Charles Newkerk & Elese Hunn child: Gertrude born June 18, 1823

August 22
Adam Thumb & Maria Shafer child: Jonathan born Febr 14, 1823

August 24
Abraham Van Alstine & Elezebeth Baud child: Nancy born August 14, 1823
Jacob Zimmerman Jun. & Elezebeth Gray child: Theoron born May 19, 1823

Sept. 13
John D. Thum & Eve Bellenger child: Lucinda born March 27, 1816 Sponsors: Jacob J. Youker Jr. &
Sina Belliner
John D. Thum & Eve Bellinger child: David born December 4, 1822 Sponsors: Joseph Shaver &
Mary Bellinger
Loville---Joseph Shaver & Mary Belliner child: Harvey born Febr 22, 1823 Sponsors: John D. Thum
& Eve Bellinger

Sept. 14
Henry House & Cornelia Mosure child: ------- born August 1823

Sept. 17
Benjamin Brown & Elezebeth Van Valkenburgh child: Hiram born March 3, 1822
Jacob Brown & Betsey Best child: Getrude born May 18, 1822 Sponsors: Christien Eigebroat & wife
Margreta
Jacob Brown & Betsey Best child: Nancy born Febr 10, 1823 Sponsors: Peter D. Fox & Polly Best

Sept. 28
Thomas Failing & Caty Klock child: Elezebeth born Sept 22, 1823
Christiaun House & Caty Hese child: Jonas born Octobr 20, 1823 Sponsors: John C. House & wife
Annah

Note. Last entry. Date of Baptism not Sept 28 or else year of birth is wrong.

October 31
Joseph Tusler & Margret Spanknble child: Harriet born Septem 17, 1823

Novm
Coonrod Flander & Elezebeth Nellis child: Cathrien born Sept 20, 1823 Sponsors: John J Kring wife Elezebeth Nelles
Christian House & Elizabeth Kring child: Delila born July 6, 1823
George J. Youker & Cathrien Cretser child: Philip born Sept. 13, 1823 Sponsors: Cathrien Youker

Novm 23
Benjamin Fox & Cathrien Staats child: Elezebeth born August 21, 1823 Sponsors: Volkert Oothout & Dolly Fox

Novm 28
John Hese Jun & Nancy Reice child: Absalom born Novm 9, 1823 Sponsors: John Hese & Elezebeth Bellenger

Novm 30
John P. Clause & Mary Van Buren child: Peter Barnhart born Apr 2, 1823 Sponsor: Peter Clause

Decembr 7
Frederick Fox & Nancy Fox child: Freerick born October 11, 1823 Sponsors: Josiah Fox & Caty Fox

Decembr 17
Urial Bauder & Caty Klock child: Elizabeth born Novm 19, 1823 Sponsors: Henry C. Klock & Elizebeth

Decembr 21
Christoffel Klock & Elizebeth Dyslin child: Mary born October 23, 1823 Sponsors: Ebenezer Fox Jr. & Mary Dylin

1824 Baptisms

January 9
John D. Thum & Eve Bellinger children: Permilia born April 13, 1818 Sponsors: Peter B. Bellinger & wife Elezebeth and Peggy born May 22, 1820 Sponsors: Androw Shaver & wife Peggy

January 25
John Failing Jun & Caty Ellwood child: Elizabeth born 1823
Jacob Failing & Guitty Tocky child: Alexander born Decembr 2, 1823 Sponsors: Jones Snell & Elizabeth Klock

Febr 4
Robert Nellis & Caty Dyslin child: Robert born Decembr 11, 1823 Sponsors: John Zimmerman & Polly Dyslin

Febr 15
Bertholomew Schram & Sally Dunn child: Ann Eliza born Novm 13, 1823 Sponsors: Seth Nellis & Harriet Lindsley

John Brown & Cathrien Woever children: Amanda Malvina born Sept 30, 1823 Sponsors: David Bellinger & Elezebeth Weever and Nancy born October 10, 1823 Sponsors: Levi Brown & Polly Weever

Febr 22
Daniel Graff & Eve Failing child: Catherien Eliza born January 3, 1823 Sponsors: Adam Failing & Nancy Shults

March 4
Jacob A Walrath & Maria Klock child: Malvina born Febr 29, 1824

March 6
Jacob Bitleman & Elezebeth Snell child: Nancy born September 28, 1823 Sponsors: Annah Elezebeth Zimmerman

March 14
William N. Shaver & Peggy Clause child: Ephraim Hudson born January 5, 1824 Sponsors: Jacob Schram & Peggy Shaver
David Heese & Rosina Bellinger child: Josiah born Febr 15, 1824
Albert Voorhese & Margreta Denison child: Ellin born Dec 18, 1823

March 24
Abraham Hese & Caty Davis child: Matilda Evelina born Febr 19, 1824 Sponsors: Robert Davis & Cathrien Hese

March 25
John F. Bellinger & Elisebeth Flander child: Lovina born Febr 11, 1824
Jacob J. Bellinger & Nancy Flander child: Lena Ann born Jan 13, 1824
Jacob H Flander & Elisebeth Groof child: Lena born Febr 29, 1824 Sponsors: Henry Flander & Caty Fox

April 18
John H Bellinger & Lena Walrath child: Margreet born Mar 15, 1824 Sponsors: Peter H. Bellinger & Margreet his wife
Adam Hillegas & Margreta Heart child: Maria born Feb 15, 1824 Sponsors: Henry C. Heart & wife Eve

April 25
Joseph W. Nellis & Polly Fox child: Mary born Jan 11, 1824 Sponsors: Elijah Nellis & Caty Fox

May 16
Christian A. Walrath & Caty Hillegas child: Ruben born April 1824

Henry Walrath & Polly Cambell child: Hiram born 1824
Casper Lodewic & Elesebeth Bellinger child: Maria born Jan 23, 1824 Sponsors: David Bellinger & Polly Nelles

June 6
Jacob Mickel & Caty Wever child: Abraham born March 24, 1824 Sponsors: Abr. Walrath & wife Nancy
Henry Kring & Guartrude Nellis child: Margreta born March 25, 1824 Sponsors: John W. Nellis &

Margrete Klock
Abraham Walrath & Nancy Wever child: Jeremiah born May 1, 1824 Sponsors: Adam Walrath &
Polly Wever

July 4
Jacob Walrath & Maria Smith child: Maria born May 11, 1824 Sponsors: Joseph Kring & anna Post
Frederic Shults & Elesebeth Herkember child: Cathrien born May 20, 1824

July 11

John G. Klock & Guity Zimmerman child: Nehemiah born May 25, 1824 Sponsors: Adam A. Walrath
& May his wife
John Shults & Nancy Nellis child: John Henry born April 18, 1824 Sponsors: John W. Nellis & wife
Margreta

July 25
John Riece & Eve Beekman child: Stephen born June 3, 1824

August 22
Daniel Loadwick & Betsey Landtman child: Charles born Febr 28, 1824 Sponsors: Daniel Shaver &
Betsey Loadwick

Sept. 3
David Walrath & Betsey Farbs child: Liza Ann born May 6, 1823 Sponsors: Anthony Walrath & wife
Cathrien

Sept. 5
David Vanslike & Betsey Hillegas child: Henry born July 31, 1824 Sponsor: Widow Caty Crouse
Charles Devoe & Caty Gray child: Cathrien Eliza born July 16, 1824

Sept. 19
George Cox & Maria Hillegas child: George born January 4, 1824

October 24
Peter Flander & Margreta Riece child: Nancy born August 24, 1824 Sponsors: David J. Flander &
Nancy Smith
Champion, Jefferson Co.
John A Cratsingbarg & Maria Grams child: Henry Grams born July 5, 1820
child: Margreeta born Sept 21, 1822
child: Coonrod born Sept 20, 1824
John Davice Jun. & Mary Eyagler child: Susannah born May 24, 1816
Aron Gray & ------ Sweet child Lucinda born December 25, 1817 Sponsors: John Cratsenbarg &
wife Anna Maria

December 5
John Hufman & Anna Bitleman child: Clorana born Sept 27, 1824 Sponsors: John P. Bellinger &
Elesebeth his wife

December 9

Henry Morselis & Maria Putman child: Daniel born June 25, 1824

1825 Baptisms
Philip Kring & Cathrien Crass child: Delia born August 30, 1824 Sponsors: Frederic Cool & Delia Cross Dilleburgh in Palatine
George Kring & Mary Cross child: James born August 24, 1824 Sponsors: Philip Kring & Cathrien his wife
John Cool & Eve Crisman child: John Henry Cool born 1824 Sponsors: George Crisman & Elisebeth Cretzer

January 20 Danube
Lutheras Walrath & Tyna Post child: Mary Cathrien born Sept. 1, 1824

January 21
David Ehle & Elsebeth House child: Elijah born Oct. 15, 1824

January 22
Jacob D. Flander & Elesebeth Flander child: Lucretia born Oct 20, 1824 Sponsors: David Devoe & Eve Devoe

January 29
Jabis Lwis & Elesebeth Young child: Charles Nelis born Nov 24, 1824

Febr. 4
Cornelius Maybee & Elesebeth Fox child: Anna Margreta born July 12, 1825 ?

Febr. 6
Adam A. Gray & Magdelena Loucks child: Androw born Dec. 18, 1824

Febr. 19
Eve Zimmerman child: Alvin born Nov. 8, 1824 Sponsor: Lena Zimmerman

March 4
John J. Klock & Anna Hillegas child: Lovina born Febr 12, 1825
Peter Jennings & Barbary Reice child: Anthony born Nov. 13, 1824

March 31
William Coony & Polly Eygebroat child: Polly born March 16, 1825

April 3
Nicholas J. Smith & Catharien Ellwood child: Elesebeth born Dec. 15, 1823

April 17 of Canajoharie
John P. Bradt & ELesebeth Dingman child: Jacob born March 21, 1825
Cornelius S Wessel & Sarah Van evera child: Isaac Norman born Sept 4, 1824

May 1
Charles Obyrns & Sarah Huffman child: Alexander Morgan born Febr. 16, 1823
Nicholas Failing & Maria Youker child: Daniel born Febr. 25, 1825

May 8
John H. Smith & Jemima Denuse child: Henry born April 1, 1825 Sponsors: Henry Smith & Elesebeth Stenbargh

May 14
Peter Heese & Polly Daniels child: Mary born April 15, 1825
Johannes Heese & Elisebeth Bellinger child: Elias born April 18, 1825 Sponsors: John Lorn & wife Polly Smith

May 15
Jacob A. Walrath Jun. & Maria Klock child: Annah born Febr. 20, 1825

May 22
(Nicholas Zimmirman & (Crhistiana Thum child: Analiza Ann born Febr. 17, 1825
May 30 Lewis County Denmark or Campion
(Androw Cratsingbarg & (Barbary Crems child: (John born May 13, 1822 child: (Peter born Mar. 31, 1825

Lowill

Bortney N. Cotell & Cathrien Cook child: Lydia Cathrien born March 1, 1824
child: Eliza Caroline born April 4, 1825

June 1
Samuel Ramsey & Jemima Cook child: Elisebeth born Sept. 19, 1824

June 5
Peter Klock & Susannah Feick child: April 21, 1825

June 8
John A. Failing & Nancy Shults child: Clinton born April 10, 1825 Sponsors: Jacob H. Failing & Gartrude his wife

June 12
Peter N. Schuyler & Nancy Dyart child: Lucinda born Sept. 15, 1823
Jacob C. Hillegas & Peggy House child: Nancy born April 11, 1825 Sponsors: John House & Nancy Hufman
Volkert Gitman & Margreta Flander child: Eve born May 2, 1825

June 26
William P Nellise & Maria Bennit child: Mary Magdelene born Oct 8, 1824
Jacob Cool & Cathrien Baum child: Philip born Jan. 11, 1825 Sponsors: Philip Sponable & Anna Baum

July 1
Isaac Ellwood & Nancy Willson child: Gideon born June 24, 1824
Cornilus Vankamp Jun. & Caty Defendorf child: Daniel born May 8, 1825

August 14
John W. Defendorf & Hanah Delong child: George born Dec. 11, 1821
Ditto child: Polly born Sept. 11, 1823
William Keller & Cathrien House child: William born Febr 13, 1825
Abraham Frelih & Margreta Defendorf child: Barbary born March 2, 1825

August 28
George Hillegas & Elesebeth Youker child: Levi born Aug. 2, 1825 Sponsors: Ludwic Haring & wife Peggy

August 14
Daniel Miller & Mary Cross child: Androw born June 23, 1825

Sept. 15
John A. Walrath & Polly Wever child: Daniel Edwin born July 14, 1825 Sponsor: Lena Walrath

Sept. 18
Warner Nellis & Betsy Obryns child: Peter born Aug. 6, 1825
Daniel Klock & Polly Klock child: Anna Maria born May 19, 1825 Sponsors: Abraham Klock & Dolly Klock

October 7
Daniel Snell & Anna Dyslin child John Henry Dyslin born Jan. 16, 1823 Sponsor: Anna Beekman
Daniel Snell & Anna Dyslin child: Peter born Oct. 8, 1824 Sponsors: Peter P. Snell & Cathrien his wife

October 5 Turin or Matinburg
William Stawring & Cathrien Iselman child: Mary born March 24, 1824
Archibel Meyers & Anna Fetterly child: Elesebeth born Oct. 2, 1825 Sponsors: Peter Fetterley & Cathrien his wife

October 6
Coonrod Cambell & Elesebeth Fetterley child: William born March 25, 1825 Sponsors: William Stawring & Cathrien his wife
Moses Seger & Elesebeth Aramstrong child: Elesebeth born May 5, 1818 Sponsors: Thomas Fetterly & Jane his wife

1825

Henry Burkdorf & Caty Morisson child: John born October 29, 1825

Note. This page was evidently started by Mr. Devoe in a fit of absentmindedness, He had forgotten fot the time, that he had already commenced the reverse side of the page; see page 89. Also refer to note on page 76.

October 9
Henry Hart & Eve Bellinger child: Jacob born July 30, 1825 Sponsors: Henry Hese & Jly Ann House

October 23
Henry Spanable & Cathrien Cool child: Sene born May 4, 1825 Sponsor: Philip Spanabl

October 30
Jacob Mickel & Caty Wever child: David born July 4, 1825

Novm 6
Phillip C. Bellinger & Caty Zimmerman child: Barbariann born Oct 9, 1825 Sponsors: John

Eygebroat & Barbary his wife
John Vedder & Caty Dayhaeh child Betsey Sponsors: Jacob Flander & wife Betsey

December 4
Anthony Walrath & Caty Davice child: Obediah born Novm 15, 1825

December 14
Daniel Ingersoll & Elesebeth Burkdorf child: Jeremiah born August 30, 1825

December 18
Daniel Borden & Polly Avery child Elenener Sponsors: Joseph J. Nellis & wife Magdelene

December 25
Henry H. Failing Jun. & Nancy Zimmerman child: Jane born 1825 Sponsors: Adam Snell & Polly his wife

1826 Baptisms

January 3
Thomas Failing & Cathrien Klock child: Stephen born Dec. 25, 1825

January 23
Henry House & Carolina Mosure child: Lise born Jan. 4, 1826

January 29--Danube James Green & Caty Dominic child: Sylvester born Sept. 17, 1825 Sponsors: Peter Dominic & wife Eve Wiselman
Henry Ostrander & Margreta Defendorf child: William Henry born Dec. 6, 1825
John Shall & Cristianna Reice child: Almire born Jan. 2, 1826 Sponsors: Jonas Reice & Eve Klock
Peter Shall & Lena Mowers child: William born Oct. 24, 1825 Sponsors: William Shall & wife Eve Kniskern

Febr. 2nd
Henry Hairling & Nancy Bankard child: Aron born Dec. 26, 1825

Febr. 8 --Martinsburgh Lewis County, Jow Flint & Polly Stawring child: Jow Ann born August 5, 1825 Sponsors: Thomas Fetherley & wife Jane Sicker
Febr 25
John J. Crouse & Cathrien Lesher child: Henry born Jan. 19, 1826 Sponsors: Henry Lesher & Elesebeth his wife

Note: Minden, Manheim, Oppenheim, Denmark, Osquack, German Flats, Danube are the names of places

Bapt. Date Parents Names Child & Birthdate Sponsors

1826

Feb 26.
Christian House & Caty Hese --- Jeremiah 9 Feb, 1826 ---- Peter Hese & Julian House

Mar 05
Daniel Stawring & Margreta Feterly--Mary Jane 12 Nov, 1825---Jacob Casler & wife Mary Cathrien
James Rankins & Elesebeth Stawring--Hariate Ann 11 Oct, 1822--George Armstrong & Almira
Stawring

Apr 02 Henry G. & Elesebeth Klock--- Nancy 13 Mar 1826 -- Christian J. Klock & Peggy Walrath
09 John Baum & Lena Ellwood-- Mary Elesebeth 10 Feb 1826--

23 Christian A. Bellinger & Nancy House-- Cathrien 13 Feb 1826-- Philip C. Bellinger & Caty
Zimmerman

30 John D. Flander & Anna Smith-- Lass 14 Mar 1826-- Nicholas Smith & wife Catharien

May 16 Casper A Loadwick & Nancy Lantman--Marget 7 Jul 1286-- Peter Loadwick & his wife Anna

21 Peter Flander & Margreet Riece-- Margreet 27 Feb 1826-- Christopher Shults & Margreet his
wife Christopher Klock & Elesebeth Dyslin--Magdalene 27 Feb 1826May 29 John Ausman &
Catharien Klock-- Maria 4 Nov 1824 -- Catharien 27 Jan 1826 Turin
June 4 Anthony Schuyler & Anna Shell-- Margaret 13 Mar 1826
Danube-- Moses Walrath & Peggy Witmosure-- Tyne 14 Nov 1825
--------- Jacob Shull & Anna Klock -- Jacob 3 May 1826
---------Bertholomew Schram & Sally Dunn-- Sally 28 Nov 1826
--------- Daniel Groff & Eve Failing-- Gertrude 8 May 1826-- Jacob Failing & wife Gertrude
June 7 Jacob Crouse & Mary Butler-- Delida 17 Mar 1826-- Charles Klock & Nancy Walrath
---------William Class & Susanna Riece-- Gedion 3 May 1826
June 11 John Defendorf & Anna Maria Ostrander-- William 15 May 1826
June 25 John Failing Jr & Catharien Ellwood-- Nancy 9 June 1826
July 01 Henry Dachsteder & Maria Casselman-- Daniel 23 Apr 1825
July 12 Simon Dreisbah & Elesebeth Crouse-- Cathrien 8 Feb 1826
July 16 Henry A. Walrath & Polly Cambell--Daniel 1 Mar 1826-- William Cambell & Elesebeth Baum
Aug 06 Jones Klock & Polly Klock-- David 3 June 1826-- David Fox & wife Elisebeth
Aug 27 Jones Reice & Eve Klock-- John 25 July 1826-- John Reice & Tyna his wife Danube
Sept 3 Robert Crouse & Nancy Shill-- Emily 24 July 1826-- John Shill & Cathrien Loucks
-- Permelia 25 July 1286-- Christian Ausman & Elisebeth Crouse
Sept 18 Nicholas Van Braukln & Polly Sheley-- Alexander 13 June 1826 Denmark
10 Markus Petrie & Kathrien Rankins-- Thomas Rankins 10 Jun 1826-- Adam Rasler & wife Dolly
Turin
12 William Swackhammer & Mary Failing-- Jacob 19 Jun 1825
24 Peter P. Smith & Elisebeth Cool-- Nathan 14 Aug 1826-- Kathrien Flander
25 Ralph Myer & Nancy Philips-- Annacha 2 Sept 1825-- Annacha Myer
Oct 02 John W. Hawn & Jemina Smades-- George 21 May 1824-- Jacob J Zoller & Wife Katharien---
-Twins -- Betsy Ann 24 June 1826 -- Sally Smades 24 June 1826
02 George W. Wheeler & Delia Hawn--Elesebeth 16 Sept 1826--Martin Smith & wife Elesebeth
06 John J. Kring & Elesebeth Nellis-- Diaane 22 Aug 1826-- Joseph P. Nellis & wife Diame Dewe
Turin- George Putman & Elesebeth Klock-- Theodore Jacob 17 Sept 1826
Oct 23 John Zimmerman & Nancy Klock--Christian Klock 11 Oct 1826--Christian Kock & wife Eve
Jacob Best & Eliza Crane-- Caroline 28 Apr 1826--10 evening
Robert Nellise & Caty Dyslin-- James Dyslin 14 July 1826
Nov 06 Peter Ginnings & Barbara Rice -- Jacob 6 Nov 1826
Peter B. Cook & Mary Fox-- Volkert J. Oothout 12 Oct 1825-- John J. Nellis & Polly Fox
Nov 12 Casper Lodwick & ELisebeth Bellinger-- Isaiah 30 Sept 1826
Nov 13 William Radley & Margreta Marks-- William Henry 4 Jul 1826
Nov 19 Christoffel Fox & Hannah Suits-- Henry 26 Aug 1826-- Henry Markle & wife Nancy Keller

Nov 21 John Krake & Rachel Sits-- Salomon Gipson 18 Oct 1826
Dec 17 Richard Putman & Nancy Shall-- Betsey 14 Apr 1826-- Jacob Shall & Betsey Van Antwerp
Danube
Peter N. Schuyler & Nancy Dygart-- Peter Wellington 13 Mar
Dec 20 George Kring & Mary Cross-- Mary 12 Jun 1826-- John Peck & wife Eve
25 John H. Heise & Ladish Provote-- James Nathan 13 Aug 1826
Charles Devoe & Caty Gray-- Mary Ann 4 Nov 1826

1827

Jan 17 John Kretser & Elesebeth Deusler-- Adam 27 Oct 1826-- Adam J. Klock & wife Cathrien
24 Henry J. Walrath & Betsey Eygabroet-- Maria 25 Jul 1826-- Adam Eygabroat & wife Rachel
Feb 19 Jacob H. Flander & Elesebeth Grott-- Simon 8 Feb 1827-- John H. Flander & wife Margreta
Jaugo
Mar 12 John F. Bellinger & Elesebeth Falander-- James 3 Feb 1827

A Record of some of the Baptisms of the Church at Snells Bush.

1819

Jan 01 David Bass & Maria Rasbah--Lucinda 26 Dec 1818--Jacob Thum & Maria his wife
Levi Abrahams & Hannah Hyde-- George 16 Dec 1818
John Young & Mary Hart-- Parents did not get their child recorded

Jan 31 Marks L. Dachstader & Lena Petre-- Lena 27 Dec 1818

Feb 14 Frederick Zimmerman & Maria Klock-- Frederic 23 May 1818
Isaac Keller & Betsey Snell-- 20 Dec 1818 No Name written Forgot

Mar 07 Valentine Staring & Margreta Hart-- Isaac 29 Aug 1818-- Henry Klock & Nancy his wife
Henry Hart & Charity House-- Joseph 2 Feb 1819-- Joseph House & Nancy his wife

Mar 27 Sufranus Snell & Eve Fryer-- Emily 31 Jan 1819-- George P. Snell & Peggy his wife
Jacob Moier & Caty Vanslike -- Peter 7 Apr 1819-- Peter Keller & Betsey Moier

Jun 20 Jacob P. Snell & Maria Helmic-- Betsey 24 May 1819
Daniel Guitman & Delia Zimmerman -- Analisa 27 Apr 1819-- John Snell & Analisa Spoon
Jul 12 Adam Zimmerman & Eve Smith-- Moses 11 Jun 1819-- Peter Zimmerman & Lena his wife
Jacob Uker & Elisebeth Spanable-- Daniel 8 Jun 1819-- John Veder & Elesebeth Uker
Joseph House & Nancy House-- Mary Ann 24 Aug 1819-- Adam House & Margreta his wife
Oct 22 John G. Klock & Guitty Dachstader-- Maria 12 Sept 1819
Nov 21 John W. Markle & Anna Helmack-- Anna 17 Sept 1819
John J. Snell & Lena Zimmerman-- Abaline 1819
Henry Tocky & Maria Failing--Guitty 1819
Leonard Dachstader & Nancy Dachstader-- Lena 3 Aug 1819-- Lena Dachstader

Papers got torn before here recorded on-- waiting for the record
Note. Entry No. 15. Date of baptism not July 12 or else year of birth is wrong.

1819

Peter Bellinger & Caty Sheal-- Levi 26 Sep 1819-- David Hase & Rosina Bellinger
Jacob Rasbah & Nancy House-- Morrise 13 Apr 1819-- Joseph House & Nancy his wife
Daniel Mackinley & Rachel Rese--John 3 Dec 1819
Frederic F Snell & Margreta Shaver-- Maria 28 Dec 1819--Abraham Shaver & Caroline his wife

1820

Jan 23 Peter Clause & Betsey Shaver-- David 10 Sep 1819
Jacob House & Caty House-- Levi 30 Nov 1819-- Abraham Snell & Caty House
Peter Van atten & Elesebeth Rasbah--Mary Ann 13 Aug 1818--John Rasbah & Margreta his wife
? Christian Bonsted & Caty Rickard--Carolina 8 Feb 1820--Joshua Snell & Lena Rickard
Mar 8 Peter A. Zimerman & Lena Guarloch-- Peggy 22 Feb 1820-- Henry Garloch & Peggy Snell
May 21 Lorence Zimmerman & Elesebeth Helmik--Martha 21 Mar 1820
Henry Zimmerman & Betsey Petrie--Gilbert 11 Apr 1820-- John Petre & Nancy Zimmerman
Richard Zimmerman & Sally Smith-- Isaac 30 Mar 1820-- Isaac Smith & Dolly Bellinger
Jacob Zimmerman & Mary Zimmerman-- Caty 24 Mar 1820--David Zimmerman & wife Mary
Parents names were torn from -- Hiram 15 Aug 1820--George Snell & wife Caty
my paper they were written on -- Ann Aliza 31 Aug 1820-- John Rickard & Ann Aliza Spoor
John J. Zimmerman & Mary Baum-- Jacob 29 Jul 1820
Oct 08 Jacob Thum & Mary Snell-- Lena 5 July 1820-- John Snell & Rebecka Leip
Peter Zimmerman & Elesebeth Wise-- Mary Ann 12 Jan 1820--William Zimmerman & Polly Wise
Henry Hose & Elesebeth Carn--Nancy 16 July 1819-- Joseph G Snell & Margreta White
Jacob Wise & Anna Hager-- Morris 17 March 1820-- Adam Snell & Eve Zimmerman
John Adam Failing & Elesebeth Zimmerman--John Adam Failing 29 Apr 1820--Peter Zimmerman&
wife Elesebeth Wise
Note. Entry No. 15 Sponsors; compare with sponsors entry no. 12, pg 93 there is doubt in this
record on more than one occasion as to whether this last name is "Spoon" or "Spoor".

Part of this page contains children from Menheim Church, some from St Johns Church .

Dec 12 Jacob W. Zimmerman & Polly Hager--John William 29 Dec 1819
John J. Zimmerman & Mary Baum--Jacob 20 July 1820
Simon D. Owins & Maria Fishback-- Ira Hamilton 6 Feb 1820 (repeat see p. 70)
John C. Zimmerman & Guitty Zimmerman-- Margreta 12 Oct 1820
Henry Hart & Guitty House-- Elias 18 Feb 1820-- John Petrie & Caty House

1821

Mar 04 Adam Zimmerman & Eve Snell-- Guity 8 Feb 1821--Richard Zimmerman & wife
Surfranus Snell & Eve Fry-- Betsey 24 Jan 1821-- Adam Kills & wife Elesebeth
Apr 16 Peter F. Snell & Caty Ellwood-- Liza 12 Mar 1821
Oct 27 William Zimmerman & Polly Wise-- Emeline 18 May 1821--Jacob Wise & wife Anna
Jacob Hart & Betsey Baum-- Barbary 27 Aug 1821-- John Young & wife Mary
Daniel Guitman & Delila Zimmerman-- Margreta 25 Feb 1821
Jacob Klock & Caty Gray-- Caty 30 Sept 1821-- Elijah Gray & Delia Klock
Abraham Owens & Sally Van Valkenburg-- Elmira 15 July 1821
William J. Enders & Nancy Leip-- Nilson Leip 26 Sept 1821
The rest of the Baptisms of Snells Bush Church are regularly recorded in this record and the reason
why the above are not is recorded on the inside of the cover of this book.

1827 Mar 27 John Heese Jr & Nancy Riece-- James Washington 27 Feb 1827
Oppenheim or St Johns Church

Apr 03 Daniel Defendorf & Margreta Merkle--Josiah 11 May 1824--Henry Merkle & wife Nancy Keller
Daniel Defendorf & Margreta Merkle --Jeremiah 11 May 1824-John Defendorf & wife Cathrien Picke
Daniel Defendorf & Margreta Markle---Adam Klock 24 Oct 1826--Adam J Klock & wife Cathrien
Apr 16 Peter Klock & Susana Feick-- Stephen 16 Jan 1827

1827

Apr 21 Joseph P. Nellis & Diadame Dewey-- Salley 16 Feb 1827-- John P Nellis & wife Nancy Nellis
23 David Heese & Rosine Bellinger-- Elisha 25 Feb 1827
May 06 Isaac Ellwood & Nancy Wilson-- Barbarian 27 Aug 1825
Minden- John Wilson & Susan Elwood-- Mary Ann 23 Dec 1826
David Vanslyke & Betsey Hillegas-- Abraham 5 Nov 1825-- Peter Hillega & wife Sally
Abraham Freileck & Peggy Defendorf-- Caty 12 Apr 1827
May 13 Henry Hairing & Nancy Banckart-- Mary 24 Jan 1827-- George Brown & Mary Hairing
Osquack
May 20 George Snow & Susannah Dillenbah--Mary 29 Mar 1827
Jacob Shaul & Eve Crisman-- Mary 5 Apr 1826-- Christian Shaul & wife Mary
Joseph Fox & Hannah Brunner-- Henry 10 Apr 1827
Jacob J Shaul & Cathrien Walter-- Levi 26 Feb 1827
Daniel Shaul & Rachel Smith--Elesebeth Ann Oct 1825-- David Shaul & wife Caty
May 27 Volkert Guitman & Margreta Flander-- Christopher 23 Mar 1827
June 04 William Nellis & Maria Bennit-- William 25 Mar 1826-- William Bennit
June 10 John A. Dingman & Margreta Krankhait--Lansing 8 Feb 1827
Minden
June 24 Henry Hase & Polly Davise-- Eve 22 May 1827-- Peter Hase & Eve Hase
July 01 Jacob D. Flander & Elezebeth Flander-- Margreta 3 Jun 1827
July 11 Abraham Walrath & Nancy Wever--Mary Ann 8 Jun 1827--Adam A Walrath & wife Maria
Zimmerman
Turin
July 15 Benjamin Fox & Cathrien Stauts--Kathrien 182-----
John H. Smith & Jemima Denuse--Peter Jay 13 Jan 1827--Peter Jay Denure & Nancy Gudermuet

1827

Aug 02 Peter Cramer & Margreta Hadcock--Loiza 30 Mar 1827
Aug 04 William Kniskern & Margreta Schuyler--Elesebeth 18 July 1827
Aug 05 Lodewick Hairing & Margreta Uker-- Margreta 7 July 1827-- Peter Wilcox & Mary Uker
Christian Walrath & Eve Haring-- Mary 28 June 1827
Aug 25 James Klock & Marsha Buel-- William 23 Mar 1827
Sept 01 William Cougnet & Elesebeth Gudermut-- John 27 1827
Sept 02 Daniel D. Hess & Elesebeth Suits-- Stephen 6 Oct 1826-- Stephen Fox & Levina Fox
Sept 03 Christian Vedder & Dority Thum-- Lorette 10 Aug 1827
Henry C. Hart & Eve Bellinger-- Mary Ann 29 Aug 1827-- John Heese & wife Nancy Riece
Oct 07 Jacob J. Klock & Nancy Nellis-- Augustus 24 Aug 1827--Augustenus Klock & July Ann Nellis
Oct 22 John A. Cratsinbarg & Maria Grems-- Asnamaria 17 Jan 1827
Denmark
Androw Cratsenbarg & Barbary Grems--George Henry 2 Feb 1827
Nov 04 Jacob Hillegas & Peggy House-- Lucinda 22 Sep 1827
Warner Nellis & Betsey Bryhes-- Analiza 11 Sep 1827
Johanes Hase & Elesebeth Bellinger-- Lucinda 24 Oct 1827
Nov 09 William Radly & Margreta March-- Susannah 13 Aug 1827-- Benjamin Clause & Clarissa
Claus
Nov 10 Adam Walrath & Polly Wever-- Aaron 27 Feb 1827-- Henry Merselia & wife Maria

Nov 22 Jacob A Walrath & Maria Smith-- Lena Ann 1826-- Benjamin Veeder & Nancy Quackenbush
Nov 28 John Brown & Katharien Wever-- Godfrey 28 July 1827-- Daniel Zimmerman & Lavina Fox
Dec 16 John J. Moyer & Elesebeth Dachsteder--Sarah 18 Aug 1827
Dec 23 Nicholas N. Weber & Elesebeth Shoemaker--Joseph Shoemaker 29 Sept 1827
German Flats-- Daniel Hess & Margreta Orendorf--Peter 6 Sept 1827--Jacob Philipse & wife Lena Orendorf
Dec 30 Thomas Failing & Katharien Klock--Nancy 9 May 1827--Henry R. J. Failing & Nancy Kern
John J. Kring & Elesebeth Nellis-- Peter 4 Oct 1827-- Peter Post & Elesebeth Shaw

1828
Jan 14 Jacob Snell & Mary Moyer-- Lewis 6 Sept 1827-- Jonas Snell & Elesebeth his wife
John W. Riggs & Maria Gross-- Mary 20 Jan 1827-- Jonas Snell & Elesebeth his wife
Jan 23 Henry P CLine & Katharien Klock-- Jeremiah 29 Jan 1825
Henry P. Cling & Katharien Klock--Katharien Ann 6 Oct 1827
Feb 05 Philip Rea & Rabeca Millard--William Hiram 16 Oct 1827
John Ausman & Katharien Klock--Magdalene 1 Jan 1827
Feb 10 Jacob H Flander & Margreta Jaugo--Henry 21 Jan 1828
Feb 17 Anthony Walrath & Caty Davice--Elesebeth 16 Nov 1827
Jacob Zimmerman & Elesebeth Gray-- Elisha & Elijah 26 Dec 1827
Peter Flander & Margreta Reese (no child listed)
John J. House & Nancy Hufman-- Walter 4 Feb 1828
Mar 08 James Safford & Lucretia Ostrom--Mary Alida 26 Nov 1826
Mar 20 Jacob Brown & Elesebeth Best-- Levi 12 Jan 1828--George Dygart & Elesebeth Shaw
Mar 21 Jacob Mack Grary & Roe Lene Barns-- John 4 April 1826
Apr 19 John Shults & Nancy Nellis-- Marget 28 Jan 1828-- John Everson & wife Margret
Coonrod Flander & Elesebeth Nellis-- Adam 1 Feb 1828-- Jacob D. Flander & wife Elesebeth

Note. Entry No. 19 The name of the mother may be written "Roesene."

Osquack Jacob Eckler & Hannah Shinholts--Jacob Frederic 18 Feb 1828
May 18 Isaac Waldron & Mary Shaull--Thomas 13 Mar 1828
May 25 David Fox & Elesebeth Klock--Jacob 18 Jan 1828--Stephen Fox & Sophia Kock
June 15 Christopher Klock & Elesebeth Dyslin--Elesebeth 4 Feb 1828--Jonas Snell & Elesebeth his wife
July 22 Abraham Walrath & Nancy Wever--Anna Maria 20 Apr 1828--Daniel Klock & wife Nancy
July 26 Jacob Crouse & Mary Butler--Eli 7 June 1828
July 27 Benjamin Veeder & Lena Walrath-- Mary Ann 17 May 1828--Adam A Walrath & wife Maria
Christian House & Caty Heese--Levi 5 July 1828-- Henry House & wife Cornelia
Christopher Flander & Mary Haring--Martin 9 June 1828
Aug 10 Jacob Prame & Nancy Prame--Peggy 21 Jul 1828-- John Prame & wife Margreta
Aug 12 Martinus Klock & Eliza Cox-- Nancy 2 Aug 1828
Aug 17 Peter Smith & Elesebeth Cool-- Jane 6 Aug 1828-- John Tobbits & wife Mary
Sept 14 Andreus Stall & Orsela Zigler--France Lodwick 20 Jul 1828
Leray
Sept 21 Benjamin Clause & Elesebeth Heese--Helen 30 Aug 1828
Sept 28 Danil Fox & Caty Klock--Nancy 12 June 1828-- Christoffel Fox & wife Nancy
Jones Klock & Polly Klock--Elesebeth 8 May 1828--Benjamin Klock & Elesebeth Klock
Sept 29 Adam Walrath & Mary Leip-- Ervin 27 Jul 1828-- Peter Graves & Mary Walrath
Cornelius Walrath & Polly Goodale-- Stephen William 4 Jul 1828--William Walrath & wife Margreta
Sept 30 Henry Burkdorf & Caty Morison--David 21 Sept 1828
Sept 30 Henry Hairing & Nancy Banker--Rue 28 Aug 1828
Sept 31 Henry McKoy & Charity Funck--Charles 18 Mar 1818
John Hawn & Jemime Smedia--Nancy 15 Aug 1828--James Wilke & wife Peggy

Oct 12 Peter Loucks & Caty Davice--Mary Ann 3 Jun 1826--Henry H Hase & wife Polly
Christian A Walrath & Cathrien Hillegas-- David 4 Sept 1828-- David Hillegas & Nancy Failing died 23 Feb 1831
John Vedder & Caty Dayhash--George 11 Jun 1828
Nov 12 Joseph Mosure & Magdelene Smith--Levi 30 Aug 1828
Dec 21 David Hadcock & Nancy Monck-- John 16 Nov 1828

1829

Jan 04 Jacob Moyer & Barbary Carnerose--James Alexander 14 July 1828
Jan 23 David Walrath & Elesebeth Farbs--Walter 28 Aug 1826
Jan 25 Abraham Heese & Kathrien Davis--Jacob 10 Jan 1829--Jacob Edle & Kathrien McKoy
Jan 26 Nicholas Houck & Rhoda Degrusla--James Nicholas 8 Nov 1020
Feb 08 Adam R Gray & Nancy Brown--John Adam 11 Apr 1828-- John W Nellis & Margret his wife
Feb 17 Luther Russel & Nancy Cox--Betsey Maria 7 Jan 1829-- Ebenezer Cox & ELesebeth Failing
Feb 22 James Safford & Lucretia Ostrom--Dolly Kathrien 7 Jan 1829
Jacob J I Klock & Kathrien Shaver--Karthrien 7 Jan 1829--Joseph Shaver & wife Maria
Mar 01 Robert Nellis & Caty Dislin--Mary 28 Sept 1828--Josiah Nellis & Elida Beekman
Mar 19 Benjamin Crouse & Caty Ann Wever--Eve 14 Mar 1829
Thomas Failing & Kathrien Klock--Josiah 24 Feb 1829
Mar 20 Henry Merselis & Maria Putnam--Aaron 23 Feb 1829--John Putnam & Kathrien Baum
May 18
Turin
April 12
Parents, Daniel Klock- Nancy Defendorf, Child & Time of Birth, Kathrien May 31, 1824
Parents, Daniel Klock- Nancy Defendorf, Child & Time of Birth, Melise June 29, 1827
April 23
Parents, John H. Smith, Jamime Denuce, Child & Time of Birth, Chancy January 2, 1829, Sponsors, Leonard Crouse & Sally his wife
Parents, Peter Nellis- Kathrien Fox, Child & Time of Birth, Stephen March 27, 1828, Sponsors, John Kring & Polly his wife
Parents, Jacob Tuesler- Margaret Snell, Child & Time of Birth, Simeon February 3, 1829, Sponsors, Christopher Fox & Nancy his wife
June 1
Parents, John H. Zimmerman- Nancy Klock, Child & Time of Birth, Elesebeth April 7, 1829
June 12
Parents, William W. Hodge- Sally Granger, Child & Time of Birth, Sarah June 5, 1829, Sponsors, David DeVoe
June 21
Parents, Jacob Hillegas- Peggy Thumb, Child & Time of Birth, Ruben March 1, 1829
Parents, David Resse- Rosina Bellinger, Child & Time of Birth, George Henry Febr 5, 1829
June 29
Parents,George Lesher- Mary Klock, Child & Time of Birth, Chestina May 17, 1829, Sponsors, Josiaha Nellis, Eve Nellis
July 12
Parents, Charles Devoe- Caty Gray, Child & Time of Birth, Irene _____, 1829
Parents, Peter Heese- Maria Dennels, Child & Time of Birth, Abner June 19, 1829, Sponsors, Robert H. Nellis, Annas Dannels
Parents, Jacob H. Flander- Elesebeth Groff, Child & Time of Birth, Mary Katharien May 16, 1829, Sponsors, Daniel Flander, Polly Groff
Parents, Jacob Moyer- Caty Vanslyck, Child & Time of Birth, Peter April 7, 1819
August 1
Parents, George Hilleges- Elesebeth Uker, Child & Time of Birth, Nancy April 26, 1829, Sponsors, Harry Hayring, wife Nancy

August 16
Parents, Warner Nelles, Child & Time of Birth, Luther August 11, 1829, Sponsors, Kathrien Flande;
Parents, Warner Nelles - Child & Time of Birth, Calvin August 11, 1829, Sponsors, Peter P. Smith & wife Elesebeth
Sept.
Parents, Nathan Snell - Nancy Fox, Child & Time of Birth, Mary Elesebeth July 27, 1829
Sept 18
Parents, Peter Heese Junr.- Betsey Dorn, Child & Time of Birth, Lovisa Sept 6, 1829, Sponsors, Peter Heese & wife Polly
Sept 27
Parents, David Van alstine -Lidia Tarpenny, Child & Time of Birth, Jonathan Hunter July 22, 1829
Parents, Jacob C. Hillegas - Margreet House, Child & Time of Birth, Rosina August 24, 1829

1829

November 2nd
Parents, Jacob A. Walrath- Maria Smith, Child & Time of Birth, Adam August 7, 1829, Sponsors, Henry 2nd J. B. Failing & wife
Parents, Jacob A. Walrath- Maria Smith, Child & Time of Birth, Eve August 7, 1829, Sponsors, Cally Kocklin
Parents, Christian Vedder- Dorothy Thum, Child & Time of Birth, Luther Sept 9, 1829
Parents, Henry I. Heese- Polly Davice, Child & Time of Birth, John Elexander Sept 18, 1829, Sponsors, John Heese, wife Elesebeth
November 7th
Parents, Isaiah Nessle- Margreta Allenburgh, Child & Time of Birth, Darlin Thompson January 15, 1826
Parents, Isaiah Nessle- Margreta Allenburgh, Child & Time of Birth, Rosinah Maria November 21, 1827
November 15th
Parents, Peter Flander – Margreta Riece, Child & Time of Birth, Almira September 16, 1829
November 22nd
Parents, Peter Hillegas – Phebe Ingeram, Child & Time of Birth, Rosina Fcbr 28, 1820
Parents, Peter Hillegas – Sally Trumble, Child & Time of Birth, Fanny Elon May 5, 1828, Sponsors, David Hillegas, Fanny Elon Failing
Parents, Peter Hillegas – Sally Trumble, Child & Time of Birth, Jane Ann September 20, 1829
December 7th
Parents, John Flander – Peggy Gaugo, Child & Time of Birth, Nancy September 13, 1829

1830

January 3rd
Parents, William Coughet – Elesebeth Oudermut, Child & Time of Birth, Garret September 30, 1829
Parents, Abraham Devoe – Maria Walrath, Child & Time of Birth, Augtin June 28, 1829
January 26th
Parents, Philip Cramer – Kathrien Hadcock, Child & Time of Birth, Samuel February 12, 1828, Sponsors, Peter Cramer, wife Margreta
Parents, Peter Cramer – Lena Casler, Child & Time of Birth, George August 19, 1829, Sponsors, Abel Nickerson, wife Cathrien
Febr 13th
Parents, Benjamin Veder – Lena Walrath, Child & Time of Birth, Nancy December 14, 1829
May 30th
Parents, Peter Klock – Susan Feock, Child & Time of Birth, Mary Ann April 19, 1830

1831

Feb 24th
Parents, Martin Klock – Lisa Cox, Child & Time of Birth, Margreet Sept 13, 1829
*Note: The last entry in the record written by Mr. Devoe was recorded on Feb 13, 1830. The last two entries on the pages are by Rev A. H. Myers.
Entry No. 17, See No. 5, on page 66, and note memorandum written in the record there, that refers to the entry above.

A Record of Baptisms Commenced by the Revd. Abraham H. Myers

1830

Nov 7th
Parents, Simeon Klock – Eunice Easterbrooks, Child & When Born, Andrew, July 14, 1830, Sponsors, Andrew Klock, Betsey Vn Allen
Parents, Daniel Zimmerman – Lavinia Fox, Child & When Born, Hannibal, Apr 7, 1830
Dec 5th
Parents, Abraham H. Myers – Hannah Blanchard, Child & When Born, Harriet Josephine, July 9, 1829
Parents, William B. Hall – Betsey Hase, Child & When Born, Mary Elizabeth, Oct 29, 1830, died March 13,

1831

Dec 22nd
Parents, John A. Snell – Mary Failing, Child & When Born, Martha, Sept 30, 1830, Sponsors, Conrad Snell, Gertrude Failing
Jany 14th
Parents, Christopher Klock – Elizabeth Dyslin, Child & When Born, Ann Catharine, July 4, 1830, died Jan 17, 1831
Jan 17
Parents, Henry Zielley – Nancy Nellis, Child & When Born, Peter, Jan 15, 1831

Febr 20th
Parents, Jacob Bellinger – Nancy Flander, Child & When Born, Nancy Maria ,June 15, 1830
Parents, James Forbes – Maria Anderson, Child & When Born, Anna Maria, July 12, 1826 and Hiram, Augt 2, 1829
April 3rd
Parents, Robert Nellis – Caty Dyslin, Child & When Born, Annah, Nov 17, 1830
Parents, Henry House – Cornelia Mosure, Child & When Born, Henry Nelson, Feb 25, 1831
April 30, John Angus, an adult
May 9
Parents, Christian House – Caty Hase, Child & When Born, John Jacob, Apr 18, 1831, Sponsors, John P. Windecker, Lana Hase
May 15th
Parents, John A. Shafer – Mary Youron, Child & When Born, Horace, March 4, 1831
June 12th
Parents Christian A. Walrath – Catharine Hellegus, Child & When Born, Nancy Catharine, May 17, 1831, died June 13, 1831, Sponsor, Nancy Hellegas
Parents, Abraham Hase – Caty Davis, Child & When Born, Isaac March 31, 1831, Sponsors Danl. Davis & wife

David Hase – Rosina Bellinger, Child & When Born, Silas, Jany 29, 1831
July 17th
Parents, Jacob J. Snell – Gertrude Eleanor Fox, Child & When Born, Eleanor, Apr 19, 1831
Parents, John A. Walrath – Margaret Reese, Child & When Born, Nathan, June 10, 1831
July 31st
Parents, David Van Slyke – Betsey Hellegas, Child & When Born, John, Sept 28, 1830
Aug 14th
Parents, George Hellegas – Elizabeth Youker, Child & When Born, David, Apr 7, 1831, Sponsors, Nancy Hellegas, Saml Timerman
Sept 4th
Parents, William Campbell – Elizabeth Baum, Child & When Born, Christiana, March 22, 1831, died Sept. 1831, Sponsors, Thos. Getman, Jr., Margaret Baum
Sept 11th
Parents, Robert J. Crouse – Nancy Shill, Child & When Born, Urilla, June 27, 1831
Sept 25th
Parents, John Angus – Julia Ann House, Child & When Born, Christiana, Aug 24, 1831
Oct 9th
Parents, John Shall – Christina Rice, Child & When Born, Malinda, Sept 9, 1831
Oct 30th
Parents, Jacob Zimmerman Jr. – Elizabeth Gray, Child & When Born, Stephen Gray, 1831
Nov 6th
Parents, Volkert Snell – Elisabeth Klock, Child & When Born, Alanzo, March 19, 1831

Records of Baptisms by Rev. Herman B. Stryker

Child's Name & When Born: _____, Parents: Jacob H. Zimmerman – Margaret Doxtader, Place: St. Johnsville
Child's Name & When Born: Alvin Feby 23, 1832, Parents: Francis Lighthall, Jr. – Margaret Klock, Place: St. Johnsville
Baptized: July 1, 1832, Child's Name & When Born: Benjamin, April 23, 1832, Parents: Henry I. Hays – Polly Davis, Sponsors: Samuel Hoffman – Polly Stanburgh, Place: Eukers Bush
Baptized: July 15, 1832, Child's Name & When Born: Cyrene, June 11, 1832, Parents: John J. House – Nancy Hoffman, Place: Euker's Bush
Baptized: July 30, 1832, Child's Name & When Born, Benjamin, Feb 11, 1831, Parents: Henry P. Kline – Catharine Klock, Place: State Road
Baptized: Oct 8, 1832, Child's Name & When Born, Nancy, June 20, 1831, Parents: Charles Nellis – Jane Frey, Place: St. Johnsville
Baptized: Nov 25, 1832, Child's Name & When Born, Horatio, Parents: Christopher Klock – Eliz. Dyslan, Place: St. Johnsville
Baptized: Dec 23, 1832, Child's Name & When Born, Eva Ann, Nov 25, 1832, Parents: Jacob C. Hellicost – Margaret House, Sponsors: Levi Hays – Rosina House, Place: Eukers Bush
Baptized: Jan 1, 1833, Child's Name & When Born, Celia, 1832, Parents: John Adam Snell – Mary Failing, Place: St. Johnsville Ch.
Baptized: Jan 15, 1833, Child's Name & When Born, Harvey, Oct 12, 1832, Parents: Isaac Garlock – Nancy Doxtader, Place: Upper St. Johnsville
Baptized: Jan 17, 1833, Child's Name & When Born, Albert March 25, 1832, Parents: Benjamin Vedder – Lany Walrath, Place: St. Johnsville,
Baptized: Jan 20, 1833, Child's Name & When Born, Lorenzo, Oct 21, 1832, Parents: Benjamin J. Clause – Nancy Flander, Place: Eukers Bush
Baptized: Jan 20, 1833, Child's Name & When Born, Mary Ann, Dec 17, 1832, Parents: Abraham Failing – Catharine Baum, Place: State Road
Child's Name and When Born: Nathan Christie, Jan 23, 1831, Baptized: Feby 3, 1833, Parents: Aaron Van Antwerp – Catharine House, Place: John C. House's, Eukers Bush
Child's Name and When Born: George Mills, Decm 4, 1831, Baptized: Feby 3, 1833, Parents:

Samuel W. Smith – Charlotte H. Mills, Place: Eukers Bush

Child's Name and When Born: Mary, June 3, 1832, Baptized: Feby 17, 1833, Parents: Joseph Deusler – Margaret Sponable, Place: Eukers Bush

Child's Name and When Born: Nathan, April 2, 1833, Baptized: May 5, 1833, Parents: Daniel Failing – Nancy Hess, Place: Crings Bush

Child's Name and When Born: Ira, Oct 15, 1832, Baptized: May 5, 1833, Parents: Josiah Getman – Sarah White, Sponsors: Josiah Orman – Lucinda Getman, Place: Eukers Bush

Child's Name and When Born: Caroline, Dec 12, 1832, Baptized: May 5, 1833, Parents: Jacob Brown – Elizabeth Best, Sponsors: James Best – Mary Getman, Place: Eukers Bush

Child's Name and When Born: Eve, Feby 6, 1833, Baptized: May 16, 1833, Parents: Jonas Deusler – Maria Hess, Place: Eukers Bush

Child's Name and When Born: Nelson, Jun 15, 1832, Baptized: July 7, 1833, Parents: Abraham Klock – Abigail Swackhammer, Sponsors: Leonard Bauder – Peggy Klock, Place: Eukers Bush

Child's Name and When Born: Charles, July 20, 1833, Baptized: Aug 18, 1833, Parents: Jacob A. Walrath – Mary Smith, Sponsors: William Campbell – Betsy Campbell, Place: Parsonage House

Child's Name and When Born: Henry, Aug 2, 1833, Baptized: Aug 18, 1833, Parents: David Venton – Maria Quackinbush, Sponsors: Nancy Walrath, Place: Parsonage House

*Child's Name and When Born: Margaret, May 11, 1833, Baptized: Septr 1, 1833, Parents: David Bellinger – Byoddi Flanders, Place: Eukers Bush

* Child's Name and When Born: Elijah, Septr 13, 1833, Baptized: Septr 15, 1833, Parents; Christian House – Catharine Hayes, Sponsors: John M. Easterly – Delia Hays, his wife, Place: Eukers Bush

*Baptized by Rev. Peter Stryker
Note: In the original record, the dates of birth and of baptisms and the name of the child, were written each in separate columns. They are arranged as above, because the page is not wide enough to do otherwise. The first date given is the date of birth; the second, the date of baptism.

Entry No. 8, the memorandum written beneath the name Peggy Klock has been so much scratched out, that it can only be read with difficulty; it may not be transcribed correctly.

Record of Baptisms Rev. Herman B. Stryker Minister
Baptized by Rev. Peter Stryker

Child's Name and When Born: Armenia, Febry 2, 1833, Baptized: October 27, 1833, Parents: Abrm. Hays – Catharine Davis, Place: Ukars Bush

Child's Name and When Born: Mary, Septr 5, 1833, Baptized: Oct 27, 1833, Parents: Dan'l Graaf – Eve Failing, Place: Eukers Bush

Child's Name and When Born: Charles Evens, Jun 12, 1833, Baptized: Novr 3, 1833, Parents: Dan'l. Zimmerman – Lovina Fox, Place: St. Johnsville

Child's Name and When Born: Melissa, April 4, 1832, Baptized: Novr 9, 1833, Parents: William Hall – Elizabeth Hays, Sponsors: David Falnders & his wife, Eva Hays, Place: Eukers Bush

Child's Name and When Born: John Alonzo, Sept 18, 1833, Baptized: Novr 9, 1833, Parents: William Hall – Elizabeth Hays, Sponsors: John Hays & his wife, Elizah Bellinger, Place: Eukers Bush

Child's Name and When Born: Elihu, Octr 7, 1833, Baptized: Novr 17, 1833, Parents: Conrad Snell – Gertrude Failing, Sponsors: Jacob E. Failing & his wife, Gertrude Dockey, Place: St. Johnsville

Child's Name and When Born: Mary Jane, Augt 20, 1833, Baptized: Decr 22, 1833, Parents: Warren Nellis – Elizah Byrnes, Place: Eukers Bush

Baptized by Rev. Herman B. Stryker

Child's Name and When Born: Lucinda, Jany 4, 1833, Baptized: Jany 2, 1834, Parents: Isaac Teusler – Elizabeth Loudewick, Place: Crings Bush
Child's Name and When Born: Nancy Margaret, July 9, 1832, Baptized: Jany 2, 1834, Parents: Peter Thumb – Caty Cosselman, Place: Crings Bush
By Rev. P. Stryker

Child's Name and When Born: Hervey, Decr 7, 1833, Baptized: Januy 18, 1834, Parents: Peter Bellinger – Lena Bellinger, Sponsors: Hervey Van driessen & Eliabeth Yuker, Place: Yukers Bush

Record of Baptisms Rev. Herman B. Stryker Minister
Baptized by Rev. P. Stryker

Child's Name and When Born: Nathan, July 16, 1833, Baptized: February 16, 1834, Parents: John A. Walradt – Peggy Reese, Place: Yukers Bush
Child's Name and When Born: Clark, January 1, 1834, Baptized: Februy 18, 1834, Parents: David Crouse – Mary Lasher, Sponsors: Wm. Crouse & his wife, Catharine, Place: St. Johnsville
Child's Name and When Born: Thomas William, May 4, 1833, Baptized: Februy 27, 1834, Parents: Thomas Henry – Maria Margaret Klock, Place: St. Johnsville

By Rev. H. B. Stryker

Child's Name and When Born: Erastus Needham, December 22, 1833, Baptized: March 2, 1834, Parents: Benjamin Booth – Mary Thumb, Place: St. Johnsville
Child's Name and When Born: Catharine Mynderse, Oct 9, 1833, Baptized: March 23, 1834, Parents: Stephen Yates – Gertrude Schemmerhorn, Place: St. Johnsville
Child's Name and When Born: Reuben, June 6, 1833, Baptized: April 27, 1834, Parents: Henry Walradt – Polly Campbell, Sponsors: David Baum – Cath. Walradt, Place: St. Johnsville
Child's Name and When Born: David Herman, May 25, 1833, Baptized: Sept 7, 1834, Parents: Benj. Vedder – Mary Walrath, Place: St. Johnsville
Child's Name and When Born: Joseph Grams, May 18, 1835, Baptized: Oct 17, 1835, Parents: Joseph H. House – Betsey Grany, Place: Eukers Bush
Note: Entry No. 8. The name transcribed as "Grams" may be "Granes". In a hurried examination, I can find nothing to compare it with, and I am now under the impression that the name comes from the "Gramps" family.

Record of Baptisms during the ministry of Rev. Jas. Murphy

Parents: Christopher Bellinger – Nancy Smith, Child & When Born: Walter Octr 28, 1834
Parents: Jacob Bellinger – Nancy Flanders, Child & When Born: Marietta May 24, 1834
Parents: David Flanders – Eva Hays, Child & When Born: Morgan, Octr 21, 1834
Parents: Richard Bellinger – Catherine Fink, Child & When Born: Frederick, July 19, 1835
Parents: Christian Failing – Nancy Veder, Child & When Born: Margaret, January 4, 1836
Parents: Simeon Snell – Margaret Bocke, Child & When Born: Hanibal, June 11, 1836
Parents: Peter Hays Jr. – Betsey Dorn, Child & When Born: Horatio, July 4, 1836, died April 11, 1844
Parents: Joseph Caltleman – Julianna Thum, Child & When Born: Peter Nichols, May 11, 1836, Witness By: Nicholas Thum & Rachel Thum, grandparents

A Record of Baptisms during the ministry of the Rev. Abraham H. Myers

1837

Baptized: Nov 19, Parents: Henry I. Hase – Polly Davis, Child's Name & When Born: Alida Ann, March 19, 1837

Baptized: Dec 17, Parents: Augustus Smith – Margaret Bellinger, Child's Name & When Born: Amelia, Oct 16, 1837

1838

Baptized: Jan 6, Parents: Christian Failing – Nancy Vedder, Child's Name & When Born: Julia Ann, Oct 12, 1837

Baptized: Jany 18, Parents: Jacob H. Zimmerman – Margaret Doxstader, Child's Name & When Born: Darwin, Oct 28, 1836, died Jan 18, 1838

Baptized: Feby 11, Parents: Levi Hase – Mary Hilts, Child's Name & When Born: Mary Ann, Aug 19, 1837

Baptized: Feby 11, Parents: David Baum – Catharine Walrath, Child's Name & When Born: Andrew, July 5, 1837

Baptized: Feby 18, Parents: Daniel Failing – Nancy Hess, Child's Name & When Born: Anna Eve, Jan 15, 1838

Baptized: March 11, Parents: Jonas Dusler – Maria Hess, Child's Name & When Born: Emeline, June 22, 1837

Baptized: April 13, Parents: Stephen Yates – Gertrude Schermerhorn, Child's Name & When Born: Henry, Dec 17, 1837, died March 24, 1844

Report to classis

Baptized: May 6, Parents: David Crouse – Polly Lasher, Child's Name & When Born: Ann Elizabeth, July 20, 1836

Baptized: May 20, Parents: Henry J. Hase – Mary Windecker, Child's Name & When Born: Amanda, March 11, 1838

Baptized: June 17, Parents: Joseph Dusler – Margaret Spontnable, Child's Name & When Born: Harvey Nelson, Oct 16, 1834

Baptized: June 24, Parents: Peter Hays, Jr. – Betsey Dorn, Child's Name & When Born: Solomon, April 28, 1838

Baptized: July 8, Parents: Jonas Klock – Polly Klock, Child's Name & When Born: Deloss, Dec 15, 1837

Baptized: Sept 2d, Parents: Benjamin Crouse, Child's Name & When Born: Oliver, October 10, 1834 and Martha, Celista Jany 15, 1837

Baptized: Oct 9, Parents: Samuel Shults – Elizabeth Shults, Child's Name & When Born: Sarah, Nov 29, 1837, Sponsors: Jas. Dillenbach- Sarah Ann Shults

Baptized: Oct 28, Parents: John Crouse – Catharine Lasher, Child's Name & When Born: Alfred, July 14, 1838, Sponsors: Adam Nellis – Harriet Kingsbury

Baptized: Dec 16, Parents: Jacob Vosseller – Rosina House, Child's Name & When Born: Harvey, Sylvanus June 29, 1838

Baptized: Dec 16, Parents: Abraham Hase – Catharine Davis, Child's Name & When Born: Annette, Aug 11, 1838

1838

Baptized: Dec 25, Parents: John Hase, Jr. – Nancy Reese, Child's Name & When Born: John Henry, Oct 12, 1838

Baptized: Dec 30, Parents: Christopher Flander – Mary Haring, Child's Name & When Born: Catharine, Sept 1, 1838

Baptized: Dec 30, Parents: Daniel Bascom – Charlotte Veghte, Child's Name & When Born: Elizabeth, Sept 13, 1831; Harriet, March 1, 1833; Wm. Chamberlain, April 30, 1837

1839

Baptized: Jan 2d, Parents: Doct. John W. Riggs – Maria Gross, Child's Name & When Born: James Oliver, Sept 11, 1830; Albert and Alfred (twins), Nov 9, 1837
Baptized: Jan 13, Parents: Peter Van Driesen – Mary Spontnable, Child's Name & When Born: John Page, Sept 12, 1838
Baptized: Jan 13, Parents: John Angus – Julia Ann House, Child's Name & When Born: John Peter, Sept 1, 1838
Baptized: Feby 10, Parents: Christian House – Caty Hase, Child's Name & When Born: Joseph William, Dec 17, 1838, Sponsors: Wm. Hase – Polly House

Report to Classis

Baptized: May 19, Parents: Alexander Ramo – Catharine Smith, Child's Name & When Born: Margaret Ursula, Jan 1, 1833; and Lucy Ann, May 7, 1835
Baptized: June 16, Parents: Daniel Failing – Nancy Hess, Child's Name & When Born: Nathaniel, March 28, 1839
Baptized: June 23, Parents: Jacob C. Helligass – Peggy House, Child's Name & When Born: David, Jan 18, 1839
Baptized: June 23, Parents: Stephen Brown – Eliza Lawton, Child's Name & When Born: Mary, Feb 28, 1839
Baptized: July 3, Parents: Henry A. Walrath – Mary Campbell, Child's Name & When Born: Jacob Henry, July 28, 1838
Baptized: Aug 2d, Parents: Christopher Bellinger – Nancy Smith, Child's Name & When Born: Julia Elizabeth, Aug 4, 1838
Baptized: Aug 4, Parents: Revd. Abraham H. Myers – Hannah Blachard, Child's Name & When Born: Henrietta Josepha, Jan 15, 1839
Baptized: Oct 27, Parents: Jonas Dusler – Maria Hess, Child's Name & When Born: Stephen, June 4, 183(?)
Baptized: Oct 27, Parents: Benjamin Booth – Mary Thumb, Child's Name & When Born: Peter, Jan 25, 1839
Baptized: Dec 22, Parents: David Flander – Eve Hays, Child's Name & When Born: Aaron, April 15, 1839

1840

Baptized: Feb 2d, Parents: Benjamin Vedder – Lena Walrath, Child's Name & When Born: Margaret Jane, April 2, 1837; and Daniel, Feb 23, 1839
Baptized: Feb 2d, Parents: William B. Hall – Betsey Hase, Child's Name & When Born: Mary Catharine, Nov 18, 1838

Record of Baptisms - A. H. Myers, V. D. M.

Baptized on Feb 16, 1840, Parents: Henry J. Hass, Polly Davis, Child: Emily Catharine, Born: Sept 1, 1839
Baptized on April 12, 1840, Parents: Peter Hase Jr, Betsey Dorn, Child: Chauncy, Born: Dec 23, 1839
Baptized on April 19, 1840, Parents: Barney Becker, Lucinda Cook, Child: Ervin, Born: May 12, 1939

Baptized on May 1, 1840, Parents: George Timerman, Lena Youron, Child: Caroline, Born: Oct 9, 1839

Baptized on July 19, 1840, Parents: David Baum, Catharine Walrod, Child: Nancy Catharine, Born: Jan 28, 1840

Baptized on Oct 4, 1840, Parents: Jacob F. Baum, Eliza Ann Lock, Child: Jacob, Born: July 9, 1840

Baptized on Oct 25, 1840, Parents: Augustine Smith, Margaret Bellinger, Child: Oliver, Born: March 7, 1840

Baptized on Dec 5, 1840, Parents: Rufus C. Willsey, Frances Ellen Failing, Child: Marvin Everett Failing, Born: June 30, 1840

Baptized on Jan 11, 1841, Parents: Jesse Smith, Catharine Thumb, Child: Laura, Born: Dec 20, 1840

Baptized on Feb 7, 1841, Parents: Joseph J. Eigenbroaat, Child: Marvin, Born: Nov 5, 1840

Baptized on Feb 21, 1841, Parents: Jacob Vosseller, Rosina House, Child: Nathan Justus, Born: March 27, 1840

Baptized on Feb 28, 1841 [Ephrata typed under date], Parents: Henry Keiner, Henriette Elizabeth Gross, Child: Mary Catherine, Born: Oct 19, 1840

Baptized on March 21, 1841, Parents: John Turner Jr, Elizabeth Failing, Child: Martha Viola, Born: Sept 18, 1840, Sponsors Wm. E. Knieskern and Jemima Fonder

Baptized on May 2, 1841, Parents: Daniel Failing, Nancy Hess, Child: Elizabeth, Born: Feb 20, , 1841

Baptized on May 2, 1841, Parents: Daniel Groff, Eve Failing, Child: Margaret Ann, Born: March 7, 1840

Baptized on June 6, 1841, Parents: Jerome Hoffman, Esther Thumb, Child: Mariette, Born: Feb 12, 1841

Baptized on June 9, 1841, Parents: John Flander, Margaret Chawgo, Child: John, Born: July 25, 1840

Baptized on June 9, 1841, Parents: John Turner jr, Elizabeth Failing, Child: Elizabeth, Born: Aug 12, 1836

Baptized on June 9, 1841, Parents: Reuben Failing, Catherine Klock, Child: Jacob Henry, Born: Jan 2, 1841

Baptized on June 20, 1841, Parents: Levi Hase, Mary Hilts, Child: John Norman, Born: March 25 , 1841

Baptized on 20 June, 1841, Parents: David Flander, Eve Hase, Child: Philip, Born: April 28, 1841

Record of Baptisms - A. H. Myers pastor

Baptized on Aug 22, 1841, Parents: Benjamin Vedder, Lana Walrath, Child: Louisa, Born: Jul 7, 1841

Baptized on Sept 19, 1841, Parents: Alanson Snell, Mary Snell, in Manheim, Child: Margaret Ann, Born: June 25, 1841

Baptized on Oct 10, 1841, Parents: Christian House, Caty Hase, Child: Daniel, Born: July 24, 1841, Sponsors John J. House and his wife

Baptized on Oct 10, 1841, Parents: Jacob C. Helligas, Margaret House, Child: Sally Ann, Born: March 8, 1841

Baptized on Nov 21, 1841, Parents: Henry J. Hase, Mary Windecker, Child: Esther, Born: June 20, 1841

Baptized on Dec 22, 1841, Parents: Hon. Stephen Yates, Gertrude Schermerhorn, Child: Susan Schermerhorn, Born: June 27, 1841

Baptized on Dec 25, 1841, Parents: John Angus, Julia Ann House, Child: Charles Henry, Born: sept 27, 1840

Baptized on Jan 2, 1842, Parents: David Crouse, Polly Lasher, Child: Aaron, Born: Dec 1, 1841

Baptized on Jan 16, 1842, Manheim, Parents: Joshua Snell, Nancy Snell, Child: Joshua, Born: Nov 4, 1841

Baptized on Feb 27, 1842, Manheim, Parents: Jacob Yoran, Mary Timerman, Child: Enos, Born: Dec

25, 1841

Baptized on Feb 27, 1842, Manheim, Parents: Robert McGinnis, Jane Shannon, Child: Sarah, Born: Mar 8, 1841

Baptized on April 8, 1842, Parents: Solomon Flander, Mary Hase, Child: John Henry, Born: Dec 4, 1841, Sponsors Henry Hase and Hannah Smith

Baptized on April 1842, Parents: Andrew R. Groot, Mary Ann Tannahill, Child: Elizabeth, Born: Jan 18, 1837

Baptized on April 1842, Parents: Andrew R. Groot, Mary Ann Tannahill, Child: Mary, Born: Dec 16, 1839

Baptized on April 21, 1842, Parents: Henry A. Walrath, Polly Campbell, Child: Wm. Andrew, Born: March 22, 1841

Baptized on April 21, 1842, Parents: Isaac Dusler, Betsey Lodawick, Child: Abram, Born: Aug 3, 1841

Baptized on April 24, 1842, Parents: Christian Failing, Nancy Vedder, Child: Mary Ann, Born: April 30, 1841

Baptized on April 24, 1842, Parents: Jonas Dusler, Maria Hass, Child: Amanzo, Born: May 12, 1841

Baptized on June 5, 1842, Manheim, Parents: Adam Smith, Enaliza Getman, Child: Asa, Born: Sept 28, 1841

Baptized on June 12, 1842, Parents: Jacob Landgrave Eacker, Child: Catharine Elisa Groff, Child: Gertrude, Born: March 27, 1842

Baptized on June 19, 1842, Parents: Peter Hase Jr, Betsey Dorn, Child: Amanzo, Born: Febr 13, 1842, Sponsors Christian House and his wife Caty Hase

Record of Baptisms - A. H. Myers

Baptized on July 5, 1842, Parents: Adam Loucks, Jane Collier, Child: Richard Henry, Born: May 10, 1841

Baptized on July 5, 1842, Parents: Benjamin H. Petree, Elizabeth Loucks, Child: Twins, William and Willard, Born: March 12, 1842

Baptized on July 31, 1842, Parents: Christopher Flander, Mary Haring, Child: Mary, Born: April 21, 1842

Baptized on Aug 7, 1842, Parents: Rev. A. H. Myers, Hannah Blanchard, Child: Florence, Born: Aug 5, 1841

Baptized on Sept 25, 1842, Manheim, Parents: Peter A. Timerman, Lany Garlock, Child: Sarah Caroline, Born: July 10, 1842

Baptized on Oct 23, 1842, Parents: Joseph Dusler, Margaret Spontnable, Child: Laura Ann, Born: March 17, 1842

Baptized on Oct 23, 1842, Parents: Jacob Vosseller, Rosina House, Child: John Sandford, Born: April 16, 1842

Baptized on Dec 11, 1842, Manheim, Parents: Simon Snell, Margaret Dockey, Child: Henry Ozias, Born: July 3, 1842

Baptized on Jan 8, 1843, Parents: Jerome Huffman, Esther Thumb, Child: Sarah, Born: Aug 26, 1842

Baptized on Jan15, 1843, Parents: John Angus, Julia Ann House, Child: David, Born: Sept 5 , 1842

Baptized on Jan 22, 1843, Parents: Henry J. Hase, Polly Davis, Child: Lovina, Born: June 11, 1842

Baptized on Feb 4, 1843, Parents: George Timerman, Lana Youron, Child: Anna Marie, Born: Nov 10, 1843, Parents:

Baptized on Feb 26, 1843, Parents: Levi Hase, Mary Hilts, Child: Sanford, Born: Dec 10, 1842

Baptized on April 2, 1843, Parents: Augustus Smith, Margaret Bellinger, Child: Helena, Born: July 19, 1842

Baptized on May 7, 1843, Parents: John Ingersoll, Margaret Klock, Child: Wm. Henry, Born: Feb 17, 1843

Baptized on May 14, 1843, Parents: Daniel Failing, Nancy Hess, Child: Henry, Born: April 8, 1843

Baptized on June 4, 1843, Parents: John A. Shafer, Mary Youron, Child: Ellen, Born: Oct 4, 1842

Baptized on June 22, 1843, Parents: Reuben Failing, Catherine Klock, Child: Adam Lorenzo, Born: Oct 12, 1842

Baptized on July 30, 1843, Parents: Doct. James D. Smith, Catherine Thumb, Child: Mary Margaret, Born: March 3, 1843

Baptized on Aug 6, 1843, Parents: Absalom Hase, Elizabeth Crane, Child: Herman, Born: June 11, 1843

Record of Baptisms - A. H. Myers, pastor

Baptized on Nov 4, 1843, Parents: Doct Francis B. Etheridge, Frances, Child: Francis, Born: Jan 20, 1842

Baptized on 1Dec 17, 1843, Parents: Jonas Duesler, Maria Hess, Child: Oliver, Born: July 9, 1843

Baptized on Jan 3, 1844, Parents: Stephen Yates, Gertrude Schermerhorn, Child: Mary, Born: April 21, 1843

Baptized on Jan 28, 1844, Parents: Abraham Haise, Catharine Davis, Child: Daniel, Born: July 4, 1843

Baptized on June 2, 1844, Parents: Peter Hase Jr, Betsey Dorn, Child: Olonzo, Born: Jany 22, 1844

Baptized on June 9, 1844, Parents: Obadiah Flander, Elizabeth Hess, Child: Oliver, Born: April 27, 1844

Baptized on June 16, 1844, Parents: David Flander, Eve Hase, Child: David Henry, Born: Dec 5, 1843

Baptized on June 16, 1844, Parents: Roswell Carpenter, Jane Sophia Hase, Child: Nancy Catharine, Born: Oct 17, 1843

Baptized on June 23, 1844, Parents: Benjamin Vedder, Lana Walrath, Child: John Henry, Born: April 1, 1844

Baptized on Aug 3, 1844, Parents: Elijah Bauder, Margaret Crouse, Child: Webster, Born: Nov 4, 1841

Baptized on Aug 3, 1844, Parents: Elijah Bauder, Margaret Crouse, Child: Livingston, Born: Aug 30, 1843

Baptized on Aug 10, 1844, Parents: Jacob Vossler, Rosina House, Child: Jesse Alfred, Born: July 1, 1844

Baptized on Aug 11, 1844, Parents: Reuben Failing, Catharine Klock, Child: Jason, Born: April 15, 1844

Baptized on Aug 11, 1844, Parents: George Dygert, Nancy Spontnable, Child: Catharine, Born: Dec 1, 1843

Baptized on Sept 15, 1844, Parents: Henry A. Walrath, Polly Campbell, Child: Sarah Elizabeth, Born: May 5, 1844, Sponsors: Seth Nellis and Elizth Baum

Baptized on Sept 25, 1844, Parents: Christian Vedder, Dorothy Thumb, Child: Christian, Born: June 15, 1844

Baptized on Sept 25, 1844, Parents: Jerome Hoffman, Esther Thumb, Child: John Adam, Born: June 9, 1844

Baptized on Oct 20, 1844, Parents: Jonas House, Nancy Helligass, Child: Adison, Born: sep 26, 1844

Baptized on Nov 3, 1844, Parents: Henry Hart, Mary Ann Morey, Child: Anna Maria, Born: Aug 3, 1844

NOTE. The record kept by the Rev A. H. Myers ends with this entry; the following are by the Rev. Joseph Knieskern

Baptized on July 27, 1845, Parents: Absalom Hayse, Elizabeth Crane, Child: George Washington, Born: May 22, 1845

Baptized on Aug 20, 1845, Parents: Elijah Bauder & Margaret Crouse, Child: De Witt, (Died Aug 20, 1845)

Baptized on Sept 4, 1845, Parents: Peter Saltsman, Polly Fox, Child: Frances, Born: March 14, 1842

Baptized on Sept 4, 1845, Parents: Peter Saltsman, Polly Fox, Child: Lewis, Born: May 14, 1844 (Died Sept 8, 1845)

Baptized on Sept 28, 1845, Parents: Daniel Failing, Nancy Hess, Child: Christian, Born: Jan 17, 1845

Baptized on Oct 4, 1845, Parents: Solomen Flander, Mary Hays, Child: Hiram, Born: Aug27, 1845

Baptized on Feb 7, 1846, Parents: Doct. F. B. Etheridge, Frances, Child: James Henry, Born: March 20, 1844

Baptized on April 5, 1846, Parents: Nellis Rockafellow, Irene Dockey, Child: Henry Irwin

Baptized on May 3, 1846, Parents: Isaac Dusler, Elizabeth Lodawick, Child: Margaret, Born: April 25, 1845

Baptized on June 6, 1846, Parents: Geo. Timerman, Lana Yoran, Child: Martha, Born: May 1, 1846 [April 20th crossed out]

Baptized on June 6, 1846, Parents: Rev. J Knieskern, Emily S. Williams, Child: Henry Williams, Born: Nov 10, 1845, Died Aug 14, 1848 Aged 2 yrs. 9 m. & 3 days

Baptized on July 12, 1846, Parents: Peter Haise Jun., Betsy Haise, Child: Horatio Deloss, Born: March 4, 1846

Baptized on Aug 24, 1846, Parents: Jerome Huffman, Esther Thumb, Child: Oliver, April 5, 1846

Baptized on Oct 10, 1846, Parents: Levi Haise, Mary Haise, Child: Lucinda, Born: Aug 16, 1846

Baptized on Oct 10, 1846, Parents: Jacob Vosseller, Roseann Vosseller, Child: George Albert, Born: Aug 9, 1846

Baptized on Nov 8, 1846, Parents: Jonas Deusler, Mary Hess, Child: Mary Martha, Born: Nov 25, 1846 [it was typed with both years as1846]

Baptized on Jan 26, 1847, Parents: Geo. Perry, Catherine Haise, Child: Geo. Washington

Baptized on Feb 18, 1847, Parents: Solomen Flander, Mary Haise, Child: Owen Deloss, Born: Nov 22, 1846

Baptized on Feb 28, 1847, Parents: Reuben Failing, Catharine Klock, Child: Joseph, Born: Sept 27, 1846

Baptized on March 7, 1847, Parents: Daniel Failing, Nancy Hess, Child: Daniel, Born: Aug 1846

Baptized on April 5, 1847, Parents: Doct F B Etheridge, Frances, Child: Mary Cornelia, Born: Aug 8, 1846, Died Oct 4, 1847

Baptized on May29, 1847, Parents: Obadiah Flander, Elizabeth Hess, Child: Daniel Obadiah, Born: May 29, 1847

Baptized on March 6, 1848, Parents: John H Nellis, Christina Klock, Child: Mary Frances, Born: Nov 28, 1846

Baptized on March 14, 1848, Parents: Christian Vedder, Dorothy Thumb, Child: Hannah, Born: July 3, 1846.Baptized on July 16, 1848, Parents: Peter Haise Jun., Betsy Dorn, Child: Wm. Welshe, Born: April 12, 1848, Sponsors: Wm W Davis and Matilda Haise

Baptized on Aug 13, 1848, Parents: Jonas House, Nancy Helligass, Child: James Almerin, Born: June 7, 1848

Baptized on Oct 15, 1848, Parents: Jonas Dusler, Maria Hess, Child: Maria, Born: Dec 16, 1847

Baptized on Nov 27, 1848, Parents: Elijah Bauder, Margaret Crouse, Child: Alfred

Baptized on Jan 7, 1849, Parents: Levi Haise, Mary Haise, Child: Levi Jacob, Born: June 13, 1848, Died Mch 17, 1853

Baptized on Feb 3, 1849, Parents: Robert Klock, Catharine Snell, Child: Marcus R., Born: Sept 19, 1841

Baptized on Feb 3, 1849, Parents: Robert Klock, Catharine Snell, Child: Mary Margaret, Born: March 28, 1846

Baptized on March 4, 1849, Parents: Geo. H Kline, Nancy M Ehle, Child: James Henry, Born: June 15, 1848

Baptized on March 4, 1849, Parents: Jerome Hoffman, Esther Thumb, Child: Dewitt, Born: Feb 27, 1848

Baptized on Oct 6, 1849, Parents: Johnathan Thumb, Clorena Hoffman, Child: Martha

Baptized on Oct 6, 1849, Parents: Jacob Haise, Margaret Kring [No entry made in child's name and birthdate column]

Baptized on Oct 6, 1849, Parents: Daniel Failing, Nancy Hess [No entry made in child's name and birthdate column]

Baptized on Jan 27, 1850, Parents: Augustus Smith, Child: Margaret, Born: Nov 16, 1847

Baptized on Jan 27, 1850, Parents: Nathaniel Helligas, Margaret Flander, Child: Martha, Born: Nov 18, 1849

Baptized on May4, 1850, Parents: George Timerman, Lana Yoran, Child: Emily

Baptized on June 2, 1850, Parents: David Flander, Eve Haise, Child: Mary Alice, Born: June 12, 1849

Baptized on June 9, 1850, Parents: Geo. H Kline, Nancy M Ehle, Child: Anson Melvin, Born: Sept 9, 1849

Baptized on Aug 31, 1850, Parents: John J Haise, Cyrene House, Child: Walter, Born: May 17, 1850

Baptized on Sept 1, 1850, Issac Hand, an adult

Baptized on Sept 1, 1850, Parents: Issac Hand, Angelina Davis, Child: Thompson B., Born: Oct 10, 1842

Baptized on Sept 1, 1850, Parents: Issac Hand, Angelina Davis, Child: Sarah Ann, Born: Aug 29, 1847

Baptized on Oct 14, 1850, Parents: John J Klock, Mary Elias, Child: Hiram Afonsor, Born: Feb 17, 1849, Died April 7. 1851

49487091R00235